940.5421 Astor, Gerald,
AST   1926-

         A blood-dimmed tide.

$28.00

DATE			

A BLOOD-DIMMED TIDE

A BLOOD-DIMMED TIDE

The Battle of the Bulge by the Men Who Fought It —by—

Gerald Astor

DONALD I. FINE, INC.

NEW YORK

Library of Congress Cataloging-in-Publication Data

Astor, Gerald, 1926–
    A blood-dimmed tide : the Battle of the Bulge by the men who fought it / by Gerald Astor.
      p. cm.
    Includes bibliographical references and index.
    ISBN 1-55611-281-5
    1. Ardennes, Battle of the, 1944–1945.   2. World War, 1939–1945—Personal narratives, American.   I. Title.
    D756.5.A7A76   1992
    940.54′21431′092—dc20   91-58657
                                                                         CIP

Manufactured in the United States of America

10 9 8 7 6 5 4 3 2 1

Designed by Irving Perkins Associates

*In memory of the men who drowned
in that bloody surge, those who resisted it
and to the special breed that seeks
to prevent its reoccurrence.*

ACKNOWLEDGMENTS

I AM GRATEFUL TO all of the survivors among the former GIs listed on pages xiii–xv, for their cooperation and answers to my interviews, letters and telephone calls. I am also indebted to them for the use of their diaries, journals, memoirs, letters and clippings.

I am also obliged to Maj. Gen. George Ruhlen, past commander of the 3rd Field Artillery Battalion, John Kline of the 106th Division Association and editor of *The Cub of the Golden Lions*, Saul Solow of the 30th Infantry Division, Dave Pergrin of the 291st Engineer Combat Battalion Association, Charles Hammer of the 285th Field Artillery Observation Battery Association and Wayne Pierce of the 325th Glider Association for locating individuals.

Eric Fisher Wood III and Pam Wood were helpful in obtaining material on Lt. Eric Wood, Jr., as was his widow Meg Bayless, his friend Ted Kiendl and his college classmate Dick Crook.

Moira MacDonald Queen furnished me with details on her late father, Charles MacDonald.

The staff of the Archives Branch of the U.S. Army Military History Institute, Carlisle Barracks, Pennsylvania, under Dr. Richard J. Sommers, efficiently directed me to valuable materials. I drew from Archives copies of an unpublished manuscript by Charles La Chaussee of the 517th Parachute Battalion, an oral history contributed by Major General William Desobry of the 10th Armored Division and the "Ethint" series—interrogations of German officers Jochen Peiper, Friederich von der Heydte, Otto Skorzeny and Sepp Dietrich. More official material came from the U.S. Army Center of Military History and the National Archives in Washington, D.C.

John Bauserman was kind enough to share with me documents he collected on war crimes attributed to German soldiers. Prof. James Weingartner of the University of Southern Illinois and author of *Crossroads of Death*, a book on the Malmédy Massacre, furnished additional information on war crimes by soldiers.

Jean Milmeister, curator of Cercle d'Études sur la Bataille des Ardennes, at Tuntange, Luxembourg, and who with his associates created the Monument of the Unknown GI in Clervaux, provided me with interviews he had conducted.

Ralph Hill supplied copies of his correspondence with various individuals involved in the Battle of the Bulge.

George Winter provided information, photographs and maps.

Clark Archer lent photographs from the archives of the 517th Parachute Regiment Combat Team Association.

Small excerpts have been drawn from an unpublished manuscript by Charles La Chaussee; from an unpublished book, *I Was No Hero* by Harry Martin and from *Voices from the Foxhole* by Dorothy Chernitsky (Uniontown, Pa.: Dorothy Chernitsky, 1991).

Quotations from *Company Commander* by Charles MacDonald (New York: Bantam Books, 1979) by permission.

CONTENTS

PREFACE

EARLY IN THE MORNING of December 16, 1944, as a winter-paled dawn reluctantly crept from its bed, a hilly, wooded section of land known as the Ardennes began to bleed again. Twice before in the past thirty years, this turf, largely belonging to Luxembourg and Belgium along the German border, had been the avenue for savage attack. Then it had been the native people who had bled. But now in December, American GI blood soaked the ground and hundreds of thousands of young Americans lost their innocence.

The attack by the forces of Nazi Germany swiftly pierced the U.S. defenses, creating a forty-mile-wide, sixty-mile-deep bulge in the U.S. lines. The Battle of the Bulge soon pitted 600,000 American soldiers and perhaps 50,000 British against the Third Reich's 550,000. What made the Bulge special was that within the span of about a six-week campaign, it featured the major components of warfare, the double-edged sword of technology, the collection and use of intelligence, the best and worst of strategy and tactics, the products of military training and experience.

Most of all, the Battle of the Bulge put the man with the gun to the test. For all of the cataclysmic bloody violence, despite the enormous numbers involved, the 1944–45 war in the wintered-over Ardennes did not turn on precisely directed, massive encounters of tanks nor on confrontations of huge phalanxes of troops. When the generals and the commentators sought to describe the situation, they resorted to the word "fluid." One brass hat's "fluid" is another soldier's military anarchy. Far more often than any commander would like to accept, the Battle of the Bulge broke down into an every man for himself.

Said then-Lt. Col. George Ruhlen, who commanded a field artillery unit, "The German attack timetable was fatally disrupted in the first four days of the Bulge, in numerous cases by squads, platoons, companies—and sometimes individual soldiers—who courageously and tenaciously held onto key terrain until killed, captured or forced to withdraw."

Whether or not the outcome truly had been decided by the end of the fourth day—the hemorrhages of the Ardennes lasted well beyond four days—the story of the Bulge is largely one of individuals thrust into the crucible of war. Their experiences and their reactions offer revelations about heroism, the ability of humans to stand fast under the most fearful onslaughts, the capacity to endure terrible deprivation and horrors as well as the reversion to brutality, murder and massacres. And their attitudes add insights into the age-old question of why men have continued to allow themselves to be plunged into the crucible. Many of the Americans who found themselves on the line those first awful days in December were true innocents of war, fresh troops brought up before the expected final push that would lead to unconditional surrender.

The voices speaking here represent an infinitesimal portion of the more than one million men caught up in the war of the Ardennes. In no way are they intended to represent a scientific sampling. Furthermore, under the best of circumstances, eyewitnesses may distort occurrences, particularly as time tends to blur some memories. Personal biases and egos influence perceptions. And given the huggermugger quality of those awful moments in the winter of 1944–45, it is not possible to determine if every event described is factually exact. Nor is this a definitive or encyclopedic account delineating the activities of all who participated or an explanation of successes and failures.

Nevertheless, while conceding some limitations, the accounts of experiences and how those involved felt then and now offer vignettes of the America from which its soldiers sprang, the battlefield dynamics of World War II, behavior under fire, what the prisoner of war endured and what it means today to have been a GI during the Battle of the Bulge.

THE SOLDIERS

Sgt. William Dunfee, Co. I, 505th Parachute Regiment, 82nd Airborne Division

Sgt. Glenn Fackler, Co. A, 38th Armored Infantry Battalion, 7th Armored Division

Pfc. Bob Hall, Ammunition & Pioneer Platoon, 3rd Battalion, 119th Infantry Regiment, 30th Division

Pfc. Philip Hannon, Co. A, 81st Engineer Combat Battalion, 106th Infantry Division

Sgt. Schuyler Jackson, Regimental Hq. Demolition Platoon, 502nd Parachute Infantry Regiment, 101st Airborne Division

1st Lt. Alan Jones, Jr., Hq. Co., 1st Battalion, 423rd Infantry Regiment, 106th Division

Capt. Charles La Chaussee, CO, Co. C, 517th Parachute Combat Team

S. Sgt. Leo Leisse, Ammunition & Pioneer Platoon, 3rd Battalion, 422nd Infantry Regiment, 106th Division

Capt. Charles MacDonald, CO, Co. I, 23rd Infantry Regiment, 2nd Division

Maj. Hal McCown, 2nd Battalion, 119th Infantry Regiment, 30th Division

Sgt. Richard McKee, Co. A, 422nd Infantry Regiment, 106th Division

S. Sgt. Curtiss Martell, Co. C, 119th Infantry Regiment, 30th Division

Pvt. Harry Martin, Co. L, 424th Infantry Regiment, 106th Division

1st Lt. Harry Mason, Co. D, 110th Infantry Regiment, 28th Division

Pvt. James Mattera, Battery B, 285th Field Artillery Observation Battalion

S. Sgt. William Merriken, Battery B, 285th Field Artillery Observation Battalion

Pvt. James Mills, Co. I, 423rd Infantry Regiment, 106th Division

1st Sgt. Ben Nawrocki, Co. B, 393rd Infantry Regiment, 99th Division

Cpl. Jerry Nelson, Co. C, 40th Tank Battalion, 7th Armored Division

1st Lt. Dee Paris, Co. A, 14th Tank Battalion, 9th Armored Division

Pvt. Frank Raila, Co. E, 423rd Infantry Regiment, 106th Division

Pfc. Alan Shapiro, Co. C, 346th Infantry Regiment, 87th
  Division
Capt. Glen Strange, Hq. Co., 27th Armored Infantry Battalion,
  9th Armored Division
Capt. Wallace Swanson, CO, Co. A, 502nd Parachute Infantry
  Regiment, 101st Airborne Division
Pfc. William James Tsakanikas, Intelligence & Reconnaissance
  Platoon, 395th Infantry Regiment, 99th Division.
Cpl. Ed Uzemack, Co. B, 110th Infantry Regiment, 28th Division
Capt. Nathan Duke Ward, Hq. Co., 81st Engineer Combat
  Battalion, 106th Division
Pvt. Leonard Weinstein, Co. G, 325th Glider Infantry Regiment,
  82nd Airborne Division
1st Lt. Eric Fisher Wood, Jr., Battery A, 589th Field Artillery
  Battalion, 106th Infantry Division

GERMANS

1st Lt. Horst Gresiak, 7 Company, 2nd SS Panzer Regiment
Cpl. Hans Hejny, 381st Armored Engineer Battalion, 2nd Panzer
  Division
Lt. Col. Friederich von der Heydte, CO, Operation Gryphon
  (Auk)
Lt. Col. Jochen Peiper, CO, *Kampfgruppe Peiper*, 1st SS Panzer
  Division
M. Sgt. Heinz Rohde, German infiltrator, part of Operation *Greif*
Pvt. Josef Schroder, 15th Company, 15th Regiment, 5th
  Parachute Division
Lt. Col. Otto Skorzeny, CO 150 Brigade, CO Operation *Greif*

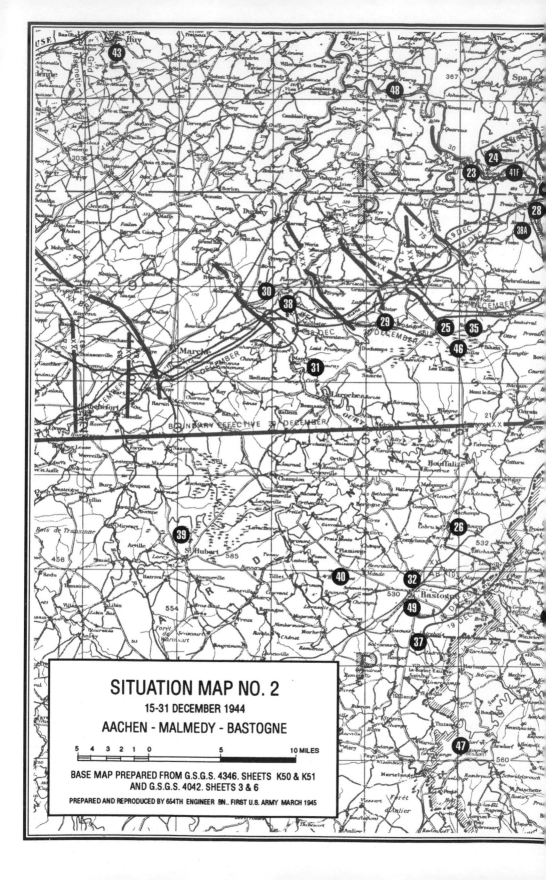

SITUATION MAP NO. 2

15-31 DECEMBER 1944

AACHEN - MALMEDY - BASTOGNE

5 4 3 2 1 0   5   10 MILES

BASE MAP PREPARED FROM G.S.G.S. 4346. SHEETS K50 & K51
AND G.S.G.S. 4042. SHEETS 3 & 6

PREPARED AND REPRODUCED BY 654TH ENGINEER BN.. FIRST U.S. ARMY MARCH 1945

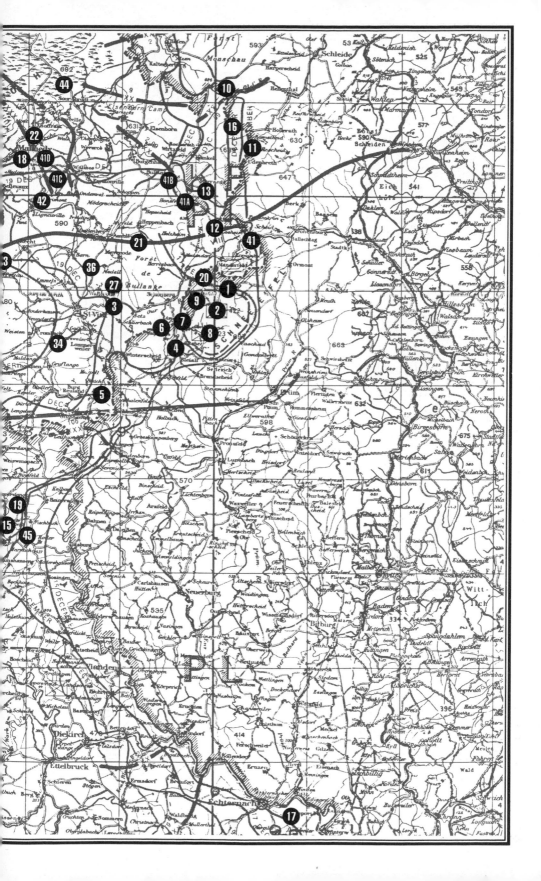

KEY TO THE U.S. FIRST ARMY SITUATION MAP NO. 2 (OVERLEAF), COVERING THE PERIOD OF DEC. 15-31, 1944. THIS MAP OFFERS A GUIDE TO WHERE THE SOLDIERS WERE DURING THE BATTLE OF THE BULGE.

1. Philip Hannon, of the 81st Engineer Combat Battalion, was in the vicinity of Auw.
2. Richard McKee, with the 422nd Infantry, was on the Schnee Eifel.
3. John Collins, of the 81st Engineer Combat Battalion, fought in the futile defense of St. Vith on the Prumerberg. Also at that site was Nathan Duke Ward.
4. Clifford Broadwater, with an antitank company, held a position near Bleialf.
5. Harry Martin, of the 424th Infantry, defended the southern flank of the 106th Division.
6. Frank Raila was part of an abortive effort to retake Schönberg.
7. Alan Jones, like Raila, was a member of the 423rd Infantry on the Schnee Eifel.
8. James Mills served with the 423rd.
9. Leo Leisse hauled ammo for the 422nd Infantry.
10. Carmen Capalbo was wounded as the 395th Infantry attacked toward the Roer.
11. Ben Nawrocki of the 393rd Infantry was among the troops of the 99th Division driven back through Rocherath-Krinkelt, until a line could be established along Elsenborn Ridge.
12. Lyle Bouck and Bill Tsakanikas, members of an Intelligence & Reconnaissance Platoon for the 395th Regiment, came under fire the first day, in front of Lanzerath.
13. Dick Byers, as a forward observer with the 371st Field Artillery Battalion, began the Bulge near Hunningen and eventually retreated to Camp Elsenborn.
14. John Chernitsky was training noncoms for the 28th Infantry Division at Wiltz when the breakthrough began.
15. Ed Uzemack was a runner with the 110th Infantry Regiment of the 28th at Clervaux.
16. Charles MacDonald and other troops from the 23rd Infantry Regiment, assigned to assault the Roer, rushed to defend against the breakthrough.
17. Marcus Dillard, with the 12th Infantry Regiment, 4th Division, held out at Dickweiler.
18. Jim Mattera and Bill Merriken, from the 285th Field Artillery Observation Battalion, survived the massacre just outside of Malmedy.
19. Harry Mason commanded machine guns at Grindhausen for the 110th Infantry Regiment.

20. Barney Alford and the 589th Field Artillery were to support the 422nd Infantry. Alford fell back through Schönberg and St. Vith to defend the Baraque de Fraiture crossroads (see No. 25).

21. Eric Wood of the 589th escaped capture at Schönberg, fleeing into the woods near Meyerode.

22. Frank Currey of the 30th Division's 120th Infantry Regiment earned his Congressional Medal of Honor in the fighting on the outskirts of Malmedy.

23. Curtiss Martell, from the 30th Division's 119th Infantry Regiment, battled for Stoumont.

24. Hal McCown and Bob Hall, from the 30th Division, became prisoners at La Gleize.

25. Joe Colmer and Leonard Weinstein, with the 325th Glider Infantry, defended the intersection of Baraque de Fraiture.

26. William Desobry, from the 10th Armored Division, tried to keep the route to Bastogne open at Noville.

27. Glenn Fackler, from the 38th Armored Infantry Battalion, 7th Armored Division, was forced to retreat near St. Vith.

28. Bill Dunfee, with the 505th Parachute Infantry, 82nd Airborne, blocked the enemy advance at the Salm River.

29. Charles La Chaussee, from the 517th Airborne Combat Team, barely escaped entrapment at Freyneux. Later, he was wounded near Bergeval (see No. 38A).

30. Melvin Biddle, from the 517th, received a Congressional Medal of Honor for feats between Soy and Hotton.

31. Arnold Albero, with Task Force Hogan of the 3rd Armored Division, was surrounded at Marcouray before a Christmas night escape.

32. Schuyler Jackson and Wallace Swanson came by truck, while Jack Agnew arrived by parachute on Dec. 23, to defend the encircled town of Bastogne.

33. Jerry Nelson manned the gun as his tank from the 7th Armored Division's 40th Tank Battalion wiped out three German tanks at Poteau.

34. Glen Strange, of the 27th Armored Infantry Battalion, 9th Armored Division, turned the tables on his captors at Neubruck.

35. Dee Paris of the 14th Tank Battalion, 9th Armored, blocked the enemy near Regne.

36. Jim Buck, from the 106th Division headquarters at St. Vith, became lost, and may have met Eric Wood near Meyerode.

37. Abe Baum led a small column from the 4th Armored Division into Bastogne via the Arlon road just before the Germans surrounded the town.

38. Bill Boyle brought his 1st Battalion of the 517th Airborne into battle between Soy and Hotton and led a force including troops from the

75th Division, through which Task Force Hogan escaped capture. Boyle was wounded near Bergeval (38A).

39. Alan Shapiro, with the 87th Division's 346th Infantry, was part of the reinforcements shipped into the Ardennes from the south.

40. Cy Blank, with the 11th Armored Division, swung up from Neufchateau around Bastogne towards Houffalize.

41. Jochen Peiper launched his task force from Losheim. His route led him through Honsfeld (41A), Bullingen (41B), through Faymonville and Thirimont (41C), by Malmedy (41D), Ligneuville (42), Stavelot (41E) to La Gleize (41F).

42. Otto Skorzeny stayed behind the lines for his Operation *Greif* but advanced to Ligneuville as his brigade tried to take Malmedy.

43. Heinz Rohde, disguised as an American for *Greif,* reached the Meuse River at Huy.

44. Friedrich von der Heydte parachuted into the Hohes Venn region as part of his ill-fated mission.

45. Hans Hejny participated in the attack on Clervaux.

46. Horst Gresiak led German panzers in a successful assault upon the Baraque de Fraiture defenders.

47. Joseph Schroder was captured by U.S. 4th Armored troops at Bigonville.

48. Three members of *Greif* were caught at Aywaille and subsequently executed.

49. Charles Boggess commanded a tank column that smashed through German defenses along the road from Assenois to open a corridor into Bastogne.

A
BLOOD-
DIMMED
TIDE

. . . Things fall apart; the centre cannot hold;
   Mere anarchy is loosed upon the world,
The blood-dimmed tide is loosed, and everywhere
   The ceremony of innocence is drowned . . .
And what rough beast, its hour come round at last,
   Slouches towards Bethlehem to be born?

—WILLIAM BUTLER YEATS
"The Second Coming"

Chapter I

THE INNOCENTS

PHIL HANNON, AGE TWENTY, had been assigned to the 81st Engineer Combat Battalion, part of the 106th Infantry Division. "I grew up in Ripon, Wisconsin, had a year at the University of Cincinnati when my family moved to College Park, Maryland. I transferred to the University of Maryland right there.

"We were all in the ROTC, and our commander told us that the unit was going to be called up and we might be better off if we enlisted while they would give us an option of the branch of service. I signed up for the engineers, since I had heard that they got to ride much more than the infantry. I took my basic training at Fort Belvoir, Virginia. It was very good, I think. I learned to handle a variety of weapons, the demolition trade using explosives, how to build bridges and roads.

"I hadn't developed any great hatred of the enemy we supposedly were about to face. When I was in high school I knew we were working up to a warlike confrontation with the Germans. President [Franklin D.] Roosevelt was leaning to the British side and had gone out of his way to head the country toward the mess. As a result it had maybe come sooner but I'm not sure there was any way to avoid it. We were well on our way to getting into the war, it was a question of when.

"I was less aware of the problems with Japan. I remember in 1941, the year I graduated from high school, that our economics teacher remarked that he would be very surprised if we were not at war with Japan in six months. We looked at him astonished. What the hell was he talking about? All of our sights were on Europe where they were already fighting. When the Japanese then jumped us at Pearl Harbor, it was upsetting. The guys I knew always had more animosity towards the Japanese than the Germans.

"I heard that some civilians had a lot more feeling about the Germans than we did. In fact, there was a family in Ripon, of

1

German background that supposedly was driven out of town by the local people.

"When the ASTP program (Army Specialized Training Program that sent soldiers to study on college campuses) opened up, I took placement exams at Georgetown. They put me in the advanced engineers' course at the University of Maryland. There were only 200 of us in the course although the total number of ASTP men at Maryland was three or four thousand. Since we were a small, tightknit unit, we had a gorgeous time, particularly with my folks living right there. Girls had to sign out from their dormitories or sororities. Our house became a place where they could sleep over the weekend.

"I was not a very good student. All of my previous courses had been ones concerned with business. I had no background in chemistry, physics, calculus. Furthermore, I didn't particularly want to be in college at the time. I wanted to be in the army and get things over with over there. My grades were so terrible I had to go before a review board to explain why I should not be thrown out. They asked me didn't I like it there in college? Why wasn't I doing the kind of work I was capable of? I had just met Jean and so I told them that I had met a girl with whom I was serious and that I was also distracted because my folks lived in College Park. They sort of accepted this as reasonable and figured I'd settle down now. They decided to let me stay, with a couple of remarks that my group wouldn't be there much longer, anyway.

"When I got back to the others and told them what was ahead, the partying started in earnest. We had one great carousing time, every night. Half of us went to the 106th Division, and the rest I think to the 87th Division. In the 81st Engineers we participated in maneuvers in Tennessee for six weeks. I enjoyed it, even though it was nasty and cold. To prepare us for any eventuality, including shipment to the Philippines, we even had to use our mosquito nets during a snowstorm.

"Our outfit stayed intact, but they gutted the infantry regiments in the summer [after D-Day and the breakout in France]. They stripped them of maybe two-thirds of their best trained guys and replaced them with newly drafted guys who had just completed their basic training.

"From Tennessee we had gone to Camp Atterbury, Indiana, and then to Miles Standish in Massachusetts in preparation for shipping out to Europe. At Miles Standish, an officer stood up and announced, 'Every other one of you will either be wounded or killed.' We just turned to the GI next to us and said, 'That's tough shit for you, fella.'

"We were eighteen, nineteen, twenty-year-old kids. None of us could believe anything that bad could happen to us. At most we thought of the million-dollar-wound, getting hit in the leg and being sent home as a hero."

On November 10, 1944, S. Sgt. John Collins from A Company of the 81st Engineer Combat Battalion, the same unit in which Phil Hannon served, sailed for Europe aboard the U.S.S. *Wakefield*. Collins grew up in an orphanage in Kansas City, Missouri. Although he had served in the National Guard from 1938 to 1940, squeezing in a year of college to boot, the Merchant Marine rejected him as physically unfit. The draft swept him up in 1942 when he was twenty-five years old and sent him to Fort Jackson and the combat engineers.

When the *Wakefield* docked, GI trucks hauled the troops to the small town of Blockely, about ninety miles north of London. It was the third week in November. He jotted down a present tense journal.

"We are about three quarters of a mile from the mess hall, located near the center of the town. The town is funny looking. It's all crammed together with very narrow streets. We try out the 'Pubs' but none of us can take the bitters (warm beer or ale) or the cider, (extremely sour). No dancing or singing in their Pubs. I did not see a woman in any of the Pubs. I like the USA style. We hike every morning. Then we clean equipment, clean our barracks, etc. The equipment [rifles, carbines and other gear made of metal] is packed with cosmoline [grease] and very hard to remove. It rains most of the time.

"Thanksgiving day!! Everyone agrees that we should be thankful we are Americans after a feast like we just had! Turkey, mashed potatoes, peas, carrots, coffee, bread, butter, sugar, cream, pumpkin pie and candy. My best dessert was a letter from home. My new son was born 6 Oct. and due to the intercession of Lt. Rutledge I had received a three-day pass. When I returned, my barracks bag was outside in formation with the rest of the platoon as we were loading for Miles Standish near Boston."

The day after Thanksgiving, the 81st prepared for transport to the mainland. "Trucks and mobile equipment is all new and everything seems to be smoothing out. The mens' spirit is exceedingly high. A great bunch to be with.

"Thursday was Pearl Harbor day. A few of us talk about it, but it seems so distant and so long ago. We slept in the truck for these two days so our blankets could dry and because it was continually raining. Miserable sleeping but dry! Left Friday in convoy travelling across Belgium. Nearly all the towns are destroyed but we were welcomed by everyone we met.

"On December 10, I was in an advance party to Auw. Our unit is replacing the 2nd Division engineers at Auw. Their lieutenant showed us around and we found where to place our platoons and equipment. We understand that our division is to cover a front line of approximately 25 miles. We will be very thin. We were made welcome by the enemy with a couple of rounds from their 88s.

"The snow is fairly deep in places and the ground is frozen, making digging very difficult. The 2nd Division is moving out and banter is going back and forth between the troops. The front is very quiet. The infantry troops are deployed just below this ridge [the Schnee Eifel] and we are just below the troops. It is also known as the Ardennes Forest. In any other movie it would be a beautiful place.

"Auw is a small town of about 600 (pre-war) people. It is almost on a hill with a valley between it and the front which is about three miles. Once in awhile we can hear rifle fire at night. The weather is sloppy, cold and snow about one foot deep or more, depending where you are. Lt. Woerner, Smitty, the jeep driver, Stanley, the toolkeeper, and myself stay with a German family of eight—five girls, ages 6 to 28, a lad of 12, their uncle and their mother. One tot was killed a few weeks previously by shelling. They seem aloof but that could be because of the language. At night, the Lt. and myself sleep between sheets—compliments of the German family.

"December 13 and 14 we are still working on repairing and building roads for the 422nd Regiment. The morale is very high and the men are having fun, so it seems. Pvt. Suckow wants to carry five rounds for shooting deer. Pvt. Skaggs stated he mistook a cow for a deer and shot it. It is against our policy to use other people's stock for beef or shoot one. However, it had been done, but Skaggs knows what a deer looks like since he hunts them in

Missouri where he hails from. How could one mistake a black and white Holstein cow for a deer?"

Three months after his eighteenth birthday, little more than a year after Pearl Harbor, on December 11, 1942, Richard McKee, a high-school grad from Akron, Ohio, volunteered for the army with the necessary signed consent forms by his parents.

"I enlisted in the Coast Artillery because my father George McKee had served in the Coast Artillery during World War I. I left Camp Perry, Ohio, for H Battery, Provisional Training Battalion at Fort Screven, Georgia, located on Tybee Island at Savannah. Two weeks later I spent my first army Christmas on KP. I also had KP on New Year's Eve. In May, 1944, after completing NCO School, attending gas training courses for coast artillery noncoms, I volunteered to transfer into the infantry. I was sent to Camp Atterbury to join the 106th Infantry Division. I qualified as an expert rifleman with an M–1 and became an assistant squad leader, 3rd Platoon, Company A, 422 Regiment.

"We sailed from New York on October 20, 1944. I was seasick before we even got out of the harbor. At our Fairford, England, camp, we were billeted in metal Quonset huts. We spent many hours in training marches over the hilly countryside while here. There was little physical evidence of the war. We did get a few passes into the city of Oxford. We took a train into the town, which was always filled with soldiers. There were only a couple of places to hang out. Most of the time was spent walking up and down the streets and having a few beers.

"Before a four-day furlough to London, our platoon took up a collection to purchase a radio so we could listen to the Glenn Miller band. After looking all over London, we finally found one in a little shop on one of the side streets near Piccadilly Square.

"On December 1 after a very rough crossing of the English Channel we arrived at Le Havre, France. We debarked from the ship on unsteady LCIs. Le Havre had been leveled to the ground during the invasion. There was little left standing. As we walked up the long steep hill out of Le Havre, we carried everything; full field packs, rifles, ammunition, gas masks, knives and grenades. We marched twelve miles to board trucks during a heavy downpour.

"We spent six days, from December 1 to December 7, near St. Laurient, France. We lived in pup tents in mud and rain. It rained at least once a day every day we were there. Our mess sergeant Bob Richardson was an excellent cook who had worked at the Court House View Cafe in Rochester, Indiana, before he enlisted in the Coast Artillery with me. He always saw that I had plenty to eat.

"We left that camp in trucks on the 'Red Ball Express' [an army quartermaster transport outfit largely composed of African-Americans]. The sight of miles and miles of destroyed German war material burned and dumped into the ditches gave us some indication that we were changing from training to the real thing.

"We began to sense the war in the faces of the old women and men as our convoy moved through the gloomy forests around Malmédy and St. Vith, Belgium. Bastogne was just another town as we moved on, jammed together like sardines in a can.

"Cold, soaked and frozen, no change of warm clothing was available because our barracks bags had not caught up to us. But, we fell from the trucks and took over, man for man, gun for gun from the troops of the 2nd Division. Our destination, which we reached on December 8, was an area in the Ardennes along the top of the Schnee Eifel twelve miles east of St. Vith near Schönberg."

The Schnee Eifel [snow mountain], mentioned by both Collins and McKee, consisted of a steep, thickly wooded half-mile-high ridge extended on a rough north-south line. A chunk of the West Wall, the German fortifications designed to bar invasion of the *Vaterland*, ran along the Schnee Eifel.

Pvt. Harry Martin, Jr., Company L, 424th Infantry Regiment, a soldier uncomfortable with authority, followed a bumpy military career before he arrived in the Ardennes. He was painfully shy, a child born out of wedlock, although his father after leaving town returned eventually to marry his mother. He describes himself as both physically and mentally abused in his early years. The death of his mother when he was only seven traumatized him; his father's difficulties as a compulsive gambler who rarely held a job further damaged his self-esteem.

Growing up in Plainfield, New Jersey, Martin watched newsreels in the movie theaters that showed the Japanese invasion of China, the bombing of cities and soldiers bayoneting civilians. The last image particularly horrified him. He says he can still see Neville Chamberlain, the British prime minister, returning home to proclaim, "Peace in our time." But as a twelve-year-old kid he believes he recognized Chamberlain as "weak and pathetic. I thought war was inevitable; just a question of Hitler choosing where and when."

With the coming of the first peacetime draft in U.S. history, Martin saw the clips in the theaters where American soldiers trained with broomsticks while awaiting the production of genuine rifles. When Pearl Harbor came, Martin listened on the radio to his favorite commentator, Gabriel Heatter, an early devotee of the happy-talk approach, who almost inevitably opened his broadcasts with "Yes, there's good news tonight."

Martin was anxious to sign up once the U.S. entered the war. "Every time we had assembly in high school we sang the songs, 'The Caissons Go Rolling Along,' 'Anchors Aweigh' and 'The Marine Hymn,' which was the most stirring of all. I hated school and was anxious to be inducted so someone else would make future decisions for me."

But when he went for his physical along with others from his North Plainfield High class, he nearly flunked the eye examination after the examiners discovered he was practically blind in his left eye and glasses did not correct his vision. When the doctor stamped his papers "Insufficient Vision," Martin despaired. He thought of his ancestral history that recorded family members in the Civil War, the Spanish-American War and his father in the American Expeditionary Forces in France during World War I.

To his delight, in spite of the physician's notation, he was accepted, albeit with the classification of "Limited Service." In army parlance that meant he would not be assigned to combat duty. However, he quickly discovered that the army was not the answer to his emotional problems.

"It was not long before I wanted to go home. I was afraid of everyone and everything. I was a typical Caspar Milquetoast, the fictional character the 'Sad Sack.' Oddly enough, hortatory letters from his father and warmer ones from his sister helped him persevere. And he also *liked* army chow, 'which was much better than what we had been getting at home, especially the meat which we could not afford often."

During basic training designed to mold him into a military policeman, he flopped dismally when he first tried to qualify as a rifleman. For five weeks, after supper and on Sundays, Martin received extra instruction. Over and over, noncoms drummed the phrase "Squeeze the trigger" into his head. He finally scored well enough on the range to achieve the middle level of proficiency, "Sharpshooter."

One day, a corporal dressed him down for failing to perform housekeeping duties around the barracks. Martin, having been given extra duties that exempted him from these tasks, lost control of his temper. As much to his own surprise as that of the noncom, he raged defiance. From then on, Martin says he no longer blindly accepted authority. In succeeding days, he increasingly voiced his opinions, no matter how exalted the person issuing the orders. He learned to drink excessively, chased women, went AWOL, goofed off while guarding prisoners and earned a reputation as a troublemaker.

But Martin was bored with his life and outraged by what he considered the pampering of the prisoners who refused to work if the temperature fell below a certain level and who insisted on a holiday to celebrate Hitler's birthday. When a notice on the bulletin board asked for infantry volunteers, Martin signed up.

He became a member of Company L, 424th Infantry Regiment, 106th Division. Forced to requalify as a rifleman, Martin shot so well he was upgraded to "Expert." However, he discovered infantry life even more unpalatable than his previous experience. He continued to rebel, goofing off, challenging orders and embarking on another absence without official leave. When he returned from his illicit holiday, he escaped a court-martial only because the 106th was now ticketed for overseas shipment.

There was, however, a final physical examination. At issue was his "Limited Service" classification. Aside from Martin's bad vision, what else was wrong with him, inquired the doctor. He explained, "My orders are to release only those who have two or more things wrong with them."

"He almost put words in my mouth. He said, 'Just tell me one other disability that you have and I will release you from the infantry.' He was definitely on my side and I was moments away from getting out of the infantry, which I wanted so much. I just could not give him the answer he was looking for. I think I felt guilty about leaving the men I had trained with for the last four months. The men of the 3rd Squad were the best there was. I guess I really did not want to leave them."

In England, talk among the members of the 3rd Squad focused on what lay ahead. "We all had to deal with our fears. One man in our platoon dealt with his by telling everyone he was absolutely certain that he would be killed. We would try to talk him out of it but that only made his conviction stronger.

"In the pubs we saw American soldiers wearing the Combat Infantryman's Badge, the Purple Heart and campaign ribbons. We looked at them with awe and thought, 'Look, there is a soldier who went through combat and survived.' We talked with them and asked what it was like. But none of them offered advice or told us what combat was like. It was as if there were no way to explain it. You sensed that they did not really want to talk about it.

"The one thing that scared me most was the thought of being run through with a German bayonet. The thought of that long steel blade going through my body was bad enough, but the worst part would be when he would violently withdraw the bayonet, taking my guts out. I would be left to die an agonizing slow death."

About six weeks after he arrived in England, Harry L. Martin, Jr., a soldier restricted to "Limited Duty," moved into a position formerly occupied by the 2nd Division, facing the Siegfried Line, inside the German border. He had been cheered by the report from his sergeant that this was a quiet sector where combat troops were sent to rest and "green troops like us were gradually broken in. There had been no real activity in this area for nearly three months. In this quiet sector, we would earn our Combat Infantryman's Badges and receive periodic passes to Paris. We felt we were lucky to be there."

Clifford Broadwater received his form letter that began, "From the President of the United States, Greetings," via the Selective Service Board in Washington, D.C., almost a year before Pearl Harbor, as the country began its first ever peacetime draft for military service.

Broadwater, an employee of the Retirement Division of the U.S. Civil Service Commission, entered an army desperately struggling to cope with the influx of rookies while maintaining some of its older graces.

"After a couple of days at Camp Lee, Virginia. where we were issued uniforms and equipment, attended a few training lectures and did some close order drill, we were loaded on a troop train. It had Pullman cars with upper and lower berths for sleeping at night, and Negro porters to make the beds for us. Soldiers had to sleep double in the lower berths and single in the uppers.

"We arrived in El Paso in the wee hours of the morning, just before daylight and unloaded to the sounds of martial music. The regimental band was there to greet us. Loaded into trucks, we rode to an area at Fort Bliss designated as the Anti-Aircraft Artillery Recruitment Training Center."

The Fort Bliss that now housed Broadwater was rapidly expanding. The desert had just been bulldozed level, streets laid out, a mess hall erected and tents pitched. Broadwater and his comrades lived in sixteen-foot square tents that held six men. They spent several days plucking stones "the size of our fists or smaller" from the pathways and parade grounds.

Between calisthenics, lectures or films, close order drill and training exercises, the men changed uniforms several times each day. The pay was twenty-one dollars a month with a nominal fee charged for clothes laundered by the quartermaster corps. The monotony of close order drill was relieved by the presence of the regimental band, blaring out marches that helped the recruits pick up the proper cadence.

Broadwater went through the drudgery of a three-day tour of kitchen police, did a stint with a 75-mm gun battery, worked in the supply room and at the motor pool.

"Then came December 7, 1941. I remember that Sunday, some time after lunch a number of us were playing volleyball in the street between the tents. When word came that Japan had attacked Pearl Harbor, the volleyball game sort of faded out. Active service was supposed to be for one year. We had started to make plans for what we would do after we got out of the army. Now everything was changed to an infinite tour of duty.

"Martha Coble of Jay, Oklahoma, and I had been engaged for quite some time and had tentative plans to be married after I got out of the army. Now I wrote to Martha and asked her if her mother would permit it, would she like to come to El Paso for a while.

"I sent her the money for the bus ticket. I met her at the bus depot and she said later that she had been wondering what sort of a greeting I would have, whether I would hug and smooch her or what. She says I shook her hand. I don't have a clear memory, but the shy, bashful country boy that I was, with dozens of other soldiers around, that seems likely.

"I took her to the Guest House at the training center and engaged a room for her. There I did smooch her; I remember that clearly and told her that if she was willing, we could get married while she was there. When she said yes, I made plans for the wedding.

"I had given this some thought and preparation. There had been military restrictions on soldiers getting married, so I had played it safe and asked my battery commander for a written, signed permission to marry. I had already bought her an engagement ring in Washington, D.C., that cost $35.00 and the wedding ring came to about $15. The wedding was held in the living room of some friends I had made in El Paso. I got two three-day passes with a four-day furlough between them to cover the time Martha was at Fort Bliss and our honeymoon.

"Someone suggested a trip to Carlsbad Caverns [New Mexico] and we borrowed a Buick from one of the sergeants. His requirements were that I be responsible for the car and we take his nine-year-old son along. With three of the other fellows, we became a party of six."

Following his honeymoon, Broadwater and his fellow GIs shipped out to Bermuda to furnish antiaircraft defenses. It was early in 1942 and Bermuda was classified as a war zone. Panicky authorities absurdly worried the enemy might seize the island. Broadwater was issued a Browning Automatic Rifle (BAR) with live ammunition. His assignment was to defend headquarters if it came under attack. Others from the antiaircraft battery manned machine guns from foxholes dug on the beaches.

The hastily thrown up barracks lacked heat and fresh water. The men showered in cold, salt water until the army improved conditions. Gradually, the atmosphere became more relaxed; there was time for picnics on the beaches, bicycle trips around the island and swimming.

After a year, the authorities decided no real threat to Bermuda existed and Broadwater, who had advanced to the rank of sergeant major, returned to Fort Bliss as part of the permanent cadre. He found a place in town for his wife, Martha. However, in June of 1944, the top brass concluded that fewer antiaircraft units were needed. Broadwater received orders transferring him to the 106th Infantry Division, now stationed at Camp Atterbury, Indiana.

"There I was, a master sergeant from antiaircraft artillery serving in the infantry, assigned to an antitank company of the 423rd

Infantry Regiment. I was excess rank, maybe excess person, and was to help 1st Sgt. Floyd Jesson with paperwork and details in his office.

"I trained with an antitank squad under a corporal and a sergeant. We had a 57-mm antitank gun which fired a cartridge weighing about 12 1/2 pounds. The fired projectile had a muzzle velocity of 3,000 feet per second with an effective range of maybe 500 yards. On the firing range you could stand behind the gun and see the course of the shell. Supposedly, it could penetrate four or five inches of armor plate. The German tanks had as much as seven inches of armor plate. But the gun was capable of knocking off a track and disabling a tank."

Broadwater shared one last furlough with Martha before he entrained to the staging area for the 106th Division at Camp Miles Standish. "We went to New York and loaded on the *Queen Mary* with all of our men, all of our equipment, trucks and guns included. There must have been 16,000 men on the ship." [While the *Queen Mary* was probably carrying approximately that many troops, some units of the 106th sailed aboard the *Aquitania* and the *Wakefield*.]

"I was on the fourth deck down. There was a large open area with a row of steel-pipe posts set just far enough apart for the length of a bunk. The steel-frame bunks had hinges and a canvas stretched over the frame to sleep on. The bunks were five tiers high and on the other side of the posts were another five bunks. There was a narrow aisle and during the day the bunks were lifted up on their hinges and tied to the posts to make space on the deck. Above the bunks were slatted platforms where we stored baggage."

Broadwater squeezed in a three-day pass to see the sights, London Bridge, the Tower of London, the changing of the guard. But along with Phil Hannon, Richard McKee and the remainder of the 106th, he soon found himself rolling over the Red Ball Highway, bound for the Ardennes.

"We moved in the positions and foxholes occupied by the 2nd Division. This was a 'quiet sector' and little action was expected. Our antitank company headquarters moved into a three-story duplex building in Bleialf, Germany. We had beds to sleep in.

"My watch post was at a window on the second story. My two-hour shift was in the middle of the night. A fellow I relieved said, 'See that tree out there? After a while it will go over and speak to the corner of the house.' One night one of the sentries was sure he had Germans coming in, so he fired away. Next morning they found a dead rabbit and a dead goat out there."

Alan Jones, Jr., traveled a different path to reach the Ardennes as a member of the 106th Division. "I was an army brat. My father, Alan Jones, Sr., was regular army, although not a graduate of West Point. I was born in the Philippines, where I've never been back, but we lived all over. I attended a different high school every year, finally graduating in Washington, D.C.

"World affairs were a regular topic at the dinner table and I was very much aware of what was happening in Europe. Since my father was in the army, naturally there was a lot of talk about the state of the military. It was in awful shape, particularly the army. There had been so little spent on it that my father spent seventeen years in grade as a captain. In fact, my future father-in-law, a graduate of West Point, was a lieutenant for fifteen years.

"Still, the only thing I ever wanted was a military career. But I had graduated at seventeen, too young to enter the Academy. Furthermore, I couldn't pass the eye test. So I went to the University of Hawaii for a year and did exercises to strengthen my eyes.

"I entered West Point in 1940 in what was to be the first of a series of three-year classes.[A consequence of the war in Europe that began in 1939.] I think I was well trained during my time at the Point. When I received my commission, I took a basic officer's course at Fort Benning [Georgia], then became a platoon leader in the 42nd Division.

"The word was that they were not going overseas but I knew from my dad, who had been the CO since its activation, that the 106th was bound for Europe. I wangled a transfer to the 106th in July of 1944. I don't think there was anything wrong with joining the division commanded by my father. He didn't like the idea, but he didn't oppose it either. It was my choice.

"They cleaned us out in August. We lost our cadre, and we had to scramble to get the troops through maneuvers and teach the replacements how to handle themselves. We received a lot of men from the ASTP. They were smarter than the average troops, mostly under twenty-five, and physically fit. But they were untrained in infantry tactics. [The official figures show that the 106th lost 3,145 men in April, 877 in May, 331 through June and July and then 2,894 in August.] I had been made S–3 for the 1st Battalion of the 423rd Infantry Regiment, which made me responsible for plans and operations.

"We got to England in November. We had about a month there and we could only engage in basic stuff, physical conditioning with a lot of road marches, firing small arms and rezeroing weapons. The weather interfered with much of the range work. Other than that we conducted classes in first aid, map reading and similar exercises.

"In the Ardennes, we relieved elements of the 38th Infantry Regiment, part of the 2nd Division. Along with a few others I went up five days before the rest of the battalion. We exchanged range cards [data for weapons and fixed points] and they told us what it was like. The troops deployed in dugouts that had been covered with logs for protection against overhead artillery bursts. The battalion command post and company headquarters occupied pillboxes that had been part of the German defensive system, the Siegfried line or West Wall.

"There was some snow atop the logs over the dugouts but it was not that cold. I wore a field jacket when I moved around to the different companies in the battalion.

"We were led to believe that this was a quiet area. We thought of it as a place where we would have combat training, learn to use patrols and become accustomed to a combat zone. We used much of our time to calibrate our radios and check all of our guns.

"Our major concern was to readjust some of our defensive positions. While the switch with the 2nd Division was on a man for man, gun for gun basis [at dug-in emplacements for everything from machine guns to artillery pieces, the newly arrived troops swapped their equipment for that of the units they relieved], the 2nd Division was a battle-seasoned outfit. They had accumulated many weapons not formally listed in the table of organization. As a result, they had a helluva lot more machine guns than we did. With fewer guns, our weapons did not conform to the kind of defensive arrangement that the 38th Regiment had.

"We were aware of some enemy activity. We could hear trains in the vicinity of Prüm [a town several miles behind the German lines]. Our patrols reported one or two sightings of isolated tanks but we did not notice any increase in enemy patrols. We reckoned some unusual activity on the other side, but we had no concern for any massive attack.

"We could see the enemy in the distance and they could see us.

Actually, they occupied other parts of the Siegfried line. There was a little bit of fire, sporadic rounds of artillery. We knew this was now serious business and you felt you had to sort of tiptoe around.

"Still, the word was this was a quiet area, it was our first experience on the line. People were a little uptight. We didn't know what it was going to be like."

Leo Leisse, a native of St. Louis, enlisted at the advanced age of thirty-three. "I wanted to be with my brother Robert, fourteen years younger, who had received his welcome from FDR on his nineteenth birthday. I started at Fort Jackson, South Carolina, with the 106th Division, which had just been activated. When I was on the rifle range, some guys warned me that if I qualified as an Expert, I'd be made a sniper, and that would be dangerous. But I was determined to do the best and got an Expert medal, which I prefer over the Combat Infantryman Badge because I had to earn the Expert medal, while just being there brought you a CIB.

"Our original cadre of noncoms and officers were very good but after they took away many of them to be replacements, we had mostly ninety-day wonders as officers when we went overseas. While at Miles Standish, one of my men tried dropping a large stone on his foot to avoid shipping out. He didn't hurt himself that badly but Colonel Bloom, the medical doctor for the regiment, ordered him left behind as unreliable."

Leisse was old enough not to look forward to combat. "I didn't think much about being killed, wounded or taken prisoner but I hoped everything would be over before we had to go." It was not and S. Sgt. Leo Leisse with an Ammunition and Pioneer Platoon for the 422nd Regiment reached the Ardennes along with the others from the 106th Division.

Frank Raila of Chicago, in contrast to Leo Leisse, had hardly passed his eighteenth birthday before being summoned to arms late in 1943. Son of a mailman and grocery checkout clerk, at the time the draft board selected him, Raila had finished high school and attended junior college for a few months. During the summer months he worked in a Studebaker factory which made engines for airplanes.

"I followed events in Europe, the stories about Hitler and his so-called master race. I was also aware of the situation in the Pacific. All of my peers knew about Hitler, the havoc of the war, his ruthlessness and the misery he inflicted upon people like the Jews. Some classmates left high school to enter service. When they came back, they had many stories to tell their friends. I knew sooner or later I'd be in the war."

After basic training and assignment to the 423rd Infantry Regiment's Company E at Camp Atterbury, Private Raila became a member of a .30-caliber, light machine gun squad. Following arrival in the Ardennes, he spent his first night in a hut, then moved into a tent erected at a spot where he cleared away the snow. "We used pine boughs to prop up the tent and pine needles to lie on. It gave reasonably good shelter and I lived that way for another three or four days. It was so cold, that only the roads where the tanks and trucks traveled were wet and slushy. Everything else was snow and frozen. I don't recall any hot food for us after we left England. After the stay in tents, we lived in the open."

Raila had little contact with the officers. With the exception of a lieutenant who received his Bronze Star while at Atterbury for bravery in Africa and seemed combat-wise, the others failed to impress the young soldier. "I thought they knew what they were doing, but they did not inform us of anything. We never were told where we were except somewhere in the mountainous part of Luxembourg and Belgium. We weren't told whom we replaced or that we were on the Schnee Eifel. They didn't seem to believe in communicating with the lowly dogfaces.

"I had contempt for the captain of my company when I saw he dug his foxhole next to the one of the captain from another company. Both appeared to lack leadership. They stuck together while we milled around without any direction. It seemed to me they should have been out directing us, advising us, encouraging us."

Things seemed quiet for the first week but then a mortar round blew the head off a major. "I didn't see it happen but news like that went around like wildfire. I dealt with my stress by recalling my home, my mother, father, sisters and my mother's family."

Jim Mills, born in November 1925, was raised by his grandparents in Des Moines, Iowa. When Mills reached his thirteenth birthday, his carpenter grandfather died and the family depended upon welfare, known as "relief" during the Depression days.

"I didn't pay a whole lot of attention to the war when I was in high school. We didn't take the newspaper for money reasons. I seldom went to the movies where there were newsreels. Mostly I heard about events on the radio and the only talk at home was about who was going into service, who had been killed.

"I turned eighteen in 1943 and three months later I was drafted, without even graduating from high school. Later, I received some credits for basic training to fulfill my high school requirements and was awarded a diploma after the War, in August 1945.

"After basic training at Camp Fannin, Texas, I joined the 106th Division at Camp Atterbury, where we were given additional instruction, spending two weeks in the field, two in barracks. I was not turned into a Rambo but I felt like I was a good soldier who could do what was required of me in combat. Hitler and his soldiers were running over everybody and it wouldn't be long before he would try to take the U.S. I thought we were good enough to beat the Germans and that I was with a good bunch of men."

Mills was assigned to Company I, 1st Platoon, 3rd Squad, 423rd Infantry Regiment. He had been trained to use the M–1 (Garand rifle issued to infantrymen), BAR, machine gun, bazooka, mortar, bangalore torpedo, flame thrower, plastic explosives and grenades. He was named assistant BAR man for the squad, which meant he carried ammunition and was expected to use the weapon if the GI designated as BAR man became incapacitated.

"Our company commander was a West Pointer and as GI as they come. We stood inspection every night in Atterbury and that was kind of a joke with the neighboring companies. But the captain did his best to see we were good soldiers."

Company I entered its Ardennes positions on December 8, occupying dugouts constructed by the troops it replaced. "These dugouts were made of logs, mostly underground, and mounded over with dirt. Each dugout held several men with bunks for sleeping and a potbellied heating unit. One corner of the dugout had gun or vision ports on both sides of the corner where we took turns all night keeping a lookout for German patrols or whatever. There was a blanket hung behind the lookout to close out light so we could see better and no light could escape, revealing our position.

"We did not know at the time but we were atop the Schnee Eifel. There was a valley in front of us and similar mountains across the valley facing us. There were firebreaks through the pines on both mountains.

"We were served hot meals from a chow line set up between

two trees, fairly close to the firebreak. We were green troops and the front in our area seemed quiet until men started to line up across the firebreak to get chow. About the second time this happened, a German tank pulled out into the firebreak on the opposite mountain. A few well placed shots messed up our chow line and prevented any further careless crossing of the firebreak.

"Cans were strung out on wires well in front of the dugout to pick up movements of German patrols trying to get through our lines. Too much shooting from any one dugout gave away its position in the dark and drew return fire.

"[One day] Captain Moe, the CO of Company I, ordered 2nd Lieutenant Blodgett, 1st Platoon leader, to take a patrol during daylight hours to see where the Germans were and see if we could obtain any information. The patrol was made up of Blodgett, Sgt. Elmer Shipman, Pfc. Robert Widdicombe and myself. There was snow on the ground and we were in olive drab uniforms so we used tree cover as much as possible.

"We got almost to the crest of the opposite mountain. There were mounds of dirt and straw with dummy poles stuck in the side to look like gun emplacements. As we got close to these dummy gun emplacements, we were spotted and drew small arms fire.

"We immediately started to withdraw and Lieutenant Blodgett instructed us to get out of the woods. We started walking through a snow-covered clearing near another woods, back deeper in no man's land. As we were crossing the clearing, mortar shells began coming down all over the woods we had just left. Meanwhile, the woods were booby-trapped. The lieutenant saw wires just under the snow and grenades tied to the trees on each side. We followed our footsteps and returned safely to our lines.

"I was on guard in our dugout at 5:30 A.M. on the morning of December 16, 1944, when all hell broke loose. For a minute I thought the world was coming to an end."

At Stalag 9B Ed Uzemack of the 28th Division (hatless, holding paper at center), Denny Murray (hatless at Uzemack's right shoulder), and Jack Dunn (eyeglasses, center)—three former newspapermen—produced the POW Daily News Bulletin. *(Courtesy Ed Uzemack)*

S/Sgt. Jack Agnew, Pathfinder team of the 506th Parachute Regiment, 101st Airborne stands in the back row, third from left. His buddy, Jake McNiece is in the front row, second from right; Lt. Schrable Williams, the squad's CO is in back row, far left. *(Courtesy John Agnew)*

Pvt. Jim Mills, Co. I, 1st Platoon, 3rd Battalion, 423rd Infantry, 106th Division, saw "all hell break loose." *(Courtesy James Mills)*

At nineteen, 1st Lieutenant Lyle Bouck already had served for two years. *(Courtesy Dr. Lyle Bouck)*

Pvt. Frank Raila, Co. E, 2nd Battalion, 423rd Infantry, 106th Division thought the German searchlights "made a pretty sight." *(Courtesy Dr. Frank Raila)*

Pfc. Philip Hannon, 1st Platoon, Co. A, 81st Combat Engineers, 106th Division, "could not believe anything bad could happen to us." *(Courtesy Philip Hannon)*

S/Sgt. Richard Byers, 371st Field Artillery Battalion, 99th Division, earned a battlefield commission as a 2nd Lt. *(Courtesy Richard Byers)*

Scout Carmen Capalbo of the 99th Division was among the first Bulge casualties. *(Photo © Maggie Hopp)*

Cpl. Jerry Nelson, Co. C., 40th Tank Battalion, 7th Armored Division, a gunner on a Sherman tank, knocked out three enemy panzers in the space of a few minutes at Poteau. *(Courtesy Gerald Nelson)*

S/Sgt. Bill Dunfee, Co. I, 505th Parachute Regiment, 82nd Airborne Division, jumped in Italy, France and the Netherlands but rode a truck to the Ardennes fighting. *(Courtesy William T. Dunfee)*

Pfc. Cy Blank, 492nd Armored Field Artillery Battalion, 11th Armored Division (front row, second from right), received a modest farewell from family and friends at the railroad depot after enlistment. *(Courtesy Seymour Blank)*

Pfc. Alan Shapiro, Co. C. 346th Regiment, 87th Division, was rushed into the Ardennes. Eight days later he was evacuated with frozen feet. *(Courtesy Alan Shapiro)*

Top Left:
1st Lt. Eric Fisher Wood, Jr.,
Battery A, 589th Field Artillery
Battalion, 106th Division, prepped
at Valley Forge Military Academy.
(Courtesy Eric Fisher Wood, III)

Top Right:
Wood graduated from Princeton
in 1942, where he played varsity
football. *(Courtesy Eric Fisher Wood, III)*

Bottom Left:
On the eve of the German
breakthrough, Lt. Eric Wood wore
the garments Belgian villagers
described as belonging to the U.S.
officer who swore to wage "his
own war." *(Courtesy Eric Fisher
Wood, III)*

Schuyler Jackson, who became a demolition expert for the 502nd Parachute Regiment, 101st Airborne, wore a football-style helmet before his very first jump and was not yet entitled to tuck his trousers into his boots. *(Courtesy Schuyler Jackson)*

S/Sgt. Francis Currey, Co. K, 120th Infantry Regiment, 30th Division, wears his Congressional Medal of Honor earned for valor near Malmedy. *(Courtesy Francis Currey)*

T/Sgt. Joe Colmer, Co. F, 325th Glider Regiment, 82nd Airborne Division, fought in the defense of Baraque de Fraiture, a strategic crossroads. *(Courtesy Joe Colmer)*

Pvt. Harry Martin's weak eyesight did not keep him from a front line position in the Ardennes with the 424th Infantry Regiment.

Major Abe Baum, 10th Armored Infantry, 4th Armored Division, took a task force 40 miles behind the German lines in a near suicide mission to liberate a prisoner-of-war camp. *(Courtesy Abe Baum)*

Lt. Dee Paris, Co. A, 14th Tank Battalion, 9th Armored Division, commanded a platoon of light tanks. *(Courtesy Demetri Paris)*

Top Left:
Leonard Weinstein, as a replacement, was "volunteered" into the 325th Glider Regiment and fought at Baraque de Fraiture. *(Courtesy Leonard Weinstein)*

Top Right:
1st/Sgt. Ben Nawrocki, Co. B, 1st Battalion, 393rd Infantry, 99th Division, helped defend the vital Elsenborn Ridge. *(Courtesy Ben Nawrocki)*

Bottom Left:
Obersturmfuhrer (1st Lt.) Horst Gresiak led a company of tanks that routed the Americans, including Joe Colmer and Leonard Weinstein, from the crossroads known as Baraque de Fraiture. *(Courtesy George Winter)*

Chapter II

CHECKERBOARDS, INDIAN HEADS AND THE BLOODY BUCKET

As NEWCOMERS TO THE former German West Wall in the Ardennes, the 106th Division occupied a jagged strip of territory roughly twenty-eight miles in length. Those in charge realized that the 14,000 troops were spread somewhat thin. However, in the mind of the Twelfth Army Group Commander, Gen. Omar Bradley, it was an acceptable risk under the circumstances.

The Golden Lions, of course, were not the sole soldiers facing the enemy across a narrow no man's land. The 1,400 men of the 14th Cavalry Group, a highly mobile outfit but ordinarily not armed heavily enough to provide a stalwart defense, guarded the left flank. Their specialty lay in reconnaissance and combat patrols characterized by light, darting attacks.

However, to the north of the 14th Cavalry was an almost mirror image of the 106th, the 99th or Checkerboard Division (so dubbed because of their shoulder patch design). It too was packed with people drawn from the ASTP and flushed out of the army air corps cadet programs or ground crews. But the 99th had come on the scene nearly a full month before the 106th. Unlike the Golden Lions, many men had already come under fire and in some instances tasted combat.

Carmen Capalbo, born in November 1925, grew up in Harrisburg, Pennsylvania. His grandfather had emigrated from Italy around the turn of the century and had been a teacher there. But in Pennsylvania he eventually started a bakery that soon thrived. Capalbo's father had worked for the family business and later owned a grocery store but died when his son was only twelve.

"I was a very close student of what was happening in Europe. As a boy in the 1930s, I remember getting up early in the morning to listen with my father and grandfather to Adolf Hitler on the radio, even though none of us spoke German. In civics and history at school, we spent a lot of time on the excesses of the dictators in Europe. Mostly it was Hitler and Mussolini. We were aware of the Japanese in China but that was more removed. Until Pearl Harbor we just didn't pay much attention to the Far East. The local newspapers were good and they reported regularly on world events. At the movies we saw newsreels that covered the leading players. We regularly tuned in to the news on the radio.

"My father had been a theater fan. He had taken me to see an Italian touring company and the minute I saw the actors, their makeup under the footlights, I knew what I wanted to do with my life. I wanted to direct plays. People would ask me what I wanted to be when I finished school and I would answer, 'a director.' They would look puzzled and ask, 'You mean of a bank?' Nobody knew about theatrical direction in those days.

"I was also a big radio freak. While I was still in high school, I became a regular radio drama producer on a local station. By the time I graduated from high school, I had produced and directed one program than ran for four years and another for two. One show was aimed at adults, a kind of "Twilight Zone" type of drama. The other was called "The Children's Playhouse." My grandfather, even though I had been groomed to take over the bakery business, was very supportive. By proxy I considered myself a protégé of Orson Welles.

"When I graduated from high school, I was still seventeen and I figured I had about six months before I would be in service. There was such a shortage of civilian manpower that radio stations couldn't staff operations. I took a job at the new station in York doing news production. I commuted from my home in Harrisburg. At the same time I put on shows at the military camps in the area.

"Harrisburg was a center of military activity. The Harrisburg Academy had been taken over by the Army Air Force. There was a big installation at Indiantown Gap, the home of the 28th Division, and another at the New Cumberland Reception Center. I produced shows at these places and got to know many of the Special Services officers. I assumed that when I did go into the army, I'd be assigned that kind of work.

"A few months after my 18th birthday I was drafted. The Special Services operations were being broken up and I was shipped to Camp Wheeler, Georgia, for seventeen weeks of basic training as an infantryman. I finished in the summer of 1944 and then joined the 99th Division at Camp Maxey, Texas. I was assigned to the First Platoon, Company A, First Battalion of the 395th Regiment.

"Most of the guys had either been in the ASTP or would have gone to college except for the war. We weren't a bunch of fuck-ups but neither were we a lot of Rambos. We did a lot of reading.

"We left Massachusetts for Europe on September 29. The voyage lasted 13-1/2 days. It was a converted tanker. I've never been so seasick in my life. The sight of Scotland, the Firth of Forth, was so beautiful after nearly two weeks at sea.

"We spent about a month at Dorchester, England, and then with our barracks bags beside us, slept for a night on the Southampton docks before boarding ships to Le Havre.

"We took off across France, jammed into open trucks. Going through the narrow streets of one small town at night, we thought it was raining on our heads. But it was the local citizens emptying their chamber pots on us and it wasn't all liquid either. When we went through Belgium, however, the people generally welcomed us.

"We passed through Malmédy, then entered the woods to replace units in the 9th Division. Our outfit was walking up one side of a road and they were coming down the other side. I'll never forget the visual difference. There was something in their eyes I can't describe. Some people talk of the 1,000 yard stare. What I saw was the look of combat. These guys were the same age as we were but they seemed 100 years older. I realized then that we were facing something different. There weren't many words exchanged, maybe a yell of the usual 'You'll be sorry,' but that was about it.

"We moved into their former positions, well-built bunkers that could hold from six to eight guys. The mouth of the bunker formed a Y shape, made out of two foxholes where we stood guard.

"The snow was very deep, particularly where it drifted on the road or in the woods and snow fell nearly every day. It was hard to avoid becoming snow-blind. The forests had that Germanic quality, everything neatly planted in perfect rows except for where an artillery blast tore up things.

"During our first days on the line there had been absolutely no activity. We had not seen any of the enemy, there had been no firing. Intelligence reports said that it had been this quiet even before we arrived. One day in mid-November, I was lead scout of a patrol led by the company commander, Captain Martin. We were a squad of maybe a dozen men and moved out along a dirt road north of our position and which ran east and west. If you stood on that road and looked up it, after about 1,000 yards it began to climb in a gentle rise to end with the horizon.

"We were to cross the road, swing through the woods to a fire-break that intersected the rise in the road and see if there was any activity in a large clearing that lay beyond. As the scout, I was in front. When it came time to cross the road, I plunged into snow-drifts well over my head. It was hard to breathe and when I tried to see in the wall of snow, I felt myself surrounded by colored lights. I climbed out, and everybody followed.

"Jack Little was the guy right behind me as the second scout when we started through the firebreak. The other men behind were deployed in a kind of semicircle in the woods. We reached a point where I could see this big open field, maybe fifty yards across to another woods. I turned to the captain to indicate that I didn't see anything. But I motioned that I would go a bit further.

"There was a big puddle of water in the pathway of the fire-break and I sort of daintily tiptoed through it, trying to keep my feet from getting wet. I reached a spot where a huge tree, perhaps fifty feet in length had fallen. I hit the ground behind it and peered over the tree trunk.

"My heart stopped! Coming out of the woods across the open field, I saw my first German. Then more and more, a never-ending column, until there may have been fifty of them. To me, it looked like the whole German army. It was a big raiding party and they were wearing white, snow camouflage uniforms. I ducked down and yanked Jack Little down with me. I signaled to the captain about the situation. Meanwhile, Little seemed ready to open fire; he unlocked the safety on his M–1. I grabbed his wrist. With my eyes I told him not to fire or we'd be wiped out.

"The Germans approached in a pyramidal shape. In the lead was a machine gun team and out on the wings I saw two more machine guns. The man in charge looked to me like a master sergeant. The troops did not seem to expect trouble. Their rifles were all slung and we could hear them talking, even laughing.

"Suddenly, the sergeant stopped, like a pointer who spots a bird. He threw up his arm. Instantly, there was dead silence. They must have been straining their eyes and ears to detect something. He lowered his arm and ordered the group to continue forward. They tramped another ten or fifteen yards when he yelled and everyone hit the ground. He moved forward and shouted at his machine gun crew. They ran up to the edge of the firebreak, parallel with us. They couldn't have been more than thirty-five or forty yards away from us. The machine gun units that had been on the wings of the pyramid also rushed up. There was an order to fire and all hell broke loose.

"But they never saw Little or me on their right flank, and they couldn't see the others from our outfit down the slope behind us. We had full cover and we wiped out the first machine gun crew. Because we were behind that big tree, the sergeant couldn't figure where the fire was coming from. When he sent up a second machine gun crew, we got them too.

"All our guys behind us were also firing but they couldn't see anyone either. The only ones able to see what they were shooting at were Little and I. The whole thing lasted maybe five or ten minutes. Ultimately, they retreated. They must have thought they had run into the entire American army. When they disappeared into the woods, Little and I pulled back on our bellies. I crawled through that puddle that I had so carefully avoided when going forward. Our guys were delighted when we showed up. They figured we'd been wiped out. Nobody on our side was even scratched. Later, I was told they found eighteen to twenty German bodies in the field.

"We came back to our positions and I was called in to headquarters, which was in a barn, to report. Until that moment in the barn where I described what had happened, I had not been aware of fear. But inside the command post, where they had an iron stove for heat, I began to shake like I had never shaken before.

"Fear was different than anything I had anticipated. I never thought of myself getting killed. Somehow, you get to believe that with the tremendous force behind you, you'll come through. In fact, my greatest fear was that I'd have to kill somebody. To me, taking another human's life was very troubling. What had happened up on the edge of the firebreak was that the training took effect. We did exactly what we were supposed to do. It's like the moments before one goes on stage when you have all that fear.

But once you get on stage, everything falls into place, the rehearsals pay off. I've talked to hundreds of actors, and not one of them ever was aware of fear one second after hitting the stage. You become so focused on carrying out the job that your awareness becomes different.

"Somebody told me this was the first actual combat for the 99th although it may have been only the first for my regiment. But whatever, the division commander, Gen. Walter Lauer pinned a Bronze Star on me and the captain for what we had done. We were credited with holding our fire to a point where we could ambush them, rather than the other way around. Jack Little did not receive any award, though he certainly deserved one.

"Success has its down side. After that, anytime there was a patrol, I was asked to lead it. I went out five times in a row. We were on a big reconnaissance sweep about ten days later. As we moved through a large field, a friend of mine tripped a booby-trap wire. He was thirty yards away from me when I saw his body thrown up in the air like a rag doll. He was dead when he hit the ground. The fellow next to him was badly wounded. The medic applied first aid and six of us began carrying him on a stretcher back to our lines, where we had radioed ahead to have an ambulance ready. When we were about a hundred yards from the ambulance, we paused for a rest. Some color came back into his face and he smiled. 'I'm fine,' he said. We were encouraged and told him to hang in there. In a few minutes we reached the ambulance where there were medics and a doctor. 'Thank God, we made it,' we said as we turned him over to them. The doctor, a captain, looked at him and said, 'This man is dead.' We were appalled. It had happened in the space of a few minutes. These were the first deaths on our side."

While "Cap" Capalbo and his associates were being blooded, other elements of the 99th also sampled combat. The 394th Infantry Regiment occupied positions along the southernmost territory defended by the Checkerboard outfit and adjacent to the 14th Cavalry. Among those involved here was the Intelligence & Reconnaissance Platoon of the 394th, under the command of twenty-year-old 1st Lt. Lyle J. Bouck, the second youngest of his eighteen-man squad up on the line.

"We were a really poor, Depression family. My father was a carpenter but there was no construction work. We moved around a lot when I was a kid and lived in houses without indoor plumbing or electricity. There were five kids and we lived in places with only one bedroom. We didn't always have enough to eat; we picked berries, ate dandelions. We didn't think anything of it. We thought everyone lived that way.

"I went to a number of different schools and I did not pay much attention during classes. But when I was in the fifth grade, I was not promoted with the other kids. They went ahead without me and that changed my attitude. I was embarrassed and disappointed. I started to work hard at my books. I'd stay up half the night to do the work and you can't believe the grades I got with the same teacher. Since then, I never had an academic subject I couldn't handle. That was a turning point in my life. I became extremely competitive. I became eager to achieve.

"In 1938, shortly before my fifteenth birthday, my father arranged for my brother and me to attend a two-week encampment of the St. Louis National Guard. The idea was that we would receive meals and get paid a dollar a day. When it was over, I heard that if you joined the Guard, you drilled once a week and got paid thirteen dollars every three months, which was a lot of money to us then. My father had been in the National Guard during the 1920s and he knew people in it. They weren't so fussy about who joined then and they bent the rules to let me in at my age.

"I was a little, skinny kid and I think my father arranged for someone to look out for me. I was assigned to the supply room, where I folded blankets and counted canteens. The training we received was good but there was a lack of equipment.

"I didn't pay any attention to what was going on in the world. On December 20, 1940, they called our outfit to active duty. I was still only seventeen but nobody paid any attention to that. My father wanted me to get out but I proposed that if he'd let me stay in, I'd finish high school when we were demobilized after a year.

"We went to Camp Robinson for training and they made me supply sergeant. I didn't think I was ready for the responsibility but the CO said let's try it. As a buck sergeant I was getting paid sixty dollars a month. Pearl Harbor came before our year was up and I stayed with the outfit. Ten days after Pearl Harbor, on December 17, I celebrated my eighteenth birthday.

"From the start, as an underage kid in the Guard, I had thought officers were special people. Now that I was eighteen I was eligible for Officer Candidate School. I applied and my CO recommended me. I had to falsify my application. I claimed I had four years of high school but I had only two.

"I graduated from OCS at Fort Benning, Georgia, on August 26, 1942. The system was in high gear. A class would graduate at 10 A.M. after seventeen weeks and at 2 P.M. the bunks would be filled with a new class. A new group arrived just about every day. The practice at Benning was to keep the top ten percent of each class to expand the infantry training cadre. How I managed to rank fourth in my class, I'll never know. But I was able to stay at Benning for two years, which gave me an opportunity to mature, to develop physically, mentally and emotionally. I learned how to deal with line infantry troops. I also developed some self-confidence. When I first became an officer at Fort Benning, I would take a roundabout route to my classes so that I could avoid meeting other soldiers where I would have to take and give salutes.

"A colonel took a liking to me and asked if I'd like to go through an advanced course. I accepted the offer and I was the only 1st Lieutenant among a group of field officers [ranks above captain through full colonel]. I also took a three-month course at Fort Hood, Texas, which was a Basic Infantry Officer Training Center.

"I was now a company commander under a regimental CO who was a screamer and behaved crazy. At a meeting, we heard that four 1st lieutenants were wanted to serve with the 99th Division. All four of us at the meeting volunteered and so I joined the 99th at Camp Maxey.

"I served as weapons platoon leader and then a company executive officer. The regiment went on maneuvers and the Intelligence & Reconnaissance platoon screwed up so badly that the regimental commander was relieved. The new CO fired the S-2 [Intelligence officer] and ordered his replacement, Maj. Robert L. Kris, to create a new I & R platoon.

"Kris had been wounded and awarded the Silver Star while serving with the 9th Division in Africa. After rehab, he volunteered for another combat outfit. Kris retained four guys from the original I & R unit and sent the rest to rifle companies. I happened to be the range officer on a 1,000-inch machine gun range the day after another lieutenant had run it very badly. I had studied the manual at Benning and when I issued some orders, Kris questioned me about them. I explained my reasons. Shortly afterwards, I got a call from him asking me if I would take over the I & R platoon. He told me he wanted this to be a handpicked unit.

"Kris and I became good friends as we put together the platoon. We looked for guys who had at least a high school education, were athletic, superior IQs, good marksmen. I interviewed about ninety soldiers before we settled on the thirty-two designated by the table of organization. We were down to twenty-four men by the time the Bulge broke out. [Half a dozen of these were occupied with duties away from the main body of the platoon.]

"A number of the group came from the ASTP and they were already disgruntled when removed from a rifle company to the I & R platoon. But the fellows we chose fitted in well. The ASTP men worked out fine. You could tell them something once and they were smart enough to get the point.

"I was 'military friendly' with the enlisted men but not buddy-buddy. My platoon sergeant, Bill Slape, was not a popular guy. He took no nonsense and he took stuff off my back. Slape got the job done. I had said we would become a well-disciplined, well-trained, physically fit bunch and we did with special exercises. We even ran maneuvers where we put some guys in German uniforms just to increase awareness during training.

"Bill Tsakanikas was nineteen, the only guy younger than I. He was very aggressive, always quick to volunteer and I used him as a scout and messenger. Corp. Aubrey McGehee was a big strong former tackle at LSU, a real tough guy. Jordan 'Pop' Robinson at thirty-seven was the oldest. Risto Milosevich, somewhat of a wild man, and Vernon Leopold, a refugee from Germany, were both from the ASTP.

"We arrived on the line the first week in November, replacing people from the 9th Infantry Division. Our I & R platoon manned observation posts and went on patrols. Kris and I took a combat patrol to Losheim to bring back prisoners. We brought home four of them and killed a gang of Germans in the process. The regimental CO chewed us out for taking chances but Kris was gung ho; he wanted to show the troops that it could be done.

"Around December 10 we moved to Lanzerath into prepared positions. The snow on the ground amounted to a few inches and the temperature, in the low thirties during the day, fell into the twenties at night with a sharp wind. Early mornings there would be a cold fog. We took over foxholes that accommodated two to three men. The positions lacked coverings but we added six- to eight-inch pine logs for protection. We dug out a place for a jeep with a machine gun. Our total fire power consisted of sixteen M–1s, two carbines and two .30-caliber machine guns.

"About 300 yards back we had a log cabin where anyone not on post could sack out. We got mail daily and a jeep brought us hot food twice a day. It seemed like a quiet zone. We operated the observation post round-the-clock. The Germans were firing V–1 rockets over our positions toward Liège far to our rear. The area was known as 'Buzz Bomb Alley' and we recorded azimuths as they passed overhead. To find the source of the rockets, we ran a patrol that penetrated eight miles into their territory. Then we watched our artillery blast away at the targets.

"I knew that the 106th had replaced the 2nd Division on the Schnee Eifel. I was aware that the strategy called for the 2nd and the 99th to attack with the objective of capturing four dams on the Roer River. I was advised that the Germans might counterattack and our mission was to serve as the eyes and ears for Division and keep in touch with the 14th Cavalry Group, which belonged to a different corps, on our right flank. They had some antitank guns and machine guns as part of their defenses. I made contact with them and so we settled into waiting and watching. Right in the town of Lanzerath in front of us, a field artillery observation team occupied a house.

"The night of December 15 started out routine. We had a couple of guys scheduled to take R & R at Honsfeld, where they'd have hot meals, showers and Marlene Dietrich was coming to put on a show December 17. The chow jeep came up with hot food and some mail. I had received my monthly liquor ration. I didn't drink, so I passed it out for the entire platoon to share. I sent back Carlos Fernandez to help draft some maps and Vernon Leopold, who had developed a case of trench foot. We heard a lot of clanging, banging and screeching of machines. We reported this to regimental headquarters."

Between the territory manned by the 395th to the north and the 394th to the south, stood the 393rd Regiment of the division. "We relieved the 9th Infantry Division troops on November 8, 1944," recalled Company B Platoon Sgt. Ben Nawrocki, a native of South Bend, Indiana, and a defense plant worker until his induction, "The foxholes and gun emplacements were really spread thin with gaps between squads, platoons, companies and other units. We had no reserve. All our men were up on the line. We were overextended in terms of a good defensive position. But the 9th Infantry guys [relieved by the 393rd] did a good job on the foxholes. They were two-men type with a slit trench adjoining and covered with pine branches and logs to protect against the weather and artillery.

"The defense line was at the edge of a wood along the International Highway, an inviting artillery target. There was quite a lot of snow and the trees were covered as well as the ground. The terrain was bad. The field of fire began with the International Highway but then it dropped into valleys studded with wooded corridors, the Siegfried line laced with barbed wire, dragon teeth concrete tank barriers, pillboxes and forts with protective crossfire. The area was heavily mined.

"It was cold, hard to keep dry and warm. We had to keep our toes moving or they would freeze. We wore a pair of socks around our stomachs and exchanged them daily. We slept with our shoes on and during the day we would take them off, rub our cold feet and change socks. Men stood on pine boughs and straw. Trench foot became a big problem. We lost quite a few men that way.

"From the first of December until December 16th, our patrols and troops reported heavy movement in front of us, even though the enemy muffled wheels and horses' hooves with straw. This was all reported back to headquarters but over the field phone we were told, 'The kids are seeing things.' The reporting went on for two weeks and no artillery or mortars were fired."

Another Midwesterner who wore the blue and white Checkerboard patch on his uniform was Dick Byers, born and raised in East Cleveland, Ohio. He graduated from Shaw High School, which he credits with an excellent English department, giving him a "better grounding in the English language than most college kids of today.

"I remember being at the dinner table and hearing of Hitler's invasion of Poland and the start of World War II. My father stated emphatically that Roosevelt would never get us into a war."

Byers came from a family of Anglophiles that listened nightly to the British Broadcasting Company and the reports of Ed Murrow recounting the Battle of Britain. While rooting for the British, Byers took a date to see the British comedienne Gracie Fields. As a high school student he had even delivered a book report on an article printed in the *Reader's Digest*, "The German Soul—The Sword." His distaste for the Germans was also heightened by an exchange student from there, "an arrogant Aryan who bragged about his military training and lauded Hitler."

After high school, Byers earned a paycheck in a defense plant but then blew his deferment in favor of hitchhiking around Ohio, Pennsylvania and West Virginia. He happened to be browsing in the phonograph record department of a Cleveland store when he listened to FDR's "Day of Infamy" speech, December 8, 1941.

"I tried to enlist in the U.S. Army Air Corps but my teeth weren't good enough, so I went next door to the Royal Canadian Air Force recruiting office. They said, 'Hell, we don't expect you to bite the Jerries!' " But he was too tall at six-four to meet their standards.

Resigned to waiting for the call from the draft board, Byers labored on a dairy farm for several months. He built up his body on chores during the day, then tore himself down nights, carousing in the local bars.

The army assigned him to the 371st Field Artillery Battalion of the 99th Division then being formed at Camp Van Dorn, Mississippi. "Early in training I was made acting or lance corporal, probably because I shouted marching commands louder than most of my companions. I had newfound self-confidence after taking the AGCT test [military IQ exam] and learning that I was well qualified for Officer Candidate School. Then I made full corporal until spring 1944, when I passed over sergeant to become staff sergeant, chief of detail section (responsible for land surveys to locate gun positions on maps). My applications for OCS and ASTP had been accepted shortly before the quotas were drastically cut on the premise that the war would soon be over."

Instead, he sailed with the Checkerboards for Europe. With the 99th in England, Byers wrote home about the picturesque scenery, the night flights of British bombers and his visit to Piccadilly Circus.

"At night the 'Piccadilly Commandos' come out into the blackout and innocents like me have to fight for their honor! They're there by the hundreds! The sidewalks are crowded with 'Commandos' accosting soldiers and trying to proposition them. 'Five pounds ($25) to spend the night; two pounds ($10) to go in a taxi; one pound ($5) to go into the alley.' You damn near have to knock them away. Several times I was grabbed by the arm and had to fight like hell to save myself from a 'fate worse than death!' At first it is amusing but eventually the novelty of their brazenness wears off. Some of them are quite nice looking and that makes it seem even more revolting. Most GIs will forget the beauty of England and the suffering and terror the English have gone through and remember only the whores in Piccadilly Circus. It is unfortunate."

Byers had become a member of a forward observer team by the time his outfit crossed the Channel and trucked to the Ardennes. "Six days were spent in the rear echelon around the guns, at battalion headquarters or doing odd jobs and just loafing. One day I borrowed an M–1 and went deer hunting through the woods and along the railroad tracks between Hünningen and Buchholz Station. I didn't see any signs of a deer but I learned the most direct route between the two places. That knowledge was invaluable a few days later.

"From the house in Hünningen we commuted east to the front and manned an observation post overlooking the town of Losheim. We happened to be right beside, in the middle and on top of the notorious 'Losheim Gap' through which the Germans poured armies that invaded Belgium in 1914 again in 1940 and finally once more in 1944. The road we used crossed the border into Germany. Naturally, the first time we entered Germany, we all lined up on the side of the road and christened the German soil. We were very careful to stay on the blacktop because we heard an infantry major had taken part in a similar ceremony a few weeks before. He stepped on a land mine and his helmet with the gold oak leaf still lay there beside the road.

"Our nighttime quarters in Losheimergraben, a crossroads village, consisted of half a duplex house, part of a small development of modern units. We assumed these were second homes, belonging to more affluent Germans, judging by the quality of the furnishing and two fur coats left behind. We used the sleeves of them to make mittens. The house still had most of the amenities, beds with mattresses, silverware, china, glasses and cooking utensils. Papers we found, indicated it belonged to Herr Fritz Rehn. There was a photograph of him in a German officer's uniform.

"While we manned the OP, one man stayed behind and prepared the evening meal. We supplemented our 10–1 rations [boxes with food to feed ten soldiers for a day] with cabbages and onions salvaged from the garden. Using the stove and bake oven, we came up with some unusual side dishes. My specialty was grinding biscuits and tropical chocolate together, into either a chocolate pudding or a cake, depending on how much clean water you were able to melt from the snow.

"After our evening meal we read, wrote letters or played cards using the jeep's headlight. We removed it nightly, hung it from the ceiling and wired it to the battery of the jeep outside. At times we enjoyed telephone music. Someone in Cannon Company had a radio. They would pick up Axis Sally's broadcasts and put them out over the phone lines to the various Cannon Company outposts. The guys next door let us patch into their phone lines and share the music. Everyone was so hungry for music and the sound of a female voice, even hers.

"On December 7, 1944, I wrote home about the comforts of our quarters. 'At first we thought living in a house was the height of luxury; then living in a house with furniture was it; then sleeping in a bed was it; then eating on a table with linen, silver and china was it; then having electric lights was it; then music via telephone was it. But now we have IT! We have a bathroom, a nice clean little bathroom with a big mirror, prints on the wall and artificial flowers in the window but that is not IT. In this bathroom is IT— an honest-to-God white porcelain toilet that actually flushes when you pull the chain! That is IT—a thing dreamed of by all our GIs as they bare their behinds to the bitter breeze and shiver in the snow. The lieutenant tells me I am to be recommended for an Oak Leaf Cluster on my Good Conduct Medal for accomplishing this miracle.' " Byers restored the fixture to working order with some deft improvisations of pipes and melting snow from the roof.

"For years afterward, the sheer hedonism of having the luxurious facility so near the front lines bothered my Puritan conscience and gave me twinges of guilt that I had been responsible for starting the Battle of the Bulge by tempting the Fates for having it too good!"

For all of his seeming insouciance, Byers was not totally carefree. Referring to the working toilet, he noted, "No longer would we have to use a thundermug or a hose out the window at night [when impelled to use a latrine] to avoid bumping into a Jerry patrol nosing around the house in the dark. We did not post sentries but depended upon the infantrymen around us to keep 'the Little Green Men' away. We had no real way to lock the front door and [because of] the things we heard go bump in the night, many nights I lay tense in my 'fart sack' with eyes and ears straining and a cocked .45 in my hand, waiting for the door to burst open."

Behind the 99th Division in December stood one of the most veteran combat organizations of the war in Europe, the 2nd Infantry Division. The men who wore its oversize Indian-head patch on their shoulders had battled from Normandy to the current positions on the Siegfried line occupied now by relief from the 99th and 106th. In the ranks of the 2nd Division was Charles MacDonald, probably the youngest company commander of World War II.

Charles MacDonald sprang from a line of South Carolina farmers. He, however, hated the life of a farmer and broke away from it as soon as possible. In fact his first escape came at age four, when he accompanied an older sister to school, decided he preferred that environment to the farm and enrolled at that tender age. Continuing to accelerate his education, MacDonald finished high school in three years and graduated from Presbyterian University in 1942, shortly before his twentieth birthday. Commissioned an officer as a result of his ROTC studies at Presbyterian, MacDonald immediately assumed command of a rifle company. At age twenty he received his captain's bars.

As a replacement officer, MacDonald took over Company I, 23rd Infantry Regiment, 2nd Infantry Division at the beginning of October 1944. On the third of that month, MacDonald and his men crossed the border into Germany, about twelve miles east of the Belgian town of St. Vith. As he nervously prepared to reconnoiter the positions his outfit would assume in place of elements of the 28th Division, his communications sergeant warned, "For God's sake, hide those damned captain's bars." MacDonald quickly stripped off the silver emblems of his rank so attractive to enemy snipers.

In succeeding weeks MacDonald coped with his tendency to tremble during artillery barrages, gradually won acceptance from his men and learned the tactics employed during a kind of stand-off. While several of his troops had been wounded, none had been killed. On December 10, headquarters informed him of an imminent assault upon the Roer River dams. The attack was to be so secret, the men were instructed to remove their trademark shoulder patches. Company I prepared to pull out and move north.

"It had begun to snow when our relief appeared the next afternoon. My men were amazed at the appearance of the men from the incoming unit. They were equipped with the maze of equipment that only replacements fresh from the States would have dared to call their own. And horror of horrors, they were wearing neckties! Shades of General Patton!"

On the front lines, south of the 106th Division, another veteran and hard-hit outfit, the 28th Division manned positions along the Luxembourg-German border. It too started its trek towards Germany in the heavy fights through the Normandy hedgerow country. Probably no infantry division endured a worse stretch in the Huertgen Forest during November than the 28th. The shoulder patch, a red keystone, denoted the origins as the Pennsylvania (the Keystone State) National Guard unit. Because of the casualties endured by the division, the insignia became popularly known as "the bloody bucket."

Like a battered boxer between rounds, the 28th during the respite from the Huertgen battles and mid-December, sought to regain its strength. Its ranks began to fill up with fresh infantry replacements from the States. Training exercises taught the newcomers infantry maneuvers and integrated them into platoons and squads. The veterans relished hot showers, hot meals, clean new clothes. There was R & R in the Luxembourg towns and cities amid civilians who joyfully welcomed their presence.

Among those who had survived Normandy and the Huertgen Forest was T. Sgt. John Chernitsky, a member of the antitank company in the 110th Infantry Regiment. A boy from a small "patch"—Juniata, Pennsylvania, a company town built and run by the company that mined coal and produced coke there—he was an early member of the 28th.

"In 1939, the Pennsylvania National Guard was recruiting, 'Join now and get your year in service before being called up in the draft,' which was being organized by Congress. I joined the National Guard shortly after graduating from high school. I made trips each weekend to the armory in Connellsville and was schooled in close order drill and other army procedures. The National Guard was called up on February 17, 1941. My antitank company was mustered into federal service with the rest of the 28th Division.

"We started to receive supplies but we still did not have a 37-mm antitank gun which was supposed to be our basic weapon. Our training started in improvising with a truck axle and a pipe fastened onto the middle of the axle, pieces of sheet metal cut to be used as shields on both sides of the pipe and two other pieces of pipe welded to the axle with hinges so they could be spread out for what appeared to be a 37-mm antitank gun. Dragging the gun behind a weapons carrier made more noise than a bunch of tin cans would on the back of an automobile after someone was married. When we got to Indiantown Gap with three of these dummy guns, the rest of the regiment tagged us 'Captain Scott and his Clang-Glangs.'

"We took our dummy guns and some of the dummy rifles that we cut out of wood, to make believe we had rifles, from Indiantown Gap to the Carolina maneuvers. While there, three 37-mm guns were delivered to the company. The dummy guns were loaded on a weapons carrier and delivered to the nearest junk dealer.

"In a large field in North Carolina, Congressman J. Buell Snyder of Pennsylvania had come to visit the troops from his district and we held a regimental review. The Congressman brought a recorded message from President Roosevelt. I'll never forget the conclusion of that address. 'No American boys will set foot on foreign soil. I hate war, Eleanor hates war' (and most of the boys added later, 'and Fala hates war')."

The maneuvers over, trucks began rolling north to home base. "On the night of December 7, 1941, we pulled into a bivouac area at A.P. Hill, Virginia. Someone had a portable radio and heard that the Japanese bombed Pearl Harbor. While traveling through the South, we Yankees were not treated too politely. The Southerners didn't appreciate Yankee soldiers floating around the South. But on December 8th that all changed. On this day, we got hot coffee, cakes, doughnuts and people couldn't treat us any better because from now on we were the soldiers who were going to protect them."

A year and a half after listening to FDR's pledge, Chernitsky stepped off a boat and placed his foot on the foreign soil of England. There he and his comrades spent seven months before the division landed in Normandy, two days after the beachheads established on June 6. By the 12th of the month, the troops of the 110th had met the enemy in bitter combat.

They fought their way through the heart of France. "Orders came for the division to assemble on the outskirts of Paris. The Free French Army was already in the city. The Allied Command decided to celebrate the freeing of Paris and the 28th Division marched twelve abreast through the Arc de Triomphe on the Champs Élysées. This was August 29, 1944.

"The Germans continued to retreat before us, with occasional skirmishes. But now we moved so fast that the antitank men slept on the trucks as they rolled. A couple of guys would stay awake as lookouts. We finally paused when we arrived at the Luxembourg border with Germany."

One day, Lt. Gen. Omar Bradley, who had actually commanded the 28th Division for a period in 1942 but now reigned over the entire Twelfth Army Group encompassing all U.S. European ground forces except those in Italy, accompanied by a captain serving as his aide, showed up in a jeep near the Siegfried line. Chernitsky recalled, "Evidently, they were lost and when they stopped to check their map pretty close to our gun positions, I approached the jeep. The general saw me and, miffed by my failure to accord him his due, asked, 'Don't you recognize who I am?' I answered, 'Yes sir, I do but we're having trouble with snipers in the area. If I salute you, you're a dead bastard.' Just then a sniper fired; everyone hit the dirt but the captain. He was hit, wounded in the shoulder. We maneuvered for cover and the general was now more appreciative of my behavior."

Then came the orders for the 28th to attack through the Huertgen Forest. "I had never seen such destruction to forest land. The German artillery kept firing at the tops of trees and artillery bursts hit the trees. The shrapnel fell just like rain and the artillery was constant—day and night. Very noticeable in the Huertgen Forest was the movement of medics and ambulances. When they had a chance, they picked up the dead. The German losses were heavy also but we could never figure out what happened to the Germans who were wounded or dead. We could hear screaming and cries for help but the next morning we couldn't see any wounded or dead.

"The only dead German I can't forget is one who infiltrated into our platoon area. I was lying in my slit trench and heard a movement outside the trench. I asked, 'Is that you, Proud?' (The runner for our platoon.)

"I heard, 'Yeah.' The voice didn't sound familiar, so I lay and listened for more movement. It wasn't long until a hand came down over my trench. The hand began to feel around my neck. I already had my .45 in a firing position and I saw the outline of a helmet, a German helmet. I fired up through his helmet and he fell into my slit trench. His knife was in his hand. I got help to take his body out of my trench, rolled it over to the side. The next morning, the body retrievers took his body away. I gathered up more leaves from the forest, cleaned out the blood left in the slit trench and didn't sleep very easily after that for the next week or so. I learned to recognize voices and, to this day, the least little movement, even around my home, wakes me at night."

Ed Uzemack, unlike Chernitsky, came to the 28th Division as an infantry replacement and at age twenty-nine was old enough for draftees now entering service within weeks of their eighteenth birthdays to have referred to him as "Pop" had he not been gifted with a boyish face.

"I grew up on Chicago's South Side, a blue collar district that to old-time Chicagoans is better known as 'Back-o'-the-Yards.' [Stockyards for the city's slaughterhouses.] The first six grades of my education were completed in a Lithuanian parochial school, where I learned to speak English almost as a foreign language.

"After transferring to a public school, I went on to high school and eventually Northwestern University's Chicago campus for training in journalism. I dropped out after four years of night school classes when I became a reporter for the tabloid *Daily Times*, 'Chicago's Picture newspaper.'

"As a budding journalist, who had also taken a college-level evening course in international affairs, I was very much interested in following the pre-World War II events in Europe and other parts of the world. I was an avid reader of newspapers even as a teenager. I often worried about the potential destruction of civilization, predicted by some, in the event of another world war. I wondered why the League of Nations was so ineffective and why Hitler was able to rise to power. Mussolini's growing strength also concerned me, although at first I thought he was a clown.

"I was able to express concerns through some of my assignments at the *Daily Times*. I participated in the newspaper's exposure of the German-American Bund and its youth camps in the States. On an undercover assignment, I joined a Chicago-based Bund, attended and then wrote about a celebration of Hitler's birthday with my Nazified fellow members at the German-American Alliance headquarters on the city's North Side. I also handled a number of other undercover assignments dealing with Nazi efforts in the U.S. My interest in what was happening was further stimulated with work on a newspaper column, 'Your Boy in the Service' and features on training, draft boards and similar stories.

"I was drafted just as my newspaper career reached new heights. I was a regularly bylined feature writer and I resented the interruption of what was shaping up as a very promising future. Later, I learned my local draft board would have granted me a deferment if my city editor had not foolishly tried to go over their heads with an appeal to the state selective service office for an exemption. To add to my unhappiness at going into the service, my bride was pregnant with our first child when I first put on a uniform in July, 1943. I didn't see my son until he was already seven months old. And the next time I saw him was eleven months later.

"After basic training I spent six months learning the skills of a radar crewman. But immediately after D-Day, June 6, 1944, any GI who had not received his second stripe as a technician was reassigned to the infantry for packaging as a rifleman replacement. I went overseas in September, 1944, with a group of 200 guys like me. We spent a few weeks in England for some brief training and reequipment.

"The packet of guys was shipped to a replacement depot at Omaha Beach in Normandy. The first thing we saw after landing at Omaha Beach was the vast array of white crosses marking the graves of the GIs killed during the D-Day invasion. With seventy-four other guys, I was assigned to the 28th Division. The second lieutenant, who acted as CO of our packet and put on a good tough guy show in ordering us around aboard ship and in England, flipped his cork as we were being assigned in small segments to the various frontline units that needed replacements. Screaming and raving about not wanting to die, etc., he was taken away by medicos, presumably for psycho evaluation. We never saw him again.

"The packet I came up with was dumped about midnight on Halloween in the Huertgen Forest with Company B of the 110th Infantry. We slept on our shelter halves that night, as ordered. When roused at dawn, I found I had placed the head part of my shelter half on a pile of feces. There were bodies of Germans killed in action scattered throughout the area we temporarily occupied. I learned that the division had enemy on three sides; we came darn near being completely surrounded.

"As we moved out on some prearranged schedule, I soon got

into the habit of watching for snipers in the treetops, as did the combat veterans guiding us. At one point I slipped on the wet ground and fell to my knees. I felt somebody reach under my arm to help me up and heard him ask, 'Are you all right, soldier?' As I turned to answer, I saw a general's stars on the man's helmet and was amazed to see the cigar in his mouth as he grinned. He was Gen. Norman Cota, the division commander. Later I would see him in combat areas several times.

"We spent the night in previously dug foxholes after being instructed to prepare to move out before dawn with only light combat packs. It was still fairly dark when we moved into an orchard and spread out. Despite orders not to, we lit cigarettes and smoked them with cupped hands to shield the glow. Suddenly, all hell broke loose. The Jerries had zeroed in on the orchard and were lobbing mortar shells and artillery fire in a continuous barrage that lasted about forty-five minutes.

"The green replacements suffered the heaviest casualties. More than half were killed or wounded. The veterans were calling to the men to keep their heads down and follow as they crawled towards the direction from which most of the shellfire originated. Although my newshawk instinct was to look and see what was going on, my many weeks of infantry training, some of it under live ammunition fire, reminded me to do as the veterans commanded. Unfortunately, not all of the replacements had similar training before being shipped overseas.

"A GI crawling ahead of me had both his legs blown off by a shell that landed on his limbs. Another shell hit so close to me that I could feel the heat on one side of me as it exploded and my ear buzzed. I kept crawling towards where I thought the shells were coming from and eventually left the orchard with the survivors, mostly combat vets. A sergeant told me to round up the guys who had come with me as replacements. I told him I didn't even know who the hell they were, but I would do my best. Somehow I managed to find about half a dozen totally frightened replacements, and suddenly I realized I was just as scared as they were. But that morning we became combat vets. I received my Combat Infantryman Badge, effective December 1, 1944, after several more weeks of fighting in that miserable forest.

"My fear throughout seemed to be mingled with curiosity about what was going to happen. I remember seeking comfort and freedom from fear during artillery barrages and combat forays by reciting the Twenty-third Psalm, repeatedly. I remember praying often for my safe return to my family, and if it so happened that I would be killed, to experience at least once more, a dry, warm room and one bright light bulb over my head to overcome the black, soggy, cold nights in the foxholes before I died."

As the third week of December 1944 began, Ed Uzemack and the others from Company B manned positions overlooking the Our [Sauer] River. "German soldiers were located on a height on the other side, doing pretty much what we were on our side of the river, hanging out personal laundry to dry, trying to see what was happening across the river."

The assaults through the Huertgen Forest gained little ground and cost the Americans heavily. According to Chernitsky, "God only knows what saved me and most of my platoon. We were ordered back to Luxembourg. The division had called for noncoms to start a noncommissioned officers' refresher school. There had been so many casualties and so many men were promoted to ranks of corporal and sergeant in the field without having understanding of the duties for noncoms. I was picked for an instructor. We were sent to Wiltz to begin the instruction. It was December 14."

Cheek to jowl of Ed Uzemack's B Company, D Company, the heavy weapons unit for the 1st Battalion of the 110th Infantry, included Lt. Harry L. Mason. An ROTC student with two and a half years of college, Mason put on army olive drab via the draft almost nine months before Pearl Harbor. "Not until we entered the war did I give the Germans any thought at all," he admits.

He considered the long training period adequate but nothing could prepare one for the reality of combat, "a hard way to make a living. I knew anything could happen, but not to me. Nobody dwelt on dying, we only hoped our luck would not run out."

A soldier who survived Normandy, Huertgen, the Bulge and close to 100 additional days of fighting, Mason appraised his immediate superiors as a mixed bag. "Some were good, some were marginal—we called them 'Colonel Comforts' because they came to us from higher headquarters to enable someone up there to be promoted. My men, a good cross section of the U.S., were the best. There was never a problem; they did what they were told with very little complaining.

"I lived through the war, so I was able to receive many decorations. My men were at least equally deserving. However, on one occasion I turned in a recommendation for a Bronze Star to an ammo bearer during the Normandy fighting. He went out of his way to put his machine gun in action after both the gunner and assistant gunner went down. Our general rejected the recommendation, saying, 'It was just a good soldier doing his part.' During this action that soldier had been killed by a shell fragment.''

Like Uzemack and Chernitsky, Mason narrowly escaped death in the Huertgen Forest. Acting on orders, he organized a force that included about 100 raw replacements and led them in an assault that recaptured a hill from which another company had been driven. ''We fought off small German counterattacks while receiving heavy artillery and mortar fire most of the time.'' In the end, the operation came for naught as Mason and his troops evacuated the position. ''I lost some of my oldest and best soldiers on that hill. I was put in for a Silver Star but in forty-seven years I haven't heard anything further about the medal.''

Although by the time he arrived in the Ardennes Mason had endured a number of ferocious battles, he maintained an even emotional keel. ''I didn't hate the enemy. I just tried to do what was expected of me as best I could. Under fire I naturally felt fright at times. However, with time you become dull, weary and lose your feelings.''

On December 16, Mason's machine gun platoon occupied positions in the small village of Grindhausen. ''We didn't expect an attack but we were almost always ready for anything with our guns prepared and in position.''

Two other major American outfits also directly faced off against the Nazis. The 4th Infantry Division, which waded ashore at Utah Beach on D-Day and then participated in the Huertgen Forest campaign, had perhaps twenty-five percent of its original complement when its Company M, 3rd Battalion of the 12th Regiment settled into the Luxembourg village of Dickweiler in the Ardennes.

Marcus Dillard, an 81-mm mortar gunner for Company M who grew up in Anderson, South Carolina, had been six weeks shy of his nineteenth birthday when he arrived at Utah Beach. ''I had followed events in Europe for several years. I had volunteered for the service immediately after I graduated from high school, but I was told I was too young.''

Like so many GIs, Dillard did not often speak of the possibility of death with his buddies. "We did talk about being captured and the favorite line was, 'Maybe I'll get that million dollar wound and be sent to the rear.'"

On the landing craft ferrying him across the English Channel on D-Day, Dillard was more seasick than scared. He actually felt better once he left the boat. He quickly adjusted to the need to hit the dirt or find cover when under fire. "I dealt with stress by praying a lot. I thought and believed the only thing that could bring me through now was to pray to God. Many, many of my comrades did the same."

In Dickweiler, Dillard and his associates bedded down in houses. The GI kitchens dished out three hot meals a day. Everything seemed quiet.

Also within small arms distance of the enemy were components of the 9th Armored Division. With the exceptions of the 1st and 2nd Armored, the mechanized U.S. divisions were organized into combat commands. These functioned in the fashion of semiindependent regimental combat teams. Because of their mobility these units frequently operated separately from their brother outfits. The 9th Armored featured Combat Command A, CCB and CCR, the latter ostensibly the reserve unit. For the 9th Armored, CCB, in the standard table of organization included the 14th Tank Battalion, the 27th Armored Infantry Battalion and the 16th Armored Field Artillery Battalion. In addition, there were engineers, medics, cavalry reconnaissance troops and a smattering of other detachments.

The 9th Armored Division's CCB deployed mostly toward the north, behind the 2nd and 99th Divisions. CCA ventured south; it owned the 60th Armored Infantry, plugging the gap between the 4th and 28th Divisions. CCR resided in the middle of the Ardennes, not far from the town of Bastogne.

Although back of the front lines, a number of heavyweight U.S. entities spotted throughout the Ardennes, like the 28th Division, were slowly refilling their depleted ranks, or else, like the 106th Division, awaiting their summons to an offensive that would sweep across the Rhine.

Chapter III

THE TEN PERCENT POSSIBILITY

THREE MONTHS AFTER D-DAY, June 6, 1944, Allied troops crashed out of the tenous beachheads on the coast of Normandy, knocking the German armies back to the prewar borders of the Third Reich. The first Free French forces rolled into Paris on August 24. The U.S. Third Army under Gen. George S. Patton drove up the middle of France. By September 11, the Allied Army troops from Operation Dragoon, which put men on the Mediterranean beaches August 15, had linked up with Patton to create a continuous front. American GIs had already begun to reside in portions of the Siegfried fortifications, whose vaunted impregnability was of a piece with that of the vulnerable French Maginot Line.

On the Eastern Front, Soviet armies applied unceasing pressure upon the *Wehrmacht,* chewing up men and materiel in enormous quantities. From the air, U.S. and RAF planes rained bombs upon German military installations, cities and towns. The explosives blasted and burned factories, railyards, supply depots and civilians without surcease. On clear days, travel along open roads or by rail during the daylight hours risked murderous thunderbolts from the sky.

While the Allied advances on both fronts frequently encountered fierce resistance, the capacity of Hitler's Germany to hold out much longer seemed doubtful. The satellite nations, Finland, Rumania and Bulgaria, read the future. The Finns broke off relations. The other two actually turned their armies against Germany. Hungarians and Yugoslavians could be counted upon only so long as Nazi armies held guns at their backs. The Allies began to plot masterstrokes that might end the fighting before Christmas.

On September 16, 1944, top German military leaders met with Adolf Hitler for the daily discussion of the war situation at his East Prussian headquarters, *Wolfschanze* (Wolf's Lair). Der Führer, a

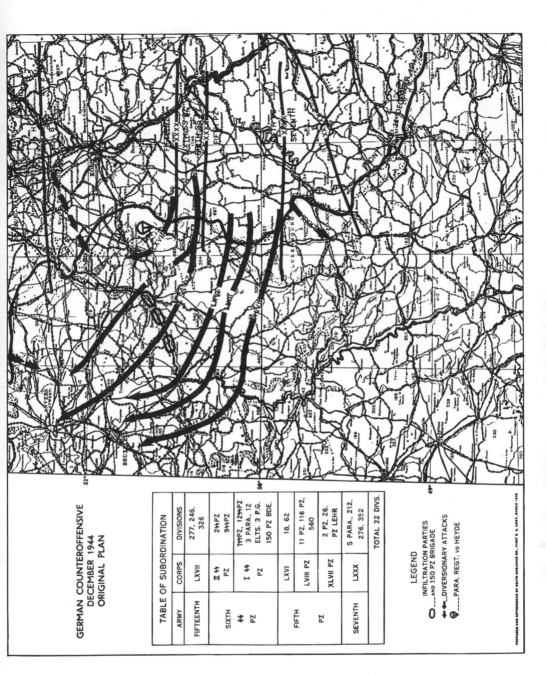

GERMAN COUNTEROFFENSIVE
DECEMBER 1944
ORIGINAL PLAN

TABLE OF SUBORDINATION		
ARMY	CORPS	DIVISIONS
FIFTEENTH	LXVII	277, 246, 326
SIXTH SS PZ	II SS PZ	2 SS PZ, 9 SS PZ
	I SS PZ	1 SS PZ, 12 SS PZ, 3 PARA., 12 ELTS. 3 P.G., 150 PZ BDE.
FIFTH PZ	LXVI	18, 62
	LVIII PZ	11 PZ, 116 PZ, 560
	XLVII PZ	2 PZ, 26, PZ LEHR
SEVENTH	LXXX	5 PARA., 212, 276, 352
		TOTAL 22 DIVS.

LEGEND
0 ----- INFILTRATION PARTIES AND 150 PZ BRIGADE
----- DIVERSIONARY ATTACKS
----- PARA. REGT. vo HEYDE

The original strategy conceived by Adolf Hitler, despite the misgivings of his top generals, called for the Sixth SS Panzer Army to drive through the Ardennes across the Meuse River to the Belgian city of Antwerp. The Fifth Panzer Army, operating on the Sixth left flank, would sweep over the Meuse as part of the pincers aimed at Antwerp. A less ambitious scheme envisioned the two armies bridging the Meuse and taking Liege. The Seventh Army's mission through Luxembourg was to seal off American reinforcements from France, to the south. The parachutists were to seize crossroads and delay U.S. units on the northern flank.

corporal during World War I, had never allowed his lack of instruction in classic military tactics to interfere with his self-taught strategic concepts. While his ignorance and inexperience dismayed his generals, the absence of a military background endowed Hitler with the ability to propose the totally unexpected.

To his astonished minions at *Wolfschanze* he announced, "I have just made a momentous decision. I shall go over to the counterattack, that is to say," as he indicated on a map, "here, out of the Ardennes with the objective Antwerp."

The grandiose plan envisioned a sweep that would cross the Meuse River and culminate in the capture of the Belgian port. The British 21st Army Group, to the north of the Ardennes, which included the Canadian expeditionary force, would be cut off and face another Dunkirk. A second evacuation like that of June 1940 could eliminate England as a serious factor. The staggering defeat might then induce a negotiated peace, enabling the Nazis to turn their full attention to the Communists in the East.

Historians point to Hitler's announcement at Wolf's Lair as evidence of his unswerving self-confidence (note his use of the first person pronoun) even after the abortive attempt to blow him up in July had cost him full use of his right arm and impaired his hearing, as well as a number of highly competent officers executed for their alleged participation in the assassination plot. As a student of history, again the product of a selective autoeducation, Hitler frequently cited incidents in the past where a single, spectacular coup changed the course of events.

Celebrated for exploiting the limited vision of opponents and his genius at discerning the vulnerable seams among *realpolitik* partners which he translated into a divide and conquer strategy, Hitler saw a victory in the west as far more than a military success. He could not accept that such disparate parties as the Western democracies and the Soviet Communist dictatorship could maintain an alliance based only upon resistance to Nazi Germany.

He lectured his generals, "Never in history was there a coalition like that of our enemies composed of such heterogeneous elements with such divergent aims . . . . Ultracapitalist states . . . ultra-Marxist states . . . If now [we] can deliver a few more heavy blows, then at any moment this artificially bolstered common front may suddenly collapse."

His reference to "a few more heavy blows" was prophetic in that the almost unchecked Allied advance that had begun with the breakout at St.-Lô on July 25 subsequently had degenerated into a series of counterpunches, several of which severely bloodied the attacking forces. Only one day after that meeting at *Wolfschanze*, a huge aerial armada left airfields in England to drop thousands of British and American paratroopers and tow gliderborne units into Holland. The daring scheme of the nominally cautious Gen. Bernard Montgomery to outflank the West Wall and open up the shortest route through Germany to Berlin turned into a disastrous defeat. Inadequately supplied and undermanned, the operation, dubbed "Market-Garden," leveled heavy casualties on the two best-known U.S. airborne divisions, the 101st and 82nd and nearly destroyed the best of their British counterparts.

The thrust through the thick woods of the Huertgen Forest had gained no turf and left the 28th and 30th Divisions badly mauled. And in the Ardennes itself, the 4th Division a few days before Hitler announced his plan took a licking along the Schnee Eifel.

In spite of these setbacks for their adversaries, however, the German high command was all too aware of the weakening of their own armies and the massive power they faced. Field Marshal Karl Gerd von Rundstedt, the crusty patrician Prussian who refused to humble himself before Hitler, had been reinstated as commander in the West. When he was informed of the audacious stroke planned by the former corporal, he growled, "Antwerp! If we reach the Meuse, we should go down on our knees and thank God—let alone trying to reach Antwerp!"

But Hitler, firm of faith in German destiny and the strength of his people, still believed the nation could rise on his command. Furthermore, in spite of the blizzard of ordnance from the skies, the country's production of things like planes and tanks had actually increased. During the September in which he revealed his plan, the factories rolled out 3,031 single-engine aircraft, 170,000 rifles, 27,000 machine guns, 1,000 antitank guns, 321,000 tons of munitions and 2,500 tanks. Fuel shortages were of far greater concern than any other lack and, for all of the achievements, limitations of ammunition hampered operations. Widening the draft to include older and younger males, combing out staffs and supernumeraries among what the dictator called "rear area swine" and boosting the workweek to sixty hours added manpower—ten million were under arms—albeit the troops of late 1944 were less effective than those who first followed the call to war in 1939. And in the months after that September, the toll exacted by the Allied aircraft had begun to reduce armament output.

The choice of the Ardennes as the point of his great strike was not arbitrary. Moves through the Ardennes were a tradition with German armies. They had struck through the Ardennes into the heart of France first in 1914 and again in the 1940 *blitzkrieg* that ended with the Germans triumphantly astride the shores of the English Channel. On the other hand, the Allies seemed to regard the Ardennes as unpromising for their forces, adopting the view expressed by Marshal Ferdinand Foch, Supreme Allied Commander of World War I, who described the terrain as "an almost impenetrable massif." Laying plans for the assault upon Germany in 1944, the Allied strategy plotted attacks north and south of the Ardennes, rather than directly through it.

There were valid reasons for generals to regard the Ardennes as unsuitable, in spite of its previous history. The turf, honeycombed with thick forests, slashed with deep gorges cut by swift coursing streams, and pimpled with precipitous hills, seemed inhospitable to a modern armored offensive during the cold, rainy, or snowy days of winter. The 1914 and 1940 onslaughts occurred during drier periods, summer and late spring. Fog, mud and ice would seriously interfere with operations. A U.S. officer who fought there described the days as filled with "a white darkness." Furthermore, the major roads of the Ardennes ran north-south, rather than east-west, hampering the swift passage of motorized units.

While the high command staff in the personages of Field Marshal Wilhelm Keitel and Gen. Alfred Jodl, out of fear and bereft of personal battleground experience, accepted the extravagant design decreed by Hitler, those in the field sought to scale down operations to something within the range of reality. But their objections were brushed aside and, except for some tactical changes, the basic plan remained.

Three German armies would be involved along a seventy-mile front. The Sixth Panzer Army, commanded by Joseph "Sepp" Dietrich, a boozy, up-from-the-ranks comrade of Hitler dating back to the 1920s, would hit in the north, bursting through the defenses of the U.S. 99th Division and parts of the 14th Cavalry Group.

The Fifth Panzer Army, under Gen. Hasso-Ecard von Manteuffel, a classically trained officer favored by *der Führer* for his previous successes, would strike through the middle of the Ardennes, over land held by the 106th Division and the battered 28th Division. And to the south, the Wehrmacht's Seventh Army would move out against portions of the 28th, elements of the 9th Armored and 4th Divisions. The Seventh's mission was basically to block any attempts to rush reinforcements to the beleaguered U.S. troops under attack by the Fifth and Sixth Panzers. At jump-off, the Germans expected to hurl nine divisions, including three armored ones, well over 100,000 troops, against considerably fewer Americans, thinly spread out with no strong reserves behind, like a crust over soft snow.

Hitler has been granted credit for divining strategy that launched the Ardennes attack against thinly held positions manned by inexperienced troops. But this is nonsense. When Supreme Commander Dwight D. Eisenhower stuck his finger on the map in September, not even a spy in Allied headquarters could have known the disposition of particular forces three months off.

Germany's evil genius also benefitted from several other factors not in his power to acquire. The German generals, including the crafty Field Marshal Gerd von Rundstedt, who had been reinstated as commander in the West, contended that the entire scheme would fail if the Allies continued their mastery of the skies. Hitler and the *Luftwaffe* chief Hermann Goering assured von Rundstedt and company that the Nazi airplanes would protect the men on the ground and their resupply. It was an empty promise. Sustained air support was beyond the capacity of the petrol-short, pilot-thin *Luftwaffe*.

The thrust into the Ardennes, however, had been postponed from its original date of November 1 several times. It was finally fixed for mid-December, when flying weather turned unusually bad. As a consequence, both reconnaissance and tactical sorties by Allied airmen were severely curtailed. (The series of delays for a period of six weeks further weaken any notions that Hitler possessed knowledge or insights into the nature of the Allied lines in the Ardennes.)

The Germans took great pains to conceal plans and operations from those seeking to divine intentions. The Nazis first designated the strike as *Wacht am Rein* (Watch on the Rhine). To even gossip about it was to risk execution. But the code name when detected by the various enemy intelligence outfits suggested a defensive strategy along the Rhine.

All movement of troops and equipment, borrowed from the

Eastern Front and Italy, occurred by night. That not only protected trains from aerial attack but it also concealed the shift of forces. Discussion of *Wacht am Rein* or *Herbstnebel* (autumn mist), a name later adopted by the military commanders, via radio was *verboten* because such messages could be intercepted. Only telephone and hand-to-hand communications were permitted.

Although it was inevitable that some information on the changes of scenery for Nazi troops and gear reached the Allies, the secrecy helped screen the German intent. But the failure to discern the strategy also stemmed from the rapid advance of the Allied soldiers and the absence of serious challenge by the *Luftwaffe* to airmen. Few seriously believed that the Germans could possibly mount any massive attack. Most were convinced they were hunkering down for a final, futile defense of the homeland.

Into the mix, Hitler tossed one more unorthodox element. On October 27, he summoned to *Wolfschanze*, SS *Hauptsturmführer*, (Lt. Col.) Otto Skorzeny. Ostensibly, the six-foot four-inch Skorzeny, his face scarred from student duels with a sabre, was to receive *der Führer*'s personal praise for leading a task force that drove Hungary's regent, Adm. Nicholas Horthy, from power after Horthy signed a separate peace with the advancing Soviet armies.

Otto Skorzeny, for all his notoriety as the archetypical Nazi officer, had neither a strong military background nor long-term membership in the party. In fact, he was not a German, but, like Hitler, an Austrian. As a young man he had developed something of a reputation as a playboy. No one considered him an ideologue; his passions centered on things like auto racing, women and getting ahead in his construction business.

When World War II broke out, Skorzeny was thirty-one and his size as well as age disqualified him when he volunteered for pilot training. At his relatively advanced years, he became an officer-cadet posted to an SS outfit. He continued to resist the mold. "I saw how some of the 'regulars' sinned against the fine human material that is brought to them, how stubbornly they bent the individual will and crushed personality. It seemed to me the reverse was what was needed for the tasks which a soldier in modern war can carry out."

He demonstrated to superiors an innovative mind. When called on to devise ramps strong enough to carry tanks aboard ships during the occupation of Holland, Skorzeny, drawing on his construction background, devised the appropriate plans. Instructed that the local people would only manufacture the ramps at the point of a gun, Skorzeny instead persuaded them to cooperate with rations of schnapps and chocolate. On the other hand, his betters were far less happy when he subsequently requisitioned some needed tires from a supply dump with a threat to assault the depot.

In April 1942, Skorzeny received his baptism of bloody fire. He served with the invaders of Yugoslavia and earned a quick promotion to first lieutenant after he ambushed a much larger number of enemy troops and convinced them to surrender. The entire campaign in Yugoslavia lasted only ten days but two months later the Germany armies headed east. Skorzeny's commanding general at the briefing for his officers announced, "Within a few weeks we will parade in Moscow."

The first few days, the *blitzkrieg* churned on schedule. The invaders raced huge distances, 300 miles into the Soviet Union in a single week. They captured staggering numbers of prisoners, more than one million in successive drives at Minsk, Smolensk and Kiev. But somewhere on the way to the Moscow parade, the enemy rallied. Counterattacks at Smolensk bogged down the German advance. Casualties began to deplete the ranks; shortages of food, water and ammunition afflicted the strung-out lines of the Germans. And then winter smashed into them with all of its Tartarian fury.

Skorzeny now sought to cope with an unceasing blizzard of horrors visited upon his men, enemy soldiers and civilians trapped in the bitter, give-no-quarter butchery. The troops, lacking cold weather gear because of the optimistic expectations, shivered and battled frostbite while dynamiting tanks out of the ice. Skorzeny credited his dueling experience with giving him the strength to survive psychologically.

"I was . . . grateful for the self-discipline we learned in our student clubs. I never felt so bad under the sharp eyes of my fellow students. My knowledge of pain, learned with the sabre, taught me not to be afraid of fear. And just as in dueling you must fix your mind on striking at the enemy's head, so, too, in war. You cannot waste time feinting and sidestepping. You must decide on your target and go in."

Skorzeny spent eighteen months practising his self-discipline in the face of an implacable foe that seemed not to count its losses. "You go into Russia, win tremendous victories, advance hundreds of miles. Prisoners flow back, an endless river of humanity with one guard to five hundred of them. The fields and forests are a graveyard of captured tanks and vehicles left to rust.

"When you retreat . . . they all rise up to meet you . . . Thousands of prisoners slip away into the forests. New leaders cross the lines to them by night. Abandoned guns and tanks are secretly patched up. A host of special troops are dropped from planes, skimming the snow, careless of broken limbs, they jump by moonlight without parachutes. And so there is a striking force where none was before."

In December 1942, only a few weeks after Pearl Harbor and the German declaration of war against the U.S., a wounded Skorzeny left the Eastern Front to recuperate in Vienna. He wore an Iron Cross for his bravery, and the medal issued to every single German soldier who had survived the first, ghastly winter in Russia.

Impressed by the elite British commandos with their dramatic raids, Hitler had decided to create his own *kommandos.* The German high command regarded such special forces with the traditional distaste of a well-organized bureaucracy for any kind of independent, unorthodox unit. The usual search of dossiers turned up the name of Otto Skorzeny as a candidate to lead the unit. As an officer seemingly without powerful champions to interfere with their prerogatives, Skorzeny was an acceptable choice to the generals.

Skorzeny set up a training base and zealously pursued information on weapons and tactics from the best teachers available, the British commandos. He studied their equipment, seized when agents who parachuted onto the Continent were captured. He pored over their documents on espionage and methods of communication.

Meanwhile, the German hierarchy kept Skorzeny and his men on a very short leash. They denied his suggestions to adopt innovative, higher tech weapons better suited to commando style operations. They bottled up proposals for raids. He could only continue to train his men and await an opportunity.

In July 1943, Skorzeny received an abrupt demand to appear at the East Prussian headquarters of Hitler, *Wolfschanze.* This was to be Skorzeny's very first meeting with the Nazi chief. Ushered into the august presence along with five others, all superior in rank, Skorzeny on request briefly recounted his career.

Hitler now asked what each officer knew of Italy and the

Italians. When Skorzeny's turn came, he mentioned that he was an Austrian. Something in the commando leader's attitude or his ethnic background evoked a positive reaction from Hitler. He dismissed the others and proceeded to lay out a mission for Skorzeny. After a preamble about his relationship with Mussolini, Hitler explained that his Axis partner had been overthrown and arrested. It would be Skorzeny's job to rescue him before treacherous Italians surrendered him to the Allies. The entire affair was, of course, to be top secret, and Skorzeny would serve under the command of paratroop chief Kurt Student.

Weeks slipped by while Skorzeny, Student and their intelligence operatives sought to pinpoint Il Duce's place of detention. After a number of false starts he was located at a small hotel on Gran Sasso, the highest of Italy's Pennines Alps. By the official and Skorzeny accounts, the penetration of the secrecy surrounding the hiding place required great guile and derring-do. Others have suggested that the simple medium of bribes in the right places supplied the vital information.

The actual rescue involved 100 German soldiers, ninety of whom were drawn from General Student's paratroopers. The remaining ten included Skorzeny and men from his outfit. According to the publicized accounts, the terrain forced the gliderborne troops to crash land on a small rocky slope near the hotel. Skorzeny was aboard a glider that pancaked onto the ground. However, while one group of men relied on gliders, two others, using the funicular, simply climbed Gran Sasso. There was no resistance; some say the *carabinieri* had been paid off.

Skorzeny's real triumph was to make it appear as if he had personally rescued Mussolini and, according to one historian, managed to have the cameras feature him. Certainly, by September 1943, with all hope of a conquest in the East abandoned, with the Germans driven out of North Africa and now retreating from a surrendered Italy, any kind of hero was welcomed by the propaganda machinery of the Third Reich.

General Student himself remarked a few years after the fact, "The liberation of Mussolini by Otto Skorzeny is an historical inexactitude. He was simply a small cog in the wheel of an operation, just like all the other soldiers who took part."

But so far as Hitler was concerned when he had Skorzeny appear in October 1944, the big SS officer had now twice pulled off magnificent feats. And now he wanted him to play a key role in the plan to sweep through the Ardennes.

Initially Hitler praised Skorzeny for removing Horthy, promoted him to lieutenant colonel and awarded him the German Cross in gold. Then when the two were alone, according to Skorzeny, Hitler confided, "The world thinks Germany is finished, with only the day and hour of the funeral to be named. I am going to show how wrong they are. The corpse will rise and hurl itself at the West."

On a map he outlined the thrust through the heart of the Western Front and on to Antwerp. He cited massive numbers for the German assault, 6,000 artillery pieces and 2,000 aircraft from the *Luftwaffe*, including the new ME 262 jets. "You, Skorzeny," continued Hitler, "will play an important part. I am going to assign you the most important mission of your life. There are several bridges between the cities of Liège and Namur on the Meuse River and your commandos will capture one or more of these bridges before they can be destroyed."

Then Hitler revealed his masterstroke. "I have decided that this can be accomplished faster and with lighter losses if your men wear American uniforms. The enemy has done us a great deal of damage by the use of our uniforms in various commando operations. Only a few days ago I received a report that the use of our uniforms by an American force had played no inconsiderable part when they captured Aachen [the first German city to be taken by the Allies]. Moreover, small detachments in enemy uniforms can cause the greatest confusion among the enemy. They can give false orders and upset their communications, sending bodies of troops in the wrong direction." Hitler, undoubtedly had fond memories of coups scored by fifth columns that helped his forces during various invasions. Skorzeny was informed he had only five or six weeks to organize his forces.

The mission for Skorzeny and his troops received the code name Operation *Greif,* the name of a mythical bird. The commander set about recruiting troops for what was officially the 150th Panzer Brigade with 3,300 men. He was promised that most would have an easy command of the English language as spoken by Americans. He also sought equipment and clothing that was American.

Right away, Skorzeny had detected one terrifying problem. He recognized that, under the rules of war, anyone from his command who was captured faced a firing squad. Indeed, the Germans had decreed execution for any commandos dropped behind the lines, regardless of what uniform they wore. The fate of members of *Greif* should they be captured in enemy uniforms generated considerable discussion. Hitler, himself, sought to allay fears with the direction that, if forced to fight, the troops should instantly shed their disguises, like so many Clark Kents ducking into telephone booths to shuck their outer garments. Hitler insisted the rules only doomed those wearing an enemy uniform while in combat. The distinction sounds like utter nonsense. But, in fact, after World War II the U.S. Department of the Army agreed that The Hague Regulations of 1907 on international warfare do not prohibit deceptive use of enemy uniforms under all circumstances except when employed to deceive during combat.

Gerd von Rundstedt, a traditionalist, stuffily questioned whether *Greif* was "fully in accordance with international law." He even had the audacity to inquire whether there was any definite proof that U.S. soldiers had put on German uniforms when attacking Aachen.

The matter went to Alfred Jodl, who reassured Skorzeny: "Since the Field Marshal has raised the problem, we have reexamined the matter. There is no question of any infringement of international law. It is merely a war stratagem such as the other side has already used on all fronts and with far greater frequency than we have. You need have no scruple.

"Moreover, all the men selected are volunteers. They are quite aware of the possibility that they may be treated as partisans. This they have accepted. No one forced them into it.

"Furthermore, there can be no question of changing the orders already given. They are as sacrosanct as all the other tactical measures laid down for the offensive."

As "sacrosanct" as *Greif* was, considering it came directly from the brain of Adolph Hitler, Skorzeny soon pondered a plea to abort the entire operation. The foremost cause of his dismay was an OKW (Army High Command) staff publication sent to all units of the *Wehrmacht*: "Report until October 10, 1944, all English-speaking officers and soldiers available for special missions. These are to be directed to Friedenthal [Skorzeny's training base] near Berlin, in view of their incorporation into the commando units of Lieutenant Colonel Skorzeny."

The chief of *Greif* was outraged by such an egregious breach of secrecy. He believed the operation hopelessly compromised. "I almost threw an apoplectic fit. I flew into a towering rage. General Fegelein, Hitler's brother-in-law, advised me, 'The business is after all incredible and incomprehensible, but that is only one more reason for you not to speak to the *Führer* about it. Consequently, it is impossible to cancel your mission.' "

Indeed, about two weeks before the offensive started, American intelligence, having obtained a copy of the message, was already attempting to interpret the import of the OKW missive. But there was no possibility that Hitler could be talked out of his scheme. Security was redoubled and, supposedly, one man was actually executed for some indiscreet comments in a letter home. Links with the world beyond the 150 Brigade were severed. Paybooks were temporarily removed. Members of the 150 Brigade who became ill could not be hospitalized.

Far more threatening to *Greif* than exposure was the almost total failure to provide the right men or equipment. The intensive search for qualified volunteers produced a pitiful total. Skorzeny recalled an interview with an officer recruit recommended for his facility with English. "I asked him to tell me about himself in English. 'Yes, Herr Oberstleutnant. I became my last order before five months.' " The candidate paused and added in German, "If you will allow, I will explain in my native tongue."

After World War II ended, Skorzeny insisted, "I had ten men who spoke the English language fluently, thirty or forty who spoke it fairly well and about 150 men who managed to make themselves understood with difficulty." His statistics, produced while he faced a war crimes tribunal, may have been understated in order to minimize the magnitude of the charges against him. But the number of *Grief* soldiers who could pass themselves off as Americans was exceedingly small.

One who could was Heinz Rohde, a sergeant who, after severe wounds, was training troops in Hamburg, a city regularly plastered by Allied bombers. Thinking he could escape the threat of the air attacks, Rohde volunteered for the special unit. He was shocked to discover the extent of security. The guards posted around the training base were Ukrainians, soldiers who did not speak German and therefore would be less able to pass along gossip. The small group eventually was called *Einheit* (unit) *Stielau* (the surname of the captain in charge). Stielau, in fact, was the last of six officers chosen to head the eighty-man company in the period between

November 10 and December 16. That fact in itself suggests the problems involved in making the scheme operational.

The best of the contingent were either sailors who had frequented the U.S. or German-Americans, men who had lived in the States for some period of time before returning to the Fatherland. Instructors tried desperately to teach the remainder the rudiments of American profanity, a couple of innocuous, all-purpose expressions and to keep their mouths shut if possible.

Thus, a soldier learned to respond, if challenged by a sentry for the password, "It's okay, Joe. It's me." While the figurative Joe paused to consider the answer, the German had an opportunity to run or shoot. Supposedly, the infiltrators were schooled in the current slang—"So's your old man,"—"Go lay an egg," or the various imprecations that employed "fuck."

Rohde remembered a diet of American movies, especially war films. (Seeing themselves portrayed as the stereotypical Nazis of World War II by Hollywood must have bemused the members of *Einheit Stielau*.) They also visited PW camps to perfect their idiom.

Behavior modification was difficult. Whenever an officer like Skorzeny appeared, the men naturally snapped to a rigid attention, uncharacteristic of GIs. If Skorzeny shouted at a group to "Relax!", instead of falling into an American slouch, the troops uniformly stamped their boots to assume a military "at ease" posture. Even such simple gestures as the right way to draw a cigarette from a pack, how to chew gum and the artful evasion of the need to salute perplexed the volunteers.

The Brigade fared only slightly better in scrounging American equipment. As a retreating army, the German opportunities to haul off heavy equipment as booty were limited. Instead of the twenty Sherman tanks requested by Skorzeny, he received only two. To make up the difference, the proprietors of *Wehrmacht* armor tried to disguise German Tiger tanks with tin sheets. The ersatz Shermans might have fooled a novice spotting them in poor light at a considerable distance.

Skorzeny asked for thirty armored cars but got a mere six. It seemed that many German officers enjoyed captured jeeps but when Skorzeny requisitioned these, they disappeared. However, a foraging party discovered fifteen hidden jeeps and peremptorily acquired them. All of the vehicles received paint coats and insignia that followed U.S. formats with a designation of the 5th Armored Division as part of the American Ninth Army.

Obtaining the proper clothing should have been less of a problem. German troops, coping with shortages from their quartermaster corps, had often supplemented their uniforms with salvage from American dead and prisoners. But to Skorzeny's dismay, the first batch he received was British. Then a shipment of U.S. field jackets arrived, with a painted triangle, a prisoner-of-war marking. No one could scare up a large enough uniform to fit Skorzeny. That was not an official problem, since Hitler had expressly forbidden him to risk his valuable life by crossing the enemy lines. To all complaints about the supplies, the form of the stock answer was, "Don't worry. Once the offensive starts, there'll be plenty left for you as the Americans run."

Much more easily accomplished were forged papers that would pass muster with Americans who inspected them. The Germans had extensive experience with manufacturing phony documents. Also, among the items distributed to the commandos were cigarette lighters with a vial of a swift-acting poison hidden in the wool wadding.

The authorities created a special set of signals to avoid situations where German troops might attack their comrades who wore enemy uniforms. As the disguised soldiers traveled towards their targets, they could indicate their route by painting white spots on houses, trees and roads. Pink or blue scarves with the second button of the blouse unbuttoned would disclose their true identity. If challenged during the day, a *Greif* agent need only tap his helmet twice to assure another German. At night, a blue torch in the left hand issued a challenge, while a red torch in the right affirmed allegiance to the Third Reich.

White letters on the hoods of jeeps, a *C, D, X, Y* or *Z*, meant the vehicle belonged to the 150 Brigade. Even the tanks bore a code message; when not engaged in firing, the turret gun pointed to nine o'clock.

The secrecy of the 150 Brigade mission—Skorzeny advised only the most senior of his officers on the job—naturally generated wild tales. On one occasion, the commander was startled by a lieutenant who confided that he was extremely familiar with Paris. When Skorzeny inquired the significance of the knowledge, the lieutenant, deducing from his leader's previous exploits, said he had guessed the nature of the operation. They would slip through the American lines and kidnap the head of the Allied armies, General Eisenhower.

Said Skorzeny, "We did not plan to capture high American officials. That was never part of the scheme. When the unit was organized, the soldiers began to spread rumors about the employment of this special unit. Naturally we censored all the mail and tried to suppress these rumors. But by the middle of November, however, I began to realize that it would be impossible to stop them, many of which were spread by officers in the units.

"I had a meeting with Folkersam, who was my chief of staff and Hardick [the brigade commander], and we decided to let the rumors go but direct them so they didn't come too close to the truth. Since the three of us were the only ones who knew the plans for our employment, this was not a difficult task.

"I recall specifically that some men were claiming that our unit single-handedly was to capture Antwerp, while others said we were to drive for Dunkirk and free German toops encircled in that town." Accordingly, when Skorzeny heard the lieutenant's "secret," he refused to commit himself but did not deny his subordinate's notion. Skorzeny was proven absolutely on the mark with his perception of the part rumor could play in spreading confusion. In fact, the wild stories about *Greif* among GIs may have been its most effective weapon.

At the suggestion of Field Marshal Walter Model, whose Army Group B encompassed the trio of armies making the assault, Hitler added another wrinkle to the plan. He ordered a paratroop drop behind the Allied lines. The airborne troops, relying on surprise, would block the arrival of American reinforcements, seize key bridges and hold them until the ground-based panzers arrived within hours. The mission would include 300 straw dummies, whose parachutes would add to the American confusion.

This operation was concocted even more hastily than *Greif*. Orders to mount the assault were issued December 8, only eight days before the actual thrust into the Ardennes would begin. The officer chosen to lead the 1,200-man contingent in Operation *Hohes Venn* [named for the target territory north of the Schnee Eifel] or Operation Auk, was Lt. Col. Friedrich A. Freiherr von der Heydte, a veteran paratrooper.

Heydte, from a Bavarian Catholic family of considerable standing, had studied law, served as an assistant professor of jurisprudence in Berlin. He left the country to study in Vienna, Paris and Italy following the Nazi takeover of the government in 1933. Immediately after the end of World War II, supporters claimed he banished himself from the Third Reich when the authorities ousted a Jewish professor. In fact, in the spring of 1933, Heydte belonged to the Catholic conservative right wing led by Franz von Papen that mistakenly thought it could penetrate the Nazi Party and transform it into its image of a law and order party. Indeed, far from any anti-Nazi sentiments, Heydte had belonged to an SA [the precursor to the SS] student outfit.

The aristocratic Heydte had returned to Germany in 1935 and joined the 15th Cavalry Regiment, known as the military home of "internal emigrees," populated mostly by fellow Catholic officers. As a captain, Heydte commanded a paratroop battalion in Crete, where he earned the Collar of Knight of the Iron Cross. He added to his background with a tour as chief of staff for a paratroop division in Italy and then headed a regiment that occupied France in 1944, before D-Day. By December he had assumed command of all paratroop training.

Despite Heydte's credentials, the German airborne flock no longer resembled the stuff of *blitzkrieg*. In fact, not since Crete in 1942, had they undertaken combat leaps. The best of them had become foot soldiers to be mauled on all fronts by the superior enemy numbers and firepower.

As an experienced soldier, Heydte was dismayed by the tools given him for any airborne mission. *Hohes Venn*, even more than *Greif*, labored under enormous handicaps. With just about one week to put together the parachute strike force, Hitler had issued an order to all parachute regiments to send the Heydte *Kampfgruppe* (task force) 100 of their best troopers. In the tradition of all armies, the various commanders seized an opportunity to rid themselves of problems, and dispatched their worst, the physical and mental misfits—the sad sacks.

Complained Heydte, "Never during my entire career with the Parachute Forces had I been in command of a unit with less fighting spirit." However, 250 members of Heydte's former unit, the 6th Parachute Regiment, on their own volunteered, and somehow Heydte managed to hang onto them. "Each one of these volunteers could be trusted implicitly.

"I quickly replaced the men whose fighting spirit appeared lowest with trustworthy volunteers from the school units, thereby including a number of men with no previous experience. They would jump for the first time on the night of 16–17 December. From what I could learn, these men stood the test amazingly well, proving that special training is not as essential as a stout heart and a dextrous body that has been trained by sports.'' But the fact was that hundreds upon hundreds of raw, inexperienced soldiers filled out the *Kampfgruppe* quota. Not only had so many never jumped before, but also this was to be a night exercise, spilling men through dark skies into woods and swampy ground.

Furthermore, Heydte was well aware that in the parachute forces of 1944 ''most of the officers had originally been part of the *Luftwaffe* ground forces or had served with antiaircraft or signal communications.'' As a consequence they had no infantry experience. ''In the last five days before the operation began, many men had to be taught the most rudimentary elements of infantry combat and behavior under fire. My company commanders were constantly amazed at the lack of knowledge of the troops.''

The quality of his troops was one of several critical weaknesses. He had carefully chosen a former flier at Stalingrad as commander of the aerial flotilla assigned to convey the paratroopers in 112 Junkers aircraft. ''Pilot and crew training, however, was still deficient. Most of the pilots and radio operators were young and many had just left school, while some of them had never even finished training. Two-thirds of the pilots did not hold the certificates required for flying a Junkers 52 aircraft. The crews were not accustomed to formation flying. Most of the crews had no front line experience. For more than half of the men the operation would be their first flight over enemy territory. [That meant their initiation into the perils of an antiaircraft attack.] Moreover, the pilots and jumpmasters were not used to cooperating with each other. In view of these conditions, [the flight commander] considered a night parachute drop, even without enemy opposition, to be extremely hazardous.''

On December 10, his troops' underwear impregnated with louse repellant, their bodies vaccinated against tetanus, gas gangrene and typhoid fever, Heydte led an advance party to the staging area, a military camp along the Senne River. He arrived at 2:00 A.M., awakened the commandant and learned that no orders had been received covering the billeting for the 1,200 paratroopers. Every building at the base was jammed with Waffen SS troops.

''I had no other choice but to telephone a pharmacist whom I had known in peacetime and who lived in the village of Oerlinghausen, about 20 kilometers north of the camp. [He] agreed to arrange for emergency billets in Oerlinghausen and other nearby villages." By 10:00 A.M. the men had all been accommodated by obliging householders. Heydte himself moved in with the friendly pharmacist.

"We were welcomed by the people of Westphalia and Lippe, who were not in sympathy with the Nazis. A short time before, units of the Waffen SS had been billeted in the same villages and the farmers made no secret of their pleasure in accommodating soldiers of the *Wehrmacht* rather than those of the unpopular SS.

Now Heydte reported to the top brass, where he received the broad outlines of the Ardennes offensive and the mission of *Hohes Venn*. "We attempted to voice our objections to the operation on the basis of the insufficient training of both the plane crews and the paratroopers. However, apparently, General [der Flieger Peppo] Schmidt had been drinking heavily, for he dismissed us rudely."

Heydte took his case to a higher court. He approached Field Marshal Model and voiced both his own doubts and that of the air transport commander. Heydte protested that, instead of a miniature regiment numbering little more than 1,000, he required division-size strength to achieve the objectives.

"After listening to my report, Field Marshal Model asked me whether I gave the parachute drop a ten percent chance of success. When I answered in the affirmative, he stated that the entire offensive had not more than a ten percent chance of success. However, it was necessary to make the attempt since it was the last remaining hope to conclude the war favorably. The field marshal concluded that if the most was not made of that ten percent chance, Germany would be faced with certain defeat."

Model informed Heydte that his outfit would fall under the control of Sepp Dietrich, commander of the Sixth Panzer Army. Now Heydte visited him. While waiting to see Dietrich, Heydte studied the operations maps. He noted, "We had thoroughly reconnoitered the American front lines and the enemy chain of command was well known. However, we were completely without knowledge of the enemy's strategic reserves. The distribution of forces within the American communications zone was unknown." The absence of such information, of course, could be devastating for the paratroopers since they would be jumping in the uncharted area.

As Dietrich continued to be tied up with other business, Heydte chatted with a garrulous clerk. For the first time the parachute colonel learned of *Kampfgruppe* Skorzeny. The role of *Greif* added one more anxiety for Heydte.

"Late in the morning I reported to Sepp Dietrich, who gave the impression of an old noncommissioned officer permanently addicted to alcohol. He had all the qualities of a first-class NCO of the old German Army. He was personally brave, tough and disciplined, and he cared for his men as though they were children and he chastised them like a stern father. He was feared, respected and even loved. But he was certainly not a commander."

The two discussed what the paratroopers might accomplish. They agreed on a drop about eleven kilometers north of the key road hub of Malmédy. Sepp Dietrich refused to permit patrols behind the U.S. lines and subsequently a plea for a personal aerial reconnaisance of the turf by Heydte was rejected by the *Luftwaffe*. The generals feared such missions might tip the German hand.

When Heydte asked for Dietrich's opinion on what kind of forces he might face, the chief of the Sixth SS Panzer Army growled, "I am not a prophet. You will learn earlier than I what forces the Americans will employ against you. Besides, behind their lines there are only Jewish hoodlums and bank managers."

Through Dietrich, Heydte arranged for bare-bones support from a long-range artillery battery. A forward observer equipped with a radio was assigned to jump with the *Kampfgruppe*. Uneasy about depending upon a single radio, Heydte requested a shipment of carrier pigeons that could carry messages if the communication equipment failed or was lost. Dietrich snapped, "I am not running a zoo. I am leading my panzer army without pigeons; you should be able to lead your *Kampfgruppe* without pigeons."

He reassured Heydte the paratroopers need only hold out for a few hours and then the special task force with its new *Jadtigers*, massive 128-mm antitank guns, would rumble to the rescue. "Don't be afraid," said Dietrich. "Be assured that I will meet you personally by 1700 on the first day of the attack."

In fact, Dietrich was unenthusiastic about *Hohes Venn*. In the course of their conversation, Dietrich growled, "A parachute drop is the one certain way of alerting the Americans about our attack." Heydte obtained from Dietrich one concession. The general's chief of staff drew a boundary line that barred any action by Skorzeny's brigade in the area of *Kampfgruppe Heydte*.

In the final few days before the launch, Heydte scrounged materials to construct his 300 dummies. The parachutes for his troops arrived so late they could not be repacked. He fretted over the possibility that foreign laborers in the factories might have sabotaged the chutes. He worked out arrangements to guide the aircraft. *Luftwaffe* searchlights between Paderborn, the main airfield, and the front lines would mark the initial path. Where the presence of German artillery beside the searchlights prevented their use, tracer bullets from antiaircraft batteries were to substitute. A guide plane from the bomber wing would pick up the flight at the front lines and lead it to the drop zone, which would be marked by incendiaries. To compensate for the deficiencies of the raw air crews, the planes would travel the final fifty kilometers with their wing lights illuminated.

On the morning of December 15, Heydte received his orders, scheduling the airdrop for between 0430 and 0500 in the predawn of the following day. Everything was in readiness for the masterstroke.

The architect of the grand strategy was even testier than usual. Hitler lashed out at his generals on December 12. He declared "The army's continuous setbacks can be tolerated no longer. The army must gain a victory. The German people can no longer endure the heavy bombing attacks. The German people are entitled to action from me."

He questioned Sepp Dietrich, "Is your army ready?"

"Not for an offensive," boldly answered the Sixth Panzer Army leader.

"You are never satisfied," *der Führer* sneered.

Privately, Sepp Dietrich forlornly muttered, "All Hitler wants me to do is to cross a river, capture Brussels, and then go on and take Antwerp! And all this in the worst time of the year through the Ardennes where the snow is waist deep and there isn't room to deploy four tanks abreast, let alone armored divisions! Where it doesn't get light until eight and it's dark again at four and with reformed divisions made up chiefly of kids and sick old men—and at Christmas!"

When Gen. Hasso von Manteuffel, head of the Fifth Panzer Army asked for additional equipment, Hitler snapped at him:

"I have given you everything I have from the production line. This offensive is absorbing eighty percent of all my tanks, my artillery and my trucks. The Sixth Panzer Army is up to strength."

At a gloomy birthday party for von Rundstedt, no one dared mention the topic uppermost in the military minds. An indiscreet word could leave one subject to the death penalty, decreed for loose lips on *Herbstnebel*.

Chapter IV

THINGS FALL APART

On Saturday, December 16, newly promoted to the rank of five-star General of the Armies, Dwight Eisenhower attended the wedding of his valet, Mickey McKeogh and Women's Army Corps Sgt. Pearlie Hargrave in the Louis XIV Chapel at Versailles, near Paris. Gen. Elwood (Pete) Quesada, the chief of the tactical air forces in Europe, Gen. Omar Bradley and Gen. Courtney Hodges, head of the U.S. 1st Army, which faced the Germans on the Siegfried line, visited with a Belgian manufacturer to arrange for custom-made shotguns.

For the past few days, Bradley, in a chauffeured staff car, had escorted actress Marlene Dietrich, performing morale-building shows for American troops. He had been somewhat bemused by her complaints about the food and accommodations. The actress was due at the Honsfeld headquarters of the 99th Division to ply her arts for the benefit of the men there, including a pair of men designated by Lt. Lyle Bouck from the I & R squad hunkered down before Lanzerath.

Hodges had devoted some of the previous day welcoming a contingent of major league baseball stars, Frank Frisch, Bucky Walters, Dutch Leonard and Mel Ott, building morale with visits to the troops. The U.S. First Army had just dispatched the 2nd and the 99th Divisions towards the Roer River dams. A pervasive fear that the enemy would release the waters behind these dams and flood out the plains between the Americans and the Rhine dictated the move. Thus, regiments containing Capt. Charles MacDonald with the 2nd, and Carmen Capalbo and Ben Nawrocki in the 99th were moving to the attack even before the Germans' intended surprise strike against them and others in the Ardennes. A situation report from the First Army Headquarters noted the enemy was defending the territory "strenuously."

Field Marshal Sir Bernard L. Montgomery, running the British Twenty-first Army Group, targeted for isolation through Hitler's

Ardennes strike strategy, relaxed on a golf course with Welsh professional Dai Rees. Well south of the Ardennes, Gen. George S. Patton urged on his Third Army, including his favorite outfit, the 4th Armored Division and the newly arrived 87th Infantry Division in a push that Patton hoped would put him across the Rhine first.

The brass supervising action through the Ardennes accepted the evaluations of their intelligence experts. Those in charge of the American apparatus groped their way through thickets of information —intercepts of enemy communications through the medium of ULTRA, the code-breaking machine, the photos and observations dervied from the air corps, gobbets of gossip and facts revealed by prisoners, tales from civilians who crossed the lines, the accounts of troops up on the line. The fodder fed to the decision makers also reflected a certain amount of competition and ego among the analysts.

While the American Office of Strategic Services (OSS), precursor to the Central Intelligence Agency, was available to supply data, there was a distinct antipathy of some military men towards civilian input into the military hopper. The irascible Col. Benjamin (Monk) Dickson, First Army G–2, when approached on the possiblity of aid from the OSS, answered, "I don't want a man from OSS, nor a dwarf, nor a pigmy, not a Goddamned soul." And to this point, the armed forces had little reason to call on the OSS. During the drive across France, Belgium and Holland, many of the local civilians gladly informed on the hated occupation troops. But now, on the border of Germany, that kind of resource dried up. The military failed to take measures to replace it.

A desire to get the job over with, by the start of the new year if possible, a sentiment heartily endorsed by the civilians and those in uniform, seemed to affect evaluations of conditions for both the civilian leaders of the Allied governments and their brasshat subordinates.

According to Gen. Edwin Sibert, the Twelfth Army Group's G–2, and a rival intelligencer to his inferior, Dickson, there had been complaints concerning the dullness of the reports from Sibert's realm. Officers allegedly failed to study them because the files read so dully. To remedy the situation, Sibert ordered Col. Ralph Ingersoll, a former newspaperman,in effect, to jazz up the memos. In retrospect, Sibert remarked the result was to deliver overoptimistic accounts, the kind of stuff the warriors enjoyed reading. Some of the happy talk undoubtedly also owed its origins to the air corps' penchant for overestimation of its results. Its top management insisted no one could possibly continue to work and produce with all the high-explosive tonnage dumped on the enemy. But in fact, as the post-World War II statistical analyses and debriefing of such Nazi officials as Albert Speer revealed, the Germans, with their slave laborers, kept right on manufacturing the tools of war in spite of all the bombing.

Field Marshal Montgomery spoke for his Twenty-first Army Group: "The enemy is at present fighting a defensive campaign on all fronts; his situation is such that he cannot stage major offensive operations. Furthermore, at all costs he has to prevent the war from entering on a mobile phase; he has not the transport or the petrol that would be necessary for mobile operations. The enemy is in a bad way."

At the Twelfth Army Group, the summary issued on December 12 followed the same line. "It is now certain that attrition is steadily sapping the strength of German forces on the Western Front and that the crust of defenses is thinner, more brittle and more vulnerable than it appears on our G–2 map or to the troops in the line." The allegedly rosy view of the "troops in the line" was made before Charles MacDonald and Cap Capalbo and their fellow GIs confronted the resistance to advances towards the Roer.

Over the next few days, qualms ruffled some military intelligence specialists. ULTRA flagged down messages that roused suspicions about the German intentions. Although poor weather interfered with flight operations, planes flew some reconnaissance missions. But for the most part, those that got off the ground focused upon the terrain near Aachen and the Roer, the area of the American attack.

On December 9, the U.S. 83rd Division took a prisoner who said there were strong rumors of an all-out attack within the next few days. A couple of deserters, as well as two men captured by the 4th and 106th Infantry Divisions, claimed they were told of an imminent big push. Monk Dickson sounded a vague alarm but at most he indicated a strengthening of the enemy defenses in the plains before the Rhine rather than indicating an assault.

On December 15, an officer from the 28th Division scrawled a pencil-smudged report, replete with military abbreviations, detailing his interrogation of a Luxembourg woman, Elise Dele-Dunkel. "A German woman [the intelligence specialist failed to distinguish her nationality], whose statements are believed to be reliable, acording to VIII Corps, has given the following info of her obsvns behind the German lines during the 3 days beginning 10 Dec. She saw many horsedrawn vehicles, pontoons, small boats and other river crossing eqpt. coming from the direction of Bitburg and moving W. through Geichlingen. In Bitburg she overhead some military personnel saying that it had taken 3 weeks to get them from Italy. There were also trps in the town w/gray uniforms and black collar patches. She also stated that she had seen many arty pieces, both horse drawn and carried on trucks.

"Comment: A very interesting rept. Buildup of trps has been confirmed by TAC/R [tactical air corps reconnaissancc] and PW statements. However, presence of large nos. of engr. w/bridging eqpt suggests preparations for offensive rather than defensive action. No div. from Italy has been reptd. on the move to the West. front by Higher Hq but possibility always exists that such a move has in fact taken place."

Elise Dele-Dunkel told her interrogators she had escaped after being held for several days by the German soldiers. The intelligence officer noted, "The woman's nerves were jarred quite a bit when . . . she struck a trip wire and exploded a mine. She had tried to creep under waist high wire and when the mine exploded, the shrapnel went over her as she bent." To the intelligence officer, her jitters added to her credibility.

Of considerable significance was the presence of the river- and stream-fording items. These definitely indicated an assault. Furthermore, the presence of SS troops, (the gray uniforms with the black collar patches) the forces drawn from Italy and the sighting of so much artillery hinted at unexpected strength.

However, while Dunkel first told her story to Americans on December 14, a full day passed before the information was forwarded to higher-ups. By then, less than twenty-four hours remained before zero hour for the Germans.

While some of the Americans on the front lines, like Lt. Alan Jones, were watchful, the complacent attitude that pervaded the uppermost echelons seemed to filter down. There was no general order insisting upon high state of alert. In fact, Gen. Hasso von Manteuffel, in command of the German Fifth Army, doffed his regular uniform, put on the garb of a simple colonel to allay suspicions from prying American eyes or gossip, and personally reconnoitered the positions in front of his army. He visited with the division commanders, battalion leaders and even men who went on patrols.

From these sources and from what he could see the *Amis* (Americans) stayed on guard one hour after dark, then returned to their huts to sleep, reappearing one hour before dawn. Their habits suggested to him something less than a state of readiness. Dick Byers, as part of a field artillery observation team, confirms Manteuffel so far as he could observe. "Before the Bulge, we were a nine to five army in the Ardennes."

Because the enemy seemed so relaxed, Manteuffel argued against the typical opening gambit of artillery barrages to launch the attack. That would only "wake up" the Americans. It would be far better simply to send infantry and armor swarming across the thinly-manned, positions. Furthermore, Manteuffel claims he proposed the use of "artificial moonlight," illuminating the path for German panzers and grenadiers by bouncing searchlights off the predawn clouds. (Others also lay claim to this innovation.)

Originally, said Manteuffel, Hitler scheduled the onslaught to begin at 11:00 A.M. However, the diminutive general (he stood only about five feet two inches) persuaded his leader that with darkness coming by 4:00 P.M. the Germans would have precious little daylight to achieve maximum success. Accordingly, the first salvos were to boom at 5:30 A.M. Furthermore, instead of a lengthy artillery preparation, Manteuffel planned for less than an hour of the big guns before sending his infantry forward. His armor would pass through the infantry at night and be in position to break out the following day.

While Manteuffel controlled the tactics of the Fifth Panzer Army, Sepp Dietrich, whom Manteuffel, like Heydte, regarded as incompetent to command a division, let alone an army, disregarded his colleague's notion. He insisted upon a full-scale softening up through artillery, and by the time his Sixth Panzer troops were to move forward, the first rays of morning sun would eliminate any benefits from searchlight reflections off clouds.

In both instances, the two German generals thought in terms of foot soldiers creating wedges for the armor, unlike Patton and Rommel, who used their tanks to crash through. Furthermore, Manteuffel's idea of maneuvering his panzers during the blackness of night was a very risky proposition under the best of circumstances and even less propitious on the narrow, twisty highways of the Ardennes.

But even before the targeted hour for the attack, the paratroopers under Heydte were scheduled to leave. He noted, "The airdrop was to take place between 0430 and 0500. Motor transport columns were to convey the troops from their billeting area to the Paderborn and Lippspringes airdromes."

However, by 8:00 P.M. on December 15, Heydte learned that most of the vehicles had not arrived. As a result, by takeoff time for the planes, not even half of the paratroopers had arrived at the airdromes. No one had authorized fuel for the trucks. The entire operation was scrubbed, to be reinstated twenty-four hours later.

In the north, the U.S. 1st Battalion, 395th Regiment, 99th Division, had held its position until December 13. Now the Checkerboards, joined with 2nd and 9th Division segments, in the thrust toward the Roer River dams. Subsequently, Ben Nawrocki in Company B of the 393rd Regiment, and Cap Capalbo and his fellows in Company A from the 395th dutifully obeyed orders to move forward. Nawrocki's 2nd Platoon carried out a diversionary attack, designed to fool the enemy on the direction of the main attack. "We had a reinforced platoon with machine guns and mortars and artillery observers. We had to cross a mined and machine gun covered area. The enemy fired about 100 rounds of artillery."

One of the very first shells ripped a hole in the back of the platoon leader, Lt. John Carnevale. He instructed Nawrocki to take charge, since he could no longer move. Under a heavy barrage, the platoon doggedly followed its prescribed route amid explosions and the cries of men, "Medic! Medic!" A runner dispatched by Carnevale ordered Nawrocki to call a retreat; the losses were too much.

"We had nineteen wounded, one dead," said Nawrocki. "I was carrying a fellow named James Crosby out. He used my rifle for a crutch, and near the International Highway, he set the butt down on a mine. It blew him off me. My clothes in front, from the knees to neck, were shredded. The veins on my body seemed as thick as my fingers. I got some help to take Crosby out. Other men went back and got those who hadn't received the word to pull out and bring back the rest of the wounded." Nawrocki was amazed that the ordeal had lasted only an hour. The survivors from the 2nd Platoon settled back into their dugouts.

* * *

Company A with Cap Capalbo pushed towards its first objective, a hill, perhaps half a mile off. The enemy resisted fiercely and the company spent the entire day taking the hill.

"When we got to the top it was 4:00 P.M. The place was heavily wooded and we were told to dig in. It's a cardinal rule not to dig a foxhole under a tree because of treebursts. But we didn't have a choice with all of the trees around. My buddy started to dig a hole. After a while, to give him a rest, I suggested he go back down the hill and bring some water and I would continue digging.

"He had just left when suddenly a massive artillery attack hit us. It went on and on. Our foxhole was maybe eighteen inches deep. There was no way I could get my entire body under ground. I lay on my stomach with my head near this huge tree trunk. At last it seemed the shelling ended. Almost miraculously, no one had been hurt. But some mystical element warned me it wasn't really over. I still had my head down, close to the tree, when this one final mortar round smashed directly into the base of the tree.

"I was sprayed with shrapnel, all along my right side, fingers, arm, buttocks and leg. The explosion turned the ground into something that resembled granulated sugar or fine sand. I knew I was hurt. It seemed like I had been hit by a train but I didn't feel any pain. My right leg was covered with debris and I could only see the heel of my right shoe. I exerted every ounce of strength I could muster to move the leg but I couldn't. The shock left me unable to do it. I said to myself, I've got to move that goddamned shoe! I had to find out if it was still attached.

"Meanwhile, the other guys saw what had happened. 'Hey, Cap, are you okay, are you okay?' they kept asking. They dug me out and immediately stripped off my field jacket. Thank God, my leg was still attached. A medic put sulfa power on my wounds and they carried me down the hill on a stretcher held over their heads. It was a very frightening sensation to be up in the air, unable to find cover. I felt completely naked. I kept thinking, another mortar round and I'm gone.

"It was dark when we got down the hill. The commander of the battalion had kind of adopted me after I got the Bronze Star. He wanted me to go to OCS. He broke down and cried, 'Cap, Cap.' He gave me a shot of brandy. [A hoary tradition for battlefield wounds that contradicts modern medical protocol.]

"I said, 'Don't worry. I'll be back.'"

Sometime during the night, Capalbo was evacuated to a temporary hospital set up at Malmédy, perhaps ten miles back.

Nawrocki's sector was anything but quiet that day and night. "We received more than the usual number of artillery and mortar rounds. They seemed to hit our automatic weapons positions. They seemed to know the location of every emplacement. After midnight, artillery cut our phone lines. Lt. Charles Kingsley went out and spliced them. I told the men to be on the alert for an attack.

"At 2:00 A.M., a patrol returned to our lines and reported they had to turn back, as Germans were laying in mass formation in the draws and valleys in front of Company B. The information was communicated to battalion headquarters and artillery requested. Not a round was fired, although the fields must have been gray with Germans."

Pfc. Nolan Williams of Haskell, Oklahoma, on patrol for Company K of the 99th Division's 394th Regiment, discovered the massing of enemy forces on the night of December 15, which led to one of the more bizarre encounters with the enemy. "Shortly after dark, we made our way around enemy outposts and bumped into an enemy patrol. There was some small arms shot but I don't remember that we returned fire. We did skirt around the patrol and move deeper into enemy territory. Soon, we were hearing mass movements of tanks, tracks and men. The sergeant tried to contact our headquarters with his hand radio but could not get a response. He believed the troop movement important enough to cut short our mission and return to report.

"We flopped down on the first floor of the Bucholz farmhouse. Very early in the morning a shell or grenade exploded in the courtyard, throwing glass on us. Someone said, 'Let's go down in the basement to get out of this shelling.' I put on my belt, hung my rifle, Jungle Jim [a 1940s comic strip figure] style across my chest, tucked a box of K rations inside my shirt and carefully picked up my new overshoes—I had only been issued them the day before.

"In the dark, I went down the hall and started down the steps. About halfway down I heard someone speaking German, very rapidly. I assumed it was just one of our interpreters. But then there were several voices, all German. In the dark, I placed my hand on the head of the person just in front of me on the steps, pulled his head over to me and whispered, 'There are Jerries in this basement.' I knew all of our helmets had netting on them and suddenly I realized that the one I was holding had no net!

"At that moment, a German officer in the basement pointed a flashlight on us and said in perfect English, 'Hands up, boys. The war is over.' I'll never forget the saucer-sized eyes of the young German into whose ears I had just whispered. He must have been as frightened as I.

"But I responded, 'Like hell it is!' And I shoved the young soldier down the steps on top of the officer. Up the stairs, down the hall out toward the courtyard I practically flew, meanwhile clutching my new overshoes in my right hand. In the doorway, silhouetted by the white snow, stood a German with a burp gun in ready position. I'm sure if that soldier is still alive, he wonders what hit him. I hit him with my overshoes, ran over him from toe to head like a freight train and on to the barn. But I dropped the overshoes. To show how important they seemed to me, I seriously considered going back to the yard to retrieve them."

"I went into the barn and began to get control of myself. I unwound myself from the rifle straps and had the butt ready to defend myself. Someone else began to enter the barn and just as I was about to smack him with the butt, I recognized the sergeant. We decided we would try to get some help.

"We made a dash for the road and I noticed a German halftrack parked by the house. Now I saw the road was bumper to bumper with tanks, troop carriers and infantrymen. We hid a long time in a ditch, then dashed between the tanks. Eventually, we were reunited with nine of the others from our original thirteen-man patrol. We became part of the general withdrawal."

About the time Carmen Capalbo reached Malmédy and Nolan Williams stumbled into the enemy, the big guns of the Sixth Panzer Army opened up all along their front. A murderous rain of everything from fourteen-inch railway pieces to mortars crashed down upon the men of 99th Division. In their log- and dirt-covered burrows, casualties were few but the cascade of high explosives tore up the network of wire lines necessary for communications. The Fifth Panzer Army, in spite of Manteuffel's fear of waking up the Americans, blasted away in some sectors and the Seventh Army contributed its share of long-range shelling.

Ben Nawrocki with a brother regiment to Williams's noted, "At 4:00 A.M. on December 16, it seemed all hell broke loose with artillery shells landing all over. The ground shook. We had a wool sock in a bottle of gasoline for a light but the artillery kept blowing it out. We could not stick our heads up. Trees and branches fell all over, and shrapnel whined around. The treebursts were very dangerous. We found it better to squat, rather than spread-eagle; squatting made a smaller target.

"When the artillery started to let up around 6:00 A.M. and we stuck our heads out of our holes, an eerie sight greeted us. There were lights of all descriptions, lighting the sky and ground. The lights pointed up into the sky and into our positions. They beamed from tanks, trucks, pill boxes, everywhere.

"This was to help the Germans see the terrain and us. The snow was hip-deep with a heavy fog. If the lights were intended to throw fear into our troops, it didn't succeed with us. The enemy were between us and the lights made them a good target. Some wore American uniforms, throwing grenades, a few were seen on skis. Some wore white snow suits. We kept cutting them down. In many places the Germans piled up on top of one another like cordwood."

The entire 990th Regiment of the 277th *Volksgrenadier* Division had hurled itself at Company B. "On the left flank of the 3rd Platoon, a rifleman with a BAR was firing at the oncoming Germans, who piled up three or four feet high in front of his foxhole. I don't know his name but he was bucktoothed, and when he looked down at his feet, I heard him yell, 'Goddamn, I'm barefoot.' He had been so busy for six hours, he never had time to put on his shoes."

The embattled soldiers in Nawrocki's sector, aided by artillery fire from the big guns to the rear, inflicted heavy casualties. The resistance stalled the enemy infantrymen, jamming up the advance of the panzers behind.

On the right flank and to the south, the impact and the immediate problems varied. George Ruhlen, then a lieutenant colonel commanding the 3rd Field Artilley of the 9th Armored Division, described events in his area, along the Luxembourg border. "At 0615 on the 16th of December, shells of 105 mm, 150 mm and 170 mm came whistling into Haller [a town on the Sauer River below its junction with the Our]. The fire increased, and as all ran for cover, the rumble of enemy guns could be heard echoing up and down the Sauer valley. It was soon apparent that this was not a local raid nor a retaliation for harassing fire delivered the previous night.

"Bells in the Haller church struck three high notes, then three low notes, and then incessantly for half an hour until the bell ringer was evicted. An estimated 800 to 900 rounds fell in and near the town between 0615 and 0715. Columns of smoke and dust from tremendous explosions were seen in the vicinity of Beaufort. *Nebelwerfer* rockets fell near gun positions with their characteristically terrifying shriek. [GIs called them 'Screaming Meemies.']

"An observer reported sixty Germans crossing the river on a small pontoon bridge near Dillingen, but they were not carrying weapons and it was believed they were coming over to surrender. A minute later came the report that these Germans were carrying machine guns and frantic calls for normal barrages came from all observers almost instantaneously. All wire lines were shot out except the liasion line to the 60th Infantry Command Post. A heavy ground mist made observation very difficult, let alone making close air support impossible. In the forward areas, vague figures appeared in the fog, unidentifiable even a hundred yards away."

In the area occupied by the 106th Division, the huge shells launched from railway guns thundered into St. Vith, division headquarters. Up front the amazed troops watched the searchlight beams carom off the low-hanging clouds to illuminate roads and open fields. More ominously, they spotted white-clad figures in the distance advancing towards them as the clatter of tracked vehicles reached their ears.

From the snow-encrusted emplacement for their light machine guns, the 423rd Infantry Regiment's Pvt. Frank Raila, as part of the squad, watched the German searchlights bounce off the cloud cover. "It was a pretty sight."

Sightseeing ended with the dawn. "We saw a Tiger tank in the trees to our front. Our machine gun fired tracers to point out the tank to the tank destroyer unit nearby. Two or three of them went out to get it. Then 88 [millimeter] shells started coming, landing in the woods behind us where we put on our back packs. Small arms fire was directed at us and we fired back, with machine guns, mortars. The tank destroyers came back. One had been hit. Its .50-caliber machine gun was at a twisted tangle. A dead crewman was strapped in front. He was the first dead American I saw.

"I could barely make out figures, far ahead of us, 500 to 1,000 yards, with dark, flapping greatcoats. As soon as people began to shoot, they disappeared.

"The place we were in apparently had become untenable. I had gone back to get ammo twice for the machine gun and the sergeant said we were going on the march. We all hit the road, passing U.S. trucks burning, with ammo exploding, an occasional shell shooting into the air, pyrotechnics!

"It got very confusing. We were not much of a company any more. There were different platoons and companies. We were told to walk down a field in front of us to the right of a road. Everything was quiet. I think the Germans let the point keep walking. Then when we reached an area of a few acres, all hell broke loose. It was very surprising. There had been no sound of incoming; mortars may make a sound but I didn't hear anything until the explosions started to rock the ground. Dirt flew up everywhere, pelting you in the chest and back.

"We all dropped down, paralyzed. People were hollering and screaming until the sergeant said, 'Get out of here!' We crawled back until the explosions didn't follow and then we ran like crazy. We straggled back to the 'front lines,' a miserably thin line of GIs, including my own machine gun platoon."

Sgt. Leo Leisse, with the 106th Division's 422nd Battalion Headquarters in the Ammunition and Pioneer Platoon, was at breakfast when he too shrank under the softening-up thunderbolts from the German 6th Army. "I had no conscious sense of fright but I was scared as hell, I'm sure. I did whatever the officers told me to." For the moment, his location, once the artillery faded out, was not immediately in peril.

Initially, there was little to even hint at a cataclysm for Phil Hannon and the others from Company A of the 81st Engineer Combat Battalion. "We were roused by 'calling cards' mailed by 88s on Saturday morning. We were 'green' and so, shrugging our shoulders, said, 'What the hell, this happens every so often.' And off to chow we went.

"Chow was good, as chow always is to guys who are in good shape, and the gang was full of laughs about the close calls that had dropped in on us. The heavy firing in the east didn't register, so the talk was about Christmas and the mail that was starting to come in. We didn't think it strange that all the German civilians were up and in their basements long before the shelling started.

"The third platoon had a couple of jobs to finish up front, so we loaded up and moved out. The same old horseplay went on. The KPs got the everyday razzing as we rode by the kitchen. We dropped off the second and third squads and mine went up farther to finish the corduroy road we had begun the day before.

"The front was quiet. The shells were going over and beyond, and we felt safer than in our little village. We felt safer until we noticed the worried looks on the faces of the officers. A major walked by with a .45 in his fist, so we woke up. No work on the road this day and we headed for home. We never got there."

John Collins, like Hannon, a member of Company A of the 81st Engineers, was somewhat less blasé about the opening salvos. "We were literally bowled out of our beds by artillery shells landing in and around our company area. We dressed quickly and went downstairs to find the German family crouched in a rear room, fully dressed. It looked as though they knew it was coming. We crouched with them until we could collect our wits and the shelling slacked off. But not much. We now knew what it feels like to be under fire and we were scared. Really scared. Maybe a better word would be frustrated. If someone is shooting at you, you can retaliate but this shelling was for the birds.

"At about 0600 we left for the mess hall to find most of the company in line for chow. When a shell would come in, everyone hit the ground. Immediately afterwards they were back in line." As Phil Hannon noted, the three platoons left the area after breakfast to perform routine chores. John Collins was temporarily left behind, assigned to bring up the outfit's equipment.

He had almost finished the task when the shelling increased. The company commander decided to recall the three platoons and dispatched Collins with a Lieutenant Coughlin to retrieve the men. They reached the 1st and 2nd Platoons without trouble and passed the word.

"We headed to the 422nd Regiment to round up my 3rd Platoon. As we neared a guard shack about 800 yards behind the lines, Lieutenant Coughlin very nonchalantly said, 'Sergeant, turn around real easy and let's get the hell out of here.' I swung the jeep around and slowly retraced our way back. It was then that I saw the white-clad enemy in a field about 800 yards to our left. At this point we were only about seventy-five yards from the guard shack and I really poured the juice to the jeep. We heard some rifle fire, but with my sliding on the snow and the lieutenant yelling 'Faster!', we made it without any hits, if they were shooting at us. The lieutenant told me that the guard at the shack had on white boots and his rifle did not look like ours. Him being an ex-ordnance man, he'd noticed."

Collins's company commander ordered everyone to pull back to the village of Heuem. Lieutenant Coughlin organized a defense from buildings behind the retreat. Accompanied by foot soldiers, a quartet of German Tiger tanks trundled up the road, and blew away the houses, scattering Coughlin and his men.

The remnants of the 81st Engineers assembled briefly at Heuem but the pressure from the enemy continued. Collins and the others would continue to fall back until they reached St. Vith, where Gen. Alan Jones, Sr., as CO of the 106th, sought to restore control.

From a hillside vantage point, the general's namesake son watched with dismay as the enemy battered the town of Bleialf, inhabited by portions of a brother regiment, the 424th. Jones, Jr., himself was not in imminent danger.

"There was very little shelling on our positions the first day, and not much on the second, either."

Jim Mills, the assistant BAR gunner with Company I of the 423rd Regiment, awake and on guard in his dugout, also watched a massive artillery barrage fall mostly upon other units of the 106th Division, near the point where the GIs of the 424th Regiment intersected with those of the 423rd. "It was still dark and the German flares would stay in the air for several minutes, lighting up the entire front. There were eerie, screaming sounds, but nobody had ever mentioned the 'Screaming Meemies' to us. We were told to be ready for an attack from our right flank and dug ourselves in to face the threat."

Clifford Broadwater, the antiaircraft artillery master sergeant transferred into an antitank company of the 423rd Infantry Regiment, had been on the line only a few days when the brass decided to form a provisional military police unit. The group set up shop in the vicinity of Bleialf, several miles behind the infantrymen on the main line of resistance.

As the senior noncom in the newly created MPs, Broadwater, along with what he calls "a seldom-seen lieutenant" and thirty GIs, had begun to take charge of the first German prisoners seized in the attack.

"We were supposed to meet some of our units and pick up more prisoners. A sergeant and I took a detail and went looking. We sallied forth, although none of us knew exactly where to go and none of us knew the country. The ground was pretty level with some scattered trees that looked stripped by artillery, quite desolate. We wandered forward, never saw anybody else nor heard anything.

"That night I heard the artillery booming. Didn't hear any landing anywhere close. Guess I was too dumb to be scared. I just turned over and went back to sleep."

On the night of December 15, the Observation Section for C Battery of the 371st Field Artillery, which included Dick Byers, slept in a house located at the center of Mürringen. According to Byers, his bedroom shared the back wall and roof in common with the barn.

"Just before dawn, on the morning of the 16th, we were awakened by a muffled explosion and a slight tremor of the house. None of us thought enough of the occurence to get out of a warm sleeping bag to investigate. But so far as our group was concerned, this was the start of the Battle of the Bulge.

"One of the guys finally went downstairs and out to the latrine. By the early light he saw that a delayed-fuse artillery shell had gone through the roof of the barn, just two feet from the wall of our bedroom. The round had buried itself in the haymow before exploding. Throughout the morning, shells struck at seeming random around the village. One exploded among a group of artillerymen lined up for breakfast and killed several. By midmorning, we realized there was a pattern to the explosions. They fell close to houses occupied by American troops. Later, we heard that a captured German artillery observer had a map marked with all of the occupied houses. The information must have been given to him by someone planted in the area by the Germans as they retreated in October.

"In the afternoon I drove an officer to a command post for a conference. I stayed with the jeep and was caught in the first and worst barrage I've ever been in. I was caught flat-footed in a pine forest without any adequate cover. The shells were hitting tree-tops and spraying the ground all around us with steel fragments. I believe I actually pressed a slit trench into the snow and frozen ground with my body, trying in my terror to become as small and flat as possible. The noise was so incredibly loud it could not be heard. It rang in my ears and vibrated my body. Just imagine putting your head up inside an enormous bell while giants pounded it with sledgehammers.

"Most young soldiers felt invulnerable even when their comrades were dropping all around them. It was when they lost that sense of invulnerability and suddenly realized the truth of their situation that terror replaced it, a shortness of breath and a pounding heart. I had a terrible feeling of my back being so vulnerable."

The quietest sector for the 106th's defenses until December 16 had been that held by elements of the 424th Regiment just inside the German border above Luxembourg. Just before dawn on the 16th, a noncom burst into the cabin where Harry F. Martin, Jr., bunked and yelled, "The Germans are coming! The Germans are coming! We will all be killed!"

Martin and Bill Williams snatched up their rifles and steel helmets. They ran to their position, a two-man foxhole on the extreme left flank. The remainder of the platoon took their stations in log bunkers.

"As soon as we got into our foxhole, Bill announced he was going to use a rifle grenade. Seconds later I could see hundreds of shadowy heads bobbing up and down, coming over the crest of the hill just before dawn. They acted like they were drunk or on drugs, screaming, shrieking. I was absolutely terrified. They had already outflanked our company and now they were coming to finish us off.

"With nothing on our left and out of sight of our platoon on the right, it felt almost like we were against the entire German Army. I was horror-stricken. There was no thought of running away or surrendering. I had an absolute conviction to fight to the death, while being certain we would be killed.

"Just about then, Bill tugged on my leg. I was vaguely aware he asked me to let him know when the Germans were close enough. Neither of us had ever fired a rifle grenade before and we did not have the slightest idea of the effective range.

"There were so many of them storming down the hill coming

right for us. There was no way of stopping all of them. I had a feeling of utter hopelessness; I was panic-stricken. I felt my entire life force had left my body. I was already dead and was fighting like a zombie. Sheer panic caused me to fire without thinking or aiming. I was unaware of my body, just terror, firing as fast as my finger could pull the trigger.

"They kept coming as though immune to death. Apparently I was not hitting a thing. I was so transfixed with fear and terror, my eyes did not focus on the individual enemy. I was firing blindly, without thinking or looking through the sights. In my terror-stricken seizure I continued to fire in the general direction of the swarming sea of terror, the huge mass of bodies charging toward me. It was as though the entire hillside was alive, moving with huge tentacles to devour me.

"Bill tugged on my leg again and yelled, 'Are they close enough?' I can remember telling him no, but my brain didn't register distance. I could not even think about what he was saying. He must have tugged my leg half a dozen times during the battle and I kept telling him no.

"In the middle of this terrifying battle I heard a very confident, calm voice inside my head say, 'Squeeze the trigger.' I calmed down instantly, took careful aim at one of the charging Germans through my gunsight and squeezed the trigger. He flung his arms up over his head and fell down dead, shot through the head. I felt a sensation surge through my whole body. I was no longer a zombie. My life force had come surging back. I was alive and for the first time I felt that I had a chance to come out of this battle.

"At this very moment I was a veteran combat soldier. I continued to shoot the attacking Germans until they finally stopped coming. The battle was over. After such intense fighting it was very strange how suddenly the battle ended. How quiet everything had become. A feeling of disbelief it was over. At the time it seemed as if it would never end.

"Later I thought about the voice I heard telling me to squeeze the trigger. I failed to qualify with the rifle in basic training. I had to go back and do everything by the numbers without live ammunition, again. For the next five weeks after supper and on Sundays, the practice continued. Over and over they drummed the procedure by the numbers into my head, always ending with 'Squeeze the trigger, do not jerk the trigger, slowly squeeze the trigger, sque-e-e-ze the trigger.' After awhile, at night I dreamt about squeezing the trigger. We had made fun of doing things by the numbers but it had saved my life."

In support of the 106th Division's 422nd Regiment and the men of A Company from the 81st Combat Engineers—Phil Hannon and John Collins—was the 589th Field Artillery. The executive officer of Battery A was Eric Fisher Wood, Jr. Within the first few hours of December 16, Eric Wood became the acting battery commander as the advancing Germans captured Battery A's nominal leader, the boyishly exhuberant Capt. Aloysius J. Mencke, in a forward observation post.

Eric Wood qualified as one of the best and brightest of his generation, with a potentially magnificent future. Born in Santa Barbara, California, the hometown of his mother, in 1919, he was the oldest child in a family of three boys and one girl. He spent most of his civilian life in parts of Pennsylvania.

His father, Eric Fisher Wood, Sr., had led an adventurous life. Back in the first decade of the twentieth century, he panned for gold in Alaska. The wedding ring he pressed on his wife's finger came from ore personally mined by him in Alaska. He distinguished himself during World War I, serving with the American Expeditionary Forces in France. Wood, Sr., managed to combine a career as an author with the profession of architecture. He polished his studies of the latter at the Sorbonne and wrote a biography of Gen. Leonard Wood. He also found time for a losing run for political office.

By the advent of World War II, after a rocky period for the family fortunes as a result of the 1929 stock market crash, Eric Wood, Sr., headed a large firm under his name and owned a profitable apartment house as well as a good-sized farm in Pennsylvania. He was regarded as a highly opinionated but intelligent man. And with mobilization for World War II, he became a brigadier general, given the task of feeding and housing the hordes of displaced persons, slave laborers, mostly from Eastern Europe, transported to work far from home and now freed by advancing Allied armies.

Eric Wood, Jr., attended a series of private schools before graduating from Valley Forge Military Academy. At the academy he played football and performed well in track and field, among other sports. He showed an entrepreneurial bent, operating the campus news agency. When Eric graduated at the top of his class, Princeton admitted him to the Class of '42.

Those who knew Eric, Jr., at that time of his life describe him as uncommonly mature for his age. As the firstborn son, he scored noteworthy academic and athletic achievements, much to the satisfaction and intense interest of his father. The son, as strong willed as his father, was also the one member of the family who refused to allow himself to be steamrollered. "Eric respected his father but felt he still thought in terms of the early years of the twentieth century. He did not appreciate that the world had changed," according to the former Margaret Wadsworth, who married Eric, Jr. "His father would occasionally ask his advice, then disregard it."

The arguments between the male parent and his offspring were not noisy but the elder Wood was unable to build rapport. Eric Wood, Sr.'s fondness for the bottle probably significantly affected relationships. Indeed, after World War II, Eric, Sr., would disown one of his boys.

However, there was also a strong bond between the firstborn and his father, a relationship strengthened by such adventures as a rugged camping trip in Alaska in 1929, just before the stock market crash crimped the family fortunes. The party included Eric's mother, who, like all of the Woodses, at the insistence of her husband, had learned to handle a rifle effectively. Young Eric bagged a moose. During the appropriate seasons, while growing up in Pennsylvania, Eric continued to hunt.

While he had been a major factor on the Valley Forge football squad, Eric never starred in a similar role at Princeton. Paul Busse, who accumulated excellent press notices for his exploits on the Palmer Stadium field in those years, describes Wood as "a very virile, masculine guy, a hard-working player without exceptional skill or natural ability for the game." Others from the period remember him as "a great softball pitcher" for the interclub competition.

Perhaps what is most remarkable about Wood's four years at Princeton is how few of his classmates really can recall him, even though he was a member of Elm Club (such "eating clubs" were the school's equivalent of Greek letter fraternities), earned a varsity P in both football and track and participated in a variety of extracurricular activities. He was at heart a loner. And his isolation was probably magnified by a ghastly hunting accident that killed his closest friend and roommate, Andrew Jones, just before the start of their final year at Princeton.

Eric Wood, Jr., had always demonstrated a touch of the rebel, the independent. He had displayed his contempt for authority along with his taste for practical jokes while a senior at Valley Forge. With several other cadets he had come to regard the commandant as an unreasoning stickler for the rules. One of the unbreakable ukases dictated that in the event of fire all cadets would assemble on a paved area some distance from the buildings. Wood and his associates poured a mix of gas and oil on the designated safety zone and started a blaze. When the alarm was duly sounded, students, faculty and commanding officer all milled about, unable to resolve the question of where to assemble. Hardly the height of wit, the stunt demonstrates Wood's resistance to unthinking power.

He graduated from Princeton with honors from the School of Public and International Affairs, but refused a commission as a second lieutenant in the field artillery, which he had earned through his enrollment in the Reserve Officers' Training Class. He apparently chose to turn down a commission after a discussion with his father. The elder Wood, now busy with his military duties, requested his son to oversee the family farm. While a resident farmer and wife actually fed the pigs, milked the cattle and grew the hay, the operation was large enough to demand some supervisory business expertise.

A second reason for Wood, Jr.'s not immediately packing himself off to the army may have been his marriage. Meg Wadsworth, from Wayne, Pennsylvania, had known Eric for some time and their courtship continued while she attended Bryn Mawr. In July 1941, before beginning his senior year, the pair took along their respective roommates and eloped to Maryland, with Andrew Jones as best man. "My parents did not want us even to be engaged and they would have tried to break us up," says the woman who married the college student. "And the reaction of Eric's father would have been the same."

Princeton rules forbade marriage for its undergraduates but the university's celebrated Dean Christian Gauss ignored the infraction. He apparently was aware that the ordinary restrictions of peacetime could not be maintained. The couple's first daughter, Pam, was born while Eric was still an undergraduate.

Eric Wood, Jr.'s delay in entering the service certainly did not reflect his sentiments about the two sides. "We were sympathetic with England," says Meg. "We were less so for the French, who folded their tents." Her husband, she says, actually spent only a small portion of his time dealing with farm matters. "There are not many young men of twenty-one or twenty-two who know what they want to do with their lives. But Eric did. He foresaw a brilliant opportunity in the plastics field. And after graduation he took a job with Fairchild Aviation in Hagerstown, Maryland. It was close enough for him to be able to commute."

Even at the defense plant, Eric Wood again demonstrated his singularity. "There were two distinct groups at the plant, the engineers and the workers," notes Eric Wood's wife. "Eric did not have an engineering degree but he managed to be accepted by both." He joined the labor union and became the shop steward.

As a scion from the conservative Pennsylvania gentility with a preppie, white-shoe education at an upperclass Ivy League university, Wood's involvement in a union smacked of rampant heresy. "I remember a wild Sunday dinner," says Meg Wood. "Eric's father certainly did not believe in unions. Nobody shouted but the language became extremely acerbic. After that one time, everyone avoided the subject." According to Eric Wood's daughter, Pamela, her father spoke of the need for unions to attract educated people such as himself in order to bridge the gap with management.

Eventually, however, the World War II demands for manpower overtook any prospects for remaining a civilian. Although he was now the father of a daughter, as well as a husband, Eric Wood, Jr., entered the service in April 1943 and soon received his commission in the field artillery. He was posted to the 589th, part of the 106th Division.

For well over a year of the 589th's stateside training, Meg Wood, with their infant daughter Pamela, was a camp follower, trailing her husband from Fort Jackson, South Carolina, through Tennessee maneuvers to Camp Atterbury, Indiana, the final home of the outfit before it left to fight.

Eric had become close friends with Lt. Ted Kiendl, the executive officer of another battery. In a wrinkle of fate, Kiendl and Wood switched units on the eve of departure for Europe, with Wood assuming Kiendl's Battery A post and Kiendl taking Eric's slot with Battery B. "Eric struck me as a man of unimpeachable character," says Kiendl. "He had a sense of himself that gave him great confidence." But, according to Kiendl, he was no prig. Occasionally he would drop a Rabelaisian remark that was all the more striking because of from whom it came. And as a soldier, he impressed Kiendl with his thoroughness, his attention to detail. "We all learned to field-strip a weapon, break it down into its basic components to clean it. But Eric taught himself how to take the entire thing apart, the kind of work ordinarily done only by the artificer, the specialist in weapons. He also carried more equipment than others, anything that he thought might enhance his performance."

When the division embarked for Europe, Meg Wood was expecting a second child. "Here I was, pregnant, and he was on his way overseas. But, being Eric, he had everything in total order to cover any possibilities."

On his way to the Ardennes, Eric met his father and his brother Peter, who was serving on the elder Wood's staff in London. A second reunion occurred on December 15 during a brief visit by brother and father to the battery gun positions near the town of Schönberg. There were no DPs in the Ardennes for General Wood to concern himself with, but it was typical of him to go where he wished without concern for regulations. Meanwhile, on December 8, Meg Wood had given birth to Eric Fisher Wood III.

The 2nd Division artillery men had dug sufficient foxholes for all of the gun crews. But Eric Wood was unhappy to discover that there was no cover over the foxholes. He ordered his cannoneers to roof-over every position. By December 14, the troops were protected from overhead bursts by pine logs. In addition, he arranged to build some flexibility into the emplacement for his Number Four gun. By this alteration, he gave the battery not only the capacity to fire in support of ground troops but also a means to defend against an enemy advance along the only paved road in his vicinity.

Among the soldiers serving with Eric Wood was a Floridian, Barney Alford. He grew up in Pensacola, where the family roots dug deep, perhaps four or five generations. "I thought about events in Europe, particularly with reference to Hitler. He seemed to me to be a madman out to rule the world and would eventually have to be defeated. Even before the U.S.A. got into the war, I followed what happened very closely."

Alford had completed a year at the University of Florida when called up by the draft. "I had field artillery ROTC in college," says

Alford. "When I entered the service, the armed forces were trying out a quota system for the different branches. I think that was because everyone seemed to want to get into the air corps. I wanted to join the marines but one had to go through the draft board and sign the papers indicating the branch you wanted. I put down my choice, but when I got to the induction center at Camp Blanding, Florida, they had lost my papers at the Marine Center. So I ended up in the 589th Field Artillery Battalion."

Because of his ROTC training, Alford was installed as the number one man on a 105-mm howitzer. He was promoted to corporal and then became a sergeant in command of Battery A's second gun section. The battery itself consisted of four sections.

Alford's section was in place southeast of the town of Auw, not far from Phil Hannon and his fellow 81st Engineers on December 16. "We were just behind a ridge in some crude log cabin-like structure which we inherited from the 2nd Division. They were the best we had during the fighting and we got hot meals regularly." At 6:05 A.M. they recorded their first piece of incoming mail. "We received about fifty rounds. I wasn't very impressed with our first shelling, as it was not very close to us. Later, as it got closer, we quickly learned to read the whistle of the rounds and knew when to take cover."

During a lull, Alford saw Eric Wood going from one gun section to another, "making sure all of the men were in the shelters that he had us build and that no one had been hurt." Subsequently, Wood personally took out a patrol to investigate a nearby building that conceivably contained enemy observers. While four or five soldiers covered him, Wood boldly entered the house by himself. It was empty.

The guns now boomed away at targets supplied by battery headquarters. "The thought occurred to me," says Alford, "that here we were shooting at each other and neither of us knew one another with no personal grudge against each other."

The war became considerably more personal for the men of Battery A when a quartet of German tanks clanked up the highway alongside their position. Bazooka and howitzer shells discouraged two tanks. Eric Wood, when he heard the tracked vehicles approaching, had sprinted to a small hill where he could actually see the oncoming tanks. He yelled commands to his gunners with the Number Four piece, the one to which he had added an extra dimension of coverage. The crew scored a direct hit. Further fire from Battery A and the adroit use of high explosive loads curtailed any budding attack by infantrymen supported by the tanks. For the moment, the 589th people had held their ground.

The forces which attacked the 589th with Eric Wood and Barney Alford, as well as the 424th Regiment, were from the Fifth Panzer Army commanded by Manteuffel. The assault resisted by Harry Martin, Jr., and others in L Company and the artillerymen was part of a pincers, designed to surround the other two regiments of the 106th Division. Theoretically, Manteuffel's troops aimed then to drive west through St. Vith, the headquarters of the 106th, and proceed through Bastogne. Both of these towns served as hubs for the few good roads through the Ardennes. From there, the German forces would strike for the Meuse.

The strategy of the Sixth Panzer Army under Sepp Dietrich envisioned a more spectacular advance. It called for a spearhead to punch through the American defenses and within two days cross the Meuse, a distance of about fifty miles from the closest point of attack. To pull off this combat coup, the commander chose SS Panzer Lt. Col. Jochen Peiper.

Only twenty-nine, son of a World War I Prussian army officer wounded in Africa, Peiper bore excellent credentials. He joined the Hitler Youth in 1933. At age nineteen, he wrote to the headquarters of the *Schutz Staffel* (protective brigade) Superior District East, whose chief was Sepp Dietrich, and requested active SS membership. He declared himself intent on making the SS his career and sought to become an officer candidate. By age twenty-one Peiper had fulfilled his wish; he received his lieutenant's commission. The training site for SS officers was at Dachau, home for Nazi Germany's first concentration camp. The glory begun at Dachau would eventually turn into sackcloth and ashes at the same site.

Peiper's baptismal name was actually Joachim, taken from the Bible. True believers in the elite *Schutz Staffel*, however, scorned the Holy Book, and Peiper changed it to Jochen. As a member of the SS, he was politically correct enough to become an aide-de-camp to Gestapo chief Heinrich Himmler. He toured conquered Poland with his boss and personally witnessed murders by gas. He never, however, actually joined the Nazi Party, explaining once that he did not wish to curry favor for his military career by using the leverage of a party member.

The beginning of World War II in 1939 recast the SS. One branch assumed responsibility for internal security matters like the concentration camps. The other half became a military force separate from the traditional *Wehrmacht*. The Waffen SS, as it was known, operated its own armor, artillery and infantry. It was Hitler's hidden ace in the event that the traditional German military establishment ever sought to overthrow him. On occasion, Waffen SS performed duties associated with their concentration camp cousins, murdering Jews, Poles, Russians and others in conquered territories with its weapons instead of poison gas.

Peiper served at Hitler's military headquarters in Poland, then joined the crack *Liebstandarte Adolf Hitler*, the 1st SS Panzer Division in France. He picked up both First and Second Class Iron Crosses for his work during the spring of 1940. In fact, he and another officer became such favorites that they were given the use of two autos seized in France and kept for their use at *der Führer's* command post. Himmler assured the pair that after the war ended the cars were theirs.

The *Liebstandarte* entered combat in the Soviet Union in July 1941, driving 600 miles to the Don River in four months. But winter brought severe casualties and the outfit retired to France for refitting. Peiper began to build a repuation for audacity and brutality. In 1943, the German 302nd Infantry Division appeared trapped on the banks of the frozen Donets River. Sepp Dietrich, commander of the 1st SS Panzer Division, acting on orders from above, dispatched Peiper with a mechanized battalion to rescue the beleaguered soldiers. Peiper led his troops in an attack that temporarily drove off the Soviet armies. The battalion formed a semicircle that shielded the 302nd from further ravages by the Red troops. When all of the infantrymen had made their escape, Peiper discovered the ice on the Donets too thin to bear the weight of his halftracks. In a brilliant maneuver, he swung the battalion around and smashed through the enemy ranks from the rear until he found a bridge capable of handling his vehicles.

An SS trooper who served with Peiper said, "In Russia, generally we did not take any prisoners at all. On various occasions we burned down whole villages with blowtorches." Near Kharkov, in 1943, the soldier understood Peiper was in command when a village was torched. The orders called for the men to "bump off all inhabitants, including women and children. It was generally known in the unit that Peiper actively participated in the action."

Promoted to the rank of major, he personally destroyed an enemy tank with a rifle grenade from only a few yards way. One comrade said Peiper grinned and remarked, "That should suffice for a close-combat badge, boys." His heroics in Russia added Oak Leaves to his Knight's Cross.

Shifted to the crumbling front in Italy, Peiper engaged in partisan control. When two of his men were captured by guerrillas in a Piedmontese town, Peiper launched a full-scale assault on the place, destroying most of the buildings and killing thirty-three inhabitants.

Such operations caused some men to refer to him as "Blowtorch Peiper." German psychiatrists reported Peiper was "intelligent, but egocentric and mistrustful of others." He habitually sought to impress his equals with his connections. They evaluated him as a critical and difficult subordinate, strong of will, inclined to attempt to achieve results in quick, impulsive thrusts. But he was thoroughly faithful to the Nazi credo. His character, his skill ful use of armor, plus his excellent command of English, made him an ideal choice for the lead element of his old outfit, the 1st SS Panzer Division, in the Ardennes.

Kampfgruppe Peiper (Task force Peiper) received official word of the strike through the Ardennes on December 14, although Peiper himself knew of it three days earlier. At that time, said Peiper, the Chief of Staff for the Sixth SS Panzer Army inquired "what I thought about the possibilities of an attack in the Eifel region and how much time it would take a tank regiment to proceed eighty kilometers at night. Feeling it was not a good idea to decide such a question merely by looking at a map, I made a fast run of eighty kilometers with a Panther tank, driving down the route Euskirchen, Münstereifel, Blankenburg. If I had a free road to myself, I could make eighty kilometers in one night. Of course with an entire division, that was a different question." Peiper did not seem to consider the problems of people shooting at him or blowing up bridges in his pathway. The exercise resembled a football player who proves he could sprint 100 yards while the other team was still in the lockerroom.

Peiper could not train his *Kampfgruppe* during the few days between hearing of his mission and the jump-off. The move of the U.S. 2nd Division and the 99th forced the German high command to make Peiper's legion a reserve in the event of a breakthrough. Nor was he permitted any kind of reconnaissance. Under the circumstances, he could only instruct the men on how to drive through mountainous terrain and on icy roads.

At a briefing, Peiper received a map that described the path for his column. It included narrow, even unpaved roads. He studied it and then complained, "This route is not for tanks but for bicycles." He pointed out that other units had been given better roads, but this was the plan approved by Hitler and no one dared change it. In fact, a standing order decreed that the troops were forbidden to encroach upon the turf assigned to others.

Kampfgruppe Peiper, with 4,000 men, was to advance in a fifteen-mile-long column. Tactically, the extended line of soldiers, tanks, halftracks, artillery, trucks and other vehicles weakened the task force's striking power. But the roads, as Sepp Dietrich noted, were too narrow for any broader movement. Furthermore, the sinuous stretch reduced maneuverability to a minimum. Peiper sought to equip his Panzer phase with the lighter Panther tanks rather than the heavy, underpowered and sluggish big Tigers.

Nevertheless, when all of the elements had been shown to Peiper, he bragged his group would reach the Meuse River first, depending on several caveats. Peiper wanted an initial infantry attack to penetrate the American lines by 7:00 A.M. and clear the mines from the road between Losheim and Losheimergraben. Then engineers would need to replace a destroyed overpass on his route by noon. If these were accomplished, the SS lieutenant colonel guaranteed he would reach the Meuse by midnight or the early hours of December 17. The commanding officer of the 12th *Volksgrenadier* Division asserted that the artillery barrage begun before dawn would easily allow Peiper's people to reach Losheim by 7:00 A.M.

The road conditions and the massive traffic for the German armies forced Peiper to place all of his combat units at the front of the column because it would be impossible to move up reinforcements rapidly, if needed. A group of halftracks carrying infantrymen led the procession. When resistance developed, the foot soldiers were to await the medium tanks. The engineers with their heavy equipment were consigned to a place far back in the ruck. Obtaining their services quickly would be a problem. *Kampfgruppe Peiper* carried enough ammunition to last it four or five days and fuel for an even shorter period, as two entire trainloads of gasoline never reached the assembly point. Additional supplies of fuel would have to be captured, taken from Allied dumps.

For all of the problems, the veteran Waffen SS soldiers under Peiper assembled in good cheer under cover of the Blankenheimer woods, where their commander lived in a forester's house. Morale remained high and their determination was supposedly bolstered after an assignment to clean up an area of Düren, devastated by an Allied bombing attack that splattered the remains of women and children on walls, sidewalks and streets. Indeed, as part of his pep talk to the men, Peiper told them to remember the "terror bombing" at Düren.

An unwelcome addition to the inflexible line of march, however, was the assignment of the 150 Brigade, the overall unit under Skorzeny that included the contingent from Operation *Greif.* Skorzeny's people, with their faintly disguised "Sherman" tanks, genuine U.S. Jeeps and trucks, were to accompany the combat team of *Kampfgruppe Peiper.* Their assignment was to race forward and seize Meuse bridges after Peiper carved a wedge through to the river.

For his part, Peiper scorned the *ersatz* Americans. "They might as well have stayed at home because they were never near the head of the column where they planned to be," said Peiper. The presence of the Skorzeny bunch undoubtedly irked Peiper because he exercised no tactical control over them.

While the bulk of Skorzeny's 150 Brigade awaited their opportunity alongside *Kampfgruppe Peiper,* forty-four men under *Greif* successfully infiltrated the Allied lines. They had been broken into three groups. Demolition teams sought to blow up bridges, munitions and gas dumps. Several small squads were to reconnoiter as far west as the Meuse River and report where the enemy troops were and their strength. In addition, as opportunities presented themselves, these men were to reverse road signs, switch mine markers and perform similar acts that would mislead the Americans. The third section focused on disruption of communications, cutting telephone wires, blowing up transmitter stations and issuing false commands.

Skorzeny described the technique that enabled his commandos to slip through the lines: "The jeeps would follow at the rear of an attacking panzer column and when the column got into a fire fight, they would move off the road and travel around the battle area on side roads until they were behind the withdrawing American troops. This was very easy in the first few days of the confused fighting."

"Very easy" was the description given by the chief of *Greif*, but for a commando like Sgt. Maj. Heinz Rohde, bearing identification as "Sgt. Morris Woodahl" of the U.S. Army, it was not a day at the beach. "At 5:15 A.M. timed to the exact second, a hellish scene sprang to life around us as virtually hundreds of dazzling searchlights around the Hohes Venn Mountains directed their ghostly fingers onto the American positions, and the artillery and rocketlauncher positions behind us unleashed an unearthly fire such as we had never yet encountered in any attack over such a narrow area. The unmistakeable whine of our own shells made it plain that we must be right in front of the enemy positions. A series of balls of light shooting up heralded a coming change of scene, brought about by the panzers, whose menace had till then lain dormant.

"After moving on barely fifty meters, the panzer which we had been closely following in our jeep came to a standstill. The leading panzers made it known that we were now in no man's land. High time to discard our para-suits [German uniforms worn to this point over the American ones]. For our driver this was a real feat of acrobatics, as it was impossible for us to stop and he had to carry out his undressing act while we were on the move. Our jeep jumped around like a young deer, and while the driver kicked frantically at the accelerator pedal, the co-driver tried to steer the vehicle around the obstacles with desperate wrenches of the wheel.

"The first burning American truck suddenly appeared. It was now that we first ran up against the strong defenses of the Yankees; directly in front of us a group of American infantry was trying to place an antitank gun in position. How relieved we were to find that apart from being splattered with mud nothing else had hit us.

"A sergeant [American] tried with shouts and signals to bring us into action; which was a quite unreasonable demand, as we had strict contrary orders and certainly didn't come under his unit." Almost immediately thereafter, an American MP confronted the party. He energetically indicated they should avoid the road as enemy shellfire was bombarding it.

Rohde noted, "the gradual coming of daylight, and the disarray of the enemy combat units, all gave us unexpected encouragement. We realized with increasing satisfaction that our disguise was fairly complete and, accordingly, felt more and more safe. We were later to learn how deceptive this feeling of safety was. How could we have known that no American jeep was manned by more than two or, at most, three soldiers [the commandos packed four men in a jeep]? Who told us that at this point we should be driving either with no lights at all or fully illuminated, but under no circumstances with coverings over headlights—the so-called blackout lighting—as we were doing?"

Ten miles behind the American lines, Rohde and company transmitted their first radio report and were overjoyed at the prompt, coded acknowledgement. As they continued on, they observed numerous roadblocks with large numbers of military police, signs that boded poorly for the espionage and sabotage teams. They were well behind schedule when daylight faded. Now Rohde noticed that the genuine American vehicles employed full headlights. The jeep was quickly pulled off the road on the pretense of a mechanical problem. The men lifted the hood while they surreptitiously ripped away the blackout covers from the headlights.

"All of a sudden, there was a jeep standing right beside us. A captain swung his long legs out of the jeep and in a stentorian voice offered to tow us to the nearest repair unit, but he was as pleased as we were when our jeep started up again. With a friendly 'thanks' and an 'O.K.' we both went on our way."

The team sent a radio message advising of the standard American use of headlights. "Later we learned that our warning was received too late; two of our commando teams had already been recognized and intercepted."

By 5:30 P.M. they reached the town of Huy on the Meuse. They had been instructed to cross the bridge and file intelligence on the nature of the American defenses. To Rohde's dismay the bridge was packed with traffic moving in both directions. Even as he and his comrades watched from perhaps 300 yards away, a huge searchlight was brought into place across the river and bathed the area in a bright beam. The spies interpreted the illumination as evidence the Americans were now aware of their mission. They reported the information to their superiors and asked permission to leave immediately. Headquarters refused at first but by morning reluctantly acquiesced. Using a different route, Rohde and company successfully made their way back to the German lines.

Initially, protected by the fog of battle and the absence of awareness of *Greif* among the Americans in the field, other teams also passed themselves off as GIs quite successfully. Said Skorzeny, " . . . a little adventure showed us how receptive the Americans then were to rumours . . . . at a village where two American companies were organized for defense, having established roadblocks and machine gun nests. It was for our men a shock when they were addressed by an Americn officer who wanted to know something about the situation at the front.

"After the team leader—who was wearing the uniform of an American sergeant—had recovered his surprise, he invented an excellent story for the benefit of this officer. The fright betrayed in the the face of the men was probably attributed to the alleged previous scuffle with German troops. The team leader solemnly assured him that the 'Krauts' had passed the village on both sides, so that it was virtually isolated. The American must have swallowed this story, as he soon gave an order to withdraw."

The advantage of American ignorance of *Greif,* however, ended mid-morning, the very first day of the German attack. In the vicinity of where Harry Martin learned to "squeeze the trigger," Lt. William Shakespeare, making sports page headlines a few years before while lugging a football for Notre Dame, captured a German captain from the 116th Panzer Division. Bagged along with the officer was a map case containing the plan of attack and papers outlining Operation *Greif.* The documents spelled out the recognition signals and the roads upon which the teams expected to operate. Within a few hours, the material circulated among the top echelons of U.S. intelligence.

Chapter V

THE CENTER DOES NOT HOLD

WHILE *KAMPFGRUPPE PEIPER* AND its impatient commander idled its engines in anticipation of the lightning strike for the Meuse, twenty-year-old 1st Lt. Lyle Bouck and the handful of others in the Intelligence & Reconnaissance platoon of the 3rd Battalion, 394th Infantry Regiment, 99th Division, remained in place on the outskirts of Lanzerath, directly in the path of the spearhead.

"We had made contact with the task force from the 14th Cav," says Bouck, "and knew they had some machine guns and antitank guns on our right flank and in Lanzerath in front of us. But they were in a different Corps, so the communication between us was limited.

"Some time before dawn, the artillery fire began. I don't know how long it lasted but it seemed like a long time. At first it went over our heads. Then they started to hit in front of Lanzerath. There was a short lull before quite a bit began to drop on our positions. I had the impression we had been bracketed. It was intermittent for more than an hour, a lot of treebursts.

"Initially, we were in a shocked, stunned state. I kept wondering when we'd start taking casualties but the log coverings over the foxholes shielded us. I called regiment when it began and they'd been half-asleep when it started. But the word was artillery fire was hitting the entire regiment. The only instructions I got were to be doubly alert.

"After about two hours, the firing lifted. I went to every foxhole to make contact. To my surprise, nobody had been hurt. But we were all scared. I told everyone that somebody would attack us soon. Yet, nothing happened. We could hear small arms fire up the road near Losheimergraben and behind us at Bucholz Station. But our sector was quiet. I contacted Kris at regiment to get in-

105

structions. I had to use the radio since the telephone lines were all gone. Kris told me to stay in place and report what's happening.

"Maybe an hour later, we suddenly heard motors, American vehicles moving. The tank destroyers pulled out, traveling towards Bucholz Station." Although Bill Tsakanikas, who shared a foxhole with Bouck, subsequently was quoted, "If they can't sign off on the phone, they might at least wave goodbye as they leave," Bouck does not remember any conversation over the abrupt exit of the 14th Cavalry. Instead, he recalls talking by radio with Kris and being told to get someone into Lanzerath to take sightings from a house previously manned by field artillery observers.

"I took Slape, my platoon sergeant, Tsak and a fellow named John Creger and we ran down the hill and into the house. Inside the place we found a civilian, using a telephone. Tsak was ready to shoot him but I said let him go. We couldn't handle prisoners and I was not going to shoot an unarmed man. From the second floor we could see where the road dipped, then crested about 600 yards away. Through my field glasses I saw German soldiers wearing the helmets of paratroopers. We had taken along a field wire and I told Slape and Creger to stay there and keep me posted.

"When I got back to my position, I tried to get artillery fire from regiment but they said they couldn't give us any. Just about then, from a nearby trail, a jeep pulled up. It carried Lt. Warren Springer and three enlisted men from a Field Artillery Observation unit."

Indeed, Springer, Sgt. Peter Gacki, Cpl. Billy Queen and T/4 Willard Wibben belonged to C Battery of the 371st Field Artillery, the outfit in which Dick Byers served. Byers remembers, "We had all been worried about them. They had reported on the night of December 15 that Losheim [behind the German lines] was lit up like a Christmas tree."

Springer volunteered to join his tiny band with the I & R Platoon. Bouck accepted and urged Springer to see if he could raise some artillery fire upon the oncoming enemy host. The newcomers adjourned to foxhole positions and Bouck never saw any of them again.

The FA observer, using a radio in his jeep, contacted the 371st gunners. Springer watched the results: "Some rounds came in on Lanzerath. I sent corrections, and there were more rounds. Then something hit the jeep, either mortar or artillery fire, and halted all communications."

Bouck was advised of a sudden emergency. "Slape called to tell me that Germans were in the house. I promised him help. I ran to the front of the platoon and picked three men. Aubrey McGehee from McComb, Mississippi, was a strong, rugged man who'd played football. McGehee knew the layout of the house, and he'd knock the crap out of anybody. Jordan 'Pop' Robinson was thirty-seven [any enlisted man over the age of thirty inevitably picked up the nickname of 'Pop'], was from Tennessee and he'd shoot anything he saw. I could count on Jim Sivola from Florida to back up McGehee.

"Slape and Creger decided not to wait. They made a break for it, ducking through a door to an adjoining barn where they hid themselves under some cows. Meanwhile, my three guys arrived at the house and quickly got into a fire fight with the Germans. Slape and Creger bolted from the barn, circled into the woods and then came back across the road, which ran north-south. A machine gun opened up and shot off the heel of Slape's left shoe. He fell hard on the road, breaking a rib and his chest bone. But he and Creger made it back to our place. McGehee, Robinson and Sivola, meanwhile, were cut off by the machine gun and isolated on the east side of the road.

"While all of this was going on, here comes a German column up the road, walking north towards us, single file on both sides of the road, their weapons slung. They were singing as they marched.

"I ordered don't fire until I give the word or I start shooting. There was an advance party of maybe thirty and then the main body of troops with the command group. That's whom I wanted to hit. I was also wondering whether they would turn left and cut us off but they kept on straight ahead, due north.

"Just as I was running all this through my head and about to open fire, Tine Scholzen, a little girl of about thirteen, ran up to three officers in a jeep at the front. She pointed up the road, in our direction. I still think she was showing them which way the tank destroyers went. I don't believe she knew we were even there. But the paratroopers suddenly dispersed.

"As they did, Tsak opened fire and so did the rest of us. McGehee, Robinson and Sivola saw no way to get back to us. They took off from the east side of the road and tried to reach the 1st Battalion. When they came to a deep railroad cut, they went down and then up the other side. German soldiers in camouflage caught them. Sivola was badly wounded in the shoulder, a bullet tore off most of the calf in Robinson's right leg and, seeing the situation was hopeless, McGehee and the other two surrendered.

"For us, the shooting stopped as the Germans retreated. We could see people crawling around to reorganize. Then after maybe an hour and a half they came screaming and yelling, in a direct frontal attack up the snow-covered hill. They were firing at us but they had no targets. And there was a typical farm fence that bisected the hill. The paratroopers had to climb over this fence. For us it was like target practice. We had a couple of BARs, a .30-caliber machine gun manned by Risto Milosevich. Tsak and Slape took turns on the .50-caliber machine gun of the jeep, until it was hit in the breech and blew up. The other guys had M-1s, while I had a carbine. I could see blood all over the snow, I heard screaming, hollering. It was a bizarre scene, hard for me to realize it was really happening.

"Then they stopped coming. Someone waved a red flag and in poor English yelled, 'Medics! Medics!' It was approaching noon. For forty-five minutes, except for the sounds of wounded men in pain, the field and woods were quiet. They tended their injured, dragged them backwards. We had our own casualties. In this second attack, a rifle grenade smashed into Lou Kahlil's face. It didn't detonate but it broke his jaw in four places, and hammered five teeth into the rest of his mouth. Someone stuffed sulfa powder in the wound, then rubbed snow on his face. Lou got back on his feet."

When the third attack came, Kahlil again was firing at the enemy. Risto Milosevich, alone in a foxhole, for a time operated a machine gun by himself. Milosevich recalled, "It was like shooting clay ducks at the amusement park. But while I was concentrating hard on a German, I didn't notice another one about fifteen yards from my hole. He had a potato masher [grenade] in his hand, cocked and ready to swing it forward. He was looking right at me. I had the machine gun in my hand and fired point-blank. He scared me so badly that I think I kept firing so long I cut him in half. But by myself I couldn't keep the gun from jamming.

"Slape came into the hole with me. He took over the machine gun while I fed the belt. He kept firing and firing and I was harping at him to shoot in bursts of three." The weapon became so hot that it cooked off rounds even when Slape released the trigger. He could only shut it down by raising the cover. The barrel finally bowed from the heat and became inoperable.

"We had to use my M–1, since Slape hadn't brought his to the foxhole. It worked out well, though I kept shouting at Slape to save one bullet until I loaded the next clip.

"I saw a German medic about thirty yards from our hole. He was working on a soldier whom I thought was dead. That made me very suspicious. The medic kept looking at us and his lips moved constantly. After the medic had appeared, mortar fire was landing right on us. I was sure he was directing it. And then as I watched him, he turned. I noticed a pistol in his belt. I asked Slape for the rifle so I could shoot him. He refused, saying there were too many other Germans in front of us. When I explained about the medic, Slape shot him." During a lull, the platoon sergeant discovered two bullet holes in his field jacket.

Springer and his three companions, from their dugouts, also poured small arms fire on the enemy. At some point, an enemy slug struck Cpl. Billy Queen in the stomach. There was nothing his companions could do for him.

Ammunition began to run low as the Germans were driven back after a third attack. Joe McConnell saw a soldier charging his foxhole. He managed to shoot him in the chest or stomach but as the man fell he discharged his weapon. Slugs struck McConnell in the upper left arm. And one of Bouck's original eighteen men in the position was now dead.

Enemy fire had destroyed the platoon radio. Bouck detailed Cpl. Sam Jenkins and Pfc. Robert Preston to carry word of the I & R platoon's plight back to headquarters and return either with reinforcements or permission for the unit to withdraw. The two sneaked back through the woods. But the area behind the platoon was now a hive of enemy soldiers, as other Americans had retreated. For thirty-six hours, Jenkins and Preston hid out, trying to reach friendly forces. They were captured on December 18.

Bouck decided to pull out. "It was late in the day, but still light, somewhere between three-thirty and four-thirty in the afternoon. I sent word that when I blew a whistle three times everyone would leave the foxholes with their weapons. We'd rendezvous at a point on the road. We would move by night through the woods. I told Slape and Tsak to remove the distributor caps from the jeeps.

" Tsak was with me in a foxhole as we prepared to take off. I heard the sound of boots and Germans hollering as they fired. I had one full magazine left in my carbine. I saw two figures running towards us. I had filed the sere off my carbine, so when I squeezed the trigger it operated like a machine gun. I emptied the clip at those two. I was satisfied that I had fired my last round.

"I saw the muzzle of a gun poke into our hole. I pushed Tsakanikas to get him out of the way and then someone yelled, 'How many of you? How many of you?' I didn't speak much German but I answered, *'Zwei! Zwei!'* With that came a burst of gunfire.

"The next thing I knew, I am lifting Bill Tsakanikas, who was making a horrible gurgling noise, out of the foxhole. There was an arm helping me and, whomever it was, he pulled Tsak out. Someone shined a flashlight on his face. *'Mein Gott! Mein Gott!'* I heard. When I saw what a bloody mess Tsak was, I couldn't recognize him. Half his face had been shot away. His right eyeball hung in the gap where his cheek had been.

"There was still some small arms fire going on. An officer who spoke very good English demanded, 'When are your men going to stop shooting?' I answered, 'Those must be your guys. We don't have any ammo left.' He didn't answer but the firing ended. I felt very hot. I had been hit in my boot."

Springer had also surrendered. "I heard a mixture of German and English. We were told to throw our guns out and come out or they would throw hand grenades in. I expected that they would shoot us when we came out, but I thought I would rather go that way than to be inside the enclosed space of the dugout when a grenade went off. So out we came and I was surprised when they didn't fire."

A soldier motioned for Bouck to pick up Tsak. "I don't know how I did it. There was a German helping me support him down the hill. We climbed over that fence past all of the bodies of the German dead.

"Another soldier was right behind us and he suddenly came around in front. He kept asking if we had been at St.-Lô. I answered, *'Nein. Nein.'* He started screaming about his comrades at St.-Lô. Shit, I didn't know what else to say. Then he stuck a gun in my back and pulled the trigger. I don't know whether it was a misfire or the gun was empty. But someone said, *'Raus. Raus.'* He disappeared and we went into Lanzerath.

"They put us in a room with a bench. They sat me there with Tsak, who leaned on my left shoulder. He'd been bandaged and only one eye and his nose were visible. Blood seeped through my field jacket and I realized I had been grazed. I could walk okay, without pain or discomfort.

"The rest of the platoon showed up. Sgt. George Redmond carried in Lou Kahlil. You could only see a nose and and eye on him also, because of the bandaging. They brought in McConnell. His field jacket had been cut away and he had a bad wound in the shoulder. There were German wounded all over the floor and it seemed like a strange combination of a command post and aid station.

"Slape whispered to me there did not seem to be any guards. He thought we could slip out the back door. I answered that I had to stick with the wounded and see that they received help. Slape said he'd stay.

"The time dragged on. It was dark. Artillery fire landed on the town but nothing struck our building. I made contact with someone of authority and after a conference he agreed to let Tsak lie on the floor next to Kahlil.

"A cuckoo clock on the wall sounded off when it reached midnight. That meant December 17. I had reached my twenty-first birthday. I had an aunt who studied astrology and when I reached thirteen, she told me that if I could live past my twenty-first birthday, I would have a very long, meaningful life. With all that had happened, I kept thinking of her prediction. Now that I was twenty-one, I actually became tough, cocky, nothing could hurt me.

"Just about this time, I realized there was a furious argument going on. An SS officer was pounding his fist as he tried to show a map on a bureau. He gave that up and stabbed the map on the wall with two bayonets. While he was shouting at another officer, messengers came and went; the SS officer spoke to them. I could hear the sounds of tanks and other heavy vehicles. This went on well after midnight, until a few hours before dawn."

Springer, Gacki and Wibben, the survivors of the observation team also spent the remainder of the night in the place. Unbeknownst to Bouck, in what was formerly the Café Scholzen, he had been an eyewitness to a bitter dispute between the commander of 9th Regiment in the 3rd Parachute Division and Jochen Peiper, who was now close to twenty-four hours behind his schedule, not having penetrated the American lines by an inch. Peiper had arrived in Lanzerath in a fury. He had been stalled for hours because a bridge blown while the Germans retreated during the autumn had not been repaired. Horse-drawn artillery from the 12th *Volksgrenadier* Division had blocked the roads, preventing engineers from bringing up their repair gear. Two detours that consumed valuable time had brought him to Lanzerath.

A decrepit relic of a once-crack unit, the 9th Parachute Regiment was led by Col. Helmut von Hofmann, whose background did not include infantry maneuvers. The attempt to overrun the I & R platoon's position was a disastrous waste of manpower. One of the experienced German noncoms, Vince Kuhlbach, had pleaded vainly against tactics that directed large groups of men across an open field into withering fire. The low quality of the parachute regiment is evident from the memories of a member who said later, "I was armed with a machine gun. When I checked the weapon, I discovered the firing pin was missing. When I asked an officer about the missing part, I was told that I should wait for someone to be killed or wounded in order to use the gun. On record we were a fully motorized troop, but there were few vehicles and less petrol. The essential pieces of equipment and ammunition were moved by handcart and pram."

Although outranked by the paratroop commander, Peiper demanded an explanation for the delay. Peiper recalled von Hofmann's response. "His answer was that the woods were heavily fortified and that scattered fire from prepared pillboxes, plus mines in the road were holding up the advance. He told me it was impossible to attack under these circumstances.

"I asked him if he had personally reconnoitered the American positions in the woods, and he replied he had received information from one of his battalion commanders. I asked the battalion commander and he said he had gotten the operation from a captain in his battalion. I called the captain and he answered that he had not personally seen the American [forces]. At this point I became very angry and ordered the paratroop regiment to give me one battalion and I would lead the breakthrough.

"The attack was set for 0400. Two Panthers would lead the column, followed by a series of armored halftracks and then a mixture of Panther and M4 [Mark IV] tanks. Strangely enough, we broke through the area without firing a shot and found it completely unoccupied."

The I & R platoon, of course, had surrendered and, in the darkness, Peiper, following the road, never saw the hundreds of bodies still lying in the fields. Estimates of the German dead, almost entirely attributable to the small arms of Bouck and company, range from 300 to 500. Later on, Peiper did not even seem to remember the many wounded Germans being treated in and around the Café Scholzen.

Although he claimed that except for occasional artillery rounds he intially encountered no Americans, Peiper realized that mines planted by the Americans and left by his countrymen when they retreated had threatened his column. With his timetable already badly disrupted, he decided simply to roll over the mines as if they were no more than speed bumps. "I ran into a German mine field which the 12th *Volksgrenadier* Division had neglected to clear. As the time factor was more important than some armored vehicles, I decided to detonate the mines by rolling over them. This way I may have lost five to seven halftracks, which could, of course, be repaired." From Lanzerath he set his sights on Honsfeld as his first objective.

At the Café Scholzen, several hours after *Kampfgruppe Peiper* clanked away, and as dawn broke, his captors informed Bouck he would be taken outside. "I asked if I could speak with Tsak and Kahlil. Tsak was conscious. I told him they were taking him to a hospital and I'd see him after the war. I said, 'I'm putting your Bible,' which he always carried, 'and that picture of your sweetheart in your pocket. I'll say a prayer for you.' He couldn't answer me but I'm sure he heard because he squeezed my hand. And as I stood there, they hauled Kahlil and Tsak to a flatbed truck and drove off with them."

Herded by guards, Bouck, his leg still oozing blood from where he was hit at the top of his boot, started a series of long hikes that marked the lives of so many American POWs.

For William James Tsakanikas a different nightmare had begun. He recalled his experiences in a first person monologue. "Am I dead and in another world?" he thought. Suddenly, as though to dispel his doubts, "the stretcher carried from darkness into light, bright blinding light, and he knew for sure he was alive. He was alive because I was that soldier."

"I had no clear idea of what happened. However, the bright light sparked the flame of hope with the realization that, while something serious befell me, in this world of warming light, everything would be all right. How comforting the light, even through the mist which hung before my eyes. The room seemed crowded with white tables, and teams of ghostlike figures clustered about each of them. The smell of ether permeated the air.

"My head ballooned. I had no pain. I sensed no body. Everything centered in my head and it drifted, about to float off into the air. The white-clad figures, murmuring among themselves, sounded congregated at the foot of my table. Finally, I realized that they spoke German, and I was their prisoner! Yet they were about to intervene surgically to save my life. New hope surged through me with this realization.

"Then, clearly, I heard a German ask, 'Ami, how old are you?'

"I imagined that I answered 'Nineteen,' but I could not hear my voice.

"While thinking about the oddity of this, a decidedly German accent slashed the silence with 'Und now you die!'

"I froze! My thoughts reeled for comprehension. Maybe I didn't hear him right. But looking directly over me, as though to emphasize his threat, stood my announced murderer with an ether mask poised ready to slam over my face.

"How sly, I thought. They were going to suffocate me with an ether mask and make it look as though I went out on the table. I shuddered. No one would know."

Tsakanikas says at this point he recalled the final moments in the foxhole, the "Brrrp! Brrrp! as a burp gun closed in." Consciousness returned briefly during the first interrogation of the survivors, a mention of St.-Lô and the mechanical responses of name, rank and serial number. He realized that the answering voice was his own. A German, on bended knee, was bandaging his head as he lay in the snow. "For the first time, I began to feel pain. Finally, he finished and in a surprisingly kind and friendly tone said, 'Ami, you and your comrades are brave men.'"

As they dragged him down the slope, the wounded man says he heard a German cry out, "*Ach, mein Kameraden!*" At that moment, Tsakanikas saw dead enemy piled up, half buried in the snow. "My foot dragged over one of the bodies, face up, a blonde kid, his eyes staring that blank stare, his lips parted as though he were asking in unbelief, 'Why?' He had not a visible mark on him. No blood. But he was dead. My thoughts went to the mothers of these boys and the worry they were enduring at the moment and the anguish they would suffer when they received the news that their sons were dead.

"I remembered my mother again and reminded Bouck that he must communicate with her if he survived. 'Bouck, Bouck, tell my mother when you get back that I love her and that I didn't suffer.' "

He remembered luxuriating in a bed, under the warmth of blankets, a shadow of a man removing his shoes with the comment, "Ami, you will not need these anymore." Then he was bumping down a dark corridor.

"Then suddenly the bright light of the operating room, the realization that I'm alive, and the burst of new hope. How can this monster standing over me, choking me with a mask, mean what he said, 'Und now you die.'

"Why? They can't be that cruel. Why all the trouble to bring me here and then kill me? Despair grew. I can't move to throw off the mask! I can't breathe! The mask is choking me! My head is swimming . . . Wait! Wait! What was that? Listen! He said '. . . in fifty years.' Listen! He was joking. He said '. . . in fifty years.' He was kidding. He was joking in order to loosen me up for the first operation in a series [necessary] to save my life after the machine gun wounds of the head and face."

While Bill Tsakanikas writhed in his semiconscious nightmares and Lyle Bouck disconsolately slogged along in a column of prisoners, Jochen Peiper's advance guard pushed towards Honsfeld. The route followed the road through Bucholz Station, a tiny cluster of houses. Earlier, Dick Byers from the 371st Field Artillery, which had already lost one forward observation quartet with Bouck's I & R platoon, was dispatched to replace the captured team. The new party amounted to three men, a lieutenant, Sgt. Curtis Fletcher and Byers.

"We pulled our jeep off the road into a barn attached to a farmhouse. It was across the road from Bucholz Station. Some GIs from the 1st and 2nd Platoons of K Company, 394th, were dug in on the side of the woods away from the road. From their holes they could see Bucholz Station and the road from Lanzerath. A few K Company men and the aid station were in the farmhouse basement.

"From midnight to one o'clock, I stood guard with an infantryman on the porch of the house. We took turns ducking into the house to warm up with a cigarette. It was a quiet, cold night. We could clearly hear the SS Panzer troops shouting back and forth, the racing of tank engines, the squeal of bogie wheels as *Kampfgruppe Peiper* worked its way from Losheim, over to Lanzerath and then on towards us. I commented that their noise sounded like a bunch of quartermaster troops on maneuvers in Louisiana." Actually, the discipline among Peiper's legion was usually very good. The loud talk may have come from the less well-trained paratroopers Peiper had acquired in Lanzerath.

When Peiper's column, guided by the paratroopers on foot, clattered up the road hard by the farmhouse, Byers was asleep. A departing GI rifleman paused long enough to shake Byers and whisper urgently, "Get up! There's tanks outside!"

"I mumbled something, rolled over and went back to sleep. Sergeant Fletcher, also asleep, never stirred. But as our lieutenant started to leave, a wounded GI called out and attracted his attention. He shone his flashlight and saw Fletcher and me, still lying there, sound asleep. He *really* woke us up! We grabbed our coats and helmets, buckled on our pistol belts and headed outside. There we pulled on our galoshes and ran for the barn, thinking we'd use the radio stashed there to call in artillery fire on the bend in the road that forced the tanks to slow down.

"As we opened the back door of the barn, we saw three German paratroopers silhouetted against the white snow, but they couldn't see us with the black courtyard behind us. Since they appeared armed with Schmeissers [burp guns] and had the backing of an entire panzer battle group, we decided not to argue over possession of the radio. We took off through the side gate into a patch of pine woods parallel to the road.

"In the woods, someone had a walkie-talkie picking up Germans speaking too-perfect English. 'Come in, come in, come in. Danger, danger, danger. We are launching a strong attack. Come in, come in, anyone on this channel.' No one responded, knowing they were using a captured radio to locate us in the dark. It shouldn't have been hard since we were only a few yards away. Over the roar of the engines we could hear the shouts of the paratroopers as they guided the tank commanders around the bend.

"I recall a feeling of exhilaration. We could hear them, thus we knew where they were and where to go to avoid them. And we knew where they were to kill them, if we had to. I thought, it's funny, but the closer you get to the Krauts, the less scared you get. That is, when you see them, you can kill them. But when you don't know where they are and what they are up to, you fear the unknown.

"Fletcher had not taken time to buckle his galoshes before going out of the gate and they were clinking. Without saying anything to the rest of us, he knelt down to fasten them while we went on. He was captured from behind before he finished.

"We wandered through the woods between the road and infantry foxholes and dugouts. A couple of times we approached a hole and the lieutenant said in a tense, still voice, 'Don't shoot, men. This is Lieutenant _____ of C Battery, 371st. Don't shoot!' Then he would remember to use the password, 'Shining.' Only then would we see the two gun barrels aimed between our eyes and hear the countersign, 'Knight.'

"Eventually, I realized this wasn't getting us anywhere. We couldn't function as artillery observers without our radio and, with .45-caliber pistols, we weren't going to be much help against paratroopers and tanks. In fact, my pistol hand felt paralyzed from gripping the weapon so tightly that I must have permanently embossed my fingerprints on the butt.

"I suggested to the lieutenant that I knew the way back to our gun positions via trails. He accepted the idea and we headed north. There was still a steady stream of tanks, halftracks and paratroopers on the road, which was lined with big, low-limbed pines. We ducked under one into a roadside ditch and waited for a break in the convoy. Enemy soldiers trudged by, just above our heads. When an opening finally came, we dashed across the road, dove into a ditch on the other side, then made our way towards Hünningen. Now my deer hunting expedition paid off, because I knew the route from that earlier trek through the woods and fields.

"Behind us, we suddenly heard gunfire. Apparently, some GI in K Company had opened fire. The flak panzers with their 20-mm cannons and quad machine guns mowed down the woods, knocking out most of what was left of the company.

"Then we looked over our left shoulders and saw a tank firing. We heard small arms from Honsfeld. When we reached the edge of Hünningen we were challenged by the 1st Battalion, 23rd Infantry Regiment of the 2nd Division. We told the men digging in what we had seen and they answered that they were old-timers sent down to save our inexperienced asses. It was dawn by the time we reached our gun positions. The 'march order' had been given and we were just in time to jump on the back of a truck and leave for our next position near the twin villages of Krinkelt and Rocherath. I managed to grab some cold pancakes from the mess truck and ate them on the way."

An essential item in the paper war waged by the U.S. Army is the Morning Report, a summary of conditions at a unit. For Battery C, 371st Field Artillery Battalion, the Morning Report covering December 16 is deceptively innocuous. "Intermittent fire on enemy targets throughout the day. Gun positions and Btry CP shelled by enemy guns. Slight damage at Btry CP. No casualties during the day. One quarter ton vehicle and equipment captured by enemy. Personnel safe. Weather cold. Morale good. Preparation for possible retreat." Only the last phrase indicates something amiss.

The December 17 Morning Report is a document of another tone. "Engaged in action with enemy. Missing, one off, 5 EM [Springer, Gacki, Wibben and Queen, plus one more man] Retreated from Mürringen, Belgium to Krinkelt Belgium. Continuous enemy shelling denying movement."

Disaster surfaces in the December 18 Report. "Retreated from Krinkelt, Belgium on foot at 0045 hrs. Destination unknown. Abandoned 80 percent of vehicles and all howitzers. Abandoned howitzers were made ineffective by removal of sights and firing mechanisms. No demolition agent available. Abandoned 300 rounds of artillery shells."

Kampfgruppe Peiper now attacked Honsfeld. Occupied by a service unit of the 99th Division detailed to provide the amenities of a near-frontline rest camp—hot showers, hot food, entertainment —Honsfeld's U.S. garrison was ill-prepared to host a confrontation with the brute power of *Kampfgruppe Peiper.* The captain in charge hastily formed a provisional rifle company out of his own men and some stragglers. A handful of antitank platoons arrived to confront the enemy and a small troop of men from the 14th Cavalry Group also had retreated to Honsfeld. Some sentries were posted but the majority of the men were instructed to bed down and await a possible attack later in the day.

In the darkness, perhaps an hour after leaving Lanzerath, the Germans rolled right past the Americans guarding the approaches to Honsfeld. Those on guard apparently failed to recognize the panzers which slyly joined the stream of U.S. vehicles traveling through the village by night. A belated discovery of the enemy on the outskirts generated brief and ineffective resistance. Peiper was pleasantly surprised by the ease with which he captured the village.

"An American reconnaissance unit was stationed at Honsfeld. The vehicles were standing in front of all the doors of all the houses in town and there were plenty of weapons around, particularly tank destroyers, but the troops were not at their weapons or in the vehicles, but were in the houses asleep. For that reason there was hardly any fighting at all."

Peiper failed to note that twenty minutes of sporadic shooting from Americans disabled a pair of flak tanks—self-propelled anti-aircraft armor. His booty, however, included fifty U.S. vehicles including recon cars, halftracks, two-and-one-half-ton trucks as well as a number of field guns. Some of those caught in Honsfeld managed to flee but others, thinking their situation hopeless, surrendered.

Pvt. Jim Foley of the 394th Regiment was among the infantrymen savoring R & R at Honsfeld. He had ignored the artillery rounds during the evening. "I wasn't going to get out of my sleeping bag until they blew me out." The level of anxiety rose slightly as recon cars pulled out and scrammed west. "We stayed in the sack until after 5:00 A.M., when we heard some heavy vehicles in the street. I decided to take a look, but before I had a chance I heard a shot outside. Wooten from G Company ran into the room. All he had on were his long johns and he looked funny as hell. He said, 'One of those silly damn guards of ours took a shot at me when I stepped out to take a piss.'

"It sounded funny at the time but what we didn't know was that the 'guard' was a Jerry. I piled back in the sack until 6:30 A.M., when I heard Kraut voices in the street. I stuck my head outside to see a few of our recon cars burning across the street and three Kraut tanks very much intact! Then some bastard opened up on me with a burp gun and I got my ass back inside quick.

"We barricaded the door and decided to make a break out the back window. We changed our mind when we saw the fields crawling with Jerry infantry. We were stuck but good. So we sat on the floor, me with my trusty .45, which couldn't hit a B-29 at ten paces, and waited. Then we heard the staff sergeant from E Company was going to surrender the whole rest camp. After a few minutes of horrible confusion, we were all lined up outside with a bunch of stupid Supermen screaming like crazy at us. I hated to give up like that but I guess it was best. We didn't have so much as a BAR in the whole place. If we had started shooting, we would have been slaughtered like a bunch of cattle."

Peiper himself barely paused in Honsfeld before rolling onward. But as the echelons behind him followed, the murderous acts associated with SS forces erupted. An officer lined up eight prisoners rousted from their beds, barefoot and in their underwear, and sprayed them with a burp gun. A group of Germans disregarded a white flag displayed by five GIs and killed four, leaving one man alive. A tank then crushed the life out of his body. There were a series of similar incidents and, at the very least, those prisoners not used for target practice endured blows from rifle butts. The Germans slaughtered civilians as well, including a pretty young girl who made the mistake of volunteering to serve as a guide to the next objective, Büllingen. Her body was found months later, seven bullets in her back.

Peiper actually disobeyed instructions with his route of march. "On account of the obviously poor road conditions, I decided to go by way of Büllingen . . . assigned to the Hitler Youth [12th SS Panzer Division] by the operational order. Since I heard the noise of combat which was due to the Hitler Youth comparatively far to the rear and up northeast, I thought it might be possible to pass through the town of Büllingen without causing a traffic jam together with the Hitler Youth Division."

He was undoubtedly also attracted to Büllingen because that village of 2,000 contained a small U.S. gas dump.

Again, *Kampfgruppe Peiper* surprised the Americans. It was 7:30 in the morning. Resistance from combat engineers and a service company was light. Neatly lined up on a pair of small airstrips on either side of the road, Piper Cubs, liaison planes for artillery observation and communication, stood with their motors warming up, props spinning. They belonged to both the 99th and 2nd Division artillery. An alarm, "the Germans are coming," had barely sounded. Most of the fliers attached to the 99th zoomed away, taking off directly at the enemy tanks as if they were dive bombers. But machine guns and cannons strafed the hapless little ships of the 2nd Division, demolishing all but one. Peiper later claimed all of the aircraft were destroyed, but he was incorrect.

The Germans ordered about fifty American PWs to fuel their

vehicles and *Kampfgruppe Peiper* continued its gallop toward the Meuse. It overran small garrisons in Moderscheid and Thirimont. While Peiper in a jeep drifted back to inspect elements in his column, his armored spearhead, the vanguard of the Sixth SS Panzer Army, rumbled toward a fateful intersection on the road between the key towns of Malmédy and St. Vith.

On the left flank of Sepp Dietrich's 6th SS Panzer Army, Hasso van Manteuffel's Fifth Panzer Army which struck the 106th and 28th Divisions applied increasing pressure. The initial impact of the shelling and advance of German infantry had halted the work crew with Phil Hannon from the 106th's engineer battalion. At regimental headquarters in Schönberg, Hannon and his mates learned they were cut off from the village they occupied.

Hannon recalled, "The men in regimental headquarters had been taking a pasting from the German artillery. Some of their nervousness got to us. A buzz bomb clattered over, rather low. The boys bolted from the truck. We deployed by instinct on the outskirts of the town. No one had to yell 'Go here' or 'Do this.' We did the right thing automatically. A rock pile here, a depression, a ditch, a manure pile—we made use of them."

No one realized how vulnerable they actually were, just a couple of noninfantry platoons, a few medics, radio operators and headquarters staff people. A jeep with a .50-caliber machine gun and rifles were all the fire power that could be mustered. For four hours they lay there, able to see their former village pounded by big guns from both sides.

"A lieutenant was in a hurry to get a German. He jumped into the jeep and opened up with the .50 at a moving spot 1,000 yards away. The gun would fire only one shot at a time. 'We've been yelling for a replacement for that gun for a week,' the supply officer yelled. The lieutenant quit in disgust. The regular gunner grabbed the machine gun. His first shot stopped the spot. It never moved again.

"My platoon of engineers was called on to unload ammunition for a platoon of tank destroyers that pulled in. The Heinies spotted us and threw 88s at us. Thank God, a number of them were duds! After the first five or six shells landed we could judge where they were hitting. We were getting battle-wise fast.

"The Heinies missed the boat when they didn't smack us that morning. Infantry companies fell back and set up a line on the outskirts of the village. Tank destroyers positioned themselves to cover the field and roads. We settled down to stick as long as possible.

"They asked for a bazooka man and since I had trained with a bazooka, I stepped out. Four of us went out on the road between the Heinies and regimental headquarters and dug in. We had one bazooka, seven rounds for it and our rifles. By the time we finished digging in, it was pitch black, getting windier and colder by the minute. About midnight two of us decided we had enough of freezing. We were wearing field jackets, no overcoats. We left the other two as the bazooka team and returned to the village. While blankets were hunted up for us, we had a chance to clean our rifles. They were coated inside and out with mud. I doubt if they would have fired. The captain told us the mess hall was serving chow all the time. We got some stew and coffee and headed back with our blankets.

"When daylight came we took a look around. We had been told the infantry was all around us when we went out the night before. Three hundred yards *behind* us we located them. We pulled back to the top of a little knoll where we could command the road and fields very well. The Heinies spotted a company of infantry that had moved into position on a hill behind us. Zing! I yanked in my head and did some worrying. Zap! Damn those 88s! The infantry on the hill behind was catching hell, but the shells sounded as if they were skinning my helmet on the way over."

Hannon gave up the bazooka slot to some infantrymen and rejoined his engineer colleagues. They had charge of a dozen or so German prisoners. But the enemy artillery continued to bedevil the Americans in Schönberg. It became apparent that the small contingent in the village was trapped. "About two o'clock Monday afternoon, we got orders to abandon the town and try to break out. Two infantry battalions were supposed to be fighting to open the way and we all left the place expecting to get out. A protective barrage of smoke and time fire laid down by our artillery accompanied our pullout."

Ed Uzemack, no longer a green replacement after his exposure to combat with the 28th Division's Company B of the 110th Infantry in the Huertgen Forest, and his comrades became uneasy toward December 15 after night patrols heard the ominous sounds of squeaking tank treads across no man's land. "The reports were dutifully transmitted to division headquarters, where they were dismissed as unlikely because the terrain supposedly did not suit tanks.

"On the morning of the sixteenth we experienced an intense and longer bombardment. The quiet that followed was soon disrupted by shouts of alarm from GI lookout posts. German infantry in large numbers were moving up the hill towards our village of Clervaux, Luxembourg. The fighting that ensued was weird. It was like shooting ducks at a carnival. With a heavy blanket of snow on the hillside, the Germans wore no camouflage and the dark uniforms made inviting targets. Besides our M–1 rifles, we had a couple of .50-caliber machine guns and perhaps a mortar or two.

"After encountering heavy fire from our vantage point, the enemy troops broke and ran for cover. The action was repeated several times during the day, in what were almost suicide missions. We retained control of our positions and retired to our quarters, in my case an inn at the intersection of three highways that served as platoon headquarters. There were about eight of us billeted at the inn, the platoon commander, a couple of noncoms and us dogfaces. Because of my poor eyesight and a cracked lens in my eyeglasses, I was assigned as runner, equipped with a walkie-talkie, between the command post and squad positions, which were spread out over a half mile in either direction along the highway. The GIs occupied abandoned homes in the village.

"The next day we got our wakeup call, a barrage, a bit late but effective. As the almost one-sided infantry battle continued, the walkie-talkie crackled with requests for more rifle ammunition, casualty reports and calls for a runner. Running zigzag along the road between GI fire and that from the enemy, loaded with bandoliers of .30-caliber ammo, I turned onto an ice-covered walk where one of our squads was housed. A German machine gun opened fire to my right as I slipped and fell on my back, sliding towards an open door. A couple of GIs grabbed my legs and dragged me inside. After they found I was not wounded, they took the ammunition and questioned me on the status of the fighting in other sectors. I knew as little as they did.

"I needed a cigarette badly after I realized how close I had come to cashing in my chips. Cigarettes were scarce and the guys suggested I get them from a guy in the next room 'who no longer needed them.' Enemy fire had killed the GI that morning. He had a nearly full pack of smokes in one of his pockets which, they felt, I was entitled to as a kind of reward for bringing the bandoliers.

"While with this squad I heard the cries of a wounded German soldier, lying a few yards away. The GIs said he'd been calling to his buddies for help for more than an hour. When the enemy retreated, though, they left the wounded man, whose cries would fade and then return, louder than ever. Finally one GI blurted, 'Why don't we put the bastard out of his misery!' He and a couple of other men slowly moved out towards the sound. We heard several bursts of fire and then no more cries from the wounded man.

"In the wake of some Sherman tanks, I returned to the platoon CP. It seemed we had successfully repulsed the enemy once more. At the inn, the platoon commander shared a bottle of Scotch with those of us there to celebrate what we figured was a victory. We mixed the Scotch with some canned grapefruit juice, for whatever reason I'll never know.

"I was in the kitchen preparing some hot chocolate when a GI sergeant burst through the main entrance to warn us of enemy tanks headed our way and only half a mile away. He left hurriedly, saying he had to warn others. We heard his jeep pull out and prepared to protect ourselves. Division HQ advised us to hold our positions.

"Our hastily formed strategy was to hide in the cellar, wait for the tanks to pass our post believing the darkened, shell-battered inn was deserted. We hoped then to join some other units and surprise the Germans from the rear. Obviously, it was both a brave and naive plan, since our heaviest weapon was a .50-caliber machine gun, not very effective against tanks.

"It wasn't long before we heard the tanks rumbling and squeaking outside our building. They moved around the perimeter of the inn but to our dismay, several shut down their engines and parked. Moments later, the sound of heavy boots came tromping on the floor overhead, gutteral voices and loud laughter followed as they found some of our personal stuff we hadn't been able to carry with us into the cellar. It dawned on us that the GI Paul Revere was probably a Jerry scout, disguised in a GI uniform and driving an American jeep. He was checking out where Americans were and at the same time encouraging them to take off.

"Around midnight, the noise upstairs quieted down to snores and barely audible talk. Sitting amid abandoned crockery, we hardly dared to move or even breathe. A muffled radio inquiry to division HQ brought the response, 'Hold your positions.' They claimed help would come but there would be no further radio contact.

"At dawn, after a seemingly endless night, the outside door of the cellar was kicked open by a heavily armed German. A sleeping GI awakened by the intruder yelled, 'Hey, guys. They found us!' We were herded out by a handful of Germans armed with burp guns. As we were marched to the front of the inn, we saw at least two huge tanks facing the building with their awesome 88s pointed towards the cellar area. They had played cat and mouse with us all night long."

As the offensive began to shred the American front, the enemy sought to move masses of men through its opening wedges. Hans Hejny, an Austrian, served with the 38th Armored Battalion of the 2nd SS Panzer Division, an outfit with a brutal reputation from its campaign against the Soviets and one severely mauled in Normandy. Its initial push thrust into Luxembourg.

Hejny's entry into the Ardennes came on the heels of a comfortable sojourn at the German town of Dreis. "We were there a short time but it seemed like home. The people were kind to us. They were extremely thoughtful. When we moved out on December 15, our driver said, 'Fuck it! I was sure that it would be quiet at Christmas time. Now I'm sure we'll have to fight. I wonder how many of us will bite the dust this time.'

"Orders were quiet and lights out. Only a thin ray of the night advance device made the road track barely visible. It was hard to see the roads and we had to concentrate to avoid falling into ditches. But we were happy, in part to escape the stupid training routine that reminded us of the barracks-square, and we were excited by the expectation of a new advance, where one always could pick up countless spoils of war.

"I knew if we continued in this direction we would come to the border of Luxembourg. We did not see any preparation from an aerial bombardment nor were there any tanks in sight. The road was empty, nobody was ahead of us in the dark. There was no snow which would have brightened the night.

"We reached the top of a hill and could see the vague outlines of Luxembourg. The road extended from a forest into a plain and there were taillights from the column ahead of us gliding downwards and disappearing into the woods.

"On December 16, just as I was lulled to sleep by the monotonous droning of the motors, there was a sudden flash. Then followed earsplitting explosions. It was a terror-fraught fire attack. As far as the eye could see there were flashes everywhere, heavy and heavier guns were fired. Everything was lit up as if by day. Conflagrations erupted and we thought we heard piercing screams, perhaps screams of death of those hit.

"We were so scared and tried to leave the trucks, but orders came not to leave them under any circumstances. All of us jumped into the vehicles without averting our eyes from the horrible spectacle. Because of the fires, the landscape seemed drenched in blood. There was so much light that one could recognize the face of each person. We had to continue forward, most unhappy as we watched the awful bombardment over our heads that brought death and destruction.

"I had looked at my watch as the firing began. It was exactly 5:30 A.M. The first shots from machine guns and rifles could be heard, and the first real enemy contact came at 6:00 A.M. The road ended at a river and we left the trucks. All of the soldiers had stopped here.

"The platoon leader informed us, 'We engineers have been given the order to quickly build a ferry so the most important vehicles and other units can cross the river until the blown-up bridge farther up the river has been sufficiently repaired. Time is scarce and it's important each platoon leader sees that everyone lends a hand and nobody dodges work. And one thing more, no one leaves this place. I don't want anyone to go in the nearby farmhouse. It has been mined and anyone who tries will be punished.'

"In the shortest possible time the company built a passable ferry, using huge flotation bags. With the same speed, a small landing pier was erected on shore, as the first ambulances arrived. Fortunately, they were only smaller vehicles. Even so, some lost traction, pressing the floation bags menacingly into the water. It took too much time to get some vehicles across the river."

Eventually, Hejny's unit moved into what was enemy country. The column advanced on Clervaux, where Ed Uzemack of the 28th Division had been trapped. "Leaving the protection of the woods behind us," said Hejny, "the street led us among the first houses. We were not yet in the middle of combat action, only the next bend of the street separated us from it. There was an indescribable combat pandemonium, every noise mixed with another, grenades, rifles shots, mortar and machine gun fire. A unique blast from hell.

"I saw Jahn cautiously moving ahead, always searching for cover, to get to the house from where one could see the situation. I kept close to him. Projectiles whistled around our ears, impacting in the walls, splintering whole portions from them, ricocheting, twittering aimlessly through the air, sounding as if they were harmless chirping birds. I reached the corner of a house to look straight ahead.

"A huge fire raged in the middle of the roadway, obstructing any passage. Dense clouds of smoke floated above our heads. Because of the dark smoke I could not make out what was burning until a gust of wind for an instant provided sight of the street. About fifty meters away, an American Sherman tank was fully aflame. Behind it some Americans sought cover, but these poor devils had no escape left. There was no possibility of flight. There were too many eyes, too many rifle barrels waiting tensely for them to step forward.

"Dense smoke clouded the scene almost completely and the enormous heat exploded the ammunition inside the tank. Now certainly the Americans could not last too long behind the tank and would have to leave the worst cover in the world. A massive detonation wave shook the street. Whole pieces of steel were hurled into the air. The windowpanes of neighboring houses burst with loud cracks. A terrible gust of fiery wind threw me back, choking and coughing.

"Then I saw for the first time an American soldier, and he was jumping for his life. Inside, I crossed my fingers for him, somehow perhaps he could make it and that would save me. But no sooner did he make his daring leap, than rifle and machine pistol shots whipped the pitiful guy. Mortally wounded, he fell to the ground. A comrade took off to help him, risking his life. As he bent down to the fallen one, he too was dropped by murderous bullets.

" 'Assassins! Dirty pigs!' a voice within me cried out. I don't know why, but at the moment I felt immense sympathy for the Americans. The cowardice and brutality toward the completely defenseless men set me aflame with wild hate. No attempts were made to take prisoners. Almost fainting with anger and helplessness, I tried to hold back my tears confronted with that horrible, ignominious deed. Another detonation wave broke. Smoking, red-hot pieces of steel from the bursting tank bounced on the ground in front of us."

Hejny slipped into one of the buildings, perhaps in search of loot, as he had mentioned. It was a coffeehouse and pastry shop but he said, "In and on the glass case were partly cut pies, appetizing pastries and other wonderful things. But they were covered with splinters of glass. Nothing useful was left."

When he returned to the streets of Clervaux he saw German tanks shoving the burning American armor aside to open passage for the attacking forces. Hejny rejoined his fellow engineers who boarded trucks dodging through the countless fires as they moved through the town.

John Chernitsky, from the antitank company of the 28th Division, had hardly arrived at Wiltz in Luxembourg to serve on the faculty instructing fledgling noncoms when orders directed teachers and pupils to rejoin their respective units. Enemy fire, however, blocked some roads. Chernitsky and others returned to Wiltz. "I stayed in Wiltz with the [newly] organized riflemen who were made up of members of the band, clerks, cooks, bakers and any men caught between Wiltz and Clervaux. After an artillery barrage, I was hit in the back with shrapnel. I covered the wound with sulfa powder from the packet on my cartridge belt and wrapped my undershirt around my back." Chernitsky and the improvised rifle troops dug in to resist the enemy advance along the southern flank.

About the same time as Lyle Bouck witnessed the confrontation between Peiper and the paratroop commander in the café, Friedrich von der Heydte's ill-trained paratroopers and their equally inexperienced pilots prepared to take off, twenty-four hours behind their original schedule. Not only was the commander fearful of the added problems of a later jump, but also the weather now became a factor.

"According to [the German air force] we were to expect a wind velocity of six meters per second above the landing area. This report, however, did not coincide with the local weather report which [said] a much higher wind velocity had to be expected above the target. Six meters per second is the highest wind velocity permissible for a night parachute drop into a wooded area. Presuming a higher wind velocity above the landing area, I would have refused to jump. Both *Luftflotte West* [the air force command] and General Peltz (top officer for the air force fighter corps) knew this." There is no mistaking Heydte's conviction that his superiors cooked the figures to insure that his outfit jumped.

Around 3:00 A.M. the chutists boarded their transports. A priest had blessed the aircraft and the men rendered the paratroopers' anthem, *Rot Scheint die Sonne* (The Sun Shines Red). The patriotic bravado trumpeted, "When Germany is in danger there is only one thing for us: to fight, to conquer and assume that we shall die. From our aircraft, my friend, there is no return."

For all his misgivings, Heydte must have been shocked by the magnitude of the mishaps subsequently endured. "The commander of the transport group based his navigation and timing for the approach flight not on the local report but on that of *Luftflotte West*. This decision proved disastrous and the task force jumped into a surface wind of seventeen meters per second [almost triple the acceptable limit for experienced parachutists].

"The error was serious, not so much because the near-gale of the wind raised the number of jump casualties and stragglers, but because the transport aircraft were unable to fly at the speed assumed by their commander. Many of the untrained and inexperienced jump-masters gave the jump order according to clock time, rather than by observing the location of the landing area on the ground. About 200 men jumped in the Bonn area [more than fifty miles away from the target zone] rather than in the Hohes Venn Mountains. Tracer and rocket signals and guide aircraft were in use only until 0330, by which time only the first echelon had reached the landing area."

Only thirty-five of the 106 planes, or less than one-third, dropped their human cargo in the right place. Some of the Junkers 52s were shot down by anti-aircraft. The extremely heavy fire dispersed the somewhat ragged formation of Junkers. Others, as Heydte indicates, simply lost their bearings, since an umarked distance of forty miles separated the last seachlight beacon and the incendiaries dropped in the landing area.

Unskilled jumpers, whipsawed by the wind, crashed into trees or the ground, breaking legs and backs. Many who floated to the earth without serious injury lost their weapons while struggling to control their chutes in the gusty, cold dark air.

Heydte himself used a new Russian chute designed to thwart the usual oscillations experienced by jumpers. He was the first German to use the device and it was almost a necessity for him. His right arm was in a splint because of an accident a few weeks earlier. Heydte landed smoothly, right on target. The only problem was, he was totally by himself. Not a single other man came to earth beside him.

By 5:00 A.M., with daylight rapidly approaching, Heydte had managed to rendezvous with less than a platoon, twenty-five members from his original 1,200-man brigade. "Only about 150 had appeared by 0800. With this pitifully small number of men who salvaged only a single medium-caliber mortar, I had only the slightest chance of success. I decided first of all to remain hidden near the road junction until the sounds of battle approached; then to come forth from the forest to open up the road in the last minutes before the arrival of the German tanks. At the same time I decided to reconnoiter the surrounding enemy territory.

"I dispatched reconnaissance patrols of from two to three men each to the roads leading to Eupen, Malmédy and Verviers. The patrols were to hide at the edge of the roads and avoid contact with the enemy, except that they were to capture any enemy messengers traveling alone and bring them to me.

"The results of this reconnaissance exceeded all expectations. By later afternoon of December 17, I had a comparatively clear picture of the enemy, including the considerable shifting of forces. This intelligence would have been of greatest value to the Sixth Panzer Army, if only I had been able to transmit it. Unfortunately, because of the high wind velocity during the airdrop, every radio set had been lost, and I had not been given any carrier pigeons."

For three days, Heydte operated in this fashion, capturing a total of thirty-six Americans in the process, while suffering only one man wounded. During this period he kept adding to his file on the U.S. deployment of forces, an achievement that merely heightened his frustration, because, thanks to Sepp Dietrich's contemptuous dismissal of a request for carrier pigeons, the information remained buried in the woods with the remnants of *Auk*.

Neither *Greif* nor *Auk* functioned according to design, but in the minds of the now-besieged Americans, both of them soon assumed formidable potential. Initially, however, the salvos fired by the three German armies along the West Wall before dawn on December 16 struck most of the top brass as, at worst, a retaliation for the attack by Carmen Capalbo's 99th Division and elements of the 2nd Infantry Division towards the Roer dams, or perhaps a gambit to relieve the pressure generated by Patton's advance into the Saar Basin.

However, as reports streamed back from the front, Field Marshal Montgomery thought it prudent to leave the golf course and return to his headquarters for more information. The first communiques did not change the social calendar for Eisenhower. After the wedding of his valet, he presided over a reception at his house, dined with associates and played several rubbers of bridge before retiring.

At the same time, he seems to have been the first to have grasped the possible seriousness of the threat. He started the process of inserting more GIs to meet the growing Ardennes challenge.

In his diary of December 16, Maj. Gen. Everett Hughes from the SHAEF staff wrote, "Brad [Omar Bradley] says Germans have started a big counterattack towards Hodges. Very calm about it. Seemed routine from his lack of emphasis." His demeanor may have seemed unruffled, but by mid-afternoon of that day, Bradley telephoned Patton and told him to send the 10th Armored Division, then in reserve near the Luxembourg-France border, into the Ardennes. The Third Army commander protested the loss of one of his outfits: "There's no major threat up there. Hell, it's probably nothing more than a spoiling attack to throw us off balance down here and make us stop this offensive." Bradley, however, was adamant. Furthermore, he arranged to shift the 7th Armored Division, which was also in reserve, to give Hodges more punch.

Kay Summersby, secretary for Eisenhower, noted, "[Hodges'] First Army is attacking, the German has advanced a little, now only twelve miles from Luxembourg."

Maj. William Sylvan, aide de camp to Courtney Hodges, entered a gloomy note in his diary on Decmember 17. "The situation developed badly during the day and may be considered by tonight to be severe if not yet critical. Captured orders show the desperate determination of the enemy. The G–2 estimate said the enemy could attempt to drive over the Meuse."

On the other side, gleeful German military radio eavesdroppers heard messages, "We have been bypassed. What shall we do?" A welter of orders instructed, "Blow up your guns," or gave new coordinates for withdrawal. A delighted Hitler telephoned Gen. *der Panzertruppen* Hermann Balck, struggling to contain Patton's Third Army. "Balck! Balck!" gushed *der Führer,* "Everything has changed in the West! Success! Success! Complete success is now in our grasp!"

Chapter VI

ANARCHY UNLOOSED

COMPANY I, 23RD INFANTRY, 2nd Division, commanded by Capt. Charles MacDonald, who a few days before gaped at the sight of the necktie-clad 106th Division, hiked into a portion of forest three miles west of Camp Elsenborn, a former Belgian army depot. The snow lay nearly a foot deep over the hard, frozen ground. "The forest, deathly silent a moment ago, was soon filled with the tramping of many men, punctuated by sharp curse words and the sound of shovels scraping against the frozen earth."

The regimental CO advised MacDonald that the division had jumped off in the attack toward the Roer dams, a combined assault that included the 99th Division and Carmen Capalbo. An anxious MacDonald learned that the advance, initially successful, now faltered. "My personal fear of being committed in the attack grew day by day. I had seen action now, but I had seen only defensive action along a sector that was listed as 'quiet.' I had yet to experience the death of one of my men, and I knew that casualties would be much higher in the attack. Would I be as paralyzingly afraid on the offense? . . . Would I personally come out alive?"

MacDonald's anxiety rose with ominous news of an enemy penetration near the twin villages of Krinkelt and Rocherath. Company I packed away spare gear, including MacDonald's typewriter and his manuscript, "Nine Days in a Pillbox," and boarded trucks that hauled them southeast, into the path of the German onslaught. ""The GIs we passed did not give us the usual happy smiles and shouted well-wishes and insults to which we had become accustomed in rear areas." Once in position, an appalled MacDonald heard orders to prepare for a nighttime attack, even though the company knew nothing of the terrain, the disposition of the enemy, and carried only a basic load of ammo. When he asked an operations officer the location of the enemy, the captain responded, ""I dunno. Nobody seems to know a goddamned thing. They say it's that way," and he gestured toward the east.

However, before the scheduled zero hour, the mission changed from one of attack to defense. The men desperately sought to protect themselves. The earth resisted shovels and picks. Sweaty hours passed before the troops could dig more than a few inches. At midday of December 17, while Dick Byers scrambled to escape the Peiper juggernaut, and Ben Nawrocki's B Company desperately fought to survive, refugees of the 99th Division retreated through MacDonald's frigid outpost.

"A ragged column of troops appeared over the wooded ridge to the front of the 2nd and 3rd Platoons. There were not over two hundred men, the remnants of nine hundred who had fought gallantly to our front since they were hit by the German attack the preceding day. Another group, the size of a platoon, withdrew along the highway, donating the few hand grenades and clips of ammunition which they possessed to my 1st Platoon. Two men stayed to fight with my company. Two enlisted men, carrying a badly wounded lieutenant, stopped, exhausted with my 3rd Platoon . . . I called for a litter squad.

"The riflemen could not be sure if the next troops that appeared over the ridge were friendly or enemy. I alerted the artillerymen to call for fire in the event the approaching troops were Germans." A few minutes later, any question of who it was ended with "a hail of small-arms fire which sounded like the crack of thousands of rifles echoing through the forest. There was no doubt now. My men could see the billed caps. They were Germans."

The assault was massive. "Wave after wave of fanatically screaming German infantry stormed the slight tree-covered rise held by the three platoons. A continuous hail of fire exuded from their weapons, answered by volley after volley from the defenders. Germans fell right and left. The few rounds of artillery we did succeed in bringing down caught the attackers in the draw to our front, and we could hear their screams of pain when the small-arms fire would slacken. But still they came!"

A seemingly endless number of reinforcements backed up the enemy and the defenders began to run low on ammunition. Seven times the enemy infantry had tried to crest the hill and seven times the American fire had driven them off. MacDonald called for resupply but none was available. He began to receive reports of casualties, including that first death he had so dreaded.

A bullet pierced the helmet of an aidman, leaping from a foxhole to attend a wounded GI. But battalion could not send stretcher bearers for the fallen. German soldiers died a scant ten yards from forward foxholes. Machine guns fell silent as the gunners emptied the last belt.

To MacDonald's plea for help the sole response was "Our orders are to hold at all costs." MacDonald pondered the meaning: *"Company I's last stand! And what is to be gained? Nothing but time. Time born of the bodies of dead men. Time."*

A bevy of Panther tanks now lumbered toward Company I. Artillery and mortar shells failed to deter them. The Sherman tanks assigned to protect the unit, figuring confrontation with the heavier, bigger-gunned panzers suicidal, fled. Reports of tank cannons firing directly into foxholes reached MacDonald. He saw elements of M Company backing away and then his own 1st Platoon. "I managed to get the men to move to my CP, but I could not stop them there. They walked slowly on toward the rear, half-dazed expressions of their faces."

On his own, MacDonald told his people to fall back to form a new defensive line. Two members of the 23rd Infantry, Pfc. Richard Eller from M Company and Sgt. Jose Lopez of Company K, stuck to their machine guns covering the retreating GIs. In the face of small arms, tank and artillery shells, they poured out withering streams of bullets. Both men subsequently received the Congressional Medal of Honor for their courage.

But nothing availed MacDonald and his soldiers. The captain found himself running, staggering, crashing through the lower branches of fir trees while bullets spattered around him. Tank shells snapped off the tops of the giant trees. It became a pell-mell rush back towards safety.

"I felt we were helpless little bugs scurrying blindly about, now that some mad monster had lifted the log under which we had been hiding. I wondered if it would not be better to be killed and perhaps that would be an end to everything."

Earlier, the ambulance carrying Carmen Capalbo had borne him to a temporary hospital in Malmédy. The Belgian town served as a hub for Allied military outfits servicing combat units along the Siegfried line. When Capalbo arrived at the temporary hospital in Malmédy, he joined an ever-increasing number of casualties awaiting treatment. As ambulances deposited more and more wounded, the medical authorities decided only to accept those patients who, if not treated immediately, would die.

Despite his grievous injuries Capalbo was diagnosed as able to travel further. An ambulance bore him some fifteen miles northwest to the city of Verviers. "They unloaded us in the gymnasium of a high school converted to a hospital. We were all laid out on the floor and told to wait. I was half knocked out from medication but I could hear airplanes overhead, bombs falling somewhere and even what sounded like strafing runs. Rumors started to spread about a huge German offensive. I saw women civilians crying out of fear.

"Ultimately, they carried me to a makeshift operating room. It was full of tables with doctors on either side and hardly any space for anyone to walk through. Klieg lights on the ceiling changed night to day, although by this point I had lost track of time. When a technician prepared to give me an anesthetic, I remembered how I had broken a leg as a boy in Pennsylvania and how sick I had been from the gas. I said, 'I hope it's not ether,' and he told me to relax. They were using sodium pentathol. He said, 'I'll make a bet with you. If you can count to three after I give you this, I'll pay you ten bucks.' I didn't make it."

Now surgeons began removing from Capalbo's torn flesh the jagged slivers and chunks of metal and wood that ripped into his body when the mortar round smashed into the tree.

Capalbo's evacuation from Malmédy seemed none too soon, for by noon of December 17, the spearhead of *Kampfgruppe Peiper* was nearing the crossroads of Baugnez, less than two miles from the outskirts of Malmédy. Throughout the day, American army traffic and civilians seeking to escape had passed through Malmédy. Noncombat units closer to the front had received orders to withdraw. The hospital personnel that had looked over Capalbo only hours before packed up and left. A small infantry replacement depot disappeared along with a tank repair shop.

The Allied strategists guessed that Malmédy, in spite of the good roads that radiated from it, could be bypassed and the greater threat was to St. Vith. Reinforcements including parts of the 7th Armored Division wended through the town bound for St. Vith to aid the 106th Infantry Division with Lt. Alan Jones, Jr., Phil Hannon, John Collins and others. Left to hold Malmédy in the event of an attack was only the 291st Engineer Combat Battalion under Lt. Col. David E. Pergrin.

Actually, the the 291st's responsibilities extended beyond the town limits. Pergrin set up roadblocks along a series of roads and intersections in the villages of Amblève, La Gleize, Stavelot and Trois Ponts. At best he could muster a squad for each outpost; in some instances only two or three soldiers guarded the approaches to the U.S. positions. The route of *Kampfgruppe Peiper* split the small forces under Pergrin, making the 291st's situation even more precarious.

Pergrin pleaded with units in transit through Malmédy to stay and help him defend the town. The commander of the 7th Armored Division's 38th Armored Infantry Battalion, part of CCB, refused to request a change in his orders and pushed on along Highway N 23, towards St. Vith. In the vanguard was Glenn Fackler, a machine gun squad sergeant. Fackler had missed exemption from the draft by only a few hours delay in the birth of his second son. Had the boy entered the world on the morning of November 27, 1943, instead of the afternoon after the deadline for induction, the father would have qualified for deferment.

Fackler underwent the course for an infantryman at Camp Blanding, Florida. By September 1944, ten months after he donned a uniform, as a replacement with the Seventh Armored, he came under fire during a siege near Overloon in the Netherlands.

"I was very scared that first time, dazed by the realization someone was trying to kill me. A staff sergeant near me received a wound from an 88. I gave him first aid and helped a medic evacuate him. I think my training was excellent and I learned to keep cool and to be careful.

"When the Germans broke through, we were near Ubach, Germany. The 38th AIB as part of CCB of the 7th Armored headed southeast towards St. Vith, via Malmédy."

As word of an oncoming phalanx of German armor reached Dave Pergrin and his combat engineers at Malmédy, another small detachment rolled into the town on the heels of the 38th AIB. This was Battery B of the 285th Field Artillery Observation Battalion and numbered about 140 soldiers. Unlike Dick Byers and observers integrated in field artillery units, the men of the 285th performed more specialized services. They not only mapped and surveyed but also used sound-and-flash—techniques to locate the sites of enemy mortars and artillery. Sound-and-flash observers would crawl as close as possible to front line positions, set up microphones and then lay wires back to an observation post. By picking up the noise of a gun, coordinating the sound and flash created by the weapon, technicians could calculate the placement of the mortar or fieldpiece. It was dangerous work; the wires to microphones had to be maintained constantly.

Pergrin made his case to the CO of Battery B but to no avail. Orders specified he proceed to St. Vith in support of artillery there. An unhappy Pergrin watched the trucks roll down the hill and towards the Baugnez crossroads from where the convoy would head south.

Shortly after the departure of Battery B, Pergrin learned from one of his patrols that a large number of enemy tanks and other armor had been spotted. Then, "We heard firing way off to the east that sounded like mortars or tank guns and machine guns." Pergrin remarked to his staff, "That little field artillery observation battery must have run into that column of German tanks."

According to Peiper, "I suddenly heard my cannons and machine guns open fire. I realized that the point had hit the main road from Malmédy to Petit Thier and I drove off to the point in the jeep. The column behind me was detached, since the piece of road was exceptionally difficult."

He met the lead element of his armored spearhead about two-thirds of a mile east of Baugnez. "About five tanks and about the same number of halftracks were standing in front of me and they were shooting with all weapons at their disposal. I saw that it was an American truck convoy. I gave an order to cease fire several times, since I was annoyed at having my armored spearhead held up, in view of the fact they had lost so much time already. Furthermore, I was annoyed at having these beautiful trucks, which we needed so badly, all shot up. It might have taken about two more minutes until I was understood everywhere. I, thereupon, loudly ordered them to continue to drive on at great speed. I then mounted the vehicle of Major Poetschke and ordered him to send a radio message that the enemy was leaving Malmédy [an erroneous interpretation by Peiper] and that we had reached the main road south of Malmédy."

Peiper said he then proceeded to the crossroads, where he found the way blocked by the American trucks. A Panther tank had begun to shove the shot-up U.S. vehicles into the ditches. "I saw a large number of American soldiers, forty or sixty according to my estimate. Some of them were standing in the road already; some were lying in the ditch; and the great majority of them were lying on the west side of the road in the open area.

"Some of the American soldiers played dead; some of them slowly crept towards the woods; some of them suddenly jumped up and ran toward the forest and some of them came towards the road. Grenadiers who were in the halftracks behind me fired on those who carried rifles and were running towards the forest."

Peiper said he motioned with his thumb for the Americans to move back under cover of the German weapons. He also reportedly yelled in English, "It's a long way to Tipperary, boys!"

Leaving Poetschke in charge, Peiper said he prepared to push on to Ligneuville. He gave his driver permission to fill up on oil. "I didn't see any vehicle in front of me and I had the impression that I was the first vehicle. We had information there was an American command post in Ligneuville. Since I knew with certainty we would meet resistance in Ligneuville, I had no desire to be the first one to enter the town. I motioned to my rear and three halftracks and the tank of 1st. Lt. Arndt Fischer, the adjutant of the 1st Battalion, passed me by. They continued towards Ligneuville at great speed and I attached myself to their heels." He said he did not see any prisoners shot.

Peiper's memory of what happened at the crossroads is considerably different from that of the GIs involved. A jeep with the Battery CO, Capt. Roger Mills and its executive officer, Lt. Virgil Lary led the small convoy. The second truck behind the jeep bore Supply Sgt. Bill Merriken with two companions. The caravan stopped abruptly as a shell exploded off to the right just in front. Successive rounds scored direct hits behind Merriken and the sound-and-flash crews scattered into a roadside ditch.

"The firing lasted maybe five or ten minutes," remembered Merriken. "There was debris flying around and none of the guys could move out. Our view was obstructed because of trees and a bend in the road, but then a tank came, with its machine gun firing at the ditches. Lt. Lary said, 'Surrender, boys.' The German in the tank said, 'Up, up, up,' and motioned us to go to the rear. As I went up the road, the tank fired. Then more vehicles passed and we were again motioned to hurry."

T/5 Jim Mattera rode in one the last of the trucks. "We hit the crossroads, heading south. All at once 88s [actually they were 75-mm guns on Mark IV Panthers] on tanks came down and they hit three vehicles behind me. Everybody jumped off, got down beside the road. In twenty minutes every vehicle gone. Blew everything up. Machine guns shooting, dut dut dut, across the road, you couldn't raise your head up. I heard tanks coming down the road, as far back as I could see were tanks with swastikas on 'em."

"The panzers turned to their left at the crossroads. German soldiers suddenly come out through the woods with their automatics. It looked like a thousand of them. They were SS troops in black. I was in the ditch and it was a high-crowned road. One tank come down the road with guy up on the machine gun. I'm laying there with my carbine and two fellows next to me. I had the carbine right on the guy's eyes and was ready to pull a sniper when they stopped me. 'You miss him, you son of a bitch, and our ass is mud.' I dropped my carbine. This SS trooper on the machine gun swung around and he directed us up to the crossroads. He spoke English.

"We walked about 200 to 300 feet. There was a whole mob of GIs up there. Here we are, hands up. They told us to line up, I had a wristwatch I got as a present while in high school. Little sawed-off officer took it off me. I wanted to hit him so bad.

"There was a Lieutenant Goffman. When they got to him, he said, 'The Geneva Convention don't allow you to take our belongings.' Boom! Down he went. First shot I heard. They shot this Lieutenant Goffman. We were on the crossroads, not in the field. Then we were ordered down to the field, I'm right in the front row, like cattle. My recollection I seen them set up three tripods facing the field. There was an officer shouting to hurry up. Then I heard an officer command, '*Machen alle kaputt!*' Kill them all. The machine gun bullets began. We all hit the ground, ten to fifteen minutes. I heard my buddies hollering. Haines, my buddy next to me on the ground, said, 'I'm hit, can you help me?' I said lay still. Then I heard him gurgle and die."

Merriken and others have slightly different memories of the first moments of the massacre. The supply sergeant, after being herded into the field, said they stood for some time. He noticed a halftrack or tank maneuvering for position, apparently trying to train its cannon on them. "I figured they were going to blow us up. But they couldn't depress the gun enough. There was a lot of shouting and I saw a man with a pistol."

The pistol wielder was subsequently identified as Pvt. Georg Fleps, a twenty-one-year-old Rumanian-born SS volunteer. He obeyed an order relayed through his tank commander, Sgt. Hans Siptrott, to shoot. His first bullet felled Lieutenant Lary's driver, who stood next to the battery's exec. The second shot killed a medic, 1st Lt. Carl Guenther. The falling bodies amid the tightly packed mass of men may have caused some movement. It is highly likely that some who had been in the front ranks desperately pushed toward the rear. But there was no massive attempt to run from the field. In any event, machine guns poured death into the crowd of nearly 100 Americans.

The shooting lasted about fifteen minutes, according to witnesses. When it stopped, those who were still alive lay there, stunned, too frightened to move or speak. "We all dropped to the ground," said Merriken. "Then we heard a number of vehicles pass. They fired at us from the road, you could hear the thud of rounds hitting bodies." There was another pause before a second line of vehicles rolled by, those aboard also shooting at the hapless victims on the ground.

"The fellow next to me," said Merriken, who had been hit twice in the back, "was delirious, moaning about being shot. I whispered to him to be still. He didn't stop. I heard footsteps of someone coming. He came to the fellow moaning and fired a pistol. The bullet went through my right knee. Part of the other man was on top of me and I figure he was shooting at him." While the German walked off to check others, Merriken kept his arm in place across his mouth to prevent his vaporized breath from showing.

Jim Mattera remembered: "I heard the tanks and halftracks winding up, rrmmmm, rrmmmm. Down the road they come. Everyone who went by opened up with a machine gun. I heard one guy yell, 'You will cross the Siegfried line, you American bastards!' Brrrp! Jesus Christ, I thought they'd never stop. Finally, no more hollering. I'm laying there, about ten degrees that afternoon. Jesus Christ, my heart is in my mouth. I couldn't feel nothing burning. I kinda surmised when you're shot you're gonna hurt. When I hit the ground, my helmet flew off. I was twenty and had plenty of hair. I'm laying there bareheaded. Finally I thought I heard somebody walking, there was maybe an inch or two of snow.

"Somebody's here, I thought. Thank God I didn't open my eyes to look. I was too scared to open them. I heard this mild voice say, 'Hey, Joe, you hurt? I'm here to help you, Joe.' Nobody answered.

Then it was, 'Hey John, you hurt?' Guy said, 'Yeah, I'm hurt, I need help.' Boom! Oh, I thought, you dirty sons of bitches. I don't know how many of them there were, maybe two or three Germans, sent them in there, while they left one machine gun on the road."

Mattera remarks that, while lying there, he realized the SS troopers knew they had done something they shouldn't have and they meant for nobody to get away to inform the world of what "it ain't supposed to know." He lay quiet as the enemy administered the coup de grâce to anyone they suspected of retaining life.

"Finally I got enough nerve to open my eyes and looked at all the bodies laying there all which away. Shaking, scared. I was looking right down the bore of the machine gun on the road. It looked like it was pointing right at me. There were three Germans standing behind it talking.

"I thought, Jesus Christ, three Germans, but I didn't have a hand grenade, nothing. How the hell was I going to get out of this mess. I'm shaking bad. I felt I gotta make a break. If you knew Jim Mattera, soldiered with me, you knew my voice. Finally, I got up and yelled, 'Let's go, you guys,' and started running. These three Krauts looked around. Oh God, they heard me. 'Halt, Amerikan soldaten! Halt! Halt!' Halt, your ass! I was jumping over top these bodies and they got down at this machine gun and she starts sawing.

"Jesus Christ, it's between my legs—ching ching ching. I might have run 100 feet, I took a big tumble. I thought they were going to cut me in half. I seen a couple guys get up on each side of me. I saw some head for a house. I figured I'd try to fool them. The MG stopped, I'm laying there like I was hit. The machine gun swung over, trying to get these other guys. I lay there, maybe couple seconds, got up and run again.

"I was getting away, they must have seen me getting away, they opened up again. I must have been 100 yards away, and I staggered up a hill and down into a woods, hid under this big brush pile. I was by myself, shaking like a dog."

When night blacked out the area, Mattera crawled along a hedgerow toward the American lines. He saw some of the enemy, in green uniforms, with a dog, apparently hunting for survivors. "The dog stuck its head through the hedge, hair up on his back. They said something to the dog and left.

"I forgot the password, I was shaking. Come down the road into

Malmédy, couldn't think of it. The outpost challenged me. 'Who goes there?' 'Cpl. Mattera from B Battery.' 'Advance and be recognized.' They asked me the password. I said, 'Hell, I don't remember no password.' They were going to shoot me. 'I'm from Lancaster County, Pa.,' I yelled. They accepted me."

When he was taken to an aid station the medics thought he had been wounded, since his entire side was saturated with blood. But it came from the man next to Mattera at the slaughter. They did find three holes in the rear end of his trousers.

"While I was there, this boy, John Cobbler, walked in. He was white as a sheet. 'How'you doing?' 'I ain't so good. I'm shot up.' They removed Cobbler's uniform and found six wounds. He died in an ambulance as he was being evacuated."

Bill Merriken heeded Mattera's call to flee. "I got up but started to wobble. My leg where they shot me was like a chunk of lead." Realizing he could not outrun his pursuers, he headed for the nearby houses, hoping to hide. He crawled into a woodshed where he escaped detection. Others had sought refuge in the Café Bodarwé at the crossroads. The SS troopers set the café ablaze, then gunned down those who ran from the flames. They also murdered the proprietress, who had witnessed their viciousness.

In the late afternoon following the butchery, an elderly farmer spotted Merriken and beckoned for him to follow him. "They put me on a bench beside the door. A woman got a pan of water, took my jacket off. I told her not to touch anything else. I tried to stop the bleeding by my knee with the canvas leggings. They made some soup and coffee for me. I had one sip of the soup and passed out. I woke up in a huge bed, feeling very bad. The woman volunteered to take a note to Malmédy to get help. I heard the motor of the ambulance as they came. They busted through the door, took me, bed sheets and all, on the stretcher. The woman kissed me and the civilians crowded around and waved to us. The ambulance was fired on but made it to Malmédy." Merriken was finally discharged from a hospital after treatment of his wounds in April, four months later.

Lt. Virgil Lary, like Merriken, survived through the charity of the civilians in the neighborhood. A farm family offered succor, bandaged a foot wound. With an improvised crutch and helped by two women, Lary hobbled to the headquarters of Col. Dave Pergrin in Malmédy. Pergrin already knew of the slaughter from several others who reached his outposts. Seventy-two men died in the killing field, another fourteen were murdered in the immediate vicinity. Several civilians who had observed the affair were also shot. The American high command quickly ordered the savagery publicized.

When the German offensive had begun, Combat Command B of the 9th Armored Division was assembling at Faymonville, close to the line of march being followed by *Kampfgruppe Peiper*, perhaps twelve miles behind the front. In the hours since then, elements of CCB fanned out. Ligneuville, where Peiper headed from the Baugnez crossroads, rather than a stronghold, contained mainly service personnel for CCB's 14th Tank Battalion.

In spite of being heavily outgunned, the Americans at Ligneuville managed to justify Peiper's fear of stiff resistance. He remembered, "Just before entering the town, I suddenly saw in front of me the tank of Lieutenant Fischer. It had been set afire. I stopped about fifty yards from that vehicle and recognized a Sherman about eighty meters to my right. He was just about to aim his cannon at my vehicle. I ordered the driver to pull back at once and we remained at a protected corner of a house. Another halftrack which followed us, passed us by and was knocked out at that moment. I, myself, took a rocket-launcher and ran into the house in order to knock out the Sherman from the rear window but it was knocked out at that very moment by another tank." In point of fact, the recalictrant American armor consisted of a tankdozer equipped with a 76-mm gun.

Besides the tankdozer, Peiper's panzers destroyed a pair of Sherman tanks left for refitting and an assault gun. The fire that consumed the lead Panther badly burned its commander, Arndt Fischer, a friend of Peiper's. His mood was not improved to discover his bag of American survivors included no top-echelon people. A number of GIs fled under cover of machine gun fire from the 14th Tank Battalion's mess sergeant, Lincoln Abraham. He gave up his life in the attempt. Peiper groused, "We got there too late and only captured their lunch." He dallied just long enough to feast on the food at the Hôtel du Moulin, left by the hastily escaping headquarters personnel of an antiaircraft brigade.

Leaving a detachment to secure Ligneuville, Peiper pressed forward, seeking to cross a natural obstacle, the Amblève River, at Stavelot. Behind him, his SS troopers dealt with their captives. Among these was M. Sgt. Paul Ochmann, leader of a reconnaissance platoon, wearing the black of the SS, a gray-green overcoat and the black hat with the death's head insignia of the SS.

Ochmann, almost thirty-one years old when the Ardennes offensive began, enlisted in the SS in 1936. His peacetime unit was the *Totenkopfstandarte Thüringen,* the unit responsible for guarding the Buchenwald concentration camp. Ochmann subsequently explained how he came upon eight American soldiers standing beside the road.

"All of these prisoners wore American uniforms; however, they did not have steel helmets on any longer. Their hands were either clasped behind the neck or raised above the head. When I saw the prisoners, I went to an SPW [German halftrack] in which sat *Untersturmführer* [2nd Lieutenant] Hering, Platoon Leader of the 9th Panzer Pioneer Company. I remembered that immediately before departing from [Ligneuville] *Sturmbannführer* [Major] Poetschke shouted something to me which I could not make out. When I saw the prisoners, the shout of Poetschke, which could have meant that prisoners of war must be bumped off, occurred to me. I recalled that *Untersturmführer* Bucheim said two days previously that we should not take any prisoners. Moreover, I was in a bad mood because I received from *Untersturmführer* Kurt Kramm, an hour before, the order to remain and guard about 30 vehicles captured in [Ligneuville], as well as eight American prisoners of war. These eight were not the ones [I saw along the road].

"For these reasons, I went to Hering and said to him, 'Here are eight prisoners, they should be shot. I need another man.' Hering told me that I should go to the next vehicle, [where] *Sturmann* [Cpl.] Suess should go with me. I went to the SPW and asked for Suess; I said he should come with me, the eight prisoners were to be shot. Suess stepped from his vehicle, taking a weapon.

"Together with Suess I led the prisoners over to the other side of the road, [about] 100 meters. In the vicinity of the cemetery where the terrain descends on the right of the street, I stopped the prisoners, who were marching one behind the other. I formed them right at the edge of the road, for I selected this location intentionally because there the bodies could drop right down the steep terrain without lying in our way.

"I indicated to the prisoners with my hand that they should place themselves with their backs towards me and face towards the slope, as I intended to kill them by a shot in the neck. I know that by a shot in the neck the victim falls forward.

"I shot the first American prisoner of war in the neck from a distance of about 20 cm. [eight inches]. The American was doubtlessly dead. From the motion he made, I saw he was hit in the neck and he fell forward. Then again with my pistol I shot the second American prisoner of war in the same manner. I knew from my service with the *Totenkopf Einheit* [the SS units assigned to guard and execute concentration camp inmates].

"All told, I myself shot and killed with my pistol in this manner four or five of these American prisoners of war. The others were shot in my presence by Suess. While I shot, Suess also shot."

Having executed the hapless PWs, the two SS men found another eight PWs as they walked back to the village. According to Ochmann, he brought these captives, including an officer, to the Hôtel du Moulin "because I was of the opinion that enough prisoners of war had already been bumped off."

Belgian civilians provided different versions of events. A farmer's wife, Mme. Marie Lochem, tending her cows, said she watched as Ochmann yanked eight prisoners from a group of twenty for a burial detail. After they dug the graves for three dead Germans, Mme. Lochem saw Ochmann line up the gravediggers and shoot them in the head. All fell over, presumably dead. But one only feigned a mortal wound. Later, with the aid of a Belgian civilian, he escaped temporarily, only to be recaptured. More than a month later, when American soldiers drove the Germans from Ligneuville, Marie Lochem pointed out the site of the atrocity. In the snow, searchers uncovered a total of eight corpses. (The discrepancy of eight actual dead and the one who slipped away remains a mystery.) One of the bodies identified by dog tags was Lincoln Abraham, the valiant mess sergeant whose efforts with a machine gun allowed so many others to escape capture. The boots had been stripped from the dead by the shoe-poor Germans. Any personal jewelry was also missing.

Hotelkeeper Peter Rupp, German by birth but Belgian in allegiance, also related a version of events that varied from Ochmann's tale. Rupp accosted Ochmann and denounced him. "Murderer!" he yelled. "You killed eight of them. I saw you put the pistol in their mouths!" (Another discrepancy with Ochmann's account.) Master Sergeant Ochmann responded to the charge with a fist to the jaw of the sixty-nine-year-old Rupp, knocking out two teeth.

An SS officer nearby instructed Ochmann to kill the remaining prisoners and Rupp, but another officer countermanded the order. The hotelkeeper decided a dose of conviviality might relax the Germans. He plied them with whiskey and wine until tension and concerns about prisoners abated. By the next day, Ochmann and others from *Kampfgruppe Peiper* had left the village to rejoin the spearhead.

On the right flank of the embattled Americans at Malmédy and the surrounding territory, the small units composing the 14th Cavalry Group had resisted the attackers in a series of small battles but, overwhelmed by enemy might, were forced to fall back constantly. The armored *Führer Begleit* Brigade and elements of the 18th *Volksgrenadier* Division thrust through the gaps left by the retreating cavalry group and threatened to encircle the U.S. 422nd Infantry Regiment. Other forces from the 18th VG, along with troops from the 62nd VG Division, hammered the southern flank of the 106th, including the 423rd (where Alan Jones, Jr., was a battalion exec.) and 424th Regiments.

The CO of the 106th, Gen. Alan Jones, Sr., had already advised higher echelons of severe problems facing his outfit. Initially, he was promised help from parts of the 9th Armored Division. Later information said the 7th Armored Division would arrive shortly. Until then, the 106th would have to fend off the foe. Word that the 7th Armored, like its antecedent cavalry, was riding to their rescue buoyed morale of enlisted men and officers under siege.

Desperate circumstances, meanwhile, threatened Battery A of the 589th Field Artillery, where Lt. Eric Wood, Jr., and Sgt. Barney Alford sought to avoid entrapment by the enemy and provide covering fire for the retreating foot soldiers. For Alford, chief of the second gun section, the first forty-eight hours must have seemed endless. "We fired steadily from about nine o'clock until about 1500 in the afternoon. We fired all the ammunition in the position, and in the battery ammunition dump, and were firing as fast as the ammunition could be unloaded from vehicles of the ammunition train." The rapid, almost continuous fire, according to one observer, was due to Wood's organization of cooks, drivers and other service people into ammunition handlers.

"That night we were ordered to displace to the rear. At about 2400 we began attempts to get the pieces out of position. We loaded eighty-three rounds in each prime mover and started trying to get out through the soft mud. Lieutenant Wood had to take one of the prime movers and help me pull one of the other howitzers out."

Alford's laconic description skimps the magnitude of the efforts demanded by the abominable conditions. Working in a darkness illuminated only by artillery shell bursts, Wood and the artillerymen coupled two and three trucks in tandem with tow ropes to winch the howitzers, inch by inch, from the sucking mud. It took about three hours to extricate the big pieces up onto the main road.

Alford noted, "During that time small arms fire was going overhead into the area where our guns had been. We finally moved out about 0400. On the way, my driver rammed the gun in front of us and caved-in the radiator of our truck. This caused us to lose water and made the truck run hot. We could only go a little ways before we had to stop. We were to get almost to the new position by running for short distances until the motor quit. When I got close to the position, I could hear firing behind us."

Eric Wood, as usual, was the last to leave. With half a dozen men he searched the abandoned position for any usable ammunition or equipment, even as occasional bullets continued to whistle by.

The shifting tide of battle required the entire battalion to move its heavyweight arsenal several times. The clumsy howitzers bogged down in a thick goo of mud and melting snow. The primmovers, two half-ton trucks, skidded precariously on the slick roads. Time started to run out. Battery C was engulfed by the German advance. Food and ammunition exhausted, the commander blew up his guns and gave the order for an every-man-for-himself cross-country dash to safety. Most were captured, some killed, including the CO. Service Battery delayed the Germans briefly before it, too, was overrun.

Maj. Arthur C. Parker, temporarily in command of the battalion, called for the two remaining outfits, A and B Batteries, to run west through Schönberg and assemble for the defense of St. Vith. Alford received the latest instructions. "Lieutenant Wood told me to set up my howitzer on the road for antitank defense and I started trying to get it into position on the road. The brakes were no good and we couldn't hold it in position, so we tried to chock the wheels with boxes. Then a jeep came by and the occupants said tanks, accompanied by infantry, were coming. Lieutenant Wood said we wouldn't be any good out in the road, so he commanded me to march order and meet him on the other side of Schönberg, 'if he got there.' "

The GIs of Battery A maneuvered two more of their guns from the muck and onto the highway to join Alford. But a fourth piece remained stubbornly mired. Wood ordered those up on the road to take off. The word from the Battery CP was "Tanks one mile from Schönberg, coming up road from Bleialf," to the south.

Wood stayed behind, struggling alongside Sergeant Scannapico and others in the eleven-man gun section, to retrieve the one remaining howitzer which mulishly refused to be hauled from the ooze. For a full thirty minutes, as the enemy drew closer and closer, the lieutenant and the enlisted men sweated and cursed as they dug, pulled, pushed and winched the piece until it finally yielded. The men piled into the back of the truck; Scannapico took his place next to the driver, T/5 Kroll, while Wood climbed into the back.

Rolling behind them were the cannoneers for Battery B with similar orders to displace near St. Vith. Wood's close friend, Ted Kiendl, with whom he swapped the post of executive officer for Battery B, was not among them. Kiendl became a casualty on the very first day. As he had trotted to aid some wounded, a shell struck a nearby tree. Wooden splinters perforated his body. Somewhat ignominiously, Kiendl had been borne to an aid station atop a mail pallet, bleeding over the letters. But Battery B, under command of Capt. Arthur C. Brown, now had abandoned all of its guns due to the imminence of German grenadiers and tanks. The stretched-out convoy rattled along the road toward Schönberg.

Alford and the other three howitzers with their crews, aided by their thirty-minute head start, had cleared Schönberg by the time Wood and company approached the village. As their truck accelerated down a steep hill, Scannapico caught sight of a light enemy tank blocking the bridge leading to the main street. Wood first yelled to Kroll to hit the gas and speed by. But one hundred feet from the panzer, Wood changed his mind. He shouted to stop. Kroll obeyed. The small troop dismounted and opened fire on the armored behemoth with carbines and a bazooka.

The tank retreated over the bridge and disappeared in the maze of town streets. The Americans boarded their truck, Wood now sat beside Kroll, while Scannapico rode the running board. They cautiously crossed the bridge. Scannapico and Pfc. Nicholas Campagna, bearing the bazooka, acted as scouts, stalking the tank. They found it lurking in an alley. The two returned to the truck, which raced forward. At the mouth of the alley, Scannapico jumped down and let fly with his carbine while Campagna fired a rocket.

Campagna scored a near miss, hitting a building close to the tank. But machine gun fire killed Scannapico. With the vehicles of Battery B still trailing them, Wood and his crew continued up a rise that led out of Schönberg. There they met an even more formidable adversary. A heavyweight German tank confronted them, cannon and machine gun leveled at the truck.

Wood barely had enough time to yell, "Halt! Dismount! Take Cover!" before the tank let fly. Machine gun bullets struck driver Kroll in the legs. A cannon shell smashed in the motor of the truck. The GIs, with Wood, as well as those from Battery B, scrambled to find shelter in a ditch beside the road or a field just beyond it. The wounded Kroll toppled into the ditch, where Cpl. J. Don Holtzmuller applied first aid. The driver did not seem badly hurt. Later his body was discovered with a bullet through the head; surivors are convinced he was executed.

The Americans tried to burrow into the dirt as German soldiers raked their area with small arms fire. Pinned down along with the soldiers from the 589th were a half-dozen members of the 333rd Field Artillery, a segregated African-American unit. Holtzmuller, huddled with two others, was overwhelmed by the fusillades. "Machine gun fire, including lots of tracers, were landing and kicking up dirt all around us. Prielozny [another GI] was hit in the left hand. The whole field, which was a couple of hundred yards wide, was blanketed by fire from all directions. It didn't look as though a man could run a yard without being shot to pieces. So the three of us decided to wait for a lull and then try to surrender. We were successful."

Although Wood and his people had made it through Schönberg with just one casualty from the brief confrontation with the light tank, those of Battery B ran into a firestorm in the village from burp guns and rifles. A few escaped but most were immediately captured. However, a number, including Captain Brown, eluded the enemy and reached the U.S. lines a few days later.

On the other hand, everyone from Wood's battery, caught on the outskirts of Schönberg, gave up. There was a single exception. "After we were lined up back of the highway beside the German tank," recalled Holtzmuller, "I said to the others, 'Where is Lieutenant Wood? I don't see him.' One of the other men said, 'He could be crumpled up on the floorboards of the cab.' But he wasn't there. Just then a small-arms shot from the edge of the woods beyond the open field barely missed one of the Germans. That made us feel better. Knowing Lieutenant Wood, we figured that was probably him shooting from the edge of the woods."

In all probability, it was not Wood. Fleeing the ambush in Schönberg, some of the men from Headquarters Company of the 589th found themselves in that same large field where the Battery A GIs sought refuge. S. Sgt. Frank Aspinwall of Headquarters Company, peering at the scene, said, "I recognized Lieutenant Wood, Lieutenant O'Toole, McIntee, Cologne, Steward, Camiscioli and Lawson headed up the mountain." The last five all became captives but Aspinwall's final sight of Wood, related to Major Elliot Goldstein, was of him disappearing into thickets of trees as bullets kicked up the snow around his heels.

Meanwhile, for the increasingly vulnerable 106th Division, CCB of the 9th Armored was the only help available. Among the elements of CCB were the 27th Armored Infantry Battalion from Combat Command B and the 14th Tank Battalion, assigned the mission to relieve pressure in the St. Vith area, opening up a corridor for the trapped regiments to escape.

The 27th was short most of its service company, caught at Ligneuville where Paul Ochsmann murdered "four or five" and its Company A, detached to support the 99th Infantry Division. On Sunday evening of December 16, with the 27th AIB committed to creating a path for the 106th's infantrymen, then Capt. Glen L. Strange, who had originally helped set up Company A, headed back to retrieve the unit.

Strange, an atavism of his Oklahoma-Colorado roots or drawn from mold of the movie vision of the old Wild West, was born in 1915. He sprang from the loins of Ringwood, Oklahoma farmers, garden variety pioneer stock. His mother Eunice had ridden a springboard wagon from Honeywell, Kansas across the infamous Cherokee Strip while her father, Frank Harman, riding his horse Prince, preceded the family to stake out a homestead patch.

"When my mother graduated from eighth grade, she started teaching school south of Ringwood, in a wooded area about two miles from where she lived. My granddad took a horse and tied a log to him and dug a footpath through the woods from the house to the school so my mother would have a trail and not get lost.

She told me one time she was walking this trail and come face to face with a mountain lion. She froze and stared at him, and he at her. In a few seconds the lion turned and moseyed off through the woods. During the summer, my mother would go to Alva, Oklahoma to a college to get a teaching certificate for the following year. She did this maybe two years and then got a lifetime teaching permit.

"I don't know how old I was at this period of my life but with my older sister Mary Alice I stayed with a neighbor family while my mother was away or teaching. I don't remember the family's name but they were Negro and had several children. From an early age I did not have or know any racial feelings. As far as I knew they were equal to us, probably just as poor. My mother said it was a good family for me to be with as the lady always was fresh with milk, since she had a child every year and didn't mind sharing the milk. I don't know if it's all true but my mother joked with me about it, and I have a faint recollection of sucking one black tit while my playmate sucked the other.

"My granddad Harman was a sheriff in Major County and I believe had three notches on his .44 revolver. I wanted that gun but a cousin got it. The story I got from an uncle is that my granddad and his deputies shot down seven outlaws in Ringwood one night."

Ringwood was "Blackjack and sand country," he says, referring to the scrawny oak trees, good mainly for fence posts and firewood, and which grow on almost beach-like ground. His was a Huck Finn-like boyhood. "I hunted quail, fished with a cane pole, string and hook, using only grasshoppers for bait and catching Blue Gills or Goggle-eyed perch. The soil where the trees have been removed grows the best watermelons and cantaloupes in the country. And you find wild blackberry vines and other berries but you don't pick them unless you are not afraid of copperhead snakes and a few rattlers."

With the family finances desperate, Strange's folks relocated to 360 acres in Colorado. "Our first home was a dugout. When I went to school it was three miles away in a one-room frame building. My sister and I shared a horse for the trip. We now had a two-room house out on the prairie. But Colorado was not a good place to farm. We returned to Oklahoma. I had started helping Dad farm at nine years of age. We bought the first combine in Kay County. But when the Depression came we were selling wheat for as little as twenty-five cents a bushel. By 1932 we were broke and moved to Tonkawa after selling all we had."

His father became an agent of an oil company, then worked at other jobs. As a stripling, Strange, like Lyle Bouck from the I & R platoon of the 99th, enlisted in the National Guard, "so I could get the $21 every three months."

After completing high school and taking some local college courses, Strange, in 1937, married the former Doris Furber, a Tonkawa belle. While the husband worked for an iron works that forged rock bits used in petroleum drilling, his wife earned a paycheck from what was then known as a "drug store." According to Glen Strange, they discussed the war in Europe. "Each day we all talked about it. I felt like we could end the war in short time if we were there. But I didn't think that'd be necessary. My opinion was that England could win it. I was disappointed in them, and France as well."

In September 1940, two months after the *blitzkrieg* that knifed through the springtime of the Ardennes swallowed up the Low Countries and France and routed the British Expeditionary Force, Strange heeded the call-up of his National Guard outfit. He climbed the enlisted man's ladder to first sergeant with the 45th Infantry Division before entering OCS at the armored school, Fort Knox, Kentucky. Upon graduation he immediately jumped one rank to first lieutenant because of his earlier National Guard service.

Positioned all along the West Wall from late October to mid-December, the 9th Armored units by dint of patrols and small counterthrusts against similar enemy operations, acquired some battle conditioning. Strange noticed a quickened heartbeat in the presence of artillery and small arms fire.

Toward the evening of the first day of the Bulge, with their armored battalion deployed to confront enemy columns poised to strike at St. Vith, Strange and the battalion exec, Maj. Murray Deevers traveled to the CP of a 99th Division regiment. To assist in the aborted attack toward the Roer Dams, the 27th AIB's Company A had been attached to the 99th's forces. Now, with their own formidible task, the 27th wanted to retrieve its men. After a considerable amount of argument that included cussing and appeals to higher authorities, the 99th's regimental commander reluctantly released Company A.

"It was one hell of an eerie feeling as we moved along the road to St. Vith. The Germans used lights bouncing off the low-hanging clouds to illuminate their path and the targets. There was also a lot of arty [artillery] fire from both sides, many buzz bombs being launched by the Germans, and they made one hell of a noise."

His 27th AIB as part of the 9th Armored's CCB encountered its first severe test near the village of Steinebrück, southeast of St. Vith, on the Our River. Supported by a preparatory artillery barrage and the 14th Tank Battalion, the 27th AIB carried out a counterstrike upon the forces of the 62nd *Volksgrenadier* Division which had sliced through elements of the U.S. 106th Division.

"We gave the 62nd VG one helluva bloody nose before getting orders to withdraw." In numbers the American losses were relatively small but these were the first of Strange's comrades to die in action. While Strange acted as an observer and self-confessed morale builder with his presence, he personally faced no immediate peril. His trials by fire lay ahead.

Strange's boss, CCB commander Gen. William Hoge, planned to follow up his success at Steinebrück with a further drive on Winterspelt. However, the 106th Division chief, Gen. Alan Jones, sent a message that while Hoge was welcome to carry out the attack, he must retreat to defensive positions with the coming of night. Hoge saw no point in conquering territory at the cost of lives and then relinquishing the land. He messaged the 27th AIB to back off under the cover of darkness. General Jones was still operating in the belief that the 7th Armored would soon arrive at St. Vith and his grand strategy envisioned a coordinated counterpunch by the elements of the two armored divisions.

Designated as the spearhead for Winterspelt under Hoge's strategy was his 14th Tank Battalion. Demetrius Paris, a lieutenant, commanded a platoon of light tanks for D Company in the 14th.

Born in 1915, Dee Paris spent his public school years in Leavenworth, Kansas. "I was active in football, track, dramatics, singing and as a cadet and cadet officer of the Junior ROTC, the only such unit in the state. It was established because of nearby Fort Leavenworth, home of the Command and General Staff College.

"I attended Ottawa University, Ottawa, Kansas, originally a Baptist Indian School, because it was a small institution and I could play football there. I dropped out after a year and a half to help my father who lost two businesses because of the Depression. While in college I had been interested in world affairs. Three of us decided we would learn to fly and become soldiers of fortune in the China situation. We took physical exams at Fort Leavenworth and I failed because they said I was underweight.

"I was working for the Veterans Administration at Wadsworth, Kansas and tried to enlist. I was informed the VA had obtained a deferment for me since I knew several jobs in the supply branch. The local draft board refused to change my status. The problem was that the law at the time provided job return rights for draftees but not volunteers. Later, the law was changed to protect volunteers as well. I got a family friend to intervene through the state draft board, which made the local board furious. Eventually, I resigned my job to enlist, scored very high on the examination as a Volunteer Officer Candidate.

"I reported for military service, September 21, 1942. During the physical, the MD examined my anus and a psychiatrist kept asking me if people hated me or did I hate anyone. I replied I was beginning to hate him for blowing his foul breath in my face. I requested assignment to the armor branch because I thought it would be more exciting than being a dogface, an infantryman.

"After thirteen weeks of basic training, I was to be interviewed by a board of officers. Approaching the hearing across the parade ground, I counted the steps to cope with my nervousness. A colonel sternly asked the first question: 'Estimate the distance to that flagpole on the parade ground.' I gave him better than an estimate. I was approved for OCS at Fort Knox.

"We had 300 students, with one-third expected to fail. I tutored Ralph Houk, the baseball player who later managed the Yankees and other teams. Houk had been playing ball at Fort Leavenworth when the post was told that the players it collected either had to go overseas or to OCS. Houk had never so much as touched a weapon up to this point in his military career.

"Upon graduation they passed out either a second lieutenant's commission in the armored infantry or in the cavalry. The old cavalry guys still didn't believe the horse had been replaced. I drew the cavalry with the MOS [Military Occupation Specialty] Tank Unit Commander. I reported to Fort Riley, Kansas, the cavalry center of the army. The 9th Armored, training there, had been made up from cavalry regiments, now mechanized. We had a a considerable number of regular army enlisted men. That was fortunate because they were accustomed to discipline and had been taught the horse came first, take care of it before anything else. That paid off when it came to maintenance of our tanks in combat.

"Our officers received their commissions from several sources, ROTC, OCS and West Point. Their personalities and backgrounds varied greatly. Some were cautious, others daredevils. Some were noisy braggarts, some were quiet. Some chased women, some were aggressive, some were meek. Some were gamblers who'd whip out the cards everytime there was a ten minute break. I've seen five men on a dark night lying face down in Louisiana mud with their heads under a pup tent, a candle perched on a helmet and cards in their hands.

"Just before we went overseas our battalion commander was hospitalized and replaced with Lt. Col. Len Engeman. That made an enormous difference. Engeman was an excellent leader who knew how to make decisions.

"The enlisted men were similarly varied. But until I got in the army I never realized how many Americans couldn't read or write. We wrote letters home for some of them. My platoon sergeant was a career man in the cavalry whom, I later learned, operated the biggest payday crap game at Fort Riley and was the major local bootlegger, bringing booze from wet Missouri to dry Kansas. He was decapitated when my platoon was caught in a trap. After his death, the man who replaced him as platoon sergeant was a quiet, religious guy. He later had the tip of his nose shot off. If I had a problem man, I'd place him in the platoon sergeant's tank crew or my own.

"However, enlisted men often did things officers never heard about or learned of only much later. For example, my platoon sergeant went to the hospital for a few days while we were at Fort Riley. Only forty years later did I learn that he had called our radio repairman a 'damned liar' and the latter damn near beat him to death. In the old army, you settled disputes with your fists.

"The history of the tank in the U.S. Army is interesting. When Americans got around to believing it might be a useful weapon, they shopped around for parts rather than design something original. They used an aircraft engine and installed a cannon adapted from the French 75. Gen. George S. Patton's wife [Beatrice] designed a suit that made you look like a space man.

"J. Walter Christie, an American, tried to sell them his suspension system but it was rejected. The Germans, the Russians and the British all used Christie's suspension. But the Americans chose the volute spring system, which gave a much poorer ride, was difficult to maintain and tended to throw tracks. We now use the Christie suspension system.

"My light tank had a patty-cake 37-mm gun that could not penetrate the German armor. Our best hope was to shoot at their tracks to immobilize them or at their lightly armored rear to disable the engine. If we came on them suddenly, we could hit them with a smoke shell and then head for cover. The smoke shell might make the enemy crew think their tank was burning and evacuate. In that case we could use the 37-mm HE (high explosive) or the machine guns.

"The tank had two of these and this was another problem. One was mounted on the turret for the commander to fire. The difficulty was it was behind him. If not fastened, it could swing wildly when moving and knock the commander's head off. If fastened, one couldn't get it free in time to use it. There were strict orders from ordnance not to modify equipment or weapons. We ignored it, welding the gun directly in front of the commander. Only then could I use mine as I did against advancing infantry.

"Our medium tanks, the Shermans, had 75-mm guns with a relatively slow muzzle velocity. The German 88 was an all-purpose weapon, good also for antitank and antiaircraft usage. Their 75-mm antitank gun had high muzzle velocity, and speed is what makes for penetration. The exception is the bazooka, where it is very slow moving but has a bigger warhead.

"All our tanks had a high silhouette compared to the Germans. We could easily be seen. In 'hull defillade' you are supposed to place your tank just below a ridge or high ground with just the top visible. But when we moved up to fire the tank cannon, we exposed far more of the tank than the enemy in its hull defillade.

"They also had smokeless powder. We did not and every time we fired, revealed our position with both smoke and flame. One of our lieutenants received one of five new tanks with the 105-mm gun. Shortly after, we were adjacent when he fired. The smoke and flame could be seen for miles. When I questioned why we did not use smokeless powder the answer was that chemical salts in that kind of explosive would corrode the barrel and damage the lands and grooves. Yet, I once went to an area in France where I saw hundreds of disabled tanks, many with a single hole in the body. They had perfect gun tubes that could have replaced any damaged by the chemical salts.

"Our tanks also could have used a small portable gasoline stove to heat rations and a canvas tie on the tank for a lean-to shelter. Soldiers are always hungry and if the service company is stuck where they can't reach you, you live on canned rations. Quite often they were cold when you'd have given anything for hot food or coffee. When it came to sleeping we had a choice of staying under cover inside the tank or else lying down outside in an exposed foxhole.

"The American .45 handgun was adopted in 1898 solely because it would knock down charging Filipinos during the Insurrection. Its muzzle velocity was only eighty-eight feet per second. You could almost see the bullet. The Belgian Browning and the German Luger were both much lighter, more accurate and easier to disassemble and clean. In fact, we used to have competitions to see how fast one could take apart and put together a Luger in total darkness. In combat, I equipped myself with both a Luger and a Belgian Browning and left my .45 in the tank.

"Our binoculars were twice as heavy as the German ones and less powerful. I used both one day from my tank turret while the morning mist was still on the ground. I could see nothing with the government issue ones, but the German pair revealed German soldiers with overcoats hanging to their knees.

"The good news was our tanks, for all of their defects, were mechanically superior. I put hundreds of miles on mine without an overhaul, while I understand the German tanks could at best make 100 miles between overhauls. The German turrets were not electrical and the crew had to hand-crank them to position the tank gun. They could not swivel nearly as far as ours."

"Just before the Bulge we were in a quiet sector of Belgium. We could see the Germans and sporadically fired in their direction, but they did not return fire. When we were in Luxembourg, within sight of the enemy also, I often visited my tanks at night. Several times I reported to the S–2 [intelligence officer] of the battalion that I heard vehicles moving in the night. I suggested the enemy might be bringing up tanks. Our S–2 was utterly useless. He paid no attention, did not forward the information to higher headquarters nor did he request an infantry patrol to reconnoiter the area.

"Although most accounts speak of snow, where we were, while it was cold, the coldest winter Europe had experienced in years, there was no snow on the ground at the start. As tankers we wore a combat suit that was like heavy coveralls. Underneath we wore our worsted uniform shirt and trousers. We had tank boots and socks with double feet. I had gloves which I wore inside my mittens.

"I've been cold all my life but never as cold as this. It just wouldn't quit. My fingers swelled and I had to remove a ring. The men learned that if they did not occasionally take off their socks and boots they would develop trench foot. A steel tank can be a miserably cold place. When the situation permitted, we tried to warm ourselves from the engine exhaust.

"When we moved to the St. Vith area after the major attack began we didn't know what was happening at the time. We were confused. We'd be sent one place to defend a road junction, then later to another place to clear a town.

"We were told there were Germans in American uniforms and vehicles. The idea scared us spitless. Everybody was jittery. You'd get stopped by someone and have to use a password several days old because you hadn't received a new one. A guard at a road crossing would interrogate you endlessly.

"Several men from the 106th Infantry Division, having thrown away their weapons, fled through us, accusing their officers of having failed them. We invited them to join our chow line. A Belgian civilian pointed to a man in the line and said he was a German in an American uniform. He was taken away and I don't know who he was or whatever happened to him.

"A Belgian told me he was surprised that we had not been informed that many people in the area favored union with Germany. One of the things I learned from my first combat experience was to take nothing for granted, that the enemy could wear a uniform or civilian dress.

"As a platoon leader, my responsibility was to give the impression of calmness under fire. I remember a young 2nd lieutenant whose infantry platoon was in foxholes just inside a forest. When I asked why he didn't have a hole, he replied, 'If I had one, I'd be in it.' That became my guiding principle.

"I nearly always kept my head and chest outside of the turret. It gave me greater visibility—tanks are really blind vehicles. When action got hot, I would crouch lower with only my head exposed. I once called for artillery fire on my position when it was about to be overrun by German infantry. I lowered the hatch cover, but did not close it completely. I wanted the men to see me. I was scared shitless but I'd get out of the tank to show myself.

"Once, while a few German artillery rounds landed in the general area, I left the tank turret, crouched on the deck and shaved, using warm water in my steel helmet. In response to a radio call to me, my gunner answered, 'He's outside the tank, shaving.' Of course every man in the platoon wearing headphones heard that. While troopers remained inside the tank for hours on end, using their helmets to relieve themselves, I would place my sleeping bag on the ground under the rear end. While they were cold and uncomfortable, I was warm and resting. I was less fearful than when inside, and it may have had a calming effect on others."

The 14th and Paris backed and filled around St. Vith, before a tank outfit from the 7th Armored relieved them. Then the 14th dropped off south and west of the town to defend a new line being established there.

While the strategists shifted Dee Paris and his battalion into another sector, Gen. Robert Hasbrouck, CO, of the 7th Armored, fearful his CCB under Bruce Clarke might be trapped, brought to bear elements from CCA under Col. Dwight A. Rosembaum, specifically the 40th Tank Battalion. Cpl. Gerald (Jerry) Nelson, a red-headed twenty-year-old gunner from Wisconsin crewed in one of the Shermans.

"My father was a millwright in a local factory and my mother a good Christian woman who raised four kids in a modest home. I graduated from high school at seventeen. After learning electric welding in the summer of '42, I began to work on the submarine program at Manitowoc.

"I could probably have obtained a deferment because of my job but I wanted to go, army all the way. I didn't follow the events in Europe or elsewhere around the world but I was moved by the patriotic songs and posters and felt I had to do my part.

"I don't think my training was very good. After basic in the summer of '43 at Fort Knox, I went to mechanics' school for three months. We never had a car in our family and I didn't know how to drive. On D-Day, June 6, while in England I began a thirty-day mechanics course. I came to France at the end of July as a replacement, joining the 7th Armored outside of Metz. I had never even been in a medium tank, and only briefly in a light one during my entire career, and now I am a gun loader outside Metz. The Sherman I was now part of packed a 75-mm cannon and three machine guns with a crew of five.

"Still, once inside the 'monster' and surrounded by the whole company, I felt we were invincible. I'm sure we all thought it was possible but we didn't talk about being killed. I found a little solace knowing that you never hear the one that hits you, so you wouldn't know it happened. My greatest strength came from the Twenty-third Psalm—'Yea, as I walk through the valley of the shadow of death, I will fear no evil: for Thou art with me, etc.' I did pray for safety and I think just as much for skill and courage to do my very best.

"Occasionally, we'd talk about the 'million dollar wound,' shot in the foot and sent home. When the day ended and we took up a position for the night, alongside a barn, in some bushes, I always asked, which way home? I meant the direction to our lines. If we had to retreat, I didn't want to go the wrong way.

"In a month, with hardly any experience, I was moved to gunner. All day long, I would practice elevation and traversing to gain speed. I was tremendously concerned about the position of our turret, in case of a bailout—fire—or whatever. If our cannon was turned a little, the guys down below wouldn't be able to open their hatch to get out, and I was the only one in a position to traverse. I didn't want them to be trapped.

"My two closest friends were the loader and the gunner in the next tank, Ace Domino and a little Jewish guy, Shorty Horowitz. They both came from New York but I lost track of them after the war. Shorty said he was a low-class entertainer in saloons. He used to sing, 'If you knew Susie . . .' In fact, my daughter is named Susie. Shorty taught me an Al Jolson song one night around a fire and I scribbled it inside the cover of my prayer book —'I'm gonna hop off a train, and slip down that lane, and jump into my Mammy's arms . . .'

"During our time in combat, I always seemed to have a lump in my stomach. My appetite wasn't much but I didn't have any hate towards the Germans. We didn't see those guys that much because in a tank you're usually at long range. You see movement or flashes in the woods, men ducking for cover, vehicles racing away. But afterwards, when I saw our people killed or wounded, I felt sickened and just hoped it would all end soon. At those moments I felt a little more scared, a little more homesick and a little more of everything we hate about war. There wasn't much conversation in my tank. We five were more quiet than talkers.

"After we left Patton's Third Army we became part of the First Army, Ninth Army and even the British Second in the northern part of Europe. During our time in Holland, we had trouble sinking in the mud, so they developed 'duck's feet,' four-inch extensions put on the outside of the tracks on both sides. According to whether you were in the mud or in woods or cold weather, every section of track had to be opened and the foot added or removed and then the track put back.

"Right before December 16, we were maybe sixty miles north of what became the Bulge. We lived in buildings, and had cut a Christmas tree from a little cemetery. We found some ornaments and paper to decorate it when word came to move out. There was mention of a breakthrough but we all thought it was a local one, small. We started out in the afternoon and drove till dark, slept in a column on the side of the road.

"In the morning it was rainy and dark. I remember this clearly because every so often I had to flip down my periscope to the position where a rubber blade would wipe off the raindrops. Ordinarily we did not like to do this because we always bore-sighted our 75 and then lined up the sights in the periscope, which you did not move again. But sometimes you just had to make the adjustment.

"Our tank, commanded by Sgt. Truman Van Tine, was in the lead, and about midafternoon as the road through the woods passed a clearing, a shot suddenly missed us. We sped across and then the same thing happened to the tanks behind us. We knew we had arrived, with a lot of shooting, small arms. The firing was not at us but to our front and side.

"Officers conferred and sent three tanks, including us, a mile ahead to an intersection with a few buildings. We were first and, as usual, Van Tine stood behind me. He always kept his hand on my shoulder, as if to reassure me. He told me to turn the gun to the right to cover us. Just as I did it, the turret was suddenly and violently hit. It spun halfway around; my face struck the padding on the sight, hard enough to stun me. Meanwhile, Van hollered, 'Shoot straight ahead!'

"I didn't know where 'ahead' was fast enough. Van jumped out and fired the .50-caliber on top of the turret, while I trained on some buildings where there were apparently German infantry. I fired several rounds from the 75 into the buildings. Van was still outside. I stood up and a round hit the ammo box of the .50 next to my ear and I saw no Van Tine. I ducked in, looked out again and he was lying on the edge of the deck, about to roll off.

"I hollered to the driver to count to six and then take off. I was going out to hold Van Tine so we wouldn't lose him. We did that and on the way back to the rest of the company I held Van in my arms and put a first-aid bandage over the hole in his forehead. I never realized part of the back of his head was gone. He was dead before I ever got to him."

Jerry Nelson and the others from his company were in the vicinity of Poteau, astride the highway that led west from St. Vith toward Vielsalm and in the path of the First SS Panzer Division seeking to link up with its spearhead *Kampfgruppe Peiper*.

Nelson spent a sad, fitful night in the woods, mourning the death of Van Tine. He heard the sounds of much shooting, saw the flashes of muzzle blasts and exploding shells, but his own tank fired not a round. "The woods were very thick, and when you cannot see the other fifteen tanks in your company, you feel a lot lonelier. At night, as always, we took turns, one guy stayed awake for two hours on guard duty. But in the woods, the tank is blind, the guns are useless ten feet to your side. We would pull out a machine gun and set it up for close cover outside."

"In the morning, a Sergeant Burris replaced Van Tine as tank commander. We had backed into the edge of a woods for cover. In front of us was an open field with a knoll. Without any warning three tanks came over that knoll. On an overcast day and in a wooded area, it can take awhile to identify vehicles. We didn't have time to decide what kind of tanks these were, but in a war the decision to shoot comes from the direction people are going. There were not supposed to be any friendly forces in front of us. So when people and machines started coming at us, they had to be the other guys. Uniforms and helmets don't always count. Uniforms get dirty and we were too far away to make out the shape of a helmet, at least half a mile or so.

"We hit the first two quick. The distance was the same for each one and all I had to do was traverse a little. The third tank sped up to get behind a small growth of brush for concealment, the same thing we were trained to do. Only his cover was to his front and we were at an angle, exposing his broadside. So we shot him, too. I don't remember any people bailing out, but some must have.

That was it, and I think the Germans decided they had better find a better area for their attack."

It was a remarkable piece of work which lasted no longer than it takes to read Nelson's brief account. But his Deadeye Dick shooting eliminated three invaluable panzers, blunting for the moment a vital German advance.

To the southeast of Nelson, however, the retreat from Schönberg had begun with Phil Hannon and the others from the motley assembly there optimistic about their chances. "We moved slowly in short jumps because no one knew what lay ahead. At one stop we found a pile of bedrolls, duffel bags, overcoats and the like, discarded by infantry troops. Those of us without overcoats or bedrolls picked them up. Five cartons of smokes were found, so everyone would have cigarettes for a while. To eat, we each received a D bar. I ate mine, labeling the three pieces of it breakfast, dinner and supper. I picked up a can of frozen meatballs and spaghetti. That completed my food for Monday, December 18.

"The convoy suddenly seemed headed into the midst of a terrific firefight but then turned parallel before we reached the tracers. I happened to be up front in the truck and could see more than the others. Between prayers, I reported in a low voice—'Looks like the road goes right into the fight. Those .30s are getting outtalked. Christ, they are throwing up a lot of stuff. Watch out for that low wire.' When we turned parallel to the firing, we all sighed with relief, and whispers about turkey for Christmas started. We were disappointed and scared when the vehicles pulled into a patch of woods and the orders were to 'de-truck.' "

Confusion dominated the pitch-black night. Officers had a tough time finding their men and bringing some order. "Muttered curses could be heard all over the place. 'Get the hell out in the open. A treeburst would kill you sure as Christ.' 'Dig in, you damn fool!' While I dug in, one guy in my platoon asked to borrow my rifle because someone had stolen his. I fell asleep and slept soundly.

"About 4:00 A.M. a patrol got to us and started shooting the place up, with tracers flying up and down the field. The firing jarred me awake and scared the sin out of me. The shelter I had dug was half full of water. I headed for a mound of dirt. When things quieted down I went looking for the guy with my rifle. I used to cuss that rifle out during training but I sure wanted it now.

I found the guy with it, and after some argument he gave it to me. He swiped one from our lieutenant.

"When daylight came, we took a look at our positions and saw they were too exposed. We drove the trucks into the woods, camouflaged them and started to dig in, ready to fight it out. What a mess. Men dug beautiful two-men foxholes but everyone seemed to crave company. The holes were too close together. We'd be firing over the shoulders of men in front of us, and if the Germans threw heavy stuff in, it would have become a bloody hill. The officer who tried to get the German with the single-shot machine gun raised hell. He was about the only officer worth anything as far as I could see. We were all dead tired and digging new holes didn't sit well. But most of us could see what would happen. We spread out and began to shovel again.

"They needed engineers to fill a watery crater hole. Since I had hip boots, I was one of them. There was a truck and two kitchen trailers stuck hub-deep in the crater. The first thing we did was raid the trailers, D bars and fruit juices were all we could find without cooking. But we didn't complain. We were working when suddenly out of the woods, trucks and men burst forth. What a scramble. Men all over the trucks, hanging any place they could. 'We're getting out! Pile on a truck!'

"It sounded good but first another raid on the kitchen trailers. I got a carton of D bars and hailed a truck. Just then, a grenade I had hooked to my jacket fell off. When it hit the ground, the pin fell out. The weight of the grenade kept the the handle from kicking off. The boys around me broke and ran, except for one GI. He reached down, picked up the darn thing, walked about five yards and threw it into a field. The surprising thing was, the kid who used his head had been the one everybody figured would be the first to crack.

"When the grenade exploded, the convoy stopped dead; men sprawled all over the place. That allowed me to jump on a truck, one that happened to be pulling a 37-mm cannon behind. It was obvious we couldn't keep up dragging that gun behind. The driver stopped and one guy jumped off and uncoupled it. Usually it takes two to heave one off but this kid practically threw it off. We lost our place in the convoy, but since there were no umpires around, as in maneuvers, we crowded back into line.

"We were moving at a good pace until the lead jeep started out of a little village. Wham! The convoy stopped and started turning around. A Royal Tiger tank was raising hell with the front of the convoy. The road was blocked. We had one more chance, going back. 'Sure doesn't sound like we're getting out.' 'Throw me that peanut butter.' 'Wish I had a spoon. It's kind of messy this way.' 'For Christ's sake, don't be particular. Give me that stuff!'

"We were still catering to our stomachs when we spun around and started to change our route. Then the jeep in front of us hit a land mine. We were stopped! Trapped! Beaten without a good fight!

"The order came down the line to throw up our hands. We destroyed our weapons, cussed and cried, felt empty and lonely inside. Our fighting was over. We were beaten, tired, hungry and cold. But we were still soldiers and Americans, and expected treatment as such."

The loss of Schönberg opened the way for a German assault on the strategically important road hub of St. Vith. To protect St. Vith, already choked with civilians and military traffic fleeing west, mostly under orders, to avoid entrapment, General Jones assigned the 81st Engineer Combat Battalion, commanded by a former University of Illinois football star, Lt. Col. Thomas Riggs. The manpower originally available to Riggs amounted to little more than 110 survivors from his own organization plus about 350 from the 168th Engineer Combat Battalion, an antitank platoon whose weapons lacked appropriate sighting mechanisms, plus some artillery support.

Riggs quickly discovered that no sooner did he pick a spot on the map to erect his defenses, than the Germans would bypass it. He finally set up shop a bare mile from St. Vith, on high ground known as "the Prümerberg."

S. Sgt. John Collins, who luckily had remained behind to bring up equipment while others in his platoon moved up into the path of the German juggernaut on December 16, in the few hours before Schönberg fell, was still wearing hip boots and desperately trying to make sense of the chaos about him.

"Things are in such a state of confusion that it's difficult to understand what, where, how or when things happen. I do know that my platoon is more than likely catching hell if this drive extends to their area. [It did.] Man for man, squad for squad and platoon for platoon I would put my money on them as well as any! I love them all and right now I wished I was with my platoon."

"Captain Harmon [the company CO] found us some food, and as soon as we were fed, he started us back to Auw [the village on the Schönberg–St. Vith road] to try and aid the ones still there of the 422nd. The shelling was too intense and we had to return to Heuem. Heuem and Schönberg were both under heavy shelling."

Weary and shaken, men of the 81st straggled back. Collins found a supply vehicle where he obtained a pair of combat boots. He and the others walked aimlessly in the direction of St. Vith, awaiting orders on Sunday, December 17.

"From nowhere or out of the sky appeared Lieutenant Colonel Riggs, who stopped us and organized us into a defensive unit along a firebreak atop a wooded hill. The firebreak separated two wooded areas by about fifteen feet. The lieutenant colonel deployed us along the hillside and we dug in—the dirt flew!"

Riggs believing the 7th Armored counterattack would pass through his area, arranged for daisy chains of mines to stretch across the road. These could be pulled away to allow friendly traffic. Around 4:00 P.M., instead of friendlies, a column of German tanks plus what Riggs estimated as a battalion of infantry advanced from a distance of 1,000 yards. The six tank destroyers failed to score any hits but at least caused the armor to back off. The concentrated fire from Riggs' engineers, converted into riflemen, drove off the opposing foot soldiers. However, a rueful Riggs remarked, "The [tank destroyer] platoon moved north and out of our sector without reporting. This was the first of several units that left our sector to join a movement to the rear. It was this kind of attitude that increased my determination to hold our position."

After a time, with his foxhole deep enough to satisfy inspection, Collins was granted permission to bring rations and coffee from the command post, a short distance back.

"While there, the enemy tried to penetrate our lines and was succeeding when Riggs grabbed me and yelled into my ear: 'Remember the Ranger training we had? Then, let's go!' I didn't have time to answer yes or no. I grabbed four or five men and we took off, following the lieutenant colonel, who went up the hill like a tank."

Riggs recalled the moment. "At about 1900 hours, an enemy combat patrol penetrated our lines and got within thirty yards of the CP. I gathered four people in the CP and ran up the hill to the point of penetration, closed the gap and ordered a clean-up of infiltrators. I found that the gap in the skirmish line had been made by men fading to the rear. From that point on I visited our front line every hour or so, particularly at night, to let the men know their commander was there."

The "Ranger" reference indeed triggered a memory in Collins. "Ranger training was given in Fort Jackson when I first joined the division. I was one of four Pfc.s who volunteered for the training. Riggs was a major then and he aided each of us. Without his physical help I am sure I would have been written off. Riggs is maybe 6' 3", 280 pounds, a large man made of muscle and bone, a real fighting machine."

Convinced of an enemy concentration of armor and artillery in a nearby woods, Riggs managed to contact the air arm. A P–47 buzzed the area and one of the enemy tanks was so incautious as to try to discourage further inspection with a burst of machine gun fire. The Thunderbolt pilot strafed the spot several times and the black smoke rose from a hit.

The combat engineer battalion remnants awaited the inevitable further assaults. A slight spark of encouragement flared with the arrival of Maj. Don Boyer and the 38th Armored Infantry from CCB of the 7th Armored. The 38th AIB, with machine gunner Glenn Fackler, was the unit that had rejected Dave Pergrin's plea for them to join the defense of Malmédy. Several other elements from the 7th Armored also reinforced the Americans in front of St. Vith. Perhaps the cavalry would yet trundle to the rescue. However, Boyer related the discouraging news that a severe case of gridlock almost paralyzed the efforts of the 7th Armored's CCB.

For Collins the period in front of St. Vith became a blur. "We stayed in our positions for the whole night and every so often the lieutenant colonel would walk up and down in front of us. I also did my part in keeeping the men awake but I doubt that any slept much. We were a bunch of frustrated, scared kids. Except for Riggs and one lieutenant, we felt our officers had deserted us. There was plenty of courage in the men who stayed on the line. Without exception, every one of us relied on the lieutenant colonel to bring us through this situation.

"You can bet they are going to attack when the shelling is intense and then stops. They will charge, yelling, screaming and firing or throwing grenades. Tanks were in the area but were stopped with chain mines and in one case our own tanks. Their tanks, though, are much larger than ours and have firepower advantage. Our tanks are no match.

"We had no blankets and we shook from the cold and the shelling. Some units seemed to fade away when the going got tough. I guess we did not have the guts or brains to leave. I didn't seem to be doing much but at least I remained and followed orders."

One officer who stuck it out in that painfully exposed line before St. Vith was Nathan Duke Ward. "I was born near Boone, North Carolina, in 1916. The family moved to Cumberland County, Tennessee, when I was about six or seven, and I grew up on a farm near Crossville. I graduated from Cumberland County High School in 1936 and followed construction work in Ohio, Minnesota and Iowa. I was in Dayton, Ohio, in 1941, when I received my draft notice and reported for army service at Fort Oglethorpe, Georgia, November 26, 1941. I was scheduled to attend construction school at Fort Lee, Virginia.

"A popular song at the time was 'I'll Be Back in a Year, Little Darling' but I didn't make it. A few days later, I was in a theater in Chattanooga when they stopped the show and said all military personnel were to report to their home station. The Japanese had bombed Pearl Harbor."

Duke Ward never got to construction school but instead attended a field artillery training center at Fort Bragg. He spent most of his time serving the army as a carpenter between occasional visits to a firing range. From there he shipped to a field artillery battalion at Cape Cod. "This was the first time I had ever seen the ocean. And being from the South, I became known as 'Little Rebel.' "

The army continued to benefit from his carpentry skills and eventually his abilities translated into selection for OCS in the engineers at Fort Belvoir, Virginia. From there he joined the 106th, as a member of the 81st Engineer Combat Battalion. He arrived in Europe as CO of the Headquarters and Service Company. And on the outskirts of St. Vith, he assisted Riggs in the patchwork defense.

Like Collins, he admits to his fear. "The 88s, mortars, burp guns and buzz bombs were very frightening. Like most of the others, I was scared stiff and wondered when one of the shells would have my number on it. At times I just resigned myself to my fate. Other times I envied those going to the rear on stretchers. Morale stayed good, although we had very little food and the weather was mighty cold."

With the arrival of Boyer and his people, Riggs rearranged his lineup. He shifted Ward and his men further south to extend the flank of the defense. It was in this area that a daisy chain blew off the track of a German tank. The explosion disabled the tank, but it continued to occupy a position where its still-operating 88-mm cannon stared down the throats of Ward and his cohorts.

Some GIs claimed to have heard the enemy shout in English, "You Yankee bastards! Kill those Yankee sons of bitches!" The fine usage of American locutions may suggest the attackers belonged to Skorzeny's 150 Brigade. However, it was Manteuffel's Fifth Panzer Army that stalked Schönberg, and the Skorzeny troops were part of the Sixth SS Panzer Army to the north. In any event, the infantrymen, supporting the disabled panzer, were driven off by rifle and machine gun fire. Still the tank menaced the embattled GIs of the headquarters company.

Some modest, rather self-effacing support in the form of medium tanks now stood behind the engineers' foxholes. Ward requested they move forward and knock out that threatening enemy behemoth. "At first," says Ward, "the officer in the tank refused and said as soon as the turret of his tank showed over the hill, the 88 would knock it off. After a second appeal, he said he would try. I volunteered to ride the turret to the top of the hill and point out the German tank.

"We moved up, and as soon as we got to the crest of the hill, the 88 opened up. The first round hit under the turret where I was sitting. The concussion knocked me off the tank. A piece of the shell pierced my helmet. I was stunned but eventually found my helmet and put it on my head. As I scrambled away, I remember seeing the German tank burst into flames. One of our officers found me wandering in the woods a little later and took me back to my CP."

Temporarily, the advance on St. Vith halted. But John Collins, Duke Ward and their leader, Colonel Riggs, were all in peril. Both the 422nd and 423rd regiments, with Alan Jones, Clifford Broadwater, Leo Leisse, Frank Raila, Richard McKee, Jim Mills and more than 7,000 others from the 106th Division, were surrounded. Those on the Prümerberg awaited the inevitable resurgence of the opposing army.

Chapter VII

SURROUNDS AND SURRENDERS

WHILE THE COMBAT ENGINEERS on the Prümerberg braced themselves for the weight of the German Fifth Panzer Army of Manteuffel, unaware of the armored forces falling back behind them, the vanguard of Sepp Dietrich's Sixth SS Panzers, the column of *Kampfgruppe Peiper* to the north, sank its punch into the solar plexus of the American forces.

He continued to detour around Malmédy, although only the tiny combat engineer outfit under Dave Pergrin and a few men from other units held the road hub. But Peiper's objectives were the bridges on the Meuse, not the conquest of towns. From Ligneuville, Peiper planned to cross the Amblève River in the village of Stavelot. The only route suitable for Peiper's tanks was a curved main road that snaked between a chasm on one side and a steep hill on the other. As the German armored column clanked toward the vital bridge shortly after dark on December 17, a lone American sentry, posted by Pergrin, Pvt. Bernard Goldstein, alerted by the rattle of tracks and voices in German, stepped onto the road. Within hailing distance of the tanks, he commanded, "Halt!"

The startled German infantrymen riding the Mark IVs leaped off and blasted away with their machine pistols. A few U.S. M–1s replied in kind. Goldstein himself scrambled up the side of the hill to escape. An American bazooka rocket slammed into the lead tank, disabling it. The German column reversed gears and backed off to consider the situation.

Unknown to the enemy, they faced only a thirteen-man team manning a roadblock. But Peiper believed Stavelot was heavily defended. An assault at night could be disastrous. Furthermore, his troops, already without sleep for at least thirty-six hours, badly needed rest. *Kampfgruppe Peiper* chose to break off the engagement until dawn. The Americans in the vicinity, including not only Pergrin's 291st but also soldiers from the 202nd and 51st Engineer Combat Battalions, prepared charges to blast a series of bridges desperately needed by the enemy to continue its penetration. Among the structures targeted was the one at Stavelot. Under cover of night, an engineer work party installed the requisite explosives.

During the night a tank destroyer platoon and an armored infantry unit reinforced the slender garrison at Stavelot. But when morning arrived, the Germans bombarded Stavelot with howitzers and mortars. However, the initial rush to the village produced twenty-five to thirty casualties among Peiper's men, albeit knocking out several U.S. tank destroyers. The SS Panzer lieutenant colonel ordered a pause while he maneuvered his infantry into position for support of his armor. Peiper said, "At dawn we launched the attack, led by two Panther tanks running at full speed. The lead one was hit and burned but its momentum carried it through the antitank obstacles where it careened off two Sherman tanks. A second Panther then seized control of the bridge and the Americans evacuated their position. We continued at top speed towards Trois Ponts, delayed briefly by a single antitank gun which was destroyed."

At an appropriate moment, before the Panther tanks reached the Stavelot bridge, the Americans sought to detonate the explosives. But nothing happened. The misfire, at first chalked up to happenstance, later was attributed to a pair of strangers in GI uniforms who assisted in placing the charges. They belonged to Operation *Greif* and sabotaged the mechanism.

Peiper later insisted that there were American tanks present, but U.S. records indicate he faced only tank destroyers, 75-mm, halftrack-towed pieces. Furthermore, the detour taken towards Trois Ponts, taken apparently because Peiper's lead armor thought the narrow main street of Stavelot threatening, veered away from the highway to Spa, site not only of First Army Headquarters, itself a bejeweled prize, but only two miles up that highway an enormous, lightly guarded fuel dump. The gas stored there was enough to keep Peiper's task force rolling for months. No one from Skorzeny's spies had informed the spearhead of its whereabouts.

Peiper noted later, "When we penetrated Stavelot, too many civilians shot at us from the windows and openings in their roofs. The only goal that I was looking for was the bridge near Trois

Ponts. I, therefore, had no time to spend on those civilians and continued driving on, although I knew that resistance in this town had not been decisively broken."

In fact, the column left behind "many wounded" in a hastily improvised aid station. They came under fire as new American forces, aided by local Belgians, according to Peiper, tried to retake Stavelot. "With the help of a few tanks which followed behind some infantry, we succeeded in the counterattack to remove our wounded."

Peiper and company arrived at Trois Ponts about 11:00 A.M. on December 18. No saboteurs in Trois Ponts prevented the U.S. engineers' destructive achievements. In rapid succession, the three crossings that give the town its name and would have enabled Peiper to speed towards the Meuse exploded in loud roars. *Kampfgruppe Peiper* hit the road towards La Gleize and Werbomont seeking alternate ways over the Salm River. Along the way, a brief break in the cloud cover enabled two coveys of P–47 Thunderbolts to swoop down on the column. The bombing and strafing further reduced Peiper's forces and slowed their pace. Peiper may not have known it at the moment but the hour had struck when predator becomes prey.

On the move to stop *Kampfrguppe Peiper* was a veteran combat organization, the 30th Infantry Division. Part of the Ninth Army involved in the drive to capture Aachen along the northern stretch of the front, the "Old Hickory" Division, nicknamed for Andrew Jackson and forged from National Guardsmen from South Carolina, North Carolina and Tennessee had begun its fighting in Normandy shortly after D-Day. It was technically in reserve during the first weeks of December, standing down in territory behind the Roer Dam assault after having participated in the seizure of Aachen.

Curtiss Martell, a platoon sergeant with Company C, 119th Infantry Regiment of the 30th, remembered "enjoying a much needed rest from combat duty" during the second week of December while billeted in the small German town called Kohlscheid. The bitter wintry weather was familiar to Martell. Born in Minot, North Dakota, in 1923, he moved to Royal Oak, Michigan, while still a toddler after his parents separated. His mother worked to support herself and her son.

Upon finishing high school in Detroit, Martell accepted a job in a factory that produced engine parts for military aircraft. He enrolled in technical training programs provided by his employer and added further knowledge through correspondence courses in civil and sturctural engineering.

"I was inducted into the army in mid-January, 1943. My thoughts on the occasion were mixed. The wars in Europe and the Pacific Islands were far away. I had little regard for them. Sometimes I thought of joining the air corps. I liked excitement and thought I could get my fill as a tail gunner.

"I was originally assigned to and took my basic training with the 26th Yankee Division and was a member of the 328th Infantry, which happened to be Sgt. Alvin York's outfit in World War I. But upon completion of training, a group of us became a cadre with the 30th, Old Hickory Division.

"We landed on Omaha Beach in Normandy on June 13. Our first nasty encounter was against SS paratroopers. We suffered many casualties, but managed to drive them back to new defensive positions. Squadrons of American bombers flew overhead, targetting the enemy at St.-Lô. Meanwhile P–47 fighter planes flew in behind us, bombed and strafed the hell out of us. Our planes knocked out our ammo-dump and also hit a field hospital. I received a cut near my temple that drew a little blood. I didn't have a medic look at it and I never reported the wound. That was a big mistake because I would have received five points for the wound. Prior to the beginning of the Ardennes campaign, people with enough points could go home to the States on furlough. I lacked three points. I would also have received another Purple Heart to go with two I did receive, along with the Bronze Star, Silver Star, Presidential Unit Citation and five major battle campaign stars.

"There were times when I thought about being wounded or killed, primarily because I saw so many casualties. I never thought I could be a prisoner of war and I can't recall ever discussing these possibilities with my comrades. When being attacked, my heart would pound, most notably during the first experiences of combat. After more and more skirmishes, that feeling subsided. Toward the end of the war I became a bit reckless because the fear of battle was almost gone. One buddy and I were even laughing once while under fire.

"In the beginning, I harbored no animosity toward the enemy. They were soldiers dedicated to the duties of combat for their country, as we were to ours. However, my attitude changed dramatically as time passed. I became a person with vengeance in his heart and at times almost vicious in nature. My leadership became more demanding.

"Battle casualties were generally high. The new replacements never really knew me. I learned not to become buddies with my men because it was difficult to accept their death, should it happen. I had a good relationship with most of my superior officers. Most enlisted men that I led were dependable. During the Ardennes campaign, the men performed admirably. On another occasion I had trouble with four men. One deserted his post; another refused to serve as point scout for the platoon [Cap Capalbo's job in the 99th] and two deserted. I saw acts that some would classify as acts of courage which to me were examples of carelessness.

"On the evening of December 16, some of our men heard a radio broadcast by Axis Sally. She said the 30th Division should pack up and prepare for combat with a strong German counteroffensive in Belgium. The report proved to be true. Within a few hours, our troops were on trucks speeding along the road late at night."

Bob Hall, a draftee from Chester, Pennsylvania, originally trained as an antitank crewman but eventually switched to an ammunition & pioneer platoon with the 3rd Battalion, Headquarters Company in the 119th Regiment. A & P soldiers toted shells and cartridges, performed light engineering tasks and served as riflemen.

"I was part of the original bunch in the 106th Infantry Division at Fort Jackson, South Carolina. We spent two and a half months on maneuvers in Tennessee, early in 1944, and sometimes that seems to me to have been worse than the war. We didn't know what a bed was, the weather was lousy, the food bad and etc. I guess they tried to make us as miserable as can be to prepare us for what was ahead.

"I never thought much about being killed, wounded or becoming a prisoner. Along with most of my buddies I figured 'If the Lord thinks it is my time to get killed, it will happen.' We learned to think of ourselves as only serial numbers instead of human beings. There was always some talk about an officer the guys didn't like. 'When we get overseas, I am going to shoot that S.O.B.' That was probably just talk. I never saw or heard of anyone doing it. My superior officer was 1st Lt. Walter J. Goodman. I can only say great things about him. I recall having to walk through a suspected mine field. He insisted on going first and told us to follow his footsteps. Unfortunately, after the war he was killed in a car accident in Paris."

One of thousands of Golden Lions stripped away from the division to fill the depleted ranks of units already in combat, Hall became a member of the 30th Infantry Division in the Normandy hedgerows in July 1944. Within a month, Hall earned a Silver Star "for gallantry in action." When his unit was pinned down by fire from an enemy artillery piece beyond the reach of friendly guns, Hall and two other GIs volunteered for an attempt to destroy the German weapon. Armed with a bazooka, Hall and his companions worked their way across open terrain while under intense fire. They gained a vantage point for a clear view at the hostile gun. All three opened up and destroyed the artillery piece.

"The saddest thing I ever saw was while in the hedgerows. We were assigned to take a trailer to a spot where eight or nine dead GIs lay. We picked up the bodies while their buddies watched and cried. We brought the dead men to a field cemetery and there were a great many American and German bodies lined up. It was a terrible sight."

In October 1944, while using mine detectors to aid in an attack on the German city of Kohlscheid, Bob Hall took a hit in his leg from a rifle bullet. Following medical treatment, he returned to the line after about ten days. A few weeks later, while Hall was sitting with buddies playing cards, an enemy shell exploded. Shrapnel pierced a card in his hand and tore up a finger. Patched up again, on December 17, Bob Hall, with others from the 119th Regiment, boarded trucks in a 30th Division rest area near Kohlscheid and motored towards the Belgian town of Stoumont. After an overnight stop in Eupen they reached their destination. On the following day, there would be a violent collision between *Kampfgruppe Peiper* and the 119th Regiment of Bob Hall.

Francis Currey, born in June 1925, had been orphaned when he barely reached his teens. He grew up in a hamlet of the Catskill Mountains, Hurleyville, New York, population perhaps 250. Immediately upon graduation from high school in 1943, Currey enlisted.

After basic training at Fort Benning and maneuvers with the 75th Division in Louisiana, he embarked for Europe to serve as an infantry replacement with the 30th, already blooded from engagements in Normandy and the drive out of St.-Lô. Currey earned his acceptance with the 30th with his baptism of fire at Kirkrode, Holland.

But on December 17, Frank Currey, elevated to sergeant and BAR man for the Third Platoon of Company K, 120th Infantry Regiment, as a member of the 30th left his foxhole and hot meals to commence a forty-mile trip southeast to halt further penetration by the German spearhead. While Curtiss Martell and Bob Hall with the 119th Regiment trekked toward the western end of the Bulge line, the 120th, claiming Frank Currey, located near Malmédy.

Just about the moment that Pvt. Bernard Goldstein singlehandedly challenged *Kampfgruppe Peiper*, Capt. Charles MacDonald, distraught by the pell-mell retreat of himself and his company, met some of his fleeing troops at a road junction near the twin villages of Krinkelt and Rocherath. He had barely lapsed into a nap before combined masses of enemy armor and infantry overwhelmed the hastily constructed defenses.

"There seemed to be no lull coming in the firing. I ran toward the rear of the farmhouse, snagging my trousers on a fence post and tearing them badly. I flattened myself against the back wall of the stone building just as a shell from an enemy tank crashed into the front. The house rocked precariously, trembling from the impact of the explosion.

"The snow-covered area to the rear of the house became the beaten zone for countless tracer bullets. Tank fire crashed around the building. Artillery fell without pattern in the snow. The night was ablaze with more noise and flame than I had thought possible for men to create. Here was a 'movie war.' Here was Armageddon."

The fallback of Captain MacDonald carried him south to the area where shattered elements of the 99th Division also tried to regroup. For better than two days, Company B, 393rd Infantry sought to drive off wave after wave of Germans. Ben Nawrocki was there.

"We were surrounded and had no contact with the rear. The officers decided to withdraw and try to fight our way to friendly lines. It was decided the two battalions [393rd Regiment, 1st Battalion and 394th, 2nd] would band together.

"It was miserable going. We headed for the town of Mürringen, that the 394th Regiment held. We came under our own artillery which mistook us for German troops. We were creeping six and eight abreast in snow, mud and water while the artillery kept taking its toll. We tried to carry all the wounded we could. There were cries and moans and screams of pain from the wounded. It was heartbreaking and hard to continue. We didn't know it was our own artillery. We had no contact whatsoever.

"Our first sergeant, Earlington Bond, was wounded, a big chunk out of his leg, but he kept on with us. We came across a lot of trucks and vehicles, strewn with wounded begging for help. It seemed like every one of them was full of wounded. I presume German artillery got them much earlier. It was a terrible scene. Here were our own troops and we were so dog-tired we could do nothing for them. We were frozen to the bone and it was cold.

"I had nothing to eat since the night of December 15 and now it was about midnight December 18th. Many were in the same position. The few who had C rations tried to keep them from freezing, holding them close to their bodies. It was hard not to give up. Men would curse and go on.

"We headed for Krinkelt. We could see a hell of a firefight going on by tracer fire and burning buildings.It was dark in the valley and all that stood out was the firefight. Finally, a small patrol under Sergeant Henderson contacted a 2nd Division outpost and they lifted the artillery fire and shifted it to our flanks for our protection. They said they had mistaken us for enemy troops.

"Sergeant Morris Finer, Sergeant Malone, Private First Class Bevins and I, along with two other men, volunteered to go out and bring in as many wounded as we could. We kept going back and forth under fire all night long. Sergeant Malone, a big massive man, had us wait until he wrapped his feet in rags as they bled badly from frostbite and trench foot.

"We used two rifles pushed through two overcoat sleeves and buttoned to improvise stretchers. It was muddy and slippery, with sniper fire as well as artillery on us."

Backing up the retreating 99th Division regiments were the field artillery battalions. Dick Byers occupied an uncomfortable ringside seat to the bloody events. He had barely found himself a comfortable basement room in a schoolhouse in the village of Krinkelt before his battery commander summoned him to join the gun crews behind the village.

"We spent most of the afternoon digging a two-man dugout on the hillside between the guns and town. We made several trips into Krinkelt, liberating mattresses to line the bottom and a door to cover the top of the dugout.

"My father-in-law, who was in France during World War I, once told me of being chased across a field by a series of enemy artillery shells. The identical thing happened to me as, alone, I returned from my last trip to town. Someone at the controls of an 88 was searching that road as I came down the hill from the village. One shell after another hit high up on the embankment to my right or left, keeping pace with me. The banks of the road flattened out at the bottom of the hill where the land turned boggy. I was completely exposed so I ducked my head and ran like hell for the dugout. The final shell whistled in closer than any I had ever heard. But it burrowed deep in the soft swampland and splattered me with mud instead of shrapnel.

"About 10:00 P.M we woke up to the sound of a firefight and tank battle in Krinkelt/Rocherath. When we came up out of the hole I saw a scene I can't forget. There was a fire blazing in front of the Krinkelt church. It was a burning Sherman tank, one of three knocked out by Panthers near the church. The flames lit the height of the church spire. Through binoculars I could see figures running back and forth, silhouetted by the fire, and watched tracers from tanks at either end of town. My melodramatic and frequent thought that evening was a line from Alan Seeger's poem, 'I have a rendezvous with Death / At midnight in some flaming town . . . ' "

Byers's sightseeing concluded abruptly with orders to haul the big guns to positions further back. The ground had been churned into thick muck by the shifting of heavy equipment. Like Eric Wood with the 589th, Byers and his companions heaved, pulled and sweated before the massive pieces reached the single road available. The first imminent danger brought unexpected and terrible results.

"We had some guys out in front of gun batteries, between them and the village. They were never trained to be so dangerously exposed and a few became extremely trigger-happy. A party of their officers came from town in the dark and were challenged. The officers responded and approached. Someone, however, opened fire and killed a major. Another officer identified himself, calmed everyone down, then got up to come forward and was shot in the leg.

"Two of our officers had reputations for being really tough, by-the-numbers soldiers. It turned out that First Lieutenant Mahaffey was just as tough as his reputation and the other was worthless, taking off well in advance of his men."

On the road, the men of the 371st Field Artillery discovered their route blocked by a pair of antiaircraft halftracks, abandoned in mud up to the tops of the tracks astride the road. "They blocked the entrance to the small bridge over the stream and there was no way around them through the swampy lowland. The order was given to abandon all equipment and get out on foot. No one issued orders to spike the guns or destroy any other equipment. On their own initiative, several soldiers dropped thermite grenades down the barrels of their howitzers. Some truck drivers left their engines running with the hand throttle pulled out and opened the petcocks to the radiators."

An all-night slog in which Byers says he was asleep on his feet brought the battery to Camp Elsenborn, the former Belgian army installation. Late in the morning, the battery commander dispatched the first sergeant to rouse the troops with an unpleasant message. All were to appear for inspection within an hour, clean-shaven and in clean uniforms. "This was really good for our morale, because we were all depressed. The captain gave us something to really bitch about, as well as something to do that was not easy. When the inspection ended, we gave the captain an 'A' for applied psychology because we all felt so much better."

Byers and a group of his comrades made an attempt to retrieve their abandoned howitzers and vehicles. But before they could reach the site, retreating GIs persuaded them that the enemy now controlled the area. Subsequently, Byers volunteered for a detail that drove west, out of reach of *Kampfgruppe Peiper*'s column, then south to pick up new jeeps and trucks.

The hamlets of Krinkelt and Rocherath, so close to one another they were known as the twin villages, witnessed fierce resistance from the Americans, mostly soldiers from Ben Nawrocki's 99th and Charles MacDonald's 2nd Divisions. In the towns no discernible front line could be drawn as troops from both sides occupied houses in a crazy quilt pattern.

The thick morning fog aided the defenders, whose bazooka-wielding infantry could approach German armor close enough to launch without being seen. When crews from disabled tanks tumbled from the turrets and escape hatches, GIs on rooftops or from building windows shot them down. Word of scattered executions of American prisoners spread. Some GIs retaliated in kind.

"It was an absolute deathtrap," said Sgt. Willi Fischer, who commanded a Panther for the 12th SS Panzer Division committed in a two-pronged thrust with the 277th *Volksgrenadier* Infantry Division. "I was positioned behind Johann Beutelhauser, my platoon commander. As I reached a point near the church [Krinkelt] Beutelhauser [caught] it right in front of me. Beutelhauser succeeding in getting out but the gunner was hit by rifle fire as he got out. Near me Brodel's panzer was burning gently, with Brodel still sitting lifeless in the turret. In front of me, further along the road, more panzers had been put out of action and were still burning."

In spite of the carnage wreaked upon the two German divisions, the Americans were forced to flee the twin villages to eventually dig in for a last desperate defense along the Elsenborn Ridge. There the survivors would be joined by the Big Red One, the 1st Infantry Division, in a desperate attempt to prevent expansion of the northern shoulder of the salient.

Two days after the Germans crashed through the front lines, the CO of A Company, 422nd Regiment, the 106th Division group on the right flank of the 99th, directed Mess Sgt. Bob Richardson, Pvt. Kenny Wines and Sgt. Richard McKee to cache the company payroll, about $70,000 in French, British and American currency. The trio packed the money into a .50-caliber machine gun ammunition container, smeared the metal can with grease and buried it between two trees near an abandoned German pillbox. "For all I know, it is still there," says McKee.

The unit moved out. McKee remembers, "While we had no idea of how devastating the German attack was, we felt we were headed for trouble. As we marched down a road, the side ditches were strewn with gas masks and equipment. Everyone was in such a hurry, they threw away everything so they could go faster and easier. No one bothered to tell us if we were advancing or retreating.

"Around mid-afternoon, we were crossing an open field when three German 88 artillery shells screamed overhead and detonated to our right. One of the fragments hit me in my right leg. We picked ourselves up and ran to the woods. I became separated from the rest of the column."

McKee joined two other soldiers and slept in the woods that night. Early in the morning, the three started to walk in the general direction taken by their fellows. They came upon a group of men digging in at the edge of a forest and began to create their own foxholes.

After they finished, a captain approached McKee. "You are now promoted to staff sergeant and squad leader." The freshly-breveted noncom immediately received an assignment to lead a patrol with the aim of determining if Germans were in the area. McKee and five others cautiously started out towards another thicket atop a hill about 500 yards off.

"We had just crossed a small stream when a couple of Germans suddenly appeared and yelled at us to throw down our rifles and surrender. I told the private who had the radio to report the Germans in the woods. He was so nervous and scared he couldn't talk. I grabbed the radio and informed the captain. He said, 'Get the hell back here, immediately.'

"We ran back, and by the time we reached the outfit, we had only enough time to jump on the last jeep in the convoy. In their haste to leave the area, some trucks had skidded into ditches and overturned. Others were stuck in the mud. A kitchen truck had rolled onto its side and a twenty-five gallon pot poured steaming hot pork chops in the middle of the road. It was panic, pure and simple. It was no withdrawal. We were running for our lives."

The convoy jerked along in starts and stops, frequently halting to wheel to the rear as German troops popped up ahead. "As we entered Schönberg, the lead jeep supposedly hit a land mine and blew up. The CO was reportedly killed. All of the vehicles stopped. It was around 9:00 A.M. and one of the officers, holding a white flag, told us to destroy our guns, other equipment and surrender. We couldn't believe it. We were not under fire and we could not see any Germans. We could not understand why we were surrendering.

"I took my M–1 apart and threw the pieces over a fence. Kenny Wines [who assisted McKee in hiding the payroll] seized his carbine by the barrel and slammed it against a tree. The gun discharged and hit him in the stomach. He died of that wound.

"We stood around a while. Everyone was told to get rid of family pictures, money, billfolds and knives. Keep only your dog tags, blankets, canteen and that stuff. A couple of us almost decided to jump into a jeep with a .50-caliber machine gun and take off across country. But we decided not to. Around 10:30 A.M. [ninety minutes approximately from the decision to surrender] the Germans came up and took over. They were like a bunch of kids with new toys, trying to start the trucks and going through them. Our captors ordered us to get rid of our helmets and put our hands on top of our heads. They took our watches and anything else they wanted. They told us that if anyone attemted to escape, they would shoot everyone.

"The war was over for me, but my battle for survival was just beginning."

Assistant BAR Gunner, Jim Mills from Company I of the 423rd Regiment, stationed on the right flank of McKee and the others in the 422nd, passed the first two days of the German attack without coming under extremely heavy artillery barrages. But he and his companions did not realize that the enemy had managed to break through on their right flank. "They went around behind us and cut us off. But I am not sure that even our leaders were aware of how serious things were.

"We were called together and told that we were going to have to go back to our rear and fight our way out. We were told to leave our duffel bags and other stuff in a common pile and not carry anything we didn't need. Most of us left our heavy overcoats and just wore field jackets because we could move better. I had my M–1 and its ammo, a light field pack with entrenching tool, canteen of water, a couple of K rations, hand grenades, belts of ammo for the BAR carried by Bob Widdicombe, and three bazooka shells which I hung on my back using a strap through the tail fins.

"That morning, as we moved through the woods, crossing a firebreak, volleys of rifle fire broke out. Sammy Pate, our physical training instructor, was shot in the head, right between the eyes. There was a burst of fire from our guys who claimed they got the German who hit Sammy. It was hard to believe that Sammy got it. He was probably in the best shape of anybody in our company. I guess he never knew what hit him.

"When all the shooting started, I hit the ground and felt a very sharp pain in my back, between the shoulders. Damn, I thought, am I hit already? I asked a buddy to check my back. He said he didn't see any hole or blood. Finally, it stopped hurting. Later, that afternoon, when we came under fire again, I hit the ground and felt the same piercing blow in my back. It suddenly dawned on me that it was the end of a bazooka shell fin driving into my back. Somebody told me I might as well throw the bazooka ammo away since the only bazooka in our group had been shot up. So I pitched them."

The Germans now zeroed in on Mills and his unit. He watched the shells exploding overhead, first on one side of the road, then the other, walking towards the area where he cowered. He stopped observing and stretched out on the ground as flat as possible. "Shrapnel fragments came ripping through the air with a rapid whooshing sound. You could hear them tearing between you and the guy next to you, all over the place. I don't know about the other guys but I prayed a bit."

They managed to scramble into the partial protection afforded by woods and started to make foxholes. Mills burrowed down a foot and struck a tree root. He shifted to a spot a few feet off and hit another root. "I was so tired it didn't make any difference. I just slept on the ground, cold and wet. In the morning I opened my last K ration, cheese and bacon. Suddenly, artillery shells began exploding in the treetops. I put my head in the deepest side of the hole I had dug, my belly over the root and my hind end sticking out."

The barrage slackened, the company resumed its effort to slip through the encirclement. To break out, they would have to capture Schönberg, now in German hands. Small arms fire crackled from an apparent fierce skirmish beyond a nearby ridge. As the wary Mills trudged along a road, an enemy tank rattled into view about 100 yards off. Five infantrymen accompanied the tank and started to set up a machine gun.

"I aimed at the group and fired my M–1. For some reason, I snapped on the safety, rolled behind a tree before flipping the safety off to fire again. The tank cut loose. The first round crashed into the embankment in front of my tree and tore out a four-foot-square hunk of earth. The second shot shattered a telephone pole, breaking it off about four feet above grade. The top spun around the wires a couple of times. Another shell plowed a trench at the ground line between me and two others. One of them took shrapnel in his right leg, the other in his left elbow.

"Widdicombe was firing away at the tank with his BAR. The tank panned the area with its cannon. A round knocked off the top of the tree I was behind and the branches fell on us. I knew if I stayed there much longer I was going to get hit. When the cannon swung away, I took off, up a hill. When I was in England, another GI and I took a short cut in order to catch up with the company after it left us behind to store some stuff. The two of us heard sounds like somebody snapping their fingers near your head. Then I saw dirt kicking up to our right and when we looked to our left we could see we had blundered onto the back side of a firing range. Now, outside of Schönberg, I heard a whole series of snaps and the bark started chipping off a tree to my right. Someone was shooting at me with a machine gun. I hit the ground, fast. I never saw it or heard the actual firing but I knew what was happening. I forgot all about the tank having a machine gun to go with that cannon. I heard my squad leader, Sgt. John Najarian, yell, 'What's the matter, Mills? Getting a little hot over there?' "

The tank backed off. During the respite, Mills foraged in the area where the armor had been and found a jeep with two cans of condensed milk and an abandoned German machine gun. Widdicombe was retrieving these when someone opened fire on him. Mills yanked him over an embankment to safety. But their war was also finished.

"Shortly after, someone came up to us and said that we had been unable to break out. We were to destroy our weapons and surrender. Very soon, Germans came through, asking the locations of their dead. We sure didn't tell them of any places; we figured they might blame us."

About the same time Richard McKee became lost in the woods near Schönberg and Jim Mills with Company I began its abortive try to break out, Johann Peter Maraite, a Belgian woodsman, walked along a dirt road through the forest near his hometown of Meyerode in search of a Christmas tree. Suddenly, around three o'clock he saw two armed American soldiers. "They beckoned me to come into the woods to join them, which I did. We of Meyerode speak only German, of which language neither American had any knowledge. But by gestures I made them understand that I was their friend and that they could trust me. They, on their side, appeared very anxious to exchange ideas with me, and they were wet, cold and tired."

Maraite convinced the two soldiers to accompany him to his home. Discreetly, the woodsman led them to the house. "It was dangerous, with German soldiers and SS troops occupying the village. But how could we do less for friends who needed help. Yes, the SS troops might have killed us if they found out about it. But as yet there were no Germans billeted in our house. They did not come until the next day, when nine were put to live with us." In the failing light of the late afternoon, Maraite posted "our good dog outside to give warning if anyone should approach."

Johann Peter Maraite, his wife Anna Maria and his daughter Eva described their American guests. "One was an officer, a big handsome man about twenty-five years old, with single silver bars on his shoulders." In fact, some months later, the Maraites looked at a photograph of Lt. Eric Fisher Wood and announced, "Yes, yes, yes, it is he."

The other soldier was smaller and wore no insignia. He carried a rifle, not a carbine, indicating he was most likely an enlisted man. The lieutenant, identified as Eric Wood, wore a knee-length overcoat and carried a pistol and a map. Both had gloves, scarves, helmets with knitted caps inside the liners, and overshoes.

After he first reached his home and gave the grateful Americans hot coffee, Maraite dispatched Eva to fetch a neighbor, Jean Schroder, who spoke English and could act as an interpreter. Eric Wood, while at Princeton, had studied French, reasoning, said his wife, that when he went to war, that would be the most valuable language. Schroder, however, was not at home and Maraite himself took a further risk, venturing out after dark to find his neighbor. Then, over supper, with Schroder translating, the Belgians conversed with the weary soldiers.

"They were very tired but were cheerful and determined, not scared or afraid. The lieutenant said funny things that made us laugh." The manner was in character with Eric Wood's penchant for wry humor and practical jokes."While sitting at our table they dried and counted their cartridges and seemed not too displeased with the number. They had evidently been doing much shooting and wished to know exactly how much ammunition they had."

The officer, according to Schroder, asked no sympathy for their plight. Speaking firmly but without bravado, he sought information about the enemy which he could coordinate with his map. While he was grateful for an opportunity to dry his clothes and eat, that seemed secondary to his interest in intelligence.

He told his hosts that he was the only one who had managed to break away. He spoke of the ambush near Schönberg where the others were either wounded, killed or captured. And he declared that he absolutely refused to surrender; he would never yield. His last orders had been to proceed to St. Vith and that was his first objective. Then he would see if it were possible to aid his comrades left behind in the snowy fields. He also explained that he had found his companion in the woods after making his own escape.

The natives explained that from what they had seen and heard, a very large battle had been started by the Germans. They warned that his chances of reaching St. Vith were probably impossible since the country between Meyerode and St. Vith teemed with enemy soldiers. Indeed, they thought St. Vith itself was a hopeless case because from their house they could see fires consuming the town. In fact, German artillery had already begun to lob shells into the village where the CO of the 106th Division, Gen. Alan Jones, Sr., father of the executive officer with the 1st Battalion, 423rd Regiment, now encircled by Nazi soldiers, made his headquarters.

The news failed to deter the lieutenant. "He said he would either fight his way back to his own outfit, or if that proved to be absolutely impossible, would collect American stragglers, of whom he had seen some in the woods and start a war of his own. He said it could start right away so far as he was concerned and that he was perfectly willing to run into SS men that very night, that he and his friend would take good care of them.

"As soon as he had obtained all the information we could give, he did not wish to jeoparadize further our safety by continuing in our home. But we persuaded him that this was unwise, because one can easily lose his way in strange woods at night. We convinced him to stay the night and start out at early dawn when the Germans would be stirring around in their bivouacs but not yet moving out of them. Under these conditions, he could see them before they saw him, which, it was agreed, was sound hunting procedure. We showed him on his map exactly where all of the bivouacs were. We also told him about the roads and landmarks and he noted these on his map. He was greatly pleased with the large amount of exact information we were able to supply and we were proud of this."

Later in the evening, the Belgians turned over a double bed to their guests. Several times the watchdog barked but it was only other neighbors paying calls. The Maraites entertained them in their kitchen without disclosing the presence of the Americans.

About 5:00 A.M., Maraite awakened the pair. They were so

sleepy that it required a second urging from the host to rouse them. Indeed, a buzz bomb plunged into Meyerode during the night with an explosion that shook the Maraite house, but the two Americans, to the amusement of the Maraites, never heard it.

"We gave them breakfast at 6:15 A.M. so they could start out just before dawn or around 7:00 A.M. We gave them a package of sandwiches, well buttered, with plenty of meat, to take along. Before they left, they carefully cleaned the rifle."

Johann Peter Maraite guided them partway. "All remained quiet, so certainly they made their way safely back into the forest, accompanied by our prayers."

For Lt. Alan Jones, Jr., with the 1st Battalion of the 423rd Infantry Regiment up on the Schnee Eifel, the first two days of the German offensive posed relatively little threat to his well-being. "We could watch some of the fighting from our hill and we received reports of the progress of the attack, the talk of a stiff battle. They didn't break through until the second day. There was no great pressure on us but we were to readjust our positions slightly after Bleialf fell around noon.

"On the third day, we received orders to attack to our rear, to move into positions along the Schönberg Highway to St. Vith and destroy the Panzer army. Then it was almost dark when the regimental commander, Colonel Cavender, received orders to attack Schönberg itself." Supposedly, Cavender, after reading the message, mumbled, "My poor men—they'll be cut to pieces."

Oddly, what may have doomed the 423rd and its companion 422nd was a strategy based upon a belief the regiments could only survive if they broke through their encirclement. To carry out the attack to the rear toward Schönberg meant that both outfits would leave the Schnee Eifel whose rugged hills and bunkers afforded them strong defensive positions. However, once the infantrymen of the 106th left the Schnee Eifel they became vulnerable to armor as well as foot soldiers. The decision perhaps turned on the vain expectations that the bulk of 7th Armored would pin the enemy from the other side.

"As night fell," says Jones, "we trekked through the Alf Valley. It was very muddy, very dark, the woods heavy, just terribly tough going. The transportation bogged down. I became increasingly concerned about our weapons carriers and command jeeps.

While I was assisting the movement I became separated from the Battalion. There was enormous confusion."

Organization broke down, partly because of failure by higher headquarters to maintain clear communications, partly as a result of the difficult conditions. The determined German attack exploited the lack of coordination. A salvo of enemy artillery fatally wounded Jones's battalion CO, Lt. Col. William H. Craig. "He was a wonderful man," says his former S–3. "The other two battalions from the regiment went on the attack but ours seemed to lose direction with Craig's death. No one seemed to know what to do; finally the exec moved them out. I gathered up some loose ends, put them into a company formation for tactical purposes. We had tankers, artillery crewmen, infantry.

"By the time we were organized and caught up to the 1st Battalion, the word was to surrender. 'Tear your weapons apart and throw the pieces about.' I couldn't believe it. My battalion just had not been in that much fighting. [Jones's outfit had been trailing the two other battalions of the 423rd, which absorbed the most punishment.] I was aware that we were low on ammunition. All we had was what we personally carried. And we had very little mortar or machine gun ammunition. We were supposed to be resupplied by air but that never happened."

In fact, the mission to drop materials to the two cut-off regiments failed because of an intractable bureaucracy and inept planning. The appeals to the air corps for help began on the afternoon of December 17. A series of telephone calls and radio messages assured a delivery that night. The first requests listed 200,000 rounds of .30-caliber machine gun ammunition, 200,000 rounds for M–1s and 1,000 bazooka rockets. Subsequent requisitions added mortar shells, bandages, wound dressings, plasma, morphine and 8,000 rations.

But those who promised the aid did not reckon with the layer upon layer of approvals required before props began to spin. Paperwork grounded the C–47 aircraft throughout the remainder of the afternoon and through the night.

Inexplicably, the air corps continued to handle all such missions to the continent from airfields in the United Kingdom. The system added flying time and interposed the volatile weather between England and the front. As a consequence of the climatic conditions, only some of the scheduled cargo planes finally left the UK on December 18. However, when they zoomed over an airfield in

Belgium where they would acquire fighter protection, the airdrome declared itself "too busy" to accomodate them. The wing commander, nevertheless, landed there, only to learn no one had advised the local airmen of details like map coordinates for the scheduled drop. Worse, no one had arranged for the fighter plane shield. The entire operation was scrubbed.

Lt. Alan Jones, Jr., of course, was not privy to an explanation for the absence of aid by air. Jones only knew he had been surrendered by higher authorities. He attempted to deal with his immediate situation. "An African-American sergeant [a refugee from one of the overrun artillery batteries], tommy gun hanging around his neck, came up to me. 'We haven't even starting fighting, lieutenant. Let's go out and kill some Germans.' It didn't strike me as a feasible action.

"A runner came to me with a message. All weapons were to be rendered inoperable. And all units were to stand fast. While the number of casualties had piled up, which concerned Colonel Cavender, I was surprised that we weren't given the option to try to scatter and infiltrate our way out. I could have done that on my own. But at the time, I mistakenly thought I should stay with the men and see they were properly treated. That was dumb. The Germans, just as we did, separated officers and noncoms from the rest of the prisoners. There is no way to take care of your men or exert any control over the situation."

Sgt. Leo Leisse, whose 3rd Battalion of the 422nd Regiment attacked toward Schönberg on the morning of December 19, soon realized the acute shortages. "Very quickly, we came under small arms and artillery fire from several directions—and the 1st Battalion was attacked by tanks—and part of it was cut off and captured."

Leisse and portions of the surviving two battalions plugged on, intent on opening the main conduit for their fodder. "We came under intense fire from several types of weapons which inflicted heavy casualties and knocked out a number of our mortars and machine guns. The 423rd on our left sustained heavy casualties and was badly disorganized. On the afternoon of 19 December, unable to get supplies of food or ammunition or to evacuate our casualties for the past four days, Col. [George] Descheneaux decided to surrender.

"We had begun to retreat, some of the men in frightful disorder, towards the wooded area when the next order came to 'Stand fast!' Presumably it came from a German officer who said that he would annihilate the battalion if we attempted to get into the woods. I passed the order to my men. I had one helluva time convincing my 'get away' man at the rear to come back. He was very reluctant to obey, figuring he could have made it. He was an atheist and many a night we would try to get him 'to see the light.' However, he did come back and I was proud of all my men, carrying out orders though scared stiff, as was I, about what would come next.

"A bit later we got another order from Colonel Descheneaux to destroy our weapons. I cautioned my men to first unload ammo and throw it into the creek, then break their rifles over rocks. All did so without injury, except Bob _____, who neglected to empty the chamber and shot himself in the heel."

A kaleidoscope of heart-stopping fear, black humor and grisly horror enveloped Pvt. Frank Raila, serving with a machine gun crew from the 423rd Battalion. "There is nothing that prepares you for combat. To get the impact through training, you'd have to have people around you killed, homes blown up, civilians killed as part of excerises. Even when you are exposed to the killing zones and all of the horrible happenings, you can never get used to it. There is this continuous fear."

He recalls the courage of Sgt. Robert Dalheim, who, despite the crackle and boom of small arms and incipient artillery, stood fully erect in front of his mortar squad. Dalheim made himself into a human aiming mechanism to point the direction for his men. "The army taught you a stance with your arm forward in lieu of the finder on the weapon. What he did was extremely dangerous. At the time we were all running, falling down, getting up, running, falling, firing. It was amazing for this guy to be standing up in the midst of this. Everybody around broke into cheers for that mortar crew.

"What made their performance all the more remarkable was that there was something wrong with the weapon. They were forced constantly to disconnect the tube from the base, tilt it and slide the round out, delicately catching it with the fingers and then replacing the pin in it. If they knocked the sensitive nose of the round without a safety pin in it, the thing would go off in their faces. Only when they used all of their shells and needed more ammunition did they pull back to fix the mortar.

"On the other hand, one sergeant from a mortar squad, very tough in the States, had no problem using his fists on people, extremely bad temper, would curse, a latrine mouth. First time we set up our line, in the snow, when we were being shot at by 88s, mortars and small arms, I was told he went completely bonkers. One of the men in his own squad became his replacement."

Raila remembers gruesome details. "I almost stepped on some-one's maxilla—upper jaw. I just happened to look down and there it was—all of the teeth, perfect, clean, shining, pink-white roof of mouth lying in the muddy road. The sight made me jump. The skins of bodies were pale white, light grey or green. Men with helmets off seemed not at all dead. Their hair blew in the breeze.

"The worst order I ever heard in my life was when Sgt. Bob McBride, who had played football for Notre Dame in 1942, turned to me and said, 'Raila, get up and run out there and help bring that man back.' There was a wounded GI ahead of McBride and Ray Russell on the machine gun; I couldn't even see him from where I was. I got out of my hole and there in the distance in front was this hobbling GI. We were under small arms fire, and oh, how I didn't want to go, but I went. It was very scary, but I brought him back. I still think of this incident several times a year."

The disorder mentioned by Leo Leisse briefly separated Raila from his unit. "We never heard that the enemy had broken through. I was only told we were attacking. Our officers didn't inform us of anything. The only thing we realized was that we were catching hell frequently, which gives you the idea you're not winning. We were on the move so much and digging so many holes, some of which would fill up with water. You had to have the stamina of an eighteen- or nineteen-year-old just to survive the weather. You're sweating like crazy inside your clothes; the outside of them are wet from snow or rain. You're being shot at and bombed. At that, even those wet holes would seem pretty comfortable when you're walking and 88s are coming in. First the shells would land behind us, then in front and finally right on top of us. The Germans were very clever, combat-wise and knew how to bracket us. One thing I think we could have done when we were marching forward, we should have advanced with fire, shooting in front, into the woods, or house or the road. A good number of bullets would have at least made it a little hot for Germans. Instead, we marched forward, guns at the ready. Then we would fall down and start to fire. On the other hand, all we had was the ammunition we carried. Maybe the officers and noncoms felt we had to conserve it. Still, if we could each have let loose one clip, it might have been better.

"Meanwhile, I could hear bullets making a hissing sound around me, and when they pierced the snow, you might see a small amount of vapor. It was a situation in which there was always something possibly worse than the misery you were currently in."

He had suddenly been handed a bazooka, a weapon with which he had only a brief acquaintance. Carrying the three rockets on his back which would "disintegrate him" if struck by shrapnel or a bullet, Raila, whenever he dug, excavated deep enough for him to lie on the bazooka ammo or cover it. Along with his bazooka and its rockets, he draped his neck with strands of electrical wire hooked to boxes of ammunition for the machine gun. "I had my .30-caliber magazines for my carbine in a belt around my waist. The bazooka was hung over my shoulder and I carried my carbine in my left hand. It was quite a load.

"We had been running through streets. Because of sniper fire we went one at a time. When I had crossed several of the streets, I found myself alone, in a lane that petered out into fields. The others must have turned to the right or left, or maybe were hiding in the buildings, who knows. I could hear some Americans yelling behind me and I thought it would be better to return from where I had come. Suddenly, a wild-eyed major came upon me and said, 'Go out there,' pointing to the fields on the outskirts of the town, 'and set up a bazooka defense because a bunch of Tiger tanks are coming through.' Then he turned around and ran back.

"I scurried forward, and there was still nobody around me. Hell, I was the only one in that field and he wants me to stop Tiger tanks with my three bazooka rounds and my carbine? It would be suicidal to stay. It was very possible Germans would come down the road and shoot me from behind. I headed in his direction but he had disappeared.

"While I was in combat, all of the systems of fight or flight syndrome were at full blast. What kept me or anyone else going, I suspect, was being among my peers, the ambience of people watching what you do or how you act. You want to be a good soldier and you accept the orders from a noncom or an officer.

There are exceptions, you're not going to follow a crazy order—walk backward toward the enemy [or try to halt oncoming Tiger tanks alone].

"There are moments when somebody freezes, unable to get going when there's a mortar barrage or artillery rounds falling. But they respond to an order from a noncom, officer or even a private. That's a case where leadership makes a difference.

"One of the things that became a real sham was the Combat Infantryman Badge. There were officers who drove into the rear of the combat zone, which could be maybe a mile wide and a mile deep. They'd stay there for a certain length of time, then fill out the papers for the CIB. That gave them the same status as the poor slobs forced to be in the equivalent of the killing zone. Less than ten percent of the whole army ends up in the front line or combat zone. Even fewer are in the first fifty or 100 yards of that killing zone, where men are killed, replaced, killed, replaced constantly."

After his experience with the wild-eyed major, Raila rejoined his machine gun squad. "The reason I was running around and getting separated from them was that officers and noncoms would come around and pick up any GIs that weren't actually firing the gun and get them together for a group to march somewhere, infiltrate somewhere. Every time it happened, it was terrible. We would come under fire from mortars, 88s and machine guns, like being given a death sentence, as it was for some of the men.

"One bunch of our guys wiped out a machine gun nest except for a German corporal who was wounded in the arm. One of our men was marching behind him. He had his rifle in his left hand, his comb under his nose, imitating Hitler, and he was goose-stepping behind this wounded, captured German. This made everyone laugh, even though we were still under small arms fire. But these crazy guys were standing up and walking.

"When this wounded German walked behind a small group of us on the front line, the GIs turned and pointed their guns at him. I thought they were going to shoot him. I yelled out, 'Don't shoot. We're Americans. We don't shoot people like that.' It was kind of naive, dumb, in the war zone but I said it. The guy didn't get shot, I don't know if anyone would have actually fired, but there were some nervous trigger fingers present. Under the circumstances, the fellow was pretty lucky. Sergeant McBride told me to help this German to an aid station, which I did until a GI came up the road and I got him to take over."

The group that included Raila, exhausted from their incessant marches, digging, exposure to enemy attacks, took cover in a cluster of buildings, awaiting an opportune moment to retreat. Raila and the others from his crew lay down, after imploring another GI to wake them from a quick nap when word to pull out came. Raila awoke thirty-five minutes later to discover himself left behind with McBride, Ray Russell and a few others.

"I saw a Red Cross flying over the last building and noticed a couple of GIs go in. I walked there and it was like an abattoir. There was blood all over the floor and two corpsmen, one of whom was injured, but no one had bandaged his wounds. In one room they put all of the dead. The wounded mostly lay on stretchers. An officer had half his face shot away. The bottom of his litter had maybe half an inch of blood in it, he was sloshing around in his own blood. There were no I.V.s or units of blood to give them, just sulpha powder and bandages.

"I recognized a fellow from our unit on a table. I tried to help him. He'd been shot through the testicles and maybe the buttocks. His clothes had been cut away and his genitals looked like bloody cantaloupes. I tried to help him but my hands were full of dirt. All I could do was dump sulpha powder and fluff bundles of bandages over his grossly swollen scrotum.

"I discovered the German corporal I'd helped, on another stretcher. I gave him some cigarettes and chocolate and he said, 'Dankershoen.'

"Suddenly, I heard hobnailed boots, and then a young guy with a skull and crossbones on his cap [SS insignia] stuck his assault rifle through the window, right by my chest. I thought I was dead." Fortunately for Raila and McBride, the German to whom they had shown compassion spoke up on their account. Their captors put them to work carrying the wounded to trucks.

"McBride and I had carried that wounded corporal about fifty or sixty feet when we paused for a rest and put down the litter. Another German soldier popped out in the street and leveled his rifle at me. I thought I was about to be killed again. But the German on the stretcher sat up and convinced him not to shoot. After we loaded him on a truck, they walked us several miles to an interrogation center, a card table where they took our names, ranks and serial numbers. There were about twenty-five of us and we were now prisoners of war."

Cavender had surrendered his 423rd Regiment after conferring with his colleague, Col. George Descheneaux, CO of the 422nd, who agreed upon similar action. The exultant German forces bagged more than 3,000 U.S. soldiers on the morning of December 19. Altogether, the captives from the 106th eventually added up to more than 7,000.

Chapter VIII

INTO THE BREACH

THE 7TH ARMORED, PREVIOUSLY REMOVED from the line for rest and refitting sixty miles from the front, now struggled to fulfill its assignment to rescue the embattled 106th Infantry Division. The failure of the mission remains one of the bitter controversies among those caught that winter in the Ardennes. According to researcher Ralph Hill, himself a captain with a military government unit at the time of the Bulge, the 7th Armored had been designated a ready reserve on December 1. At 5:30 P.M. on December 16, Omar Bradley, acting at the direction of Eisenhower, telephoned Brig. Gen. Robert Hasbrouck, CO of the 7th to "Alert your division for immediate move . . ." Unfortunately, the communique from Bradley failed to spell out details for such matters as the disposition of the division's artillery battalions. Hasbrouck certainly does not appear to have been impressed with the gravity of the situation. Instead of immediately requesting clarification, Hasbrouck directed the CO of the 7th's CCB, Brig. Gen. Bruce Clarke to personally ascertain the details.

"Bruce, the 7th Armored has just been ordered to move to Bastogne. I have no idea why . . . . I want you to get your combat command going as soon as road clearance can be obtained. In the meantime, I'd like you to go to Bastogne yourself. Find out what you can from General Middleton [the VIII Corps Commander]." Clarke abandoned plans for a respite in Paris. Three and a half hours after Bradley sent his order, Clarke began a slow, arduous jeep trip to Bastogne. The men and equipment of CCB were expected to follow.

At Bastogne, when Clarke arrived at 4:00 A.M., the same lack of urgency infected Middleton and his staff. The CO of the VIII Corps told Clarke of a penetration that menaced the 106th Division, but he apparently did not recognize the magnitude of the breakthrough. Clarke caught a few hours of sleep and then supposedly learned for the first time that his troops had not commenced their march until just before dawn. Any rescue by CCB could not possibly occur until late on December 17.

Thus, a full twelve hours elapsed before Clarke contacted his superior, Hasbrouck, and straightened out the disposition of the artillery and the actual mission. Ralph Hill suggests that the slow reaction of the 7th to the emergency may have resulted from an inability to actually have men and machines on "ready reserve," really prepared to move out on short notice. Many of the 7th Armored troops, who had engaged in hard fighting near Metz and the lowlands, were sampling the pleasures of Holland that weekend.

By himself, Clarke pushed on to St. Vith. Lt. Alan Jones's father, the CO of the 106th, greeted him enthusiastically and instructed Clarke to counterattack towards Schönberg with CCB and "break that ring that these people have closed around the Schnee Eifel." Clarke revealed that, at the moment, the extent of CCB in St. Vith amounted to himself, two aides and a driver. The possibilities for saving the embattled 106th Division regiments atop the Schnee Eifel dimmed further from the gridlock that bogged down reinforcements. A dubious dance of rank further complicated the situation. While Alan Jones, Sr., was a major general, Hasbrouck and Clarke wore only the single stars of brigadiers. However, both men had extensive experience in combat. Clarke, in fact, had only recently joined the 7th Armored after distinguishing himself with Patton's favorite mechanized outfit, the 4th Armored. On the other hand, Jones, like his soldiers, absorbing terrible punishment from the enemy, had never directed actual operations.

Clarke formed a low opinion of his nominal commander at St. Vith, an appraisal seemingly shared by Hasbrouck. And the facts indicate that Jones vacillated between depression and optimism. He had confided to Clarke, "I've lost a division quicker than any other division commander in the U.S. Army. I've got two regiments out on the Schnee Eifel, and my son is in one of them. I don't know whether we'll get to him at all."

However, a short time later, Jones, by telephone, reassured General Middleton, "Don't worry about us. We'll be in good shape. Clarke's troops will be here soon." Clarke was astonished at Jones's upbeat talk. Along with the anguish over the fate of Alan Jones, Jr., and the others under his command, General Jones, although only fifty years old, also suffered from serious heart disease.

His tactics and strategy paralleled his mood swings. He delayed, perhaps fatally, permitting a battalion in reserve to reinforce the units under attack. For hours he refused to see the CO of the 14th Cavalry Group, who had left his command post to confer with Jones. And about 2:30 on the afternoon of December 17, he seemed to give up. "General Clarke," he said, "I've thrown in my last chips. I haven't got much, but your combat command is the one that will defend this position. You take over command of St. Vith now." Headquarters staff for the 106th evacuated the town on the19th and headed for Vielsalm.

The nonplussed Clarke, an irascible man with his own medical problems—a nagging gallbladder condition—must have felt as if he were being handed the helm of the Titanic. His own CCB was still trying to get through. The regiments on the Schnee Eifel no longer responded to radio messages. All he could command for the moment was that miscellaneous collection of combat engineers— John Collins and Duke Ward, plus a handful of antitankers—under Lt. Col. Tom Riggs. The 38th AIB was still crawling towards St. Vith.

Nearly three days before, during the afternoon of December 16, it was Dwight Eisenhower, the SHAEF boss, who seemed to be the first member of the brass that recognized the seriousness of the breakthrough. He had flatly announced to Omar Bradley, "That's no spoiling attack." After study of an operations map, Eisenhower had directed Bradley to send the 10th Armored Division, which belonged to George S. Patton's Third Army, and the 7th Armored Division to help stem the enemy advance. When Bradley remarked that Patton might be miffed at the shift of one of his divisions to another command, Eisenhower snarled, "Tell him that Ike is running this damn war."

Between issuance and fulfillment of an order that involves logistics for 14,000 men, guns, ammunition, vehicles, cannons and armor, time stretches with fateful force. The bulk of the 10th Armored had arrived by the afternoon of the second day of the Ardennes offensive. Most of the division joined in the defense of the southern shoulder of the Bulge, working with the understrength 4th Infantry Division and a patch quilt of people from the 28th Division, whose battered riflemen included former typewriter-bound soldiers, cooks, bakers and band members that replaced their horns, drums and woodwinds with M–1s. But Combat Command B of the 10th Armored headed north to resist a possible surge towards the vital road junction of Bastogne.

On December 17, the disquiet from the previous day's reports had deepened into full-scale anxiety. An ULTRA intercept of a message from von Rundstedt to the German commanders now received wide dissemination. "Mighty offensive armies face the Allies. Everything is at stake. More than mortal deeds are required as a holy duty of the Fatherland."

Kay Summersby noted, "The German is dropping paratroops in the Liège area [not true]. The going is still heavy. Bradley is leaving for Luxembourg."

Omar Bradley, who had been somewhat skeptical of Eisenhower's reaction the day before, looked at a situation map that showed fourteen German divisions invested and wondered, "Just where in the hell has this sonuvabitch gotten all this strength?"

That evening the Allied strategists decided to throw several more valuable assets into the fray. Operation Market Garden in September, a high-risk parachute and glider operation championed by Montgomery, dropped the U.S. 82nd and 101st Airbornes into Holland along with the British 1st Airborne. Altogether about 28,000 soldiers reached the scene but it proved truly "a bridge too far." The Brits in particular absorbed a brutal hammering and the U.S. forces emerged considerably battered.

Still licking their wounds from the disaster, the 82nd and 101st were out of the line for refitting and replacements. While both were understrength they were still formidable fighting units. The pair received march orders into the Ardennes on the evening of December 17.

William T. Dunfee, born in Columbus, Ohio, a high-school dropout, briefly managed a filling station in Sarasota, Florida, then became a truck driver for a Columbus lumber company. In 1942, Dunfee, nineteen, enlisted in the army. A volunteer for the parachute infantry when he signed up, Dunfee received his basic training in heavy weapons at Camp Roberts, California, before attending paratroop school at Fort Benning, Georgia.

"When I enlisted in the army, the base pay was $21 a month. My reasons for choosing the paratroops were two. There was $50 a month extra as hazardous duty pay and there was the challenge of jumping. Until this time I had never even been in an airplane.

"The paratroopers were tough kids. Many were from the Canton, Youngstown areas, eastern Ohio and western Pennsylvania. They were from coal mine and steel mill backgrounds. Boozing and brawling were an accepted way of life."

Having earned his wings, Dunfee joined the 505th Parachute being formed at Benning under then Lt. Col. James M. Gavin, a stick-thin West Pointer. "Slim Jim Gavin was respected and loved by every man who served in his command. We of the 505 were very proud to have served him in his first and last combat missions. With tongue in cheek, we claim to have given him his basic training.

"In the paratroops you were intentionally stretched to your maximum physical and emotional endurance. In parachute school and subsequently in the 505th's training, you were allowed two positions, Attention and Parade Rest. No leaning on anything or hands in your pockets. Any minor deviation from the rules was punished by additional pushups. In July 1942, in Georgia, it was *very hot.* When you were in ranks and a man fell over from heat exhaustion, if you bent over to help him, you were told, 'Leave him lay, soldier. He ain't dead.' The idea was to wash out as many faint hearts as possible.

"With few exceptions, our officers were capable to excellent. Gavin weeded out most of the goofballs, or stuck them in rear echelon where they couldn't get anyone killed. There was one company commander who took over after our CO was killed. He truly was incompetent. My group had captured a platoon of Germans. Their officer spoke English. I had him line up the men and have them drop their packs. About this time, this dumb-assed captain came running up. He was completely out of control. He had no idea where the rest of his company was. He had lost his helmet, his radio and the runner assigned to him. The German officer asked me, 'Who is that?' When I told him it was our CO, he inquired, 'Is he an officer?' When I responded yes, he just shook his head."

Bill Dunfee and his comrades of the 505th endured their combat baptism July 9 and 10, 1943, near Gela, Sicily. He grew to "accept the fact of friends being killed and wounded, but it's something you will never forget. At times I felt satisfaction when I saw a good friend slightly wounded but injured enough to get him evacuated. We also accepted the possibility of capture but treated it in a light vein. Before we jumped in Sicily a buddy wanted to learn how to sing 'I Surrender, Dear' in German."

The typical reaction to danger was the bravado of humor. "In Normandy, DiGiralamo was dug in near me. We had just received a horrendous artillery barrage over an extended period. When it let up, I yelled, 'Are you okay, Di G?' His response was. 'If blood smells like shit, I'm bleeding to death.' DiGiralamo would be a KIA in the Ardennes.

Restoration of the 82nd Airborne went on at Camp Suippes, Suippes Marne, France, near the Belgian border. Sgt. Bill Dunfee, a squad leader now, and the others "were quite comfortable and would have been content to sit out the rest of the war there. The night of December 17–18 sometime after lights out, we were awakened by Lieutenant Vande Vegt, exec officer of I Company. We thought he was either drunk or had lost his mind. He was sounding off how the Germans had broken through and we were to move out before daylight. By the time we were fully awake, we realized he was neither drunk nor kidding. We were up and dressed within half an hour.

"Everyone got their combat gear together, including unauthorized ordnance, mine being a Colt .45 I kept near my heart in combat. While in Naples, I had a shoulder holster made and under a jacket it was practically undetectable. I slipped it under a blanket on my bunk. One of the new men saw me hide it and asked if he could see it. I nodded yes. Before I could stop him, he pulled the slide back, popping a round in the chamber and pulled the trigger. The bullet went through my combat pants, the woolen O.D. pants beneath but not through my long johns. No harm done, except it got Vande Vegt back. Someone told him it was a firecracker. I told the shooter that if he survived the operation, we had a date on our return. This was my usual reaction to being endangered. First came fear, followed by violent anger.

"We were issued K rations for two days, one fragmentation grenade and a bandolier of ammunition. We were assured we would get more before contacting the enemy. We had neither mortar nor machine gun ammo, and a bandolier wouldn't last a rifleman very long in a good fire fight.

"We loaded onto semitrailers and headed for Belgium. It was early in the A.M. and a very cold ride. The semis had sides about four feet high with nothing to cover the top. Packed in like the proverbial sardines, we arrived at Werbomont, Belgium, while it was still morning. We were issued more ammo and K rations. My regiment, commanded by Col. William E. Ekman, moved into

Trois Ponts. We found some engineers who had remained in the town. There was occasional fire but no major German forces moved through." The stage was set for a collision between Dunfee's regiment and Peiper's task force which had recently passed through Trois Ponts and traveled up the road to La Gleize.

Into the many breaches of the American lines came another element of the 82nd Airborne, the 325th Glider Infantry Regiment. The military glider attracted strategists because it could insert directly into enemy territory bunches of combat infantrymen who had not undergone the time-consuming, specialized training of paratroopers. Seemingly, parachute-drop injuries would be reduced and light artillery pieces and vehicles like jeeps could land with the soldiers. In practice, however, gliderborne forces often were at greater risk than those jumping out of planes. The flimsy, unarmed, unarmored gliders were highly vulnerable to enemy ground and air attack. Landing the sailplanes under combat conditions, on uncertain terrain, frequently small muddy patches studded with trees, became at best a kind of controlled crash. Consequently, casualty rates among the glider troops rose above those who relied on nylon to deliver them to the battlefield. To add insult to grievous injury, paratroopers at Fort Benning needled their gliderborne colleagues, running around with bodies tilted, and arms spread at an angle shouting, "Look, Herman, no motor, no motor!" The indignities heaped on the men who rode gliders were later ameliorated when they also received extra pay for hazardous duty and the right to wear wings.

But on December 18, the men of the 325th, like Bill Dunfee from the 505th Regiment, moved toward the enemy not by air but by semitrailer. Platoon Sgt. Joe Colmer of Company F, who had been a member of the 82nd Division even before its transformation into an airborne division, actually ought never have been in the army. The family farm in Illinois was struggling through the Great Depression when he graduated from high school in 1936. "There were no jobs to be had. I joined the C.C.C. [the New Deal's Civilian Conservation Corps that planted trees, constructed dams and sought to preserve natural resources]. After a year I enlisted in the navy and when I was discharged in October 1941, we had been convoying British freighters from Boston to Iceland. After Pearl Harbor, while working for the Army Corps of Engineers in Charleston, South Carolina, I registered for the draft.

"At the time they would call you several times for interviews. After my third meeting I went to the navy, which said they of course wanted me. But the draft board now had me on its quota for the month and would not release me. However, I was told that once in an army camp, I could ask the commanding officer to transfer me to the navy. When I requested the switch at Fort Jackson, they asked me, didn't I like the army? I said I guessed it was okay and they told me to stick around for a while and I'd get to liking it. I stuck around until July 1945 and never did get to liking it.

"While we were training at Camp Claiborne, Louisiana, they decided to make the 82nd an airborne outfit. Anyone who wanted to go to jump school signed up and went to Fort Benning. The rest of us, including me, who remained behind, became glider troops."

Colmer received his introduction to combat in Italy. "I guess I felt like most everyone else, pounding heart, dry mouth and sweaty palms. I wasn't too afraid the first few times but as the war wore on, I became more cautious and took fewer chances. When you take fewer chances you may become less effective against the enemy, but you just begin to think that maybe your luck is running out.

"After we lost so many gliders and men in Normandy, I decided to volunteer as a pathfinder and went to jump school in England. Before I could finish the course, they pulled us out and sent us on the glider mission to Holland [Operation Market Garden].

"At time of the breakthrough, we were in Sissone, France, billeted in buildings the Germans had used for barracks. There was hot food and I was in town the night of the 17th when we got word of German paratroopers dropped behind our lines. We were to return to our units immediately. Back at camp, they were already loading our gear on the trucks. Before daybreak, we were on our way to the front."

Leonard Weinstein, like Ed Uzemack in the 28th Division, was an infantry replacement assigned to G Company of the 325th Glider Regiment when as part of the 82nd Airborne it returned from its bloody participation in Normandy. Cleveland-born in 1921, Weinstein, again like Uzemack, was slightly older than the ordinary run-of-1944 infantry replacements. Since his high-school graduation, he had been working at a manufacturing and printing plant with government contracts. His draft board exempted him from military service both for a vital occupational position and for support of his family.

"With most of my friends entering service I did not feel comfortable with my deferment. I asked for a transfer back to the composing room, which I was advised would end my occupational deferment. That's what happened but I rather welcomed it. At various times afterwards I considered this a damn-fool, stupid decision but, whatever, I was inducted in 1943.

"I was aware of the events of the time, Hitler and Nazi Germany, as well as the war in both the Pacific and Europe. How serious my interest is difficult to say. My days and nights were occupied with working and when not on the job I was out drinking with the few friends still around or those on pass or furlough. Female companionship was plentiful. Being Jewish and aware of the Nazi attitudes probably was a contributing factor to giving up my deferment."

Weinstein underwent infantry training in the soft sandy stretches of Camp Blanding, Florida. Like the others swept up in a shooting war, he considered the preparation extremely helpful in toughening him up but nothing could approximate the impact of combat. "One fellow said he always tried to lay on his left side in his foxhole to protect his heart. I remember one guy telling me he had a plan to blow off a foot with a grenade, which, of course, he never did." But the fact is, self-inflicted wounds, a bullet in the foot being the usual method, vexed commanders throughout the war, and the temptation was clearly heightened by the reverses of the Bulge.

"Being Jewish, I didn't know what would happen if taken prisoner, so I kept my dog tags in my pocket to be able to discard them in a hurry. After a while, I stopped doing this, and began carrying my GI Prayer Book in my left shirt pocket." (Dog tags bore a letter designating religion for the benefit of chaplains. "P" signified Protestant, "RC" meant Catholic and an "H" indicated Hebrew.) The prayer book mentioned by Weinstein was non denominational and Christian-oriented.

As a recruit to the 82nd Airborne, Weinstein had no parachute background and so became part of the 325th. "None of us volunteered for the glider troops. My impression is that the first time we signed a glider-ride manifest constituted 'volunteering.'"

Just prior to the alert for Market Garden, Weinstein required minor surgery and he missed out on the disaster in Holland. Like

Joe Colmer, Weinstein was comfortably ensconced in a solid barracks building at Sissone when march orders arrived. "We drew extra ammunition and grenades, received K rations and maybe D bars [a kind of enriched chocolate candy], cleaned our weapons and had what turned out to be our last hot meal for quite a while. Some of the men had been away on pass and returned just in time to board the open semis. A few were still in their Class A-uniforms [dress uniforms with blouse-over-shirt and perhaps low shoes]."

"We were told we were going to Belgium to help stop the attack and hold open a corridor that would allow some trapped American forces to withdraw." Weinstein, unlike many others in the Bulge, apparently was informed of his unit's mission.

"We crowded onto these long, low-bed semis, cattle cars. It was cold, wet and snowing. There was no room to sit. The roads were crowded and it was a long, miserable ride with only short stops for piss-call. It was night before we were ordered off the trucks. There seemed to be much confusion about where we were and where we were to go. Finally, we assembled in a wooded area and were told to take a break, but no smoking. I plopped down in the snow with my pack still on my back. When we were awakened, it was just beginning to get light. We did not know if anyone had been awake to stand guard."

According to historian Forest Pogue, when Eisenhower's chief of staff, Gen. Walter Bedell (pronounced "Beedle") Smith met with the Supreme Commander's top intelligence aide, Gen. Kenneth Strong to choose places for the airborne units, they studied a map spread out on the floor. "There is a place here called Bastogne which looks all right," said Strong, pointing out the location with a captured German sword. Smith agreed that it was a "good road junction" worth defending. He asked how soon the troops could be there and Strong ventured an estimate. In fact, the 101st Airborne's men arrived for their moment of destiny in Bastogne six hours ahead of the targeted time, no small factor in curtailing the success of the enemy advance.

The little drama with the German sword, described by Pogue after an interview with Bedell Smith, makes the choice of Bastogne sound almost fortuitous. But in fact, any strategist, aware of the road net in the Ardennes, would have recognized that Bastogne, along with St. Vith and Malmédy, was a valuable asset, as the nexus for five major and three secondary highways that fanned out to the goals of the Meuse River and Liège. Gen. Troy Middleton operated his VIII Corps (code name Monarch) headquarters in Bastogne, which in 1944 contained a population of 4,000. It was there that intelligence officers studied the interrogation of Elise Dele-Dunkel and her account of a heavy German mobilization and forwarded it, two days before the crunch. However, by December 18, only General Middleton and few members of his staff remained in the town. Most of the personnel had left for Neufchâteau, eighteen miles southwest.

In fact, Gen. James Gavin, in charge of the 82nd, 101st and affiliated airborne units at that period of December, recounted a session with First Army chief Courtney Hodges and his staff that pointed to Bastogne as essential to the Germans. Gavin was acting commander of the XVIII Corps only because the actual CO, Gen. Matthew Ridgway, was in England reviewing Market Garden. Ridgway's absence from the continent was another indication of the feeling that the front would be quiet that winter. Indeed, the 101st's CO, Gen. Maxwell Taylor, was back in the U.S. lobbying for more airborne soldiers while his artillery commander, Gen. Anthony McAuliffe, ran the division.

Which Americans went to Bastogne and which headed for the other less defined sector around the village of Werbomont, north of Bastogne and west of Malmédy, was a matter of logistics rather than precise plotting. The 82nd happened to be located farther from Bastogne but it was much readier to hit the road. It was agreed that Gavin's own division could arrive to block the Germans around Werbomont quicker than the 101st upon whose back, accordingly, responsibility for Bastogne dropped.

High anxiety rattled the people of Bastogne itself. Middleton's VIIIth Corps had authorized a full-fledged ball at the French Franciscan monastery. But on December 16, rumors raced through the town as the citizens watched the ominous flashes of light to the east, mighty artillery blasts heralding the return of the German armies. On Sunday the 17th, a local priest denounced the frivolity of the local people and the current military occupiers. He thundered, "Heaven has already punished the soldiers. As I speak to you, the German troops have reached Clervaux" (where Ed Uzemack of the 28th Division was captured and where Hans Hejny of the German armored engineers sympathized with hapless Americans).

At 5:00 P.M. that Sunday, the townsfolk planned to celebrate the rehanging of the church bells, silenced during the German occupation. A curfew instituted by the military command canceled the fete and deepened the gloom. Genuine panic pinched the civilians as they witnessed the departure of the VIII Corps staff and gaped at the combat-shredded shards of outfits straggling into Bastogne.

The troops consigned to hold Bastogne, the 101st Airborne "Screaming Eagles," were living in Mourmelon, near the French city of Reims. It was a frantic scramble to organize the men and scrounge enough trucks to haul them to Bastogne.

"It was forty-six degrees when we drove through the night of the 17th," recalls Schuyler Jackson, a sergeant with the 502nd Parachute Infantry. "Three days later in Bastogne the temperature hit zero. It was the coldest, most miserable time I've ever been through."

The husky Jackson—"I was a hell-raiser, broken seven times during my four years of service"—personified a stereotype of the paratrooper, hard-fighting, hard-drinking, a rebel against ordinary authority. "My father was a U.S. Navy captain, commander of a destroyer during World War I. He was a retread in World War II, called back to serve on the prisoner of war board.

" The family lived in Washington, D.C., in 1921, and I was born in a residential apartment of the Wardman Park Hotel. My father wanted me to go to the naval academy but I just couldn't put up with their honor system. I played football in high school and I figured things ought to follow the football system. If a guy is going to produce, he'll show it. I didn't see any point in keeping tabs on the other guys.

"Instead of trying for Annapolis, I went to the University of North Carolina. I was there for about a month, having a great time, just goofing off, not studying. But I was in the National Guard and we were called up February 6, 1941, ten months before Pearl Harbor. I was made an MP and on December 7th I was directing traffic during maneuvers. But I didn't want to be a policeman. I wanted excitement and that's why I volunteered for the paratroopers.

"The truth is, though, I've always been scared of heights. I can't look down from a tall building. When I was on the jump towers during training, I would get goose bumps. Once I used my chute, I was okay. The training was excellent, physical conditioning, crawling under wire with live machine gun fire overhead. We often jumped twice in one day, and made night drops also. After parachute training, I went to demolition school. The 502nd had a platoon with three squads charged with clearing mines, blowing up bridges using a composite explosive, C–2 and then C–4.

"Ninety percent of the officers we had were very good. I admire the West Pointers. They knew their stuff. I was really surprised at some of the recruits that came to our outfit. There were guys who were illiterate, unable to read or write, and some had never even used a toothbrush.

"I was broken twice at Fort Meade while in the military police, then two more times while training with the 29th Division. When I was a buck sergeant on the ship taking us to England, a captain took away my rank for gambling with the privates on the boat.

"My old man had distinguished himself in World War I, getting a Navy Cross. Before we left the States, I wrote him, 'Don't worry, I won't disgrace the family. I'll make you proud.'

"Just before we left for the drop on Normandy, Eisenhower inspected us. The photograph of him includes me. When they printed a postage stamp to commemorate the event, they put helmets on us.

"On the night of June 5th, the eve of D-Day, I went with the first batch of twenty-three planes, which included two demolition men. The packs we carried weighed more than 100 pounds. We took off at eight o'clock at night and circled for more than four hours. Some guys went to sleep. I wasn't nervous but it was a jolt to see all of those beautiful tracers coming up. They made a slapping noise when they hit the wing. We went in so low we took off the emergency chute. There wouldn't have been time to use it. We didn't jump until after midnight and I was never so glad to get out of a plane.

"It was a miserable drop with guys coming down all over the place. We were nowhere near our target, a gun emplacement. But we were not immediately under fire. We had crickets [like a child's toy that makes a clicking sound] to locate one another in the dark. That first night, all I heard were the sounds of the crickets. When the naval bombardment began, we heard that behind us. Our first objective was the Carentan Causeway."

But before they could approach there, Jackson and a companion crept up on an antiaircraft gun, still shooting at the C–47s. A few grenades silenced the weapon. Subsequently, Jackson rescued the regimental commander, Col. George Moseley, who broke his leg in the jump. Jackson and another trooper had just started to carry the colonel to safety when they spotted a furtive figure. They dropped their burden and gave chase. A spurt from Jackson's machine gun into a hedgerow produced a dozen prisoners, several seriously wounded. Turning over the Germans to the other trooper, Jackson loaded Moseley on a wheelbarrow and trundled him to an aid station.

"The enemy was SS. I didn't hate them but they were tough bastards. The colonel actually ordered us to fix bayonets but nobody actually had to use one. We lost a helluva lot of men taking the causeway.

"I was never religious and I lost any feeling for it right after the battle of the causeway. During a break I was sitting with a guy whose brother was a priest and his sister a nun. He was always talking up religion. He never cursed and his one sin was he chased women without a pause. He took his Bible out and told me, 'This is what saved us.' The words were no sooner out of his mouth then a treeburst shell snapped his neck. I've been an atheist since then.

"During the fighting in France I saw a German throw away a sack just before he surrendered. I retrieved the bag and found 88,000 French francs inside. It was the payroll for the soldiers. Later, five us went to Paris and had ourselves a time. We blew $10,000. On another occasion, we had a lot of casualties after we overran a gin factory and the guys got drunk and raised hell."

As a member of the 101st, Jackson, having survived the Normandy campaign and then leaped into the inferno of Market Garden. He continued to be impressed with the ferocity of the SS prisoners, one of whom spat in his face during an interrogation.

By the time he reached Bastogne, versions of the Malmédy Massacre had begun to circulate. "I was not that surprised. I'd been aware of atrocities by Germans and Americans. While in Normandy, I saw a soldier in my platoon shoot a prisoner. I told him to cut it out. They were in a war, just the way we were. You had to maintain some feelings as a human being. The guy became a very good soldier after that. Then at Bastogne, an artillery officer ordered me to take some prisoners into a field and shoot them. I said if you want it done, you'll have to do it. He was relieved for his actions."

*   *   *

Capt. Wallace Swanson, CO of Company A, 502nd Parachute Regiment of the Screaming Eagles, on December 16 was in the midst of a short break, coaching the regiment's football team in a game against an air force unit at Nancy on December 17. Until he took on the temporary posts of general manager, coach and trainer for the football team, the captain had been involved in preparing the hard-hit troopers at a base in France for their next encounter with the Germans.

"We lived in tents, received hot meals regularly. While socializing and romance were discouraged, a certain amount of contact with civilians occurred. My first information about the massive German attack came from our regimental commander, Lt. Col. Steve Chappuis. He, along with some others, had come to Nancy to see the game—we won by a touchdown or two. We knew something was up. The game was at an air corps base and some of our fighter planes came in low, giving what we thought were victory rolls. Our after-game meal was scuttled and Chappuis asked me to ride back with him.

"In the car with Chappuis, I had a sandwich and learned of the breakthrough in the Ardennes. At the briefing, he was told the 101st would move out on the 18th. When I got back to our camp, I found the Company A officers and noncoms issuing the SOP [Standard Operating Procedure] supplies and equipment. Our supply people had requisitioned replacement quantities for what was missing well in advance. They were under orders to keep SOP items ready. Sometimes it might be necessary to get weapons on the field of battle. That was possible but we did not rely on it. Our movement to Bastogne was quick and decisive."

Swanson, while a big-time football player, was cut from far different cloth than paratroopers Dunfee and Swanson. He sprang from the American heartland. "I grew up on a farm-ranch seven miles north-northeast of Sharon Springs, Kansas, near the border of Colorado. I had four years of college and needed one more semester to obtain my B.S. degree. I was alert to the world situation and what was happening in Europe with Hitler. I was aware of the outlandish actions and inhuman treatment of some of his own citizens, Christians and Jews alike. I also kept abreast of things in the Far East.

"I had always been interested in military preparedness. Way back in my high school days, I tried to join the Civilian Military

Training Corps but was rejected because of an ear infection and perhaps my red-green color blindness."

Shortly after graduation from Kansas State University in June 1941, Swanson, having completed the ROTC course there, was summoned to active duty. He learned the craft of an infantry officer in and around Fort Sam Houston at San Antonio. "I chose the paratroops for a number of reasons. While at college in a pilot training program, I wondered what it would be like to jump with a parachute. The airborne troops also were receiving PR as an elite army unit, special physically and mentally, and that attracted me. The pay was better than in other outfits. And I'd concluded I'd rather jump into a combat or battle situation than have to walk or ride in with more danger because of confronting the enemy real estate by real estate."

In 1942, an armed forces telegram ordered him to report for special, two to three month duty with the Eastern Armed Forces All-Star Football team on the Yale University campus. Gen. Bob Neyland, the former University of Tennesee coach, assisted by Herman Hickman, coached the squad. (There was also a Western Armed Forces team.) From all branches including the navy, marines and air corps, originally about 125 men received invitations. Some had played pro football before entering the service, others, like Swanson, had only a collegiate background. Swanson had played well enough at Kansas State University to merit a contract from the Philadelphia Eagles in the National Football League when he graduated in 1941. However, as an ROTC grad he had donned his second lieutenant's uniform that July before he had a chance to wear pads and cleats for the Eagles. At Yale, Neyland and Hickman winnowed down the team to fifty-five.

"After training for five weeks, with grueling two-a-day practices, we played three pro teams in eight days. We won two, lost to the Chicago Bears 7–0. Then the team disbanded and we all returned to our separate units."

Swanson praises the training and discipline up and down the line of his military experience, starting with his "excellent ROTC instructors" through the initial phases when he was with the 2nd Infantry Division, then the 82nd Division at Camp Claiborne, Louisiana, the infantry communication school and paratroop instruction at Fort Benning. He is also enthusiastic about his commanders, his fellow officers and the enlisted men during his time under fire.

He rejects the stereotype of the paratroooper as a kid from the wrong side of the tracks. "They came from all walks of life. In my own case, I was an individual with a responsibility to my men and comrades I associated with and to get a job done. My approach had a lot to do with my family and upbringing on the western plains of Kansas.

"The language I used was appropriate to my style. I never let foul language, demeaning words and expressions become part of my vocabulary. Nor did I permit people around me to feel free to use it without constructive criticism.

"If drinks were present, I expected equal amounts of soft drinks, not just beer or hard liquor. I found when this was handled in a proper manner, men more often than not ended up content with a soft drink. I often had displinary problems when alcohol was prevalent."

While at Fort Bragg, North Carolina, Swanson met Thelma Jeanne Combs, a Duke University graduate and a member of the army nurse corps stationed at Fort Bragg. The couple married and, to their delight, both embarked to England, where occasionally they could grab a few days together. "We visited each other at the sites of our respective camps and in English houses. The British folks were generous about opening their homes to us, including home-cooked meals they shared."

The Swansons squeezed-in sightseeing trips to London. Swanson remembers their glimpses of Madame Tussaud's Wax Museum, Trafalgar Square, Big Ben and London Bridge, as well as the more bucolic side of the country. By the spring of 1944, Jeanne was pregnant and returned to the States. Her husband readied himself for the 101st's baptism of fire, the D-Day drop.

He survived the adventure of the night drop into France and the subsequent successful, but bloody, battle to capture Foucarville and even a few painful hours as a captive of the Germans until a brief truce brought him freedom. "The Holland action [Market Garden] was a daylight jump, almost a parade-ground-like jump. But like France, it involved offensive and defensive maneuvering for the best position against an enemy trying to regroup and push us out.

"The Ardennes was different. After initial offensive action, we worked at improving our defensive line. There was a basic problem of fog and darkness at times there. The bitter cold weather meant mechanical gun parts of rifles and machine guns had to be kept free of moisture from hands or breath. Otherwise, these liquids would freeze on the weapons. Even though they had been warned and the NCOs constantly told them to be careful, more than once soldiers found themselves with unusable ones. Men told me it was a weird, hopeless feeling when they could not use their rifles or machine guns.''

A third member of the 101st destined for Bastogne was Sgt. Jack Agnew. ''I was born in Belfast, Ireland, in 1922 and came to America with my mother, sister and brother in 1926. My father preceded us to establish a home and find a job.'' The family setttled in Burkholme, a northeast Philadelphia area, where Jack attended the local public schools, graduating from Olney High School in 1940.

''Being from the British Isles, I had great concern about Hitler's activities. I lost a cousin in the Royal Air Force, and another cousin served with the Royal Canadian Air Force. I tried to join the RCAF and had my papers for it when Pearl Harbor came. After that they couldn't accept Americans.

''Then I tried to sign up with the navy air corps but they required a college education. I took the test for the Army Air Corps and they wanted me as a bombardier-navigator, a specialty in great demand then. I didn't like the idea of dropping bombs on people. We had relatives in the British Isles and I knew the hardships bombs wrought on civilians. I got mad because I couldn't fly and enlisted in the paratroops.''

Agnew received his instruction at Toccoa, Georgia. Assigned to regimental headquarters after testing, Agnew, who'd been a junior member of the National Rifle Association, also scored so well on the target range that he was issued the sniper's weapon, the bolt action Springfield '03.

''I volunteered for the demolition platoon and trained with all the available weapons, carbine, M–1, rifle grenade, bazooka, flame thrower and every type of explosive we could find or improvise. We trained most of the others in the regiment in demolition, running them through battle courses. We harassed them during their forty-five-mile marches with booby traps and simulated mortar fire, using TNT and other explosives. One of our men was killed while preparing a training area, and I myself was blown up from a predetonated charge of two dynamite sticks.

''The physical training was rough. Up 1,300 foot Mt. Currahee every morning, three miles up and three miles down. If you fell out, you were out of the 506th Parachute Regiment. We hit the obstacle course daily. Our platoon leader volunteered us for every detail, including fighting forest fires and blasting stumps out of a lake filled with cottonmouth snakes. It was good survival training. One battalion at Toccoa had marched to Atlanta, 136 miles. We at regimental headquarters and the 3rd Battalion marched from Fort McPherson, Atlanta to Fort Benning, 156 miles in seventy-eight hours."

In England, Agnew continued his military education, attending signal school where he learned to operate a telephone switchboard while doubling as a motorcycle dispatch rider. The bike was also handy for trips to a nearby pub where water cans could be filled with beer. Agnew fished for trout in streams that belonged to peers and "killed a few of the King's deer at Littlecote. Scotland Yard is still looking for that deer." Occasionally, during a close-order drill, to add zest to their menu, the men scurried after rabbits with sticks. Agnew also spent weeks training with British paratroopers for whom he developed great admiration.

His introduction to combat, like Swanson's and Jackson's, came in the vicinity of Carentan, early on the morning of June 6. "Some of the ground fire came up through the floor and seats of the plane during the trip. We had been given the command to stand up and hook up during our approach to the DZ, to make us less of a target than if we sat. I landed at the edge of a field where a German battalion was stationed. I got out of my chute and backed up to a hedge at the roadside. The German soldiers were running up and down the road, yelling *Amerikanisch Fallschirmjäger,* American paratroops. The first of ours I met was so scared he was whimpering and crying. He made so much noise I threatened to shoot him.

"The first guy from my own group I found was Mike Marquozi. He stepped into a drainage ditch and when I pulled him out, he'd lost the trigger assembly for his M–1. They'd told us the ditches were two feet deep; they were twelve feet. I gave him my Springfield '03 and I still had my .45 pistol which I bought before going overseas. I couldn't have used my rifle anyway, since I'd hurt my shoulder on landing, ramming the stock of the rifle up under it. We kept on towards our objective. We didn't have time to be frightened. We'd been told that if we didn't destroy that bridge a lot of American lives would be lost."

Agnew and associates began their demolition spree with power lines and telephone cables. Pinned down on one side of a bridge with Germans laying down a blizzard of bullets from the opposite end, Agnew blew a channel in the earth that enabled troopers to crawl through an otherwise exposed area to unite with more GIs.

"We lost more than a dozen men, including some to snipers. Newcomers wandered into the area. We yelled for them to get down but in some cases it was too late. We had no contact with headquarters; we even got bombed by our own planes, who did not realize we had advanced to our objective, the bridge. I finally managed to kill the sniper who was giving us the most trouble. I was so delighted I jumped up on a dike and gave all the Germans hell. Jake McNeice pulled me down just in time as a machine gun raked the place. When I see Jake today, he still ribs me about the scene on the dike. But eventually we managed to blow the bridge."

After his baptism of battle in Normandy, Agnew, like the others, endured Market Garden. "Those of us who survived from the beginning seemed to last the longest. Replacements appeared to have more casualties than the original guys." But when the 101st boarded the trucks bound for Bastogne, Jack Agnew was not among the troops. He had volunteered as a demolition expert to learn the art of the pathfinder. Along with twenty others, he was receiving instruction in England during December.

The 101st, with Schuyler Jackson and Wallace Swanson, was not the first U.S. fighting unit to assemble at Bastogne. Earlier, teams from the 10th Armored Division's CCB milled about the town, looking to halt thrusts from Hasso Manteuffel's divisions. Maj. William Desobry, age twenty-six, commanded a team bearing his surname. On the night of December 18, the CCB commander, Col. William Roberts, instructed Desobry to take his small force of 400 men, including half a dozen Sherman tanks, some four miles northeast to the village of Noville, chosen as an outpost for the defense of Bastogne.

"You are young," said Roberts. "And by tomorrow morning you will probably be nervous. By midmorning the idea will probably come to you that it would be better to withdraw from Noville. When you begin thinking that, remember that I told you it would be best not to withdraw until I order you to do so."

The man assigned to retain the critical outpost came from a

military background. William Desobry's father, a 1908 West Point graduate, served as Pershing's aide and with then Capt. Douglas MacArthur, whom he confided to his son he disliked as "pompous." Born in the Philippines, William Desobry, like Alan Jones, Jr., followed his father to a variety of army posts—Fort Leavenworth, Kansas, Fort Bliss, San Antonio, Hawaii and Washington, D.C., where he recalled watching the great Walter Johnson in his final days pitching for the Senators.

"There was an antimilitary period during the 1930s and when I graduated from high school in 1936 I wanted to go to Georgetown University, for the foreign service. I was stood at attention by many a colonel and told I was no damn good. That only got my back up."

Actually, the six foot, four inch, 160-pound Desobry was offered a basketball scholarship to the University of Southern California. However, he stuck to his goals with Georgetown. His father accepted his son's decision with the proviso that he enlist in the school's ROTC program. Desobry graduated in June 1941. He now accepted the military as at least his temporary destiny. After rejection by the paratroops because of his height he became an officer in the armored forces.

According to Desobry, Gen. Hasso Manteuffel crashed through the American positions of Ed Uzemack's 28th Division with one infantry and two panzer divisions. "The 28th had a terribly broad front and was still refitting after losses in the Huertgen. It fought a magnificent defensive battle, a delaying action because they didn't have the strength to stop two armored divisions and an infantry division.

"The desperate fights by essentially small units, company-size units took tremendous casualties, diverted the Germans, slowed them down. Instead of their armored divisions being able to move rapidly to the west, they would have to turn off, to this flank and that and go back and forth to help somebody. The 28th not only slowed them down time-wise but also chewed them up and gave them losses they couldn't really afford."

Nevertheless, by December 17, one day before Desobry marched off towards Noville, one of the German legions, the Panzer Lehr Division under Gen. Fritz Bayerlein, was closing in on Bastogne. "Bayerlein was a very aggressive man, had been Rommel's G–4 in North Africa and was the type who led his division from the front. Bayerlein decided the best way to get into Bastogne was not down a high-speed road which he thought would be blocked but essentially to go cross-country.

"He checked with some Belgian civilians on various roads and was informed the roads through small towns, Oberwampach and Niederwampach, were good. The Belgians gave him bad information. He started down these roads at night with tanks and himself in the lead tank. After they went a few thousand meters, the roads turned into mud. They were dirt roads which the tanks chewed up and the going was terribly slow." Still, by the 18th, the Panzer Lehr confronted the U.S. perimeter around Bastogne from due east and the southeast. The 26th *Volksgrenadiers* spread out from the south of the town to further the envelopment. And to the northeast, the 2nd Panzer Division aproached Noville, where Team Desobry awaited an attack.

Without adequate maps or intelligence from patrols, Team Desobry groped through a thick fog that did not abate with dawn. The entire area, including the billets, struck Desobry as pacific. "You could see an American unit had been there, abandoned all their stuff, their bedding, their bunks and had written on the wall, 'We shall return,' like MacArthur. We all laughed and wondered why in the hell they ran in the first place. It was very quiet, a little sleepy village. The weather, contrary to what one reads, was delightfully warm. We had no overshoes on and wore either a wool shirt or a light field jacket." During the night the two sides exchanged grenades in a brief encounter between U.S. foot soldiers and Germans on halftracks before the combatants both retreated.

"We could hear in the darkness a large number of German tanks maneuvering off the road and to the north. We all stood around the town listening to this horrendous, raucous noise of tracks and stuff going around. We knew there was something big out there and that isn't all that encouraging, particularly in the dark.

"Just before daylight we were hit again. We pulled in all of our outposts and buttoned up for the fight. We didn't know what we were fighting, maybe a reinforced tank battalion. By three o'clock in the afternoon, we knocked out thirty-two German tanks that we could see, and that doesn't include the halftracks. When daylight came, we noted the town was in low ground, surrounded by high ground on three sides. The Germans really had a shooting gallery. Because of the fog some of the attacks were fought at ranges of anywhere from twenty-five to fifty meters up to 1,200 meters."

Just as Colonel Roberts had predicted, the urge to retreat grew in Desobry. He radioed a request to abandon the outpost. Roberts conferred with the brass from the arriving 101st. Instead of granting permission to withdraw, the strategists dispatched the 1st Battalion of the 101st's 506th Parachute Regiment to bolster Desobry's defenses. "They were commanded by a Lt. Col. James LaPrade. I was told the parachute guys were walking up from Bastogne, since they had no transportation. I sent a jeep back to get LaPrade. He was a big, tall guy and very confident.

"We agreed that we couldn't stay in Noville and we ought to launch an attack and take the ridgeline. We sent more vehicles back and brought up his [La Prade's] company commanders and I took them on a reconnaissance of the area. That was real hairy. We jumped from one building to the other, dodging artillery barrages and mortar fire.

"We completed the reconnaissances with the troops still marching up. I learned from LaPrade these guys had come out of Holland and been back at a rest area to be refitted. They had lost a lot of equipment. A lot of their guys had been on pass in Paris, and came back off leave to jump on trucks for Bastogne. Many of their guys still needed equipment and some didn't have weapons. A lot who had weapons had no ammunition. Some of their officers on reconnaissance with me and some who came up later were even in pinks and greens [dress uniforms]; they didn't have time to get into their battle uniforms. Some had low quarter shoes.

"Before we had come up here, we had been getting set for the big offensive on the Rhine River. Having had considerable combat experience, we didn't have all that much confidence in the supply system. Our service company overloaded the two-and-one-half-ton trucks with spare weapons, ammunition, fuel, you name it. We sent for the service company, moved their vehicles up in the vicinity of the town of Foy in front of the paratrooper column.

"They parked the vehicles on each side of the road. As these paratroopers marched in single columns on either side of the road, a guy would come by a truck and yell he needed an M–1 rifle, he needed a BAR, or he needed a carbine or whatever or ammo, and my guys would toss him the weapons, the ammunition and maybe a helmet, whatever the heck they wanted. That's the way we reequipped the battalion. Here is a battalion coming out of

Bastogne on the approach march to make an attack and this is how they were getting some of their equipment.

"We convinced the combat command to fire a brief artillery preparation along the ridgeline since it was exposed and the fog was lifting, coming back, then lifting again. We figured we needed to smoke that ridgeline to get out of town. The paratroopers came on and, instead of going into an assembly area, went on the attack right off the approach march. They hit it just about on the nose in conjunction with the artillery preparation.

"They spread out across the fields and those guys when they attacked did it on the dead run. None of this fooling around like you see on television—walking and so on. These guys went on the dead run. They would sprint for fifty meters, hit the ground, get up and run, on and on. Our tanks moved out with them.

"Much to our surprise, the Germans also picked 1400 [hours] to launch a major attack. So when we came boiling out of town, when the smoke cleared from our artillery preparation, out of the smoke came the Germans over the ridgeline. We were engaged in a head-on clash with whatever was out there.

"The fight lasted from 1400 into about 1600. A very desperate fight. Towards the end of it, LaPrade and I realized that even if we did take the ridgeline we were fighting too big a force to actually hold it. We were taking a lot of casualties with guys exposed out there, and the men to the northeast who had the ridgeline were radioing they were under severe attack by tanks and panzer grenadiers and didn't think they could hold it."

Instead of a reinforced tank battalion, Desobry and his people were up against the massed might of the entire 2nd Panzer Division. "We said, 'Okay, good try, but let's pull back into town.' They worked their way back, which takes time. You don't just get up and turn around in the face of the enemy and walk back."

From the east towards the town of Bourcey, German tanks now threatened the ravaged ranks commanded by Desobry and La Prade."I went out there and fought them with my tank destroyers. We would sneak out from behind a building in a village, see the German tanks, take a couple of shots at them, get back behind the building. The Germans were doing the same thing.

"It started to get fairly dark and hard to see. We were tired. We had been fighting since four o'clock in the morning. When you're tired, you lose your zip. I said, 'Okay, let's just knock this off. Stay in your defensive position, keep them under fire and when it gets daylight, we'll go back at them when you can see them better.

"I got word that La Prade wanted to talk to me in the CP back in town. Unfortunately, my guys had put the CP in a house alongside the road in the middle of the town, a very small house on the first floor. When I got there and saw it, I was a bit worried. We took a huge Belgian *schrank* [cupboard] and put it against the wall to the north for added protection. I guess that would not protect us much but I thought it might help.

"La Prade and I pored over a map on a little table. He was showing me where he intended to put his paratroopers, and I agreed and indicated if he put a company there, I'd locate some tanks there. While we were working on this defense, the maintenance officer drove up in a VTR, a recovery vehicle that looks like a tank and parked it outside the CP. He came to tell me his job had been completed and he was returning to his company in Bastogne. But he made a fundamental mistake, something we were all taught not to do; drive a vehicle right up to the CP, because that just shows whomever might be watching the location of the CP.

"The Germans whom I had been fighting to the north of town shortly before saw the VTR and started shooting. They missed the VTR and hit the CP building. They really took it down. They killed La Prade, probably ten or twelve other guys. I was badly wounded, hit in the face, head and the eyes.

"The guys carried me into a cellar. When I came to, they told me I was severely injured. The medic said I had to be evacuated back to a hospital. I answered I wanted to see Colonel Roberts, because I was convinced we couldn't stay in Noville. He hadn't come up to see us. The only ones that did show up that day were from the 101st, Gen. [Gerry] Higgins and Col. [Robert] Sink, the regimental commander. Nobody from the 10th Armored."

Desobry ordered his driver to bring around the jeep. But the soldier disappeared. The vehicle was discovered overturned and Desobry never learned what happened to the missing man. An ambulance from the 101st carted Desobry off, destination Bastogne. Half-blinded, he sat next to the driver while other wounded men lay in back.

"When we got to the little town of Foy, to where I had wanted to pull back, we were stopped by what apparently was a German patrol. When they saw the wounded, we were all bloody, they said, "Aw, go on . . .' and we continued back. But this tipped me the Germans were behind us and in Foy."

In Bastogne, the regimental medics passed Desobry along to the division's forward hospital, the equivalent of the Korean War's MASH unit. He remembered going into a tent where doctors talked to him before administering anesthesia and performing an operation.

"When I came to I was in an ambulance moving down a road. The ambulance would move, stop, go, then halt. Then I heard Germans. My first reaction was, 'My gosh, we sure captured a lot of German prisoners.' Then I heard more Germans and, instead of just conversation, they were yelling *'Achtung-Halt!'* That didn't sound like prisoners.

"I asked the driver what was going on. He said, 'Oh, gee, we've been captured for about seven hours.' He explained we were moving between German units, a lot of tanks and soldiers. I asked him if he knew where Bastogne was. He said he saw signs for it. I told him, 'The next time you come to a road that says Bastogne left or right, just pull onto the road and get going.' He refused, saying there were too many Germans around."

While the ambulance bearing Desobry and a trio of other desperately mauled American prisoners jolted along the roads east towards Germany and a stalag, more U.S. soldiers slogged west. The arrival of the Screaming Eagles swelled the population of Bastogne. Individuals and small groups of men trickled in from the infantry divisions shattered by the enemy advance. Harry Kinnard, then a lieutenant colonel and operations chief under acting CO McAuliffe, said, "We had gotten permission from General Middleton before he even left Bastogne to stop any American units that were withdrawing through the town.

"We stopped every unit and we had some really good finds. We stopped several units with really big artillery with plenty of ammunition in their ammo trains. As a result we were much heavier in artillery than we could normally have expected to be. We had a portion of an armored combat command and a CCB of the 10th Armored Division. They were a splendid unit and full of fight, and of course we were not used to the luxury of that many tanks fighting with us. We had a super-fine tank destroyer unit, the 605th, which had the very newest tank destroyer and plenty of ammunition."

Artillery elements commandeered as they arrived in Bastogne included both the 969th Field Artillery and the 333rd Field Artillery, two of the very few combat units composed of African-Americans or Negroes in the lexicon of the day. A similar outfit, the 578th Field Artillery, had fired 774 rounds while carrying out twenty-three missions on December 16, near Heckhuschied. As enemy infantry closed in, the crews picked up M–1s, killed half a dozen enemy soldiers and captured twelve others before being overwhelmed.

When Kinnard spoke of refugees from an armored command, he was referring to a handful from the 9th Armored Division's 52nd Armored Infantry. Maj. Eugene Watts led a covey of seventy men blocking the sweep towards Bastogne from the northeast. They routed a convoy of enemy armored personnel carriers, inflicting heavy casualties. But suddenly, tank, rocket, artillery, mortar and small arms fire erupted to their rear as a main element of 9th Armored task force exploded in flames. Watts and company broke into small bands and infiltrated their way back to Bastogne, moving only under the cover of darkness. It took two nights for the refugees, including Watts, to cover the four miles.

Upon reporting, Watts was assigned to lead Team SNAFU, a force made up of the residue from wrecked outfits. "We collected about 175, including guys from the 106th and 28th Divisions. As more and more men came through, they downed a hot meal, cleaned themselves up and became part of SNAFU. We lived in foxholes in Bastogne. The Germans bombed the hell out of the place, their planes dropped 500-pounders at night. You had to fight the soldier's natural inclination to be warm and feel safe in a house. But that was not safe. It was safer in a hole. There were hundreds of people killed in Bastogne, and a lot of them because they stayed in houses."

The kernel of Bastogne hardened. Even before Bayerlein arrived within a short drive of the town, there had come a moment, said Kinnard, when a German recon unit in strength arrived on a hill overlooking an intersection of the roads connecting Bastogne and Werbomont. The officer saw only a single MP directing the sparse traffic. The main body from the 101st Airbone was still en route. The recon officer immediately recommended his troops plunge into Bastogne. But his headquarters scolded him for having left his assigned sector and told him to return to his proper area.

"One important thing," said Kinnard. "We had the town and

the Germans were out there in the snow. Even our outposts, by and large, had small villages where you could get a guy warm, dry his socks and feed him some hot coffee. The Germans had none of this. We simply were not going to let them run us out of the houses."

Jochen Peiper's task force, after breaking through the defenses of the 99th Division, had encountered mostly small, scattered American forces. But now, the two veteran divisions, the 82nd Airborne and the 30th Infantry, applied pressure while Peiper frantically hunted for his water crossings. A critical series of encounters centered around Stoumont, on the north bank of the Ambleve River. The American presence there would block a link-up of the 1st and 2nd SS Panzer Divisions. The defenders were unaware, however, of the critical shortage of fuel for the enemy. In fact, Peiper no longer thought in terms of the Meuse River and Liège but only the most expeditious route of withdrawal.

Initially, however, the situation for the Americans arriving at Stoumont seemed dicey. After a sleepless night aboard trucks, the infantrymen from the 1st Battalion of the 119th Infantry continued their journey on foot. Curtiss Martell remembered, "It was well past the noon hour and a steep hill could be seen to our front. As we climbed up it, our eyes fixed on a scene of American troops who were running down the hill towards us. The sight was one of utter panic and confusion as these troops ran towards us. They were fleeing the 1st SS Panzer Division and obviously were badly shaken.

"Our unit was very much concerned. We were on our way to confront this enemy and we lacked armor back-up. The only message from the fleeing soldiers was 'Get the hell out of here!' We continued our march toward Stoumont when we realized further efforts would be fruitless, especially when you're looking down the barrel of an 88-mm gun mounted on a German tank. An orderly retreat was executed while the German tanks fired their missiles at our rear ends.

"I received word for my platoon to dig in and hold a position on the high side of the hill, overlooking the bend in the road. We were told an American tank unit was on the way to provide the armor support so desperately needed. It was dusk and our tanks and TDs arrived—the 740th Tank Battalion—and occupied strategic firepower points behind the bend. We still had no sleep.

"Darkness fell and we heard the rumble of three German tanks. At that moment, we expected to engage enemy infantry with the tanks, but none came. (Of course, I was greatly disappointed by that, Ha!) The lead tank silhouetted itself against the skyline as it turned into the bend of the road. A TD fired and scored a direct hit, the German tank blazed up, ammo popped inside it. A Mark V tank tried to swing around the crippled one and it, too, was knocked out. One of our tanks then pulled up where it could see the 3rd enemy tank and it, too, was destroyed. The entire road area was blocked and the sky lit by the fires."

The main objective in the struggle for Stoumont was the St. Edouard Sanitorium, a four-story brick building that commanded the hill mentioned by Curtiss Martell. "At the crack of dawn, we were back on the road. A German tank was pushed aside so our tanks could pass to give us armor support as we headed for the high ground on the way to Stoumont. It was nightfall before we reached the top of the hill. Casualites were high and some of our men had been captured.

"Three furious counterattacks were launched against us with the enemy screaming, 'Heil Hitler!' Our ammo was running low and we were being battered. But the Germans were getting hit harder. Confusion was rampant because some Germans wore American uniforms. I saw one captured American tank with 'SS' markings painted on the sides. My messenger, who carried the maps and walkie-talkie, grabbed me, 'Listen to this!' I heard a German speaking in English, 'Hello, Joe. We have captured a lot of your buddies.' "

St. Edouard's changed hands several times after intense fighting before finally being secured on December 21 by the elements of the 119th Infantry. Martell confesses his memory fails him as he tries to recall the specific details of the final conquest of the brick building "that held nuns and American prisoners."

As the Germans retreated, they left some of their wounded, along with injured Americans for whom they had provided medical care. Later, the use of the sanitorium would become a sore point for Peiper, now holed up in La Gleize.

Chapter IX

PATTON TO THE RESCUE, NECESSARY LOSSES

By December 18, no one doubted the extent of the threat to the entire Allied operation. Eisenhower convened a council of strategy. Patton, who must have relished the appeal to him from all of those whom he regarded as his inferiors—Eisenhower for his puny intelligence, Bradley as inexperienced, Montgomery as pusillanimous, "a tired little fart"—gave them a bravura performance.

The demands upon Patton played to his strengths. As a tactical combat commander he never displayed any great brilliance, although he understood the cardinal tenet of *blitzkrieg* and modern armored warfare—the infantry support the tanks rather than the other way around. But his true genius lay in his ability to put the show on the road, to move men and machines.

On the morning of December 19, Eisenhower convened his top commanders and staff officers at Verdun, the site of terrible Allied battle debacles in World War I. The choice of Verdun served as an unspoken symbol of the current crisis. The strategy seemed obvious; shift Patton's Third Army to attack the Bulge from the south. Eisenhower turned to the man-of-the-hour. "When will you be able to attack?"

"The morning of December 21st," answered the ever-cocky Patton. "With three divisions."

"Don't be fatuous, George," reproved Eisenhower, well aware of Patton's habitual overflow of confidence. "If you try to go that early, you won't have all three divisions ready and you'll go piecemeal. You will start on the 22nd." Eisenhower added that, if necessary, the Third Army assault could come even a day later. Patton's enthusiasm, however, quickly infected those at the meeting, depressed by news of American losses and the German advances. "There was a stir, a shuffling of feet, as those present straightened up in their chairs. In some faces, skepticism. But through the room the current of excitement leaped like a flame," said Col. Charles Codman, Patton's aide, an obviously biased eyewitness.

Actually, Eisenhower sought to set an upbeat tone to the session with his opening remark, "The present situation is to be regarded as an opportunity for us and not of disaster." Patton, at least verbally, considered the enemy strategy fatally wrongheaded. "Hell, let's have the guts to let the sons of bitches go all the way to Paris. Then we'll really cut 'em and chew 'em up!" Given the inclination of most American generals not to yield turf already conquered, his pronouncement may have been tailored for his audience. However, the breakthrough existed and to Bradley, Patton chortled, "This time the Kraut has stuck his head [some believe Patton referred to another part of the body] in the meat grinder and I've got the handle."

Patton immediately pivoted his 4th Armored Division along with the 26th and 80th Infantry Divisions towards the objective. Later he would ante up two more outfits, the 87th Infantry Division, and the 11th Armored assigned to him while still in England.

Of all of his combat forces, Patton favored the 4th Armored. After coming ashore in July 1944, the 4th earned the approval of Patton first in Normandy, then the Lorraine and in the months before the Ardennes breakthrough, the campaign through the Saar region. The route of the 4th Armored from its positions on the Saar River ended with the point of the arrow in Bastogne.

"We started out December 19 at 2300," says Abe Baum, then a captain and the intelligence officer for the 4th's 10th Armored Infantry Battalion. "We were in the lead with the 8th Tank Battalion. The roads were frozen over, the metal tracks of tanks kept sliding badly. But we didn't meet any resistance and we covered 151 miles in nineteen hours."

The rapid transit, however, cost machines. The 8th Tank Battalion listed thirty-three of its machines falling by the wayside from mechanical failures. For the troops it was an endurance contest, with tankers forced to take turns standing in their turrets in order to pee. They had hardly arrived at the outskirts of the Ardennes before the brass picked Abe Baum and tanker Capt. Burt Ezell to lead a task force of about 400 men, infantry and armor into Bastogne.

Abe Baum, born in 1921, grew up in New York City's East Bronx, then a haven for Jews who'd escaped the periodic pogroms of Eastern Europe and Russia. "My father was a dress contractor. After the 1929 crash, his business folded and he went to work for other companies. Because of the economic conditions at home, I never expected to attend college. We were observant Jews but I did not pay much attention to what was happening in Europe. I dropped out of James Monroe High School to take a job as a pattern cutter."

Although Baum worked for the same firm where his father was production manager, he soon displayed an innate feisty streak. Angered because his weekly pay of seventeen dollars, up from his initial salary of twelve dollars, fell far short of the prevailing wage of ninety dollars for a skilled operator, Baum locked his boss in the designing room and refused to release him until granted an additional twenty dollars a week.

The day after Pearl Harbor, in the first flush of patriotic zeal, Baum joined the throngs eager to enlist. He flunked the eye test for the air corps. The sergeant who scrutinized the applicants' job experience noted Baum listed himself as a "pattern maker." To the army man that meant tool and die expertise and qualified Baum for a technical branch, the engineers.

"I had never so much as used a hammer to drive in a nail," remembers Baum. "But I was sent to Fort Belvoir, Virginia, for training with the engineers. When I finished the course, I gained new respect for laborers, people as talented in their field as I was in mine."

As a young man who had lived and worked in a heavily Jewish community, Baum was not well acquainted with the virulence of anti-Semitism. However, when he received his assignment to an engineer battalion with the 2nd Armored Division, that ugly phenomenon literally smote him in the testicles and face.

"It was a regular army unit and had few draftees. They were not friendly to either big city boys or ethnics like myself. It was a shock to me. I had never been out of New York. Part of the routine included boxing matches as physical training. They put me in with a 250-pounder who didn't like the idea any more than I did. When we didn't go at each other, one of the noncoms put on the gloves. I broke his jaw."

The tormentors took their revenge by matching Baum with a former professional. Baum managed to fend off the fighter for a round before the experienced pugilist slipped in a punch to Baum's privates and then hammered him in the face. The following day, the head of the division boxing program, introduced to Baum as the former wrestling headliner, Man Mountain Dean, invited the Bronx soldier to join the boxing team. Baum refused. "I came to fight the enemy, not other Americans." The refusal led to further animosity and unpleasant work details from his superiors.

"I had met up with another fellow, Ralph Combs, a graduate of City College. We agreed we had to get out of the outfit. He said OCS was the way. I said no way, I didn't even have a high-school diploma. Combs insisted I had a decent IQ and could pass the exam. When I submitted my application, the first sergeant laughed at me. I answered, 'If it's such a big joke, then why not let me try?' He said okay.

"But the day I was supposed to appear before the officer board that interviewed candidates, the first sergeant sent me on a garbage detail, three miles away. You were supposed to wear a Class A uniform when you saw the board. I had to show up in my fatigues, still smelling of garbage." Baum, however, passed muster, probably because his original six-foot two-inch, 160-pound frame had begun to fill out into more impressive stature and he demonstrated a naturally booming voice well suited to the stereotype of command.

"I had a lot of trouble in OCS, though. I flunked two of three exams in a week. One more failing grade and I was out. A classmate, a college graduate, tipped me off that I was making the mistake of studying to learn the subject, when what I should do was to study in terms of the exams."

As a second lieutenant in the armored infantry, Baum received a posting to the 4th Armored Division and participated in the first engagements among the hedgerows of St.-Lô. The hedgerows, dirt packed eight to ten feet high with roots at the base making them formidable barriers and defensive positions, forced armored infantry, like Baum's, to battle on foot while the armor flailed away at the stubborn earthworks.

"Naturally, I was afraid. But there was so much to do that you didn't have time to think about your fear. My father had always taught me to discipline myself, to exert self-control and not to let emotions interfere.

"We had received good training. The officers in the 4th were first rate, from Gen. John Wood, who commanded the division, Bruce Clarke, CO for one of the combat commands, Creighton Abrams, who led the 37th Tank Battalion, and my own superior, Harold Cohen. Ours was a particularly strong bunch because we had the will to fight. If you look at a division of 10,000 to 14,000 men, there are maybe only 150 who have that real will to fight in the manner required. But if the division commander has that capacity, and he has one similarly inclined combat commander, a battalion commander, company commander, down through individuals in the platoons and squads, the other men feel forced to follow.

"The 4th Armored had mostly people from the Northeast and, while there was occasional anti-Semitism, it wasn't prevalent. In fact, when someone from the Inspector General's office in Washington checked our rosters, he said to General Wood, 'You've got a lotta Hebes.' Wood answered, 'I wouldn't have as good a division if I didn't have these men.' There was a mistaken impression that Creighton Abrams was Jewish. He wasn't. We all had a laugh when the Yiddish-language newspaper the *Forvitz* listed a Jewish all-American football team and named Abrams as a member from West Point.

"Our equipment wasn't usually as good as the Germans'. But we had more of it. When something was shot out or broke down, we could replace it."

Plowing a steady course east, the 4th Armored operated north of the Loire. After the fall of Orléans, the division reached the key town of Troyes, on the banks of the Seine southeast of Paris, late in August. Part of the assault team seeking to wrest the town from the Germans became trapped. Abe Baum in his capacity as an intelligence specialist discovered from the local French authorities a baker who routinely delivered his wares to the local German garrisons. This information, plotted on a town map, enabled Baum and the combat command staff to pinpoint the location of enemy forces. The Americans relieved their comrades and nearly annihilated the opposition.

By the time Abe Baum, in a jeep, and the small task force started up the road to Bastogne, he had already collected a pair of Bronze Stars for the fighting in France and a Silver Star as a reward for Troyes. The first scenes along the way to the town were disquieting, abandoned American vehicles and artillery pieces, soldiers, some of them unarmed, disconsolately walking towards the rear.

Although Baum heard small arms fire in the distance, no one opposed the task force's movement. "When we got there, Ezell remained in his tank to keep in touch with our headquarters. I was told to see Kinnard. I announced, 'We're here. What do you want us to do?' He sent me to see Roberts, the commander of the armored troops. 'Where would you like to deploy us?' I asked. He had no idea of why we were there or what to do with us. To me, it looked as if the only thing he wanted was for me to hold his hand.

"Meanwhile, Ezell heard from division. They wanted us back. In my opinion, Patton decided that he did not want to pass one of his units over to control of somebody else."

That would seem to square with the bluster of Patton at the time of the recall. "I want that son of a bitch back here. I want him back as fast as shit goes through a sick duck." John Wood, whom Baum profoundly respected, no longer commanded the 4th Armored, officially because of stress problems but possibly because of independence that angered Patton. In place of Wood, Patton chose Gen. Hugh Gaffey, a former subordinate who could be expected to accept the ukases from Old Blood and Guts. Gaffey also feared dilution of his forces if the task force remained in Bastogne and the probability that more personnel would have been directed there in support.

"We were the last to get out of Bastogne before the Germans surrounded it," says Baum. "There's no chance that our two companies could have kept open the road. But if a full combat command, 4,000 men and armor, had been sent to hold the way in, the Germans might not have been able to shut off Bastogne. And there wouldn't have been the need to fight through the woods to relieve the 101st."

When Baum returned to his headquarters, his unit was put in reserve while the two other combat commands now jumped to the front of the columns. For Baum, the most harrowing experiences in relief of the men in the Ardennes would now come months later.

On the Prümerberg, there could be no help from Patton and there was no escape for the assemblage of combat engineers—John Collins, Duke Ward and their leader, Lt. Col. Tom Riggs. Collins remembered Tuesday, December 19. "They started early, all down the line. They had us keeping our heads down, but as soon as the shelling stopped, up they came. I understood that Lieutenant Rutledge was killed during one of these battles. Rutledge would be sorely missed. He was an excellent officer. Lieutenant Coughlin told me the 7th Armored Division was on the way to relieve us. I had heard this three days earlier."

According to Tom Riggs, Rutledge, refused first aid for a wound, led a counterattack and was killed while still in pursuit of the foe. With troops of the 7th Armored's 38th Armored Infantry now on the scene, that outfit's CO, Lt. Col. William Fuller, superseded Riggs. "I was to be his executive officer," recalled Riggs. "I felt a personal letdown in the change of responsibility, but I did get my first sleep since the early morning of the 16th."

On the following day, Collins noted, "I heard that Lieutenant Colonel Riggs was to be relieved but, so far as I could see, he still controlled us. I am sure that no one could have done as good a job as our lieutenant colonel. Either Coughlin or Riggs came up the hill and told me to go down and get some rations for the men. While there I had a good meal. I sent the rations back and lay down to sleep. When I went back on the line my hands were full of rabbit and bread. Where the rabbit came from beats me. But we owed our thanks to the two officers with us through the entire ordeal, Riggs and Coughlin. If Rutledge had remained alive, he would have stayed too. If there were other officers from our Battalion, I sure didn't see them. I heard there were sixty-three Jerries killed [Tuesday]."

On December 21, conditions deteriorated badly. Riggs noted, "At about 1800 hours, Lieutenant Colonel Fuller announced he was placing me in charge of the position while he reported back to Headquarters to plan alternative defensive positions. He never returned and our orders stood to defend St. Vith." In fact, Fuller reported to CCB's Gen. Bruce Clarke he could not cope any longer, and an uncharacteristically magnanimous Clarke allowed him to take what amounted to medical leave. Meanwhile, the 106th Division Headquarters had evacuated the town two days before in favor of Vielsalm, about eight miles to the west on the Salm River.

Collins broke down briefly after a fusillade of bullets perforated a five-gallon can of hot coffee and smashed his carbine. "I became frustrated, shaky, mad, scared like an old hen trying to protect her baby chicks from a hawk. I went into a house and retrieved a German machine gun I had previously found and hid. I loaded and cocked it, went out the door cursing like a sailor and ran into Lieutenant Colonel Riggs. He said not a word, only looked at me and then I threw the gun back into the house, sat down on the steps. For the next ten minutes I did a lot of mumbling and cursing. I am not sure what I accomplished but I sure felt better and relieved after the blowup. I hope the lieutenant colonel didn't think I was going to shoot him.

"In the afternoon, the barrage really started. Screaming Meemies, mortars, 88s, big stuff and little stuff. Previous shelling was a drizzle compared to this downpour. Smoke was thick, limbs and leaves on pine and fir trees disappeared. I was hit in the hand, almost the same place as an earlier scratch. Riggs came by and told us to hold the ridge and cover the road. But we were too thin and split up to be effective. At about 2100 they more or less ran over us. Many, many tanks came down the road. Flares lit up the area like daylight, the infantry riding or walking in droves behind the tanks."

Some of those flares mentioned by Collins helped devastate the last hopes of the Americans. Six massive Tigers from a heavy panzer battalion lumbered up the highway while five smaller American tanks maneuvered into a solid defensive position. But at the last moment, the Tigers lofted high intensity flares that burst behind the American tanks. The brilliant light temporarily blinded the U.S. gunners while silhouetting their vehicles. Within seconds, accurate cannon fire from the Tigers wrecked all five American tanks, killing or wounding the crews.

For Collins, Riggs and the several hundred left, all resistance ended. "We split up into three- or four-man groups to try and reach our rear lines. Every man was on his own." Blindly fleeing, the exhausted Collins "lost contact with myself. When I finally came around, I was beside a chimney and had manure all over me, like I was dragged through it. I had sprained my ankle, and had another wound on my leg. I crept up the hill to the foxholes but they were all empty. In the distance at St. Vith, the flares and firing were working overtime.

"I made my way into the old CP and the basement where I found many others hiding. I tried to retrace my steps and get into the open. I ran smack into a German who motioned me back into the basement. We had a guard, and another German, wearing a red cross on his helmet told us, in English, we were now prisoners."

Riggs similarly fell into the clutches of the enemy. Duke Ward, who'd earlier been blasted off a tank while helping to man the outpost in front of St. Vith, had already left the scene when the final attack came. He was able to make his way back to the safety of division headquarters.

Sgt. Glenn Fackler, a machine gunner with the 38th Armored Infantry Battalion from the 7th Armored Division, had passed down the road from Malmédy to St. Vith shortly before the ill-fated 285th Field Artillery Observation Battalion troops ran into Peiper's column and were slaughtered. Fackler had been positioned on the northern flank of the defenses between Schönberg and St. Vith. Fackler was dug in behind a tree overlooking an open field on the afternoon of December 21.

"From my position at St. Vith, I spotted a German tank, about 500 yards in front of me, with just his turret showing. I crawled back to a tank battalion forward observer and related what I saw. He came up to check it out and said, 'From where it is, it would knock me out before I could get a round off.' Just before dark, we were instructed to pull back 100 yards and dig in. Then all hell broke loose, with armor-piercing and treebursts in the area we had just left. My platoon sergeant was wounded by a treeburst and turned over to me his sidearm belt.

"When the shelling let up, we were ordered to resume our original position. At my foxhole I found the tree in front of it had taken a direct hit about six feet above the ground. That tank must have had me in his sights during the day and let go after dark.

"I set the tripod up, mounted my .30-caliber gun to traverse the area to my front and waited. It was so dark we couldn't see anything around us. I heard noises out in front, indicating troops with ammo boxes coming towards us. I waited for my squad leader, S. Sgt. Alphonse Alpino, to start shooting. After I felt those troops coming at us were no more than 100 yards off, I opened up and traversed the whole area to my front. I had only fired the first couple of rounds when the gun on my left also opened up. We crisscrossed the whole area with a full box of ammo. We never heard another sound and within minutes were ordered out, not knowing what had happened out front."

Fackler and Alpino had sprayed a large contingent of soldiers from the 18th *Volksgrenadier* Division, part of a two-division pincer advancing on St. Vith. After-action reports subsequently described the field covered by the two American machine guns as "strewn with bodies." "We must have killed everyone," says Fackler.

Nevertheless, the Germans continued to advance in waves, and the men from the 38th Armored Infantry Battalion also abandoned their foxholes and tried to escape. With Milton Baxter, a member of his gun crew, Fackler sifted through the forest. "We held hands to keep together. It was so black you literally could not see a hand in front of your face. We groped through the woods all night. We bumped into a sergeant just beyond St. Vith. He had a white phosphorous grenade and he said, 'I have the pin out and if we get stopped, I'll throw it.' Ten minutes later we heard a German call, 'Achtung,' I heard the grenade pop and then no more words from the German.

"In the belt given to me by the platoon sergeant I had found a compass. I argued with the sergeant we should head to the right while he wanted to move to the left. I was sure the Germans were there. We split up, and as far as I can figure he was captured. But Baxter and I found a field artillery unit ready to pull out and they took us along.

"Two days later we found the halftracks from 38th and T. Sgt. James Long. I asked him, 'Where is everybody, Long?' 'You're it, Fackler,' he answered. It would take a lot of replacements to rebuild our unit."

As the situation had worsened in the first days of the Ardennes campaign, desperation measures demanded the use of men technically capable of handling an M–1 but ordinarily well removed from the battlefield. Among these was a lanky youth from Pennsylvania, James Buck.

"When I attended Philadelphia Catholic High School, I was a brilliant shorthand student. Then I graduated on my seventeenth birthday in 1938 and couldn't find a job using shorthand. Instead I worked as a dishwasher and then as an office boy in a local retail credit company office.

"After Pearl Harbor, I tried to enlist in the marines, but at 6'4" and 160 pounds I couldn't qualify. I enlisted in the army. At the induction center, they took note of my stenography skills. Five days after I entered the army, instead of going for basic training, I was transferred back to Philadelphia to become a secretary to a brigadier general.

"I took my basic training in the corridors and rooms of the Adelphia Hotel from a staff sergeant. I learned the rudiments for handling an M–1 and they did take me out to a range somewhere to qualify with the weapon.

"I was bored in Philadelphia working for the general. I got into the ASTP program but I was still unhappy when they sent me to Georgetown. I applied for air cadet training and I was accepted for navigation school. But while I waited at an airbase to actually enter training, they decided the need for more infantrymen was much more pressing. I found myself at Camp Atterbury, as part of the 106th Division.

"Almost immediately on my arrival there, instead of going to a rifle company, they picked up on my stenographic ability and assigned me to the judge advocate's office. That meant I became part of division headquarters company, and while I had qualified with a rifle, I never received any field instruction in infantry tactics.

"I spent my working hours taking notes during court-martials. When the division received orders to go overseas, a number of guys mistakenly figured if they went AWOL or got into a fight, the court-martial would keep them in the States. Instead, they were tried but kept with the division when it embarked.

"After we moved into the Ardennes, I was in a farmhouse with my typewriter and about a three-foot-high stack of notebooks from trials which I kept transcribing. It was rainy, wet and cold, but I had a bed and warm food. I was happy to be where I was and I was oblivious to what was happening.

"But one night, and it must have been shortly after the German attack began, I was put on guard duty, at a bunker on a hill that overlooked farm land and gorgeous trees. I was a nice young boy from Philadelphia who never intended to be a soldier. Now on guard duty on this country road, my orders were to stop anyone coming up the road. If they couldn't give the password, I was to shoot to kill.

"A guy came along in an American uniform. 'Halt!' I yelled. 'What's the password?'

" 'I don't know any fucking password!' I was supposed to shoot him dead for that kind of answer. But I knew he had to be an American. He kept going up the road.

"The following night I was back in the dugout; this time with another soldier who had very little infantry training, an older guy who was an armorer-artificer. We were so stupid that when we saw our first buzz bombs fly overhead we shot at them, giving away our location. Some mortars dropped in but we were well dug in and not hurt.

"The next morning, someone ran up and shouted, 'We're abandoning this place. Get on a truck.' Someone handed me the tripod of a machine gun to carry, the armorer-artificer carried the gun. To reach the vehicles we had to walk down a steep, muddy hill. We kept slipping and sliding. The armorer-artificer threw away the gun. I dumped the tripod.

"We joined a convoy of maybe ten trucks, traveling up a back road. I sat in the back and looked out. I had no fears of being killed or wounded. I just looked out admiring the valley, seeing beautiful small villages with church steeples. Suddenly, the trucks halted and someone yelled the front of the column was being strafed by a plane. It was about 11:00 A.M. when we were told to take off into the pine forest beside the road.

"The trees were very small, maybe three feet high but very thick, so to keep under cover we had to crawl. Each man was supposed to maintain touch with the fellow in front to keep from becoming lost. Maybe an hour passed when the soldier ahead of me turned and said, 'I lost the person in front.' I turned around and saw there were four of us at the tail end of the chain, now separated from everyone else. None of us had much rifleman training. There was my buddy from guard duty, a mail clerk and some other headquarters type.

"The armorer-artificer had a compass with him and we agreed he should lead us. He struck a course in a westerly direction. For the rest of the day we slowly made our way through the woods; the trees became bigger and bigger. Towards dusk we climbed a hill and came upon a clearing. There we met this lieutenant. He was about five feet ten inches tall, husky, clean cut, good-looking. He had a bunch of men with him, maybe as many as twenty, but it was difficult to tell how many were there." The description matches well with the general appearance of Eric Wood, last identified as escaping to the woods while the others from A Battery of the 589th Field Artillery surrendered.

"I didn't speak with the lieutenant but our leader did. The next morning, the officer called a meeting. It seemed that the group expected to make some sort of attack. We were welcome to join them. We responded that our orders were to head for St. Vith. He did not order us to follow him, which he could have done if he wanted more bodies.

"We left them and continued our journey through the woods. As we crossed an open field, someone started to shoot at us. I lost my helmet leaping over a small stream. We decided it would be safer to move only at night. That slowed us down even more. Nobody said anything; I doubt if we exchanged a hundred words in a single night. We found an abandoned truck. The K rations tempted us since we hadn't eaten for several days. But because of possible booby traps we did not try to retrieve the food. We all had Halazone tablets to purify water, so at least there was something to drink.

"On our third night since the strafing drove us from the trucks into the woods, we heard voices speaking in English commanding us, 'Halt!' We'd been gone three days and had no idea of the password. We insisted we were Americans, from the 106th Division, trying to get back to our unit. They made us flop down on our bellies, throw out the one rifle among us. They were tankers, and after frisking us, stuck us on a tank. I hadn't even eaten for three days and to me it seemed as if we were sitting on top of a tank heading for battle.

"However, the tanks pulled back, through St. Vith. The town was in flames; it reminded me of the burning of Atlanta in *Gone With the Wind,* stone buildings with flames shooting out of the windows but no crumbling walls. After passing through St. Vith, we left the tanks. I joined a mixed bag of guys, strung out along a little dirt road, behind trucks. They warned us to stay on the road because of mines and booby traps.

"By now I had also lost my three companions from the woods. Still unfed since I left the bunker outpost, I noticed that right in front of me a jeep was pulling a small trailer. I thought it might carry rations and I lifted the tarp. It was full of dead GIs. I remember also passing a snowy field with barbed wire. There were GIs hung up on the wire where they'd been shot.

"When we finally halted, I was designated again to pull guard duty. I protested I didn't even have a helmet anymore. A cook agreed to lend me his. I did my shift and had my first meal in days, beans and a blob of hamburger meat. It was a brown mess but hot, not a K ration. I gobbled it up. Exhausted, I lay down to sleep in a bombed-out Belgian house. Half an hour later I was sick. Instead of going outside to throw up on the ground, I puked in my helmet and put it outside. When I got up in the morning, the vomit was frozen solid. Again, I had no helmet.

"The retreat continued. Somewhere I obtained a blanket but I must have been a pitiful sight, because one night while I pretended to sleep, I heard a discussion by those in charge. 'Don't use Buck. He's a nice kid but he's absolutely useless.' "

Eventually, Buck reached the safety of a village well behind the combat zone. There he rejoined elements from the judge advocate's office. He continued recording military justice until the end of the war.

The original timetable for the entire *blitzkreig* and in particular for Peiper's spearhead had fallen apart within the first two days. The German legions planned to overrun St. Vith after a single day; yet it was not until December 21, on the sixth day of the campaign, that Manteuffel's troops entered the rubble. *Kampfgruppe Peiper*, whose leader boasted he would travel the sixty miles to the Meuse by the end of the second day, now kicked and scratched at the maze formed by swift-flowing creeks and rivers whose bridges lay in ruins. The original objective still lay thirty miles away after four days that brought ever-increasing losses of men and machines. Peiper had no sooner pulled his main force out of Stavelot, for example, than American infantrymen supported by tank destroyers and tanks took back the town. Other German units failed to regain Stavelot.

After being frustrated at Trois Ponts by the demolitions of the American combat engineers, Peiper had swung north, seeking an outlet at La Gleize and then Stoumont. His spearhead continued to trail the bodies of murder victims. After the war, the Belgian authorities counted 138 civilians executed. For his part, Peiper insisted local citizens harassed his column with sniper fire from rooftops and windows.

He encountered little military resistance in La Gleize, but at the approach to Stoumont he faced off against the 119th Infantry, Bob Hall's regiment. Rallying his forces, the appalled Peiper noticed some of his tanks in reverse. He directed Maj. Werner Poetschke to summarily stop the retreat. Poetschke, toting a *panzerfaust* (German bazooka), went from tank to tank, warning the commanders that if they so much as backed up one meter he would blast them.

Bob Hall, with headquarters company of the 119th's 3rd Battalion, received a risky assignment. "The Germans were in the next town, La Gleize. Lieutenant Goodman sent me, Ellis 'Jim' Aldridge, from Hagerstown, Maryland, who had been right next to me both times when I was wounded, and a third guy to a hilly area to observe any movement. When dawn broke, we could see what looked like the whole German army coming, infantry and tanks." The oncoming hordes, in fact, were from *Kampfgruppe Peiper*, intent on capturing Stoumont.

"Aldridge and the other man took off. I hesitated and then ran down the hill and ducked into a house. That was as far as I could get because the Germans had cut off the way back to my platoon. In the cellar I found about thirty guys. I looked out a cellar window and saw a tank pass and then a German came right up to the window. I could have reached out and touched him. He was less than a foot away from me but at the moment he didn't realize we were there.

"I ran away from the window but there was no way to escape. Within a few minutes they discovered us and we all gave up. They herded us into the middle of the street and took whatever we had in our pockets. My mother had just sent me a new fountain pen, which they snatched. Some of us were taken to a castle which they used as a first-aid station. We were made to move the dead ones to another room. They used one of our jeeps with a stretcher to bring in wounded.

"The doctor spoke English. One German soldier, whom the doctor said was dead, made a noise while we were carrying him. I said, 'This guy isn't dead. He made a noise.' The doctor answered that it was only his lungs that caused the sound.

"We stayed there four to six hours when they began to move us up towards La Gleize. En route, our artillery opened up. We and the guards ran and ducked. It was one of the worst shellings I was ever in. I usually wasn't scared but nothing is more scary or worse than being caught in an artillery barrage. My heart would pound and pound.

"They jammed us all together in a large cellar. Every once in a while they would call for three or four of us to do something. My buddy, Max Levine, of Providence, Rhode Island, being Jewish, could speak the German language. He stayed at the door, interpreting what they wanted. The guys who went out said they were made to move ammunition.

"I was at the back of the cellar and a lot more men would be called before me, but for some reason, when they asked for six men, I volunteered. This was a mistake. We had to dig graves for a couple of dead German soldiers. They had received terrible head wounds and while we dug, here came another U.S. barrage. I dug so fast I had blisters on my hand. Naturally, this being December, the ground was good and hard. Luckily, no one was hurt."

The fighting around Stoumont and La Gleize settled into a bloody stalemate. The two sides exchanged punches that inflicted heavy damage on both. The Americans pressed their case near La Gleize with the 2nd battalion from the 119th under Maj. Hal Mc-Cown. An ROTC graduate from Louisiana State University, Mc-Cown made the mistake of attempting to reconnoiter the area. In a brief firefight McCown killed an enemy soldier with a machine gun burst, but when faced with a strong force of Germans, became a prisoner.

As a major, McCown seemed a prize catch. But he stubbornly refused to offer more than name, rank and serial number to interrogators. Peiper, at first eager to question him, temporarily lost interest. McCown joined the bunch, including Bob Hall and what was to become about 300 Americans, picked up by *Kampfgruppe Peiper* during its rampage through the Ardennes. Some of the Americans who were wounded received medical attention from German doctors and aidmen. Local priests also tried to care for the maimed on both sides.

Major McCown saw *Kampfgruppe Peiper* close up and their demeanor impressed him. "An amazing fact to me was the youth of members of this organization—the bulk of the enlisted men were either eighteen or nineteen years of age, recently recruited but, from my observations, thoroughly trained. There was a good sprinkling of both privates and NCOs from years of Russian fighting. The officers for the most part were veterans but were also very young. Col. Peiper was twenty-nine, his tank battalion commander was thirty; his captains and lieutenants ran from nineteen to twenty-seven.

"The morale was high throughout the entire period I was with them, despite the extremely trying conditions. The discipline was very good. The noise discipline on the night movements was so perfect that I could hardly believe that they could accomplish it. The physical condition of all personnel was good, except for a lack of proper food, which was more strongly apparent just before I escaped from the unit. The equipment was good and complete, with the exception of some reconditioned halftracks among the motorized equipment. All men wore practically new boots and had adequate clothing. Some of them wore parts of American uniforms, mainly the knit cap, gloves, sweaters, overshoes and one or two overcoats. I saw no one, however, in American uniforms or in civilian clothes.

"The relationship between officers and men, particularly the commanding officer—Colonel Peiper—was closer and friendlier than I would have expected. On several occasions Colonel Peiper visited his wounded and many times I saw him give a slap of encouragement on the back of heavily loaded men . . . and speak a couple of cheering words."

In one of the more bizarre episodes of the Ardennes, Peiper invited McCown to his headquarters for an extended bull session. "We talked together from 2300 until 0500 the next morning, our subject being mainly his defense of Naziism and why Germany was fighting. I have met few men who impressed me in as short a space of time as did this German officer. He was approximately 5 ft. 8 inches in height, 140 lbs in weight, long dark hair combed straight back, straight well-shaped features, with remarkable facial resemblance to the actor Ray Milland. He was completely confident of Germany's ability to whip the Allies. He spoke of Himmler's new reserve army quite at length, saying it contained so many new divisions, both armored and otherwise, that our G–2s [intelligence officers] would wonder where they all came from.

"He did his best to find out from me of the success V–1 and V–2 [rockets] were having and told me that more secret weapons like those would be unloosed. He said a new submarine campaign [was] opening up and they had been told that there had been considerable tonnage sunk in the English Channel just recently by the latest underwater attack.

"The German air force, he said, would now come forth with many new types which, although inferior in number to the Allies, would be superior in quality and would suffice their needs to cover their breakthrough in Belgium and Holland, and later to the French coast."

Considering that *Kampfgruppe Peiper* now cowered under the awesome weight of incessant bombardment and that he had abandoned all hope of carrying out his mission, Peiper's comments to McCown perhaps testify to the willingness of the true believer to accept even the most gossamer-light claims of his superiors. At this point in the war, it was becoming difficult enough for many German soldiers to resist with the sole hope of preserving the soil of the *Vaterland*. To think in terms of victory was the mark of callow boys stuffed with propaganda or fanatics divorced from realism.

McCown's memoir of his time in captivity, however, also included what would later be regarded as a significant statement about the conduct of *Kampfgruppe Peiper*. "Concerning treatment of prisoners by the SS, I can state that at no time were the prisoners of this organization mistreated. Food was scarce but it was nearly as good as that used by the Germans themselves. The American prisoners were always given cellar space to protect them from the exceedingly heavy American artillery barrages. I was taken briefly to the main prisoner enclosure, which was a large, two-room, well-constructed cellar. The men were considerably overcrowded and were allowing the guards to bully them a little. I organized the entire group of some 130 into sections, appointed a first sergeant and laid down a few rules concerning rotation sleeping, urinating, equality and distribution of food, and got the German warrant officer in charge settled upon a fairer method of giving water to prisoners and providing ventilation."

McCown himself was segregated with four other officers in a smaller cellar. The American shelling drove their five guards down into the tiny quarters. On the afternoon of December 22, a 105-mm round scored a direct hit on the wall, hurling the German sitting next to McCown halfway across the room. Two U.S. lieutenants helped pull the guard from beneath the rubble. But a few moments later, a second explosion showered the inhabitants with shrapnel, killing one of the U.S. officers and wounding three Germans. One of them died in spite of first aid.

Otto Skorzeny's Operation *Greif* never even chalked up the early successes of the now bogged-down *Kampfgruppe Peiper*. The scheme for disguised commandos, for all of its imagination, derring-do and paper potential, actually proved only a slight annoyance in itself. But the awareness that Germans might be masquerading as Americans manufactured considerable mischief, some of it fatal.

There was talk of a coup by sixty infiltrators who would gather at the Café de la Paix in Paris and meet with German sympathizers who could furnish information on Eisenhower's movements and then either assassinate or kidnap him.

U.S. military intelligence notified various commands, "Interrogation of prisoners of war indicates from two different SS sources that Skorzeny led small groups through the lines with six vehicles, presumably command cars. They were carrying forged letters of recommendation and identification papers, wearing English uniforms. Interview with Gen. Eisenhower will be attempted by the party. They will use the cover story that they have returned from the front and have vital information regarding operations and an attempt on general's life. Possibility exists that a change of vehicles may be made before reaching Paris for the purpose of covering their tracks. It is possible that they may have one officer with them in German uniform, claiming that they are taking him to higher headquarters."

Skorzeny had never scripted a plot of this nature. But the rumor was strong enough for the U.S. command to wrap Eisenhower in a cocoon of armored vehicles and a personal bodyguard wherever he went. The arrangements annoyed Ike, who relished opportunities to personally visit American units and chat with soldiers.

By December 20, aides had taken the precaution of changing Bradley's hotel room, removing plates from his jeep indicating his rank and covering over the stars decorating his helmet.

Orders for strict security discomfited the high and mighty, as MPs, perhaps enjoying an unchallengeable right to play cat and mouse with the brass, entrapped the likes of Omar Bradley, Field Marshall Bernard Montgomery and Gen. Bruce Clarke. Bradley said, "Three times I was ordered to prove my identity by cautious GIs. The first time by identifying Springfield as the capital of Illinois (my questioner held out for Chicago); the second time by locating the guard between the center and tackle on a line of scrimmage; the third time by naming the then-current spouse of a blonde named Betty Grable. Grable stopped me [the correct answer was bandleader Harry James] but the sentry did not. Pleased at having stopped me, he nevertheless passed me on."

Montgomery, when halted, imperiously directed his driver to ignore the sentry. The guards shot out the tires of his car and held the British commander for several hours. When he heard of the incident, Eisenhower enjoyed one of his few laughs during the Bulge, remarking that Skorzeny had achieved at least one memorable service. Clarke also spent an uncomfortable time locked up until he could establish his bona fides.

The grim side of the obsession with infiltrators was quick trigger fingers. A German refugee who found a home in the U.S. and became a soldier assigned to interrogate prisoners correctly responded to the request for the password. But because he retained the accent of his native tongue, the fearful sentry instantly shot him dead. It was not an isolated incident.

On December 17, one day into the offensive, suspicious African-American MPs stopped a jeep at Aywaille, on a bridge across the Amblève River. They challenged the trio of soldiers in the vehicle for the password, but none of them knew it. The riders produced identification as Pfc.s Charles W. Lawrence, George Sensenbach and Clarence van der Werth. The suspicious MPs searched the jeep. Tucked away under the seat, they discovered a wad of $900 in U.S. currency and one thousand British pound notes. To add to the suspicions of the roadblock sentries, the jeep also carried a variety of pistols, plastic explosives, half a dozen American grenades, a radio transmitter and some peculiar cigarette lighters.

A personal search turned up German paybooks. The occupants of the jeep broke down and admitted they were neither deserters nor civilian black marketeers but members of an elite German unit. They gave their actual names, Gunter Billing, Wilhelm Schmidt and Manfred Pernass. Schmidt, in fact, passed on the rumor that others from *Greif,* led by Skorzeny, were intent on capturing or murdering Eisenhower.

The trio was removed to the Henri Chapelle barracks, fifteen miles from Liège, to face a military court. The verdict was swift and the sentence summary. For venturing behind the Allied lines in American uniforms, they were considered to be spies and to be executed by a firing squad six days after their capture. On the evening before the judgment was to be carried out, they perhaps drew some solace from *Wehrmacht* nurses, imprisoned next door, singing Christmas carols.

In June 1944, the Allies issued regulations to cover the "Procedure for Military Executions: At the designated time the prisoner, accompanied by the chaplain, will be removed by the prisoner guard . . . The escort will then proceed toward the scene of the execution, the band playing the 'Dead March.' " No musicians attended this execution.

Veteran British correspondent Richard McMillan witnessed

their deaths on an intensely cold morning. "The firing squad shuffled in the snow, their rifles ready. They did not look at one another and they seemed very white of face, and when they spoke it was rather haltingly, as if something stuck in the throat, as it surely did. Because they were so constrained, few spoke, but one was more garrulous and spat from time to time and repeated:

"'Why should they give us this ****?' using a coarse American oath.

"The American padre [Col. P. Schroder] had come out, just ahead of the condemned. Then walked the three men. With their guards, they marched, head high, to the . . . shooting posts . . .

"The three men marched in slow military step down the path from their detention room. Their American uniforms discarded for an adaptation of fatigue dress (rather like a convict's garb, it seemed), they looked blue with cold—or was it the imminence of sudden death? They must have seen the firing-squad—they could not help it—but they looked not at all at it. They marched on in step.

"One, the first, was tall and thin, almost cadaverous [*Unteroffizier* Manfred Pernass], and his hair was black and awry. The second [*Oberfähnrich* Gunter Billing], blue eyes unblinking through his spectacles. The third [*Gefreiter* Wilhelm Schmidt] had nothing particular to distinguish him—meek and rather insignificant he looked.

"The first German looked hard at the ground during those suspensive seconds as the three passed in front of the waiting firing-party. He looked at the ground, we soon realized, for one reason only. He wanted to die like a soldier. At least, that was our guess. He could not understand English, could not understand the orders given to the guard 'right turn' and 'left turn' so he watched their feet. As the guard turned to the right or left, he was ready. Smartly, he swung round." Briton McMillan apparently did not know that in the U.S. Army the commands, instead of using the word "turn," employ "face."

"The condemned men came to the stakes. The first in line came abreast of the left-hand stake, passed on past the second stake and came almost in line with the third. His eyes watched his guards' feet. Their officer gave an order. They left turned. Smartly, the first of the condemned did the same. His gaze now faced the post. He walked steadily to it, turned his back to it, put his hands behind him. Calmly, he placed them behind the post. He waited there for them to tie him. The other two walked to their places. Soon the three were tied."

At this point, Chaplain Schroder, in a long overcoat and steel helmet, approached the trio. With half a dozen fieldjacketed MPs in steel helmets a step behind the Germans, Colonel Schroder offered a blessing and made the sign of the cross.

The chaplain later informed McMillan the trio had told him, "They did not require my aid to speak to their God. They could address themselves to him if they wished, directly."

McMillan wrote, "Then they were blindfolded. Black masks were placed around their eyes. Billing did not move or blink as they removed his glasses. But he blinked as the feeble sun came through."

Capt. J. Eiser, a doctor with the 633rd Medical Clearing Station, pinned four-inch white aiming marks on their shirts, over their hearts.

"No one said a word now," McMillan wrote. "The wind rustled the hedges. Under the feet of the restless shooting-squad, the snow crunched. All was now ready.

"Prepare the execution!" The order came in a clear, firm voice from the officer in command.

"He was a captain, youngish, very efficient. He belonged to the Military Police. A man used to tough assignments. What were his sensations? His lips were tight and he looked not at the shooting-posts. We could guess he, too, was tense. But it was his duty.

"The young captain gave another command. The firing-party raised their rifles.

" 'Ready!'

"A brief pause, a few seconds only. Silence, an awful silence. A piping voice broke it. It was Billing. Obviously by prearrangement between the three he had been chosen as the one to speak, to utter the last word to the world they were about to leave.

"His words came clear and steady in German: '*Es lebe unser Führer, Adolf Hitler.*' [Long live our leader, Adolf Hitler.]

"Not another sound. The other two stood straight and mute, tied. Straightest, sturdiest, though smallest of all, stood Billing.

" 'Fire!' the officer cried."

Twelve M–1s, four rifles apiece, targeted each of the condemned. After perhaps fifteen seconds, the bodies began to slump, then loll from side to side. Their heads fell forward as blood gushed in the snow.

They were buried in a temporary cemetery. After V-E Day, the bodies were transferred to a massive German military burial grounds, among 39,000 other fallen soldiers.

The paratroopers led by Colonel Heydte in Operation *Hohes Venn* inflicted even less tactical damage than the members of *Greif*. The rumors of a drop near Liège mentioned by Eisenhower's secretary quickly proved erroneous, and American intelligence, after interrogation of the first chutists captured, realized Heydte and his people posed no major threat.

Although *Auk* bagged about thirty GI prisoners—solitary message-bearers or GIs traveling in groups of no more than two or three—and destroyed a few light vehicles, Heydte's circumstances prevented him from capitalizing on his minor victories. He soon released his first batch of prisoners, giving them custody of his own injured and wounded.

Within two days, his resources quickly petered out. "Each paratrooper brought with him only enough food for twenty-four hours, which at best could be stretched to last for forty-eight hours. Probably only a few men actually did so. For each machine gun there were only four boxes of ammunition, enough only for a single engagement. Almost all of the ammunition carriers had been lost in the airdrop.

"From the night of December 16 to the evening of December 19, we received almost no food or ammunition from the air. We recognized only a single attempt to resupply by a few aircraft during the night of December 18. Only a few containers were retrieved and those held mostly nonessential items, cigarettes and fresh water—the Hohes Venn Mountains abound in fresh water.

"On December 19, I realized I could not hold the *Kampfgruppe* together for longer than one or at the very most two days. I could only carry out a single engagement, after which the ammunition for the machine guns would be exhausted. In one or two days the men would be badly weakened from hunger and cold. Originally I had intended to fight this single action to open the Eupen–Malmédy road just before the approaching German armored point reached our hiding place. But the Sixth SS Panzer Army's attack apparently had bogged down. I decided to abandon my original mission and break through to the German lines. The single action possible would be fought not for the Eupen–Malmédy road but for the road leading towards the east." Heydte released the remainder of his prisoners and left with them one of his severely injured casualties.

"About midnight between December 19 and 20, we reached the 'Helle,' a stream running towards Eupen; its icy waters reached up to our hips. While climbing the hill on the opposite side, we encountered a line of American sentries. A few shots were fired and one of our men was seriously wounded."

Heydte withdrew to the west bank of the creek, seeking to avoid a nighttime engagement in uncharted woods against an enemy whose strength he could not estimate. When morning arrived, he saw American reconnaissance patrols picking their way across steep slopes on the east bank of the stream, searching for his troops. A scout for the *Kampfgruppe* reported American tanks approaching along a clearing directly towards their hideout.

"Faced with this situation and with the ever-decreasing fighting strength of my hungry, shivering men, I decided at noon on December 20 to disband the task force. I gave orders for the entire unit to split up into groups of three and to strike out for the German lines to the east. Unnoticed by the American patrols, the men proceeded to slip quietly from the position." About one third of the ragged band, perhaps one hundred of the original contingent that made up the *Hohes Venn* force, actually managed to reach the *Wehrmacht* positions.

Heydte, however, was not among them. "On the morning of December 21, after a tiring night tramp through forests and swamps, I reached the embankment of the rail line between Monschau and St. Vith. My executive officer and personal runner accompanied me. We slept the rest of the day in some dense undergrowth next to the rail line. In the evening we continued toward Monschau, crossing the Roer River.

"Upon reaching Monschau, I left my companions and hid myself in one of the first houses at the outskirts of the town. Completely exhausted, mentally and physically, I was taken prisoner by the Americans on the morning of December 22."

His official account, taken by interrogators after the war, omits a significant detail. Still nursing the painful broken arm with which he made the jump, he also froze his feet during the few days of the operation. He was not discovered in a house-to-house search, however. The worn-out colonel, instead, actually sent a note to the Americans advising them he would surrender. His captors were soldiers from the 395th Regiment, Cap Capalbo's alma mater.

While Heydte slept his final day of freedom on December 21, Otto Skorzeny's 150 Brigade on the outskirts of Malmédy anted up its 3,500 soldiers in a futile, blunderbuss strike against (presumably) numerically weaker Americans. The disastrous miscalculation was based upon the earlier infiltration of the town by *Greif* commandos. They visited Malmédy during the first days of the breakthrough and reported only a handful of Americans present. But since then, close to four battalions of infantrymen, backed by another in reserve, artillery and antitank outfits had reinforced the combat engineers headed by Dave Pergrin.

Skorzeny, aware that his small band of operatives in American uniforms could not hope to fulfill Hitler's dream of seizing the Meuse River bridges, had offered his brigade for a conventional role. Sepp Dietrich, in charge of the Sixth SS Panzer Army, handed the troops to a 1st SS Panzer Division colonel, preparing to storm Malmédy. Seizure of the town would open up a roadnet for resupply of *Kampfgruppe Peiper.*

At 3:30 A.M. about 120 Germans advanced on a pathway that included the Five Points intersection of Baugnez, where the Malmédy massacre occurred. Unfortunately for the enemy, a soldier captured the day before revealed the schedule for the onslaught. A mine blew up the lead halftrack and the alert defenders slaughtered the infantrymen. The lifting of the morning fog displayed a mass of German corpses, most of whom wore all or parts of U.S. uniforms.

Some time after midnight, Frank Currey, of Company K, 120th Infantry Regiment, 30th Division, readied his BAR from a position on the edge of Malmédy. "Just before daylight, their tanks overran the tank destroyers and antitank weapons and we withdrew to a factory. The place had been used as a military hospital [it was the building to which the ambulance carried Carmen Capalbo almost a week earlier] but all of the personnel had pulled out. The operating tables, the instruments; everything had been left behind, including the Christmas presents mailed to the doctors.

"Adam Lucero and I ducked some small arms fire from German infantrymen nearby and a couple of tanks to get some bazooka rockets and antitank grenades from a smashed antitank halftrack.

I aimed the bazooka at a tank and it was a lucky hit, struck where the turret joined the chassis.

"We saw some enemy soldiers in the doorway of a house and I managed to knock all three down with bursts from the BAR. While other guys covered me, I used the bazooka to wreck part of the wall for the house. From where I stood, I now could see a bunch of GIs pinned down by three enemy tanks a couple of hundred feet away.

"I started firing the grenades at the tanks. The antitank grenades couldn't do much damage but they make a helluva lot of noise and smoke. The crews probably thought they were on fire and all three abandoned their tanks and fled into the house. The GIs I had seen still couldn't get away. Now I climbed onto the halftrack and used its machine gun on the house."

When the enemy stubbornly refused to back off, Currey shifted to another machine gun whose crew had been killed. He poured another fusillade into the shattered building and the Germans finally retreated, allowing the quintet of Americans to reach safety. Although hostile fire spattered all about them, Currey and Lucero picked up two wounded Americans and drove them back to the regimental aid station. All of this action stretched over a period of about twenty-four hours. In recognition of Currey's valor and contribution to the defense of Malmédy, his superiors wrote him up for a Congressional Medal of Honor which he received in August 1945. But that would come eight months in the future. A few weeks later, Currey would face what he considers an even greater threat.

The 150 Brigade actually outflanked the men of Currey's Company K and some of Pergrin's engineers. But they could not exploit their advance after losing four tanks to Currey plus several others to tank destroyer missiles and mines.

The 1st SS Panzer Division strategy consisted of a two-pronged attack. To the right flank of the column that struck at Frank Currey and the 120th Infantry Regiment marched a heavier concentration. It foundered on a railroad embankment that provided plentiful cover for the Americans. The killing field numbered 500 enemy dead from small arms and artillery. The attackers retreated.

The Americans inflicted some of the heavy damage upon the enemy with a new element in the arsenal, the VT or POZIT fuse on artillery shells. Commonly known as the "proximity fuse," it detonated when close to the target. While some military historians credit the device with reversing the German tide during the Ardennes campaign, no less an expert than 82nd Airborne commander James Gavin considered it an overvalued toy whose chief accomplishment was to strip the branches off trees. Alone it did not defeat the Nazi armies but, on the other hand, the VT added to the damage.

Far more potent was the "Time On Target" (TOT) tactic developed by American artillery. In a TOT barrage, the shells from all of the field pieces arrived simultaneously, irrespective of their distance from a target, their caliber, their muzzle velocity or range. The effect was devastating in intensity and it prevented the enemy from shifting positions between bursts.

A frustrated Skorzeny, forbidden by *der Führer* to jeopardize himself by participating in engagements, observed the action in front of Malmédy. He met members of his brigade as, in total disarray, they careened back to the protection of their own lines. His closest associate, Adrian von Foelkersam, arrived, limping from a bullet wound in his backside, bloody testimony to a pell-mell retreat. Skorzeny set out for division headquarters now at Ligneuville.

"I heard the sound of shells dropping. I leaped out of the car just as it hit an oncoming truck. I felt my face very flush, blood running down my face. I thought I'd lost my eye but I felt it still in its socket. But above the right eye, I could feel loose shreds of flesh." Doctors stitched the wound tight until surgeons could perform proper repair. On New Year's Eve, Hitler awarded him the Mention clasp of the German Army for his Malmédy efforts. But within a few days, the leavings of the 150th Brigade disbanded for assignment elsewhere. And the High Command posted Skorzeny to the Eastern front.

The 62nd *Volksgrenadier* Division, a re-creation of an outfit annihilated in the Eastern front meat grinder, having pushed the American 424th Infantry Regiment back, tangled with the 27th Armored Infantry and Glen Strange, the Oklahoman from the blackjack and sand country.

Strange's battalion, yielding to the fury of the grenadiers, had withdrawn deeper into Belgium. On the night of December 21, as a heavy snow started to close in the area, the CP bedded down in a house at Neubrueck. Strange fell asleep. "Shortly after daylight, our communications officer awakened me and said we were being attacked. I immediately went to the windows and realized we were under heavy fire. Some German soldiers lay dead just outside the back door. Lt. Col. Fred Cummings, the battalion commander, and I ran out that back door and retrieved a .30-caliber machine gun from a halftrack. I carried some ammo up the stairs and Major Deevers and Colonel Cummings manned the machine gun, killing maybe twenty of the enemy attacking us from the rear and the woods.

"I thought I could get some help from the 14th Tank Battalion, which was only 200 yards away. But because it was snowing so hard, they could not see what was happening. We had lost radio communication and when I couldn't reach the tanks, I rushed back into the house, thinking we still had the situation in hand. I did not know that an SS captain and several other enemy troops had reached the basement, throwing hand grenades. When Colonel Cummings went to investigate, they captured him. And when I burst back into the place, the first thing I saw was Cummings coming up from the basement with the SS captain and about a dozen other Germans.

"'Captain Strange, throw down your gun. We have surrendered,' said the colonel. As I dumped my carbine and .45 pistol, the SS captain threw up his right hand in a Nazi salute and said, 'Heil Hitler.'

"I don't know what impulse came over me but I answered, 'Fuck Hitler!' The officer spoke excellent English, apparently, because he smacked me on the jaw with his right fist; he held a pistol in his other hand. He damn near knocked me out and stripped me of my wristwatch.

"There were a lot of German and American wounded and the SS captain told us to move them all to the basement and send for our medics. Our doctor, Paul Russomano, whom I accompanied when he delivered a baby for a local civilian just before the Bulge, arrived with his staff to treat the men who were hurt.

"The German officer apparently realized he could not occupy the position long unless reinforcements came soon. He decided to keep Colonel Cummings and a few others in the house with the medical boys. The rest of us, twenty to thirty, were herded out the front door to be marched back. There were only about five guards. The rest of the Germans were in the house.

"Outside, as they lined us up, my S–2, T. Sgt. George Griesenger, who spoke German, whispered to me, 'Captain, let's take them right now. We can overpower them and some of us will get away.' It was a tempting idea, and I still had on me a present from my brother-in-law, a razor sharp knife shaped like a dagger, with the sheath pushed around to my back and covered by my combat jacket. He was right and I often wish we would have made our move at this time. But I was worried that they might have automatic weapons trained on us from inside. And I felt we must obey Colonel Cummings and so I told him the time was not right. George was a friend and a helluva good soldier. Because he was of German parentage, he suffered horribly in a prison camp. A number of the others died from wounds or mistreatment.

"As we started down the same trail that brought us to Neubrueck, I lagged behind as much as I could. One German soldier stayed back with me, prodding me to keep up. The snow had let up a bit and the 14th's tanks could see us. They had received word we were in trouble and figured the column was German infantry because they opened fire with machine guns. We all hit the ground.

"My guard was a young German soldier with a burp gun. Both of us had rolled under a halftrack for protection. He was laying on his gun with its muzzle pointed at me. I don't know if he had his finger on the trigger or not. But I was able to get my knife free. It is not something I want to talk about.

"I rolled out from underneath the vehicle, which was only about five yards from the bank of the Braunlauf Creek and I tumbled down into the water. It was only a small stream, maybe three or four feet wide and not too deep. Ice floated in the current but I did not even feel the cold. I was angry, scared, my heart beating like mad. I figured I would be shot at any moment.

"I came up out of the creek on the other side of the house, across the road and headed toward town to find some troops. I figured we might be able to recapture the CP with our wounded and the handful held prisoner there. I met Capt. Samuel March who'd only recently joined the 27th AIB. He carried a .45-caliber grease gun and a .45 pistol, which he gave me. The two of us sneaked down a ditch and trained our guns on a big, gangling Kraut posted at the door of the house. We yelled at him to surrender but he kept motioning for us to come in, with his weapon trained on us. Neither side would budge. We could probably have dropped him but he could also have gotten at least one of us. And there could have been other guns aiming at us.

"An artillery shell or mortar suddenly slammed into the side of the house; shrapnel struck March. I crawled to March, dragged him into the ditch for first aid. But he was dead. Wet, cold and, I think, crying, I climbed a fence, made my way through a woods to the only place I felt I might get help, the 14th Tank Battalion. I assumed our infantry companies had all been wiped out.

"The CO of the 14th, Lt. Col. Leonard Engeman, chewed my ass out for allowing headquarters to be captured and, I believe, for crying while I told him of our fate. He told me that some Americans had been murdered at Malmédy. (He was confused; our guys had been killed at Stavelot.) And I had to go back, recapture the headquarters and free the men and officers there.

" I realize now that Engeman got on my case to bring me back to reality. Engeman made me very angry. Wet and cold as I was, I was ready for anything. I rounded up a couple of dozen of our infantry wandering around, looking for battalion headquarters and someone to tell them what was happening. Engeman detailed some of his tanks to accompany us. Lt. David Duck, a tank platoon leader received the assignment. I knew Duck from our days at Fort Riley, Kansas, when we would occasionally meet at the Officers Club to down a few. He encouraged, 'Come on, Glen. We'll get them bastards and your men back.' We loaded up the GIs on the tanks and set off.

"Going down a hill, German tanks tried to take us. We lost two Shermans in a helluva tank battle, but forced them to withdraw. Lieutenant Duck and I, with some men, continued to the headquarters building. I rode on the back of Duck's tank, talking to him part of the time through a small hatch on the rear of the turret. He blasted a truck outside and it started to burn. He put several rounds into the roof of the house, and then laid down some smoke to cover me and the infantrymen who moved right up to the building. Lo and behold, they stuck a white flag out the door.

"I shouted for the Americans inside to take the enemy weapons and for everyone to come up from the basement where they were all hiding. Cummings, Deevers and the other Americans, carrying the weapons, escorted their prisoners outside. The SS captain was no longer there. I wanted to kill him but there was a lower ranking SS officer on hand. I kicked hell out of his shins."

The 27th AIB reorganized itself, setting up a new CP and, since Neubrueck itself now seemed a lost cause, the remnants of the combat command deployed on a line to the west. Strange led a party that salvaged supplies and equipment from the town. He also volunteered to head a sorty that sought to liberate his friend Dr. Paul Russomano. In the course of his forays, an artillery round imbedded fragments in his hip. Again, he did not bother to seek medical attention.

When the Germans first overran the CP, they had taken Russomano to minister to the wounded. In the melees that followed, his captors freed him to drive an ambulance, flying the Geneva Red Cross flag, back to the aid station he ran in Neubrueck, a village temporarily deserted by both sides. He discovered a building packed with wounded Americans and no way to remove them. "Having returned from the German lines, I found too many casualties. I could not leave them stranded. My duty as a doctor and loyalty to my buddies demanded I remain with them until provisions for evacuating them became available." Unfortunately, the enemy returned to control Neubrueck. Russomano spent several months as a prisoner.

Chapter X

HIGH WATER MARKS

A MOTLEY OF GERMAN troops, some in standard field gray, some wearing white snow camouflage garments, and still others dressed in pieces of American uniforms with boots stripped from prisoners or yanked from dead men's feet, battered the GIs ensconced along Elsenborn Ridge on the northern shoulder of the German salient. The Germans brought to bear whatever armor and artillery they could muster. Victory here would open up a northern road route to the Meuse.

The Americans enjoyed the advantage of favorable terrain to entrench the troops and an ever-increasing superiority of artillery. Ben Nawrocki, with the handful of men left from B Company, labored over his foxhole along the crest of the ridge. "We had only our rifles and the ammo we could carry. The ground was frozen hard, like rock. There weren't any entrenching tools. We used mess kits, mess knives, bayonets and helmets to dig in. It was frantic, hard work, but with shells flying all the time, we had to have shelter.

"We could see them shelling and attacking to our right rear in the Malmédy–St. Vith area. They were coming at us through the deep draws leading to Elsenborn Ridge. We kept beating them off. We had a good open field of fire and a lot of artillery to help us. A day or two after the 99th dug in on Elsenborn Ridge, two hundred Germans with tanks came toward our lines. The 394th Regiment was in front. The Germans carried their arms in sling position on their shoulders and waved white handkerchief flags as if to signal surrender. They were told to drop their arms. They refused and kept coming. Obviously they wanted to get closer and overrun us.

"Our officers readied all our firepower along with artillery. After they didn't respond to repeated demands to drop arms and surrender, all of the firepower on the front opened up. They tried to and did run over some of the foxholes with their tanks. But our firepower and artillery really chewed them up. There were pieces

257

of bodies and tanks flying all over. When the fire lifted, nothing moved. They all died. The tanks and equipment destroyed."

The only surviving platoon sergeant from his company, Nawrocki became first sergeant. "I made my first morning report on a piece of toilet paper on December 21. It accounted for one officer and thirteen men of Co. B, 393rd Infantry. We had 210 men on the morning of December 16th. Later, we started to get back some of Co. B who had mixed in with other troops and fought. But there still weren't many left.

"We received replacements almost daily. One batch of about fifty arrived, flown to Europe from the States. Some had very little training. I told them to dig in and they just stood there in the open when a few rounds of 88s struck nearby, wounding six. The rest started to dig in, as we used sticks of dynamite to break through the frozen crust."

The U.S. big guns continued to exact a huge toll. On December 21, they dumped a cloudburst of 10,000 rounds. The German dead piled up in awesome numbers; an early count by a Graves Registration unit added up 782 corpses in the Elsenborn area. Furthermore, as the enemy backed off from its assault that day, it left behind the broken remains of forty-seven tanks and tank destroyers.

The stalwart efforts of the 1st Division squelched a pivotal series of assaults around the village of Butgenbach. The Big Red One was the most battle-experienced American outfit, having started in North Africa, landed in Sicily and Normandy, fought in the Huertgen Forest and won the first city on German soil, Aachen. The combat savvy, however, cost enormous amounts of humanity. Much of the 1st Division, by the time of the Ardennes, consisted of replacements brought in since the first North African beachhead.

At Dom Butgenbach, two miles south of the town of Butgenbach, members of the division's 26th Infantry Antitank Company, wielding their underpowered, undersized, 57-mm cannons, blew away a number of tanks. In particular, Cpl. Henry "Red" Warner, a gunner, steadfastly manned his weapon as Panzers, accompanied by foot soldiers, bore down upon him. Warner put four shells into the first tank of a trio, setting it ablaze. Three more rounds destroyed a second tank. A third hove into sight, training its machine guns on Warner's crew, who dove into their foxholes. Meanwhile, Warner wrestled with a balky breechblock. The German armor poked forward, until it halted only ten feet off. Its commander popped the turret and stuck his head out, the better to aim at the stubborn Warner. The gunner saw the enemy appear, pulled his .45 pistol and squeezed off a couple of quick shots before burrowing into his gun pit, hoping not to be crushed when the Panther rolled over the emplacement.

Warner heard the driver gun the motor and the tank tracked towards him. Just as it was about to crush the 57-mm cannon, and perhaps Warner, the driver reversed gears. The tank backed off. Warner stole a peek in the early morning fog. The vehicle's commander lay slumped over the turret where a bullet from the corporal's .45 struck him. The crew, apparently confused by the death of its leader, decided to retreat.

On the following day, enemy forces again attempted to overwhelm the antitankers. A gun squad commanded by S. Sgt. Noah Collier took on an attack by infantrymen and tanks. Collier retrieved a BAR dropped by two wounded soldiers from the 1st Division and sprayed the advancing troops. They came supported by two more tanks. Gunner Irwin Schwartz crippled one with an armor-piercing round smashing the left track and then set it aflame with a second round into the side.

Schwartz and his assistant gunner, Donald Rose, then used an M–1 and a carbine to add firepower. But another tank rumbled up. Schwartz dropped his rifle and plugged the Panzer with three deadly shots from his cannon. When a hit on their 57 rendered it inoperable, the crew slowly retreated, hurling grenades and using their small arms until down to their last rounds.

Another antitank unit halted an enemy tank using a bazooka. A huge 150-mm self-propelled piece also fell victim to the sharpshooting antitank men. However, Red Warner, who escaped the day before, now ran out of luck. He had scored a hit on a tank but it remained capable of firing. Its machine gun killed him. But because of his efforts and those of his colleagues, plus riflemen from the 2nd Battalion, Butgenbach remained in U.S. hands, protecting the vital Elsenborn Ridge. Eventually, a posthumous Congressional Medal of Honor was awarded to Warner.

The veteran U.S. 9th Division added its forces to the strength along the northern shoulder. The Germans, although they would try one more massive but futile attack, could not fracture the line. In that direction, they would advance no further.

However, to the immediate south of the stalled elements of

Sepp Dietrich's Sixth SS Panzer Army, the situation threatened disaster for the Americans. While the skirmishes along the Salm River blocked passage west for *Kampfgruppe Peiper* as the 82nd Airborne, in conjunction with the 30th Division, applied increasing pressure, SS Panzers and Volksgrenadiers from Manteuffel's army rapidly exploited their breakthrough of the line manned by elements of the 106th and 28th Divisions. They swept on a west-northwest course that would both widen and deepen the bulge.

Falling back before the onslaught was Sgt. Barney Alford of the 589th FA with the three 105 mm howitzers that he, Eric Wood and other gun crew members saved before the truck bearing the lieutenant came a cropper on the outskirts of Schönberg. Maj. Arthur C. Parker III now commanded the battalion, whose entire arsenal consisted of those three guns. The strategists behind the front lines had located an intersection of N 15, the main highway north from Bastogne to Liège, with another well-surfaced road carrying traffic south to the Swiss border. Arteries of supply for the Americans, both routes also enabled GIs to escape encirclement. Capture of the crossroads would grant the enemy easier access to its objectives. In addition, the intersection anchored a sensitive corridor that joined the 82nd Airborne and the 3rd Armored.

The local people knew the small clump of houses at the junction as Baraque de Fraiture. Parker was told to organize a roadblock at Baraque de Fraiture with his meager artillery. He dutifully obeyed orders, enlisted the remnants of the battalion's service troops to provide a perimeter infantry defense. A detachment from the 203rd Antiaircraft Battalion, toting some multiple .50-caliber machine guns and a single 37-mm cannon, fell back to the roadblock. Parker invited them to join him and they accepted his offer. A platoon from the 87th Recon Squad, a piece of the 7th Armored appeared, and they too were recruited. The first troops in place, those of the 589th, abandoned attempts to properly pronounce the official name of the place and started to call the site ''Parker's Crossroads.''

Whatever its name, the reinforcements of the Americans were paltry considering the opposition, the elite 2nd SS Panzer Division which, in spite of heavy losses six months earlier at Normandy, retained a strong cadre of veterans and packed plenty of armor. Alongside the Panzers, the 560th *Volksgrenadier* Division consisted of less well trained infantrymen, but they alone far outnumbered the defenders. When the enemy squandered an eighty-man patrol that wandered up the road into a hail of machine gun and artillery fire, it was a victory for the defenders. But the skirmish indicated just how sizable a foe they faced.

On December 21, a mortar round during an afternoon barrage seriously wounded Parker. He tried to continue directing the defense but he lapsed into unconsciousness. Maj. Elliot Goldstein took charge. Barney Alford, in command of one howitzer, continued to bombard targets selected by observers.

As the German tide flowed around St. Vith and Bastogne towards Parker's Crossroads, the desperate U.S. commanders tossed in more blue chips. Gen. James Gavin, concerned that the loss of the crossroads could allow the enemy armor his 82nd Airborne held at bay at Trois Ponts to bypass the paratroopers and the soldiers pulling back from St. Vith, typically made his own personal reconnaissance.

"Quite a number of armored vehicles were in the vicinity of Manhay and some were on the ridge one and a half miles south. The 3rd Armored Division CP was in Manhay, and a conversation with the division commander made it apparent they were incapable of committing sufficient strength to the crossroads to guarantee retention by our troops."

As a result of his survey, Gavin dispatched the 2nd Battalion of the 82nd Airborne's 325th Glider Regiment to strengthen the defenses. Company F, led by Capt. Junior Woodruff, drew the major assigment for the defense. Since Woodruff commanded the only complete tactical unit on the scene, he assumed direction for the overall strategy. To the GIs from the 325th, the battlefield now became known as "Woody's Crossroads." Some of Woodruff's GIs took instant courses in the operation of the weapons shared with nine other fragmented outfits. They learned to operate AA guns, the 75-mms on the tanks and the 76-mms of tank destroyers.

"Captain Woody was a fine officer in both garrison and combat," remembers Joe Colmer, the ex-navy man who found himself drafted into the army and a member of Company F. "He was a natural leader and the kind of guy you wanted to follow. His people had such faith in him that, while we were in Holland, there was a fellow close to me who had his arm blown off. I gave him his shot of morphine but he asked me to tell Woody to come talk to him. Most guys in his shape would have been hollering for a medic instead.

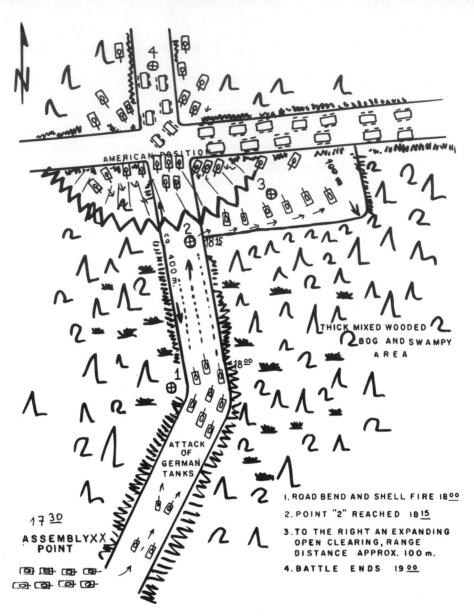

AMERICAN POSITION

THICK MIXED WOODED
BOG AND SWAMPY
AREA

ATTACK
OF
GERMAN
TANKS

1730

ASSEMBLY XX
POINT

1. ROAD BEND AND SHELL FIRE 18⁰⁰

2. POINT "2" REACHED 18¹⁵

3. TO THE RIGHT AN EXPANDING
OPEN CLEARING, RANGE
DISTANCE APPROX. 100 m.

4. BATTLE ENDS 19⁰⁰

Horst Gresiak, who led a company of German tanks that overwhelmed the American defenders at the critical Baraque de Fraiture crossroads, drew this map of the scene which shows the panzer assault from the south. Joe Colmer, as a member of Co. F, 325th Glider Infantry Regiment, places his position in a farm house to the left, just below the east-west highway over which U.S. truck traffic fled the German breakthrough. Leonard Weinstein with Co. G was on the other side of the same road. Colmer says there were far fewer U.S. tanks than depicted. The Germans exploited their success by driving north, where they wiped out most of the Co. C armor from the 40th Tank Battalion, including Jerry Nelson's Sherman.

"When we moved into the crossroads, around noon of December 22, there were only a few troops around, a couple of Sherman tanks and some halftracks. The soldiers were mostly from the 106th and they struck me as really tired and beaten. My platoon dug foxholes in an arc around the farmhouses from the northwest to southeast, about fifty yards out front. It was fairly quiet that night. The next morning, however, the Germans began dropping occasional mortar rounds, a few artillery shells, and stepped up their probes with patrols."

Along with Woodruff's crew, Companies E and G also assumed responsibility for holding the crossroads, backing up those at the pivot point from a ridge three-quarters of a mile to the northeast. Leonard Weinstein, whose minor surgery saved him from Operation Market Garden, was in G Company as it hiked down an almost impassable trail choked with rocks, thick roots and mud. "Our positions were basically two lines of foxholes. There were no hot meals and we rotated, taking turns to go back to a nearby small building where you could warm up before a small fire they kept going.

"I was in the second line of foxholes on slightly higher ground. One night the enemy slipped in close enough to the first line to kill two of our men with either a bayonet or knife. The victims were the oldest and youngest guys in the company who occupied a single hole." Obviously, the entire U.S. contingent holding Baraque de Fraiture was in danger of being surrounded.

Gavin again gave the scene his personal attention. He was dismayed by what he saw, in spite of his best efforts. "I checked the troops on the Fraiture ridge. The riflemen were 100 to 200 yards apart. There was little in the way of antitank defense." Gavin ventured into Fraiture to the CP of the 2nd Battalion commander where he witnessed a hail of mortars and small arms. He heard a message radioed by Woodruff of an all-out attack by a regiment of the 2nd SS Panzers.

Combat Command A of the 7th Armored Division, the outfit that include the 40th Tank Battalion, with gunner Jerry Nelson, committed a platoon from the 643rd Tank Destroyer Battalion (Towed). The unit of four three-inch guns pulled by halftracks and forty crewmen faced its combat debut. When some 3rd Armored Divsion Sherman tanks, headed in the opposite direction, passed the tank destroyers, ammunition handler Edgar Kreft heard one of the men on the Shermans holler there was "nobody between you and the Germans." The platoon reached its assigned spot and dug in. At dawn, the enemy blanketed the hapless antitank crews with mortars and artillery, killing and wounding a number of men. Permission to fall back was delayed until German grenadiers over-ran the Americans, who lost eighteen killed, wounded and miss-ing. Kreft became a PW.

Actually, the Germans were poised to overwhelm the small gar-rison for two days. Only an acute shortage of fuel for their half-tracks and other armor delayed the launch. But supplies arrived on the night of December 22, within hours after Colmer and Weinstein put in their appearances.

The German soldiers, like their adversaries, were nearly running on empty. Getting to the scene had been "a long exhausting night march," according to SS tank commander Horst Gresiak, then a twenty-four-year-old heavily decorated veteran. "I went at once to regiment," said Gresiak, recalling his arrival in the area. "Head-quarters had ordered, 'Immediately seize and hold the Baraque de Fraiture crossroads.' This order I opposed, since my men were dead tired, had nothing to eat, and I knew nothing of the terrain. My objections were noted and then, with two subordinates, I re-connoitered towards the crossroads. We could see nothing until we worked our way forward and from there had a glimpse into the fortified interior of the crossroads. At first we were able to see three tanks at the juncture. They were dug in, well camouflaged with only the tank cupolas showing. We scouted the area further and recognized more tanks, antitank guns and mounted machine guns. I thought, 'Holy Mother of God! We can't carry out these orders.' "

When the Germans struck the following day, the attack battered the thin ranks of GIs. Alford's gun received credit for blasting a pair of tanks before they exhausted their ammunition. The 589th artillerymen got the word to get out any way they could. Two assaults by foot soldiers were beaten off but the 2nd SS Panzer tanks, in a fierce encounter, devastated the American armor.

Gresiak called the engagement "although brief, the most violent and toughest battle I experienced during the entire war." As he progressed toward the center of the maelstrom, he noted, "In rapid succession from right to left, eight trucks were shot up in flames. Tank turrets flew in the air. It was hell, an inferno. It was like a terrible storm, like the end of the world."

As he reached the crossroads itself, Gresiak looked out upon a junkyard of wrecked, flaming vehicles. "I saw in front, in the darkness, infantry. At first I thought they were German troops." Then he noticed the steel helmets and realized they were Americans, offering to surrender. "I immediately stopped the fire, climbing out of my tank. All that remained for me was a radio communication, 'The crossroads of Baraque de Fraiture is firmly in our hands.'"

"I think it was about five in the afternoon," says Colmer, "when they started the all-out drive. We were completely overrun in thirty minutes. They had our tanks on fire. I was in a barn with three or four others and we were firing out of windows when the place started to burn. We stepped out when the place started to cave in. Someone mentioned the idea of trying to surrender, but from what we could see, they were shooting at everyone. I told the guys they could either try to give up or make a run for it.

"I headed across the road and was hit in the leg. I dove under a blown-down pine tree. Hiding next to me was a man from the 106th. His name was Cook. We lay there for about twenty minutes as the Germans walked all around us. By this time it was getting dark. It had been hazy every day and that decreased visibility also.

"The shooting died down and the Germans began taking their tanks across an open field towards a wooded area about 1,000 yards off. Foot soldiers followed the tanks in small groups of two or three, and the tanks were spread out with spaces of maybe fifty yards or so between each. After the last group passed, Cook and I took off our helmets, turned up our overcoat collars and followed the Germans across the field. Some of the Germans were wearing GI overcoats, so they paid no attention to us. We passed one of our tanks, still burning with its ammo exploding.

"I was limping badly but could still walk. Once we entered the woods, we angled off to our right in the direction of some artillery flashes we took to be friendly. After about two hours, we came upon one of our engineering outfits. They were occupying a barn and some houses. They bandaged my leg, gave us food. We stayed the night with them, then caught a jeep that took us right to the 82nd command post in Spa. I was sent to a hospital and then to England. I never learned what became of Cook." Only forty-four men, including Captain Woodruff and Colmer, from the original

116 in Company F at the crossroads escaped. The rest were KIA or added to the bag of prisoners.

On the same night that Joe Colmer, posing as a German soldier, sneaked to safety, Leonard Weinstein went out on a four-man patrol with Sgt. Woodrow Wilson. "Our mission was to get near the crossroads, observe and report back. We got close enough for a terrifying sight. Enemy tanks had advanced and at least one was firing point-blank at a farmhouse occupied by Company F. The building was ablaze, and we could see in silhouette the gunning down of our troops as they tried to escape the inferno."

By morning, the foxholes to which Weinstein retreated were untenable. "We left our positions, one at a time. While crossing some open ground I was bombed and strafed by a plane. Fortunately, they were all near misses, although fragments bounced off my boots. The depth of the snow varied but in places it was ass-deep. There was plenty of daylight as we made our way through a wooded section. I don't know who spotted the enemy first as they came towards us, but I probably shouted something like, 'Kill those fuckin' Krauts!'

"I fired at one. I can still see that hole in his forehead, from a round out of my M–1. Shortly after, I noticed two Krauts emerging from a foxhole to my right. One had his hands up, his rifle slung. The other was slightly behind him. I believe Chester [Adland] shouted something like 'Let's kill these Kraut bastards!' Chester started jabbering in Norwegian. I reminded him we were supposed to take prisoners if possible. He finally agreed after much arguing, we disarmed them, escorted them to a nearby holding area. Then we caught up with our column. But this firefight at such close quarters turned out to be the last straw for our CO, who'd been in charge since the Normandy campaign.

"We reached what was to be our 'rest area' late in the day or early in the morning.It was a rock-strewn, lightly wooded hillside. We received a few hot meals, a resupply of K rations, no new clothes. You had to sleep up against a tree to avoid sliding downhill. But we were totally exhausted and thankful to be there."

The GIs assembled at the crossroads, enjoined not to retreat, were committed to a hopeless mission. But their sacrifice, like that of Lyle Bouck with his I & R platoon in front of Lanzerath and Col. Tom Riggs's ragtag band atop the Prümerberg in front of St. Vith, bought the time, hours or days that saved tens of thousands of their fellow Americans. Baraque de Fraiture, like many similar engagements in the Ardennes, was a kind of Bunker Hill; the enemy conquered the turf but at an exhorbitant cost. Indeed, Horst Gresiak, awarded a Knight's Cross for his performance, could savor his victory only briefly. On December 24, the skies cleared and U.S. fighter bombers caught him in the open at Baraque de Fraiture. A shell fragment pierced his chest and he would be in need of medical treatment for the wound for nearly fifty years.

The fall of Baraque de Fraiture opened N 15 to maneuvers by the 2nd SS Panzer Division. While it clanked up the highway towards Liège, its companion at the crossroads, the 560th *Volksgrenadiers* continued in the same direction on the left flank. Joining this broad-based front was another Panzer division, the 116th. In their path as the trio surged northwest, lay some tankers from the 7th Armored Division, and a portion of the 3rd Armored Division.

Arnold Albero, a native of Pelham, a New York City suburb, belonged to Task Force Hogan, one of the 3rd Armored Division's roving 400-man units designed by the 3rd's CO, Gen. Maurice Rose, to provide flexibility and deflect thrusts by the enemy. " My father worked as a mason and laborer when I was born in January 1925. I took some interest as the war went on because one brother, as a member of the naval reserve, had been called up even before Pearl Harbor. Eventually, four of the five brothers in my family entered military service.

"After high school, I worked for a company making electrical equipment. My employer obtained a deferment for me but then I saw people looking at me, young, healthy, not in service. I gave up my deferment and was drafted."

Albero learned the trade of tank gunner at Fort Knox after completing the first eight weeks of basic infantry instruction. "Right after this training, I was shipped out. I couldn't believe I was actually on the way to fight. I didn't feel my training was enough. Everything was jammed down your throat. I was to be a replacement and it isn't the same as training with an outfit, working with the same fellows day in, day out. Knowing that they would be your actual buddies makes a big difference. The one thing instilled at Fort Knox was the motto 'Kill or be killed!'

"Replacements in the army were considered bastards. I joined the 3rd Armored at St.-Lô. At the armored school I had qualified as a gunner, but when I joined the division, they said I wasn't good enough. So I became a rifleman, a member of the 83rd Recon, just after its first combat engagement.

"St.-Lô was also my introduction to enemy artillery fire. The intensity of those barrages, the shells screaming through the air, the piercing sound when one came in close, I cannot forget. I was stunned by the ferocity of it all. But the words of encouragement hollered by our noncoms kept me alert, helped me gather my wits and wait it out. It was also terrifying to hear the screams of those hit . . . 'Medic!' 'Medic!' That's when I would become enraged and think only of getting back at them, kill the bastards! I felt alone at first and it took a while before they accepted me. There was Charlie, a corporal who'd been in North Africa. He'd come around at night while you were digging in and talk. He never showed he was scared and it helped. We were the first replacements received and we had to prove ourselves. But eventually you felt the camaraderie build up.

"The days before December 16, we were in Stolberg, Germany, billeted in bombed-out houses. Mostly the food consisted of C or K rations but occasionally the kitchens supplied hot meals. My buddies and I would go back to Verviers to visit friends we had made in September 1944. In fact, I'd lost my T/5 stripes for a visit that wasn't authorized. There was talk about a Christmas party and we were trying to get the Red Cross girls to bring up donuts for us.

"We moved out on December 19 in three columns. I was with the one led by Col. Sam Hogan. I think it must have been the coldest winter in my life. The roads were icy, muddy, the weather foggy in spots and always numbing cold. We lost vehicles that became stuck in the mud and all we could do was just push them to the side. We kept bitching that the column didn't seem to know where it was going. We sure as hell didn't know. On the way we picked up stragglers from other outfits which had been overrun. We also heard rumors that Germans in American uniforms were trying to disrupt our operations. It was a wild and crazy night. When dawn came we were relieved to have daylight but still confused about where we were and what was happening.

"We were now told to head towards Houffalize [a crossroads town on the Ourthe River between Bastogne and Liège] and secure the roads leading to it. But we were beaten back by a good, strong defense and retreated as our gas and ammo ran low. We moved into the town of Beffe, further west. The enemy [the 116th

Panzers] engaged us with tanks, infantry supported by artillery and mortars.

"Forced further to the west, Task Force Hogan settled in at Marcouray, an Ourthe River village on high ground. We could look out and see the Germans moving around us. Gradually, they enveloped us while we fought back attacks and beat off their patrols."

Task Force Hogan, with Arnold Albero, was completely surrounded once the Germans forded the Ourthe behind the Americans. A state of siege commenced. Instead of thwarting the enemy advance after the conquest of Baraque de Fraiture, Arnold Albero and his 3rd Armored GIs faced their own destruction. Food, ammunition and medical supplies dwindled. Task Force Hogan tightened its cartridge belts and waited for air resupply and a promise that division would try to relieve the beleaguered garrison.

Although the hoped-for dash to the Meuse was far behind schedule, the German breakthrough continued to expand, inflicting massive casualties, swallowing up chunks of territory and forcing the insertion of more defenders. Into the growingly critical arena menaced by the 2nd SS Panzer, the 116th Panzer and the 560th *Volksgrenadiers,* the American strategists pitched another veteran outfit, the 517th Parachute Regiment Combat Team.

The 517th began its existence as part of the 17th Airborne Division, activated in March 1943. Housed at Camp Toccoa, Georgia, the regiment initially received and screened parachute recruits. In the early days, the new volunteers, often half-groggy from their train ride to Toccoa, still in civvies, climbed aboard trucks for a quick trip to a thirty-five-foot high, mock parachute tower. (The actual training platform stood 250 feet above the earth.) The cadre strapped parachutes on the newcomers and then observed their demeanor during their first fall.

What was to come was far more of a test of resolve and toughness and in the role of straw boss was a prickly West Pointer, William J. Boyle. "I grew up in Brooklyn, living at 869 Sterling Place from age six until I entered West Point. As a child I attended St. Gregory's Elementary School and St. Augustine High School.

"During 1933 and 1934, some students in St. Augustine's looked at the possibilities for college. One of them asked me if I had ever thought about West Point. I checked into it and then started a weekly parade to my congressman's home, every Sunday after the 9 o'clock Mass. I was told 'not this year' in 1935 but I continued to visit my congressman's house every Sunday. When a special exam was held in May, my persistence was rewarded by an appointment. But rather than a career, the fact is, I was seeking a college education.

"In my mind, the education at West Point prepared me largely because it taught me self-discipline—although many who've known me may question this. The emphasis was on engineering and sciences. But the study of economics and history led us to recognize Japan as a potential opponent. In fact, the professor of that course clearly stated we would be forced to fight Japan.

"After graduating from West Point I was assigned to the 33rd Infantry in Panama. For the most part I trained people instead of being trained. I had learned enough about tactics at West Point to be able to handle the job but I lacked knowledge of administration. My company commander, Carl Herndon, saw to it that I obtained this skill. He was a major good influence on me, teaching me to know my job and to look out for my troops.

"I was with the 24th Infantry at Fort Benning in 1940 and my duties mainly concerned service, rather than tactics. My solution was to volunteer for the paratroops. They assigned me to a regiment without my ever going to jump school. The CO, Col. Robert Sink [who became commander for the 506th Parachute Regiment, Jack Agnew's outfit in the 101st Airborne], could not get a special quota for jump school to cover people in my situation, so he ran his own instruction at Toccoa. Sink understood troops better than any senior officer I had ever know then or since. [Agnew concurred, noting his buddies frequently referred to themselves as 'the Five-oh-Sink'.]

"Our training was vigorous, especially the physical conditioning. We qualified eight officers and some NCOs each week. The officers were chosen on the basis of a physical competition. My group, which was a later one, made the five qualifying jumps October 19, 1942. In the interest of speed, we did not pack our own chutes. That first jump I was in the middle of an eight-man stick and I remember now only the command 'Go!' My feelings that first time, I don't recall. I always had some fear before a jump and a feeling of relief when my chute opened, but the emotions were nothing spectacular. However, on the first jump, I hurt a knee. Two hours later, on jump number two, I injured my other knee. When the surgeon called me over after my second jump, I walked without a limp. There was no way he was going to put me back."

Boyle became a devout believer in the efficacy of physical conditioning and was convinced that men could perform well beyond normal expectations. "We were working up to carrying not only our own weapons but also the crew-served ones. When one company commander read the next week's schedule and saw it said machine guns would be carried on speed marches, he called me and said it was impossible. I ordered him to have a machine gun at his formation for the speed march that afternoon. I arrived with full individual equipment one minute early, and picked up the machine gun. I traveled beside this company commander all the way. He marched faster than usual, five miles in fifty minutes. I carried the machine gun the full distance. When he dismissed the company, I threw the machine gun at him, saying, 'Don't ever tell me anything is impossible again.'

"That demonstrates the best way to imbue troops with the proper spirit. Let them know you can and will do everything that you ask them to do, and the best way to get that across is to let the men see you do it, not just tell them."

The 517th separated from its original parent, the 17th Airborne, and added an artillery battalion and an engineer company to its complement, making the organization into an independent regimental combat team numbering well over 2,000 men.

Bill Boyle received command of one of the three parachute infantry battalions. "I was not really a spit-and-polish officer," says Boyle, a description backed up by men who served with him.

One of his company commanders, Charles La Chaussee, said, "Wild Bill Boyle was a large man, more than six feet. Boyle usually looked as though he had just gotten out of bed, where he'd slept in his clothes. But he was completely honest and painfully direct. The men of the battalion loved him and would cheerfully have followed him into hell. Boyle insisted every enlisted man go through the mess line before the officers and he made it a point to be last himself. His officers trod very warily in his presence and only God could help the captain or lieutenant who tried to be less than honest with him."

Charles La Chaussee started his military career as a sergeant in a federalized National Guard engineer unit. La Chaussee became bored with his job of manufacturing machine gun emplacements at Mitchell Field, Long Island, New York, and other construction duties. "I was assigned to calculate the explosives needed to destroy each bridge and culvert on the island. We were steadily working our way toward the Brooklyn Bridge when, one day, a notice appeared on a bulletin board seeking volunteers for parachute duty. It sounded more interesting than grading roads and digging ditches."

Two weeks later, La Chaussee reported to Camp Croft, South Carolina, reduced in rank to private, while he underwent basic infantry training. From there he traveled to Benning for a four-week course in parachute mechanics and physical conditioning. For the U.S. Army, the airborne forces, when La Chaussee studied the art, was in swaddling clothes. "I was in class eleven at the parachute school and everyone was learning the trade. Men dropped dead in the heat from physical exhaustion, including a doctor during a five-mile run. The landing style they taught at first was wrong and we had numerous injuries. At the same time we had a lot of practical jokers. We packed our own chutes and sometimes someone slipped lead shot in a guy's chute. He'd get conked on the head when the chute opened. When they made parachute-rigger a specialty, it took away the fear and fun of practical jokes."

By the fall of 1942, La Chaussee was in the 82nd Airborne's 504th Regiment at Fort Bragg. In November he successfully applied to OCS. "The course was thorough but in retrospect it is difficult to say just which war it prepared us for. A lot of time was devoted to drill, ceremonies and customs of the service. We spent many hours learning long-range indirect fire with machine guns, as if they were artillery pieces, a World War I hangover. Lots of time went on techniques of crawling on your back through barbed wire, again suitable for World War I. There was nothing on the psychology of command or tank and infantry teamwork." The absence of the latter La Chaussee would deeply regret during the Bulge. La Chaussee's commanding officer, Boyle, remembers him as "a serious man, something of a loner."

Ed Johnson, a trooper under La Chaussee, describes him as two quite different soldiers. "In a barracks situation, he was very GI, no nonsense, everything had to be done by the book. He was very strict on cleanliness and deportment. Some guys disliked him for this. But he was a great combat commander, fearless, always up front, careful, and didn't needlessly push us."

Nolan Powell, who earned a Distinguished Service Cross as a member of La Chaussee's company, considers his former CO as "almost the Patton of our group. He seemed to relish his time in the Service."

Although both Boyle and La Chaussee would insist that the cliché of the paratrooper as the town rowdy distorts the character, their regiment did its share to give the breed a reputation for free spirits. While at Toccoa, a benighted St. Louis zookeeper, responding to a company commander's lament about the lack of a mascot, dispatched a large lion cub to Boyle's battalion.

The beast, locked up in a hut, chewed and clawed a pile of bedding into a ragged mess. The men warily exercised the animal on a long, thick chain. An uneasy truce between humans and the cub broke down the night of a regimental "Prop Blast" party. As the official on-post ceremonies petered out, Boyle proposed they continue at a saloon in Toccoa. He and several others had jammed themselves into his elderly Ford when the regimental exec, a colonel, suggested the lion join the party. At that stage, no one was inclined to debate the issue with the ranking officer.

The sleeping cub did not appreciate being roused from its slumber and the ride in the back seat of the Ford only exacerbated its ill humor. Several swipes with a paw severely lacerated Boyle. When he arrived at the rifle range the following day, his head swathed in bandages, the regimental commander, Col. Louis A. Walsh, demanded an explanation. Boyle supplied an honest answer.

Walsh, who had tolerated the presence of the mascot, decided to dispense with its contribution to morale. But rather than simply offer the cub to a zoo, Walsh convinced the 515th Parachute Infantry at Benning that it sorely needed a mascot.

A third member of the 517th, Melvin Biddle, hailed from Daleville, Indiana. Born in November 1923, Biddle graduated from high school without giving much thought to the war in Europe. "Pearl Harbor forced me to become aware. I was employed at a grocery store and the people with whom I worked kidded me about being taken into service—soon. I told them I was too young and the war would be over before I was old enough to fight— famous last words."

Subsequently drafted, Biddle was already fascinated with the image of the paratrooper when he sat down for a last civilian lunch with a girlfriend—who eventually became his wife. "She asked me if I would write her a letter in case I decided to become a paratrooper. That clinched it and when the army asked for volunteers, I said, 'Why not?'

"During the medical exam, the doctor asked me if I had ever had any physical training such as football camp, track, etc. I told him I had been to football camp but the training to be a paratrooper proved about three times harder than I thought it would be.

"I don't remember leaving the plane for my first jump but I recall looking up to see the beautiful silk of the chute. I had a headache, however, and I presume the buckles on the risers hit me as the chute opened. One fear I had was whether I would be in position to open the reserve if the main one didn't work. I practiced remembering the exact position of my body and a buddy confirmed the position, satisfying me that I could use the reserve on my chest if necessary.

"We had a lot of tough guys in our outfit, including one from a Georgia chain gang. Most of us had a fondness for boozing and brawling. But we also had many athletes, guys with high IQs and college training. After the war many became professional men, doctors, lawyers, dentists, engineers, solid citizens.

"Jump training, field work and combat exercises helped ready us but nothing can prepare you for the actual fighting, seeing people killed and wounded. Many of my fellow troopers thought I would never live through the war. They said they'd tell my parents how I got it.

"Jump training, however, helped overcome the fear of falling. They said if you can conquer one fear, it helps you cope with other fears. To me, this seems true.

"Our officers were good. They had to be because they jumped with us and they fought alongside of us, going through the same combat conditions we enlisted men did. Colonel Boyle was one of the bravest. He was a superior tactician, a leader and a skillful soldier. I remember a time in Italy when he was hit with some shrapnel. Someone started hollering for a medic, yelling, 'Colonel Boyle's been hit.' Boyle growled, 'Shut up! We don't need any medics hurt coming to aid me.' "

Col. Rupert Graves replaced Louis Walsh, the original CO of the 517th, and the regiment went to war, June 18, 1944, during the Italian campaign. They traveled on foot for this first encounter, north of Grosseto on the road to Siena. A storm of machine gun fire pelted Boyle's 1st Battalion. A shocked Biddle saw "a young sergeant [Andrew Murphy] shot through the head and blood was spurting five or six feet in the air. You have an awful reaction when you see nice people killed right in front of you. You also fear it could happen to you. It angered many of our guys. I think I accepted it, though, as a part of war."

Boyle recalls that in front of Grosseto he initially detected no enemy and the battalion adopted an approach-march type of formation. "After the lead company received fire, I rushed forward. There was machine gun fire from seventy-five to 100 yards on my right flank. I reached for my pistol, and cussed a little at the inadequacy of a pistol at that range. My runner was better equipped and picked off the entire machine gun crew."

Like Biddle, he was taken aback by the first casualty. "When I saw my first dead man, Sergeant Murphy, I had a funny feeling, not exactly nausea but close. There wasn't any horror but I had already built up some anger against the enemy.

"We lost two officers, Lt. Howard Bacon was lucky to survive chest wounds, and nerves in another lieutenant's arm were severed. Our weapons, except for items like my pistol, were effective on the occasion and so was the training. But we needed this relatively light combat so that our small unit commanders, especially squad leaders, could learn to take charge. Previously, they had not been alloted enough responsibility. For my part, I learned to carry a carbine instead of a .45."

During these first encounters with the enemy, Nolan Powell won a Distinguished Service Cross, and La Chaussee organized an uphill charge that Powell swears seemed inspired by a Hollywood film on the cavalry.

After several further engagements, the 517th, along with a brother regiment, the 509th, and a British team, loaded up 396 C–47s at ten separate airfields in Italy for a night attack in southern France. The lead aircraft with the pathfinder paratroopers, who guide successive chutists, lost its way in a thick fog, and the mission was further hampered by navigational errors, excessive airspeeds and lack of practice in formation flying, critical to such an enterprise.

The flights, or serials (in military parlance) bearing the 517th dropped most of the troops well off the mark, although the air corps troop carrier command bragged this was "the most accurate of the war." Mel Biddle's B Company was among those scattered a distance from the DZ. "It was a stroke of luck for us. Had we landed on the target, we probably would have been wiped out. On the other hand, right after the jump there was a bad feeling of being alone in a strange country. But within a few hours when the outfit got together, that anxiety evaporated."

The 517th had racked up more than 100 days of combat experience from the tour in Italy and the campaign through southern France. In mid-November, fresh U.S. troops had relieved the regiment. Some months later, while the upper echelons rode jeeps and an advance party traveled in other vehicles, the rank and file jammed themselves into the 40-and-8 (forty men or eight horses) boxcars of the French railroad. They endured a miserable three-day trip, sitting or lying on straw while men, weapons and gear competed, often painfully, for space. Each boxcar dined on cases of ten-in-one or C rations, heated on Coleman burners. The trains lurched 500 miles with no opportunities to wash or visit toilets.

When the grungy troopers debarked at Soissons they seemed a sorry lot. Much of the equipment, including weapons, required repair or new issues. Five hundred replacements added to the confusion. The regiment began to recreate itself with parade-ground drills, training exercises that would prepare the men for an expected airborne operation over the Rhine River in the spring.

The brass considered the appearance of the soldiers a disgrace and insisted upon improvements in dress and decorum. The effort to bring back a semblance of spit-and-polish climaxed with formalization of the evening meal for officers at the Hôtel Lion D'Or. The order of the day required dress uniforms for commissioned ranks. At the dinner hour, the captains and lieutenants filed into place at long tables, and upon the entry of the regimental commander or the exec, everyone took a seat. Then the waiters served C rations, slightly disguised but, nevertheless, clearly identifiable.

Maintaining discipline in the first days of December strained the limits of the MPs. The area was brimming with paratroopers—the encampments of the 82nd and 101st Airborne and other regiments, like the 517th, lay nearby. The official history of the 517th speaks of "raucous reunions . . . held in local bistros . . . stories swapped of battlefields from Phenix City [the Alabama sin town close to Fort Benning] to the bridge at Nijmegen [a key objective during Operation Market Garden]." Alarmed by the high rate of venereal disease among the troops while in Italy and southern France, some of the 517th's medical officers tried to establish an "Idle Hour Athletic Club" with women certified as healthy by the doctors. The chaplains duly complained and the issue was still in doubt when the 517th received its marching orders a few days after December 16.

Bill Boyle, the 1st Battalion CO, heard the unpleasant news early. "I was visiting a friend with the 506th [from the 101st Division] when they were alerted."

Melvin Biddle, from B Company, quartered in an old military barracks, learned of the German breakthrough from "a Berlin radio broadcast by Axis Sally. She said we were not going home for Christmas but would be thrown into the fighting real soon."

Charles La Chaussee, C Company commander, found the first reports difficult to believe. "It was common knowledge that the Germans had been beaten and the war was as good as over. We wondered why the silly bastards continued to fight. We had been at Soissons for ten days when it was announced that we were on a two-hour alert for possible movement. That puzzled us but it didn't worry anyone very much. We packed and stored nonessential equipment and continued our program of training and rehabilitation.

"Two nights later I had a terrifying and realistic dream. It seemed that the company was moving in an approach-march formation along a small trail through a woods covered with a light snow. One platoon was leading as advance guard, followed by the company headquarters and the balance of the outfit. The ground was frozen hard and I had to sidestep occasionally to avoid slipping on icy puddles.

"Going around a bend in the trail, the leading platoon disappeared from sight temporarily. At that instant a racket of small arms fire broke out. I called by radio to find out what was happening but could get no clear response. With a runner, I trotted forward toward the fire fight. As I rounded the bend, three shots rang out and I saw dust puffs on my jacket. The slugs tore into me. Then I was falling, falling. I awoke on the floor of the bedroom, badly shaken."

In fact, as La Chaussee discovered, orders to move up had come. The date was December 21. "Colonel Boyle assembled his staff and company commanders. 'The Germans have made a breakthrough in the First Army area. Where and how deep we don't know. The 82nd and the 101st have been sent up and we're leaving at 6:00 P.M. We travel by the route Charleroi-Sedan-Namur to a place called Werbomont. I'm going ahead to Namur to report to someone from the XVIII Airborne Corps for further orders. One last thing. If anybody gets separated from the rest of the convoy, avoid a place called Bastogne!'

"Trucks had been assembled by the transportation corps and the military police, who simply pulled them off the highway regardless of their origin or their mission. There was no organizational control over the drivers. They were simply so many men with trucks from a variety of units." The spontaneous recruitment of vehicles and drivers, a matter of necessary expedience, inevitably invited disaster, as La Chaussee soon learned.

The company commanders, like La Chaussee, supervised the loading of troopers, twenty men to a truck with bedrolls, weapons, ammunition and other gear. At 6:00 P.M. as they rolled away from Soissons, a mix of snow, sleet and freezing rain fell. Canvas tops covered only a few trucks. Without protection from the elements, the troopers huddled together. Several times the convoy paused briefly for the men to relieve bladders and bowels.

La Chaussee remembered, "During one halt, I walked down the line of trucks carrying C Company. At the taillight of a truck a young replacement said, 'Captain, I don't even have a rifle. What am I supposed to fight with?' I could only tell him there would probably be plenty of rifles where we were going.

"Dawn came and then daylight broke through the gray sky. Around noon, we passed the outskirts of a city. It must have been Namur. Maps had not been issued. We didn't stop. No orders were received. We continued east, into increasingly hilly countryside. The monotony got to me and, although trying desperately to stay awake in the truck cab, I nodded off. Finally, I sensed we had stopped at a fork in the road with no trucks ahead.

"I asked the driver, 'Where's the convoy?'

" 'I don't know, sir. They were going too fast for me and I lost them. I don't know which way they took.' " It struck La Chaussee as an unpleasant reminder of his dream.

La Chaussee took inventory and counted six trucks containing almost two complete rifle platoons and a mortar section. He directed everyone to climb out and seek protection in the brush. The Company C leader then flagged down a jeep with an artillery observer, ousted a somewhat unhappy but junior lieutenant and sped off until he found an MP at a crossroads who directed him to the XVIII Airborne Corps CP. Advised the battalion now was attached to the 3rd Armored Division, operating out of Manhay, La Chaussee retrieved his infantrymen and six trucks.

"I mounted up the troopers and rode to Manhay, about seven miles south. Traffic struck me as heavy with tanks and trucks racing in both directions. Many of the tanks had sandbags on their frontal armor, held in place by chicken wire.

"At Manhay the division staff was very jumpy. One captain drew his pistol on me. Somehow, my story of having a company of paratroops outside waiting employment didn't seem too believable. But they calmed down and ushered me in to see the division commander, Maj. Gen. Maurice Rose."

A rabbi's son, Rose, seemingly born on a different galaxy than George Patton, in some ways strikingly resembled the flamboyant Third Army chief. A military dandy sporting riding breeches and brightly burnished boots, a stern disciplinarian, Rose pushed his armor aggressively and frequently risked his own safety with personal inspections up front. That penchant would eventually bring his death. But at Manhay, when La Chaussee called on Rose, the 3rd Armored was hanging on the ropes, frantically looking for means to divert the assaults upon it.

"He was a short man," remembered the paratroop captain, "a little below medium height. He was immaculately dressed in gray riding breeches with a Sam Browne belt and boots as befitted a cavalry officer. He was cool, self-possessed and seemed fully in control of the situation. He produced a small map encased in plastic and covered with red and blue arrows. He briefed me on the situation but most of what the general told me went completely over my head. I was totally disoriented. Although I knew we were in Belgium, I didn't know exactly where, or even which way the front faced.

"The gist of his briefing was that he had several task forces out [including the now-surrounded Task Force Hogan, with Arnold Albero, at Marcouray] and they were meeting heavy opposition. He was sending me 'to the hottest spot on the Western Front tonight,' to join Task Force Kane. It wasn't the time or place to ask a lot of questions. I knew I could pick up what I needed a little further down the line. I saluted and left."

Outside the CP, La Chaussee met Task Force Kane's executive officer and in his jeep headed south from Manhay while the trucks with his platoons followed. Just before dark, they halted two and a half miles from Rose's CP in the village of Freyneux. It was already dark, twenty-four hours had passed since they started from Soissons with eight officers and 154 men. "Now," noted La Chaussee, "we were God knows where with six officers and 100 men."

Chapter XI

HOLDING ON

WHILE THE 517TH JOURNEYED to its designated sector, those who had delayed but not halted the enemy advance through St. Vith, backed up towards an avenue of escape temporarily secured by the 30th Infantry and 82nd Airborne Divisions. Among the units engaged in the fluid defense, designed to slow the Germans while preserving their own hides, was the 14th Tank Battalion from the 9th Armored Division. It had been at St. Vith, then Ligneuville, and staved off significant gains for a day and a half before the elements of the 7th Armored replaced the 14th and the rest of CCB.

Dee Paris, the tank platoon leader from the 14th, coped with a maelstrom of confusion. "We'd be told what unit was on our flanks but couldn't establish any contact with the alleged units there. At one point my tanks were at least 200 yards apart. You could have driven an army between them. We were told there were Germans in American uniforms. When members of the 106th, fleeing from the front, reached us, we invited them to eat with us. A Belgian civilian pointed out a man in our chow line and said he was a German in American uniform. They took him away but I don't know what happened to him.

"I didn't see any German prisoners killed. But there is a moment when they start to surrender and you keep firing. There are at least two reasons. You don't trust them and you are so hyped on killing someone before they kill you that you just keep firing. There is a fine line between killing prisoners and killing men who would become prisoners if they weren't shot down.

"I lost one tank in the Bulge. I was ordered to proceed to a place to defend against an attack. I objected that the area wasn't suitable for tanks but was overruled. On my way there, the tank was knocked out with a bazooka. I wasn't initially aware we'd lost the tank. I found out only later. Just before spring arrived, Lt. Paul Fisher, from our first platoon, and I returned to the area and we found the tank. Nearby was a cleared area with a wooden cross bearing the legend, in German, 'three unknown American soldiers.' We also found two bodies still in the tank turret. They hadn't thawed yet. We reported the information to a graves registration unit. They told us about finding many dead American soldiers in the forest. All had one thing in common—their boots had been taken."

By December 22, the enemy seemed on the verge of swallowing up Dee Paris and his platoon. "One night I heard a noise on a nearby road. I contacted Paul Fisher and we jointly investigated. We found a horse-drawn wagon with straw in the back, driven by a man dressed as a farmer. I was suspicious; why would anyone be there at midnight? When I pulled the straw aside, I found a large army thermos container used to take hot food to the troops. That was my first knowledge that there were German soldiers in our rear. We shot the driver."

They prepared for a sprint to a more secure area. Paris had parked his tank in a barnyard, alongside a manure pile, disguising his silhouette with poles, while the others from the platoon sat on the road, 100 to 150 yards apart. "During the night, we had to take care of the occupant of the house who had insisted on repeatedly going to the barn with a lantern. When daylight came, I gave the order to pull out. I then discovered that we had sunk into the ground; the tank was frozen in the earth. We couldn't move. I radioed one of my tanks to swing into the barnyard and knock us loose. I alerted the crew to hang on. It took two good hits to get us free.

"Out on the road I started to lead the platoon. Suddenly a round passed a yard behind my tank. I wondered how long it would take the antitank gunner to reload. I waited a few seconds, and then shouted on the intercom, 'Stop!' My driver, Ray Waelchi, immediately halted and the next round passed a yard in front of the tank. I waited briefly and shouted, 'Kick it in the ass—give her hell!' Another round missed us. I still don't know how an antitank gunner only about 200 yards away could miss hitting a tank broadside." For Dee Paris, and others in his combat command, the Bulge soon became history as his outfit pulled back until given a reserve status.

The ordeal of the Ardennes, however, for the paratroopers led by Charles La Chaussee had just begun. Reaching the destination for support of Task Force Kane, the troopers dismounted, stacked their bedrolls and took cover behind bombed-out buildings. Two flights down into a deep cellar, with squawking radios in the background, La Chaussee received his assignment from Col. Matthew Kane, the task force boss. "Our orders are to take Dochamps [a tiny enclave of buildings] and link up with Task Force Orr coming in from the west. You are to make a night attack to capture Dochamps." To find their objective at night, Kane suggested the infantrymen follow the railroad line from Freyneux to Dochamps, two miles away.

Kane promised tank support directed by the 3rd Armored's Lt. Eldon MacDonald to buttress defenses once Dochamps fell. La Chaussee conferred with the tank commander and MacDonald agreed to provide a diversionary action, firing machine guns and shifting the tanks, to disguise the avenue of attack.

At zero hour, the rifle squads formed up and started hiking along the narrow-gauge track. "It was a clear night with an exceptionally bright moon, almost bright enough to read by," recalled La Chaussee. "A light crust of snow crunched under our boots. When we had cleared the village, I checked the column. One man had a cough which he could not control. I had him fall out. He was a young sergeant who was bitter about being left out of his first action. He was killed two weeks later."

In a cluster of wooden buildings, they came upon two artillery men from the 7th Armored who apparently had fled in the face of the enemy. One, an officer, could tell La Chaussee nothing of the situation other than, "the whole German army is out there. You don't know what you're getting into." The paratroop captain invited the pair to join his detachment but they declined. "I could have put them under arrest but there were other things to do."

A few minutes later, "a tremendous racket of machine guns broke out from the road about 300 yards to our left. This was MacDonald's diversion but his tracer bullets were streaking straight up into the sky. It surely was obvious to the Germans that we had either lost our minds or were trying to attract their attention. The firing stopped after a few minutes and I could only hope it hadn't done too much harm."

The party entered an open field. The moonlight allowed one to see as much as 100 yards ahead, forcing the Americans to proceed slowly with great care. Near the woods at the far edge, the scout signaled a halt, and he dropped silently to the ground.

"Getting his weapon ready, he called, 'Coleman?' There was no reply and he repeated, 'Coleman?'

"From the underbrush a voice now responded, 'Vass?' And the fight was on. That night the password and countersign were 'Coleman' and 'Burner,' for the small heaters to cook food. But when the scout called out 'Coleman,' a German-sounding word, maybe there was a German there named Kohlmann, which explains the 'Vass.'

"The scout fired his submachine gun and others fanned out to the flanks. The familar bark of a German machine gun began. In a few minutes it was all over, with three Germans killed, the weapon silenced."

Between MacDonald's bogus signal and the brief Coleman exchange, any hope of surprise had died. In the woods, a fierce firefight erupted. "That December 23 had a nightmarish quality, like something being acted out in a dream. There was a platoon of twenty to thirty Germans in the wooded patch and they fought stubbornly with rifles, submachine guns and grenades.

Said La Chaussee, "Control of more than five of six men was impossible due to the darkness and thick vegetation. Sgts. Jack Burns and Bill Delaney did most of the work with their squads. They played cat and mouse to draw fire, crawling from tree to tree, calling, 'Oh Herman, where are you? Come out, Herman, where we can see you.'

"By two in the morning we finally cleared the woods. Eight or ten Germans were killed while the rest took off. We lost one dead, four wounded, including one very seriously." Any sense of triumph soon vanished. A substantial, well-armed enemy force started a counterattack. Even as the GIs tried to repel the challenge, Lt. Tom De Coste reported the grim news of an enemy column advancing on his flank.

La Chaussee noted, "It was a miserable situation and a decision had to be made quickly. There were simply too many Germans. They were everywhere. The lieutenant from the 7th Armored had been exaggerating only slightly when he said the whole German army was out there. Major elements of the German 560th *Volksgrenadiers* [the same that helped overrun Baraque de Fraiture], including an engineer battalion, were in and around Dochamps that night. We had never before failed to take an objective and had never withdrawn. Unless I was ready to throw away a hundred men, it looked as though we were going to have to start now.

"It was hard to swallow but I ordered De Coste to bring his platoon back to our position and withdraw along the railroad." The men of C Company retreated, leaving their single dead comrade behind. In the darkness and mist, a four-man stretcher party lugged the most seriously wounded soldier towards Freyneux. On the way, the quartet almost bumped into a large German force but managed to decoy the enemy by falling to the ground before being spotted and playing dead.

The moon had disappeared, a thick fog smothered the area as daylight approached. La Chaussee settled his men into the wooden buildings where they had met the pair from the 7th Armored. Waiting for daylight, La Chaussee became distracted by long bursts of machine guns streaking the sky in the direction of Freyneux. As he pondered the significance of an apparently highly wasteful exercise, he suddenly saw a long double column of men carrying rifles, with fixed bayonets, in the high-port position.

"They emerged from the fog thirty feet away. My immediate reaction was they were friendly troops coming to reinforce us. Then I noticed their ankle-length overcoats sweeping the ground. American troops did not have overcoats like those. I raised my carbine to fire. At that moment, one of our machine guns opened up in a long continuous burst from the house across the tracks. Lt. Roland Beaudoin had spotted the enemy at the same time as I. Sticking his weapon out of the window, he held the trigger down and the German column was ripped apart at point-blank range.

"The next few minutes were pandemonium as our men and the Germans, equally surprised, exchanged fire and grenades. I looked desperately for a place to deploy to make a stand. The fog was thinning fast. I saw a group of stone farm buildings a hundred yards to the northwest. Firing and running, we fell back into these. The Germans were in strength and followed closely. We lost tactical coherence as we scrambled for positions in the farmhouses. I charged into a large building in the center of the village with a machine gun spraying bullets close behind. I found a family —man, wife and children calmly eating breakfast.

"Without a word, we raced upstairs to an attic and opened fire from a window. The German attack went on for about two hours. It was a very near thing. They seemed to be in battalion strength, snaking along hedges and fences, using all available cover and keeping up a heavy volume of rifle and machine gun fire. We had not had so many targets on our first fight in Italy.

"In the attic, Sgt. Arthur Purser blasted away with a machine gun from a window sill. It occurred to me he would present less of a target if he were further back in the attic and I told him so. Just as he pulled his gun from the sill, a bullet ripped through, barely missing both of us but knocking the carbine from my hands. We smashed a hole in the roof and continued shooting.

"When the German fire seemed to slow a little, I descended to the ground floor. The Belgian family had gone, leaving their breakfast on the table. I was drinking a cup of chicory coffee when a column of Sherman tanks roared down the street, firing their machine guns. They were from MacDonald's company, on a reconnaissance patrol. They were indeed the cavalry to the rescue.

"With their .50-caliber machine guns they began raking the hedgerow that ran diagonally across our front. German infantry were advancing behind the hedgerow, stooped over and running in short spurts. Our weapons could not penetrate the earthen embankment. The .50s punched through it, bowling the Germans over as the slugs tore into them. Within a half-hour of the arrival of the tanks, the German fire ceased altogether.

"I went up and down the village, Lamorménil, adjusting positions, assigning sectors. Lamorménil consisted of fifteen to twenty thick-walled stone and masonry buildings along a single street. Suddenly, I saw a squadron of C–47s pass overhead, flying west at 400 feet. There were twelve aircraft, equipped for parachute drop with bundles slung from the wings and bellies. For a moment I thought they were going to make a drop to us but they passed on. As I later learned, this was an attempt to air supply Task Force Hogan at Marcouray, five miles southwest."

The cargo carriers observed by La Chaussee represented the first of two attempts to aid Task Force Hogan and Arnold Albero. The initial requisitions from Colonel Hogan asked for gasoline and medical supplies. A second message added, "Request Xmas turkey be dropped by parachute." Unlike the case of resupply for the cutoff regiments of the 106th, the military bureaucracy completed the paperwork on schedule for the first try. Although the authorities forwarded confusing information for the flight plans, the troop carrier command correctly identified the precise location.

As the C–47s approached the vicinity of Marcouray and began to unload, the guns of the enemy ground forces remained silent. The reticence to shoot was not an act of mercy; instead the gleeful

Germans restrained themselves because the stuff was falling on turf they controlled. Once the supplies struck the ground, an effective antiaircraft defense knocked down three ships and damaged several others.

The net addition to the resources of Task Force Hogan from the December 23 drop consisted of S. Sgt. Andre Mongeau, a radioman from one of the shattered C–47s, whose parachute carried him inside the perimeter of the 400 men from the 3rd Armored. On the following day, the air corps made a second and equally unsuccessful drop; the fault seemed to lie with the crews' errors.

On the ground, Arnold Albero continued to live in a hole with some wreckage from a wall around him. "We made deeper and bigger pits for the tanks and artillery. But unlike the Huertgen Forest, there was nothing to cover the foxholes. My fear occasionally made me nauseous. I drank a lot of water, ate the snow. The thing was there was no place to run and hide. The noncoms had a lot to do with keeping us going. But nobody pulled rank. There was no saluting. Everyone knew what had to be done.

"We knew that the Germans had sent a surrender ultimatum to Colonel Hogan and he rejected it. We didn't expect to surrender. We'd picked up rumors that the Germans were shooting their prisoners at random. The unspoken word was to go down fighting and take as many of the bastards as you can with you."

Having been rebuffed by Hogan, the opposition charged upon defenders huddled in Marcouray. "The first time they came at us up a slope. I was working a .50-caliber machine gun mounted in a jeep. I had an open view and I saw them fall. Luckily, we fended them off.

"To me the most terrifying moment was an attack with armored vehicles that broke through a roadblock where our tank's gun was frozen and couldn't shoot. Once they passed beyond that point, they started shooting like crazy while driving through the town. However, one of our other tanks knocked them out, scattering German soldiers all over the place. We captured the ones who weren't wounded.

"After that incident, they pounded us mainly with artillery fire, guns of all calibers. We couldn't understand why they did not continue to go all-out against us. We would have been overrun; our ammunition was running low, we were out of gasoline. It may be that they were being hit from other areas than ours. Also they may not have wanted to slow their advance, so they just rolled around us and waited for us to give up.

"The stalemate dragged on. Finally, through radio contact the word came, no help was on the way. We were on our own; we'd have to fight our way out, leave on foot. When they told us to destroy our vehicles and the weapons we couldn't take, rather than let the enemy use them, that's when I learned what it is to be really scared."

There were, of course, far more Americans encircled in Bastogne. Since Abe Baum and the small task force had briefly visited the town, no other Americans had been able to get through by land. The Germans strengthened their band of infantrymen, armor and artillery around the Belgian village and on December 22, two German officers from the 26th *Volksgrenadier* Division drove up the same road from Arlon used by Baum, with a white flag flying. Stopped at an outpost manned by the 327th Glider Infantry of the 101st Airborne, they announced themselves as *Parlamentärs*— negotiators bearing a surrender demand.

While the *Wehrmacht* major and captain awaited a response, their formal paper inscribed "Call for Capitulation" was brought to Gen. Anthony McAuliffe at the CP. The document from the commander of the 26th *Volksgrenadier* Division stated: "Unconditional surrender is the only method of avoiding complete annihilation of the surrounded American units. Two hours grace is granted hereby. Should this offer be refused, an artillery corps and six groups of heavy antiaircraft guns stand ready to annihilate the American forces." The message also appealed to the American commander to avoid further suffering for the 3,500 civilians as well as his own troops.

McAuliffe's chief of staff, Col. Ned Moore, broke the news. "We have a surrender ultimatum from the Germans."

McAuliffe asked, "You mean they want us to surrender?"

When Moore confirmed that was indeed the message, McAuliffe, with a number of pressing problems, matter-of-factly reacted, "Oh, nuts," according to Harry Kinnard, present at the moment. McAuliffe initiated a discussion about an appropriate response. No one suggested they acquiesce but McAuliffe asked, "What should I say?"

Kinnard claimed, "I piped up and said, 'Well, General, I think what you said when we first told you about the message would be hard to beat.' "

Seemingly puzzled, McAuliffe inquired, "What do you mean?"

"You said nuts." According to Kinnard, the others smiled and agreed.

McAuliffe took a plain piece of paper and scrawled: "To the German Commander: Nuts!" and appended his signature, "A.C. McAuliffe, American Commander."

The message confounded the emissaries. They asked whether "Nuts" meant an affirmative or negative reply. Col. Bud Harper, regimental commander of the glider troops, informed them, "It's decidedly negative. It means go to hell."

When the men of Bastogne heard of their leader's response, they were almost universally enthusiastic. For paratroopers, trained to drop behind enemy lines and fight their way out, the situation in Bastogne was not extraordinary. In addition to the full complement of the 101st, as Kinnard noted, the holders of Bastogne had recruited additional people from those passing through, whether in disorderly retreat or on the basis of orders. The terrain provided adequate defensive protection and there was an unusually heavy concentration of artillery available to pound the enemy.

Word that Patton's Third Army hoped to break through in time to celebrate Christmas boosted morale in Bastogne further. The major problems for the Bastogne forces were shortages of supplies and the inability to evacuate a growing number of casualties from air raids, artillery and assaults. Poor flying weather interfered with air drops and protection against *Luftwaffe* marauders.

The skies began to clear, however. And on December 23, Pathfinder Sgt. Jack Agnew parachuted into Bastogne to join his fellow Screaming Eagles. He had not been along when Schuyler Jackson, Wallace Swanson and the other members of the 101st started their hasty trip to Bastogne. The pathfinder teams of the division had requested volunteers from the demolition squads. With several companions, Agnew had been sent back to England to participate in experimental techniques and equipment analyses.

Agnew noted, "When we were first alerted to the problems in the Ardennes, it was nothing new to us. Starting in the Normandy campaign, the 101st was surrounded every time it jumped. We happened to be training with a Pathfinder Troop Carrier Group attached to the Air Corps. The living conditions were great, the food great and we had passes to London.

"But on December 22, we drew chutes and all the armament we could get from the air corps people. We left on a jump mission to land in the Bastogne encirclement and guide in vital supplies. Just as we were ready to stand up, the mission was recalled. I was quite concerned about our friends in the 506th, since we heard they had gone into Bastogne with no more than two or three clips of ammo, little clothing and food.

"We left England again on the following day and completed our combat jump into Bastogne. We started to set up our pathfinder headquarters and were blown out of the first two locations. We finally established ourselves and prepared to guide the first resupply planes in." Agnew was now back with his buddies, in time for the approaching Christmas holiday.

A few miles off, the handful of men from C Company, 517th Parachute Infantry Regiment, and their leader, Charles La Chaussee, received disheartening news. The captain had borrowed a jeep from the tank outfit and motored half a mile to Freyneux. He checked in with the task force commander, Matthew Kane. "He was impatient, critical as I made my report. Corps and division wanted Dochamps taken, he said, and the attack should be resumed at two o'clock in the afternoon, with tanks and infantry combined. I suggested we'd be doing well to hold what we had but he was adamant and repeated the order."

Full of dread at what he considered a hopeless assignment, La Chaussee conferred with MacDonald and the infantry platoon leaders. He was now agonizingly aware of the deficiencies in his training. "If we had possessed some experience working with tanks, we might conceivably have devised a plan that had a chance to work, for a little while at least, although that seems doubtful in view of the enemy strength. But these were the first American tanks we had ever seen so close up. The terrain was hilly and wooded. With only a few cleared fields, there wasn't much choice of route. It did not look very promising and we were not enthused. But those were orders and they were to be obeyed."

A bare half-hour before the march hour, even as he assembled his men in the Lamorménil street, La Chaussee, to his immense relief, received word canceling the foray. C Company of the 517th and the small armored force under MacDonald spent the remainder of December 23 improving their fields of fire, erecting protection for the small force.

La Chaussee expected the enemy to storm his redoubt at dawn the following morning, the day before Christmas. The American tankers skirmished briefly with enemy armor, destroying three Mark IVs. But about ten o'clock in the morning, second-story watchers saw a sizable force of infantry in a skirmish line. Many more hidden from view by the natural roll of the land.

The eight improvised machine gun squads created by the paratroop captain homed in on the advancing foe. "As the tracers looked in, we could see Germans dropping. Eight machine guns, each firing 150 rounds per minute, totals 1,200 bullets arriving within a small area each sixty seconds. Even if only one percent found targets, the Germans had to be badly hurt. Furthermore, it was a beautifully clear day. Soon after the shooting started, American planes appeared in strength. They strafed and bombed the area of the German attack.

"We were displaying orange panels on our vehicles but the pilots still must have had difficulty telling friend from enemy. There were at least thirty planes overhead and they did not lack for targets. Explosions and columns of smoke rose as the fighter bombers scored upon enemy vehicles.

"The German effort petered out. We ceased fire and waited for new developments. German aircraft arrived. A truly epic dogfight took place. This was the only aerial dogfight I saw during the war and it was a dandy. Ground action came to a halt. German infantry was as engrossed in watching the air battle as we were. Planes from both sides were going down but the Americans seemed to be getting the better of it. While the dogfight swarmed above us, a large formation of B–17s passed far to the north, bound eastward. Winnow-strips of metal foil to jam enemy radar—dropped like snow. The bombers came under heavy antiaircraft fire and as we watched, two went down in smoke."

The recess ended and the attackers pressed their case again. "I had just returned to the command post when small arms fire broke out from the buildings I had left. It sounded as though it might be another infantry attack. Everyone was committed and the only reserve available consisted of 1st Sgt. Eldon Bolin and myself. The two of us ran down the street to find out what was happening. Troopers on the near side of the railroad embankment were firing into a cloud of smoke beside the house in which I had last seen Lt. Roland Beaudoin. The men told me they had seen several Germans enter the house. Smoke was coming from a burning German Volkswagen jeep.

"I ran across the street and into the house. Lieutenant Beaudoin, Sgt. Bill Delaney and a German lay dead, sprawled out inside the doorway. Moving past them, I fired my submachine gun into the ceiling on the chance the Germans might be on the seond floor. No return fire came and I ran up the stairway.

"Sergeant Brown was on his back near a window and appeared stunned. I lifted his head and my hands came away covered with blood. Apart from the dead, the house was empty. I recrossed the track to find out what had occurred. I learned that while Lieutenant Beaudoin and Sergeant Delaney were entering the building, the German jeep suddenly raced up, approaching the house on its windowless, blind side. An SS captain and another man dismounted, raced around the place, firing as they went. They killed Sergeant Brown. At the doorway, the pair met Lieutenant Beaudoin and Sergeant Delaney. All were killed in a point-blank exchange. The driver of the vehicle had been shot up by other men nearby. It all happened in seconds. After I calmed down and repositioned the troopers in the area, I returned to the CP. It was a very bad moment. Beaudoin, Delaney and Brown were three of my best men."

From the dead SS captain's body, La Chaussee retrieved a dispatch case which included a map overlay. The officer had been from the 2nd SS Panzer Division, known as *Das Reich*. It was committed to an attack upon Manhay, the 3rd Armored headquarters from where C Company had been consigned to "the hottest spot on the Western Front."

In fact, the XVIII Corps, commanded by Maj. Gen. Matthew B. Ridgway, had recognized that the loss of Baraque de Fraiture imperiled Manhay and then Liège itself. To plug the gap on Highway N 15 from the crossroads to the village, Ridgway arranged for a group of units from the 7th Armored's CCA to assume responsibility for Manhay and its environs.

The task force's most potent weapon was its 40th Tank Battalion. A bit more than a mile southeast of Manhay, the Shermans from C Company deployed along the critical road. Their view down the highway from which the enemy would come was blocked after a short distance by a curve that disappeared into the trees.

In one of the C Company tanks, gunner Jerry Nelson, still grieving over the death of his tank commander, Truman Van Tine, felt the loss even more keenly as he developed an active dislike for the replacement. "Burris was friendly enough but that's all. For example, in a Sherman, two guys can lay on their sides in the loader's area and try to sleep. Against the wall there is a small gas engine that runs at night to charge the batteries. Somehow the gas leaked out on Burris, who was sleeping there. Actually, it was probably because he moved a lever. But whatever, he woke me and made me take the wet spot while he took my dry one. I could live with that but he showed himself to be an asshole later."

In the distance, the American forces could hear artillery and the faint bark of small arms as the 517th Parachute Regiment's Charles La Chaussee and other GIs at Freyneux and Lamorménil grappled with the foe. But members of the CCA task force faced their own destruction. Toward evening on December 23, Panzers clambered up the road towards the spot occupied by the tank with Jerry Nelson.

Nelson recalled, "At dusk, Sergeant Freeman's tank and ours (under Burris) were set up, with us slightly behind Freeman and on the opposite side of the road, looking straight down it. Around 10:00 P.M. we heard them coming, mostly track noise. On the radio, we listened to Freeman, who would see them first, say to his gunner, 'I'll tell you when to shoot. Just a little more—Okay. Shoot! Shoot! Shoot!'

"But there was no shot. We never found out why. Burris asked me, 'Can you see them?' I answered no. He said, 'I'll jump out and fire the .50-caliber on top of the turret. Watch the tracers. You're already pointing right anyway.'

"The .50 was only half-loaded, as most of the guns were before they were really needed. Burris yelled, 'It's frozen.' He couldn't pull back the bolt. He told me to start firing and we did. Right into the blackness at point-blank. We were hitting something with our cannon. We got off six or seven rounds, traversing a little each time so we didn't always shoot in the same hole. I looked around for Burris for direction but he was gone. So were the two guys down below, the drivers. I yelled to the loader to bail out.

"As I hit the road, a tank appeared from the brush to the side. I thought it was a German who somehow got through the woods, but then a flare went up and I knew he was one of us. I tried to run fast and grab on from behind. But I couldn't. Then a single round, probably from the lead German tank let loose at the one I'd tried to jump on. I'll never know how close it was to me, but it seemed to me that I could feel something go by me and I can't describe the kind of noise it made. If that had hit me I would be, as Paul Harvey says, 'twenty years old, forever.'"

The 4th Armored Division, striving to reach Bastogne by Christmas bucked up against a wall of resistance from the German 5th Parachute Division. The Teutonic *Fallschirmjäger* could only defend themselves with bazookas, small arms and light mortars. Their artillery support was now limited to seven rounds per howitzer daily.

Josef Schroder, a native of Frankfurt, participated in the fight at Bondorf, or Bigonville, as the Belgians knew it. "We had passed the night from December 23rd to 24th in Bondorf, first in the house of the bürgermeister. We withdrew to the home owned by Gillen, a local family, because of constant fire from American panzers, especially incendiary grenades. Our resistance practially ceased as early as the late afternoon or evening of the 23d because of the superiority of the American forces, and all our ammunition was spent.

"On the 24th the order was to remain as quiet as possible and, since we were surrounded, to make the attempt to breakout on Christmas Eve. But the Americans gave us no chance. They occupied Bondorf step by step, and took the Gillen house while we were still in the cellar. The order to cease firing had come about 10:00 A.M. My buddy, Bernd Platzer, wanted to slip away on his own and left the cellar about noon. When he tried to reach the other side of the street, Americans standing only a few meters away saw him and wounded him so badly with a grenade that he lost one arm.

"When they captured Platzer, they guessed there were still more Germans in the Gillen house. They surrounded it, threw hand grenades in the yard. After that, they fired wildly, entered the house, opened the cellar door and shouted, 'Hands up!' We had seen them coming and realized we had no chance to resist.

"I screamed, 'Stop firing!', put my hands up and was the first to climb the stairs towards the Americans at the top. Together with me, another three or four German soldiers left the house. We were frisked in the yard and literally left without anything. Another man and I were brought by two Americans to the dungheap of the yard. They gestured for us to turn our faces toward the wall. Then they fired wildly, seemingly in an effort to frighten us by making it appear they were going to shoot us. Naturally, we were beset by fear and terror. But after a few minutes a first lieutenant came on foot and hollered something that I understood to mean they should let us alone.

"He asked whether one of us spoke English. I answered yes. While my comrade was led away, the officer took me with him. He brought me to a house and into its cellar. There was a woman with a newborn child. She spoke only German and she told me she had asked the first lieutenant to get milk and a bottle for the child but he didn't understand.

"Apparently, the officer went to find a German prisoner who could act as an interpreter. I did so and the officer ordered me to find milk. I led him to the closest farmhouse, entered the stable and milked the first cow I found standing there. With the milk in a bowl and followed by the officer, I returned to the woman with the baby. Meanwhile, she had found an old baby bottle in the kitchen. Together, we warmed the milk on the stove. She gave the bottle to the baby and drank the rest of the milk herself.

"After taking care of the child, the woman also made a sandwich for me. I was allowed to eat it in the presence of the officer. Afterwards, he took me to an assembly center at the edge of Bondorf. There I met my comrades and others taken prisoner around Bondorf." (The 4th Armored bagged more than 300 Germans in the town.)

"We marched about three to five kilometers along the highway. We were all quite exhausted when a truck picked us up and drove us to Arlon. Five of us, me among them, were imprisoned in a wire-mesh enclosed dungeon only about one meter high. There we spent Christmas Eve, 1944, in a bent position or on the floor. It was very cold. I remember that late in the evening we heard Christmas songs and the pealing of church bells. Only then the war was over for us. But the better part of two years would pass before we were back home."

Just before the nightdrop on the eve of D-Day in France, Eisenhower visited members of the 101st Airborne. The helmetless trooper just to the right of Ike is then Pfc. Schuyler Jackson, who lost his sergeant's stripes for gambling with lower ranks. *(Courtesy U.S. Military History Institute)*

Third Army Commander Lt. Gen. George S. Patton, Jr. (left), Gen. of the Armies Dwight D. Eisenhower (center) and 12th U.S. Army Group chief Lt. Gen. Omar Bradley plotted the strategy to contain the Bulge. *(Courtesy U.S. Military History Institute)*

Patton (right) detested British Field Marshal Sir Bernard Montgomery, who assumed much of the responsibility for halting the enemy. *(Courtesy U.S. Military History Institute)*

Waffen SS General Sepp Dietrich commanded the German 6th Panzer Army that hit the northern flank of the U.S. defenses. *(Courtesy U.S. Military History Institute)*

Brig. Gen. Anthony McAuliffe, commander in Bastogne, gave a new luster to the expression, "Nuts," making it the most famous World War II quote from the brass with the possible exception of "I shall return." *(Courtesy U.S. Military History Institute)*

GIs from the 2nd Battalion of the 325th Glider Regiment hike·into the fog-shrouded woods near Werbomont. *(Courtesy U.S. Military History Institute)*

Lt. Col. Jochen Peiper (left) initially spearheaded the drive into Belgium. *(Courtesy U.S. Military History Institute)*

Triumphant Germans from the 62nd Voldsgrenadier Division show off a captured U.S. jeep during the advance on St. Vith. *(Courtesy U.S. Military History Institute)*

Bombed out civilians in Bastogne seek refuge. *(Courtesy U.S. Military History Institute)*

On Christmas Eve, Screaming Eagles at Bastogne sing carols. *(Courtesy U.S. Military History Institute)*

A Panther tank from the 2nd Panzer Division protected itself with the side of a house. *(Courtesy E. Barkmann)*

German crewmen load ammunition on a Panther. *(Courtesy E. Barkmann)*

The shattered hulks of Sherman tanks from C Company, 40th Tank Battalion, 7th Armored Division, littered a meadow south of Manhay after the pre-Christmas battle.

Major Gen. James Gavin, CO of the 82nd Airborne, wearing white camouflage jacket and toting his M-1 rifle, communicates by field phone. *(Courtesy U.S. Military History Institute)*

An 84th Division jeep carries a stretcher with a wounded soldier as the American forces begin to push the enemy back. *(Courtesy U.S. Military History Institute)*

Arm still extended, a dead German soldier lies frozen in the snow. *(Courtesy U.S. Military History Institute)*

hird Armored Division tankers scour the landscape from an observa-
on post. *(Courtesy U.S. Military History Institute)*

hree members of *Operation Greif,* caught infiltrating U.S. lines in
merican uniforms, died before a firing squad. *(Courtesy U.S. Military History
nstitute)*

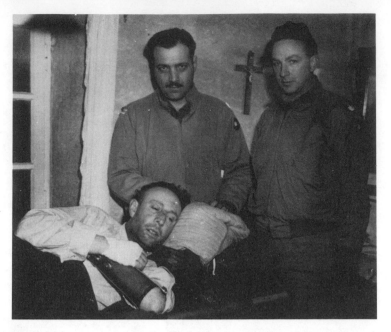

Sick and wounded, Col. Friedrich von der Heydte, commander of the ill-fated parachutists in *Operation Auk* became a U.S. prisoner. *(Courtesy U.S. Military History Institute)*

Georg Fleps, the Rumanian-born member of *Kampfgruppe Peiper* accused of firing the first shot of the Malmedy Massacre, stands before the tribunal at Dachau in 1946. *(Courtesy U.S. Military History Institute)*

Chapter XII

CHRISTMAS EVE

BLEAK AS PROSPECTS MAY have appeared to the cold, hungry, embattled GIs, the situation for the enemy was rapidly deteriorating. In the all-out sprint towards the Meuse, the crack 2nd Panzer Division, bypassing Bastogne, had by December 22 advanced to within five miles of Dinant, to positions where binoculars could pick out the objects of the *Führer*'s desires, the Meuse bridges.

Guarding these strategic spans were a pair of British armored brigades. Peter Elstob commanded one of the units from the 3rd Royal Tank Regiment, stationed on the east side of the river. He recalled the desperate strategy of the day: "Orders were that if Germans appeared in strength, the bridge at Dinant would be blown and the tanks on the wrong side of the river would hold up the advance as long as possible, placed in such position as to form a roadblock when they were knocked out. None was to come back."

To Elstob the orders spelled a "death or glory operation," but instead the panzers fell victims to a combination of luck, skill, superior artillery and their own deprivations. Elstob recalled a probe by a column of tanks and vehicles along the road to the Meuse. An exhausted British Sherman crew, napping as dawn yawned, awoke to the sound of the enemy. The tank commander immediately directed the gunner to blast away. He hastily aimed at the lead armored car but still somewhat befuddled at the sudden awakening, failed to adjust the range. A high-explosive shell in the gun chamber thus fell in the middle of the column, detonating a truck apparently filled with munitions. That effectively split the German column. The British tankers went to work methodically, knocking out a Mark IV, a halftrack and an armored car. Others from the 3rd Royal Tank Regiment wiped out three more enemy Panthers.

The 2nd Panzer Division elements pulled back. But the British big guns west of the Meuse began to hammer them. Furthermore, the acute shortage of fuel left the Panzers without the resources to maneuver. The German armored division could count on little more than forty tanks and even fewer than half the number in self-propelled guns. It was still a potent outfit but ticketed for destruction.

On the southern shoulder of the Bulge, the German Seventh Army had never accomplished its mission, to protect the left flank of von Manteuffel's Fifth Army. The weakest of the German forces, lacking any panzer division, the Seventh stumbled upon the rock of the 4th Infantry Division, whose isolated units, Marcus Dillard among them, refused to yield key sites. As a consequence, the German Seventh Army failed to push far enough to deter the reinforcements from Patton's Third Army charging out of the south. And by December 22, in fact, two Third Army contributions, the 26th and 80th Divisions had begun to pummel the German infantrymen from the Seventh Army.

To the northwest, while the lost section of Company C commanded by La Chaussee endured its trial by punishing fire, the remainder of the 1st Battalion, under Bill Boyle, attached also to the 3rd Armored, sparred with the enemy. Only a short time after they had arrived in the area, they had exchanged sporadic lead with the Germans. Boyle's units, sandwiched between a pair of regiments belonging to the 75th Infantry Division, moved against the 560th *Volksgrenadier* Division, which surrounded Task Force Hogan and Arnold Albero at Marcouray.

The line taken by Boyle's paratroopers stretched between the towns of Hotton and Soy. The battalion counterattacked towards Hotton to relieve some Americans trapped there and to ensure the safety of rear echelon units bunked at Soy. Plans and Operations picked B Company, with Pfc. Mel Biddle to lead. According to Biddle's memory, the action commenced on the morning of December 23.

"My platoon leader said, 'Biddle, out front.'" That simple order made Mel Biddle lead scout for the advance on Hotton through the dense woods and underbrush that dominated, with occasional stretches of open ground. The snow lay eight inches deep.

Slowly, in the frigid air and crawling over the snow amid the vegetation, Biddle inched forward, getting to his feet when he could detect no enemy. As he tried to travel over a field with less cover, several Germans, concealed in the brush, fired at him. Biddle flopped to the snow and wriggled towards the enemy position. From only twenty yards away, Biddle used his M–1 to kill the trio who had shot at him. This was the start of a harrowing, twenty-hour adventure.

Biddle doggedly pushed forward another 200 yards. He ambushed a hostile machine gun position, dispatching the two-man crew with his rifle. Still further on, the Anderson, Indiana, twenty-one-year-old crept up until he could lob hand grenades into another automatic-weapon nest.

Biddle signaled his mates that it was somewhat safer to advance. As they backed him up, the enemy focused on him with rifles and a machine gun. Again Biddle, rapidly reloading, dropped one infantryman, scooted to another position as bullets ripped into the spot he'd just left and killed a second adversary thirty yards away. A desperate grenadier swung his machine pistol in a 360-degree arc, spraying the brush with bullets. Biddle, face down, waited until the fusillade swung by, then slew his eleventh enemy. He tossed his final grenade at the machine gunners and followed up with a successful one-man charge, leaving the gunner and assistant dead, while an ammo bearer managed to escape.

Remembered Biddle, "There was plenty of light during the day. I had great vision. I saw the faces of all of the German soldiers. I saw each of them, before they saw me and from a very short range. That was especially true in several instances when I was only about six feet away in the underbrush."

The scout heard the sounds of armor and volunteered, with three others, to investigate. Bursts from an enemy patrol convinced others in the group it would be folly to continue. But Biddle chose to infiltrate the enemy positions under the cover of darkness.

For several hours he crept about, determining the enemy weapon emplacements, the deployment of the troops and the location of a pair of supporting tanks. During the course of his nocturnal prowl, Nazi sentries and patrols challenged the paratrooper but their shots missed. In one instance, a searcher actually stepped on the interloper's hand. Biddle stifled the urge to cry out and after the enemy moved on, slunk away.

"I was out there for a very long time but I never thought about eating. I thought how cold I was, especially my fingers. I wasn't sure I could pull the trigger of my rifle. I thought I would try sticking a finger through and pull it with my left hand. The Germans at night came extremely close. They would say 'Halt!' Then another would reply, 'Hottentot' [most likely the password]."

In the early hours of the morning on December 24, the companies of the 517th, acting on the intelligence gathered by Biddle, struck again, with Biddle repeating his role as the point. American armor, aware of the precise location of the pair of German tanks, knocked them both out. When a machine gun threatened to wither the attack, Biddle maneuvered himself to within fifty yards and killed the crew and two soldiers in support. Christmas Eve descended, with Hotton's garrison preserved. Biddle was credited with having killed seventeen Germans after firing only twenty-nine rounds from his M-1. The performance eventually won him a Congressional Medal of Honor.

"I had reached a point where I would rather die than be thought of as a coward. I was terrified most of the time but there were two or three moments when I had no fear. That's when you can really operate."

From his elevated position at Lamorménil, the 517th Parachute Infantry's Charles La Chaussee could see the road to Manhay. "Just before sunset, MacDonald called me to a rooftop and pointed to a string of tiny dots moving along about two miles to the northeast. I stared through binoculars. They were vehicles, lots of them. Although it was too far to distinguish tanks and trucks, it looked like several battalions heading straight for Manhay. The information was reported and acknowledged. But no visible action, air or artillery followed."

Having lost their tank, Jerry Nelson and the rest of his crew sat out an engagement on Christmas Eve, a total debacle for C Company. The opposition now hurled themselves upon the smaller and outnumbered American armor along the Manhay road. Part of the German force included the Mark V, a forty-five-ton monster with a huge gun and extremely thick armor plate.

Command and control, the watchwords of military tacticians, evaporated for the Americans that night in front of Manhay. Aware of the weight being hurled at the defenses, the strategists reluctantly agreed to pull back the outposts. But in the darkness, orders failed to reach some units. Others confused German armor with American or thought only infantrymen with rockets threatened them, rather than highly effective tankers.

A bulldozer had neatly dug deep holes for the Shermans

manned by Nelson's comrades. Theoretically, the emplacements in the snow lowered the silhouettes. But according to one of the tank commanders, Sgt. Donald Hondorp, the Shermans "were standing out like black targets on a sheet of white because the rich black dirt excavated was in stark contrast." Furthermore, the pits curtailed swift maneuvering for the tanks. The enemy armor surprised C Company; some crews evacuated their tanks without getting off a round. Others left, then returned to gamely resist. A German tank commander borrowed from the American lexicon: "It was a turkey shoot." In the end, the nine Shermans from C Company lay wrecked and burning while the Germans overran Manhay.

It would prove worse than a Pyrrhic victory, however. Cooler heads dissuaded General Ridgway from an almost suicidal counterattack. The winners, occupying Manhay, discovered themselves pinned by incessant artillery. Only those huddled beneath thick armor would survive.

But while Jerry Nelson awaited assignment to a new tank and 2nd SS Panzers effectively destroyed much of the armor that denoted his division, the Germans also pounded the parachute infantrymen under Charles La Chaussee, a few miles to the southwest. The captain scrounged for added firepower to repel the inevitable onslaught.

"It occurred to me that the tanks ought to have some surplus machine guns. MacDonald had lost some men and his crews were down to three or four each. None of his tanks had assistant drivers anymore and, therefore, the bow guns [normally fired by the second driver] were surplus. The guns had no pistol grips but were usable with tripods. These gave us an improvised machine gun platoon which could be shifted to places where needed. Combined with the ones we had as company equipment, the troopers manned a total of twelve for ground fire.

"In the late afternoon, the Germans brought down tank fire from a range of 600 to 1,000 yards. Tank cannon fire can be demoralizing because the projectile travels at ultrasonic speed and strikes before the report of the gun is heard. The enemy had Mark IVs or better and our Shermans, with the 75-mm howitzer, were no match. MacDonald tried to keep his tanks close to buildings and behind wood piles, waiting for a chance at a shot within their range. The Germans methodically smashed the buildings, beginning with those nearest them, then working towards the center of town. They first fired armor-piercing shot to break down the walls, then high-explosive ones to burst within the houses. One by one, houses caught fire, became untenable. As each began to crumble, the riflemen fell back to the next one.

"By dark, the southern part of the town was reduced to burning rubble. Power lines had been shredded and hung from the poles like spaghetti. Each of the remaining buildings had been hit at least once. One tank was damaged beyond repair; five paratroopers and eight tankers had been wounded.

"We set out listening posts a few hundred yards from the village. The tankers rigged electric light in our command post building from a generator in a tank outside. I called in the platoon leaders and gave them what little information I had. We were cut off without contact on either flan, but, lacking other orders, we were going to defend this place come hell or high water. Somebody reported to MacDonald that the crew from one of his attached antitank guns had stripped the breechblock and thrown the parts away. [To destroy the weapon.] This brought on one of the most picturesque outbursts it has ever been my privilege to hear. MacDonald concluded, 'Tell those sons a bitches to find those parts and put the goddamn thing together or I'll stomp mudholes in their asses and kick 'em dry!' "

The scene was strangely quiet. "We settled in for another long night. It was Christmas Eve and our radio played appropriate music, *Stille Nacht* from a German station, as well as other tunes over the BBC. MacDonald returned from the CP in Freyneux and spread out a map. Odeigne, Le Batty, Granménil and La Fosse—everything to our east and northeast had been taken by the Germans and Manhay had not been heard from.

"We were, effectively, cut off. There was no information on what the rest of the U.S. Army was up to. That night, General Eisenhower came on the air with his Christmas message for the troops. As far as we were concerned, it was the wrong speech at the wrong time in the wrong place. The Supreme Commander used such phrases as 'Congratulations! At last the German has come out of his fortifications to fight in the open. Good luck! Good hunting!'

"It was fatuous in view of who, at the moment, was doing the hunting. MacDonald went out to his tank and returned with a bottle under each arm. It was Scotch and crème de menthe. He said, 'It's a helluva mixture. I was saving it for New Year's Eve. But it looks as though we might not be around come New Year's.' Five of us shared it, becoming pleasantly numb, and slept."

On the other side, however, *Kampfgruppe Peiper* no longer doubted its reversal of fortunes, becoming the prey. Unable to ford or bridge the Salm River and Lienne Creek with his panzers, Peiper, in a farm house at La Gleize, watched in despair as the American artillery shattered his redoubts, blasted his armor and killed or wounded his troops. Several U.S. counterattacks, notably at Cheneux, wreaked heavy casualties on both sides.

Kampfgruppe Peiper reeled under constant American blows. Said Peiper, "Our position in La Gleize had become very difficult. The town is surrounded by mountains and offers very excellent artillery observation points to the enemy. The forest is very close to the town and offers very good lines of approach for infantry. In view of the great enemy artillery superiority, it was only a matter of days before the whole town would be shot to rubble. It was hardly possible to move in the streets. All squares of the streets were under direct machine gun and tank destroyer fire.

"There was a very great increase in our casualty rate. The town hardly had any cellars. The few which were available were for prisoners and wounded exclusively. The prisoners represented a terrific burden to me. And it happened constantly that the guards standing outside the cellars with the prisoners ran away during artillery fire. While inspecting, I saw a number of Americans, about eight, lying on the edge of town, shot. I wasn't able to make an investigation since it was dark and there was very lively firing. I asked Major Poetschke whether he knew anything about those American soldiers I had seen. He said, 'Yes, they had been shot in the course of an escape attempt in the afternoon of the 22nd.' "

On that afternoon, Peiper recalled, "the enemy attacked with very strong infantry, very strong tank concentrations. They penetrated the outermost houses. The whole town was filled with fog and the impression one has was that the infantrymen were in front of our doors. I myself jumped out of my cellar with a machine pistol while my adjutant began burning the secret matter."

Peiper's morale was hardly boosted by nagging demands from superiors that he "punctually report his supply situation" if he wished to receive ammunition and fuel. Nor was he heartened by a query of what should be done with his six Tiger tanks blocked off at Stavelot. To the last he responded, "Send them by air to La

Gleize." Peiper had become convinced as early as December 22 his dash to the Meuse was not simply a lost cause; unless the task force retreated the entire unit would be crushed.

Perhaps the single most deadly force brought to bear on the hapless SS troopers was a Long Tom, a 155-mm self-propelled cannon. Foragers from a tank battalion scrounged the piece, which launched huge missiles into La Gleize from a range safely beyond the best the enemy could muster.

During the afternoon, Peiper summoned his highest-ranking prisoner, the 30th Division's Maj. Hal McCown and expressed outrage at the use of the 155. "He protested to me that the Americans were using a heavy-caliber direct-fire weapon to fire on the houses in La Gleize and knock out his tanks. It was his belief that the direct-fire weapon had been placed on the chateau at Stoumont, on the ledge, which had been used as a hospital by Colonel Peiper [then recaptured by GIs]. He said he would not have his gunners fire on the direct-fire weapon because he could not be sure that his wounded and the American wounded had been removed from the chateau. I told him it was the American [policy] to evacuate casualties when they were overrun and he could be reasonably sure there were no casualties in the castle."

Indeed, considering Peiper's record and reputation as well as the desperateness of his situation, it is difficult to believe he would have refrained from retaliating against the offending direct-fire weapon out of concern for wounded, including his own. The complaint indicates rather that Peiper was hanging on to the raw end of his tether.

Shortly after dark, McCown was hauled to the CP for his fourth face-to-face encounter with the leader of the 6th SS Panzer Army's run for the Meuse. Peiper was neither the cold interrogator of their first meeting nor was he the warmer, personable brother officer exchanging viewpoints of their second meeting. Nor did he whine about U.S. tactics. On this occasion, he played the role of a trader.

"He told me he had received orders from the commanding general to give up his position and withdraw to the east, to the nearest German troops. He knew it to be impossible to save any of his vehicles, that it would have to be a foot withdrawal. His immediate concern was what to do with the American prisoners, of which he had nearly 150 as well as his own wounded. He dictated to me a plan of exchange whereby he would leave all American prisoners under the command of the senior PW, a captain, to be turned over to the American commander as the Americans entered the town the next day. He said his wounded would also be left in the cellars of La Gleize and he would leave a German medical officer in charge of them. He had previously left a considerable number of wounded in the chateau at Stoumont. In exchange for the American prisoners, all German wounded would be turned over to the 1st SS Panzer Division, wherever they might be when the wounded were assembled. I would then be released back to the American lines, as I would be the only prisoner retained during the foot movement of the Germans east from La Gleize."

McCown informed Peiper he could not assure him the exchange would be carried out as outlined, since the decision lay with higher headquarters. Peiper said he understood. The proposed agreement undoubtedly was a fig leaf to cover any recriminations hurled at Peiper for abandoning his soldiers.

The SS man also reported to McCown that during the American attack that day, nine PWs on work details were killed when they tried to run off.

Sometime after midnight, in the early hours of December 24, *Kampfgruppe Peiper* flak tank section leader Sgt. Karl Wortmann was awakened by a messenger insistently crying "Merry Christmas, Merry Christmas." Befuddled at first by the greeting, Wortmann learned it was a codeword directing him to blow up his vehicles and follow the escape column.

Around 3:00 A.M. on the 24th, the *Kampfgruppe* actually decamped. McCown had signed the agreement as spelled out by him, as did American antitank captain, Bruce Crissinger, who assumed responsibility for the GI prisoners and wounded left in the cellars. Since he would be the man to greet the liberating American forces, Crissinger retained the signed treaty. McCown became part of the column led by Peiper. There were only 800 men, from the original 4,000 that had jumped off at Lanzerath after the capture of Lyle Bouck. In addition, Peiper had added about 1,800 from two other units, such as the paratroop regiment at Lanzerath.

"At 0500," said McCown, "we heard the first tank blow up and inside of thirty minutes the entire area formerly occupied by Colonel Peiper's command was a sea of fiercely burning vehicles, the work of the small detachment he left behind to complete destruction of all of his equipment."

They moved slowly as Peiper, his staff and McCown, with his two guards, reconnoitered for a route through the American lines. The American was greatly impressed by the discipline of the troops. "The noise made by the entire 800-man group was so little that we could have passed within 200 yards of an outpost without detection." There was no food. McCown subsisted on four small pieces of dried biscuit and two gulps of cognac from a junior officer. A regimental surgeon gave him a piece of Charms candy. McCown believed the sugar helped him during what became a very lengthy march.

As they neared the bottom of a hill, McCown heard an American yell, "Halt! Who is there?" The sentry repeated his challenge three times and then fired three times. The column turned about and trudged back up the hill. A German passed McCown, limping from a bullet through the leg. He obviously had been the point man closest to the GI challenger. Peiper refused to permit the medics to apply a dressing. The former point fell into the column and hobbled on.

About two hours before midnight, as they slogged up hills, crossed small streams and pushed through thick undergrowth, always avoiding towns and villages, Peiper and his immediate staff vanished from McCown's sight. A young captain now controlled the group closest to McCown. "I heard him tell my guards to shoot me if I showed the slightest intention of escaping, particularly when we neared Americans. Whereas Colonel Peiper had given a rest break every hour or so, there were no breaks given under the new command. The country we were now passing through was the most rugged yet encountered. All of the officers continuously exhorted the men to greater effort and to laugh at weakness. I was not carrying anything except my canteen, which was empty, but knew from my own physical reaction how tired the men with heavy weapons must have been.

"I heard repeated again and again the warning that if any man fell behind the tail of the column he would be shot. I saw some men crawling on hands and knees. I saw others who were wounded but who were supported by comrades on either sides up the steep slopes. There were fully two dozen wounded in the column, the majority of whom were going along quite well by themselves. There was one captain who was rather severely wounded who moved along supported by another officer and a medical NCO. He was still with the unit the last I saw of him."

While Major McCown marched off as the sole hostage for the bargain struck by Peiper, with him, Bob Hall, from an ammunition and pioneer outfit with the 30th Infantry Division captured at Stoumont on December 19, began to believe he would be freed. McCown, the top officer among the prisoners, had spoken to the American PWs. Some forty-seven years later, McCown wrote to Hall, "I had you count off, appointed a first sergeant and platoon sergeants and reminded you that you all were still under the Articles of War. I remember telling you that we would probably be set free as the German captors were cut off from their own lines."

Hall had spent four days in a large cellar and then shifted to another house. "They tried to give us something to eat, but they didn't have much either for themselves. For three days, we had nothing, maybe an apple or a raw potato the other days. During the night, our artillery hit again and set our house on fire. The Germans called us to come up and moved us to a church. They could have kept us locked in that burning cellar.

"In the church there were fifteen to twenty of us, and one young German guarding us with a rifle. During the night and early morning, heavy shelling by the U.S. was heard. I knew they were coming close. Finally, the German soldier put his gun down and our troops got us. When I walked around, I noticed the German who took my pen. I went over to him and took two or three pens from him." No Christmas Eve could have presented a more relished gift than the freedom Hall now enjoyed.

Bill Dunfee, as part of the 505th Parachute Regiment, from the moment of arrival east of the Salm River near Trois Ponts on December 21, was, in his words, "having a very hard time with the remainder of the 1st SS Panzer Division"—*Kampfgruppe Peiper*. The American paratroopers initially ventured east of the Salm but the sheer force of numbers drove them back to a few yards of river line. For several days, the brass strategists correctly guessed the local *Schwerpunkt* (pivotal point of attack) and managed to shift men about to beat off the attacks.

To break out Peiper, the 2nd SS Panzer Division advanced towards the Salm from the south. The Americans had planned to blow a key bridge near Petite-Langlier but the enemy seized the span before it could be destroyed, making it available for the oncoming panzers. A daring raid by engineers under the leadership of Maj. J. C. H. Lee, Jr., penetrated enemy lines, hooked up explosives and detonated the bridge while German vehicles crossed it. Says Dunfee, ''We were told that a German motorcycle, sidecar, officer and driver went airborne along with the bridge. We 'doggies' loved it, we were more than a little jealous of anyone who rode into battle.

''About this time my platoon leader, Lieutenant Carter, ordered me to provide riflemen to accompany a patrol led by an armored officer. We would be riding a four-wheeled armored scout car mounting a .50-caliber machine gun, pulling a two-wheeled trailer loaded with land mines. The mission was to mine an approach to a bridge. I decided Oscar Mewborn and I would volunteer, since we both had BARs—never my authorized weapon but in combat you picked the weapon you liked best. My feeling was there was no point endangering others; between us we had the firepower of four riflemen.

''We took off about midnight with the lieutenant, driver and gunner in the scout car, Oscar and I on the trailer. We moved rather slowly, watching for German land mines. Oscar cussed me all the way, first for volunteering him and then endangering him further by riding on top of a load of mines. I tried logic with him, explaining we were dead if the scout car hit a mine anyway, whether the trailer blew up or not. He was neither reassured nor amused.

''We made it to the bridge; it was laying in the river. Someone had already blown it. Since that bridge did not show destroyed on the lieutenant's map, he insisted we go to the next bridge, a mile further. We were rounding a curve when we heard the crunching cadence of marching men. We knew they couldn't be friendlies. Oscar and I hopped off the trailer and headed towards the river and the oncoming troops. From there we could cover the turnabout of the scout car. That required unhooking the trailer because the road was so narrow.

''Crossing the road, I pulled back the bolt on the BAR. Not wanting to goof off a shot, I slid my finger forward in the trigger guard, hit the magazine release and dumped a loaded magazine in the middle of the road. The sound was deafening. We stopped and listened but there was no interruption in the cadence of the marchers. When the car finally turned around, we mounted up and took off. Back at the defensive perimeter, we could relax and laugh. Oscar especially enjoyed describing me crawling around the middle of the road trying to locate the magazine I dropped. In the dark I could only feel for it and, besides, I had a full belt of loaded magazines. It wasn't my finest hour."

Two days later, the situation became far more dicey. Dunfee and associates were spread out very thin. The 2nd SS Panzers approached. "It was most difficult at night. Half our people were awake at all time, mostly. We patrolled between foxholes. There was little grousing, only about being cold and hungry. Our primary concern was staying alive. We had been exposed to German SS troops in Sicily. We did not find them to be supermen. They were well trained, armed and led. But they bled and died, just like us."

By the afternoon of December 24, there was a firm decision to withdraw after dark. Tactically, the move would reduce the sector assigned to the 82nd Airborne drastically, by fifty percent. The new defensive position appeared far superior in terms of fields of fire and cover for defenders. The 82nd commander, Jim Gavin, had reservations. "Morale is just as important. The fact is that the troopers did not like to withdraw in front of the Germans. The memories of all the older veterans went back to North Africa and Sicily. Stories too numerous to mention came from troopers who were wounded, captured and who later escaped, about how badly they were treated by the Germans. We know that troopers in their parachute harnesses had been shot while hanging from the branches of trees in Normandy instead of being taken prisoner."

Gavin insisted, "Rather than withdraw, if the troopers had had their way they would have much preferred to attack." He noted the division's boast after Normandy, "No ground gained was ever relinquished."

On the scene, Dunfee's reaction to the withdrawal order differed in some respects. "Maybe Gavin was ready to attack but we would have been content to hold what we had and let Jerry attack. Every time he tried, we cleaned his clock. We were dug in on the Salm in good position. The one bridge in our area was rigged for demolition. If the enemy tried to get armor across, the first one would have gone airborne. We didn't consider their infantry a problem.

"Our withdrawal was reluctant; we hated like hell to give up what we had fought so hard to take and keep, to think of fighting over the same ground a second time. The division had never withdrawn in its combat history. We knew the withdrawal wouldn't be easy either, espcially at night. We were very much aware of German presence in our rear, and that some spoke English and had American uniforms and vehicles. One time while on patrol I stopped a jeep with three men wearing American clothes. I passed them on, telling them where to go so our guys could pick them up. On returning, I found they had been sent back to Battalion HQ under guard. But with our flanks exposed, we understood we could be cut off by a pincers movement. The American GI is pretty resilient. A well-disciplined unit like ours followed orders—an 'ours not to reason why' approach.

"About 2100 on Christmas Eve, we were all packed up awaiting orders to move out. Fortunately, our machine guns were still dug in, covering the shallows of the Salm to our immediate front. We were lying back on our backs, dozing, when all hell broke loose. The Germans came from our rear, shooting and yelling like a bunch of Indians. I didn't have to see them to know who it was, the rapid rate of fire of the German machine gun and the pink tracers told me. They wanted to go home for Christmas, too.

"We immediately hit our foxholes and started firing. I would estimate a company-strength group started through our area. Some made it to the river, some didn't. I would guess less than half made it to the far bank. Our machine guns, being in place and sighted, really chewed them up as they attempted to ford the river. When the smoke cleared away, we realized we were attempting to withdraw through an enemy force that was withdrawing through us. This may not be unique in military history but it was a new experience for us. When we finally pulled out around 2230 hours, we moved as if attacking to our rear."

The momentum of the Fifth Panzer Army swept up Harry Martin, the former Sad Sack of the 424th Infantry Regiment, who, during the initial attack, had recalled the dictum, "Squeeze the trigger." Beyond St. Vith, Martin, along with pieces of the disintegrated 424th, the 28th Division, the combat commands of the 7th and 9th Armored, became GI flotsam flowing through a narrow corridor of escape. The route was northwest, across the Salm River where the 82nd Airborne, including Bill Dunfee, held the way open.

Martin remembered, "On the morning of December 23, we met up with CCB of the 9th Armored in the snowbound hills west of Beho. We were still not aware of what was going on. Suddenly, to our surprise, Captain Bartel gave the frantic order to withdraw.

'Jump on anything that's moving out! Every minute counts! Every man for himself!' I climbed on top of a light tank.

"The tank I was on was going full speed for quite some time. Just when I felt confident that we had outrun the Germans and they were left far behind, the hatch on the tank opened and the tank commander said, 'We've just received word on the radio that there is small arms fire ahead. Come on and get inside where you will be safer.' I was very happy to get inside the tank where it was much warmer. I sat back and relaxed. I was out of the cold and I was protected by armor all around me. I thought, 'What a difference between the infantry and the armored divisions. They carry warm clothing, blankets and food with them.'

"A few minutes later, machine gun bullets bounced off the tank and I was thankful to be inside. I might not be alive if it were not for the tank commander."

After a time, the armor drew beyond enemy fire and halted. The tankers invited the infantrymen to share their food. Martin, who had not eaten for several days, gladly accepted. He began to make plans to stay under their protection for as long as possible. But before he could even settle down for a bite, an officer rounded up the foot soldiers and led them into a wooded area.

"One of the men grabbed a chicken and cut its head off with his bayonet. While the chicken was being plucked, we started a small fire. Just as the chicken was put over the fire, word came that the Germans were closing in once again. We quickly stamped out the fire. We ran down the road, passing the chicken around with each man ripping off a piece. We were so hungry that, like wild animals, we ate the chicken raw."

The small group continued to trek northwest, veering from the direct path a number of times as they detected the advancing enemy. After the lieutenant roused them from their fourth barn in a single night, the exhausted Martin, burdened with two bandoliers of ammunition, a canteen, mess kit, first-aid kit, bayonet, hand grenades, rifle and steel helmet, shivering with his outer wear of ordinary army shoes and a field jacket, felt he could not go on. At the last barn, when the others walked off, he slipped back and bedded down in the loft.

At mid-morning, Martin awoke, cautiously stuck his head outdoors and saw no one. But when he sallied forth and rounded the corner of the barn, to his horror, a huge German tank's cannon pointed straight at him. Somehow, no one noticed the lone American and he fled through the woods. He traveled in the direction of gunfire, figuring he would outflank the German lines and circle to safety.

Walking for hours, Martin lightened his load, tossing away first his grenades and then his pair of bandoliers of .30-caliber bullets. "As I crossed a snow-covered road, I saw a C ration biscuit wrapped in cellophane. It looked like it had been run over by a dozen tanks, but I picked it up anyway. I sat down next to a small frozen brook where water flowed over the ice. I found a small package of powdered lemonade in my pocket. I filled my canteen with ice water, mixed in the lemonade powder. I opened the crushed biscuit, taking just a nibble with small sips of my drink. I savored each little nibble and sip. I was having a banquet. All of my senses were centered on this very special meal. I was no longer cold or tired; the war was completely out of my mind. I got more pleasure out of that little biscuit than any meal I have ever had. When I finished, I said aloud, 'Well, let's go and find the war and the 106th Division.' "

Miraculously, Martin apparently passed through the broken lines of the warring armies. He reached a town with American soldiers and trucks. He asked an MP, "Which way did the 106th Division go?" The soldier flatly answered he had never heard of the outfit. Martin did not pause to eat, rest or warm himself. He trudged on, intent on meeting up with his unit. Toward nightfall, he prepared to give up his hunt and return to the town.

As he staggered back, he suddenly heard someone call his name. To his delight, the voice belonged to a sergeant from his own 3rd Platoon in L Company. The noncom led Martin to a reunion with six others from the company. "It felt good to be back with friends and just in time for Christmas Eve. I had a lot to be thankful for, to have made it back from that dreadful ordeal, back with members of my platoon, in a warm building and finally safe from the enemy. We were with a heavy artillery outfit. The commander invited us to stay for Christmas Eve and for Christmas Day with a promise of a special turkey dinner.

"All that evening and through the night, the 240-mm artillery fire sent huge shells into enemy territory. The firing shook the building, but they were on our side, giving us a sense of security.

"Even though I was starving, I was too sick to eat. After talking to the men for awhile, I curled up in the corner on the floor and went to sleep."

On the Elsenborn Ridge, the 99th and 2nd Infantry Divisions denied the German drive to widen the salient. Mortar man Rex Whitehead, from the 99th and who had been at Honsfeld only a few hours before Peiper's column captured the town and several of his buddies, had gone through a bad patch until meeting up with elements of the 2nd Division, awoke to a pleasant sight on December 24. "We got up and saw there wasn't a cloud in the sky, and soon we could see vapor trails coming from behind our lines. Soon we could hear and see the formations of bombers going over, and you wouldn't believe anything could make a bunch of guys so happy as that sight did. Judge was waving his arms and shouting something about who said we didn't have an air corps. Formations came over for about five hours and it was a beautiful sight, the vapor trails streaming behind each motor and then the escorts weaving back and forth above them, making the sky look like a giant jigsaw puzzle. Some were shot down as they approached the front, the Kraut AA would open up and there were some fighters to meet them. More than anything else, we were happy to have them up there, because we didn't draw any fire since the 88s were dual, and were firing at the planes. As soon as they were gone, we started to get it though."

Dick Byers, with the 371st Field Artillery of the Checkerboards, lived in a farmhouse. "The Germans had captured thousands of pounds of our mail and all the normal supply lines were disrupted. By Christmas Eve, we were feeling really low down and depressed without any mail for a week.

"A bunch of us, Cleon Janos, Bill Johnson, Gerald Krueger, Smith Eads, Henry Dewey, Paul Blackburn and Joe Peruzzi, were on the second floor gathered around a canteen full of gasoline with a rope wick that gave out twice as much soot as light. We were trying to get high on one bottle of terribly oily cognac. Downstairs, there were about five or six young children. Some of them were the farmer's, others were orphans the farm had taken in to shelter. A battery of 240-mm heavy artillery howitzers was out in the field beyond the farmhouse.

"The children were singing Christmas carols in their clear soprano voices and the sound effects went something like, 'Silent night'—BLAMM! 'Holy night'—BLAMMM! Somebody would get up and put the cardboard back in the window after the house stopped shaking from each blast. We were all just about ready to give it up as a bad job and go to bed when someone downstairs yelled, 'Mail Call!'

"There was our Christmas mail. I received two boxes from my wife [to be]. In each box was a can of candy corn and in each can was a two-ounce medicine bottle filled with good whiskey. I shared the fruitcake and the cookies with the boys, gave most of the candy to the kids. I gave just a taste of the whiskey to each man and managed to go to bed on Christmas Eve with the customary glow on."

Christmas Eve brought more death and destruction to the stubborn inhabitants of Bastogne. One bomb struck a makeshift hospital, killing a Belgian woman nurse and burying twenty patients in debris. Another token from the *Luftwaffe* badly damaged a command post, knocking down the Christmas tree in the message center. The GIs patiently resurrected the tree and a sergeant pinned a Purple Heart on a mangled doll.

All of the command posts received a special "Sitrep," a map of the drama in which the defenders of Bastogne played the starring roles. Red dominated the overlay, as it outlined the location of the German forces. Against the white background, in the territory still controlled by the Americans, appeared the green lettering, "Merry Christmas."

There were religious services at the tenth century chapel of the Rolle Chateau, CP for the 502nd Parachute Infantry. And there was a pre-Christmas mess for officers, featuring delectables created out of flour and beef contributed by the local Belgian farmers. Those not on duty retired at about one-thirty in the morning. They would get very little sleep. But, at that, they ate better and slept more than the paratroopers manning the perimeter.

Chapter XIII

CHRISTMAS DAY, 1944

THE WOULD-BE RESCUERS of Bastogne, the 4th Armored vanguard, stalled only four miles away due to heavy resistance. The architect of the relief effort, Lt. Gen. George S. Patton, chafed at the delay. His diary entry for the previous day noted: "This has been a very bad Christmas Eve. All along our line we have received violent counterattacks, one of which forced . . . the 4th Armored back some miles with the loss of ten tanks. This was probably my fault because I had been insisting on day and night attacks. This is all right on the first or second day of the battle and when we had the enemy surprised but after that the men get too tired."

Patton had supplied everyone in his Third Army with a wallet-sized Christmas prayer. It read, "Almighty and most merciful Father, we humbly beseech Thee of Thy great goodness, to restrain these immoderate rains with which we have to contend. Grant us fair weather for battle. Graciously harken to us as soldiers who call upon Thee that armed with Thy power we may advance from victory to victory and crush the oppression and wickedness of our enemies, and establish Thy justice among men and nations. Amen."

The origins of the prayer, however, lay not in the events of the Ardennes. Patton, frustrated earlier by conditions in his Third Army sector, had summoned his chaplain two days before the German breakthrough. Patton's deputy chief of staff, Col. Paul Harkins, remembers the general telling the priest, "Chaplain, I want you to publish a prayer for good weather. I'm tired of these soldiers having to fight mud and floods as well as Germans. See if we can't get God to work on our side."

The chaplain demurred, "May I say, General, that it isn't a customary thing among men of my profession to pray for clear weather to kill fellow men."

Patton snarled, "Chaplain, are you teaching me theology or are you the Chaplain of the Third Army? I want a prayer."

What he wanted was eventually printed, but with the passage of time, the flip side of the card bore a holiday greeting. And on the sacred morning, Patton rose and approved of the Lord's performance. In his diary he wrote: "A clear, cold Christmas, lovely weather for killing Germans, which seems a bit queer, seeing Whose birthday it is."

While Patton drew satisfaction from his prayer, Bob Hall, over whom Peiper's legion relinquished its captivity on Christmas Eve, traveled to Spa, headquarters of the U.S. 1st Army. There he wallowed in a hot bath in a large copper tub, amused by the appearance of a "girl with a thermometer who had came to check the temperature before we bathed." While Hall indulged himself for the moment and enjoyed the traditional Christmas turkey meal, Maj. Hal McCown, his commanding officer as a PW in the cellars of La Gleize, stumbled along for a final few hours with *Kampfgruppe Peiper,* as it sought escape.

"We approached very close to where artillery fire was landing and the point pushed into American lines three times and turned back. I believe the Germans had several killed in these attempts. I am firmly convinced by this time they did not know where they were on the map, as there were continuous arguments from among the junior officers as they held their conferences.

"Around midnight, the condition of the men was such that a halt would have to be given, as well as warmth and food provided. I heard the captain say he would attempt to locate a small village where the unit could hole up for the rest of the night. At about 0100 I heard word come back that a small town was to the front, which would suffice.

"The outpost had already moved into position when firing broke out not very far from where I was standing. My guards and I hit the ground, tracer bullets flashed all around us and we could hear the machine gun bullets cutting the trees very close to us. The American unit, which I later found out was a company, drove forward again to clear out what it obviously thought was a stray patrol, this time using mortar fire as well. The mortars fell all around the German position. I don't know if my guards were injured or not, shrapnel cut the trees all around us. The American machine gun fire was very superior to the covering force. I heard commands being shouted in both German and English with the latter predominating. There was considerable movement around me in the darkness. I lay still for some time, waiting for one of my guards to give me a command. After some time, I arose cautiously and began to move at right angles from the direction of the American attack, watching carefully to my rear to see if anyone was covering or following me. After approximately 100 yards, I turned and moved directly toward the direction from which the American attack had come. I whistled some American tune ['Yankee Doodle' according to one account]. I had not gone more than 200 yards before I was challenged by an American outpost of the 82nd Airborne Division. From there I went to their battalion CP, the 82nd Division CP, the XVIII Corps CP and finally my own division CP and to rejoin my unit."

In fact, the American paratroopers who challenged McCown belonged to I Company, Bill Dunfee's outfit. He remembered, "It was a cold, moonlit night with good visibility. It was too light to suit us. Ray (Mike) Maikowski was out with the point. Mike noticed movement alongside the road and eased the safety off his M–1. The man hiding there made his presence known, claiming to be an American.

"Mike told him, 'Put your hands behind your head and get your ass out here where I can see you.' It was an American, Maj. Hal McCown of the 30th Infantry Division. After he got over his fright —he was sure Maikowski was about to shoot him, and, knowing Mike, his fright was justified—he told us he had been a prisoner of the 500 to 800 Germans that charged through our lines earlier.

"By daylight, we had reached our new positions. It was bitterly cold and windy. We were told to dig in and establish a line we could defend until the end of the war, if necessary. Charles Lupoli and I selected a spot just below the high ground to our rear. It jutted out far enough to give us a clear field of fire to our right and left and across a valley.

"During the day of December 25, we dug a cave and covered it with tree limbs and the dirt we removed. We had three firing openings and felt we would be safe from anything but a direct hit from an 88. That evening the roof began to sag. We were outside cutting down a tree to reinforce it when a mortar round landed betwen us. Lupoli caught shrapnel in his foot and I was knocked down, but uninjured. I carried Lupoli back to the company CP and he was evacuated.

"While at the CP, they brought the mail forward. I got a box of Christmas cookies. I tried to get Lupoli to take some of the cookies

with him but he refused. We shared everything and were insepa-
rable. I would miss him. His godmother owned a bar and sent him
boxes of Ritz crackers with a pint of whiskey securely imbedded
among the crackers. It took a long time for our guys to figure out
how we got so happy on Ritz crackers."

Dunfee settled in his new home for the following few days.
There was no special meal for him December 25. "We went back,
a day or two later, a squad at a time, for our warm Christmas
dinners. It was really appreciated. After all those K rations, our
bellies felt like our throats had been cut."

There was, of course, no feast for Charles La Chaussee at
Lamorménil. "Christmas was cold, clear and a little quiet, although occasional artillery rounds were thrown in to let us know
we were being closely watched. There were fifteen wounded at
the aid station in Freyneux. The 3rd Armored Division attempted
to deliver blood plasma to us by artillery shells. This proved ineffective. The containers smashed on ground impact.

"Patrolling in our immediate locale, we found one German still
alive from those hit by machine gun fire from Lt. Roland Beaudoin two days before. Somehow, he had survived forty-eight
hours in the severe, near-zero cold. We carried him into a stable
near the command post. Aid men did what they could for him.
From the litter he gasped, 'You are so goot to me.'

"I thought, brother, you don't know the half of it. We were
prepared to fight beyond the last round, with bayonets. But if we
were not withdrawn or reinforced, it seemed only a question of
time before the enemy would overrun us, provided they wanted
to pay the price.

"Several men who had been wearing *gottmituns* belts [trophy
buckles taken from dead or prisoners with the inscription 'God be
with us'] now seemed to have difficulty holding their pants up.
German Luger and P-38 pistols lost all souvenir value. [No one
wanted to be captured with any loot taken from German soldiers.]
During the lull we became aware of things we hadn't noticed. A
small herd of cows grazed on the northern edge of Lamorménil.
Each day, a sturdy, young peasant girl arrived to milk them. Perhaps she was a German spy and we should have arrested her. But
then, that didn't seem likely. It could not have been news to the
Germans that we held the two villages. She returned each day,

passing through American and German positions each way. War or no war, the cows had to be milked."

McCown and Hall's captor, Peiper, in spite of the firefight and proximity to strong enemy concentrations, escaped. Sometime after the 30th Division major contacted the 82nd Airborne, the survivors of the task force reached a forty-foot-wide section of the Salm River, the last barrier between them and their comrades holding the town of Wanne. The SS soldiers linked themselves into a human chain stretched across the icy stream to provide passage. Except for a few unfortunates who fell and were swept away to a drowning death, the remnants of *Kampfgruppe Peiper* and their leader reached Wanne. Peiper himself had been grazed by an American bullet during the retreat. He also claimed to have suffered a violent heart attack but that seems unlikely since he continued, after a brief recuperation, to serve the Third Reich.

Instead of the glory of conquering the Meuse bridges, Peiper's venture cost the Germans 5,000 casualties, mostly veteran, superior soldiers, almost ninety tanks and an invaluable assortment of artillery, trucks and small arms. On the other hand, he had inflicted heavy casualties upon the American forces and driven a wedge exploited by other German forces.

Christmas in Bastogne was a mixed bag. The relief column, spearheaded by the 4th Armored Division, had not crashed through the ring around the 101st and their associates. Jack Agnew, operating a Eureka radio signal set, picked out a spot atop a pile of bricks as he and his comrades started to guide in planes bearing vital supplies. German 88s attempted to disrupt the operation. A direct hit on an artillery outfit near Agnew killed eight men in a dugout.

"The cold weather was the worst," says Agnew. "We only had field jackets we borrowed from an air corps pathfinder group. We were always hungry and thirsty but existed on very little food and drink. Our Christmas dinner consisted of hot C rations, an improvement over Ks with cow beets and onions. It was so cold that I remember finding a pig a tank had run over and which was frozen stiff. I stuck it up against a tree and it looked like a bread cutting-board. Many of the dead on both sides lay frozen stiff where they had fallen. Burial details had problems putting them on stretchers and, in places where the snow piled deep, were obliged to carry the litters shoulder-high.

"But in spite of the shells from the Germans, we managed to

guide in enough supplies to fight off the enemy. It was a great Christmas present delivered by air."

At Bastogne, the greatest price was paid by members of the 101st. Schuyler Jackson earned himself a Purple Heart. "I got hit when a shell landed nearby, ripped a strip off my field glasses. I had a concussion, and my left arm was slashed. They put a little bandage on it and half an hour later I was fine. But when I saw all of the wounded, it was tough. Goddamn, I give those doctors credit. They would work for forty-eight hours straight taking care of Americans and Germans."

On Christmas Eve, the *Luftwaffe*, taking advantage of the blackness of night, dumped two tons of high explosives, inflicting severe casualties. And it got darker before the dawn, as Manteuffel, thinking the Americans might relax their vigilance on Christmas, sprang an intense frontal assault. Beginning a few hours after midnight with a massive artillery downpour, the enemy came on with soldiers hidden by white camouflage capes and white-painted tanks, difficult to spot in moonlight or even by day.

Wallace Swanson, CO for Company A of the 502nd Parachute Infantry Regiment, had also suffered a minor wound at Bastogne, after rifle fire apparently ricocheted off a tank and nicked his right thigh. Sulfa powder and iodine prevented any complications, and he returned to duty without loss of time.

"We were at Champs [in the northwestern perimeter of the donut-shaped defense around Bastogne] and about 2:30 A.M. there was an all-out barrage, artillery, cannon, mortar and other firepower. It was raining, snowing, hailing down on our Company A positions. This was the strongest, most extensive, continuous barrage I was ever in. Their goal was to devastate our main line of resistance and all connection from the front to the back and around our strong points."

While Company B backed up Swanson's outfit, the enemy struck directly at the Rolle Chateau, site of the regimental HQ. Officers rallied a mixed bag of cooks, clerks, radiomen and even chaplains for a defense. The regimental surgeon collected his walking wounded from the stable that served as a temporary hospital, issued them rifles and led them to defensive posts, adding their numbers. The 327th Glider Infantry also became committed along its front.

The rifle and machine gun fire from all sources pitched dead and wounded foot soldiers off the German tanks and into the snow.

Fortunately, there were also tank destroyers on the scene and, along with bazooka-wielding troopers, they broke up the panzer assault.

Swanson had reported to battalion HQ, the enemy on top of him, and was still talking when all communications lines to him were obliterated. Hand-to-hand fighting in the buildings and houses of Champs followed. After several hours, Swanson could say, "The men held their positions on Christmas Day, securing protection and the enemy who infiltrated the forward positions were taken prisoners. Hot meals were provided by the battalion and regimental kitchen cooks by late afternoon and evening."

Schuyler Jackson was also at Champs. "They hadn't come at our area during the first days there. The temperature, though, was around zero. There were a couple of replacements who actually froze to death while on duty. I would always have two guys go out there to keep the men awake and prevent them from freezing. When one of our planes was shot down, I took a fleece-lined jacket from the body of one of the crew. It sounds terrible but he had no more use for it.

"There was a bridge in front of us. We had planted explosives but the detonator froze when they hit us on Christmas Day. Their infantry rode on the tanks and we were picking them off. I got myself a bazooka and hit one in the motor. The crew came out fighting. They did not surrender. We had to shoot them.

"We had originally put mines in the road but, because we expected the relief column, we pulled them off to the side of the road. When the German tanks came, some of the commanders must have thought the road mined. They drove off on the side and exploded our mines.

"We had enough ammo at our spot and stopped them cold. The last tank was turning back and going up a rise. I fired the bazooka and it was a one-in-a-million shot, dropped right down the turret. Except it didn't explode. The loader had forgotten to pull the pin on the rocket. He got some fancy cussing from me. But the tank didn't get away. Somebody else destroyed it."

The Christmas Day offensive was the closest call for the defenders at Bastogne. There would be one more half-hearted push on December 26 but the enemy was now very short of men and the tools of war. During the three days beginning with Agnew and company's descent into Bastogne, a total of 962 aircraft dropped 850 tons of supplies. On the day after the holiday, eleven gliders landed with doctors and fuel. The airmen paid in blood, 102 crewmen killed, with nineteen C–47s shot down and fifty-one other planes badly damaged. On the other hand, with the improvement of visibility, American fighter bombers struck increasingly hard at the enemy, whose vehicles often left telltale tracks in the snow that lead to seemingly concealed positions. Toward the rear of the Germans, the aerial attacks blasted any endeavor to reinforce or refurbish the German forces.

On Christmas morning, with the enemy attack halted, McAuliffe himself toured the local cemetery, where he saw German prisoners laboriously chopping holes in the frozen dirt for temporary interment of the stiffened bodies of dead paratroopers. He commented to the guards they should make certain the PWs were properly fed. Earlier, he had distributed to his men a mimeographed message. (Even under the most desperate siege conditions, the U.S. Army seemed to regard this preelectronic copying machine as vital as any weapon.)

McAuliffe's communique recounted the details of the German demand for surrender and his pithy response. His Christmas message then said: "What's merry about all this, you ask? We're fighting—it's cold—we aren't home. All true, but what has the proud Eagle Division accomplished with its worthy comrades of the 10th Armored Division, the 705th Tank Destroyer Battalion and all the rest? Just this: We have stopped cold everything that has been thrown at us from the north, east, south and west. We have identifications from four German panzer divisions, two German infantry divisions and one German parachute division. These units, spearheading the last desperate German lunge, were heading straight west for key points when the Eagle Division was hurriedly ordered to stem the advance. How effectively this was done will be written history, not alone in our division's glorious history but world history. The Germans actually did surround us, the radios blared our doom. Allied troops are counterattacking in force. We continue to hold Bastogne. By holding Bastogne, we assure the success of the Allied Armies. We know that our division commander, General Taylor, will say: Well done! We are giving our country and our loved ones at home a worthy Christmas present and being privileged to take part in this gallant feat of arms are making for ourselves a merry Christmas."

McAuliffe had caroled a less cheery tune to the VIII Corps Commander, Gen. Troy Middleton, on the eve. "The finest Christmas present the 101st could get would be a relief tomorrow."

As part of the final assault at Stoumont with Company C of the 30th Division's 119th Regiment, Curtiss Martell enjoyed a day of relative quiet while keeping a wary eye on the roads and woods below. "We were served a hot meal and it sure tasted good, having not eaten for some time. While we were dining and licking our wounds, one of our men went beserk and began to fire a .30-caliber machine gun from an outpost. He screamed as he was firing, 'The Germans are coming!' Three men subdued him and he was sent back to a hospital. He never returned."

Another nut that the enemy offensive had failed to crack was the stronghold on Elsenborn Ridge, manned by the 99th and 2nd Divisions. Sgt. Ben Nawrocki found Christmas Day painful, "it was a day of sadness. The mail delivery came in. We were asked to send a detail of men to the chaplain to open individual packages of those lost in each company. We were to take out all the perishable foods and eat them ourselves. The valuables were sent back to the families in the States. Most of Company B was dead, captured or wounded. We had a lot of food which came in handy, nutrition for half-frozen soldiers.

"We were receiving picked-over C rations, cans of of hash and beans. Men were angry at people in the rear who gave us the leftovers. The crates were obviously opened and then repacked. The food we took from the Christmas packages boosted morale and health. The sweets gave us warmth. We took the hard candy, melted it and added prune bars begged from the armored troops, along with crackers, to make a jelly.

"The Army promised us a good, full Christmas dinner and made good with all the trimmings. It was served cold, but darn good, turkey and all. I could not understand how they did it with the biggest battle ever going on."

Capt. Charles MacDonald of the 23rd Infantry Regiment, 2nd Division, with the remnants of his company, following the withdrawal from Krinkelt-Rocherath, settled into a defensive posture covering an Elsenborn section. Because so many men had been lost, the troops were first organized into provisional companies.

With the 99th and 1st Division units standing firm, MacDonald and his fellows began to pick up word on the status of their missing men. Initially, the company listed eighty unaccounted for. But each day brought word of soldiers now located at hospitals in the rear, with wounds or trench foot. Eventually, the casualty list totaled twenty-four, severe enough but not quite as catastrophic as originally feared.

"We had turkey on Christmas Day and New Year's Day," wrote MacDonald. "The division post office held up all packages that were not delivered during the breakthrough and delivered them on Christmas morning. Two feet of snow covered the ground but we were situated comfortably. Many attended special Christmas and New Year religious services held in the town creamery and thanked God for the blessings of which we were fully conscious."

The German offensive had also been frustrated on the southern flank of the Bulge, the Luxembourg turf defended by the 4th Infantry Division. Wave after wave struck at the positions in the village of Dickweiler, occupied by Marcus Dillard with Company M of the 12th Infantry. The enemy surrounded Dickweiler but their efforts to overrun the town were repulsed. "We ran out of anything to eat," says Dillard. "We killed a small calf and cooked it." Eventually, a relief force broke through to reinforce the detachment at Dickweiler. When Christmas Day arrived, Dillard and his buddies received a hot dinner.

While deliverance of Bastogne appeared at hand as Christmas Day drew to a close, Bill Boyle with the 1st Battalion of the 517th was engaged in his own form of rescue. Regiments of the newly arrived 75th Division, attached to General Rose's 3rd Armored jumped off in a Christmas Eve attack. There had been no daylight reconnaissance, the map studies were inadequate and the infantrymen short of ammunition. It was an unmitigated disaster. In the confusion, delays kept the troops from charging their objectives before daylight arrived. German weapons wreaked death and injury. Boyle's battalion surgeon told him of 900 casualties from a single regiment. The Americans floundered, short of their goals.

The 3rd Armored brass instructed Boyle to take charge. "We attacked up Le Roumiere, a hill, and swept it clean. I received orders to assume command of all American troops in the vicinity. With two of my staff, I undertook to put the assorted groups into positions and cover gaps with patrols. I knew the people from Task Force Hogan were supposed to come through that night and they would not have the password." While putting some of the men from the 75th in position, Boyle saw a column of soldiers, 200 or more, marching right towards him. He thought they might be Task Force Hogan. "I challenged them. I received no answer. On the third repeat, I said, 'Say something in English.' There was no answer. I commanded fire. But no one fired except me. My carbine jammed. I fired again and it jammed once more. I worked it by hand and fired. The column, which was German, now fled. And all of the troops in the area started shooting at the column."

As a result of his efforts during the first four days the battalion was in the Bulge, Boyle received a Distinguished Service Cross and his outfit was awarded a Presidential Distinguished Unit Citation.

Glen Strange, with the 27th AIB, had steadily withdrawn towards the west. On December 25, he was dispatched to 3rd Armored Division headquarters with orders to report the strength, position and other details of the 27th. He was ushered into the presence of General Rose. "I had not shaved since the 16th of December and had worn the same clothes since then, having lost all my others, along with my toilet articles. I began, 'Captain Glen L. Strange, with the 27th Armored Infantry Battalion, 9th Armored Division, part of Combat Command B, to make a report, sir.'

"He asked, 'Captain, are you an officer in the United States Army?'

"I answered him, 'Hell, yes, and we've been through hell, sir.'

"His reply was, 'Well, you don't look like it. Give me your report,' and he turned to his aide and said, 'See to it this Captain gets a bath, in my bathroom, uses my toilet articles, gets shaved and, Major, find him some clothes to wear, even if you have to give him some of mine.'

"After I gave him the report, I did take a bath in his bathroom with hot water, used his razor. By the time I was cleaned up, the Major had rounded up new underwear, clean O.D.s, and an almost new combat jacket and pants. The jacket was the General's, as it was too big and had the stars cut off the shoulder straps—you could see where they had been. This was the best Christmas present I could have received. I reported back to the Battalion and was envied by many for being cleaned up and having new clothes."

Like the 27th AIB, Dee Paris's 14th Tank Battalion was also in transit. There were no Christmas dinners, only C rations for rear echelon men like Casey Casebeer, a 2nd Lt. in charge of maintenance. Paris, himself, dimly recalls a special meal a day or so later. Not far from St. Vith, from D Company of the 14th paused in an open field. Tank driver Harold Lemmenes remembers, "We were washing our feet in warm water when Lt. Paris came by and looked at our feet and ordered us to go to the medics." Paris explains, "I made it a point to order a number of men to remove their boots and socks, particularly when I saw a man limping. I was no expert on trench foot—just figured that anyone having his boots and socks on for several days [Lemmenes said he hadn't taken his off for four days] should air his feet."

Lemmenes and others with sore feet lay at one end of a tent with their bare feet exposed to the cold air. Most of the bunks were filled with wounded men, groaning in pain. "That night," said Lemmenes, " happened to be Christmas. The next day we had our Christmas dinner. Jack Soukup, our radio man and gunner, and I convinced them to let us return to our company and we did that evening."

The 14th's Commander, Col. Engeman, arrived at the 82nd Airborne's headquarters in Werbermont after a harrowing odyssey through areas largely in German hands around dawn of Christmas Day. He enjoyed complete turkey dinners with both of his tank companies and his headquarters unit. The 14th elements in the vicinity of Werbermont now enjoyed a brief respite.

As Christmas Day drew to an end, Task Force Hogan, the 400-man task force from the 3rd Armored, at Marcouray, broke into small groups in an attempt to sneak through the enemy encirclement. "We put dirt in the gas tanks, dismantled weapons and buried pieces," recalled Arnold Albero. "We were told that friendly troops were to the north. I looked up into the black, dark sky trying to find the North Star. Suddenly, I wished I had paid more attention in basic training when they tried to teach compass reading at night. At dusk we started to leave, in small groups at ten minute intervals. As each left his position, they were wished well by those to follow.

"The march through the woods and hills was rough and I mean rough. We crawled across open fields with some snow on the ground, waded cold streams. When we stopped to rest, I could not only feel but also hear my heart pounding. Then when I looked back to see if the GI behind me was still there, I was relieved to see he was relatively closer than he should have been. He actually should have been at least thirty to fifty yards behind me.

"When you couldn't see anyone behind, you left a trail, a cartridge belt, musette bag, anything. I prayed that the guy in front of me knew where he was going, because I did not. The success of our infiltration rested on our lead man, whom I did not know. He was a lieutenant and I don't know which one, but to this day I pray for that man.

"At times we were so close to the Germans, you could hear them singing Christmas carols. To my knowledge, we were challenged only once during our march. After about fourteen hours, we reached friendly infantry."

In fact, the entire group of about 400, including the flier shot down while trying to airlift supplies, passed into the positions set up by Bill Boyle. The paratroop commander was told some of the task force did not contact any front line soldiers, probably because "in that fluid situation it was impossible to establish solid lines."

Harry Martin, the private with the 424th Infantry, who had become flotsam in the disorganized retreat until finding comrades, temporarily staying with a heavy artillery unit, fell asleep Christmas Eve with the promises of a feast the following day. He had been too sick to eat when he first joined his buddies in a former schoolhouse.

"All Christmas morning, we anxiously awaited our turkey dinner. They finally brought it to the schoolhouse. I felt like I could eat a whole turkey, I was so starved. I picked up a turkey leg, took one bite and spit it out. I suddenly became sick to my stomach. I guess the ordeal of the last four days took its toll. I spent all Christmas Day just lying on the floor. I was too sick to stand up or to even move."

Even those not directly engaged with the enemy experienced a dubious holiday. Lt. Harry Mason, who had been part of the retreat from Clervaux, now commanded an outpost in the vicinity of Neufchâteau, several miles west of the front. The day passed without noticeable celebration. "I was very cold and our food was K rations."

During the nine days from the start of the Ardennes offensive to Christmas night, the Allied High Command had been shifting about its responsibilities. The Americans wavered over the size of the portion rightfully due the British plate. The German approach clearly menaced that nation's army. Field Marshal Montgomery suggested to Eisenhower that he now command all of the troops on the northern half of the front, taking charge of both the U.S. First and Ninth Armies.

In his memoirs, Montgomery can hardly contain his satisfaction at the discomfort of the other Allied chiefs. "This could not have been pleasant for my critics at Supreme Headquarters. Morale was very low. They seemed delighted to have someone to give them firm orders. I have every hope the situation can be put right, now that we have a properly organized set-up for Command and proper supervision and control can be kept over the battle."

To associates he confided, "Personally, I am enjoying a very interesting battle; but one ought really to burst into tears at the tragedy of the whole thing. Possibly in years to come, certain people will turn in their graves when they think back on the past. There are some good sharp rocks ahead even now. At the moment, I do not see how this is going to turn into what Ike calls 'our greatest victory.' "

On Christmas Day, Montgomery, whose philosophy of the moment called for "tidying up our lines," reported he told Gen. Omar Bradley, " . . . the Germans had given us a real bloody nose. It was useless to pretend that we were going to turn this quickly into a great victory. It was a proper defeat, and we had much better admit it. Bradley had allowed Patton to go too far. The enemy saw his chance and took it." The statements seem myopic hindsight in light of Hitler's proposal for the offensive back in September, well before Patton had gone "too far." It is, however, a good indicator of the bickering in the high command.

Indeed, Patton scorned, "If Ike put Bradley back in command of the First and Ninth Armies, we can bag the whole German army. I wish Ike were more of a gambler, but he is certainly a lion compared to Montgomery, and Bradley is better than Ike as far as nerve is concerned." His diary notes of Christmas Day exclaimed, "Monty says that the First Army cannot attack for three months and that the only attack that can be made is by me, but that I am too weak. I feel this is disgusting and might remove the valor of our army and the confidence of our people . . . . If ordered to fall back, I think I will ask to be relieved."

In at least one instance on that Christmas Day, the two Allies combined their forces in an effective action. The 2nd Armored

Division, joined by the 3rd Royal Tank Regiment, smashed a significant piece of the 2nd SS Panzer Division toward the western end of the Bulge.

For many American GIs, the squabbles over command as well as the courageous defensive efforts at Elsenborn Ridge, Bastogne, and the approaches to the Meuse meant nothing. For these men, their role as active soldiers was over. They were prisoners of war.

Lt. Lyle Bouck, with the I & R Platoon of the 394th Infantry Regiment, stunned by a gun blast into his foxhole, had been among the first on December 16 to suffer capture. The following morning, after he bade goodbye to the frightfully wounded Bill Tsakanikas and only slightly less hurt Lou Kahlil, Bouck, with other PWs started a long journey to the east.

"On the second day as we were walking, we came to a line of pillboxes. It was snowing, there was German armor, bumper to bumper. The Germans were making fun of us and one of them came off a tank. He wanted my overshoes. I told him I was an officer. He started to scream at me. Sergeant Slape, who was still with me, said, 'Give him the overshoes. You're not in charge here. We'll all get killed.'

"I got my right boot about three-quarters off and I kicked it off. It sailed behind me. Another soldier jumped off the tank, hit me in the neck with a huge screwdriver and sent me rolling in the snow. They took me in a pillbox, where there was a German major and two soldiers with fixed bayonets. The major spoke impeccable English. At his request, I gave him my name, rank, serial number. He asked, 'What unit?'

"I replied, 'I'm a replacement. I don't know what my unit is.'

"He smiled. ''You're a 1st lieutenant and you don't know? Who is your regimental commander?' I said I didn't know. ''You're going to be difficult?'

"He told me to hold my hands up and he noticed my ring. I said something about it being from the infantry school at Fort Benning. 'Columbus, Georgia,' he remarked. 'I was there in 1938. It's a beautiful place.' Goddammit, I thought, he's got me talking about Benning.

'' 'You're from the 99th Division.'

'' 'I don't know my division.'

'' 'You're from the 394th Regiment and your Regimental Commander is Don Reilly.' I didn't answer. 'You see all those tanks out there? Do you have any idea how your army is going to stop this attack? We have jet airplanes that will knock out your air corps. We have secret weapons which will end the war quickly. We'll be in Paris by Christmas. You'll go home, not a winner.' "

The interrogation concluded on that note. "We walked until we reached a town with a railroad station. The next morning, December 18, they gave us a portion of a loaf of black bread, some tin cans with hot, bitter coffee and then loaded us into boxcars, like the 40-and-8, with seventy-two men counted off for each car. We stayed in those cars until Christmas Eve. For the more than six days, all we received to eat were two slabs of bread. The guys on the perimeter scraped frost off the metal to moisten their tongues.

"Four men died during the trip. It was a good thing it was so cold because it kept the bodies from decomposing. We were full of anger, hatred, cursing, punching one another as people started to die. I'd gotten over my shock at what happened, my personal embarrassment at what seemed like a failure. I thought of how we had such good people and yet this had happened. There was no remorse.

"On Christmas Day, the train reached Nuremberg and we received more bread. We were taken to the prison camp at Hammelburg. There they separated the enlisted men from the officers."

For Phil Hannon of the 81st Combat Engineers, the war had not ended with much of a bang, but his initial experience with the life of a PW mirrored Bouck's. "The Germans walked us into the square of a small village. They were too busy to bother with us. They were learning to drive our trucks and eat our chow. The gear shift on our trucks puzzled some of them, so we had a few laughs. One Kraut got a jeep going in reverse and couldn't shift it into forward. Another seemed to think second gear was the way a truck should run. It was funny but it hurt. We should have burned our vehicles.

"We were herded into a courtyard with a few apple trees. I was lucky and got one of the frozen apples. They told us: 'You will spend the night, here. This is where your latrine will be,' designating a corner. 'If anyone tries to escape, all will be shot.'

"For a time we sang. Christmas was just a few days off, so Christmas carols filled our minds with thoughts of home. We sang until the Germans complained that we kept them awake and if we didn't cease, we'd be shot. We lay next to and atop one another to keep warm. It drizzled all night and we were soaked by morning. None of us slept much, even though we were all dead tired.

"At 6:00 A.M. we were lined up four abreast in groups of 100 and told we'd get a break at the end of eighteen kilometers. About noon, after steady walking, we stopped in a village full of a Panzer grenadier outfit. We were supposed to get food and water. Instead, they stripped us of the overshoes we had. About six spuds were thrown from a window for better than 1,000 men. The men fought for them and the Germans laughed.

"All of us were thirsty. I gathered a couple of canteens and two helmets and let some guards know I wanted '*Wasser*.' Luckily, he was Polish. He took half a dozen others and me up the street to a house where he was billeted. While we filled our containers, he brought a bucket of boiled potatoes and motioned for us to stuff our pockets for our comrades. I had on my overcoat and loaded both pockets to the rim. When we rejoined the others, I had enough to hand two to each man in my platoon, which had stayed together."

The march continued, becoming increasingly more difficult as hunger, thirst and weariness gnawed at the hapless prisoners. They slaked their parched throats from dirty puddles, gobbled raw potatoes thrown to them by French laborers, felt briefly cheered when they passed through the German city of Prüm and observed the damage inflicted by the air corps.

Day passed into night; the men stumbled along. They sought to raise flagging spirits with song but that died out. "Most of us needed all our breath to 'pick 'em up and lay 'em down.' " The march finally ended at a railhead around 2:00A.M., nearly twenty hours after it began.

Water became an obsession. From a nearby stream, the PWs filled their canteens, then dumped in Halazone tablets for purification. But instead of waiting for the chemical to kill bacteria, the GIs gulped down the mixture instantly. At 11:00 A.M. the guards issued food, two bags of hardtack per man and a can of cheese to be split among seven persons. Hannon squirreled away some of his ration for future use.

As they milled about, Hannon spotted an acquaintance from B Company and yelled at him, " 'Where's Ben?' (One of my best buddies.) He shook his head and shouted, 'I think he got it.' That jolted me more than any of the shells that had been falling around me during the battle. Ben, dead! The best buddy a guy could ever have, dead! If I had a brother, I would have wanted him to be Ben, and the dirty bastards got him. That brought the war home to me. Sure, I'd seen guys get it. I'd seen dead bodies frozen in the stiff attitude of the dead and smelled their stink. I'd been shot at. I'd been scared until I wanted to run and hide my head and cry, but I didn't know what war meant until then.''

From the B Company soldier, Hannon learned that his friend Ben had received the classic "Dear John" letter breaking his engagement the night before the battle. Torn up, according to the informant, Ben seemed to have courted death. "He got some of the bastards before he went." He was last seen falling, as a "burp gun chased him over the hill."

Hannon said he was left with a "red rage" in his head and "my heart shriveled up in me. In a crowd of 1,000 men I was alone, lost and beaten. Time went by while my memory ran wild. Thoughts of times Ben and I had gotten drunk together, been cold together and dreamed out loud to each other. He was going to be my best man at my wedding and I at his, and now he was dead— the guy saw him fall. The guy saw him fall! Other guys had fallen with lead around them. I had and I was still all right. It will take a better army than the German one to get Ben. I saluted him with a little prayer, shook myself mentally, and went looking for my outfit.''

He found his platoon and soon they were hustled toward the rail yards. "Somehow we made it known we were thirsty and an old man and his wife started giving us water. Those old souls worked themselves like horses hauling water for us until the guards stopped them. Those people were helping us as best they could because they were built that way. We were their enemies but they were helping us. They weren't doing it because they knew Germany was going to be beaten. They did it because they were people, not puppets. Germany as a nation was rotten but its people are human beings with hearts and minds open to good things.''

The boxcars for Hannon and the others arrived, apparently fresh from carrying horses. The straw with the droppings remained as the men boarded. Jammed together, the prisoners' body heat thawed Hannon's feet. He removed his boots and twenty-four hours would pass before he could bear to touch his tender feet.

The trip descended into the depths of a nightmare. Dysentery afflicted many. Hannon, with a position beside one of the small windows, would hear a yell for "the helmet, for Christ's sake, quick!" Within a few moments, a helmet passed hand to hand would arrive at his spot and he would empty it out the window. To urinate, the men used a discarded cheese can. There was pushing and shoving, cursing, cries of pain as someone trod on another's foot. A few soldiers became delirious. Pleas for *wasser* or *essen* passed unheeded by the guards.

On December 23, the train halted in a railyard alongside another load of PWs, wearing the patches of the 28th Infantry Division. That night an engine chugging by suddenly stopped. The engineer and fireman jumped out and ran. Hannon heard the drone of a flight of planes. "We sat there and sweated. I watched from the window and saw my Christmas tree. The lead plane dropped a flare. It burst about 200 feet in the air, took the shape of a pine tree. The burning lights were red, purple, orange and yellow, looking quite like Christmas tree lights. Then things started to happen.

"Whomp! The first one hit and jarred us around. The engine on the track next to us kept blowing off steam like a giant hippopotamus. We prayed. Each time a bomb hit, I dropped to the floor. Guys were yelling. 'Crawl out the window.' 'If this damn train ever gets hit and starts burning . . .' I couldn't get out of the window and wasn't about to try. I couldn't see myself half in and half out when one of those babies hit nearby.

"Down at the other end of the car, they had better results with their helmet man. It was Corporal Stone, I think, who climbed out. A guard lying in a ditch, scared to death, spotted him and pleaded, 'Good soldier, don't run.' He ignored the guard, burrowed under our car, and unwired the door. We scrambled out as men from other cars did the same. We started looking for water and found a frozen ditch. We managed to get our fill. The bombing had stopped; the guards were worked up, shooting occasionally. We loaded back in the cars. Later, we learned eight men had been killed and thirty-six wounded during the air raid.

"On the day before Christmas, we were allowed to get water and they fed us, one-twelfth of a loaf of black bread and a daub of jam. It was more than we could handle in our weakened condition. A few of the boys were too sick to even bite it. Two of our chaplains came by and told us the bombers had wrecked the track ahead. Until it was fixed, we couldn't move. They wished us a Merry Christmas and moved on to the next car.

"When night came, we were still in the yards and worried about being bombed again. 'They won't bomb on Christmas Eve.' 'Hell they won't! They're out to win this war. Christmas won't be celebrated this year.' So we waited. From somewhere along the line of cars came a Christmas carol. Back and forth the carols went, first from our train, then from the other—'Little Town of Bethlehem,' 'Silent Night,' 'Deck the Halls,' and the rest of the favorites. That lasted for an hour or so. Then the Catholic boys in our car said their rosary while the rest of us were silent with our own kinds of prayers. The air-raid siren sounded once but we weren't bother by the bombers again."

On Christmas Day, during the morning, the journey resumed. They reached Frankfurt, where another old man sought to alleviate the perpetual thirst with buckets of water. But after a dozen trips with a bucket, it proved too much for him. Hannon's car received two helmets of water before the good Samaritan quit. The train rolled on and the prisoners reached the end of the line on Christmas Day.

As they unloaded, the GIs caught a glimpse of newspaper headlines that read 35,000 AMERICANS CAPTURED. The prisoners felt far fewer had been taken. Civilians gawked at them without expression. "We drew ourselves up and tried our best to look like U.S. soldiers and did right well, considering the condition of our clothes and bodies."

They disembarked in the village of Bad Orb, then walked the final three kilometers to Stalag IX–B. "The column came to a halt and the gates opened. We walked in prisoners, Christmas Day— and the gates of freedom had closed behind us. As we walked in, faces peered out of barbed-wire windows. They smiled and yelled, 'Russkies! Russkies!' Russian troops, allies were greeting us. We smiled and feebly waved as we marched by."

Sgt. Richard McKee, the assistant squad leader, who'd volunteered for the infantry and then been surrendered at Schönberg by his superior officers on December 18, began his odyssey to a PW camp with a 137-mile hike. The actual trip began on the twentieth. His notes for December 22 show: "Marched through Prüm, Germany. On the way we met only horse-drawn German guns and soup kitchens headed to the front. On the road we saw many

GIs killed a day or so earlier. They were still in their long overcoats and were frozen where they died. Only their shoes were missing."

A day later the column passed through Gerolstein, where their captors provided cheese and crackers. McKee endured nights locked up in chicken coops, or in stationary freight cars, and strafing from Allied aircraft. He began to lose track of time.

On Christmas Eve, McKee and his companions found a barrel of molasses in a farmer's shed. It became their Christmas dinner the following day. He noted for December 25: "Christmas Day we marched all day. It snowed."

Leo Leisse, the thirty-three-year-old graybeard enlistee and the ammunition sergeant for the 3rd Battalion of the 422nd Regiment, was among the GIs bagged in the abortive attempt to retake Schönberg. He recreated his experiences in the form of a diary while his memories were fresh. "We were marched a short distance to Auw after burial of some of our boys. The German dead were placed on top of their tanks and taken elsewhere. There were about 1,700 of us, assembled in several barns. The wounded were all placed in one large building and given what first aid could be obtained from a few medics and volunteer helpers. Many of us had held onto our first-aid kits but one of the German officers explained that our own men needed them. However, the Germans would not take them from us if we didn't wish to give them up. We then parted with the packets willingly."

Marched first to Prüm and then another twenty kilometers to Gerolstein by December 21, the GIs remained on a very short leash. When the urge for natural functions arose, the "men had no alternative but to go to the end of the building alongside of an embankment to do their duty, in full view of civilian, German onlookers, even young girls and children."

During a brief stay at an abandoned camp with wooden barracks, the GIs started to burn chairs and pieces of the walls for warmth until guards threatened to shoot anyone caught around a fire using such items. Leisse had already noticed some of his fellows adopting an "every-dog-for-himself" attitude while bartering personal articles with their captors for food and water. He saw more signs of the breakdown of fraternity as some prisoners went through a food line more than once, while others were shut out.

Like Phil Hannon, he soon found himself crammed into a boxcar with seventy others, necessitating turns to sit and stand. At least, Leisse's car had a slop bucket at one door. When it filled, the guards were called to empty it. They did not always come before it overflowed.

The train never left the station, however. On the morning of December 24, everyone hiked back to the camp—"presumably because the railroad tracks had been blown up by air raids. Upon leaving the cars, [we] took note of the twisted rails. Hurrah! Stayed all day at the camp, most of the time in unheated barracks, huddled together to keep warm. At 1700, again given some ersatz tea and bowl of weak potato soup, our feast for Christmas Eve."

Leisse endured Christmas Day there, soup and crackers in the afternoon, his holiday fare. "If we live through this, this will be the worst Christmas we've ever had or will have. About 8:00 P.M., they lined us up to move out and we stood in the cold while they counted and re-counted us before marching us out. It was a beautiful night but cold and the roads slippery with frozen, caked snow." About thirteen kilometers later, the prisoners were dispersed in barns and vacant buildings. "Could not have marched much further, so cold, tired, weak and mostly out of morale. Many already have been beaten with rifle butts because they lagged behind on marches, also fired upon for running off the road to grab a frozen vegetable such as a carrot, cabbage head, even cow beets, onions, spuds. To think this was Christmas, maybe our last, from the looks of the way the heartless bastards were treating us. Nothing will ever be this bad again."

Lt. Alan Jones, Jr., his commanding general father now aware his son was among the missing, followed the route on foot through Prüm and then Gerolstein. "Christmas Day I was in a boxcar. Several of them received direct hits. Many of us were already suffering from frostbite." He, like Hannon, was bound for Bad Orb. But there, they separated officers from enlisted men. Jones joined the group including Lyle Bouck at Hammelburg.

Jim Mills, the assistant BAR gunner from Company I of the 423 Regiment, along with Alan Jones, Jr., one of those surrendered en masse by their CO, began his descent into the misery of a prisoner with the march through the German lines. "The Germans would come along and take things they wanted, coats, overshoes, watches. I was walking alongside of Bob Holden. As we started to pass a parked tank, a German checked out Bob and indicated he wanted his watch. Bob undid the strap, then smashed it against the side of the tank. Man, was that German mad. Screaming and yelling, I thought he was going to shoot Bob. Another German came along and told him to shut up and move out.

"It got dark about that time and the tank started up. Somebody, Bob, I think, yelled, 'Let's push it in the ditch.' The road was muddy from the traffic and a whole bunch of us leaned against it. We couldn't budge it until it began to move forward. As it did, we shoved it into a really deep ditch. There wasn't much said but the idea caught on around us. A number of big trucks and other mobile equipment also went into the trench. We couldn't push things like jeeps or food kettles, which were horse drawn. There the drivers could see us. But we did our little part to slow down the Germans.

"We came to an American tank just off the road with a burnt shell hole in the side of the turret. A short way in front was an American ambulance. Just behind it lay two medics who had been carrying a stretcher with a wounded man. They had all been shot dead. The Germans had taken their combat boots and socks.

"We were on a train, sitting on a siding Christmas Eve. (Others say it was the 23rd.) It was dark and I saw what looked like fireworks out in a clearing. I thought maybe the war had ended and they were celebrating. Then bombs started falling. Somebody ran down the line of boxcars unlocking the doors and told us there was a bomb shelter across the clearing. The fellow close to the door said, 'Anybody who wants can try for the bomb shelter,' but since they were missing the tracks, he would stay. We remained in our boxcar.

"After the raid was over, you could hear moaning out in the clearing. One fellow was begging, 'Please shoot me, I can't stand the pain.' He kept screaming over and over. Finally, we heard no more. The reports were about fifteen men killed. The fellow who was screaming to be shot, we were told, had his legs and one arm blown off.

"We spent a total of ten days in the boxcars. From December 21 to 23 we received neither food or water, except the small amount when we were first loaded. On Christmas Day, I was locked in with about sixty other men. I believe we received a little food and water on Monday, the 25th."

Sgt. John Chernitsky, nursing a back wound, and who tried to rally resistance out of trumpet players, company clerks, cooks, bakers and service personnel trapped by the sudden advance, had immersed himself in the flow of U.S. soldiers to the rear. He met an American squad car, manned by Germans in U.S. uniforms. Thus duped, Chernitsky fell into the enemy bag.

Marched to Stalag XII-A at Limburg, Chernitsky was incarcerated in a civilian jail because the PW camp could not accommodate the hordes already packed into it. After the authorities dished out a two-inch-thick slab of baloney and a slice of bread, a German noncom announced in English, this was their Christmas dinner. By mid-afternoon of the holiday, Chernitsky's journey resumed aboard a boxcar. In addition to the feast earlier, the forty men in the car received a milk can of water, with a warning this would have to last them at least two days.

Pfc. Ed Uzemack, the reporter from Chicago who had become a veteran after surviving the bloody Huertgen Forest campaign as a replacement in the 28th Division, lost his freedom on December 17. "We could see that their tanks were in excellent condition and that the enemy soldiers were pretty sharp. Our immediate captors behaved a bit like gentlemen. The black-uniformed Panzer men were young, cleanshaven and very smart in appearance. They were efficient and cocky in their attitude towards us. They had captured us and quite naturally attributed this feat to their 'Aryan superiority.'

"The small group of men captured with me was permitted to secure blankets and overcoats before setting out on the march. Very few other prisoners had a similar break."

Things deteriorated rapidly, however. "We were forced to march several kilometers to a hillside air-raid shelter. We went through our first real shakedown as PWs. The German guards stripped us of every grain of tobacco and every ounce of food we carried. Many of the guards took from the GIs their watches, pens, billfolds, personal letters and other items of souvenir value. A good many of our men lost pictures of their loved ones."

Along with 400 others, Uzemack was forced inside the air-raid shelter, designed to accommodate only half that number. As he entered, an English-speaking guard warned, "Take a good deep breath, Yankee. It will be the last fresh air you'll get for some time." For almost two days Uzemack lived in the "pitch-black, damp, foul cave in the side of a hill. We lay in this dungeon with no food and little water. The air grew foul with the cave smell and the men became extremely irritable and hungry."

On returning to sunlight after almost forty-eight hours, Uzemack noticed a change in the quality of the traffic. "The Nazi column was still rolling down the road. Their equipment looked like something out of a junkyard. Vehicles that had to be towed, horse-drawn vehicles and other decrepit pieces rolled past us all day." He also marked the passage toward the front of a number of well-marked ambulances, carrying heavily armed troops.

Uzemack's group, as did the other PWs, frantically hunted for food and water. Uzemack, to his own horror, scratched in the mud to retrieve the remains of an apple tossed away by one of the Germans. To their surprise, almost a feast of half a loaf of sour bread plus marmalade and a small piece of cheese greeted them at a stop on December 20. Unfortunately, the guards failed to instruct the GIs that this was to last several days. Furthermore, the excess, such as it was, proved more than many roiling stomachs could handle. Quartered in a church and unable to leave the premises, Uzemack noted, "In the morning, the vestibule was almost ankle-deep in vomit and other excreta. A great many of the men had become ill."

The following three days they marched, finally stopping, after 100 kilometers, at Gerolstein. The convoy was commanded by "a monocled son of a bitch, with natty breeches, swagger stick and boots." He forced a twenty-man party to clean up an improvised latrine with their bare hands. He also relieved the men of all of their money, a collection that stuffed several thousand dollars in various currencies into his personal pockets.

Locked in boxcars at Gerolstein, the Americans heard the ominous hum of approaching U.S. aircraft. "One plane swept low over the train, zoomed up—and then came back. This time he meant business. We heard machine gun fire strafe an objective. Men pounded on the walls of the cars, screaming to be let out. A few medics in the car behind managed to get out. They waved their Red Cross helmets at the planes overhead and opened a few of the cars. Men streamed out in droves.

"Despite their fright, pain and weakness, most headed for a vegetable patch some distance away, fell on their knees in the furrows and began grubbing out the carrots and turnips, jamming them in their hungry mouths."

When the raid ended, the Germans rounded up the prisoners, firing warning shots over their heads and hitting one GI in the back. Subsequently, he died from the wound due to a lack of medical care and the hardship of the trip. Christmas Eve brought no surcease. The men abandoned efforts at caroling; the will to carry on appeared to be evaporating.

Late on Christmas Day, shortly before midnight on a siding at Bad Orb, the authorities relented and dumped eight loaves of bread and seven meat tins in amongst the nearly sixty Americans with Uzemack. "Despite the darkness, we managed to divide the food. Like many of the others, I decided that this was the best Christmas dinner of my life."

Clifford Broadwater, assigned to an antitank company in the 106th, had already arrived at Bad Orb and been marched off to the stalag. His train trip had been slightly less onerous than some of the others. He estimated only fifty men per car. Heat was provided by small wood-burning stoves, fired up by the prisoners who whittled scraps of fuel from a couple of pieces of lumber.

On Christmas Day, he took up residence in a barracks. Their bunks consisted of board bottoms wide enough for two men to lie flat on their backs. Each man received either a blanket or parts of a blanket and drew an armful of straw to serve as a mattress.

Sgt. John Collins of the 81st Combat Engineers, captured on the Prümerberg as part of the defenses improvised under Col. Tom Riggs in a futile attempt to preserve St. Vith, started his journey to a stalag on foot. "I was dressed fairly good with long john underwear, wool shirt and pants and a field jacket. No gloves, but I had my wool cap with liner and helmet. But we were all cold. After pleading and begging, two of us were allowed to entered the bombed house of the CP, found a number of blankets and some rations, which we gave away. I kept one ten-lb. can of bacon and one blanket.

"We marched all day and finally reached Auw, from where I had started on the 16th. Now it looked empty and bleak. As we continued on, we saw several dead GIs lying along the road and in ditches. We had a chance to inspect the Germany Army. It stinks! Mules and wagons—trucks pulling trucks and trucks with steam boilers in the rear using wood and coal. Soldiers in our uniforms (partially) and some of our vehicles."

On the third day he reached an interrogation site. He refused to answer a number of questions, providing only name, rank and serial number. His captors removed his watch and wedding ring. Collins spent the night in a barn. On the day before Christmas, wondering about the fate of others in his platoon, Collins hiked through Prüm.

"We have been accumulating more prisoners. We must have 900 or more. I am in the rear of the column and cannot get to the front where I had seen Lieutenant Colonel Riggs. He had a blanket draped around his shoulders. Some dogfighting going on in the air and we are all rooting for our planes. My feet are wet and extremely cold."

On Christmas Eve, the mob of disconsolate prisoners shuffled into Gerolstein. Collins reflected on the holiday: "We received one slice of bread. First food since Dec. 21. When we were being interrogated, I left my can of bacon with a Lt. whom I didn't know. I was afraid they would take it when they questioned me. Never trust a hungry GI! That was the last I seen of my bacon. I was told they made him go with the officers in the front of the column, so maybe it could not be helped.

"I seen some Jerries eating our rations—both K and C. I hope they choke! The more I see of the German Army, wonder what keeps it going."

Maj. William Desobry, seized while unconscious in an ambulance after being wounded outside of Bastogne, had recovered somewhat, thanks to the skill of a German surgeon. Shortly before Christmas, trucks deposited him and fellow prisoners in a railraod station. "I, along with about five American wounded, were standing there, all bloody, gory, torn up. The Germans were curious as hell. There were mobs of them in the station. They would come over, look at us and talk excitedly. Every doggone one of them had swastika arm bands and nine out of ten were in uniforms. They were doing this silly 'Heil Hitler' business. We stood there, watching it and all we could think of was, 'Gee, this is exactly like old Charlie Chaplin's movie [*The Great Dictator*].' "

Instead of a train ride, however, Desobry was driven to a large hospital in Andernach, on the Rhine near the Remagen Bridge. The facility housed hundreds of German and American wounded, most of the latter from the 28th and 106th Infantry Divisions and his own 10th Armored.

"The American doctors who were captured didn't do much. They were in a state of shock, just like we were. A German medical officer spoke English and he was one of the finest, kindest men I ever met. He came to see the Americans, and those who were still badly wounded and needing help were taken to the operating room. He was far more effective than any of the five or six American doctors who were captured. He was kind of disgusted with them and tried to get them to do more."

During one night, bombers flew over, apparently intent on wrecking the Rhine bridges. Desobry and others were rushed out of the hospital and sheltered, under guard, deep in the railroad station. "I was sitting next to a German guard, an old fellow, and he had been in the States. All during this bombing, he and I argued who was the better boxer, Joe Louis or Max Schmeling."

On the day after the air raid, Desobry boarded a German Red Cross train. "It was the most plush thing I had been on in years. Doctors and nurses were on board and they had music playing in the cars. We learned it was the 24th of December and they played Christmas music, the most popular was Bing Crosby singing 'White Christmas.' German and American wounded were all mixed together. At one end of the train there was an operating room."

Desobry's improving fortunes continued. His train halted in the marshalling yards near Münster as British aircraft pelted the area. The German travelers were allowed to leave for shelter but the prisoners stayed aboard. However, the attackers failed even to scratch any of the cars. When the all-clear sounded, the German travelers returned. The engine puffed a few miles further to deposit wounded from both sides at a huge *Luftwaffe* hospital in Ibbenbüren on Christmas Day. Desobry would spend the following month there, in relative comfort.

For still others, Christmas Day was a time of transition, a moment in the passage to the Ardennes. Pvt. Alan Shapiro, from the 2nd Battalion of the 346th Infantry Regiment, 87th Division, was nursing a bad cold, painful feet and the shocks of his combat initiation in Reims, about 100 miles from Bastogne on Christmas Day. Still almost a month shy of his nineteenth birthday, Shapiro grew up in a suburb of New York City, Mount Vernon, and as the son of a magazine publishing executive, assumed the right to a college education and a professional career.

When the University of Illinois, his father's *alma mater*, and like all U.S. colleges in the war years, starved for civilian undergraduates, offered academically qualified students admission even before they obtained high-school diplomas, Shapiro enrolled. It was an opportunity to tuck away a year of higher education before the inevitable notice from Selective Service.

"I don't see how anyone approaching eighteen in 1944, unless he was a sure 4–F or a pacifist, could have doubted that soldiering was his fate. I had no special animosity for 'Mr. Hitler,' just the generalized one that everyone I knew had. It was clear to us that Hitler was an extremely dangerous lunatic who had to be stopped and destroyed."

At Illinois, Shapiro enthusiastically soaked himself into what remained of campus life, joining a fraternity, striving to smoke a pipe and pursuing both the standard scholastic and extra curricular experiences. "I thought of myself as a budding sportswriter, having earlier typed up reams of baseball, basketball and football summaries, statistics, articles and features that I produced for my own pleasure. I could hardly believe that they paid people to watch ball games and write them up. As a reporter for the *Daily Illini* and a freshman, I was relegated to high-school track meets, but it felt like pretty important work to me then. I enjoyed doing it. Just as I had liked being a go-fer for the *New York Daily News* at $18.75 a week during the summer of 1943 and having the chance to run photos from Madison Square Garden to the *News* office when the Golden Gloves were on."

Plucked off the campus shortly after his eighteenth birthday by his draft board, Shapiro reported to Fort Jackson, South Carolina to train as a rifleman with the 87th Infantry Division. In mid-October, the Division shipped out from Camp Kilmer, New Jersey, bound for Europe. Assigned to E Company, Shapiro had developed close friendships with two other members of his twelve-man squad, Elmer Straka and Johnny Sirko. Straka was first scout for the squad, Shapiro the second. Sirko carried the BAR.

Aboard the *Queen Elizabeth*, Shapiro gaped at the extensive gambling. "There were several recreation rooms in our area which were exclusively used, day and night, for shooting craps, poker and blackjack games. In the aisles between the tiers of bunks and in almost every clear space, some form of gambling was going on. All of it was out in the open without any interference from the officers." After he succumbed to temptation and lost almost every dollar he had, Shapiro retired to penny-ante poker with his friends. He admits his one pleasure while pulling guard duty was to order officers to return to their cabins for their lifejackets, which were mandatory at all times.

In England, Shapiro, Straka and Sirko when off duty stuck together for an occasional pub crawl, or a visit to a theater that showed "movies made before I was born." They spent most of their leisure time in the barracks, writing letters back home to girlfriends and parents. A mild training regimen involved conditioning hikes and classroom lectures.

Around Thanksgiving, the 87th crossed the Channel to France. A few days in an open field, exposed to constant rain with the forlorn injunction to find shelter if you can, then a jolting two days packed into the 40-and-8s and, finally, after a truck ride from Metz, Shapiro, his companions and the other 4,000 members of the regiment marched, single file, an interminable column, through the mud towards the front.

On December 11, now part of Patton's Third Army, the 346th Regiment launched the first attack for the 87th Division. Moving up, Shapiro and his mates came upon "grimy tankers and artillerymen. One Joe leaned out the door of his halftrack and pointed to my gloves, which were nothing more than shreds. 'No gloves,' he said. Without another word he took off his gloves and handed them to me, also giving his scarf to Elmer. 'You guys need them more than me.'"

Shapiro plodded forward, dropped to the mud to dig in, "It was like taffy. My hole was a foot deep. I quit and lay down in the mess. Jerry shells came in and landed a few hundred yards to my left. Nobody was there. Everything was confusion. Nobody seemed to know what to do. I was fifteen yards in front of everyone. Dietrich called for a light machine gun. I doubled myself up in the mud and our machine gun fired over my head.

"Two tanks silhouetted themselves against the sky 100 yards away atop a hill. They started shooting. A pattern of bullets ran up to Max Wechter, the platoon runner, next to me. The bullets stopped in time. I laughed at Max. It wasn't funny but I laughed. An antitank gun fired at the tanks. They hit one four times. We could hear the clang of the shells bouncing off the metal. Firing a 57-mm at a Tiger is like hitting the Empire State Building with a golf club."

They dug in for the night but the rain of shot and shell from the enemy poured down harder. They tried to erect a wall of grass sod around the foxholes. Shapiro heard his mates gripe, "That won't stop a goddamn tank from running over us." "The Kraut tank was still clanking up and down. It was getting to me. That SOB is coming over this hill the minute it's completely dark."

To Shapiro's immense relief, word passed to his squad leader, S. Sgt. Dick Pusatieri, to tell the men to retreat. "I grabbed my rifle and pack. Elmer and Johnny right behind me. I took ten steps and, God almighty, here it comes. WHAM! Five yards from me. I hit the ground and somebody screamed behind me, 'Medic! Medic!'

"WHAM! I burrowed my face in the mud and prayed to Whomever is up there. I heard Elmer. 'I'm hit, Al. Al. Dick. Dick. Medic. Medic.' I was paralyzed. The shells kept landing in the middle of our platoon. They were screaming, moaning groans that I won't forget until the day I die."

When the avalanche of high explosions and shrapnel subsided, Shapiro rejoined what was left of his unit. He learned Pusatieri had assisted a wounded Elmer Straka from the field. Johnny Sirko appeared and Shapiro hugged him. But many others were already dead or badly wounded. In the morning he learned that Company E was down to 110 men from its original 189 and at that it had suffered less than any other outfit in the regiment.

Taken out of the line temporarily, its commander relieved for the botched attack, the 346th recuperated from the trauma of its first combat day before returning to the maw of war. For the former Illinois student, it was another diet of artillery shelling, tank and small arms fire while he tried to preserve his life groveling in muddy holes.

Shapiro had also begun to have serious problems walking. "I was at the point where it didn't matter how far we marched or what we did. My feet ached so badly that I just moved mechanically without thinking and only during breaks did I realize how my feet hurt. We pulled into a dinky town filled with trucks and GIs hopping on board. Each of us were given two blankets to wrap around our bodies during the ride. The trucks didn't have cover over them and the cold wind played hell with our faces. None of us knew where we were going and I don't think anyone cared much. At least there weren't shells coming over."

In fact, the 87th Division had been designated as one of the pieces of Patton's Third Army to smash the German salient. Thus it was that in mid-passage to the Ardennes, Shapiro and the others, after a nine hour ride, arrived in Reims on Christmas Eve. "We had a complete night's sleep, a wonderful Christmas present. Midway through the morning, many went to Christmas services given by the chaplains. We also received a chicken dinner, with fresh vegetables for lunch. For the first time in many weeks I felt as if I had really eaten."

Shapiro spent the remaining hours before dusk standing around warming fires, wondering what was to come next. After night fell, the men of the 346th once again readied themselves for a journey. "We piled onto the trucks which were covered and packed them to the limit. The whole platoon was in one truck and there was plenty of bitching. I had my legs doubled up under my chin, and I couldn't move without annoying somebody. I was luckier than most, since my back was against the side of the truck. The fellows in the middle rested against the knees of the person behind them.

"It was impossible to sleep. There was nothing to see so we just sat there. The ride seemed interminable. Guys hollered for the trucks to stop and allow us to relieve ourselves. But during the entire twelve-hour ride, we didn't stop once to allow us to stretch or anything else. Some men were afflicted with a bit more than kidney trouble and a lot of us suffered from bad cases of the GIs [diarrhea]. We pissed in the gas cans and shit in a pile of straw. Peeing was a delicate situation, since the nozzles on the gas cans were the size of a quarter and you had to be careful not to squirt all over everyone. It didn't seem funny to us and the truck hardly smelled like a rose garden. But there wasn't anything we could do.

"When we finally stopped and left the trucks, we didn't know where we were or even what country we were in. There were woods all around us. We marched off into them a few hundred yards away and dug in."

Chapter XIV

REVERSING THE TIDE

At Lamorménil, Capt. Charles La Chaussee of the 517th Regiment looked for a way to slip through the enemy positions that surrounded him. An indefatigable Sgt. Jack Burns led eleven patrols in search of a safe route, finally discovering an old logging path free of Germans. La Chaussee and the tank commander Eldon MacDonald agreed to mount all of the parachutists on the vehicles. "The tank turrets could not be traversed with the troopers on the decks, so the armament would be unusable. We decided the best solution in an ambush would be to hang on tight and go like hell. Riding the deck of a Sherman tank over logging trails and hilly terrain is very much like being in a small boat in a heavy sea. We managed to hang on; the alternative would not have been pleasant. And we arrived within an hour in the position held by the 289th Infantry, 75th Division."

In a footnote to his memoirs, La Chausse remarked, "The SS Officer who had been captured at Freyneux met with a fatal accident and failed to survive the trip." It is unclear whether or not La Chaussee meant the enemy officer was killed to prevent him sounding an alert as the Americans sneaked to safety under the guns of the Germans.

Gen. Tony McAuliffe and the besieged 101st Airborne lamented the failure of the 4th Armored to celebrate Christmas with them at Bastogne. But on the day after, the sledgehammer approach of the 4th Armored cleft a liberating wedge through to the Belgian town that came to symbolize the Bulge. Lt. Col. Creighton Abrams, CO of the 37th Tank Battalion, who frequently partnered with the 10th Armored Infantry Battalion, Abe Baum's unit under Maj. Harold Cohen, for combined operations, on this occasion directed a company of his tanks to lead the breakthrough.

To prepare the way, Abrams coordinated his schedule with field artillery batteries. As the dusk gathered towards four-thirty in the afternoon, six Sherman tanks, led by 1st Lt. Charles Boggess and followed by halftracks with infantrymen, started their run towards the Bastogne outposts. Abrams, perched on the turret of his tank cresting a hill three short miles from Bastogne, radioed the big guns, "Concentration Number Nine. Play it soft and sweet." The musical injunction referred to a common nickname for Time-on-Target action, "Serenade." Notwithstanding the gentle instruction, the TOT bombardment of 420 rounds smashed into the Germans hunkered down in the buildings of several villages en route.

"Let 'er roll!" messaged Abrams to Boggess, whose tank, "Cobra King," now raced forward. Boggess recalled, "The Germans had these two little towns of Clochimont and Assenois on this secondary road we were using to get to Bastogne. Beyond Assenois, the road ran up a ridge through a woods. There were lots of Germans there, too.

"We were going through fast, all guns firing, straight up the road to bust through before they had time to get set. I thought of a lot of things as we took off. I thought of whether the road would be mined, whether the bridge in Assenois would be blown, whether they would be ready at their antitank guns. Then we charged. I didn't have time to wonder."

Inside Cobra King, Cpl. Milton Dickerman, the 75-mm gunner, "used the 75 like it was a machine gun. Murphy [loader Pvt. James G.] was throwing in the shells. We shot twenty-one rounds in a few minutes and I don't know how much machine gun stuff. As we got to Assenois, an antitank gun in a halftrack fired at us. The shell hit the road in front of the tank and threw dirt all over. I got the halftrack in my sight and hit it with high explosives. It blew up."

Boggess's driver, Pvt. Hubert J. Smith, contended with a dirt-smeared periscope. "I sorta guessed at the road. Had a little trouble when my left brake locked and the tank turned up a road where we didn't want to go. So I just stopped her, backed her up and went on again."

The tanks, barreling through Assenois, running a gauntlet that included their own artillery lobbing in rounds dangerously close, destroyed what was left of the village. From the ruins and warrens beneath buildings, perhaps 100 Germans from the Fifth Parachute Division, comrades of the already-captured Josef Schroder, taken at Bondorf, sprang up to confront the American infantrymen in the halftracks. A nineteen-year-old rifleman, Pvt. James Hendrix from the 53rd Armored Battalion, silenced two 88-mm gun crews, aided a pair of wounded GIs and muted several enemy machine guns, deeds sufficient for a Congressional Medal of Honor.

Meanwhile, the tiny column led by Boggess bowled on at thirty mph, climbing the road through the forest. The machine gunners on the Shermans sprayed bullets right and left. Dickerman slammed three shells into a pillbox—later the Americans found twelve bodies inside. They raced by red, yellow, and blue colored parachutes still hanging from trees, mute evidence of fuel, food and ammo drops. When a gap briefly opened in the American armor traffic, several Germans seized the chance to strew mines across the road. The lone halftrack accompanying Boggess hit one, disabling the vehicle. Tank crewmen leaped from their steel vaults to the road, tugged the explosives from their path and the caravan bowled on.

Said Boggess, "I spotted some foxholes filled with men in GI uniforms. I yelled for them to come out because we thought the Germans might have men in our uniforms around Bastogne, ready to knock us off. Nobody moved, so I called again. After I said we were from the 4th Armored, a lieutenant from the engineers [Lt. Duane Webster] climbed out of his hole and said he was glad to see us. They had me covered, too." Little more than five minutes had passed since the TOT barrage.

Four of Boggess's six tanks actually made it to the outposts of the 101st Airborne. But Boggess and company never got an opportunity to see the sights of Bastogne. Instead, the tankers immediately established a perimeter defense to allow supply vehicles to reach the town. Some 400 enemy soldiers surrendered to the units of the 4th Armored that now swarmed through the breach. Shortly after five o'clock in the afternoon, Creighton Abrams shook the hand of Tony McAuliffe. The siege of Bastogne was officially lifted.

The relief by land began as a trickle; indeed, the manna from C–47s continued to fall. Five doctors and four enlisted medics arrived by glider on December 26 to set up a hospital. The enemy, however, did not melt away. Germans would continue to attack the town for several more days.

Success at Bastogne under his belt, Patton chafed at the decision by Eisenhower to hand over command of the First and Ninth U.S. Armies to Montgomery. He shared the unhappiness with Omar Bradley, temporarily bereft of a major hunk of his forces as a consequence of the SHAEF shifts. "Bradley and I had a long talk during which he told me that Montgomery stated the First Army could not attack for three months and that the only attacks that could be made would be by me, but that I was too weak. Hence, we should have to fall back."

To "Old Blood and Guts" the notion of retreat was unacceptable and he sounded the call to "Charge!" for all of his command. Along with the already committed 4th Armored, he brought to bear the 26th and 80th Infantry Divisions, the 11th Armored and the newly arrived 17th Airborne fresh from England. And the 87th, Golden Acorn, following its journey from Reims, entered the stage.

Pvt. Alan Shapiro, with the 87th Division, had clambered down from a truck after his miserable twelve-hour journey, ignorant of even the name of the country in whose snow-covered dirt he plunged his entrenching tool. In fact, he was now in Belgium, west of Bastogne, to take part in the offensive designed to dissolve the Bulge.

Adjoining the 87th was another newcomer to the area, the 11th Armored Division, whose troops had never been in combat before. Pfc. Seymour Blank, an observer for the 492nd Armored Field Artillery, a component of the Thunderbolt Division—so denoted by the jagged strip of lightning on its triangular patch—like Shapiro, was a native of Mount Vernon, New York.

A graduate of A.B. Davis High School, Blank attended Columbia in New York City for a year before enlisting, the day after Pearl Harbor. Following basic training, he enrolled in the ASTP program at the University of Oregon. "I studied, of all things, Spanish and the Mediterranean area, culture, history, geography. We worked quite hard, six hours of classes daily, an hour of physical education and an hour of drill. There was reveille every morning and taps every night, but except that we wore uniforms, one hardly felt that one was performing military service.

"I'm not sure why I applied for ASTP. I don't think it was to avoid combat. I was a Jewish kid and I enlisted because I wanted to get rid of Hitler. I don't think I hated all Germans, but mainly their leaders. Like many Jewish soldiers, I took off my dog tags, which had my religion stamped on them, in case I was ever captured.

"We all spoke very little about combat because no one could

project what we knew we faced. And the common fatalistic approach, "if a bullet has your name on it, there's nothing you can do," was constantly reiterated.

"I didn't analyze my fears at the time. Most of us had a feeling that we would make it, somehow, that all those awful statistics involved other, nameless soldiers. This changed radically when the real thing became a 24-hours-a-day part of our lives and we dug the deepest foxholes, blacked out everything in sight at night, gave no exceptions to someone who didn't know the proper password. We became very careful soldiers, who were looking at lots of death around us and were scared witless. I don't believe I had ever seen a dead body until some of my closest buddies were killed our first day of combat."

Blank's introduction to violent death came alongside Shapiro's 87th Division, committed to clearing the highway from St. Hubert due west of Bastogne.

The U.S. Army official history of the War in the Ardennes declares the 87th Division was at full strength when hurled at the Nazi forces toward the end of December. The historians were plainly in error. Says Shapiro of the division's status when it shifted to the Ardennes, "We hadn't received any replacements and some companies were down to a handful of men. As we were the best-off of all the companies with 100 men [compared to a normal rifle company complement of 193], thirty-five from E were to be sent to another company to even up the regiment."

Getting the troops into position, even the thinned ranks of the 87th Division, became a tortuous process. Shapiro, one of the transferees to C Company, labored over a series of foxholes in the unyielding, frozen dirt, huddled around fires that could never compensate for the frigid temperatures, vainly tried to shake incipient dysentery, fretted over festering sores on his hands and feet, while his outfit shifted, seemingly aimlessly, from place to place. "The war still appeared peculiar to me. None of us had the slightest knowledge as to how the overall picture of the war appeared. With all of our constant confusion, I couldn't see how we were winning and the Germans were retreating. I wasn't killing anybody. I didn't see any Germans and their only manifestation was in their shells and machine guns."

The soldier paired with him was slowly losing his grip. "He was always complaining, and every shell seized him with an agony of terror, no matter how far off the explosion. He had a dreary morbidness which affected us all. I couldn't blame him, for I felt much the same most of the time, but his talk bothered me."

Even in these dire moments, a suggestion of nature's ominous power struck Shapiro. "There was something oppressive but beautiful about the forest in the morning. The sky was dull but the snow-covered trees, as far as you could see, were enchanting. Nevertheless, I felt as if the trees were bearing down on me. A person with claustrophobia would have found it unbearable."

After one short trip by truck, the company halted in front of a house with a stone facade and lace curtains. The executive officer warned the soldiers to be careful, since the inhabitants, an elderly couple, had been kind enough to offer their hospitality. Shapiro removed his shoes and stretched out in front of a small fire. When an officer asked if anyone knew French, Shapiro volunteered to exploit his high school knowledge. "I understood phrases and sometimes sentences and made up the rest for the benefit of the officer. We learned finally that we were in Belgium. To our surprise, from somewhere batter appeared and the woman began making waffles. Where she had gotten all the flour and eggs, I shall never know, but I shall also never forget them. All afternoon she continued to make waffles and pots of coffee. I had at least a dozen with numerous cups of coffee. She refused to accept any money, although we had no place else to spend what we had. We realized that it was New Year's Eve sometime that afternoon."

Shapiro visited an aid station for treatment of his hands and feet. A doctor rebandaged the affected parts. Shapiro asked the physician for overshoes. After the medico angrily declared he would not release his patient for duty without overshoes, a pair was found. "They were Young's. He had been evacuated that morning and, though there was a bullet hole in the center of one, I took them gladly, even though they were about two sizes too large.

"New Year's Day was beautiful as the dazzling brightness of the sun nearly blinded me while reflecting off the snow. It was warm enough walking that we didn't need to wear our overcoats. We looped them over our front pack straps and set out. Due to somebody's brainy idea, we were even lugging gas masks now. Previously we hadn't carried them but a truckload had been brought to the company. They were the old black rubber masks and because of the intense cold, nearly frozen solid. By thawing them out over a fire, they could be used. They wouldn't have done a bit of good in a gas attack."

Shapiro's feet pained him with each step in what became another six-hour hike into the wilderness. He fell behind his comrades. A captain from another company dressed him down.

"My feet hurt," protested the private.

"Our feet hurt, too," snapped the captain.

"I don't notice you carrying a pack and, even if you were, I wouldn't give a God damn. My feet hurt, and I don't give a fuck what you say or think." The officer let it pass and Shapiro slipped even farther back in the ruck of marching men.

On the morning of January 3, the CO of C Company, obviously angry over the constant tramping about that seemed to have no purpose, advised the platoon leaders that anyone who felt physically unable to continue should report to the aid station, "but Christ help anyone who was faking."

Some twenty-five soldiers, including Shapiro, dropped out to take advantage of the offer, leaving a bare twenty-five, half of a platoon, from an entire company, to forge ahead. At the aid station, men with problems similar to Shapiro's agonizingly sore feet were shunted aside. There were too many wounded from other companies requiring immediate medical attention at the makeshift aid station.

The foot-pained private and his similarly complaining buddies enjoyed a night of rest, except for stints of guard duty. In the morning they discovered that, because of a threatened attack, the aid station had retreated several towns. While waiting for transportation to the facility, Shapiro stayed with a "colored tank bunch." These men belonged to the 761st Tank Battalion, the first African-American armored outfit to fight in the European Theater of Operations. Over the next few days, the black tankers would work with infantrymen of the 87th Division in a savage series of battles to retake the town of Tillet from the Germans.

When he finally reached the medics, Shapiro said, "The doctors examined us quickly, letting most of the boys stay for the night. I was hoping I would get the same. Some fellows, despite their vehement protests, were packed off to the company.

"I took off my shoes. My feet were very swollen. I started telling the doctor my story. He didn't listen. He just kept studying my feet.

" 'We're evacuating you, soldier.'

"I was in seventh heaven; Banks, Vitrano and others there were green with envy."

Shapiro was diagnosed as suffering from frozen feet. He had incurred a variety of the million-dollar wound, even though his malady had deteriorated to the point where he could no longer bear to set foot on the floor. By ambulance, swathed in blankets, he traveled west, until a further exam at a hospital tagged him "UK litter." He was on his way out of the ZI, the zone of the interior, where men were shot at and shelled. Thousands of other U.S. soldiers developed the same disability or its more serious kissing kin, trench foot.

Meanwhile, the 11th Armored Division on the flank of the 87th staggered through its first encounters with the enemy. Patton pronounced himself appalled at the high rate of casualties in both of those divisions as well as the newly committed 17th Airborne, which he attributed to combat inexperience. In his diary for January 4, he commented, "The 11th Armored is very green and took some unnecessary losses to no effect. There were also some unfortunate incidents in the shooting of prisoners. (I hope we can conceal this)." If indeed such executions occurred, they were kept secret.

Certainly, as the killing dragged on, amid the frightful living conditions, the mood of soldiers turned increasingly vicious. George Graves, a corporal in headquarters company of the 504th Parachute Regiment of the 82nd Airborne recalled, "After a month in the Ardennes, our old vets were punch-drunk and didn't give a damn what happened to them. They had nothing to look forward to—except a wound that would evacuate them or a coffin . . . . fighting mad after wading through waist-high snowdrifts for twelve hours to get to Herresbach. Some of our boys ran wild, shooting everything that moved in the town. The Krauts used up all their ammo shooting at our guys, then came out yelling, 'Kamerad!' Our troopers would reply with 'Kamerad, hell!' and a burst from a tommy gun."

The sights of combat overwhelmed Cy Blank. "I suppose I will never forget seeing a hand-painted road sign that read 'Bastogne, 4 Km' on a dirt road in Belgium. But I really cannot describe some of the awful things we saw as we got closer. I still, almost fifty years later, am unable to bring myself to put into words what I saw and smelled and touched."

Patton was more bemused than appalled by what he saw. "I drove to visit the troops attacking Houffalize. At one point we came across a German machine gunner who had been killed and apparently instantly frozen, as he was in a half sitting position with his arms extended, holding a loaded belt of ammunition.

"I saw a lot of black objects sticking out of the snow and, on investigating, found they were the toes of dead men. Another phenomemon resulting from the quick freezing of men killed in battle is that they turn a sort of claret color—a nasty sight."

After Arnold Albero with Task Force Hogan infiltrated through the German positions on Christmas night, he hoped for at least a few weeks out of harm's way. But by December 30, the outfit had been reequipped with halftracks, jeeps and trucks. The 3rd Armored Division began to move south towards Houffalize, a key town in the hands of the Nazi armies.

"We were ambushed by enemy infantry. Our lead vehicle was knocked out. A fierce firefight ensued. I jumped off the halftrack. I suddenly felt weak, stunned, shocked. I couldn't believe it had happened to me. I tried to get up but I could not. I put my hand on my leg and felt my pants stick to my skin because of the bleeding. This is a moment when you feel alone, helpless and scared. I don't know how long I lay there, ten minutes or an hour. A buddy stayed with me until a medic finally gave me a shot of morphine. The next thing I remember, I was in a field hospital for my first operation."

On the same day that Alan Shapiro's limping walk-on role in the Ardennes ended, the 517th Parachute Regiment returned to the fray. Regiments from the 62nd *Volksgrenadier* Division, poorly trained recruits blessed with positions on the high ground, and pieces of the 1st SS Panzer Division, along with other German units, occupied the turf designated as the 517th's objective. From the southwest, the 551st Parachute Battalion, previously attached to Jim Gavin's 82nd Airborne, expected to subject the enemy to a two-pronged blow.

Lt. Col. Bill Boyle, his 1st Battalion in reserve, followed the initial attack by the 517th's 2nd Battalion from his CP, situated on a slope offering Boyle an excellent view of the battle. He watched the American paratroopers slam into a stonewall defense that left 100 GIs dead and wounded in the snow. Without waiting for the summons from above, Boyle instructed his exec to prepare troops for movement and on his own rushed to the regimental CP. "From where I was I saw that something would have to be done and I wanted to influence the orders I would receive."

In charge of the overall operations, the 82nd Airborne chief, Gen. James Gavin, personally reconnoitered the area. He was highly dissatisfied with the lack of progress.(Later, he blamed the "limited experience" of the 517th, which was erroneous, considering its participation in Italy, southern France and the Ardennes only a few days earlier.) The plain truth is the German soldiers, motley as they were, resisted stoutly and a counterattack in which they forded the shallows of the Salm River, further harrassed the Americans. Gavin chewed out the 517th Regimental Commander, Col. Rupert Graves, stabbing a finger into a map. He pointed at the villages of St. Jacques and Bergeval. "I want those towns by daylight tomorrow."

As soon as Gavin quit the scene, Graves said, "Get Boyle," who, anticipating the call, was right at the door. The 1st Battalion leader and his chief studied the map. Graves proposed that Boyle's outfit pass through the battered 2nd Battalion and advance up the bare, sparse covering of the hill in front of the two objectives. "Feeling that this could only result in having two battalions chopped up, I argued and eventually persuaded Graves to let me follow the 551st, using the woods for cover."

They worked out a plan and Boyle led a force of perhaps 250 to rendezvous with the 551st Battalion. Charles La Chaussee's C Company was among those on hand. A Company, taking five on a hillside nearby, was to join the battalion when possible.

Boyle had hoped to travel through at least part of the woods before dusk and maybe even reach St. Jacques before dark. But by the time the column started out, night had already fallen. Boyle navigated in the darkness by a compass and with a guide from the 551st. The mile-and-a-half hike to St. Jacques dragged on for five hours. In the black of night and through the thick underbrush, the paratroopers could stay together only by each man keeping a hand upon the backpack of the trooper ahead of him.

In spite of the presence of a guide, Boyle and his mates never located the soldiers of the 551st. However, they maneuvered right to the outskirts of St. Jacques before discovery. "It was going on midnight and we asked for artillery to help us in. We had already lost our surprise. The 82nd Division artillery advised us that the quota for the day had been used. I could have blown up but I told B Company to wait a few minutes, then call for artillery right after midnight and to go at that time. This worked out well."

B Company swiftly overcame the enemy, mowing down soldiers seeking to form up in the street and crushing all resistance in thirty minutes by working house to house with rifles and grenades.

A captive told Boyle that the other objective, Bergeval, had all but been abandoned, with perhaps fifteen men who desired to surrender still there. Boyle, cautiously sent La Chaussee's C Company to establish the American presence. Working into position, C Company killed five German sentries. Then artillery prepared the ground for a full-scale American assault. The supposedly tiny German band, allegedly ready to run up the white flag, responded with automatic weapons. That drew more salvos from big guns.

La Chaussee's people charged, three platoons abreast, whooping, shooting from the hip. When the skirmish ended shortly before daybreak, not a single GI casualty was recorded but 121 Germans gave up, twelve to fifteen lay dead and another twenty escaped. In the street stood two jeeps and a halftrack, all in good operating condition and bearing the insignia of the U.S. 106th Infantry Division. Boyle made certain to speak with his support-artillery battalion commander, who assured him that, rationing or not, the 517th would receive its barrages in the future.

Boyle's expedition bagged a total of 150 enemy soldiers and killed thirty to forty. An additional seventy-five men in the vicinity surrendered to another unit passing by that day. The total cost to the 517th was two troopers. The success, of course, stemmed not only from the skillful disposition of forces by Boyle but also the actions of the 517th's 2nd Battalion and the 551st Battalion troopers that pinned down the German units.

The CO of the 517th's 1st Battalion credits his battle achievements to lessons learned from his first CO after graduating from West Point, Capt. Carl Herndon. "During tactical problems and discussions he emphasized the principle of 'Fire and maneuver,' often preached at the infantry school at Leavenworth but frequently forgotten in the field. It combined to keep me on my toes mentally in combat. Maneuver is not just for armor. In fact, Gen. Norman Schwarzkopf demonstrated in Iraq the importance of maneuver in battle."

On the following day, regimental headquarters urged Boyle to cross an open area and take high ground beyond Bergeval overlooking the Salm River. Boyle advised Graves that it would be better to delay until the cover of night. "Actually, I hated night fighting and as I believed that a leader leads by doing, I was forward, not rearward, during attacks. I convinced Graves to go along with my ideas, even though he did so reluctantly. I am sure he was pressured by General Gavin. But I know in my heart that we did the job better than if I had relented to the pressure, and surely with less casualties."

But among those casualties was Boyle himself. The swift ebb and flow of units during the period frequently cut contact between outfits. That night, after his people struggled eastward through the snow and darkness to new positions, Boyle began to worry about his inability to locate the 551st Battalion. He dispatched a patrol to look for the missing troops but it reported no contact. Boyle himself then led a probe to seek the 551st, again finding no one.

Accompanied by his intelligence specialist, S. Sgt. Robert Steele, and two troopers, Boyle decided to retrace his steps to Bergeval in hopes of learning the whereabouts of the 551st. He had been warned enemy soldiers might be roaming the area.

"Near the bottom of the slope in the open area, there was a bush about fifty feet from a lone tree. The field was snow-covered and there was bright moonlight. We were a few feet beyond the bush when we were challenged in German. I dove toward the bush as a machine gun fired." Three bullets from the burst of automatic fire smashed into Boyle. Steele and the two others answered back with their weapons, checked to make certain their assailants had left the scene and then returned to their fallen commander.

Meanwhile, as Boyle lay bleeding in the snow, he heard a tremendous racket of gunfire on the ridge where he had left his main body of troops. "I prayed, God, don't let me die. This was a moment when I experienced fear. I knew my brachial artery [in the arm] was severed and that I could not stop the bleeding. By the time Steele and the others got to me, I accepted that I was dying and must do what I could for my outfit. It seemed that the brief prayer had given me peace and I was now calm."

He gasped to Steele, "Get back to Bergeval. Tell [Maj. Donald] Fraser that all hell's broken loose up there, and that I'm hurt and for him to take command." The three walked away, but Steele returned alone.

"They will deliver the message. I'm not leaving without you," Steele answered.

"Goddammit!" swore Boyle. "There's nothing you can do for me—I'm dying."

Boyle was far too big and heavy for Steele to haul through the snow and up the slope to Bergeval. Measuring his words to fit the man, he said, "The trouble with you, Colonel, is that you don't have enough guts to try to help yourself."

Desperately wounded as he was, Boyle was infuriated by the remark. "Damn it, Steele, give me your hand." Boyle pulled himself from the ground and, leaning on his intelligence noncom, hobbled nearly a mile to Bergeval. Before he would consent to entering the aid station, he insisted on briefing Fraser, his exec.

Still conscious despite his terrible wounds, Boyle heard Capt. Ben Sullivan, the battalion surgeon, instruct his assistant to stop working on Boyle, arrange for his evacuation and ply his art on someone whom he could help. "I knew he was right. They were unable to put plasma into me, as badly as I needed it. Later, Sullivan visited me when I was recuperating in a hospital in the States and told me he did not think I would live to get to a hospital.

"I never had an opportunity to ask Steele, 'Why did you stay with me and get me to come in at some considerable risk, when by simply obeying my order, you would have been relatively safe?' I believe the explanation is that when men live, eat, train, gripe and suffer together, they stick together."

Even as the physicians all but gave up on Boyle, his subordinate La Chaussee with C Company, as Boyle realized while lying in the snow, also was in desperate straits. La Chaussee had been instructed to take his men at night to those heights near the Salm. Plowing through the snow in the dark, fatigue and poor visibility caused the captain to convert a tree into an enemy soldier in full battle regalia. When the apparition vanished, La Chausee plodded on.

One of his platoons halted where an east-west trail crossed their front. A lieutenant informed his CO the men heard motors on the trail and glimpsed a communications wire. "I sensed something moving down the trail, a few feet to our right. I brought the carbine to my hip and said, 'Halt!' The movement continued and I fired. In the same split second a voice called, 'Nicht schüttenzie!'

[stop shooting] and a bullet snarled by. I had intended to fire several rounds but the damned thing missed fire on the second trigger pull. Nearby a trooper cocked his arm back to throw a grenade. He'd already pulled the pin and the grenade would have bounced off the trees back into us. I caught his arm, forcing him to roll it down the trail, underhanded.

"The grenade exploded and Allison and another man ran down the trail, returning with a German soldier and a small sled he had been pulling. It was loaded with supplies."

Deciding an enemy force was close at hand, La Chaussee saw no way to organize an attack through unexplored an uncharted ground in the dark. The troopers began to dig in, apathetically, by La Chaussee's account. He considered a strong defensive posture urgent and, as forcibly as possible, so informed the platoon leaders. He had barely finished when a firefight erupted. Out of the gloom a halftrack lumbered straight towards La Chaussee and the strung-out company. The captain briefly trained his carbine at it, then realized the weapon had jammmed. The armor passed without a shot exchanged. On its side the troopers observed a big white American star, one more piece of booty now in the service of the enemy.

The shooting now instensified. Troopers died and were wounded in their foxholes. La Chaussee sent a runner to inform Boyle at Bergeval (the captain knew nothing of his leader's fate). But the message bearer fell into a hole in his path. The arms that grabbed him were not friendly. He was a prisoner.

Shivering in the cold night air, the two sides exchanged artillery and mortars. Only one of C Company's six machine guns still functioned. The other five ran out of ammunition or froze. The troopers who had kept their gun operating urinated on it to prevent sticking. With his radio shot to pieces, La Chaussee communicated through runners and shouts. At one point he yelled, "Has the A Company platoon gotten here, yet?"

In the dark a voice inquired, "How many platoons has A Company got?"

"They've got sixteen platoons and they're all coming at you bastards!" shouted La Chaussee. "Suddenly overhead there was a blinding explosion, and a streak of white light reached down and struck me just below the right knee. It was as though someone had walloped me with a baseball bat, although there was no immediate pain. Five other men around me were hit by the same shell. Aidman Hugh Webb was very busy. He crawled to me, cut away the pants leg, and before I knew what was happening, shot an injection of morphine into the leg. The morphine finished what fatigue and exposure had started. For an hour I was unconscious."

While he was out, reinforcements from A Company made their way to the scene. The Germans relinquished the field. As a day-break fog lifted, La Chaussee awoke from his stupor to look out on an eerie scene. A scant fifty yards away from his position lay the shattered hulks of two antitank guns, and a halftrack rested in the snow. Enemy dead and wounded spread over an acre of killing ground and in some spots pairs of bodies lay heaped upon one another. But his company had twenty-three casualties, two dead, one missing, twenty wounded.

When the moment for La Chaussee to leave came, he grabbed for his gear, web belt, canteen, ammunition pouches, binoculars—placed earlier beside his foxhole—the stuff disintegrated in his hands, shredded by shot "as though an army of giant ants had been at it."

"Leaning on an aidman on one side, I began to hobble down the hill. Along the way, we passed several foxholes. A German popped out of one of them, hands held high. 'Me Polski, Kamerad,' he said.

" 'All right, Polski,' I said. 'Give us a hand here,' and with him on the other side, I limped to Bergeval."

La Chaussee was in shock by the time he reached the same aid station where Boyle had come a few hours earlier. On the morning of January 5 there were thirty-five casualties from the First Battalion and twenty from the Third. Since La Chaussee appeared likely to survive his injuries, he was temporarily consigned to a nearby stable. The captain remembered protesting, "Don't put me out here with the horseshit."

Several hours later he reached an operating table in a surgical hospital serving the 82nd Airborne. The shell fragment that walloped his leg had struck about two inches below the knee and close to the shinbone. Either it was believed anesthetic was unnecessary or because of a shortage of time, the surgeons worked on La Chaussee without dispensing painkillers. Four men held him down while the scalpel probed the wound. The pain was excruciating but the fragment, one-quarter the size of a fingernail, was removed in two minutes and the wound closed with twelve stitches.

Evacuated to a hospital in Liège, La Chaussee luxuriated in a ward bed atop the five-story building. He was puzzled at the empty beds around him until a man stuck his head out from underneath one. La Chaussee inquired what he was doing down there.

"You'd better get down here, too. This place is under buzz-bomb attack and if they hit the roof you're dead unless you're under cover."

"I had been out in the cold too long to pass up a chance to stay in bed and figured that if a buzz bomb did hit the top floor we were all gone anyway, whether in bed or under it. So I remained happily beneath the covers."

Others in the Ardennes, taking the offensive to eliminate the Bulge, encountered similar stiff resistance. All along the southern shoulder, where the German Seventh Army had failed in achieving its goals while on the offensive, the Nazi infantrymen refused to cut and run, exacting a high price for every yard yielded.

The 84th Division, whose CO, Gen. Alexander Bolling, had a lieutenant son in the same stalag as Bouck and Jones, worked with the 2nd Armored Division to knock the enemy out of a series of towns. These included Dochamps, where La Chaussee was routed, Marcouray where Task Force Hogan had been trapped, and Bolling's soldiers recovered the crossroads of Baraque de Fraiture, site of the rout of the remnants of the 589th FA, and F and G Companies of the 325th Glider Regiment with Barney Alford, Joe Colmer, Leonard Weinstein.

Stubborn refusal to withdraw marked the confrontations for the 30th Division. Heavily engaged almost from the start of the breakthrough, the Old Hickory soldiers began the task of expelling the enemy. A few days after Christmas, the company commander asked Platoon Sgt. Curtiss Martell to lead a patrol into no man's land, a stretch of hills, trees and fields blanketed with snow.

"I selected five men to go with me. We were given white capes so that we would blend into snow. At nightfall, we proceeded from the edge of town on a hill where several of our tanks were parked. The weather was bitter cold, the snow almost a foot deep.

"We came to a large chalet and entered to warm ourselves. We found several GIs and a couple of women in a festive mood. The sight of us in white capes caught them by surprise. They were fearful that we could be Germans. I quickly identified us and our mission. They felt at ease but I was very upset that no sentry was posted outside. I considered talking to the man in charge but dismissed the thought because we needed time to complete our mission.

"As we headed toward enemy territory, flares lit the sky periodically. We traveled through the heavy snow for about two miles, when we were stopped by barbed wire. Covering the wire cutters with my gloved hand to deaden the sound of the cutters was not enough. The noise carried in the crisp, cold air and could be heard distinctly. Several flares again illuminated the sky. We lay still in the snow.

"Once past the barbed wire, we continued toward enemy lines. We came to a road, which I was not about to walk down. I heard Germans talking, a machine gun bolt slam shut and more flares shot up. Evidently a German outpost was located nearby and they must have sensed our presence. Our mission was not to engage in combat but to locate the enemy. I motioned for us to get the hell out of there.

"We failed to gain knowledge of the enemy's strength. But I had taken into consideration the possibility of being captured and executed, as had other GIs and civilians been. We had heard of the Malmédy Massacre. I also heard words to the effect of take no prisoners. That was just troop talk, because I do not believe such an order would come from high echelon. [A fellow survivor of the 30th insists there was official sanction for a no-prisoner policy.]

"Two days later, our troops launched a new attack. Our unit didn't gain much ground because of rocket and mortar fire by the enemy. The dark of night came quickly, so we held our positions. It was so cold that we crawled under the tanks, to absorb some of the heat emitted from the engines. My feet felt like I was walking on blocks of wood and I thought about some guys who lost their feet because of trench foot.

"The following day, I saw some German prisoners, walking barefoot on the road. They had been wearing American combat boots and the guys who took them as prisoners made them remove the boots. This was in retaliation for the massacre. Soon after, I was wounded in the knee by shrapnel from a mortar. Medics ripped off my pant leg, dressed the wound. A jeep picked me up along with some others and took us to a field hospital. I was sent to a hospital in Paris where the shrapnel was removed. The wound kept me out of action for about a month."

The strategy deposited an equally onerous burden, ousting a determined enemy from the town of Thirimont, between Malmédy and St. Vith, upon Frank Currey, elevated to platoon sergeant with the 120th Regiment, a brother to Martell's outfit. "It was a disaster, the result of poor planning. We should have bypassed it. What a screwup! The place was supposed to be defended by the Hermann Goering Division, made up of parachute troops.

"With Adam Lucero and a fellow named Gould, the three of us got into the building that was a regimental headquarters. They were upstairs, while we were on the ground floor. Lucero kept lobbbing hand grenades over our heads, but a bullet through the throat killed Gould. A couple more from the company, including the CO, joined us. He got a few Germans himself. Eventually, we set fire to the building and got out. Years later, I came across an article a German officer wrote about the 'crazy' Americans who set that house on fire."

Nicked in front of Malmédy for a Purple Heart, a slug passed cleanly through Currey's arm at Thirimont. "I put a patch on it and back you go." For his actions at Thirimont, Currey was awarded a Silver Star to go along with the Congressional Medal of Honor earned through his previous exploits.

Like Martell, he does not believe anyone in a position of authority encouraged the killing of those who surrendered. "In fact, orders came down expressly directing us to take prisoners. They weren't seeing enough people to interrogate."

Working along the 30th's left flank, the 2nd Division foot soldiers left the redoubts of Elsenborn. Capt. Charles MacDonald brought his I Company forward and light German mortars boomed, wafting puffs of black smoke, kicking up snow. "One man from the 2nd Platoon lay in a crumpled heap and did not rise. His face was buried impassively in the snow as I passed. He was a new man, a replacement received the week before . . . a mixed feeling of horror and piety swept over me, but there was no time to stop and think. I did not even know the man's name.

"How strange is war. Some of us can go for days, and weeks, and months in war and never be killed or wounded, but another man is killed in his first taste of war." A few hours later, MacDonald felt as if someone hit him in the calf of his right leg with a giant club. The bullet carved a three-inch gash before coming to rest just short of passing completely through his calf. The Battle of the Ardennes

had ended for MacDonald, although he would return to the 2nd Division in time for the final two months of shooting.

Like the 30th Infantry Division, the 82nd Airborne enjoyed only a bare respite before resuming the job of evicting German forces from the Ardennes. The 325th Glider Regiment received the dubious honor of leading an assault in the vicinity of Vielsalm.

Leonard Weinstein of G Company had been among those who successfully withdrew from their support positions around Baraque de Fraiture just before Christmas. He had spent almost ten days living on a rocky, lightly wooded hillside, exposed to the worst of the Ardennes winter. Occasionally, the kitchens rustled up heated food but the men sustained themselves largely with K rations. Fires warmed the troopers and dried their clothes.

"Chester Idland, my closest buddy, and I were the point men in our sector for the attacking front. We were pinned down by heavy enemy fire when we got up to resume the advance. We discovered that our BAR wouldn't work. Then Chester was hit, right after Rodney Cole, with his machine gun squad about ten yards behind us, was killed. I can still see the blood spurting from his face and neck, almost fifty years later. Sgt. Dean Foss, a machine gunner and the closest ranking noncom, ordered me to get Chester back to the aid station. I had intended to do this anyway.

"I asked Chester if he could move and possibly walk. He answered, 'I don't know, but I'll try.' Under cover of outgoing artillery we started toward the rear. There was a barrage of both incoming and outgoing fire. I never knew a wounded man could move so fast. I don't know how many times we were knocked down by concussion, nor how many times we slipped and fell. We would run and walk until exhausted, then fall onto the snow-covered ground to rest for a moment. Along the way, I asked GIs for directions to the aid station.

"At one point during our dash through this terrible barrage, the sky seemed to brighten as the clouds parted. This caused me to look upward toward the sky, and there in a ray of light, it appeared as if God was looking down on me. However, he seemed to be the image of my maternal grandfather, the only one of my grandparents I had ever known. Then this vision disappeared and the skies darkened again.

"When we finally reached the aid station, Chester was evacuated first. I guess I was pretty well messed up, as I was evacuated shortly thereafter. After a few days in the hospital, I was back with the company and Chester rejoined us shortly.''

The 82nd Airborne's Sgt. Bill Dunfee, having survived the strange experience of retreating through the retreating remnants of *Kampfgruppe Peiper*, along with others from the 505th Regiment, traveled to a reserve status at Theux, Belgium.

"The good people of Theux took us into their homes and treated us royally. We had hot meals and being warm again sure felt good. We were told prior to being turned loose on the civilian population that if any man screwed up, he and his whole company would be back in the snow in pup tents. I assure you, nobody goofed. The Belgians were concerned with our loaded guns and grenades, so we when we entered their homes, we unloaded the weapons, stashed the grenades in our packs.''

In a snow storm, during the second week of January, Dunfee and his companions returned to the front. As they proceeded along a road a treeburst, that no one heard coming, showered shrapnel. Dunfee's pal, DiGiralamo, the man who joked about his immersion in dung after the Normandy jump, died instantly. The blast felled another fellow across the road from Dunfee, slashing the man's leg and foot. "I was knocked down and the butt of my BAR slammed my middle finger, putting a permanent kink in it. Shrapnel tore away my left breast pocket, mangling hell out of my toothbrush and toothpaste. There was just this one round and we continued on our way. Later, I cussed the entire German Army everytime I tried to brush my teeth with half a toothbrush, using salt as a dentifrice.''

Three companies of paratroopers struck at the Belgian town of Fosse, with Dunfee's outfit, I Company, mounting a frontal assault. Success depended upon all three hitting the mark in unison, since the company would traverse a pasture with no cover except a hedgerow only fifty yards from the objective.

"Within seventy-five yards of our objective, the Germans opened up with a vengeance. We were pinned down by rifle and machine gun fire from our front as well as the woods to our left. I found a roll in the ground and bellied down. I tried to get to the hedgerow about twenty yards in front of me, but every time I attempted to move from the trough I was in, I drew fire. In my mind's eye I could visualize the German just begging me to raise up just a little more, so he could blow off my head. I had done that very thing when the shoe was on the other foot. I was very scared and frustrated."

From his place, Dunfee could see one of the other companies "catching hell from German mortar and artillery fire. I noticed mortar rounds hitting between them and myself. I thought I was seeing mortar rounds hit the ground, bounce back up and explode. That didn't make sense. I must have been seeing them before they struck the earth. I had compassion for the poor 'doggies' trapped below. I was really ticked off at their dumb-assed company commander who had his men in the wrong place, leaving us to draw fire from an exposed flank. You take things damned personally when you're being shot at.

"After an hour or so, a Sherman tank rattled up the hill and with his help we secured our objective. It was an expensive outing for us, as we lost several more of our original men. Dick Cutler and I had been friends since basic training. He had made it to the hedgerow and raised up his BAR to fire on a sniper in a barn loft. His last words were, 'I'll get that son of a bitch.' The sniper was waiting for him to raise up. Dick took a bullet through the chest, groaned and died. Our CO, Captain McPheeters, on my right at the hedgerow, was killed at this time. He had replaced a CO killed in Normandy.

"It hurts to take any casualties, but as the original men are taken out, you become even more aware of your chances with the law of averages."

During those days in January, according to Dunfee, he was the coldest he had ever been. The fierce skirmishes, the need to carry only weapons and ammo left him without food for twenty-four hours. "During this campaign I learned there is a point where you get so fatigued, cold and hungry that you almost lose the fear of death. You fight and scratch with all the energy you have to survive, but you are animal-like in your will to live."

On a combat patrol that shot up a German battalion headquarters and bagged a prisoner, Dunfee says he saw Germans shooting their own people as they attempted to surrender. On this occasion, having completed its mission, Dunfee instructed his squad to fall back while he covered them with his BAR. "There was a young German soldier crawling up to within a few feet of where I was firing, holding his hand out, pleading. He was bleeding in several places. I motioned for him to stay away from me, and continued firing over his head. The thought crossed my mind to finish him off but I hadn't sunk that low yet."

His outfit had sustained a casualty and improvised a litter. A German first sergeant prisoner, who spoke English, was ordered to serve as a stretcher bearer. "He started quoting the Geneva Convention and refused. I became unglued and took a swing at the insolent bastard. My swing was so violent, and the footing so slick, I missed him and tumbled to the ground. I looked up and he was laughing at me. I started to pull the bolt back on my BAR. As I did, Oscar Newborn blindsided the German with a right hand that decked him. To this day, I'm indebted to Oscar. Had he not hit that German, I would have killed him. I am thankful I don't have that on my conscience. When the German came around, he was very cooperative.

"At the time, one of our men had been shot through the chest and lung. Our medic radioed the battalion aid station and was told there was no help available. Walk him out or he could stay there and die. Another man had tangled with an artillery shell. His right hand and forearm were blown away, his left arm badly mangled. Both men managed to walk out, so none of us were in any mood to discuss the Geneva or any other Convention, especially with a German version of a guardhouse lawyer. I don't know if the German realized how close he came to death. I know it bothered me that I had become so callous that I would have killed an unarmed man."

After Christmas and during the first half of December, Dick Byers filled the role of an officer in charge of an observation team from various points along the Elsenborn Ridge on behalf of the 99th Division's 371st Field Artillery. He wrote home of his "unhappy lot and duty to arise at 5:30 in the godawful morning from my warm bed in the snug snow-covered dugout and struggle 300 yards up Elsenborn Ridge through three-foot snow against a hurricane wind blowing stinging sleet and sit for four hours in a snow-filled hole while the wind covered me quickly and completely with a three-inch layer of snow. Miller, my radio operator, and I started out at six A.M. in the worst storm I have ever seen. We became lost three times and had to start over again, gaining no more than fifty yards each time. Finally, we called for a guide to come down from the O.P. and lead us up. By sheer luck we met him and he led us back to the vicinity of the dugout where he became lost. We wandered around in the blizzard within twenty-five yards of the hole for half an hour before his partner inside happened to see us and yelled us in."

But Byers recognized that hardship is relative. "I'm back in the nice warm dugout far behind the lines and the poor doughs are still out there and have been out there for a long time and will be out there for a longer time. Compared to them, I live in luxury, 99 percent of the time. They have been living on C and K rations for months, while we have been eating B rations cooked in a kitchen. Once when I was up forward, we gave four of them a can of corned beef, a can of peas, a can of butter and it was really pathetic to see how grateful they were to receive them. To them it was a banquet.

"I thank God that I am an artilleryman! Yet, in spite of their hardships, their morale is a lot higher than it is among us in the rear. They make a joke out of everything. The rougher it is, the bigger the joke. They *have* to laugh or else they go crazy. Once I was in a forward O.P. and platoon headquarters with a group of doughs. I didn't know who was whom. I watched them horse around, having a roughouse time. Later, I learned one was a private and the other a 1st Lieutenant and his platoon leader. After they go through so much hell together, they are closer than a bunch of brothers. They have a mutual trust and confidence in each other and they dispense with formalities."

While directing the 371st guns, Byers was not immune to being on the receiving end of German cannons and mortars, some of which lay no more than a few hundred yards off. However, he became acutely aware of the difference in power when a German prisoner, an observer like Byers, bitterly complained about the unfairness of it all. "Anytime his side shot anything bigger than a machine gun, it was answered by an entire battalion or at least a battery of our artillery. He would only go into 'fire for effect' with more than one big gun when there was a big fat target in front of him."

Ben Nawrocki was one of those doughs upon whom Byers lavished his sympathy. "Our faces were all bearded and black from the soot which the small gasoline fires cause. Some men would cover the foxholes with a blanket or rain poncho and some died from carbon monoxide poisoning. It was a fight all the way around. We lived like animals in a hole. Trench foot was a continuing problem and took its toll of troops. The snow kept blowing. The cold was there to stay. We had to keep moving our toes and feet all the time to prevent them from freezing.

"The forward units kept sending out patrols into the German lines. I'm not sure of the date but the skies cleared and we saw thousands of our planes in the air dropping bombs and strafing the Germans. The ground shook like an earthquake. At least we had air support. Our morale really went up. The massive air attack relieved the pressure on us some.

"We kept our positions. They would pull some troops out into the houses in the village of Elsenborn to wash up, shave and stay overnight before returning.

"But we had them stopped and we held them. We held the North Shoulder."

Jean Pauels, the bürgermeister of the village of Meyerode, counted fifty-one houses and 280 inhabitants as his domain in the winter of 1944–45. From Schönberg to Meyerode a direct route added up to about seven kilometers. But for a human on foot, or even by tracked vehicle, it was considerably farther, due to the thickly wooded terrain. Meyerode was, of course, the community where an American officer resembling Lt. Eric Wood, who escaped capture on the outskirts of Schönberg, enjoyed the hospitality of the Maraite family and where he had vowed to conduct his own war if he could not reach the American lines.

Bürgermeister Pauels said the invaders from the east entered his hamlet on December 17. "For a few days thereafter, there were several groups of bypassed Americans holding out nearby. Some at first, disorganized stragglers, were in the forests which closely surround our village in an arc. Two other groups, organized bodies, were eventually rounded up by the Germans." Pauels noted that one substantial contingent, as many as 120, tried to conceal themselves in the area and attempted to maintain radio contact with American forces falling back to the west. But, using artillery and infantry, Pauels said, the Germans eliminated every single member of the bunch by Christmas time. The villagers found no bodies, nor did prisoners ever show up in Meyerode being paraded by the victors.

For a time, Meyerode housed a German antiaircraft battery that downed or hit a number of Allied planes. But eventually, bombs from the air silenced some and, in Pauel's words, "others were exterminated by American soldiers in the woods."

The air now belonged to the Allied Forces who preyed on traffic along the major highways with such deadly results that the Germans were forced to rely on the secondary roads, the ones that snaked through the dark, forbidding forests. "But," said Pauels, "eventually, they became so frightened that they preferred to use even these roads at night. At any rate, the American and British planes blocked the two main highways with their strafing while the Americans in the woods raised daily hell along the two alternate concealed routes through the forests."

Pauels reported that, beginning about December 20 and for the next three or four weeks, villagers like himself became aware of gun battles in the nearby woods, the classic sounds of guerrilla warfare. "Everyone in the village, German or Belgian, could hear them clearly across the still, cold winter weather. Any time we saw a German patrol or transport column, or anything else, except a large body of combat troops, pass from our village and start towards the forests, we could count on hearing a fight sooner or later after the Germans had disappeared into the woods. The Americans seemed to have plenty of arms and, at any rate, they had a great deal of ammunition, which they expended very freely.

"The sounds of fighting always started suddenly with a tremendous burst of fire, and then gradually tapered off in volume to single shots and then to silence. These Americans also had a medium trench mortar which they used freely. We now suppose they got shells for it from an abandoned American ammunition dump in their area, which, even today [July 1945], has good American mortar ammunition left.

"Upwards of a hundred badly wounded Germans at one time or another hobbled back to Meyerode from the woods or were carried in on the backs of their fleeing comrades from December 20 to the middle of January. From the many things we heard the Germans say, we think their losses in killed in the woods must have been a couple of hundred."

Pauels was privy to talk at the highest levels among the Nazi occupiers, as he suffered the dubious pleasure of quartering Gen. Sepp Dietrich, the Sixth SS Panzer Army commander, and several of his staff in his own home. Meyerode also played host to the Army Group commander Gen. Walter Model and the Belgian Nazi Rex Degrelle. According to Pauels, Dietrich "was angry at the

Americans in the woods. He said words to the effect that they were criminal scoundrels and bandits. Whenever Gen. von Model's duties required him to go to the front or wherever, he generally went out by the north, away from the woods, risking the Allied planes in the air rather than go through the forests." Model also traveled under heavy guard, with two or three combat vehicles surrounding him, special units dispatched ahead to provide outposts and moving swiftly.

While all death and destruction continued to permeate the Ardennes, the Allied brass engaged in their own verbal skirmishes, fueled by offended egos and zealous protection of public image. The sniping continued between the Americans and British Field Marshal Bernard Montgomery, whose appearance upon taking command of the First Army on December 20 struck some U.S. officers as like "Christ coming to cleanse the temple." Montgomery had not endeared himself with a statement: "Gen. Eisenhower placed me in command of the whole Northern Front. I employed the whole available power of the British Group of Armies . . . and finally it was put into battle with a bang and today British divisions are fighting hard on the right flank of the First U.S. Army."

But the Britons, while rendering valuable aid covering the Meuse bridges and protecting the flank of the Americans, amounted to less than one-tenth of the soldiers fighting under the Stars and Stripes. Furthermore, the worst of the campaign was absorbed by U.S. forces. German propagandists grabbed Montgomery's remarks and tried to foment more hostility between American and British command echelons.

Prime Minister Winston Churchill initiated damage control. He told his House of Commons: "Care must be taken in telling our proud tale not to claim for the British Army an undue share of what is undoubtedly the greatest American battle of the war and will, I believe, be regarded as an ever-famous American victory." He growled a final rotund, oratorical warning to anyone tempted to exploit the rift. "Let no one lend himself to the chatter of mischief makers when issues of this momentous consequence are being successfully decided by the sword."

Montgomery temporarily defused some ire with his tribute to the Americans retreating from St. Vith, "They come back in all honor. They come back to more secure positions. They put up a wonderful show."

Nevertheless, behind the united front, the two sides continued to peg darts at one another. Some elements of the British press hinted that the fault for the Ardennes disaster fell on Eisenhower and he should be replaced as European land commander by a Briton. And aside from the personalities, a very substantive debate raged over future strategy, with Montgomery seeking to delay an offensive while the Americans lusted for immediate revenge for their "bloody nose."

On January 7 at a press conference, Montgomery tossed gasoline on the flames of discord. After reminding everyone that von Rundstedt achieved "tactical surprise," he thumped his chest, "As soon as I saw what was happening, I took certain steps myself to ensure that *if* the Germans got to the Meuse, they would certainly not get over the river . . . Then the situation began to deteriorate. But the whole Allied team rallied to meet the danger; national considerations were thrown overboard . . . Gen. Eisenhower placed me in command of the whole Northern front . . . You have thus the picture of British troops fighting on both sides of American forces who have suffered a hard blow. This is a fine Allied picture. I would say that anyone who tries to break up the team spirit of the Allies is definitely helping the enemy. Let me tell you that the captain of our team is Eisenhower."

He urged his audience to cease reports of friction. "I would ask all of you to lend a hand to stop that sort of thing. Let us rally round the captain of the team and so help win the match." Interspersed with these comments was praise for the American valor, but neither homage, nor sporting analogy, nor fealty to the supreme commander salved wounds rubbed raw. His remarks, particularly when he described the battle as "one of the most interesting and tricky that I have ever handled," were interpreted as a maneuver to extend and prolong his control over American troops. They seemed to ignore the basically U.S. role in both coordinating and fighting the holding actions that limited the enemy offensive.

Gen. J. Lawton Collins, U.S. VII Corps commander, commented that "Monty really got under my skin . . . downgrading American troops at the time of the Battle of the Bulge . . . . He held that press conference that so irritated Bradley and Patton and many of us who fought on the northern front of the Bulge that it left a sour note to what actually was a great cooperative Allied army and air effort."

Even within the American forces, squabbles of the top brass threatened operations. On the night of December 23, after the American pullback from St. Vith, Gen. Matthew Ridgway, as head of the XVIII Corps, summoned Brig. Gen. Bruce Clarke to a meeting. Ridgway's command, for the moment included CCB of the 7th Armored Division and, therefore, Clarke was his subordinate.

The CCB commander, however, nagged by stomach problems and under severe stress from the blows to his units, had been given a potion by a surgeon. Instead of responding to Ridgway, Clarke rolled over in his sack and went back to sleep. The following day a furious Ridgway upbraided Clarke for insubordination. "I'm not used to having brigadiers tell me they won't report to me." Clarke has said he explained about the drug he swallowed and his exhaustion, but Ridgway would have none of it. Instead, the superior officer lectured Clarke on Army discipline with the implication of a possible court-martial.

Unfazed, Clarke interrupted his commander. "General, I came to this command against my wishes. I got nine decorations for bravery in my old outfit [the 4th Armored]. I've got a record in the Third Army that I can go back there tomorrow morning and General Patton will be glad to see me . . . I've done my job up here. History will give our unit credit for the job we did at St. Vith. I'd like your permission to leave."

Clarke escaped further reprimand but hard feelings persisted. The men of the 82nd Airborne in their drive against the German salient reached the outskirts of St. Vith and could have occupied the town. However, someone on top decreed that the honor of being the first to return to St. Vith would go to Clarke and CCB. The paratroopers groused about the insinuation of concerns for image denying them their due. Clarke himself left the scene shortly thereafter, driven from battle by the slings and arrows of a malfunctioning gall bladder.

A rather frivolous business attended the pages of *Stars and Stripes*, the official U.S. Army newspaper. Stories about the heroic stand at Bastogne and the feats of Patton annoyed the pooh-bahs of the First Army so much that they successfully insisted on a separate edition which would focus more on their exploits. At the same time, Patton was no more enthusiastic about the newspaper. His diary for January 13 records, "Wrote the Editor of the *Stars and*

Stripes protesting against his paper as subversive of discipline. I sent a copy of my letter to General Lee . . . I stated that unless there is an improvement, I will not permit the paper to be issued in this Army, nor permit his reporters or photographers in the Army area. It is a scurrilous sheet." Patton was particularly furious at Sgt. Bill Mauldin's GIs, Willie and Joe, dirty and unshaven. One famous Mauldin cartoon showed them about to embark on a time-wasting detour rather than pass through the fief of the Third Army, where men were to wear neckties, shine their shoes, clean their faces and shave. The notion that Patton decreed proper uniform even during the zenith of battle is a considerable exaggeration but the perception persisted, making delicious fodder for Mauldin.

Within the German High Command, the disarray that inevitably attends defeat infected the decision makers. Indeed, von Rundstedt had urged an end to offensive operations after two or three days, arguing that consolidation of the limited gains would be the best the Nazi forces could achieve. Hitler and his staff ignored von Rundstedt's advice, although the generals bickered over strategy— a major issue was the unwillingness to shift emphasis to van Manteuffel's Fifth Panzer Army once Dietrich's Sixth SS Panzers collided with the northern shoulder. But on January 8, even though his troops remained in control of a considerable chunk of the Ardennes, *der führer* agreed on a withdrawal east of Houffalize, rather than see the remainder of his panzers chewed up. On January 14, the War Diary of the German High Command recorded that the initiative in the area of the offensive had passed to the enemy. The entire Sixth SS Panzer Army of Sepp Dietrich pulled out, minus well over 40,000 casualties, to hold off a forthcoming Soviet attack on the Eastern Front. German officers still enmeshed in the Ardennes expressed concern about the morale of those still expected to fight while the Waffen SS headed elsewhere.

The war of the Allied generals ended in a truce with the return of the First Army to Bradley's Group, while Montgomery retained control of the U.S. Ninth Army. The disputes would be renewed after V-E Day when the principals sowed their memoirs and the historians and analysts rooted through fields of After Action Reports, Combat Interviews, the recollections of participants to dig up truffles of controversy.

There is no firm date to cite as the end of the War in the Ardennes. Men would endure hard, terrible fighting for weeks, and not until the end of January did the Americans finally manage to establish positions roughly similar to those that existed on December 16. Whatever date one sets, the casualties were enormous for both sides. The statisticians listed 15,000 captured, 19,000 killed and more than 40,000 wounded among the 600,000 Americans in the Ardennes. British casualties totaled 1,400, with just over 200 KIA. For the Germans, who fielded more than 500,000 soldiers, the figures vary from 100,000 to 120,000 dead, wounded and captured.

Chapter XV

LIFE AND DEATH IN THE STALAGS

As THEIR COMRADES PUNCHED deeper and deeper into Germany, the Americans taken prisoner in the first days of the Bulge waged their own wars of survival. Early in January, Sgt. John Collins, the combat engineer who fought with Lt. Col. Tom Riggs's improvised defense on the Prümerberg in front of Schönberg, arrived at Stalag IV B in Muhlburg.

"The barracks are crummy and very unsanitary. About 250 of us sleep on the floor of a 60 x 30 foot room, no light, crowded, very lttle heat. I understand this was officially an English and Russian camp before we came. The British don't have it so bad, but it's not home. Most have been PWs for quite a long time. The Russians are treated like dogs; they go around scraping cans and foraging for pieces of food. There is no difference between a general or one of their privates. They are all treated the same."

Collins noted the sparse rations available. "Seven men to a 12 inch loaf of bread, a little oleo, a spoonful of sugar, one cup of soup called 'scilly'—good for shaving or washing your face—and their coffee—hot water. Also we receive a few potatoes at noon, if available. About three times weekly we have a can of bully beef or maybe horsemeat, for six men." Cigarettes served as the currency of the camp: forty to fifty bought a small can of Nescafé, seventy to eighty bartered for bread, a seventeen-jewel watch might earn 250 to 650 smokes.

The captors segregated their prisoners into three groups, officers, noncoms and the bottom ranks. Transported to Stalag VIII A at Görlitz, close to the border of Czechoslovakia and Poland, Collins and more than 1,600 Americans joined an encampment of Britons, South Africans and Serbians. Collins noted, "Ninety percent are men and the rest are ????. I sat with our little group and watched in disgust as this 10 percent in our barracks actually attacked and fought over food when seconds were announced. I understand starving people will do almost anything for food but some things are almost unbelievable. Our barracks NCO was M. Sgt. Ray Davis, with 17 years of service and he saw to it that everyone received their fair share. A good man on any job."

Collins and his mates slept on tiers of boards. The cobblestone floor was filthy from the dirt tracked in from a latrine across the street. Beneath the latrine, a full basement trapped the sewage. When it filled near capacity, the Germans sent Russian prisoners to empty it but the waste spread all over the floor and never was cleaned up. "The people with dysentery didn't help much, as they often didn't reach the latrine.

"M. Sgt. Davis did get some medicine for bad cases of dysentery. He also tried to quote the Geneva Convention rules. They cared less about these. But we understood that if you stuck your head outside after 1900 hours and until 0500 there was a good possiblity that you would be shot!

"I suppose if I had been able to keep my ring and watch I would have sold them by now. Most of the food comes from parcels which have been sent by the Red Cross. They are now only given to those who work. Noncoms do not work—at least we don't. The Germans are the biggest traders as they steal clothing and cigarettes from Red Cross packages."

In his new prison, Collins reported the wood supplies reduced. The snow piled to a depth of six feet and French prisoners labored to clear the road. The Germans came to Collins' barracks for men but no one would volunteer, or if someone did, M. Sgt. Davis vetoed the offer. "The French are the only ones getting Red Cross parcels, since they work. The English and Russians do not. The English say to watch for the French since they collaborate. However, it is hard to believe. We are all in the same boat. By them getting parcels we have a means to trade items for food."

Collins was appointed librarian, custodian of eighty books for 2,000 men. Since he could not find more books, the job demanded little. The Soviet armies appeared to be approaching and there was talk of shifting the prisoners. "The word is that we would be dead men if we should escape to the Russian front. So I hope we sit still. Come on Joe!—our nickname for the Russians.

"The barracks are infested with lice and fleas. All of us are infested with body lice. The big fat ones stay in all tight places of the clothing. You cannot get rid of them, so you try to educate them by ignoring them. Used to be called 'cooties.' My weight must be down to about 110; I was 150. I have been fortunate, inasmuch as I have not had dysentery except for one light case."

The exchange of cigarettes and personal articles for food intensified. "Some of the fellows are nearly starved but do nothing to help themselves. I'll eat as long as the Germans do, may not be much but I think I can hold out." He joined a small group that performed as middlemen, taking commissions when not acting for themselves. "We steal from the Jerries by diverting their attention and cheating on trades. Sometimes we trade our ration of bread and oleo for an item we will try to trade later. I swapped my blanket and one loaf of bread with a few spuds for an overcoat. This was a personal deal and cost me six days of bread rationing. I borrowed the bread from our kitty.

"Nearly every night we have services and one can tell that everyone is praying and trusting God to get us out of this mess. I am no different. I pray also for my family, asking God to take care of them but most of all I pray for my fellowmen."

On February 14, St. Valentine's Day, as "Uncle Joe" closed in and the prisoners marched off to the west, the count of American PWs showed a decline of twenty since Collins arrived. He remarked that he expected that a lot more than a score would have died. "They say we will be marching four days. This is the end of the first one and many men cannot walk. A wagon at the rear picks them up. Wonder what happens to them?" At the end of the four-day hike, the guards declared they would continued for four more.

Quartered in a barn one night during the march, Collins and a few companions discovered a cache of food and tobacco. A search by guards at 4:00 A.M. found much of the purloined edibles, but the tobacco escaped notice. To Collins it was as valuable as gold when it came to bartering for food.

The trek west continued. The prisoners tried to steal sugar beets from the fields by a subterfuge in which two men distracted the guards by running off while another pair harvested the beets. The guards chased the runners with dogs. "If you laid down, the dogs would stand over you until the guard got there and gave you a couple of swift kicks. But one guard clobbered me in the back with his rifle and I could hardly walk. The others took turns helping me, but it was all I could do to stand, let alone walk. They gave me a stick which helped support me, massaged my legs and feet, carried me, tried to make me walk whether I wanted to or not. I think they also gave me more food than my share. T/4 Elmer George said he would kill me first before placing me in the wagon." It was believed that the Germans disposed of anyone who sought refuge in the wagon.

Along the way, Collins saw what he was told were Jews, dressed in stripes, "skin and bones. After hearing the stories of mistreatment of prisoners and ourselves being on the short end, it isn't hard to believe anything about their actions towards prisoners."

As the ragged column walked through the edge of Duderstadt, Collins says people spat at them. "You could feel the hate. This was the first time this had happened, but they were younger people and mostly women. Previous towns usually had persons who helped us or at least just stood idly by."

What had been announced as a four-day march had turned into a marathon lasting more than a month.

Phil Hannon, from the 81st Combat Engineer Battalion in the 106th Division, after detraining from his cramped 40-and-8 ride, had entered Stalag IX B, Bad Orb, Germany, near Frankfurt. His engineer group stuck together and occupied space in a huge, barn-like building, about 100 feet in length and forty feet wide. Triple-decker wooden bunks lined the walls, in groups of four or five, with a narrow aisle separating the sections. For mattresses, the Germans supplied excelsior. There were windows every ten feet, covered with barbed wire. The prisoners ate meals at a long pine-board table with a few benches in the middle of the room. Two brick ovens provided very little heat. "The place was dark and dreary but it was better than being in the freezing wind outside.

"We picked out bunks and climbed into them, laid there and waited for the next move. Our barracks guard came in and introduced himself. He was a sergeant and I should judge about 50 years old. He explained to us, through one of our men who spoke and understood German, the rules and regulations. We could not use the inside toilet during the day or when the barracks were unlocked. We were not to lay on the bunks with our shoes on. We were to salute all German officers, stand count twice a day and many other minor rules." On the surface, the regimen did not sound much different from that demanded in a U.S. military camp.

The facilities and the operations, however, were far removed. For starters, the outside latrine was nothing more than a huge hole in the ground with strategically placed logs for support during a bowel movement. The mess kit issued Hannon was a rusty tin can with a wire handle. The basic meal consisted of a watery green "soup" which engendered an ongoing debate on the nature of the green element. Hannon, who fashioned himself a utensil from a .30-caliber bullet casing and a strip of wood ripped off his bunk, skimmed the solid elements from his portion and drank the fluid.

Beginning January 1, he kept a diary, making his entries on the backs of some photographs he did not destroy when captured. For New Year's Day, he inscribed, "Most of day in bed. Greens and little meat in soup." January 3, he noted, "Snowed. Greens. Spud soup. Thoughts of food tough. Got 3 bars of soap." The next day's entry: "Seconds in chow. Pea soup. Meat for supper. Stood hour and half in the cold. Started list of chow for home."

Apart from daily listing of food, Hannon reported religious observances on Sundays, Bible classes, the sounds of air raids, and weather conditions. During the first two months at Stalag IX B, he noted fresh infusions of prisoners and, later, the rising hopes for liberation.

The terse jottings of his diary were dictated by the limited space on the backs of his pictures. Several decades later, Hannon reconstructed more lengthy descriptions of life in the stalag. He explained how the prisoners organized themselves. "The Pvts. and Pfcs. were put in their own barracks and were left to rule themselves without benefit of any rank imposed upon them by any system. I think the Germans felt that without any leaders, the Pvts. and Pfcs. would be easy to handle and rather cowed. We were not unhappy about the set-up because this allowed us to run our barracks as we saw fit. We soon had an election for a barracks leader. His job was to act as a go-between for all of us in Barracks 24 and the Germans. I recall one of the reasons the man was elected was his ability to speak and understand German."

The prisoners exercised their own stern discipline. "Any man caught stealing from another prisoner was automatically put in the 'outcasts barracks.' First, he was thrown into the open latrine pit, and men from the quarters where he stole stood around the pit and urinated on him. Theft from the Germans was accepted practice, so long as it didn't endanger anyone else. Others who ended up in the outcast barracks were those who fought constantly or had such disgusting habits that their associates voted them out. The outcast barracks GIs pulled the 'honey dipping detail,' emptying out the latrine and hauling the mess away. The punishment deterred a lot of thieves, I am sure.

"We broke ourselves into six-man units. The meals were responsible for the number because the average daily ration of bread was six men to a loaf. The loaf was about 11 inches long, four inches square, very heavy and usually soggy in the middle. Its main ingredient we all swore was sawdust and the ever present pine needles. Each day when we got our bread, we would inspect it, compare it with the one the next section got, lift it to feel the weight, comment on our luck or bad luck.

"Each man had been issued one half of a blanket. My bunk mate and I found that one half blanket under us and one half blanket and my overcoat on top of us was the warmest way to sleep. The straw that made up our mattress was infested with lice and fleas. Every night they would go on maneuvers. Anytime during the night, you could hear someone swearing at the lice. Wherever your clothes were tight around the body, the wrists, the ankles, and under the belt was where they congregated and ate their meals. The fleas had no favorite spot—they'd bite wherever they landed. If there was any humor in this infestation, it was watching a man sneak up to his bunk, gently take hold of his blanket, fling it back and flail frantically at the fleas as they hopped about.

"We were given a hot shower and our clothes steamed about the third day in camp. On February 23, I got another shower and delousing. These were the only two times I had my clothes off while there. A major pastime was searching the seams of our clothes, killing lice. As it warmed up towards spring, you could look anywhere around the camp and find groups of men searching their clothes while gossiping like a bunch of old women at a quilting bee.

"We were counted twice each day, once before breakfast and once before lights out. On February 4th, our stove, the one closest to my bunk, exploded. The stove blew up while we were outside being counted. It seems that Bullock had hung his GI canteen inside the stove to heat some water. The canteen exploded and left the stove pieces of junk. Until the mangled pieces of the canteen were found, the Germans were like mad hornets. They thought we had grenades. Bullock was put in solitary confinement [for almost two weeks] for destroying German property and throwing a fright into our guards.''

There were weak attempts to divert themselves. Hannon mentions several talks given by prisoners. There were a few books available but he remarks, ''All my life I have been an avid reader, but while in camp I managed to read only two books. Hunger destroys all desire to read and ruins any ability to concentrate. There are many things our Federal Government does that I don't agree with, but I'm all for breakfasts and lunches in schools for any children who want them. It's difficult to learn if your stomach is empty.''

One of the prisoners formerly sang with the New York Metropolitan Opera. With the aid of a captured chaplain, he formed a choir. ''We all felt it was extra good,'' said Hannon. ''However, they gave only one performance that day because they didn't have the strength to do more.'' The group sang once more and then decided they were too weak to exert themselves that much.

Hannon and his companions developed unquenchable cravings for food. ''I remember dreaming of a roast beef dinner with mashed potatoes and gravy. I could actually smell the gravy but I couldn't eat it and I woke myself up, crying. Each of us would make up elaborate meals we would have when we got home and we tried to outdo each other. One guy said as soon as he got home (there was never any doubt in most of our minds about getting home, the only question was when) he was going to get a wash tub, bake a cake in it, smother it with ice cream and peaches and eat it all by himself.'' About thirty years later Hannon spoke to the fellow inmate for the first time since their imprisonment and asked if had carried out his culinary vision. Like most, including Hannon, he had not.

''When we first became prisoners, we felt cheated, being out of the war. For a while we were hard on ourselves, as if we had been captured because we hadn't done our job properly. The attitude changed after a few days of walking and starving. We became much more individually oriented, thinking of ourselves, instead of what we failed to do for the army. We became selfish, worrying no longer what we hadn't done but mainly what we were going to do. We stopped thinking about the big picture. Sometimes I would think of my father. I had always felt that if I got in trouble he could handle it for me.

''Some of the men were loners. They didn't team up or seem to need cozying up. They were self reliant, able to make it on their own. There were those rejected by everyone else because of the ways they acted or for their personal habits. They couldn't cozy up and had a difficult time. Then there were those, a very few, who literally gave up in the PW camp. They'd roll over and in a couple of days they were dead. That was their escape but their behavior was totally beyond my comprehension. I was just amazed when a person would shrivel up and die; they were not being treated any worse than anyone else."

Only a few days after their arrival at Stalag IX B, the prisoners went through an interrogation. Assembled outdoors in the frigid weather, the men individually entered a barracks where the inquisitors asked not only about military data but also the names of parents and grandparents. Failure to respond meant return to the formation in the subfreezing temperatures. Said Hannon, "Most of us objected to giving anything but name, rank and serial number, but after some time in the cold, most of us gave up and answered the questions, which were in direct violation of all international agreements.

"The queries about our parents and grandparents were the German way of checking to determine who among us was Jewish. Some weeks later, the Jewish men were removed from the camp. I don't know to this day where they were taken or what became of them."

Another PW from the 106th, Milt Massgren, said that he met two Jewish former GIs who had been held at a stalag before being sent with 350 other Jewish soldiers to a concentration camp. Only forty-seven of them were rescued by American troops before their turn in the gas chambers.

Red Cross inspectors toured Hannon's camp late in February. Hannon and his fellows hoped for improvements in food and heat, but he could discern no impact from the visit. However, he had been allowed to write home via the German Red Cross. Verne and Ann Hannon, Phil's parents, began to correspond regularly with the families of other men listed as missing since December 16 and whom they had met during their son's participation in the ASTP program at the University of Maryland. A network of PW parents developed. They shared communications from their sons, official information and tried to boost one another's morale.

On the day following Christmas, after Ed Uzemack of the 28th Division had "the best Christmas dinner of my life"—his portion from eight loaves of bread and seven cans of meat divided among fifty-seven starving prisoners in a 40-and-8,—he, too, disembarked at Stalag IX B.

"Got our first hot meal at the Russian kitchen—it was carrot, turnip top and grass soup. Ate it from my helmet, the only mess gear available for two months. Used my grimy fingers as eating utensils. Most men immediately became sick."

Food became an obsession with the PWs. Uzemack witnessed the same sort of frenzied commodities market in which John Collins participated, with a sixty-five-dollar watch bringing a loaf of bread, 2,000 francs the price of two cigarettes—an equivalent of $400 a pack. On "Black Sunday," January 28, a pair of GIs raided the kitchen and slugged a guard with a meat cleaver.

"We were assembled out in the snow and told the details. We were also told we would have no food or fuel until the guilty ones were found." Uzemack's diary notes: "The incident is closed. This afternoon, Barracks 42A turned over the two men responsible for slugging the guard. We received our bread and soup ration for the tonight."

On the last day of the month, the Americans enjoyed a windfall, Red Cross packages containing chocolate bars, packs of cigarettes, meat, fish, crackers, butter, raisins, sugar, coffee, powdered milk, vitamin pills and soap. "It was explained that the boxes came as a loan from Serbian prisoners—God bless them—who had a surplus. We got one box for each four men. Even so, it was enough." The men gobbled the most delectable items and then engaged in an orgy of trading with what remained. Uzemack became giddy after puffing on his first cigarette in forty-five days.

In spite of the horrendous sanitary conditions, a bare subsistence diet and the constant cold, Uzemack says only three of the 4,000 prisoners died during their first month at IX B. He credits the survival rate to the efforts of Lt. Joshua P. Sutherland, a medical officer in charge of the PW dispensary. "He really deserves the DSC," Uzemack noted in his diary.

Nothing could save the Americans when, during a dogfight in the skies, "Yank planes, chasing the Heinies, shot over the camp and accidently strafed our barracks. Val Casados, my last buddy here, was killed. He was standing beside our bunk talking to me when bullets sprayed all around us. How those .50-caliber slugs missed me I'll never know. One hit my bedpost a few inches from my head. Two other men were killed and twelve more wounded."

With two other newspapermen, Jack Dunn of the Federated Press and Denny Murray from the Chicago *Tribune* created a camp newspaper posted on an improvised bulletin board. Uzemack constituted the mechanical staff, using a pencil and paper. (One of Phil Hannon's diary notations mentions a lecture by Jack Dunn on "Sports in the Golden 20s.")

Fatalities in the camp increased rapidly with the arrival of American and British prisoners, marched from as far as 325 miles away. "Poor guys," wrote Uzemack. "They are dying fast—they are so weakened by their march and the starvation diet. Was a witness of the improvised ceremony. The funeral procession was preceded by a German guard of honor, then came the chaplain and two German officers. The pallbearers carried the plain coffins one kilometer to the burial plot. Twenty Yanks formed a Guard of Honor. The men were buried in a common grave. Saw Val's grave. Sight left me depressed all day."

Uzemack's musing over the bizarre spectacle of formal military interments turned into outrage. Toward the end of March he wrote, "Men have been dying from malnutrition and pneumonia at the rate of one or two daily. The God-damned Nazis murdered them just as surely as if they had shot them. It's the enforced march on the starvation diet that is killng most of them."

Sgt. Leo Leisse, of the 3rd Battalion, 422 Infantry Regiment, surrendered by his commanding officer, had decided on Christmas Day, "Nothing will ever be this bad again." But over the next few days the conditions worsened. Two days passed without food or water as the hapless prisoners were marched through the rubble of towns, over crater-pocked roads and snowy waste lands. He recollected, "Understand we were not to march this far but towns where we were to have been quartered had been bombed and it would not have been safe for us to stop there, for fear of trouble with the villagers."

They trudged as far as Koblenz, seeking shelter in garrison buildings while Allied aircraft dumped bombs in a series of raids. "There were several killed, and many injured by flying glass during the raids, some almost unable to walk any further. We all felt sure we would never see home again."

They continued to hike east, crossing the Rhine. When they

finally halted after a seventeen-hour, sixty-kilometer march, at Limburg, Leisse saw many prisoners of war, mostly "Poles, Frenchies and some English," working in the fields, driving teams or hauling logs. A German officer, speaking excellent English, surprised the Americans with a meticulous listing of the different divisions and approximate numbers of men captured from each unit. It was suggested that they line up on this basis; otherwise they would neither be fed nor assigned quarters. Leisse and most of his companions refused to cooperate.

The enemy relented at last and Leisse entered Stalag XII A. "We were given good soup—thick barley—put in large tents that held 100 men on each side. There was straw on the ground but no heat. Later, we were given three blankets each and an overcoat (I got a Russsian one)." He observed the start of bartering of watches, pens and rings for bread and cigarettes with guards and English NCOs in a compound on the other side of barbed wire.

New Year's Eve was ushered in with a treat of a cup of warm powdered milk, a small ration of cheese and raw meat. Leisse and the others dropped off to sleep well before midnight, "freezing our tails off."

A day later, however, the captors took away the blankets and overcoats. The prisoners once more were in transit, this time by boxcar. Leisse noted that Cpl. Bruce Schwalm was not feeling well, even though he was among the few who happened to have retained his overcoat. Leisse fell victim to the "GIs" (diarrhea), and noticed Schwalm and a fellow sergeant similarly afflicted.

Leisse recounted, "The train rolled and stopped, rolled and stopped all day because of air raids. Another night of standing or sitting in cramped position, knees under chin. Many threatened fights because of being worn out, frayed nerves. We were packed so tight and unable to move without disturbing one or more. Also men at both ends of the car had to get back and forth to the honey bucket. Sometimes those who had dysentery didn't make it in time, especially at night when one could not keep track of which way he was headed.

"What a nightmare. Cannot sleep at night for lack of room nor during the day because of those who had slept had no consideration for the men who did not. Nine more men put in our car and they were filthy as if they had been riding in a coal car, black as Negroes. Bruce feeling worse today, pains in back. Not very good, me thinks to myself."

A Red Cross parcel, from which the guards apparently removed the cigarettes, offered a tiny addition to the meager rations. On their third night in the box car, the guard refused all pleas for an opportunity to empty the slop can. There was then even less room for the men as it overflowed. They traveled a final day without food or water before arriving at Stalag IV B to be registered, deloused, showered and searched. Leisse joined 350 men in his new home.

Like all the other men who kept diaries, Leisse's commentaries focused heavily on food, constantly spelling out just what he received and what he did to make it palatable. The deprivation wreaked havoc with digestions. Those who gobbled their gruel or bread too quickly soon doubled over with cramps. His friend Bruce Schwalm continued to decline. Schwalm was excused from roll call. Leisse tried to persuade him to drag himself outside for fresh air and excercise. Leisse himself walked around the compound several times, breathing deeply, and enjoyed his first shave since before his capture.

On January 11, preparatory to another move, Leisse found himself locked up in a huge coal shed, with perhaps 1,700 Americans and English. He was pleasantly surprised to find several GIs from his outfit who had been lodged with the British and fared well, thanks to Red Cross packages and the issuance of sleeping bags and overcoats.

The next camp for Leisse was Stalag VIII A on the outskirts of Görlitz. Once in the barracks, Leisse pleaded with the now very ill Bruce Schwalm to answer sick call, but he refused. When they were not using their blankets, all of the men from Leisse's section donated theirs to cover Schwalm.

At roll call, Leisse and others carried Schwalm outside. A German officer told them to return the sick man to the barracks. Leisse and two others complied, cleaning up after Schwalm when a sudden attack of the GIs racked his body. "Pleaded with Schwalm again to get to medics in next barracks but wouldn't listen. In fact, got sore because of my insisting. Guess I'll leave him be, realizing all tempers on edge." On January 15, Schwalm entered sick bay.

Leisse visited him the following day. "Found he wasn't eating and the fellow next to him gladly accepting his rations. Asked English Major [a doctor] to check him over, as he was getting worse and certainly wouldn't improve if he couldn't eat. Later the

1st Sgt. barracks leader announced that Schwalm had been removed to a hospital. The section leader would see to it that he
received his belongings as well as take him off ration count for our
section. Felt that I accomplished something for Bruce by talking
with the English Major."

Leisse spoke of the war news that promised he and his comrades
would soon be on their way home. He relished a meal of mashed
potatoes mixed with powdered milk and butter, salt and pepper.
"Plenty of books and games loaned to compound by English."

Serenity did not always mark the roost. "Had to split S's rations
from ours, as he was too quarrelsome, always comparing others'
shares with his, as if he wouldn't get as much. We took turns
dividing to assure everyone received fair treatment but S is just
short of crazy."

The diary account of January 20 says: "Notified of Schwalm's
passing to his reward. Had tea 0900, grass soup and potatoes at
1200. Mashed with butter, salt and pepper. Dry rations included
one seventh loaf of bread, one twentieth lb of butter and one roll
cheese. Made sandwiches of toasted bread and cheese and corn
beef. Holland still sick. Don't feel so well myself last few days."

Even the entry that remarks on his preparations for attending
Schwalm's funeral includes the ingredients of the day's meal.
Leisse himself was now suffering from a severe cold with a deep
chest cough. The English physician gave him a few pills, but when
the American complained he had never felt as bad before, the
doctor commented, "You've never been this weak from starvation
before."

Borrowing items from others, the volunteers for Schwalm's funeral detail, including Leisse, put together "a uniformed appearance, combat boots, overcoats, overseas caps." At 10:00 A.M., four
days after the unfortunate corporal died, Leisse and more than a
dozen others fell out for the ceremonies. "Terribly cold, must be
below zero, walked to gate and stood there a good while awaiting
further orders—almost froze before being allowed to move into
nearby building. Then formed in column of threes and marched
about two miles to a cemetery. Almost too weak to walk and no
body heat to withstand the severe cold. Overcoat I borrowed sure
felt good—could not have done without it.

"Boys all marched proudly, with heads held high when passing
German civilians or troops on road. Chaplain had American flag
wrapped up with wreath. On arrival cemetery were led to small

stone building, might have been a tool shed or work room. When we got into basement room, out of sight of guards, we quickly removed flag and draped it over the wooden box coffin. We carried it out, fully expecting the Germans to take it off.

"To our astonishment, the German officer called, 'Achtung!' and gave a Nazi salute. The guards lined up on both sides of the walkway, gave rifle salute while we carried Schwalm between them. Coffin couldn't have been very heavy but we were already very weak and could hardly bear up under the weight, carrying the coffin about a block to the grave, already dug.

"A Nazi photographer took several shots including the officer rendering military honors. It seemed like I was dreaming all this. Next we were ordered to cover the grave. We couldn't refuse, for to do so would be to leave Bruce uncovered. However, the ground was frozen and very hard to handle. We could see how terribly weak we were when the cemetery attendent tried to show us how; the stupid jackass couldn't see or didn't realize what an effect lack of food had on us. We then marched back and to our further surprise, were allowed to keep the flag. The Nazi officer must have been an exception, not mean enough for the front lines." Leisse concluded his narrative of the funeral with a description of his next meal.

The rumors of the Soviet advances fired up hopes, and early in February, British, French and Russian prisoners were transported west. Soon Leisse himself struggled along the roads away from the onrushing Red Army. On the second day of a march, he fell to the rear and then was ordered to ride in a cart full of the guards' field packs. The following morning, medicated with some liniment, Leisse was back on his feet. The column, pausing in towns or in farm buildings, trudged for more than forty days, with only an occasional layover. So weak he could barely pull himself erect when the order to march came, tottering hour after hour, Leisse traveled 395 miles, on foot, except for an occasional short stretch in a wagon.

Sgt. Richard McKee, of A Company, 422nd Regiment of the 106th, like Leo Leisse, was among the prisoners yielded by Colonel Descheneaux on December 19. He, too, walked the 137 miles that ended at Stalag XII A in Limburg, Germany, then the grim boxcar ride to Stalag IV B at Muhlburg before transfer to VIII A at Goṛlitz, eighty miles east of Dresden.

He remembered crossing the Rhine at Koblenz. "The German civilians threw rocks at us and shook their fists. The Hitler Youth kids were especially mean. They kicked us and threw rocks at us." When they opened the box cars at IV B, McKee saw Germans "loading the GIs who had died on the trip onto wagons pulled by horses."

At IV B in early January, McKee was registered with the Red Cross as a PW and, subsequently, the War Department notified his parents that he was a prisoner. Previously, they, like the next-of-kin of other captives, had received the standard telegram stating the son or husband was missing.

McKee wrote a postcard home: "Dear Folks, I am well and feeling fine, hope all is the same back home. Bob [Sgt. Bob Richardson, who enlisted with McKee] and I are still together. He is all right too. I didn't get any of my Christmas packages you sent me. I don't suppose I will either. If you send me anything, please send hard or chocolate candy. I hope you haven't been too worried about me as it has been quite a while since you have heard from me. Write often and tell the rest the same. Dick."

McKee and his mates whiled away time discussing food. "Richardson was the best at preparing our imaginary meals, since he was a cook. The Germans played American records over the loud speakers in the huts. One song they played over and over was Bing Crosby singing 'White Christmas.' I think everyone cried when they heard it. The Germans did this, of course, to torment us."

He, too, saw rude justice enforced. "You always had to sleep on top of your possessions. If you didn't, someone would steal them at night. One night someone started yelling that a GI had stolen his shoes. The thief was caught, stripped of his clothes and shoes and forced out into the zero and snow weather, naked. I don't know what became of him."

On February 14, he left Görlitz as part of the long column of prisoners driven away from the Soviet forces. To McKee the two-month journey became the "Death March."

Pvt. Jim Mills, from Company I of the 423rd Regiment, was spared the initial long trek endured by Leisse and McKee. Instead, he spent roughly ten days locked up in a boxcar, starting December 21, with little food or water, never being able to get off to relieve himself before entering Stalag IV B.

"We were instructed to throw our steel helmets into a pile alongside the gate. We had to strip completely, line up to give our names, get our PW dog tags, a shot of some kind in the left breast and finally were given one set of clothing by the women and men running the operation. I received a British uniform with a small red triangle, the PW symbol.

"We were divided up in various barracks. In ours, most were British soldiers. They welcomed us almost like a party. They shared their food and were anxious for news about the war. We didn't know it at the time, but for them to share their food was a real sacrifice."

A few weeks after coming to Stalag IV B, Mills was one of about 100 assigned to *Werk Kommando # 557*. He was not given any choice in the matter and the men were taken to Dresden, "where we were billeted in a slaughterhouse, later to be known as 'Slaughterhouse V.'" The abattoir was located away from the center of the city on a stretch of underutilized ground. There were actually two buildings, surrounded by high brick walls. There was a potbellied stove but no firewood or coal.

At daybreak, the men were awakened, counted and issued a cup of *ersatz* coffee. They worked until dusk when they returned to a meal of a slice of bread, a bowl of thin soup and another cup of the fake coffee. Occasionally, a small piece of meat, potatoes or other items supplemented the meager diet.

The first work assignment involved clearing a roadway blocked by rubble from buildings during a Christmas bombing. One of the structures had housed a grocery store. Mills noted, "You would find an occasional cookie or other item with dirt and or glass all over it. A little cleaning made it edible, even if it did crunch some."

One day, the guards caught some prisoners taking items and there was a lineup of about a dozen men in the street. "The best we could tell was that they were going to shoot several of us to prove they were serious about plundering. Finally, they cooled down. Our interpreter [a GI who understood the language] said they really were intending to shoot us but decided to give us another chance.

"Sometimes older women would come out and leave something on the rubble half a block away. We found out they were leaving a sandwich or something to eat. One day when they laid an item down and left, yelling German soldiers chased them. I hope they got away."

In mid-January bombers dropped leaflets that warned the Germans to stop using the railroad lines around Dresden for shipment of war supplies. "On the night of February 13, 1945, the air raid sirens went off about 10:00 P.M. We got up and marched to another part of the slaughter house complex, then down a few flights of stairs into a sub-basement, two or three levels below the grade. Even in a bomb shelter you worry, because you know a direct hit will get you. After it was over, we went outside to get back to our building. We could see fires with a major part of the city really burning. One of our guys had slept through the raid and the glass of every window in the place was blown out."

About 1:00 A.M. bombers renewed their attacks. Even the slaughterhouse area took some heavy blows. "The top two or three stairs had taken a direct hit, making it pretty tough to get out. The refrigerated rooms were torn open. A lot of our guys were taking meat and hiding it inside their field jackets. The German officer and guards brought a farm wagon. We loaded it with meat, then threw blankets and miscellaneous items on top to look like we were moving our belongings, which we were, since our former home had been destroyed. The guards couldn't get our guys to stop taking meat. They were afraid that someone would come and catch us and everyone would be shot for plundering. The officer fired his pistol into the air several times to gain control.

"We pushed this large wagon through the burning streets of the town, over the fire hoses and debris. Everyone was so involved with fighting the fires that no one paid attention to us. We pushed it out to the edge of Dresden, up a long hill to Görlitz, a South African prison[ers] camp."

On February 14, the *Werk Kommando* hiked into Dresden while houses still blazed. Mills saw residents lining both sides of the streets but, other than threats, no one engaged in hostile actions toward the prisoners. Some of the men received the assignment of retrieving furniture and other possessions from the burning buildings, but the smoke and heat drove them out. The work party now headed toward the slaughterhouse to salvage any meat. On the way, through an open park area, wild animals freed from their confines at the zoo roamed the open land. When a guard pointed out a llama and jokingly remarked, *"Essen,"* a prisoner took him at his word. He chased down the beast and wrestled it to the ground.

According to Mills, he was furious when the guard forced him to set the animal loose.

As they passed through Dresden, the Americans spotted ominous vapor trails in the sky. There were no air-raid sirens to sound an alarm. The earlier raids had destroyed the warning system. "We started running toward the Elbe River, hoping to get below the river bank for protection against explosions and flying debris. About two blocks from the river, I heard the bombs falling, whistling on their way down. I looked up to see if I could spot the big ones, hoping to get out of their way if possible. But I couldn't see any.

"I could see incendiaries coming down from all over the sky in clusters. They appeared to drop until they gained too much speed, at which point they tumbled, making it possible to see them, briefly.

"I was running through a large garden. A big bomb went off about half a block in front of me. I turned and started running back the way I had come, when another went off behind me. It blew me down on my stomach. I looked around to see how close it had come. I saw one of the incendiaries sticking in the ground between my legs, at the knees. I don't know whether it was a dud or a time delay.

"There was a concrete outhouse toilet in the garden. I ran for it. There was already another PW and two guards there. After the raid, I joined some other PWs gathered on a road beside the river. Although we were caught in the open and bombs rained down all around the area, none had been killed. Some were injured but none seriously."

Mills and the others reached the slaughterhouse and began removing meat from the burning buildings. The heat was intense because a fire raged in the basement below the cold room that contained the meat. "As we grabbed hams, we tore off pieces to eat. This proved a mistake, since soon after I developed a severe case of diarrhea." The tar of the floor began to bubble from the conflagration below. The authorities decided the floor might collapse at any moment and halted the work.

After another night at the *lager* (camp) that held the South African prisoners, Mills joined a work detail to dig through the shattered brick buildings connected by a warren of tunnels. "They sent us into the basement to remove bodies. As I went down the ramp, I stepped on something that gave a little. I could see part of a shirt or dress. There was a body buried in the ramp, which you would not notice unless you stepped on it.

"In the basement, the corridor opened to a larger room. When I entered, I saw a card table which had some bottles of liquor on it. To the right was a whole pile of bodies. There was a body laying on the floor where a hall led to the next building, and it had been hit right at the waistline with one of the incendiary bombs. The body was almost burnt in half.

"The guard pointed at the corpse as one I should remove. He indicated I take a belt off another body and put it around the one I was to remove. It's surprising how much could be communicated by hand motions. I put a belt around the neck of this man and started to drag it towards the ramp, but it broke in half. That was too much for me. I sort of lost it for a bit. I began to scream, yell and dance around. I tried to get out of there but they wouldn't let me. They got me quieted down, pointed to one of the bottles on the table and insisted I have a few swallows. That was the first I ever tasted liquor of any kind.

"The guards forced me to pick up the top half of the body, put it on a stretcher at the base of the ramp. They made another man pick up the bottom half. He didn't like it any better than I did and told me so. We carried the remains out and put them on the street alongside several others.

"We then got back at the end of the line. As we neared the head of it, we would slip out of the line and go to the rear, trying to avoid going back into the basement. Finally, the guards caught us and put us at the front.

"In the cellar again, I thought I would be smart. I picked a fellow who had on a gas mask. I thought all I would need do is drag him by the mask to the stretcher. But when I grabbed the mask and pulled, it popped off his head. His eyes looked like they were almost out of their sockets. His mouth was wide open and the whole face and mouth was covered with blood.

"I lost my cool again and the guards had me drink more liquor. I remember taking out the body to the pile but the rest of the day is no longer part of my memory. From there on, this was our daily job. We cleaned up the rubble and removed any bodies found. This continued the rest of February, March and into April."

During the two nights and two days that created the destruction Mills was assigned to clean, the British Royal Air Force and the American Air Corps obliterated the historical "old town" center of

Dresden, a nonmilitary target, raining down more than 2,400 tons of high explosives and almost 1,500 tons of incendiaries. The results, said novelist Kurt Vonnegut, Jr., another 106th Division contribution to the work force, created a "corpse mine."

With the passage of time, the bodies decomposed, and, in Mills's words, "after a month it's a mess." Cleaning up bricks and rubble, the PWs, upon seeing a corpse, would try to move to another pile of debris. But as soon as their guards noticed a gap opening up between workers, they would pick a man and make him excavate the corpse. "We would dig out a body after it had been buried for days. It would be swollen, appear to be filled with pus under the skin. I will never forget the stench of burnt flesh. Years later, back in the States, I was with my wife at the time, and we passed a building where there had been a fire. I said to her, 'There's a body in there.' Sure enough, they found the charred remains of a child later."

At the end of a day's work, the laborers washed their hands in a bucket of lime water and went back to the *lager* shared with the South Africans. The camaraderie of their first encounter had dissipated. The veterans of El Alamein and Tobruk considered the American newcomers unreliable and a threat to escape plans. They worried that the foraging and stealing of food by the Americans would lead to a barracks-search by the SS. That might disclose implements and plots to escape. They successfully petitioned for separation from them. Mills says many of the South Africans, after four years as prisoners, could speak German and had been assigned to less onerous jobs, like the post office.

Conditions at the camp were terrible. Overcrowding forced two men to share each single bed. "We slept back to back and there was no room to turn over. There were no pillows, mattresses or blankets. You slept right on the wood board bottom. We were locked in for the night. Our toilet was a large metal barrel with a wood slat to sit on. There was no toilet paper, ever. I don't ever remember seeing a bar of soap or hot water to wash. Many of us had developed severe diarrhea, either from the uncooked ham at the slaughter house or the unsanitary conditions in which we lived and worked. Our *lager* stunk."

The stomach problems plagued Mills for weeks after he bolted down the raw ham. "It was terribly embarrassing and would strike at any moment. Frequently while marching down a street, I would have to step to the side of the road, drop my pants, squat and shit, usually with civilians walking along. I would walk a few blocks further and then the same thing. I am sure the people thought we were disgusting, but we had no choice, nor did we have toilet paper."

The prisoners schemed to delay their work programs. "We soon found that if we could screw up the count, the guards would keep counting until they got it right. We would sometimes kill almost an hour, stepping into a line already counted, causing the guard to come up short. We would step backward after already being counted, causing the guard to come up with an excess. Finally, they started to put a guard at the end of each line to make sure nobody moved.

"Some guards were sympathetic to our problems. We were on a starvation diet and you had to steal food whenever you got a chance. We had been warned that if we were caught, we could be shot. But I didn't think I would make it if I didn't. I might as well get as much food as I could, without being too careless. One day I found some potatoes and put them in the edge of some hot coals. When I went to get them out, the guard pushed them back in. When they were all burnt and charred, he made me eat them.

"I told our interpreter that it looked as if the guard was getting mean. He said he knew that one pretty well and would see what was upsetting him. Later, the interpreter said the guard knew I had a bad case of diarrhea and thought charred potatoes would help."

While the usual complement of guards displayed no great vigilance, there were SS troopers around who were much stricter. "They caught a fellow from Company I, 423rd Regiment. Two of our men had to go to his trial, which was very short. He was shot by a firing squad and the two at the trial had to dig his grave. We became very careful for a couple of days."

Mills himself came close to the same fate. Temporarily assigned to peel kohlrabi in a building in which bread baked, he weighed himself on a scale in the factory. He was down forty pounds and could see all of his ribs clearly. "The smell of fresh bread was just too much. As I made one of my trips past the fresh bread, I took a loaf and stuck it under my field jacket, and headed down the stairs. I had just passed the landing when a man coming up the stairs stopped me and found the bread—from the smell I guess. I got a lecture in German but he didn't take the bread. I knew that meant trouble. But I went back to the toilet and ate the whole loaf.

"When we lined up to leave, here came the man who caught me with the bread. He spoke to our interpreter, who said the owner of the factory had caught one of the prisoners stealing a loaf of bread. If this happened again, every one of us would be shot. Every prisoner in that line was looking for the stupid jerk who took the bread."

On another occasion, Mills and a companion were clearing out a garage blown apart by the bombing. The job required them to push a wheelbarrow over a wooden plank to a field. The prisoners performed in slow-motion but the guards seemed unconcerned. Prowling for food, Mills discovered a cellar full of bottles. He sampled a few but didn't like the taste. "I found a large bottle with gold tin foil on top. It tasted like 7-Up, so I drank about half of it and went back up and told my friend.

"He took his turn to check out the cellar. He told me that it was champagne, not 7-Up, and I had better get busy working, because I was going to be drunk. Our slow motion suddenly changed. I started loading and actually running across the plank with the loaded wheelbarrow. We started giggling and I got to weaving badly as I crossed the plank. The guards thought the sudden activity was funny also. They laughed at the crazy Americans and never came over to inspect the building."

Like the other prisoners housed in eastern Germany, Mills became aware of the Russians approaching. He heard artillery fire in the distance. "Our food began to improve. This was all the more indication that the Russians were getting closer."

Stalag IV B, after the same horrendous train ride, also became the temporary home of Pvt. Frank Raila. Like Mills, he was chosen for a work crew. But his assignment—which involved laying track and hammering spikes for the rail lines, filling craters, hauling out bomb duds—was close enough to IV B for him to spend his nights behind the barbed wire of the camp.

Raila saw a potentially limited future pulling alleged bomb duds out of the earth and considered escape. On the walks to and from his labor, he saw things that would fit into a plan. He noticed small sheds, more like roofed-over mounds, where farmers stored their vegetables close to the barbed-wire fence. It was possible to shinny up onto the sheds, climb down and steal some of the stored food. Some of it was cooked and eaten, but he also began to cache carrots, rutabagas and other vegetables in his pockets to sustain him once he left the camp. He observed that the guards were becoming lax, allowing a visit to the outdoor privy while leaving the door ajar.

He had not found Americans who seemed inclined to join him in such a risky endeavor, but among the British he met kindred souls. Half a dozen times they scheduled a breakout. Then, perhaps anticipating escape tries, the camp officials cracked down. They installed a crude pair of indoor toilets. The door to the outside now stayed locked at night. Raila looked for another opportunity.

Sgt. John Chernitsky, the antitank crewman from the Twenty-eighth Division, spent brief periods at both Stalags XII A and IV B before being lodged at II B, which was at Hammerstein near the Polish border. According to Chernitsky, "While we were at II B, diphtheria was reported in the Russian prison compound, and details from French, British and American PWs were digging a ditch. We could see from the compound that it was quite large. Two or three days later, while all other prisoners were confined to the barracks, we heard machine gun fire and thought the Russians or somebody had made a breakthrough, but we found that all able-bodied men, no matter what rank, were given shovels and marched out to the ditch and ordered to cover the ditch. The Germans had covered what was in the ditch with straw, but as you threw dirt on the straw, you could see arms and legs. That's when we knew the sick Russians were executed and covered in this ditch."

Subsequently shifted to a prison camp farther west, Chernitsky and his fellows were surprised to find themselves on still another march in early February. Once out of sight of the gates, an old German guard addressed them. He told them Hitler had given orders to do away with all prisoners. To protect the inmates, the camp commandant had directed the guards to move them away from the execution-minded SS. Supposedly, the commandant would cover his good deed by showing inspectors from the SS the bodies of Russian prisoners, machine-gunned and dumped in trenches. The guard, who had spent time in the U.S. during the 1930s and who, Chernitsky assumed, had some feeling for the Americans, asked that no one try to escape while he carried out the scheme to protect the PWs. Without question, he asserted, anyone who fled and was caught would be executed.

There is no evidence that Hitler ever demanded all prisoners be killed. Rumors of this nature, however, could have come to the guards, or it may have been a subterfuge designed to ensure that no one attempted to escape. Chernitsky wound up at Stalag X C, at Nienburg on the Weser River.

When Sgt. Clifford Broadwater climbed down from the 40-and-8 with the other antitankers taken prisoner, he, too, was initially lodged at Stalag IX B, near Bad Orb. After a few weeks, he moved to IX A, designated for noncoms. Broadwater's incarceration was relatively comfortable, compared to the ordeal of Collins, Leisse, Hannon and McKee. A pot of hot soup arrrived daily around noon. Every man received a quart of the mixture, usually extracted from potatoes, and on rare occasions it contained small pieces of meat, quite likely from a horse. Evenings brought a loaf of black bread to be divided among six men. Twice, small Red Cross parcels added a tiny bit of meat, candy, crackers and cigarettes to the larder.

Broadwater's contingent apparently exercised discipline through several top sergeants. There were no demands for work parties; the men received showers and delousing on two or three occasions.

Lt. Lyle Bouck, whose I & R platoon delayed *Kampfgruppe Peiper's* jumpoff for a number of hours, became part of the officers' group imprisoned at Hammelburg. The condition of the commissioned ranks confined at Stalag XIII B when Bouck arrived was, in his words, "pretty slovenly." The resident senior American officers seemed either demoralized or so beset by pettiness that they were unable to organize the prisoners along the lines of military discipline. According to then-Lt. Richard Baron, a member of the 45th Division, who was captured before the Bulge, much of the the failure was due to the "weak and vacillating leadership exercised by Col. Charles Cavender," who had surrendered his 423rd Infantry Regiment en masse. Baron reported that, while at Bad Orb, a Cavender aide came to the officers' barracks and said the Germans wanted a list of Jewish officers. Lt. Col. Joseph Matthews, who had been executive officer in the 424th, snapped, "You just tell

Colonel Cavender that every officer in this barracks is Jewish, and from now on tell him to stay the hell out of here."

The situation changed with the arrival of Col. Paul R. Goode, captured in Normandy while serving with the 29th Infantry Division, and Lt. Col. John Waters of the 1st Armored Division, taken by Rommel's Afrika Korps early in 1943. Waters, a West Pointer, was married to George Patton's daughter, which would prove a significant factor at Hammelburg. Both Goode and Waters survived a 300-mile, forty-five-day ordeal in which they trekked from a PW camp in Poland before reaching XIII B.

As the senior American at the Hammelburg installation, Goode, with Waters as his chief associate, instituted a chain of command with as much military discipline as he could muster. He demanded the men shave, dress themselves properly and conduct themselves as officers. The *kriegies,* as the inmates called themselves, organized teams to cleanse barracks, combat the vermin, distribute news and even hold classes to sustain morale.

"Not everyone was happy with Goode," said Bouck, "and some told him to take that stuff and shove it. But it was necessary to be organized." According to Bouck, there were no committees to develop escape plans, a phenomenon that was endemic among the British PWs.

Frostbite nipped both hands of Lt. Alan Jones, Jr., during his journey to Stalag XIII B. There was not much to eat on the trip and sometimes he drank from streams or ditches. Mild dysentery gripped his stomach occasionally. But once at XIII B, unlike the NCOs and, particularly, the men without rank, the officers were not expected to work while prisoners. The camp also held many Yugoslavian captives, officers in white uniforms with jackboots.

Jones witnessed the arrival of the colonel who instilled some organization in life at Hammelburg. "Pop Goode [as he was known behind his back] came in with bagpipes under his arm. [The instrument was a present from the YMCA to Goode while he was a prisoner in Poland; he was a less than accomplished artist with the wind bag.] But inside the pipes, Goode carried parts of a radio and we started to get BBC reports on the war.

"There was a lack of food. Supposedly they fed us 1,087 calories a day. I had started out at 130 pounds and I lost 20 while there. The basic problem was survival. The daily issue of food brought great concern and the cutting of the bread was viewed with intense interest. The two main topics of conversation were food and what one would do after the war. I never was aware of any organized escape plans.

"Lack of food leads to lethargy, physical and mental. Add the cold—we had no heat—and the men became weaker every day. Through a great voluntary effort we started class lessons, in languages and the Bible, for example. Anyone who had the energy could teach.

"I knew John Waters. He had been an instructor in tactics at West Point when I was there. At Hammelburg, I did what was traditional in the military, made my formal call on him as my senior officer. I scraped the mud off my boots, cleaned myself up as well as possible and went to see him. The visit lasted for the time to smoke a cigarette together, one that was cut into thirds for us to share."

Having recovered sufficiently from his wounds incurred at Noville during the first days in defense of Bastogne, Major William Desobry, with other healed prisoners, rode several trains until he reached a camp near Bergen. The place was an enormous repository of prisoners. Desobry estimated 75,000 Russians, 5,000 Americans, from 10,000 to 15,000 British, including many paratroopers captured during Market Garden, and thousands of Frenchmen. In addition, the PW *lager* bordered the infamous Bergen-Belsen concentration camp.

Shortly after Desobry became part of a very small group of Allied officers—fifty or so—British Sergeant Major Lord advised him that, as senior officer in the camp, Desobry was the boss. Desobry began to exert command, particularly over the Americans who gave Lord difficulties.

"It suddenly dawned on me. We were always trying to make as much trouble as we could for the German camp authorities. That was the only way we could have fun and still feel like we were in the war. I was demanding to have weekly meetings with the authorities. We pulled the Geneva Convention bit and every trick we could think of to make life miserable for those in charge."

Desobry managed to meet regularly with Lord by slipping out of Mass every Sunday and making his way to the enlisted men's compound. There he would also dispense justice to those soldiers considered derelict in their actions.

He also arranged to distribute Red Cross packages stored in

warehouses, where they would help those most in need, the wounded and sick in a hospital. Using cigarettes removed from the parcels, Desobry and associates bribed German soldiers to drive trucks to the port of Lübeck on the Baltic Sea, where huge amounts of Red Cross packages were held because of no transportation to the German interior. The contents sustained many of the men declining from the poor nutrition ordinarily dished out to them.

The PWs assigned to loading the trucks making the run to Lübeck brought news of vast numbers of prisoners being marched west from the Russians. Americans and Britons were hiking away from the advancing Red Army. Secret radios in the camp tuned in to the BBC with further encouraging news. Desobry knew liberation was close at hand when he learned the Allies had crossed the Rhine.

Chapter XVI

FINAL BATTLES

WHILE THE BATTLE OF the Bulge ended in January, 1945, leaving in its wake fearsome numbers of dead, wounded and captured, the Third Reich refused to accept unconditional surrender and instead tenaciously defended its native turf.

Late in February, well after his unwelcome guests—Sepp Dietrich and Rex Degrelle—checked out, Bürgermeister Jean Pauels dispatched Servatius Maraite (brother of Peter Maraite, who offered hospitality to a lone American officer and an enlisted man companion two days after the German breakthrough), along with August Pauels, the bürgermeister's cousin, as guides for an American burial detachment.

The Belgian woodsmen led the U.S. soldiers to a spot in the forest near Meyerode where, some weeks earlier, Peter Maraite said he had come across the body of the American officer whom he befriended shortly after the German breakthrough. (Some accounts declare that Servatius originally discovered the corpse.)

The group located the remains of an American officer, lieutenant's bars still on his shoulder straps, and seven dead Germans nearby. According to Servatius Maraite, "The officer's outer garment was an overcoat, and he had a wool muffler. He was without weapons, shoes, arctics or headgear. But the Americans found all his papers and much money on him. This makes me think that his weapons, shoes and arctics had been taken from him by comrades instead of the enemy, who would also have taken his money and his papers."

In a signed statement, Maraite noted that the seven Germans were only a small part of the total number of dead Germans in the vicinity. There were hastily-dug graves scattered through the area, and Maraite would not quarrel with the bürgermeister's estimate of about two hundred such victims.

From the papers, the graves registration people identified the dead officer as Eric Fisher Wood, Jr., the acting commander of

Battery A, 589th Field Artillery, last seen running into the woods to escape the enemy at Schönberg. In addition to Wood, the searchers found the body of a GI, some 250 to 300 yards yards away, with his still-loaded weapon. He was identified as Pfc. Lehman M. Wilson of the 82nd Airborne.

As near as the experts could determine, Wood had perished around January 22, which was the approximate time that the villagers claimed that firefights in the woods, cited by Bürgermeister Pauels, ceased. The physical and circumstantial evidence composed an image of Wood carrying on guerrilla warfare, as had been vowed by the officer whom Peter Maraite entertained two days after the German breakthrough. The issue of Eric Wood's heroism would eventually generate an often acrimonious controvery.

Rather than heroics, for Dee Paris with the 14th Tank Battalion, the period following the Ardennes campaign revealed war at its nastiest. The Ninth Armored, of which his tank unit was an element, had regrouped following the Bulge and become an integral part of the 1st Army's drive toward the Rhine. But faulty intelligence continued to dog his tracks.

"Originally, since horses do not have radios, the cavalry used motorcyclists to carry messages. When they did away with this method, our cyclist was devastated. I made him a gunner in my platoon sergeant's tank. We received some incorrect information and were caught in direct antitank fire. I was in the lead tank on a road approaching a village when an AT round passed just above my head. The weapon fired two or three more times, each time the round just about a yard over me. I figured he had the gun dug in and couldn't lower his gun tube enough to hit me. The shell passing overhead made a fluttering sound—like when you expel air through your mouth, fluttering your lips.

"The shells missed me. But my platoon sergeant, looking out his turret, was decapitated by a round. When the motorcyclist made gunner turned to him for orders, he saw the headless body and just about lost his mind. We got the tank back to safety but now the gunner was a mental case.

"He couldn't face that experience again, so he was assigned as a driver, which placed him in the lower, left part of the chassis. Subsequently, his tank came under fire and was struck by a round. I neutralized the German gun and went forward to survey the damage. The shell from a German 75-mm antitank piece had hit the pavement in front of the tank and pierced the thin bottom of the tank. It split the body of the driver. I was devastated. I leaned against the tank and cried.

"The battalion commander and an officer from higher headquarters arrived. This officer peered into the hatch and I lost my temper, shouting, 'If you want to see blood, why don't you come up here and fight!' My commander restrained me until I calmed down.

"But no matter what you've been through before, you can still feel a loss to the point where you ignore discipline and verbally attack a senior officer. I understand that, as a result of my behavior, he disapproved a valor award recommendation.

"Then there was an officer who had been wounded and evacuated during the Bulge. He returned just as we left on the mission that ended in the death of my platoon sergeant. He, too, was killed. At the time, however, he was carried as missing in action. His wife, who'd lost a baby just before we went overseas, wrote, saying, 'God couldn't be so mean as to take my child and my husband at the same time. He can't be dead.' Against all regulations, I wrote back telling her not to prolong her grief with hope. Her husband, my friend, was dead. It was another terrible moment.

"I never heard the wounded men make sounds. I saw the looks on their faces, and it tears you up. It is fear, sadness, shock and surprise. Injuries, on the other hand, may be a different matter. I once had my clothes catch fire and was told my screams could be heard a mile away. And you scream when you tell your crew to evacuate a tank so they will respond instantly."

As the tankers battered their way forward, Paris himself received several wounds. Fragments from an aerial torpedo ripped the flesh under his eyes. Taken back to an aid station, Paris was attended by a grumpy surgeon whose lunch had been interrupted. "He kept chewing his food and he sewed me up without an anesthetic. I couldn't stand the pain. Our casualties ran high. At one point we'd lost seventy percent of our officers and seventeen percent of the enlisted men."

The 27th Armored Infantry Battalion, with Maj. Glen Strange, who had escaped from the enemy during the first days of their advance and recruited some tankers to free his commanding officer, regrouped in France for nearly two months before returning to confront the enemy. CCB of the 9th Armored Division, with the 27th AIB as a component, stretched into an eighteen-mile-long column as it wound its way through Belgium, into Germany and across the Roer River on the last day of February.

According to Strange, the Command then slowed perceptibly. "Some of the companies had lost too much leadership. I had been told many times not to volunteer in the army but something made me feel these wonderful men whom I had helped train and been through so much needed me. I told Major Deevers, 'Give me a task force and we will move.'"

Deevers arranged for Strange to lead two companies of the 27th AIB, one from the 14th Tank Battalion, artillery support, and a platoon from the 89th Recon Battalion. "The Commander of the 89th was Maj. Ralph Houk, the major league player and manager. He was a guy I thought a great deal of and a good officer, but I should have killed the bastard when we were back in Kansas. At that time I had an operation for an appendix. Afterwards I was put in a ward next to Ralph, who had the same sort of operation three days before. He was reading a book, *Low Man on a Totem Pole*, which is very funny. About the second day after my operation he started quoting passages to me, causing me to laugh so hard I damn near ripped out my stiches. I cussed a few times but he kept it up. I felt like killing him."

The task force under Strange achieved its first objective, Lommersum, on the Erft Canal, only a few hours after its creation. "On the morning of March 4, a sergeant who piloted an L–5 [observation plane] landed in a turnip patch just behind my lines. I had flown with him before and he took me up. It was a hazy day but we could see the Rhine River and the Ludendorff Bridge at Remagen. I reported this to Gen. William Hoge, CCB commander, and his comment was, 'It won't be there when we reach it.'"

From Lommersum, Strange's task force assaulted Bodenheim. "I took A Company from the 27th AIB and a platoon of the 14th tanks and captured it with some losses in about one hour. The history books say Gen. Hoge led this attack. He did show up and was right with me to the end of it. But I gave all the orders and directed the attack. He never countermanded anything I said and it was nice to have him there, although he had no business being on the scene and his aide was killed during the fight."

On the following day, Strange was part of a party attempting to capture the village of Esch. "About 2:00 P.M. I was on foot and with the leading element. I was shot by a .30-caliber machine gun located in a church on the outskirts of Esch. My military career was over. I was evacuated and reached a field hospital in Liège on the morning of March 6." The bullet severely damaged Strange's spine and he was now to suffer through nearly two years of hospitalization with a prognosis that declared he'd never walk again.

Glen Strange, his task force and CCB of the Ninth Armored were engaged in a race to cross the Rhine, the last substantial natural barrier in the west. In the vanguard of CCB was Dee Paris with the 14th Tank Battalion. On March 6, "Colonel Engeman [Paris's CO] called me, 'Squirrel'—that was my radio code name, he was 'Gopher'—'Go up there and look at that bridge.' I tried to tell him we didn't have enough gas but he ignored me. I did not want to go in the worst way. I hated night operations, you can't see and the tanks roll off into ditches and crash into trees. At five minutes to nine, just as I told the guys to crank up the engines, I received a call to cancel the mission.

"The Ludendorff Bridge at Remagen, on the west side of the Rhine, was still standing but there was a big hole in front of it. Meanwhile, there were these German guns up on a hill that was actually behind us. We'd be sitting ducks for them if we tried to reach the bridge. I was told to take some tanks and knock out those guns. I couldn't get close enough with the tanks, so we dismounted and swept the hill like we were infantry. That silenced the guns.

"We moved into Remagen. At this point, the hole in front of the Bridge prevented tanks from moving across it. But about three in the afternoon, I saw the troops from the 27th Armored Infantry Battalion [Strange's outfit] go across, the first ones over the Rhine."

The law of averages seemed to catch up with many of the soldiers. Melvin Biddle, with the 517th Parachute Regiment, recommended for a Congressional Medal of Honor because of valor outside of Hotton, came out of that engagement unscratched. But three days after Christmas, an 88 shell struck a house behind him. Shrapnel penetrated his neck and small pieces stuck in his hairline and lips.

While the wounds were not painful, according to Biddle, he

spent a week recuperating in a hospital and then enjoyed a week-long furlough in England. On his way back to the 517th, Biddle met a fellow soldier, recovering from injuries in the Ardennes, who remarked, "That guy in the Bulge who shot all those people, between Soy and Hotton—my God, it was littered with Germans —I think they're going to put the guy in for the Medal of Honor."

"I rejoined the outfit," says Biddle. "There was a plan for another parachute drop, but I was told I couldn't be sent into combat —too many men had been killed after they were put in for the Medal. As a result, there was now a regulation that forbade combat for anyone recommended.

"It drove me silly worrying my buddies would go without me. However, the area where they were supposed to be dropped was taken by ground troops and the jump cancelled. But for me, the war was now over."

Pfc. Harry Martin, with L Company in the sole surviving regiment of the 106th Division, the 424th, had become part of the reserve. He thought he had recovered from the shock of that initial assault when waves of German attackers sent him reeling in retreat. But the first week in January, he learned they would move out the following morning, back to the front. "My face turned white. I felt exactly as though a judge had just sentenced me to death and I was going to die tomorrow."

Martin had mixed feelings about the news that the 517th Parachute Regiment, the unit of Bill Boyle, Charles LaChaussee and Mel Biddle, would act in concert with the 424th. "I had a feeling of confidence being with one of the best outfits. But also a little disconcerted, knowing they see a lot of action."

Several weeks later, still in the Ardennes, Martin was part of a force attempting to climb a snowy slope. Machine gun fire and artillery pinned them down. "Word was passed that someone was wounded and a medic needed. I raised up on my left arm, turned my head to the right and yelled, 'Medic!' Just at that moment there was a thunderous roar. I could feel my body lift up and then violently twist and slam to the ground. I was suddenly in a different state of consciousness. I no longer had a body. I no longer had thoughts, just an awareness of a perfect bliss, surrounded by a loving, protective, hazy, soft light. I knew I was dead but death was beautiful.

"But then I felt myself slowly leaving this perfect state of bliss, going back to the physical world I thought I had left forever. I suddenly realized I was not dead and went from the best feeling anyone could ever have to the worst one. My right shoulder felt as if it were crushed. Next, I felt as if half of my right foot were gone. There was pain in about five places in my right thigh, pain in the lower part of my right leg, my right arm, pain under my left knee and pain in my back. Both of my ears hurt. I felt so helpless I lost all of my confidence. I was scared shitless."

Mike Mueller, the Company L medic, worked his way to Martin in spite of the continuing drizzle of shells. He exposed his bare hands to the frigid air and laboriously cut through Martin's uniform and two pairs of long john underwear. Mueller not only tended the wounds but he shielded Martin from further damage with his body. The freezing air stopped blood from oozing from Martin's wounds and Mueller moved on to succor other men.

Meanwhile, Martin lay there for seven hours, by his estimate, as his buddies continued their attack up the hill. A compassionate GI draped a blanket over him as he passed, probably making the difference between survival and death from exposure. Martin was eventually carried from the field and now began a four-month hospitalization.

Dick Byers with the 371st Field Artillery of the 99th Division received a battlefield commission as a second lieutenant in January. "On January 27th we [Byers and five others] reported to the Unit Personnel Section to be discharged as enlisted men and sent up the street to Division headquarters, where we were sworn in as officers. From the time we left Personnel until we took the oath we were civilians, but no place to go."

The colonel who swore them in congratulated Byers and the others for making it the hard way. "When he said this, I smiled inwardly because, to me, it was a lot easier to make 2nd Lt. in the field instead of going through three months of rigorous Officer Candidate School. Above all I couldn't be tagged with the pejorative '90-day wonder.'

"I was now earning the princely sum of $276 a month. I sent $200 home, spent $25 on meals and uniforms and $7.00 for GI insurance. The rest was mine to blow as I saw fit. New officers got a $250 initial uniform allowance but the only clothing I could find in the combat zone to fit me was a couple of wool shirts and a British army officer's trench coat."

Away from the front, Byers celebrated on weak Belgian beer spiked with 190-proof medical alcohol donated by amiable air corps officers. After filling out a multitude of forms, Byers relaxed, sledding with kids from a Liège neighborhood.

When he returned to duty with the 371st, there was a brief display of military courtesy from his former colleagues among the enlisted men before relations returned to their former easy association. Byers's career as an officer in the combat zone lasted just a week after he was commissioned.

He was sitting beside his driver in a jeep with three other men packed into the back, a radio operator, a visiting Captain Christman from headquarters company hunched over an ammunition box, and a hitchiking infantryman who dangled his legs over the left rear wheel. Skidding up a long narrow trail, the jeep detonated a mine. "With a stunning explosion it blew the rear end of the jeep straight up in the air. The infantryman flew up in the air and came down in the mine crater. He soon died from the shock of his mangled legs. My driver, Joe Santirocco, was blown straight forward in front of the jeep and died within minutes from internal injuries. My radio operator, Charles Markshaffel, was blown out to the side of the road and broke his back against a tree. I landed face down, sideways, directly in front of the jeep. It flipped up on its front bumper, paused, then crashed upside down on top of Captain Christman and me."

During the brief moment before the vehicle rolled over on him, Byers glimpsed it teetering and then starting to fall. "The ridiculous thought that flashed through my mind was. 'Christ, I hope it doesn't tear my trench coat!' " Relief flooded through him after the jeep crashed down and he realized he was still alive. The cutout in the side by the front seat neatly arched over the small of his back. Six inches either way could have crushed his spine.

Byers used his elbows to dig himself free and staggered to his feet. Men in another jeep following the Byers party lifted the wrecked vehicle enough to haul out Captain Christman. Byers admits that at this point the shock of it all befuddled him. Instead of sending one of the soldiers from the second jeep for help, he started to run in search of aid. He came upon a soldier in a foxhole. "This is when I gave my first and last combat order: 'Get your ass out of that hole! Go and get the medics back here, quick!' "

Two 82nd Airborne aidmen soon reached the scene. They provided what help they could. Byers was on his feet but the other four were all down. In these moments, Santirocco asked for help because he couldn't breathe, and then expired.

"A lone infantryman, carrying his rifle at port, plodded around the bend from the front, following a single Waffen SS prisoner with his hands clasped behind his head. As the SS man threaded his way through the four wounded, he got just the hint of a smirk on his face. One of the Airborne medics sitting on a log saw the expression. He glanced at the infantryman and very quietly said, 'Shoot the son of a bitch!' The infantryman just looked away and kept moving toward the rear. About ten minutes later he trudged back alone. No words were exchanged but we all knew there was no way he could have taken his prisoner back to Battalion HQ through the deep snow and returned in that short a time."

When 82nd Airborne medics drove up in a pair of Weasels, vehicles able to navigate through the snow, they carried off the dead and wounded. Although Byers thought he was only suffering from the concussion, he accepted a stretcher ride back to the battalion aid station. During the trip, Byers says, "Knowing the trail was mined, I tried to levitate myself one inch above the floor and never took a deep breath, trying to keep my weight reduced." Months later he learned from an engineer that they had discovered half a dozen more mines along the trail which his jeep rode over and which the Weasels passed without detonating.

Technically, a Purple Heart, worth five points towards a discharge, could be awarded only if one spilled blood in combat. Although Byers's main complaint was a pain in his groin, he pointed out a spot on his knee with a few drops of blood caused when he flipped to the ground. The doctor then authorized the Purple Heart. Three weeks later, at a hospital outside of Paris, X-rays finally determined the cause of Byers's discomfort, a fractured pelvis.

The route taken by the 82nd Airborne as it began its advance in January covered the terrain where the 28th Infantry Division in the late autumn absorbed terrible punishment before retreating. Sgt. Bill Dunfee of the 505th Parachute Regiment says, "The area became known to us as 'Death Valley.' There were trucks, tanks, jeeps, trailers, tank destroyers, bumper to bumper and all shot to hell. Tanks had thrown their tracks, trucks, jeeps and trailers turned over, some burned. I had been exposed to the carnage of war in four Airborne operations—Sicily, Italy, Normandy and Holland—but I never saw anything that could compare. Freshly killed troops in various stages of dismemberment are gruesome enough for the average stomach. But these men had been through a freeze and thaw. They had lain there since November and their flesh had rotted and was peeling from the skeletons. Some were on litters. I hoped they were killed outright and not abandoned to freeze to death. There was complete silence in our column, each man handling this horror in his own way. For me, it was the most shocking single experience of the war. If anyone needed an incentive to fight, this gave him ample reason."

In mid-February, the 82nd left the front and wallowed in the comparative luxury of a pyramidal tent city at Camp Suippes, France. "Mud and all, it sure beat hell out of where we had been." When the 82nd returned to the war it served much but not all of its time in an occupation role around Cologne. At the end of April, Dunfee with the 505th crossed the Elbe in a daring night assault that caught the German defenders completely by surprise. For Dunfee, World War II ceased while near the town of Neuhaus.

Lt. Harry Mason, a member of the ill-fated 28th Division's disastrous days in the Huertgen Forest, and then forced into a helter-skelter retreat from positions at Grindhausen and Luxembourg, had finally reached Neufchâteau, a town just beyond the outer limits of the Bulge. Of the approximately 4,000 members from his 110th Regiment, there were about fifty officers and 450 enlisted men.

Mason manned an outpost at Neufchâteau with eight soldiers starting two days before Christmas. Through his post poured the reinforcements to break the siege of Bastogne and drive the enemy out of the Ardennes.

As part of a reorganized and restocked regiment, Mason, now an 81-mm mortar platoon leader, participated in the Vosges Mountains campaign, the capture of Colmar and various points near the Rhine. On April 10, he was given a forty-five-day furlough. His boat docked in the States on V-E Day, May 12.

Jack Agnew, the pathfinder who dropped into Bastogne two days before Christmas to guide in relief from the air, traveled by truck into Germany. As part of the 506th Parachute Regiment, he was among those who opened up two Nazi concentration camps. "We made the people from nearby towns walk through the camp and see what unbelievable atrocities had taken place, the incomprehensible inhumanity of man to his own. Our unit took photographs of the camp, showing how we made the people look at the piles of bodies, stacked like firewood. It would have been God's mercy upon the German army if we had found these places before Normandy. There would have been mighty few prisoners taken.

"Landsberg was one of the camps. I will never forget the man who hung onto me as if I were the Lord come to save him. Others just ran around with nowhere to go, just ran till they were out of sight. Some, at last free, just died with a kind of smile with their final bit of strength."

Pfc. Cy Blank of the 11th Armored had a subdued celebration of New Year's Eve in Bastogne before the outfit commenced to push into Germany and to the southwest. He was wounded when a mine blew up under his jeep, killing the driver, with whom he had exchanged places not too long before the explosion.

"Beginning in mid April, we began to come into contact with what had been rumored but not believed by most of us. The existence of the concentration camps became a stark, awful reality when we overran first the camp at Flossenburg, and then Dachau. The examples of barbarism we saw go beyond my ability to describe. Thirty years later while my daughter was studying the Holocaust in Sunday School, I gave her some of the photos I took. I realized that everyone must know it happened and 'Never again' is most important.

Like Cy Blank, Barney Alford, the section chief sergeant with Eric Wood who escaped to man the remaining artillery pieces at Baraque de Fraiture, professes a blurred memory of events after the Bulge. He remembers receiving a battlefield commission, assignment to a 155-mm howitzer and receiving a Silver Star.

Joe Colmer of the 325th Glider Regiment and part of the defense at Baraque de Fraiture, where he was wounded, was treated for his injury in England. He rejoined the regiment in France sometime in March and in April reached Cologne by truck. On his second night there, he went on a patrol across the Rhine. He stepped on a booby trap and soon was back in England, his fighting days over.

In the same fashion as Colmer and Dick Byers, Bill Boyle of the 517th was finishing out the war in a hospital bed. Alan Shapiro, his frozen feet slowly responding to treatment, had been in a facility in England. "The big fear among the guys was to be ZI'd— classified fit for the Zone of the Interior, which meant back to combat." In fact, Shapiro received his official walking papers in April and was in transit through the replacement depots that supplied new fodder and returned men to their units.

The continuing casualties and the constant inflow of replacements cost the 30th Division's Frank Currey, Medal of Honor and Silver Star winner, his ability to develop bonds. "I was made platoon leader and from my original platoon [forty-eight enlisted men] there were only four or five left. I couldn't buddy up with anyone outside of them. A guy in the platoon was killed and it was horrible, I couldn't remember his name."

Currey's Company K of the 120th Regiment participated in both the Roer River and Rhine River crossings. His unit eventually reached the Elbe River where they met up with Soviet troops as the war ended.

Bob Hall, a prisoner of *Kampfgruppe Peiper* for several days along with Maj. Hal McCown, from the 30th Division's 119th Regiment also crossed the Rhine. "During the night we snuck up and I was in a deserted house when our artillery opened up. It had to be the best artillery barrage since D-Day. We went over the Rhine in Navy attack boats and not a shot was fired at us.

"We went on to Magdeburg, about seventy miles from Berlin and stopped there. We knew the war was coming to an end in a week or so. We weren't even excited as one might expect. It was anticlimactic because our fighting had already ended. At the Elbe River, we met the Russians and quite a few of them were Mongolians."

After the 7th Armored, with Gen. Bruce Clarke leading it, triumphantly returned to St. Vith, the outfit pushed into the Ruhr. Glenn Fackler, with a machine gun squad during the defense of that town at the outset of the breakthrough, was with his friend Milton Baxter in Germany when a mortar round felled Baxter. A 20-mm high-explosive shell aimed at Baxter wounded Fackler.

But with the help of two other GIs, both men made it to an aid station and survived the war.

Marcus Dillard, with the 4th Infantry Division, also was among those on their feet when the final shots were fired. His outfit crossed the Rhine at Worms then drove south of Munich and on to Nuremberg.

More than two weeks after the 27th AIB jounced across the Ludendorff Bridge at Remagen, General Patton boasted that his Third Army had been the first successful assault crossing. He celebrated with several histrionic gestures, peeing into the river from a pontoon span thrown up by his engineers, grabbing handfuls of dirt on the eastern bank in emulation of William the Conqueror and topping off his performance with a telephone call to Omar Bradley. "For God's sake, tell the world we're across. I want the world to know Third Army made it before Monty starts across!" Of course the First Army with the 9th Armored was truly first over the Rhine.

Two days later, March 25, the 4th Armored Division, with Capt. Abe Baum of the 10th Armored Infantry Battalion, who had been the part of the last ground force to reach Bastogne before the Germans closed the ring, had advanced to the Main River, capturing bridgeheads at Hanau and Aschaffenburg.

Now Patton proposed to send men of the 4th Armored on a daring rescue mission, the liberation of Stalag XIII B at Hammelburg, forty miles away, where Lts. Lyle Bouck and Alan Jones, Jr., with 1,500 other U.S. officers, were confined. Patton would say on March 30, "I felt I could not sleep during the night if I got within sixty miles and made no attempt to get that place." He claimed the inhabitants were in dire peril, since the Nazis were murdering PWs.

Patton handed the mission to Gen. Manton Eddy, Commander of the XII Corps, and Gen. William Hoge, the former CO of CCB, now commanding the 4th Armored. Both of them objected strenuously to the concept of a foray of 3,000 men, 150 tanks plus artillery and other support. Nor was Omar Bradley in favor of the raid either. In the end, Patton yielded on the numbers but his persistence brought a deadly compromise. Instead of the equivalent of a full combat command, the strike force would be little more than one tenth that size, about two companies of troops.

Although Patton professed his motivation was the welfare of all of the officers confined at Hammelburg, there is strong evidence he was concerned about one individual in particular, his son-in-law, John Waters. Intelligence material indicated Waters had been moved from the prison camp in Poland and most likely was at Hammelburg. Indeed, while the task force was being assembled, Maj. Al Stiller, a bantam-size aide of Patton, who had served with him during World War I, and subsequently earned a reputation with the Texas Rangers, arrived at the 4th Armored positions and announced he had been assigned to accompany the raid because, "The General wants me to get a taste of combat. I'm only going along for a high old time and the laughs."

Harold Cohen, the CO of the 10th AIB, whom Abe Baum says had an unbelievably thick southern accent, drawled, "This isn't my idea of a high old time." However, to a supply officer, Stiller confided his role was to identify John Waters.

The idea of a sudden dramatic strike to liberate American prisoners also appealed to Patton as a way to glorify his image. His rival for publicity, the Pacific theater commander, Gen. Douglas MacArthur, had scored huge headlines with January operations that freed 5,000 U.S. prisoners in the Philippines. While lobbying for support with the 4th Armored's new CO, William Hoge, Patton boasted, "This is going to make MacArthur's raid on Cabanatuan [site where 500 were liberated] peanuts." Al Stiller repeated Patton's comparison with the MacArthur feat, changing the "peanuts" to "look like a Boy Scout hike."

The obnoxious burden of designating who would go on what he perceived as a near suicide mission fell upon Col. Creighton Abrams, newly elevated to lead the 4th Armored CCB. Actually, his first choice would have been Abrams's former regular partner on missions, Harold Cohen, and members of the 10th AIB. But Cohen was still recovering from a painful case of hemorrhoids. Indeed, he had been hospitalized with the ailment and was only on hand because of an incident involving Baum.

While Cohen received medical treatment at a hospital, his temporary successor launched 10th AIB troops at a village which proved empty of Germans. But in his zeal, the substitute directed the men into a minefield, resulting in a number of casualties. Baum, on his own, altered the operation to preserve lives. The superior officer, outraged at the captain's temerity, sought to have him transferred. Before his adversary could execute the order,

Baum drove more than sixty-five miles at night to Cohen's hospital, and convinced him to return to the division immediately and ask Abrams to rescind papers shipping Baum to the rear in disgrace.

With Cohen not available because of his painful rear end, which underwent personal inspection by General Patton, Baum became an obvious choice, not the least because it was politic to make him disappear while his friends in high places soothed a ruffled ego.

After Baum heard the bare essentials of the mission at a meeting, Patton drew him aside and in a conspiratorial whisper said, "Listen, Abe—it is Abe, isn't it? You pull this off and I'll see to it that you get the Congressional Medal of Honor." Baum has mixed feelings about the mercurial Patton.

"The important thing about Patton was he believed that infantry should support tanks rather than vice versa. He had the foresight to take a stand, lose a lot of personnel in a short period of time, where in the long haul it wouldn't be as noticeable, but you would have even more casualties as the enemy built up its forces.

"The press ridiculed him as flamboyant and he could put Barnum and Bailey to shame. But he was ideal for the war we fought. He had a feeling for the terrain, he was the most aggressive of all of the generals.

"If anybody should hate him, it would be me. But I believe he shortened the war. On the other hand, I would not want him as a father."

The two officers that Baum most admired were Abrams and Cohen. Of the tanker, Baum says, "He was sincere, honest, didn't speak down to people. In eight or ten words he could put more emphasis than someone who spoke for an hour. He led his troops, he didn't have a headquarters out there in his lead tank. Instead, he was another gun in the tank.

"Harold Cohen came up through the ranks, with battlefield promotions. He knew how to pick people and he was smart enough to marry up with Abrams."

When he learned what was expected of him, Baum says he never considered refusing the orders—perhaps a consequence of being an aggressive twenty-four-year-old. He remarked to Abrams and Cohen, "You won't get rid of me this easy. I'll be back." In retrospect he noted, "When a mission is created, nobody says this or that might happen to you. There usually isn't the intelligence available to say what could occur."

Al Stiller actually supplied the details of the operation. He spoke of 300 officers being held at Hammelburg, a monumental miscalculation that would make the affair even more bizarre. He reassured Baum there would be air cover where possible and that since Patton's Third Army was headed for another sector, the Seventh Army would be prepared to render assistance once Task Force Baum broke away from Hammelburg to return to the U.S. lines. Stiller, however, did not mention Patton's son-in-law to Baum.

Selection of which units would compose the task force was based upon those with the most equipment and men in good working order. The column that jumped off on the night of March 26 with ten Shermans, six light tanks, twenty-seven halftracks, three 105-mm assault guns, a medic Weasel for evacuation of wounded, seven jeeps, all loaded with extra fuel and ammunition, bore 293 soldiers, most of whom had slept only one night out of the previous four days of movement and battle.

The initial obstacle to Task Force Baum lay in the town of Schweinheim, through which began the most direct route to the objective. A TOT artillery cannonade opened the proceedings around 8:30 P.M. Then, a tank company accompanied by armored infantry sought to clear the main road through Schweinheim. But the enemy refused to buckle.

The farm village erupted into an inferno, fueled by exploding bazooka shells, burp guns, rifle fire and the heavier stuff from the Americans. The abundance of enemy rocketry led some to call Schweinheim "Bazooka City." A *Panzerfaust* blast disabled the lead tank, blocking the avenue for other Shermans and their lighter kin. A company clerk, Cpl. Lester Powell, gunned his jeep and pulled up beside the flaming wreck. He climbed over the tread and entered through the turret. Four crewmen were dead, the one survivor lay unconscious with his leg blown off. Powell managed to steer the tank up onto the sidewalk out of the way. He dragged the wounded man through a hatch and dropped to the ground behind him. As he headed for his jeep, Powell himself received a serious wound. But he draped the injured soldier over the hood and clambered into his jeep to make a getaway in the blood-soaked vehicle. For his efforts Powell earned both a Purple Heart and a Silver Star.

With the road open, a second tank then clattered to the end of the half-mile-long street, hosing down both sides of the narrow avenue with machine gun bullets and 76-mm cannon rounds. The fighting in Schweinheim raged on, however. When a German grenade exploded against the turret of one Sherman, the crew, following standard procedure, bailed out to avoid incineration from what could have been a *Panzerfaust*. Usually, when the men saw their tank was undamaged, they would quickly return. But in this case, an alert German beat them to it. He hijacked the tank and turned its cannon on the Americans.

Baum had hoped to break through Schweinheim one hour after the way had been cleared. Instead, the gun fights were still raging, three hours after the first shots. The town, according to one observer, resembled a vision of the great Chicago fire, a conflagration of intense heat and thick smoke. Anxious to travel as far as possible before daylight, Baum instructed the tankers in town to haul themselves up at intervals along the sidewalks, the foot soldiers were told to put down covering fire up the side streets and into the houses while his column ran the gauntlet.

With their path brightly outlined by burning buildings, and snaking between the parked tanks down the narrow street, Baum's column bolted through Schweinheim. Once beyond the fires and in the blackness of night, the column navigated by follow-the-leader, relying on the glow of exhausts and specks of illumination from blackout lights.

The swifter light tanks assumed the head of the mile-long column, which now hurried through the darkness at fifteen miles per hour. Overhead, a liaison plane dallied long enough to relay radio messages from Baum. In his jeep, the captain moved up and down the convoy, checking progress, consulting with the lead vehicles on roads to follow.

At the Berlin headquarters of the *Wehrmacht*, news of the fight at Schweinheim trickled in. In the dark, the defenders could not accurately determine the size of the American force. The Germans concluded Patton had engineered another daring thrust with a contingent of considerable size, rather than the small self-contained task force under Baum. The foe began to mobilize units to meet this threat.

To limit intelligence on his whereabouts, Baum directed the tankers to knock down telephone poles and men to snip the wires. Some of the fear of discovery was relieved by the sight of German officers, soldiers and civilians unconcernedly going about their business as the column hurtled along. The Germans seemed to assume the task force was their own. Before starting out, the Americans had smeared mud over the big white star, as much to eliminate an aiming point for enemy antitank weapons as to conceal their identity.

The Americans revealed their true colors as dawn broke near a German military camp where troops, having neatly stacked their rifles, engaged in calisthenics. The voice of the officer shouting commands died out under a blistering spray of machine gun fire from the tanks and halftracks.

Without pausing, the armor led the task force ever deeper. Two detachments of Germans soldiers marching on the highway, instantly perceiving themselves outgunned, flung their weapons down in surrender. They were told to travel west and turn themselves over to the advancing American armies. While they moved off, the tankers rolled over their abandoned rifles and machine guns, crushing them useless. When these Germans reached the military camp, they would have to explain their failure to fight but that hardly bothered the GIs.

Since leaving Schweinheim around midnight, Task Force Baum had met no organized opposition. But approaching Lohr, a larger town, nine hours later, Baum expected trouble. He shifted the heavier Shermans to the fore and prepared for battle. They bore down on a roadblock from which a German rocket shattered the lead Sherman. Its successor blew away the obstacle but there were some casualties in the shattered tank and from small arms fire.

Continuing to roll, the tanks in front spotted a German truck convoy with antiaircraft 88s. Again the American firepower overwhelmed the opposition, leaving wrecked equipment, dead and wounded strewn about. Obedient to Baum's orders to keep going rather than mopping up survivors, the column swept on. Only as they passed the carnage did the Americans realize that the antiaircraft unit was manned by German flak girls. Because of the shortages in personnel, the Third Reich had begun to use females on their antiaircraft weapons. Task Force Baum rolled on, the GIs trying to ignore the sight of shattered blonde-haired girls hanging lifeless from their smashed vehicles.

Baum swung his group around to bypass Lohr but the German commandant there learned of their presence and heard their engines. He called for reconnaissance aircraft and alerted the garrison at Gemünden, the next town on the route. He directed troops at Gemünden to prepare the bridge over the Saale River for demolition.

A railroad line loomed up; almost parallel to the invaders, tandem locomotives, hauling German troops and equipment, chugged alongside Task Force Baum. The tankers opened fire; the boiler of the steam engine blew and then a boxcar containing ammunition exploded in smoke and flame. A second train derailed and its cargo started to burn as the task force poured high explosives and incendiaries into it. Similar action destroyed a tugboat with its barges. Still on the move, Baum communicated to the Piper Cub overhead, suggesting an air strike on the concentration of rolling stock, military hardware and troops marshaled in the Gemünden railyards. Fighter bombers soon completed the demolition begun by the task force.

However, the wake-up call from Lohr to Gemünden seriously crimped Baum's plans. The bridge over the Saale River in Gemünden would put the column on the shortest route to Hammelburg. But as the task force advanced, mines lay all about the bridge approaches and the alerted enemy opened up on the Americans from across the river.

A recon platoon destroyed the mines but a German rocket disabled a Sherman as it started over the bridge, blocking access to other vehicles. As Baum and his tank commander, Lt. William Nutto, pondered their next move, another shell crashed in their midst. Nutto went down, wounded seriously enough for him to be unable to participate further. He was packed off to the medic Weasel, to be a passenger for the remainder of the trip. The task force commander himself did not escape unscathed. He dropped to his knees in shock and pain as fragments penetrated one hand to the bone and ripped a deep gash near a knee. A medic cut away pieces of his bloody uniform and bandaged his injuries.

Undeterred by the stalled tank on the bridge, a handful of infantrymen scrambled across the span. Three men, including a platoon lieutenant, reached the opposite bank before the Germans pressed the detonator. The structure collapsed into the water, carrying with it a pair of GIs.

His chosen path blocked, Baum decided to head north in search of another bridge. He sent off a last message to the Piper Cub spotter, listing two tanks lost, two officers, eighteen enlisted men wounded or killed. Back at headquarters, casualty list aside, it seemed like good news. The task force was halfway to its objective.

Traveling parallel with the Saale, Baum lost another tank as it threw a track and had to be put out of its misery with thermite grenades. A quick conference with his medics convinced him that four of the wounded could not survive the expedition. He directed that the four be placed alongside the road, a rifle with a white bandage attached jammed into the ground. He hoped the Germans would be merciful.

Farther on, the column intercepted a lone soldier on a motorcycle. When Baum's interpreter, Pfc. Irving Solotoff, a Jewish refugee from Vienna, drew from the captive that he was a Hammelburg native, the task-force leader pointed a bayonet at the terror-stricken soldier's throat. "Tell him I need a bridge to Hammelburg. If he doesn't know where there's a bridge, I'll . . ." The German quickly pointed out a site on Baum's map.

As they followed the way shown by their prisoner, he rode atop a tank with the interpreter. Passing through a woods, he spoke to Solotoff, and the American told the tank commander to halt. The German leaped off, flourished a white scarf and yelled, "*Alles kaputt. Amerikanische Panzer kommen.*" From out of the trees streamed about twenty German soldiers, who threw down their weapons. A bit farther on, the prisoner reprised his act and this time two antitank crews with their cannons surrendered. In both instances, the task force destroyed the armaments and sent the soldiers walking west.

From over the rim of a hill rattled a German staff car with three occupants. It abruptly halted as it came abreast of what the appalled driver recognized as a Sherman. One of the trio turned out to be a general. Dismissing the other two captives, Baum stuck the officer on the hood of a halftrack with the vague notion that enemy troops might withhold fire if they recognized him.

In the fields outside the village of Gräfendorf, the task force came upon 700 Russians, slave laborers for the Third Reich. Their guards quickly dropped their weapons. Baum told the Russians they were now free and, if interested in preserving their liberty, should raid the local police station to obtain more firepower. He also relinquished his general to their care.

A spotter plane appeared, but this one was German. Every man in the task force, including some of the wounded, began firing. But the plane swooped down twice to make its observations and then flew off to deliver precise information on the whereabouts and size of Task Force Baum.

Towards evening, with further guidance through the country roads from local peasants, Baum reached the vicinity of the Hammelburg camp. Some tank destroyers offered resistance and damaged or destroyed more of the armor, inflicting a number of casualties. But with his assault guns laying down a barrage, Baum extricated his dwindling task force and prepared to break into the Hammelburg Stalag itself. Lt. Nutto, supposedly *hors de combat*, left his place among the disabled and, while limping badly, joined Baum for the attack.

The actual defense of the camp relied on troops in foxholes and other concealed positions with rifles and machine guns. As the task force poured its much heavier fire upon the Germans, the camp commandant, obedient to orders from Berlin, arranged for 3,000 enlisted men, Russian PWs, to be marched eastward. At all costs, the authorities wished to avoid liberation of Soviet soldiers, who were expected to murder, rape and pillage. With his Red soldiers gone, the camp commandant agreed to yield.

Amid the confusion and shooting, however, it was necessary to dispatch a truce team from the camp. John Waters volunteered and, with several other Americans plus a German officer, set out, carrying a white flag manufactured from a bed sheet. When the party passed through the gate, a German soldier suddenly appeared, leveled his rifle and squeezed off a shot. The bullet hit Waters below the right hip, smashed off bone and then chipped his coccyx as it exited from his left buttock. The German officer with Waters and the others engaged in a furious discussion with the soldier who seemed inclined to shoot everyone. But at last he understood his commandant had agreed to the surrender. The badly wounded Waters was carried in a blanket to the PW hospital operated by Serbian prisoners. The task force battered down the barbed wire, then parked in a field just beyond the camp.

Lt. Alan Jones, Jr., from the 106th Division, says, "The attack on the camp was totally unexpected by me. I was sitting there when suddenly I heard the firing. We moved quickly to another barracks which was made of stone and would protect us better. But we were all at the windows watching, cheering our guys on. I saw Lt. Col. Waters go out with the others and I saw him being shot. Then as darkness came, the tanks moved into the camp."

Baum was dismayed to learn that, instead of the 300 officers

Stiller claimed were held at Hammelburg, the number was about 1,500. He could not possibly accommodate that many in his half-tracks or on his tanks.

As a *kriegie*—derived from the German word for PW, *Kriegs-gefangener*—Lyle Bouck thought the battle heralded the Allied advance rather than a raid to engineer his liberation. "Early in the morning, I heard small arms fire. We thought it meant that the front lines were approaching. Somewhere before dark, we saw tanks and the next thing I heard stories that a task force had come to get us.

"There was much confusion. A lot of people were standing around, Yugoslavs and Americans, amid the tanks and halftracks. I was with Lt. Matthew Reid, a 2nd Lt. from C Company of the 99th. I had learned early on that if you want to know what is happening, go to the head of the column. Reid and I found Col. Goode. We found the task force couldn't take all of us. The Yugo-slavs were told they could either go back into the camp or head west."

Actually, Baum had asked Goode to pick the limited number of lucky ones who could ride with him, a number that would be even less than 300 because of his losses. When Goode failed to make a selection, rumors circulated. "There was a story that only field grade officers would go," remembered Bouck. "Some of the guys said to one another, 'I'm promoting you to major,' and the other would reciprocate."

Baum never sought to limit the rescue to field grade officers. But he was forced to make a discouraging announcement to the crowd of *kriegies*. He explained that there were far more men than had been expected. He could take some but the rest would have to decide whether to take their chances walking westward toward the advancing Seventh Army or remain in the camp until the front lines swept past them. Those who accompanied his column would risk attacks directed at the task force. The frustrated Baum, aware of his losses in what was clearly a long shot with no real payoff, says he fought back his tears as he spoke to the prisoners.

While Baum dealt with the main body of *kriegies*, Al Stiller sought out the one man for whom the entire operation was designed. He found Waters recovering from emergency surgery performed by Serbian physicians. He obviously was in no condition to be moved and he still faced the danger of infection or paralysis.

Stiller visited with Patton's son-in-law for a few minutes, then made his way to the task force.

Baum hurriedly ordered engines cranked up for the start back, knowing the Germans would come after his task force and its cargo. Hundreds of *kriegies,* evaluating the poor odds of survival or considering themselves too weak to attempt to travel the forty to sixty miles to the American lines, shuffled back into the camp. Hundreds walked off on their own, hoping to remain free. And still others clambered aboard the tanks and halftracks.

Alan Jones and a buddy, Lt. Bud Bolling, whose father commanded the 84th Division, hauled themselves on a tank but the crowd of *kriegies* was too much for the Sherman's commander. He couldn't traverse his gun and he ordered a bunch off, including Jones and Bolling. "Bolling and I started to walk. My feet were still bothering me and I couldn't go very fast. In the morning they found me and brought me back to camp. But Bolling got away."

Lyle Bouck and Matthew Reid stuck together, clambering atop the second tank in the column. The convoy started off, trying to follow a different path home to avoid discovery and roadblocks. Recalled Bouck, "One of the guys gave each of us a grease gun. We were making pretty good progress when the tank in front of us exploded and started to burn. I see that I'm in the middle of a sea of tracer bullets. I'm hit in the left knee. It felt very hot and I couldn't tell whether I could move. Reid and I ducked into some small saplings. From there we could see where the stuff was coming from, crew-served weapons. I hollered, 'Let's charge 'em,' and we did, firing the grease guns. We could see them dropping.

"I yelled to the tankers to call the commander and tell him we knocked out the roadblock and he could move around it. We climbed on the last tank and then pulled up in an area where they put out a perimeter defense. We had some wounded and they were all put in a kind of outbuilding made of stone. They put a white flag on the rocks."

The task force commander, aware his men had had no sleep for forty-eight hours, decided to wait until dawn to make a last desperate dash to evade his pursuers. He ordered gasoline siphoned from some halftracks to fill the vehicles that would make the final run. Reid and Bouck entered a halftrack. But during the night, the Germans had brought a substantial force into position.

Bouck remembers, "All of a sudden we were hit. We took off for the woods. But they had goddamn dogs all around us and they began rounding us up. Some of the tankers took off their coveralls and the Germans got angry because they couldn't tell who was from the task force and who had been a prisoner. They went around looking at faces, trying to see who was well fed."

A salvo crashed into the building with the wounded. The walls collapsed on the hapless victims; none survived. As if in a shooting gallery, the Germans methodically destroyed every vehicle in a firestorm of shells. Baum with Stiller and another man fled to the forest. But the dogs picked up their trail.

The enemy closed in. Baum was prepared to shoot his way out, if possible. "I tried to pull up my mackinaw to reach my .45 and I saw this German. While I watched him, he pulled out his P38 [pistol] and shot me inside the thigh of my right leg. 'You son of a bitch, you nearly shot off my balls,' I said. He laughed. He understood English; he was from Bridgeport and serving in the *Volksturm*, the home guard.' Baum managed to discard his dog tags, which identified him as Jewish. Along with Stiller and the other man, he was now a prisoner, a seriously wounded one at that.

Other prisoners, who knew the ropes, persuaded the Germans that Baum was just another *kriegie* caught in the crossfire. They half-carried him back into camp and placed him in the care of the Serbian medics.

When the 14th Armored Division overran Hammelburg little more than a week later, it rescued both Baum and Waters. While they recuperated in a hospital at Gotha, Patton visited them both, presenting each with a Distinguished Service Cross. Waters earned his in North Africa and Baum's was the payoff for the task-force operation. An intelligence officer had already warned Baum that the mission must remain top secret. He then realized that Patton could not afford to recommend a Congressional Medal of Honor, for that would require a public airing of the circumstances.

The great Hammelburg raid failed to free John Waters and only a few *kriegies* and members of the task force slipped through the Germans to safety. Every piece of equipment was lost; nine men were officially identified as dead and an additional sixteen were never accounted for. Some military historians point out that, whatever the motivation behind it, the mission wreaked havoc upon a substantial number of German troops and caused a diversion of forces that the Americans exploited.

Patton never conceded that the purpose of the expedition was the liberation of his son-in-law. Abe Baum, who became friendly with Waters, asked him at the time if he had ever discussed the matter with Patton. "He said he had asked his father-in-law, who answered, 'If I did know, I wouldn't tell you because that would jeopardize our intelligence.'" Baum has no doubts that Patton was aware of Waters's location.

Little more than two weeks later Baum caught up with the 4th Armored Division. To Abrams and Cohen he announced, "I told you you couldn't get rid of me." And in the next few days he made himself conspicuous, showing up in the midst of artillery barrages as the unit prepared to advance into Czechoslovakia."Whenever I was wounded, I always wanted to come back. Other guys never wanted to return. It would piss me off only if a Jew didn't want to return and fight."

The fire fight on the premises had rendered most of the Hammelburg camp uninhabitable. Prisoners able to walk were formed into a column and marched off. Among them were both Alan Jones, Jr., and Lyle Bouck. "We thought we were headed for the Bavarian redoubt where Hitler was supposed to make his last stand," said Jones, "with us as possible hostages. My feet were in terrible shape. It was very painful and the skin split open. But after a while that seemed to make them less sore. The Germans had issued me a French soldier's overcoat into which I sewed pockets. There was an air force officer next to me on the march and he had a filthy leather flying jacket. I wanted warmth and he wanted pockets, so we traded lice-ridden garments.

"We reached Nuremberg on April 5th. It had been badly bombed and the citizens spit on us and yelled epithets. We looked up and saw B-17s filling the horizon. The last ones in the group dropped a stick near us, killing the captain of our guards, wounding fifty or sixty prisoners, including Col. Cavender, who was with us.

"During the march we traveled mostly at night because fighter planes patrolled the skies like police. We organized ourselves into syndicates of two and three to divide responsibilities. Just before daybreak one man would get us sleeping space in a barn, another would look for food to steal and a third might try to pick up material that could be fashioned into weapons for use during an escape try.

"Our chance came between Nuremberg and the Danube. We were in a barnyard, and the air force man and I noticed there were no guards around. We nodded to one another and then hid in a ditch. When the others moved out, we beat it, going east one day, then south and west to outguess the Germans.

"We became very hungry and knocked on a farmhouse door. The woman let us in, fed us bread, jam and milk. There was a German staff sergeant, recuperating from the Russian front there. We all talked in English, and I still had on my lieutenant's bars and insignia but nobody tried to turn us in. When we left, they gave us each half a loaf of bread.

"Still trying to reach our own lines, we heard artillery far off to the west. Late at night we reached a little town, jammed with SS troops. Before we could pass through, they caught us. We were marched about two miles and met the same column from which we escaped. The guards simply accepted us, stuck us back in line and off we went.

"On May 2, we came to a place with signs in German which said, in effect, this is a restricted town. Any German who remains four hours must turn in his weapon to the provost. Our senior officers told us it can't be much further. But some, like me, said, 'To hell with it. We're not going on.' We sat down on the curb. I wasn't there for more than a few hours when I looked up and there was a young kid, carrying an M–1, chewing gum. Then I saw more and more of our kind of steel helmets.

"They rounded us all up. We looked more like displaced persons than officers. They threw some K rations to us and two-and-a-half-ton trucks carried us off to a regimental field hospital. I washed for the first time in months. The GIs who found us went off to a bitter fight with those SS troops who had picked us up.

"Seventeen days later, I was aboard a steamer, bound for the U.S."

Lyle Bouck, held in a riding stable after being seized with the remnants of the task force, received two pieces of sausage and a chunk of bread before a brief train ride. From there he went on the road, through Nuremberg, escaping the B–17s that clobbered the column, with Alan Jones. With Reid, he sought to escape as they approached the Danube. Caught again, Bouck was incarcerated at Moosburg with thousands of others until April 29, when elements of the 14th Armored, which had freed Abe Baum, brought his release.

A day or so after being cleaned up and reunited with the 99th Division, Bouck began throwing up his food. A surgeon examined him, diagnosed hepatitis, and Bouck finished his European tour at a Paris general hospital.

Even as Task Force Baum had gunned its motors to scoot through Schweinheim, all over Germany the men captured during the Bulge could sense their freedom in the air. Bouck's foxhole companion, Bill Tsakanikas, had been convalescing in a German hospital near the Rhine. As early as March 4, he tried to escape but a hospital guard apprehended him. Three weeks later, a recon squad from the 9th Armored Division rescued him and other Americans from a camp across the River.

Clifford Broadwater was aware deliverance was imminent. "The camp leadership developed some outside sources of information and kept us pretty well informed on the progress of the war. Near the end, they held assemblies in our barracks, showed us where our Allied forces were.

"We knew our Army was coming closer. We could hear artillery fire occasionally but no action near us. Then the Germans decided to try to evacuate us to other camps. On March 29th, they assembled us on the athletic field for marching. We planned delays to confuse them. The French and British were first to march away. We were next but some guys collapsed on the ground. The rest of us were slow, limping. Most were acting but one fellow had a ruptured appendix and suffered some before receiving proper attention.

"The guards knew we were stalling. But we didn't get out of the camp before we stopped, waited around for a while, then were sent back to the barracks. The guards called for volunteers to make the march, first twenty, then thirty and then back to twenty. Finally they called it all off. Some of the British and French prisoners returned that evening. On Good Friday, March 30, we were holding services with the British chaplain when our GIs marched in."

The prisoners gorged themselves on a store of French food packages, rations from the GIs and what they could scavenge in town. Many became sick with diarrhea and vomiting, from both gluttony on empty stomachs and, perhaps, contaminated items from the French packages, some of which were years old. Given an orange, Broadwater downed every bit of it, including the peel.

After a week, Broadwater prepared for evacuation with a

shower and delousing. The former prisoners flew to Le Havre, France, where Leisse stuffed himself with two cups of coffee and a dozen donuts from the Red Cross. He received close scrutiny from a medical team which hospitalized him for frozen feet and malnutrition. When he recovered sufficiently, a series of flights lifted him to the U.S. and to his beloved Martha.

At the end of March, John Collins and his PW companions were laboring at a brick factory. After an air raid on the railroad next to their camp, Collins watched "Jerries whipping some prisoners dressed in stripes and I mean whipping them! We were standing by the fence and yelled at the guards but they ignored us.

"In one of the bombings, the planes dropped leaflets stating they intended to bomb the place off the map. Four of us decided we couldn't take any more of this and formed an escape plan. Very simple—wait until dark, enter the big crater by the fence and crawl through, digging if required. Sometimes the guards walked the path between the fences but we would take our chances. During the bombing, the smoke was so thick you could not see a damn thing."

On April 1 at 9:30 P.M. they made their break. "We made it through some small brush and into the city streets where we separated as planned. Sgt. Vernon Hunt, who spoke four or five German dialects plus some Polish and Italian, and myself—English only—took one side of the street. T/4 Elmer George, almost deaf in one ear from concussion but seemed not to know what fear was, and Cpl. Thomas Keneshea, a nice kid who could steal the Jerries blind, went down the other side.

"We had almost gotten through town when we heard marching troops and ducked into a doorway. They came down the street, a light flashed and a lot of yelling started. A German came out of the door to see what the commotion was about. He and Hunt had quite a conversation. Hunt told him we were *kriegies,* and we were going home. The fellow did not question us and I kept my mouth shut."

Outside of the town Collins and Hunt headed for a a previously designated area where they hoped to rendezvous with the others. The pair spent the day in a hayloft but their companions failed to appear. To allay hunger, Hunt milked a cow and Collins throttled a large duck with a blanket. After dark they tramped on, pausing to try to cook the fowl over a small fire, but giving up for lack of time and consuming the meat half raw. "It was delicious, although occasionally feathers stuck in our throats."

Three days later, they were caught while attempting to cross a bridge. "The commander in charge asked this guard why he did not put us in the canal like they did the airman. They were *Volk-sturm*-civilian guards. They seated us against the wall, everyone returned to their posts except for seven or eight sleeping on the floor. Hunt and I stayed awake, placing lice on our knees and flipping them on the sleeping guards."

He and Hunt were taken to Stalag XI B. The guard who accompanied them gave them his food as he put them aboard the train to the camp, largely inhabited by French and British PWs. On April 11, Collins noted, "We were unofficially liberated. All the guards left their posts and the gates were torn off their hinges." The captives did not pour out of the camp but awaited Allied troops.

On April 13, the senior British officer at the stalag sent around a message stating that President Franklin Delano Roosevelt had died and that the British wanted to share in the grief of the Americans. On April 16 the "Irish army" (Irish members of the British forces) liberated Collins. "Men who have gone through hell for many months, in some case years, are like wild men. Grown men crying and giving thanks to their God".

The Britons included Collins and any other Americans in the evacuation, flying them to an RAF base in England. "The English treated us royally, feeding us one meal a day, a continuous meal from the time we arose till we left." Collins was designated a malnutrition case, having lost just about one-third of his original 150 pounds.

Turned over to American authorities, Collins plunged into a hospital regimen of clean sheets, showers (which he believes he took about every three hours) and soft foods to accomodate a stomach grown accustomed to deprivation. In mid-May he had recovered sufficiently to sail home.

Frank Raila also finally engineered his own freedom. Towards the beginning of April he was in a group of prisoners that included both Americans and Britons. Temporarily, they were held in a soccer field, surrounded by a low barbed-wire fence. Raila fell into conversation with two Welshmen, one of whom was named Dave Cashman, and they were game for an escape try.

"The guards were patrolling but some of the Brits stopped them and offered cigarettes along with conversation. While they were distracted, it gave us time to slip away. We went separately, crawling under the wire, then running. We had planned to meet under a haystack we'd seen at dusk but couldn't find it. We hid ourselves as best we could, and when the sun came up, the haystack was only about fifty feet away. There was a large woods nearby, and we slept there the first day.

"At night we saw in the distance the glow from Leipzig being bombed. We headed in a direction which kept it on our right. Then we heard voices. They were eight to ten Russian slave laborers. At first we were scared of each other but then they hugged us. They had made a homemade brew, a kind of vodka. Everyone was stewed, some lay on the ground puking.

"They shared some food with us, potatoes, and then they stole a rabbit and cooked it. I ate pieces of the head, eyeballs, tongue, even the brains. It was the first protein I had since being captured. We stayed with them several days. They told us the Germans were shooting anyone they found on the roads.

"Then a couple of the Russians ran into an American patrol. We approached them and they trained the .50s on the half-tracks at us. Once they realized we were escaped prisoners, I took off my overcoat and threw it to the slave laborers. The GIs also tossed them some Spam they were carrying."

Shortly thereafter, Raila flew to Camp Lucky Strike, a depot near Le Havre for replacements and troops being shipped home. He quickly learned that overeating after a starvation diet adds complications. "One guy who stuffed himself with donuts died." He also found the interrogators suspicious of his claim to have escaped. Raila's anger increased with the boredom of Lucky Strike. "Four or five of us saw a jeep with the name 'My Buddy' on it and we stole the thing, drove into town. We ate eggs in a restaurant but there was still nothing to do but drink in the bar." Fortunately, Raila and his associates noticed MPs checking out their jeep. They slipped away and hitched a ride on a truck back to camp. Within a month, Raila shipped out for the States.

Maj. William Desobry was at Braunswchweig, in the officers' compound next to the stalag from which John Collins made his escape. Freed by a cavalry outfit, Desobry and his companions remained in place for a few days. "Some of us wandered around the countryside—why we didn't get shot, I will never know. We were looking for food and places to get cleaned up. We were all lousy and afraid they wouldn't evacuate us in this condition. The American hospitals weren't equipped to do anything but give us food."

After some travail, the officer prisoner group flew to Le Havre and Camp Lucky Strike. "We experienced a degrading business that got us mad. They called us RAMPS, Recovered Allied Military Personnel. They deloused us and organized us into companies with a company commander from the cadre of Camp Lucky Strike. A black captain came in one morning and said, 'Gentlemen, the camp commander has decided that everybody is going to have to stand reveille, and he has sent me to tell you that you will have to stand reveille every morning and have an inspection.'

"I weighed 130 pounds, stood 6'4" and had dysentery. We were majors, lieutenant colonels, colonels. We were mad at the world, insulted at being called RAMPS. Judge Hoban, a full colonel from the 28th Division, took on that guy something fierce. He told him to tell that camp commander he could go you know where and everything else. The captain answered, 'After listening to you gentlemen, I would rather have the camp commander mad at me than you mad at me, so nobody need stand reveille.' "

The RAMPs' sense of outrage overflowed at feeding time. The men stood in line outside mess tents, in pouring rains, waiting to get their meals. Frequently, the food ran out before the last ten to thirty percent of the former prisoners received their portions, even though the camp received double rations to handle the burgeoning numbers of men.

Desobry and a companion decided to attend the Officers Mess, which served cadre. They were served at lunch and in the evening returned. "There were an awful lot of officers, also girls, Red Cross girls, obviously French girls without dates. A sergeant came to us and said the mess officer sent him to tell us we wouldn't be served. I answered, 'You better go get that mess officer in here because we intend to be served. We are officers and we didn't spend the war back here at Camp Lucky Strike stealing rations from the troops and chasing French girls. We fought the war and are going to be served. Get that guy out here and tell him if he doesn't serve us I am going to bust him right in the mouth.' The sergeant, all shook up, returned and said the mess officer decided we could eat there."

As Frank Raila and Desobry noted, many of those at Lucky

Strike became bored. With the war still on, some tried to return to their units. Desobry understood that the Allies made at least a tacit agreement with the Germans that if they would stop moving PWS out of the way of the liberating forces, then the Allies would not permit the freed men to take up the tools of war again. (The Geneva Convention forbids repatriated prisoners becoming combatants again.)

Complaints from the likes of Desobry and others to congressmen and to top brass on his return to the States brought dismissal of most of the Lucky Strike staff and an improvement in conditions.

Spring brought a boost to the morale of Pfc. Phil Hannon at the stalag outside of Bad Orb. "The Germans were less strict in taking the correct count and were not insisting on our saluting them. On March 30, one of the older German guards remarked to me, 'Pretty soon,' and raised his hands in the air indicating he would soon be the prisoner."

Easter Sunday, April 1, the sounds of small arms fire and even the smells of war, says Hannon, reached Bad Orb. "We couldn't see the fighting. But none of us were in a hurry to go looking for it. We had lived this long and didn't want a stray bullet to get us. That day, most of the Germans melted away and by evening, there were no Germans around. The following morning, three American tanks rode over the gates of the camp and we were liberated!"

To his delight, Hannon learned that his friend Ben Tousey did not die in the Ardennes. Instead, Tousey, who had indeed received a "Dear John" letter in the confusion of the German attack, fell in behind a column of GIs. As they stumbled along in the gloom, he poked one man and asked where the officer in charge was. The fellow looked at Tousey and trained his rifle on him. Tousey had been traveling with a bunch of Germans wearing American garb. He thus became a prisoner, doing his captive time in East Germany until liberated.

Ed Uzemack was also incarcerated at the camp near Bad Orb. An outbreak of spinal meningitis early in March placed the stalag under quarantine. And by the middle of the month, the sound of American artillery fire could be heard. "Liberation fever was mounting. Because of the quarantine, the Germans made no effort to move the prionsers to another camp. Bets were freely made [that] the men would be free by Easter Sunday."

On that holiday, Uzemack jotted in his diary, "Our boys may come up tonight. The men are all excited—now they are tearing the wire off the windows. We are sure to be liberated tomorrow—Happy Easter."

Uzemack roused himself at two o'clock the next morning to work in the kitchen and see freedom come. An inmate MP draped a white flag on the clock towers. And at 8:12 A.M. Uzemack scrawled, "The first American recon car rolls into the camp. Holy Smokes!"

Sgt. Leo Leisse, after the 395-mile, six-week march from Görlitz to the stalag at Braunschweig, kept his spirits up with word of the approaching American army. But on April 10, beset by continuing bouts of the GIs, sustaining himself mainly on tiny increments from Red Cross parcels and the ubiquitous trading, Leisse plodded out of the camp under guard. His captors were still bent on keeping the prisoners.

In his diary he noted: "Fell out after 15 kms for last time. Syl went on, leaving me with RC package, although very little left in it. We talked many times of escaping but everytime, he chickened out. I feigned passing out and stayed in a ravine by the roadside until the last guard passed. Met another escapee, Joseph Desits."

In the morning, as they consumed a breakfast of one slice of bread, hardtack, oleo and sugar, a German soldier shepherding a handful of Russian prisoners surprised Leisse and Desits. Subsequently, Leisse found himself aboard a tractor-pulled wagon with Russians and Poles.

"When we slowed because of craters in the road, I jumped over the side of the wagon. The guard started ranting and raving, raised his rifle. Don't know what made me do it, but I took down my trousers to indicate I had to go bad, no matter what. The guard signaled the driver to go on."

Several other Americans now sneaked away from the wagon. They hid in a smokehouse overnight. In the morning, desperate for water, Leisse knocked on the door of a farmhouse. The others understood that if he failed to return after a reasonable length of time, they should head westward without him.

"The people in the house were swell. The woman's name was Mrs. Riemann. First they thought I was British because I [had] traded my combat jacket for a British air force blouse, trousers and woolen cap. My original pants had most of the seat out from being hit by spent shrapnel right before I was captured. The wound had required only sulfa powder.

"I explained we were Americans and it seemed I was more welcome. They took me into their kitchen and we communicated with help from an English-German dictionary. They gave me *ersatz* coffee and a piece of bread with a lard spread. They apologized, said German soldiers passing through earlier had taken all they could spare. After I explained about others with me, one of whom was too weak to walk, Mrs. Riemann got a wagon and went with me. We helped Desits into it and it's a good bet that Mrs. Reiman did more of the work than any of the three of us weaklings."

The escapees bunked down in a vegetable cellar overnight. In the morning their host supplied toast while her sister-in-law quizzed them about conditions for her husband, a PW in the States. American troops had reached nearby Koenigsleiter. The women supplied bicycles and guided Leisse to the town. "Actually, I could pull the bike up a hill, which any kid could have taken with ease." But in Koenigsleiter, the PWs located a medical unit and their rehabilitation began.

He reached Camp Lucky Strike on April 14. Here Leisse met a number of his old buddies who had also been rescued from the stalags. His persistent intestinal problems and swollen legs led to a diagnosis of severe malnutrition. Consigned to a bed, Leisse attacked his meals with a fervor just shy of gluttony. His diary notes are as heavily focused on the subject of food as were those he wrote while a prisoner—for example, "came back and finished corn flakes I had brought back from breakfast of flakes, scrambled eggs, bacon and coffee. Dinner consisted of good beef, spinach and mashed potatoes, bread and butter, also good GI coffee. Brought back more corn flakes and half of my beef as sandwich. More eggnog in afternoon. For supper had more beef, also corn and peas."

On May 2, Leo Leisse walked up the ramp to the S.S. *Sea Robin* for the voyage home which ended thirteen days later. Before getting on a train for home, he spent a day at Camp Kilmer, New Jersey, visiting the PX for four chocolate sundaes plus a pint of ice cream.

Sgt. Richard McKee had also been at the Braunschweig camp and, like Leisse, walked east under guard, to avoid the Allied armies. After they passed through Koenigsleiter, he and Sgt. Bob Richardson decided to escape. "Bob went first. He pretended to pass out and fell to the road. The guard came up, kicked and beat him, but he just lay there. The guard went on. Next, it was my turn. I strayed off to the side of the road behind some bushes."

Like Leisse, McKee and Richardson approached a farmhouse. The farmer permitted them to stay the night in his barn. In the morning, "his wife and daughter brought out a cooked breakfast for us. We had eggs, potatoes and bread. It was the first real food we had since December 19. After thanking the farmer, we headed down the road. We met hundreds of German troops, on foot, riding bicycles and running away from the advancing Americans. The Germans did not pay any attention to us. One German officer stopped and drew his Luger, but we ignored him and continued on. He did the same.

"We walked back to Koenigsleiter. As we entered the place, sirens began to blow at the town square. We met an American tank column coming into the town. After talking to the commander and convincing him we were Americans, he ordered the three of us to take charge of Koenigsleiter. The tanks had the Germans on the run and wanted to continue their drive.

"We looked up the mayor's office and had him issue orders to the residents to turn in all of their guns, knives, swords, etc., to the office. The people brought wagons full of guns and knives. We stacked them in a pile in a room at the office. There were hundreds of pieces. We took our pick for souvenirs. I had a matched set of German Lugers.

"After looking the town over, we went to the outskirts where there was a small PW camp with some British soldiers. We freed them. Later, we took over a hotel vacated by the Germans. Bob, who was our company mess sergeant, found a completely stocked kitchen. He cooked up a big pot of hash for us. We ate until we got sick. We slept in real beds in the hotel but I came down with dysentery and was vomiting the rich food we had eaten. During the night, the British ex-PWs wrecked and smashed everything downstairs in the hotel."

McKee and his companions tried to find transportation back to what remained of the 106th Division. The first vehicle available was a large diesel fire truck. As they drove off in it, its tank ruptured and spewed fuel over them. The trio bailed out and their last sight of the driverless fire truck was as it rolled down a hill. They managed to borrow a car liberated by some of the British PWs. It bore them to an airfield, where they hitched a ride to Paris. There McKee entered a hospital for treatment of his illness. He had lost fifty-three of his original 190 pounds. "They had me in bed for a week with I.V.s in both arms, giving me glucose and plasma."

On May 4, McKee, on a stretcher, became a passenger aboard a hospital ship. While at sea, an officer confiscated McKee's pair of matched Lugers for his own use. McKee would spend the next five months hospitalized or on sick leave.

Jim Mills, part of the Slaughterhouse V contingent at Dresden, remained a prisoner until the final week of the war. The artillery noise boomed from the east as Russian forces surged ever deeper into Germany. On May 7, the guards led them out to the road with the objective of surrendering themselves and their captives to the Americans. German civilians, soldiers and PWs clogged the highway.

Suddenly, out of the sky a flight of a dozen Soviet planes peeled off and started to strafe the refugees. Mills saw one of the aircraft coming in his direction. He spotted an earthen ramp to a hayloft that might provide some protection.

"I had just gotten to the edge of it when the plane started firing its machine guns. Shells were hitting the ground all around me, then up the side of the barn. The plane banked right, hit a cow in the hind end."

That threat passed and Mills started down the road again. Another plane dove towards him and released a bomb. "The screaming and whistling noises got even louder, we knew it was coming right down on us." The target, crouched in a small stream, amounted to a woman, a child, one German soldier and two prisoners. Showered with dirt and debris from the blast, they escaped injury.

In the disorder, Mills, with another man, crossed a field where a pair of drunken German soldiers were playing with a *Panzerfaust*. "They were laughing and cutting up, then they pointed it at us and fired it. The shell was so large, we could easily see it coming in a wobbling trajectory. We just stepped out of the way and let it go by. It hit at such a low angle it never even exploded."

The area was now overrun by Russian troops. "We saw Russians carrying buckets of beer in each hand. The Russian soldiers indicated that if we wanted anything we should simply take it." Mills heard reports of rape by the Russians, and suicides. "Women would stop you on the street and want two fellows to spend the night. The Russians would not bother them if a fellow was present."

The route back to American lines was perilous. Slave laborers who picked up abandoned machine guns amused themselves with random bursts. Anarchy governed. Some British prisoners arranged for a train to haul PWs to their own forces. Mills, other prisoners, slave laborers and their female friends piled on. But the engine soon shunted off to a sidetrack. The famished prisoners stole some chickens and that aroused a mob of angry farmers. A Soviet officer quieted them, then secured some larger live animals to feed the train passengers. "Our group was given a bull. One of our people had a pistol and shot the animal five times in the head. It got real mad, but finally staggered and fell. In a matter of minutes the bull was cut up and shared. The meat was still warm, when I got my piece [raw]."

Mills gave up on the train and started walking. He reached Pilsen and from there was directed to American troops. It was well after the last shots had been fired. At Lucky Strike he followed the pattern of food binges. Issued meal tickets, Mills and his colleagues gorged themselves at meals, then sought out mess tents where no coupon was needed. "Even after eating, we had such desire for food that we would go to the rear of the food tents, scrape the jelly cans and get enough sugar to make a form of candy." In June, Mills headed for home on the S.S. *Admiral Benson.*

Capt. Charles MacDonald, wounded in mid-January with I Company of the 2nd Division's 23rd Infantry Regiment, returned the first week of March to a new command, G Company. They crossed the Rhine in boats uneventfully. The division was part of a combined operation of the U.S. Ninth and First Armies that snared 317,000 prisoners in the Ruhr Pocket. Said MacDonald, "As infantrymen, we would have many another anxious moment in the war, but never again would we face a cohesive enemy front."

MacDonald's people pressed on against sporadic resistance, crossing the old German border with the Sudetenland first annexed by Hitler and then Czechoslovakia proper. The stream of surrendering enemy swelled to flood stage. "As our column advanced down one side of the highway, a ragged column of Germans in horse-drawn wagons, dilapidated German Army vehicles, civilian automobiles, bicycles and on foot met us coming down the other side. Some had their families with them. All had thrown away their weapons . . . The Germans were running from the Russians to surrender to the Americans.

"The traffic became almost a hopeless mass of milling people. Regiment would take no more PWs—division said their PW cages were overflowing and would accept no more from regiment." His colonel invited MacDonald to ride with him into Pilsen, amid a deliriously joyful celebration. "The news came by radio that the war was over. There ws no defining our joy. Sergeant Quinn brought out the treasured keg of cognac. The next day, May 8, would be VE-Day."

Chapter XVII

HONORS AND
DISHONORS

THE PERIOD FOLLOWING V-E Day witnessed chaos not only for the defeated but also, in a limited way, for the victors. Discipline crumbled as citizen-soldiers rebelled against the strictures of military life. The opportunity to turn fast, big dollars tempted many to larceny.

Alan Shapiro never made it back to his 87th Infantry Division. He was becalmed in a replacement depot at Bremen. "Few of my friends went home. Elmer died from his wounds. Pusatieri was killed. Hanson was run over by a tank. Moscoe dead, Miller missing, Franzen, Vosseler, Meyer, Eckleberry and countless others wounded. Only Johnny Sirko and a few others came through unscathed. The Division took 6,000 casualties during its five months in combat."

He had come to the replacement depot with hundreds of other GIs who were handed their personnel records and told to report. A number of them, instead, checked into quarters but never turned in their papers. They ate in the mess, had a place to sleep but otherwise lived on their own. Some engaged in the huge black market operations that blossomed with peace. They sold gasoline, clothing, cigarettes, food, any commodity stored or issued by the military. As the business boomed, enterprising crooks imported items like cigarettes, clothes and other valued items from their friends and relatives in the U.S.

For the civilian population and the Russian occupiers everything was in short supply. The conquerors appropriated cameras, radios, watches and house furnishings. Those with access to trucks hauled goods to places, like Berlin, where the Red Army swapped loot or liberated German marks.

The criminality bothered Shapiro less than the behavior of those with whom he bunked. There were drunken brawls every night.

He decided he had to leave one set of quarters after his fellow residents tossed a lit woodstove down the staircase.

Soldiers who had accumulated eight-five points or more by V-E Day were to return to the States first. (The formula credited points for length of service, time overseas, campaigns, battle stars, wounds and medals. PW status, however, earned an instant trip home.) Shapiro's point score fell far enough below for him to fill assignments at the Bremen G–2 office, in PR, and attend school in England while awaiting the point requirement to drop to his level.

Cy Blank, with the 11th Armored, another soldier well under the magic figure of eighty-five, went to work in military government for three months. He was bemused by the contrasts in the behavior of Europeans. "There were many instances in France and Belgium where, although we were greeted magnificently and treated like saviors, this initial euphoria towards us slowly disappeared, primarily, I believe, because we spent much of our time telling them how grateful they should be. That caused significant friction. The Germans, on the other hand, realizing they were conquered, did a lot of brown nosing, and in general went out of their way to be friendly."

Dick Byers, now a lieutenant and recovering from his wound, damaged the provost marshal's jeep near the hospital in Paris in a boozy incident. He had been saved from potential punishment by a transfer to England for physical rehab by a friendly doctor. And when he finally started to sail back to the Continent, his passage was halted on V-E Day. Instead of going on to rejoin the artillery battalion, Byers traveled only as far as Camp Lucky Strike for temporary duty with the port engineers.

On May 31, while Byers was riding a bike at the camp, "Somebody yelled, 'Byers!' I damned near fell off the bike. It was Gacki and Wibben [both members of the observation team captured along with Bouck's I & R platoon on December 16]. They took me to Fletcher's tent. [He was seized while trying to put on his overshoes when Byers escaped near Lanzerath.] My God, what a reunion!" Every member of the unfortunate 371st observation party received the Silver Star. Honors for Bouck and his men did not come until much later.

By August, the points necessary to go home had dropped to seventy-five. Byers squabbled with the military accountants who allowed him only seventy, while he insisted his score should be eighty. The army stuck him on a slow boat for duty in Manila, although V-J Day had come. Even with a forty-five-day furlough sandwiched into the trip, Byers brooded over his fate. He took personal charge of his situation during his time at home. Having custody of his personnel records, Byers said, "I used a scratchy pen and black ink as a sword to cut Army red tape. With this incredibly sharp weapon I inked in on my 201 record card the chapter and verse of the Army Regs authorizing the three battle stars that were rightfully mine. When I presented this file to Personnel at Camp Plauche [Louisiana] on my return to duty, I casually mentioned that I was an 80-point man. They checked my file, agreed I was indeed there by mistake and I was on my way back to civilian life."

Schuyler Jackson of the 101st Airborne was among the few in no hurry to be demobilized. "I was made the regimental noncom for athletics in the Alps. We were near a medical facility with lots of nurses. It was a very good deal. I was living like a king." The good thing came to an end and Jackson headed to the States. But, he carried with him the $8,000 remaining from the sack of francs discarded by the German soldier.

Carmen Capalbo, the scout for the 99th Division, who went down on the eve of the War in the Ardennes, reached the States well before V-E Day. In January 1945, surgeons at a hospital in Caen operated on him to remove more of the shell fragments embedded in his lower body. "My feet finally thawed out but I couldn't put a shoe on because my toes pained me so much. One night I woke up with a sharp pain in my butt. I called a nurse and told her I felt something sharp. She gave me a shot. A major examined me the next day and he was skeptical, but eventually they took out a bolt-size piece of shrapnel.

"I next went to a hospital in Bristol, England. There I developed a blood clot in my calf. It refused to heal. On the S.S. *Dogwood* back to the States in April, I learned of Roosevelt's death. My other memory of that three-week voyage is the big song hit of the day, 'Rum and Coca Cola.' It was played incessantly, night and day over the ship's loudspeakers. I spent some time in Camp Pickett, Virginia, and in the hospital at White Sulphur Springs, West Virginia. One day they called me and said, 'here's your discharge.

You're out now.' It was so unexpected that I didn't want to go. It's difficult to understand but this was June, and while V-E Day had come, the Japanese had not yet quit. I wanted to get back to my outfit, not to do any fighting, but to see my friends.

"In the fall of 1945 I entered the Yale Drama School under the GI Bill. I had a pension of $75 a month, which at that time wasn't bad money. Then in the early 1950s, in New York, I developed carbuncles and boils in my groin. Tiny filaments of shrapnel worked their way to the surface and I'd pick 'em out with a tweezers.

"One day, about noon, I was on Park Avenue near 56th Street when I experienced a tremendous burning pain between my legs. It felt like I had something the size of a golf ball there. I staggered into the Drake Hotel and they called an ambulance. My doctor cut out a piece of metal between my scrotum and anus." That surgery expunged Capalbo's last souvenir from the Ardennes.

President Harry S. Truman personally presented the Congressional Medal of Honor to Melvin Biddle of the 517th Paratroopers in a White House ceremony that summer. Biddle recalled the day. "President Truman said, 'People don't believe me when I say I would rather have this medal than be president.' I wanted to say, I would trade him but I was afraid to open my mouth for fear I'd be court-martialled."

To Gen. Eric Wood, the end of the shooting presented an opportunity to bury his grief under monuments to his son. While Eric, Jr., was interred with 7,000 others at the U.S. Military Cemetery at Henri Chapelle, Belgium, General Wood financed a small memorial cross at Meyerode. At the end of July 1945, General Wood obtained statements from Bürgermeister Jean Pauels and the two woodsmen, Peter Maraite and Servatius Maraite. Peter Maraite described his encounter with the big, young officer on December 18. Servatius told of leading the graves registration soldiers to the bodies in the woods in February, and Pauels detailed his convictions on guerrillas operating in the woods around Meyerode and his memories of the reactions of Sepp Dietrich and other Germans.

Wood also elicited sworn statements from a number of members of the 589th. These included enlisted men, like Barney Alford, who served under Wood's son, and other battery mates present when the unit's guns were extricated and saved from capture or destruction. Some rode with Eric Wood, Jr., on the last wild race through Schönberg, where most were captured but Eric escaped. Maj. Elliot Goldstein, who had helped direct fire at Baraque de Fraiture with the cannons preserved by Eric Wood and the 106th Division Field Artillery commander, Gen. Leo McMahon, added encomiums on the dead officer's performance.

Eric Fisher Wood, Jr., received posthumously the Bronze Star, Silver Star, Distinguished Service Cross, Purple Heart, Croix de Guerre and Belgian Order of Leopold I with Gold Palm—the only American in World War II to earn the award. In a handwritten biography of his first-born, General Wood remarked that the Belgian citation included the words "He died weapons in hand. He had lived as an outstanding example of audacity, tenacity and of heroism, not only to the American Army but also to the Belgian population of all that region."

General Wood in a long letter to a friend noted that the Belgian decoration was the equivalent of the U.S. Congressional Medal of Honor. This was the final tribute the father sought as a memorial to his son. Under the signature of McMahon, and with the approval of Gen. Alan Jones, Sr. appended, a 16-page memorandum, accompanied by supportive documents, recommended the CMOH award for Wood. The application was disapproved by the War Department. The terms for eligibility require incontestible evidence, eyewitness accounts. There were none to document what Eric Wood, Jr., did from the time of his disappearance until the official identification of his body nine weeks later. As a concession to Gen. Wood, arrangements were made for General of the Armies Eisenhower to personally present Meg Wood a posthumous Distinguished Service Cross in honor of her husband.

In 1947, an article in the *Saturday Evening Post* by Col. R. E. Dupuy painted a florid picture of Eric Wood, Jr., and his exploits. It embellished the facts, baldly stating, "How these three howitzers for four days saved the right flank of the 82nd Airborne Division of the Army at 'Parker's Crossroads' is another story." Indeed, it is another story, for, while the three artillery pieces contributed, they were but one component of a combined effort, with major input from the 325th Glider Regiment—Joe Colmer and Leonard Weinstein—which still calls Baraque "Woody's Crossroads" for their leader.

Furthermore, Dupuy wrote that Wood was found with seven dead enemy soldiers strewn around his body, like an end to a

John Wayne epic, thus gilding the actual scene described by Peter and Servatius Maraite.

For at least one man, the entire business jammed his craw. Frank Aspinwall, the sergeant with headquarters company of the 589th and the last man to positively identify Eric Fisher Wood, Jr., as alive and fleeing capture, according to a statement from Major Goldstein, objected to the canonization of the dead officer. Aspinwall said he began simply trying to report the history of the battalion during the Bulge. Apparently brooding over the image of Wood and beset by his own doubts, Aspinwall hand-wrote a number of letters in the early 1980s based on notes he recorded shortly after the Battle of the Bulge. He suggested that General Wood browbeat enlisted men and junior officers into statements that lionized the general's son during the initial phases of the attack. Aspinwall, relying on what he called "deductions" and "the law of probability," called the tale of Wood and his irregulars fighting behind the lines implausible.

Carefully asserting he did not want to disparage the dead man's character, Aspinwall insisted Wood was among a group of fifteen men who "fell out of [3] jeeps and ran up a steep wooded hill on the right." That does not square with the sworn accounts of four enlisted men who insist Wood was aboard the truck pulling a howitzer at the denouement.

Aspinall claimed that the official records listed Wood KIA on December 17. That is flatly contradicted by the statements of the two soldiers from the graves registration unit who retrieved the body identified as Wood's on February 25th, 1945. Furthermore, Wood and the other American discovered by the Maraites lay across the Our River, six or seven miles from Schönberg. Any record that states Wood died December 17 on the outskirts of Schönberg must explain the travels of his corpse. Furthermore, although the climatic conditions made certain determination of death a guess, the best estimate placed Wood's demise around the third week in January, a period that coincided neatly with Bürgermeister Pauel's recollection that the skirmishes in the forest ended about that time.

The doubts raised by Frank Aspinwall became a tempest in the teacups of people intimately connected with the 589th. Some defenders of Eric Wood, Jr.'s reputation imputed that Aspinwall, a onetime Southerner had a grudge against a Yankee officer. Others scorned him as an enlisted man who, denied a battlefield commission he felt he deserved, focused his frustration on Wood. There were angry face-to-face confrontations, including a memorable one with an Alabama-born wife of a colonel, and acrimonious correspondence was exchanged.

Ted Kiendl, living in Paris, brother-in-arms with the long-dead Wood, sent Aspinwall a nine-page, single-spaced letter countering his arguments, citing such facts as the location of the body and the time of death.

Aspinwall had wondered how it was possible that men who approached Wood's "wolf pack" in the forest and refused to join did not report its existence when they reached the U.S. lines. Kiendl rebutted, "What about those who did not join but simply never made it back to American lines?" Jim Buck, the court stenographer lost in the woods near Schönberg, and who stumbled into a group of Americans engaged in guerrilla operations, in fact did report a guerrilla group. However, when Buck looked at a blurry photograph of Wood taken in the Ardennes almost fifty years earlier, he could not say whether or not the officer he met was the man in the picture. The other soldiers with Buck during this encounter have never been located.

In his letter to Aspinwall, Kiendl argued that a convincing piece of evidence making Eric Wood, Jr., the man who spent the night with Peter Maraite lay in the woodsman's account of how the two Americans "cleaned their rifle." Said Kiendl, "This typifies Eric, and only Eric, among all my army acquaintances."

It is a slender reed on which to make the case for Wood. But in the absence of any other individual, he seems the likely choice. And strong evidence of some kind of behind-the-lines action lies in the denunciation by Sepp Dietrich of Americans in the woods— the "criminal scoundrels and bandits," in his words. Author Charles Whiting, who wrote extensively on World War II, did intensive research around St. Vith and located a number of Belgian civilians who supported the account given by Bürgermeister Pauels.

Furthermore, Ralph Hill, who was a captain with the 1st Division during the Bulge, noted that German reports spoke of heavy opposition in the woods around Meyerode. Since no U.S. units were deployed there, Hill concluded it was likely the guerrillas under Wood who worried the enemy.

That none of the force allegedly organized by Wood ever surfaced to claim honors is not surprising. They could easily have all been wiped out while the Germans occupied the area. There are many men from the Ardennes campaign still listed as missing in action, their remains never recovered, no witnesses to their demise.

As Kiendl remarked to Aspinwall, the controversy was really moot. The sanctity of the Congressional Medal of Honor, which Aspinwall claimed was jeopardized by the nomination of Wood, had been preserved. The proposal to award it to Wood was rejected. With General Wood now long dead, there was no further effort to obtain the honor for his son.

Eventually, all parties agreed to a cease-fire on the subject. The honor accorded Eric Fisher Wood, Jr., by the local Belgians near Meyerode is a stone cross erected in the Ommerscheid Forest, north of St. Vith and Schönberg, near the spot where Peter Maraite found his body. The inscription declares, "In January 1945 died here in heroic struggles by the German Offensive, Eric Fisher Wood, Capt. U.S. Army." Aspinwall suggested that the tribute was financed and erected by Gen. Wood. While Eric's father may have contributed gifts to the Meyerode villagers, the error in rank accorded the dead man and the muddled English indicate a homegrown product.

The process that meted out decorations was almost as muddled as the actual Ardennes campaign. Pvt. James Buck, the military court recorder whose brief stint as a combat soldier lost in the woods near St. Vith brought him in contact with an officer who might well have been Eric Wood and irregulars, prepared papers covering recommendations for medals. "I saw headquarters guys who had done nothing put in for Bronze Stars, for Combat Infantryman's Badges. I started adding stuff on some of the more legitimate recommendations for GIs, bumping them up from a Bronze Star to a Silver Star."

After V-E Day, Buck was transferred to a special unit, to serve as court reporter for the big Nuremberg trials of the top Nazis accused of war crimes."After seeing many of the German people in a near-starvation state, having listened to court-martials that covered atrocities committed by individual American soldiers and hearing how we in the States locked up people of Japanese descent in camps and took their property, I was never convinced that we should be putting anyone on trial. We should have simply shot people like Goering and other major figures."

A second round of war crimes trials targeted Jochen Peiper and other men from his task force. American investigators, well before V-E Day, had already identified *Kampfgruppe Peiper* and its commander as the participants in the Malmédy massacre and as the alleged perpetrators of a number of other atrocities. Peiper was twelve miles from his home in Bavaria when captured. With his name on the list for war crimes, he was soon imprisoned at Dachau, the first Nazi concentration camp, to await trial.

The former SS officer oozed self-pity. "As the world of barbed wire closed about us, we were children who had lost their mother overnight. We had been brought up under the clear rules of the front and we weren't capable of understanding the new rules of the game."

He resorted to the hoary stab-in-the-back theory and wildly exaggerated the mood of his countrymen. "Our innocence was boundless. The state had taught its youth only how to handle weapons. We hadn't been trained in how to handle treachery. Yesterday, we had been part of the Greater German Army. Today we were scorned and avoided, surrounded by the howling mobs as the whipping boys of the nation."

In May 1946, a military court, presided over by Brig. Gen. Josiah T. Dalbey, convened to hear *U.S.* v. *Bersin*. Valentin Bersin, a twenty-five-year-old tank commander of *Kampfgruppe Peiper*, had the dubious honor of having his name affixed to the case, since he led the alphabetical listing of the seventy men in the dock. To identify the defendants, they wore numbers. Peiper was designated 42, Sepp Dietrich 11, and Paul Ochmann, who in custody confessed to shooting prisoners near the village of Engelsdorf, bore 41 on his chest. The alleged war crimes included not only the killings at the Baugnez crossroads near Malmédy but also incidents at Stoumont, La Gleize, Stavelot and other places along the route of march.

The prosecution's exhibits included numerous autopsy reports on the dead Americans. Some detailed horrific mutilation of the victims of the Malmédy slaughter. Among the more ghastly, "presence of blood in the region of the sockets and the ragged appearance of skin substantiates the opinion it [eyeball removal] was performed while soldier was still alive." Other post-mortem studies found powder burns on foreheads, indicating use of pistols at close range, and raised arms when fatal bullets were fired.

A handful of American survivors from the killing field outside of Malmédy testified. Virgil Lary, the lieutenant who had since become a college student in Kentucky, was the one person who positively identified a participant. He pointed his finger at Pvt. Georg Fleps, the Rumanian recruit, and said, "This is the man who fired two shots into an American prisoner of war." Samuel Dobyns, Carl Daub, Kenneth Kingston, Henry Zach and Homer Ford, while unable to pick out anyone from among the accused, supported Lary's testimony that the firing began before any attempt to escape.

Dobyns introduced an equivocation. He said he heard an American voice yell, "Stand fast." That, according to Dobyns, was followed by the first pistol shot, after which he and others fled and the machine guns opened up. The defense, and some revisionist historians, attempted to make Dobyns's testimony, which in this respect differed from that of his comrades, proof that a mass escape triggered the slaughter. However, none of the other Americans confirmed Dobyns's account. Furthermore, Dobyns hardly aided the defense when he added he saw Germans "shoot the wounded who were crying for help." The image of brutality was strengthened by Ford, who heard rifle butts batter the injured, and Lary, who spoke of laughter from the Germans as they shot up their prisoners.

The prosecution produced a parade of *Kampfgruppe Peiper* members crying *mea culpa* or accusing their associates. The court heard a sworn statement from Pvt. Gustav Sprenger, in which he admitted firing thirty-two rounds at five of the wounded at the Baugnez crossroads. Sprenger also described how he followed orders to kill two Americans prisoners who carried a wounded German to shelter at Stoumont. "As one of the two American prisoners was half turned towards me, I shot him in the chest with a burst of three or four shots from my machine pistol. Thereupon, the other prisoner turned toward me and I shot him in the chest with a similar burst."

Marcel Boltz, a nineteen-year-old Alsatian, told the court he thought the last rounds of shooting at Malmédy were in the nature of mercy killings. However, he insisted he deliberately missed when told to murder eight U.S. PWs at Büllingen. Another soldier fingered fourteen separate individuals whom he saw shooting into the Americans at the crossroads.

The prosecution argued that the murders of the Americans were premeditated, plotted by the brass from Sepp Dietrich through Peiper and his subordinates. The cue for their approach came from Hitler's admonition, repeated at the conference, setting the strategy for the Ardennes thrust, "The battle will decide whether Germany is to live or die. You soldiers must fight hard and ruthlessly. There must be no pity. The battle must be fought with brutality and all resistance must be broken in a wave of terror."

In support of the prosecution's position, the lead figure for military justice, Lt. Col. Burton Ellis, declared, "Some troops were told to excel in the killing of prisoners of war as well as in fighting. Others were told to make plenty of *rabatz*, which in SS parlance means to have plenty of fun by killing everything that comes in sight. Others were told to 'bump off' everything that comes within sight of their guns."

A company commander, ironically named Friedrich Christ, claimed he was told, "Remember the terror bombings by the Americans, which have killed many of our women and children. Now is the time for revenge. In this offensive, no prisoners will be taken." Christ claimed the now-dead Maj. Werner Poetschke, the officer in command at the scene when the shooting began at Malmédy, had reiterated, "No prisoners."

Valentin Bersin, the titular figure on trial, allegedly supervised murders at Stavelot. He insisted he received his orders from a superior. In fact, the tribunal listened to a number of the accused attest to orders: "You will not take any prisoners of war. Civilians who show themselves on the street and also in the windows will be bumped off."

A prosecution exhibit quoted one company commander who issued a precombat pep talk with an injunction to "fight in the old SS spirit. I am not giving you any order to shoot prisoners of war, but you are well-trained SS soldiers. You know what you should do with prisoners without me telling you that."

Four former SS troopers, themselves not under indictment, claimed Peiper instructed the men to "drive on recklessly, give no quarter and take no prisoners."

Untersturmführer (second lieutenant in the Waffen SS) Rolf Reiser offered damning words about Peiper while trapped at La Gleize. Reiser said he heard Peiper tell Poetschke, "I am going to have part of the prisoners of war shot." Reiser testified he observed Poetschke and Peiper chatting with Major McCown. "It was comical; they took care of him while Poetschke told an interpreter not to tell McCown that fellow prisoners were shot." Another officer stated he heard Peiper say he had ordered some prisoners at La Gleize shot because they refused to work.

There was also evidence offered of an incident in which a solider presented a frostbitten prisoner to Peiper and his regimental surgeon. The physician, supposedly reaching the instant diagnosis that the captive could not survive outside of a medical facility, instructed the prisoner be shot. Peiper made no move to save him.

The opening statement of the defense pleaded not guilty, "because these actions occurred during the most desperate combat situation of the war." The heat-of-battle excuse would become the theme of those seeking exculpation of the accused.

Maj. Hal McCown testified as a witness for the defense. He advised the judges of the circumstances of his time in captivity, the humane behavior of Peiper and his men towards the prisoners such as himself. He related that Peiper had informed him several American PWs on work details had tried to escape during an attack and "approximately nine had been killed." Some of the force of McCown's testimony was deflated as he spoke of his night-long bull session with Peiper. It was still close enough to the bloody Ardennes for many to feel such camaraderie misplaced.

Defenders of Peiper pointed out that he had as much to gain by murdering the 150 or so captives at La Gleize, whom he spared, as those at Malmédy, if the purpose was to prevent prisoners from taking up arms again. However, when *Kampfgruppe Peiper* arrived at the Baugnez crossroads, it was the vanguard of an attack. But by the time it was necessary to decamp from La Gleize, the spearhead was a shattered remnant, 800 left from the original 4,000. Peiper knew he and the offensive were defeated. Winners can bury their guilt along with victims of their atrocities. Losers face retribution for their acts and, conceivably, Peiper's show of mercy could be attributed to recognition of possible future consequences.

On his own behalf Sepp Dietrich advised the court, "I ordered . . . that every resistance is to be broken by terror. However, I certainly did not order the PWs should be shot." And some material indicated German authorities requested an investigation when word of the massacre reached higher echelons.

The question of legal culpability ostensibly turned upon interpretation of directives. The prosecution placed in evidence an account taken from Peiper. In it he explained how he received the papers covering his operation. Included was "an order" from Sepp Dietrich's Sixth SS Panzer Army. It noted, "considering the desperate situation of the German people, a wave of terror and fright should precede our troops . . . the German soldier should . . . recall innumerable German victims of the bombing terror."

The words must have resonated with Peiper, who only a few weeks before had been assigned with his men to aid civil defense cleaning up after a raid upon the Rhenish town of Düren. He had said, "I could have castrated the swine who did that to those innocent people of Düren—with a blunt piece of glass." (Why the German civilians were any more innocent than those noncombatants who came under the destructive fire of Peiper's legions in his campaigns all over Europe is a testament to the ability of humans to exclude consideration for all but their own acts.)

Peiper in a statement recorded by his interrogators said, "I am nearly certain . . . it was expressly stated that prisoners of war must be shot where the local conditions should so require it . . ." When he passed along this information to his staff, he said, "I did not mention anything that prisoners of war should be shot when local conditions of combat should so require it, because those present were all experienced officers to whom this was obvious."

He thus admitted accepting orders which directed the execution of prisoners, albeit on a basis of when "conditions of combat should so require it." But for all of this, Peiper, while on the stand, steadfastly denied he had ever expressly commanded the execution of a prisoner. Colonel Ellis inquired how it was that such disciplined, well-trained troops as Peiper led could have resorted to random killing without orders. The SS officer dodged the question: "During combat there are desperate situations, the answer to which is given out very fast to main reactions and which do not have anything to do with education and teaching"—the heat-of-battle defense.

Peiper, who testified in German even though he had an excellent command of English, raised a new issue with a complaint that he had been maltreated by his captors. "When an American sergeant left the room to get other prisoners, I was struck several times." He spoke of a night spent in a "hot box"—a cell with extreme heat and no ventilation—and having been subjected to psychological pressure techniques.

Other defendants told the court of being coerced into confessions and accusations through mock trials, sham rituals prior to apparent execution, fake witnesses, beatings.

Peiper confounded the court further with an encomium he had drawn from Ellis himself. The prosecutor had remarked during one meeting, "I admire you and hardly know another soldier I esteem as highly. But you are sacrificing yourself for an ideal which no longer exists. The men whom you think you have to cover up for are bums and criminals. I'll prove that to you in the course of the trial. We are now parting as friends and when we see each other again . . . [we will be enemies] and I'll have to paint you in the worst bloody colors but you'll understand that I will only be doing my duty."

Peiper thus sought to persuade the court that the praise heaped upon him by his chief antagonist suggested Ellis really did not believe all of the charges leveled against him. But the prosecutor's remarks may also be interpreted as a clumsy try to play the role of the "good cop" who seeks the confidence of the accused.

Clearly, some of the original charges against the defendants reflected a grab bag of accusations. Indeed, a number were summarily dismissed, others dropped. However, the verdicts acquitted only one defendant, while condemning forty-three men to death by hanging, calling for lifetime imprisonment for twenty-two of the accused and sentences of ten to twenty-five years for the remainder. Among those given a red jacket to wear, symbolic of execution, were Peiper and Paul Ochmann. Dietrich received a life term. Peiper requested that, as a soldier, he be accorded the courtesy of a firing squad instead of the hangman.

Conviction by the U.S. military hardly convinced Jochen Peiper of the error of his ways. To his defense counsel he wrote a letter calling the war "a proud and heroic time. Where we were standing was Germany and as far as my tank gun reached was my kingdom." His chief regret seemed to be that he and his comrades had been unable to save Hitler. "When the Führer was needing his *Leibstandarte* most . . . fate had separated us from him."

He dismissed those at Dachau with him. "When seeing today the defendants in the dock, don't believe them to be the old combat group Peiper . . . . The real outfit is waiting for me in Valhalla." The swashbuckling youthful officer had never joined the Nazi party; ideology meant less to him than a belief in his leader and war glory wrapped around greater Germany.

A series of appeals to higher military authorities followed. Much was made of the roles in the investigation and prosecution by several Jewish refugees, suggesting a revenge motive on any German unlucky enough to be accused. The heavy-handed methods, hardly distinguishable from police third-degree interrogations conducted with rubber hoses, added weight to appeals for clemency. Furthermore, some rulings by the panel on the bench troubled authorities. By 1948, no execution yet had been carried out and the commander of the American zone of occupation, Gen. Lucius Clay, commuted many of the thirty death sentences and tossed out thirteen convictions altogether. However, Peiper continued to wear a red jacket and Sepp Dietrich remained destined to finish his life in the Landsberg fortress.

The battle to save the condemned continued. Peiper's defense counsel, Col. Willis M. Everett, Jr., having returned to civilian life, railed against the irregularities of the trial and the thirst for blood by Peiper's most virulent accusers. The publicity generated brought a Senate Armed Services Committee investigation. A new champion for Peiper and those still in jail appeared, the freshly-minted junior senator from Wisconsin, Joseph McCarthy, possessor of a dubious war record that he inflated, facing indictment for unethical acts as an attorney and judge in his home state.

McCarthy flailed away in the inimitable style that would grab him headlines as a Communist hunter in future years. He fulminated about the awful behavior of the American soldiers who guarded the SS troopers at Dachau, voicing his horror that "sixteen- or seventeen-year-old boys [should be] kicked in the testicles, crippled for life." Not that age should have been a requisite for the right to bash genitalia, but none of those on trial were that tender in years; a good number of veterans, like Ochmann, were well past their thirtieth year.

When one of the prosecutors being questioned by McCarthy responded that the senator perhaps did not fully understand the meaning of the "heat of combat"—a major issue around which justification for conduct revolved—McCarthy haughtily answered, "I don't know whether you saw any combat or not; but don't tell me I don't know what the heat of combat is." McCarthy had falsely depicted himself as manning a machine gun on naval attack planes. Those who looked into his record laughed at him as "Tail-Gunner Joe."

McCarthy hit a parodic high when he questioned a guard about the access of the accused to clergymen. "Did you ever see a priest or a minister or a *rabbi* [my italics)] in the Malmédy section of the prison?" When the answer was negative, McCarthy incredibly said of the SS troopers, "And you knew there was some sizable number of Protestants, Catholics, or *Jewish* [my italics] boys. I understand there was no chaplain assigned to these boys."

In the end, the authorities capitulated to the uproar. All death sentences were commuted. Granted clemency, many of the prisoners were released as the 1950s began. Paul Ochmann disappeared into obscurity, taking up the trade of a tailor. The last two to receive their freedom were Sepp Dietrich in 1955 and Jochen Peiper just before Christmas of the following year.

The killing of the soldier who no longer offers resistance is an obvious breach of the few rules that govern modern warfare. But in practice the offense is not so easy to establish. For example, is it reasonable to expect instant clemency for someone who ceased shooting only after having run out of ammunition, and having succeeded in killing a man's closest friends moments before? A number of soldiers admit to pumping bullets into individuals under such circumstances—"the heat of combat"—being the rationale for ignoring the absence of further resistance.

At times during World War II, the enemy was castigated for firing upon aircrews dangling from parachutes after their planes went down. But while the fliers at the moment no longer posed a threat, if they landed in their own territory, they would soon return to combat. Were they any different than soldiers forced to abandon a tank and considered fair game for their enemy because, if they escaped, they would man another tank?

The crimes for which Peiper and the others were held accountable fell beyond these bounds. They were accused of murdering men well after the "heat of combat" cooled and who, as prisoners, would not return to fight them. But the testimony raises the matter of "only following orders," the basic Nuremberg defense, to a level beyond that of a concentration camp guard or official. The latter could obtain transfers if they did not accept the policies that murdered inmates of a camp, granting that in the Third Reich that usually meant assignment to the deadly Russian front. Soldiers in combat units do not ordinarily enjoy the prerogative of shifting to other commands because they disagree with the immediate orders from superiors.

And certainly, when Poetschke, or whoever, directed Fleps to turn his pistol on the prisoners, the young soldier may well have believed refusal might have brought his death. Well removed from the scene, anyone judging him can insist on Fleps's moral responsibility, even at the cost of a summary execution. Paul Ochmann also explained away his atrocities as obedience to a higher authority. The military court that convicted him seemingly believed he could have refused or at least evaded the task.

It is, however, difficult to excuse the enthusiastic orgy of murder and maiming by Fleps's comrades at the crossroads. Those who participated would appear to have gone beyond "only following orders."

While no firm proof exists that Sepp Dietrich actually dictated a "take no prisoners" policy, the climate created certainly encouraged the atrocities. Thus, the guilt begins with Hitler's call for a campaign laced with terror and the echoes of it in the statements from Dietrich down through Peiper and his junior officers.

In the European theater, while there were unsubstantiated rumors of mass murders of prisoners by Allies, only one case was documented. On July 14, 1943, after a bitter fight for control of an airfield near Biscari, Sicily, several dozen, mostly Italian and a few German, soldiers apparently were shot down after they surrendered. An investigation identified the perpetrators, in what were two separate events, as a sergeant and a captain from the 45th Infantry Division, although it was obvious that other men participated in the second incident. A chaplain who spoke to American soldiers in the vicinity claimed several complained to him against the treatment of prisoners and said they would not care to continue fighting if such brutal treatment continued. (No one from *Kampfgruppe Peiper* was shown to have protested its actions to a chaplain.)

A monograph by Professor James Weingartner, published in *The Historian* in 1989, recounts what happened. The sergeant faced a court-martial six weeks after the Biscari shootings. He relied on a defense that combined an excuse of extreme emotional stress from four days of combat and his impression, based upon statements attributed to General Patton and lesser officers that U.S. troops were to take prisoners only under limited circumstances. He was found guilty and sentenced to life imprisonment.

At the subsequent court-martial of the captain, the defense rested only on his understanding of instructions from his superiors. On the stand, the officer insisted he recalled a Patton speech verbatim and recited it: "When we land against the enemy, don't forget to hit him and hit him hard. We will bring the fight home to him. When we meet the enemy, we will kill him. We will show him no mercy. He has killed thousands of your comrades, and he must die. If you company officers in leading your men against the enemy find him shooting at you, and, when you get within two hundred yards of him he wishes to surrender, oh no! That bastard will die. You will kill him. Stick him between the third and fourth ribs. You will tell your men that. They must have the killer instinct. Tell them to stick him . . . We will get the names of killers and killers are immortal. When word reaches him that he is being faced by a killer battalion, a killer outfit, he will fight less. Particularly, we must build up that name as killers and you will get that down to your troops in time for the invasion [of Sicily]."

Other men supported the captain's assertion that a "take no prisoners" attitude emanated from the brass. And the defendant summarized his position: "I ordered them shot because I thought it came directly under the general's instructions. Right or wrong, a three star general's advice, who has had combat experience, is good enough for me and I took him at his word." The court acquitted the captain. Later, he died in combat, and higher authorities released the sergeant from prison, albeit reduced in rank to private.

Subsequently, Patton denied exhorting the troops to murder prisoners. Associates defused possible charges against him, saying his remarks were only inflated rhetoric designed to steel the troops for the rigors of combat. But there is no significant difference between his remarks and those of the Germans creating the climate for the atrocities of *Kampfgruppe Peiper*.

Unlike Peiper, Skorzeny, although also listed as a war criminal, evaded capture. In fact, he decided to turn himself in to the authorities nearly two weeks after V-E Day. His Dachau trial, held more than a year after Peiper's, was anticlimactic. Already the Allies had begun to tire in their pursuit of Nazis. Furthermore, there were no obvious atrocities to be blamed on Skorzeny. When his defenders introduced testimony that his tactics differed in no way from those sometimes employed by British commandos and agents, Hitler's favorite won an acquittal.

However, new charges surfaced from other countries. For close to a year, the accused man was held before he decided to escape, stowing his considerable bulk in the trunk of a car. With the assistance of friends, he reached Germany. Eventually, the Allied authorities dropped their case and he pursued his business career. He established a prosperous firm in Spain and was gratified with official de-Nazification by a German court in 1952. For the remainder of his life, he would be regarded by many as a sinister go-between for neo-Nazi elements and netherworld commercial adventurers. He died peacefully in Spain in 1975.

Friedrich von der Heydte, the parachute commander, also spent a considerable time locked up as a potential defendant. Released and de-Nazified, von der Heydte followed a career in law, eventually becoming a judge in West Germany.

Most of the soldiers who supplied reminiscences for this book had heard of the Malmédy incident even while they were still battling to reduce the German penetration. Their reactions seem to fall in no pattern, not differing because of personal experiences with the enemy. And in their zeal to get on with their lives after V-E Day, some actually took no notice of the Dachau trials. While there were many stories in the media in the first months after the killings, the coverage of the trials in 1946, even in the New York *Times,* was haphazard and superficial.

Bill Boyle, the battalion commander from the 517th, was one who was aware of the proceedings at the former concentration camp. "My reactions were mixed. We established a precedent saying that there was law that transcended the laws of a nation. I think of that in connection with our current Congressmen who have severely criticized Judge Thomas for having such ideas."

Alan Jones, Jr., another professional soldier, had no qualms about the Dachau proceedings. "I thought it was done properly." Dick Byers, an officer by virtue of a battlefield commission, says he paid little attention to the case, trusting that the army would properly handle the matter.

Wallace Swanson, the CO of a 101st Airborne infantry Company, had entered the oil industry upon his return home. He followed the prosecution of Peiper, *et al.,* closely. "The verdicts could have been even stronger," indicating he disagreed with the clemency eventually accorded.

During the time Peiper and his people had their days in court, Glen Strange occupied a hospital bed, still trying to recover from the spine injury [from] near the Rhine. "I followed the trials as best I could with a radio and the papers, but it really wasn't much

I could learn. I thought the trials went on far too long and they should have put many of them before firing squads. I guess you would have to say I was not satisfied completely."

Tank commander Dee Paris remembered being, at most, vaguely aware of charges of atrocities while serving in the Ardennes. However, he kept current with the proceedings at Dachau. "I remember my reaction when Sen. Joe McCarthy used a U.S. Senate hearing to spread lies. I was infuriated! I could not understand why everyone, including the U.S. president, was in fear of this bastard."

Jim Mills of the 106th, who witnessed the carnage of the Dresden firestorms, gave the trials only cursory attention. "I paid attention only to the end results. But I was glad that some of the Germans had to pay for the terrible crimes they did against innocent people. Combat is one thing, murder of unarmed people is totally different, and the murders at Malmédy were not a combat situation.

"What happened in Dresden did not change my attitudes. The Germans started the war. They killed thousands of people during their conquests. All the Germans cheered Hitler while they were winning. At Dresden they just got back a sample of what they had been dishing out. Even though the bombings at Dresden were very frightening and I knew I might get killed, I hoped our bombers did a lot of damage because that was the only way the war would end."

John Collins, who had fought on the Prümerberg hill in front of St. Vith and then was taken prisoner, was "elated then I heard the verdicts."

Phil Hannon, from the same engineer battalion, undoubtedly spoke for many when he remarked, "I did not pay much attention to the trials at Dachau. I wanted to get back into my life, to college and other things. I wasn't greatly interested in punishing the enemy. I thought it needed to be done but that was somebody else's job."

As far as atrocities by Americans were concerned, Wallace Swanson of the 101st Airborne insisted, "I never saw any prisoners killed although I heard stories, some of which were factual and some questionable until investigated. I would not have allowed any PW to be killed if it was within my power to prevent it. We took many prisoners to be interrogated, not shot or killed later. The Geneva Convention laws meant a lot to me, no matter what some ill-tempered leader or soldier did in the past. Anyone should hold human life a valuable facet of God's creation."

"I was shocked by word of the Malmédy massacre," remembered Dick Byers. "I was still enough of a Boy Scout to believe that our side would never do anything like that. I rationalized and excused the execution that happened when I was wounded, with the idea that the infantryman was an 82nd AB paratrooper and paratroopers were different. To this day it bothers me to hear some of our guys admit to killing prisoners. First, I don't believe in it morally. Second, it is legally wrong. But above all it is damn foolish because, after word gets around or the enemy sees prisoners being shot, it deprives him of hope of survival, so he fights to the end. You or your buddy then get killed or wounded unnecessarily. I was wounded and out of it before the push through Germany. I might have come to think differently if I'd seen more combat, more casualties."

1st Lt. Alan Jones, Jr. Hq. Co. 1st Battalion, 423rd Infantry, 106th Division, survived to fight in Korea and become a colonel. *(Courtesy U.S. Army)*

Major Glen Strange, 27th Armored Infantry Battalion, 9th Armored Division, borrowed a general's uniform during the Bulge. *(Courtesy Glen L. Strange)*

Frank Raila, a stalag escapee, studied medicine, becoming a radiologist in Mississippi where he also served in the reserves. *(Courtesy Dr. Frank Raila)*

Survivors of the Intelligence and Reconnaisance Platoon that held up the German advance near Lanzerath convened for the medal ceremony in 1981. *(Courtesy Dr. Lyle Bouck)*

Phil Hannon, after more than four months as a POW, came home to Maryland to embark on a career in business. *(Courtesy Philip Hannon)*

Joe Colmer (with grandson Adam), twice wounded, plied the trade of a welder in Illinois. *(Courtesy Joe Colmer)*

Bill Dunfee became a lumber company executive in Ohio and savored a reunion of the 82nd Airborne at Fort Bragg, NC. *(Courtesy William T. Dunfee)*

Ben Nawrocki, a proud member of the 99th Division Association, returned to his pre-war job in Indiana. *(Courtesy Ben Nawrocki)*

Ed Uzemack (with wife Pat visiting Arizona) left journalism for public relations stints in Illinois and Pennsylvania. *(Courtesy Ed Uzemack)*

Frank Currey deserted upstate New York for the South Carolina of his 30th Division buddies. *(Courtesy Francis Currey)*

As a civilian, Leonard Weinstein, with his wife Jeanette, followed his pre-war occupation in the field of typography. *(Courtesy Leonard Weinstein)*

Jim Mills, among the last of the POWs to find freedom, used the GI bill to study the arts and business of construction in Ohio. *(Courtesy James Mills)*

Jerry Nelson (with daughter) operated a barber shop in Wisconsin and was active in fish and wildlife preservation programs. *(Courtesy Gerald Nelson)*

Dee Paris, a Maryland resident, ranked as a colonel in the reserves while laboring for the Veterans Adminstration. *(Courtesy Gerald Astor)*

Schuyler Jackson, scared of heights while a paratrooper, became a pilot and established a trucking business in Virginia. *(Courtesy Gerald Astor)*

Abe Baum advised the Israeli Military, started a clothing manufacturing firm, hit the road as a saleman, and retired to California. *(Courtesy Gerald Astor)*

Jim Buck exploited his stenographic skills with companies outside the U.S., and set up a retail chain and travel business in California. *(Courtesy Gerald Astor)*

Jack Agnew (far left) who installed telephones in Pennsylvania met with former Bastogne pathfinders (left to right from Agnew) Schrable Williams, Jake McNeice, and Martin Majewski. *(Courtesy John Agnew)*

Dick Byers used GI Bill benefits to learn to fly, then pursued a grounded life in an Ohio heating and air conditioning enterprise. *(Courtesy Richard H. Byers)*

Discharged because of wounds suffered in the Ardennes, Carmen Capalbo embarked on a career as a theatrical director and producer. *(Courtesy of Hillyer C. Warlick)*

Glen Strange needed twenty two months of hospitalization after his wounds near the Rhine and then served as postmaster and a local judge in Oklahoma. *(Courtesy Glen L. Strange)*

Harry Martin returned to New Jersey where he came a tax consultant.

Chapter XVIII

CORRECTING THE RECORDS

OUT OF THE LANDSBERG prison after more than eleven years of incarceration, Jochen Peiper, who had known nothing but the SS as an adult, started his life as a civilian, working for Porsche in Stuttgart. Back in the U.S., Lyle Bouck, the young lieutenant who celebrated his twenty-first birthday at the Café Scholzen, watching his captors and an angry SS Lieutenant Colonel Peiper peer at a bayonet-impaled map, had already immersed himself in a new profession.

Bouck had been rotated back to the U.S., still debilitated by acute hepatitis contracted while a PW. He could not shake the aches and pains. While he was a boy, his aunt, a masseuse, helped him heal from a back injury. When several men at his post decided to take their physical complaints to a chiropractor, Bouck, recalling his aunt's manipulations, went along. After six weeks of treatment, he felt better.

"I was now on recruiting duty at Cape Girardeau, married and living in a one-room rental. I intended to remain in the army and filed all of the papers for permanent rank as a lieutenant. I also applied for the accumulated leave pay due me. I received notification that I had been accepted into the regular army as a second lieutenant. All I had to do was sign the form. That same day, there was a second letter. It contained my leave pay and it was much less than I anticipated. I called up and was informed that regulations stated that if you were an enlisted man for any period of time, you'd be compensated at that pay scale. I was so pissed off that I said to hell with it, tore up my commission and told my wife I was going to law school."

But at a party, Bouck met a graduate of a chiropractic school. Recalling his benefits from that form of therapy, Bouck abandoned jurisprudence for a course in chiropractics. Once he graduated, he slowly built up a clientele and, after struggling for several years, achieved considerable success with an office in St. Louis.

In December 1965, Bouck received a letter from his companion at Lanzerath, Bill Tsakanikas. Because of his wounds, Tsak endured a series of operations and a lifetime of pain. Nevertheless, he had attended the University of Pennsylvania's Wharton School of Business, married, changed his name to William James and entered local politics in Port Chester, New York.

The note to Bouck was inspired by the publication of the official U.S. Army history, *The Ardennes: Battle of the Bulge* by Hugh M. Cole. Tsak wrote: "Bouck—We were responsible for blunting the main spearhead of the whole German offensive for that whole first 24 hour period. However, you would never know it without having been there and then reading the account from the American position and the German position.

"Listen, Bouck, I would like to see our unit cited, but more importantly, I want the world to know, but for your calm determination, it could have been another story.

"Remember when you used to say Fuck the torpedos, straight ahead. What are your orders this time?" The letter concluded, exhorting Bouck to approach members of the U.S. Senate.

The St. Louis chiropractor was reluctant to bestir himself. But Tsak refused to let the matter rest. He telephoned Bouck and vigorously expressed his anger over the Cole book's failure to acknowledge the I & R platoon's contribution. Seemingly obsessed, Tsak flew to St. Louis, bringing Cole's volume, in which he outlined passages, and urged Bouck to campaign for redress. To add to the commotion, John Eisenhower, son of the general and president, had started to research a book about the campaign in the Ardennes and had started to look into the operations of the I & R platoon.

In June 1966, Bouck opened a letter and discovered he had been awarded a Silver Star by the 99th Division commander, Gen. Walter Lauer, more than 20 years earlier. The medal only reached him apparently because, as part of his effort to aid John Eisenhower, Bouck had requested a copy of his official records.

"I decided to cooperate with Eisenhower," said Bouck, "because I was concerned about accuracy. Once I get involved in something, I can't just do it, I have to make it the best I can. For that reason I can't play golf without competing. My nephew said to me, 'Why the hell do you feel you always have to win?' I can't even cut the grass unless I do it just right. It probably goes back to the struggles of my family, my father being a loser.

"I also believed I had been derelict in my responsibilities right after the war. I was sick, we had survived, it was over. What was the point in talking about what happened anymore? In that sense I should have done more to get recognition for the I & R platoon but at the time I felt we hadn't done any more than anyone else. But now I knew differently.

"It eventually became a personal crusade with me to see that these men received the recognition for what they had done as youngsters."

John Eisenhower interviewed Bouck on the events surrounding the December 16 stand and invited the chiropractor to accompany him on a research mission in the Ardennes. Bouck begged off because of demands of his practice and the author turned to Tsakanikas. He initially declined because of the expense but Bouck volunteered to pay his way. Bouck recalled, "John Eisenhower told me when Tsak got up there on the hill and reenacted what happened, running back and forth, John was afraid he'd have to ship him home as a corpse."

Eisenhower also mentioned to Bouck that he had been unable to draw a response from Jochen Peiper. "It may have been because of his name, being the son of Dwight," said Bouck, "but I agreed to write Peiper based on our brief meeting at the Café."

After summarizing the action at Lanzerath and asking for Peiper's view of what happened, Bouck wrote: "I know you faced charges of having your men shoot prisoners of war at Honsfeld, Büllingen and Malmédy. Because we were not molested after a day of severe battle with the best German troops, I have always thought you had been accused of something for which you had no control. It is well known that in the heat of battle tempers flare and men will do things they normally would not do. Many situations like this happened also with our troops."

Peiper answered promptly, in English, explaining the delay in his penetration was not because of American resistance but a traffic jam caused by two divisions of a different nature—horse-drawn artillery, heavy trucks, tanks and armored infantry, which had only one road to share and also to pass through "one needle's eye." (Peiper was delayed between Losheim and Lanzerath by another division that relied on horse-drawn heavy equipment).

The former SS lieutenant colonel described the scene where

Bouck first saw him. "It was pitch dark. No shots rang out, and I had the disgusted impression that the whole front had gone to bed instead of waging war. The commanding officer (9th Regiment, 3rd Parachute Division), a full colonel without any combat experience, who had just been skimmed out from the ministry of the *Luftwaffe*, briefed me to the effect that the forest behind Lanzerath and Honsfeld was full of pillboxes, snipers and other obstacles. Three probing attacks had been repelled and a prepared attack could not be launched before daybreak. The room was full of soldiers, mostly officers, a great number of them asleep."

Peiper then related to Bouck how he had plunged ahead from Losheim to Lanzerath, using his halftracks to detonate mines. The material was welcome grist for John Eisenhower's mill.

Bouck subsequently inquired whether Peiper would be amenable to a meeting of veterans from both sides in Belgium. The American was apparently not aware of how Peiper's notorious reputation had dogged him, driven him from several promising positions. Union officials at Porsche had convinced the company to dismiss Peiper. He had then gone to work for Volkswagen, training sales people. But an assembly line, increasingly manned by Italian immigrants desperately grabbing the lowest paid jobs in Germany, learned Peiper occupied an executive position. The accusation of atrocities in Italy surfaced. Again Peiper lost his post.

In clumsy syntax Peiper replied to Bouck's proposal of a reunion. "When lacking your enthusiasm as to a veteran's meeting in Belgium. This is not poor cooperation but rather more experience and realism. Public opinion and certain forces behind the press and propaganda would not tolerate such a 'cease fire' as too many people still live on the unsettled past and prosper on wounds artificially kept open.

"A U.S. Lt. Colonel, permanent rank, who dared to disregard the positive picture, your 'psychological warfare division' had drawn of us, by taking the witness stand in the Malmédy Trial, testifying that no violations of the Geneva Convention had occurred, was later accused of treason and court martialled. It would be naive not to realize that the world still today is strongly influenced by certain organizations you had better not provoke, at least not openly."

Peiper could only have been referring to Hal McCown as the officer who spoke on his behalf at Malmédy, and far from any punishment for his participation in the trial, he successfully pursued a career that ended with retirement as a major general.

Bouck, meanwhile, continued to ponder his own actions. "We were at Gettysburg, Bill James, his wife, my wife and I, visiting with John Eisenhower and his wife Barbara. We started to talk about what happened. I remarked that I was now much more mature, employed common sense. If the same thing happened now, I'd have taken off when the tank destroyers left.

"Barbara Eisenhower said, 'But you're not twenty-one today.' No one touched what was really the heart of what happened in front of Lanzerath. There wasn't any thought of bravery or courage. We were frightened and we wanted to get the hell out of there. But we were afraid to go against an order. An older person would have left."

Bouck, with Barbara Eisenhower's prompting, hits on what appears to be a prime ingredient in many acts of courage—youth. The men who actually fought in the Ardennes were often little more than boys, still bearing vestiges of the adolescent sense of omnipotence, that "it can't happen to me because I am indestructible." Ed Johnson of the 517th, for example, insists the average age of his fellows was nineteen. Mostly out of the line of fire were the over-thirties, the brass hats who demand, capture of a heavily defended objective or order, the men in the field to "hold at all costs."

The Bitter Woods, the John Eisenhower account, appeared in 1969, with almost nine pages devoted to the I & R platoon at Lanzerath. Bouck disclaims some of the quotes apparently supplied by Tsak, but the narrative squared with his knowledge of the facts.

In the same year his book reached the stores, Eisenhower, appointed U.S. ambassador to Belgium, arranged with Bouck to bring a party of American veterans to meet with almost seventy former German paratroopers, men who had been at Lanzerath. "We spent three days together. We had lunch at St. Vith, but when I wanted to get off the bus at Lanzerath and see the room where I was held, the German in charge of the tour refused. 'Stay on the bus,' he ordered. 'You can see that later. We're behind schedule.' I never did get there. Later, after some drinking, he tried to tell me we were all the same sort. We all hated war. I didn't believe him."

At one point, one of the former paratroopers came up to Bouck and put his arm around him. "Lyle, we haven't talked since that day. Do you remember someone who asked, 'Who is the commandant?' It was me."

"My hair stood on end as I realized this was the guy who first spoke to me when I was captured. His name was Vince Kuhlbach, and he was now an accountant." (In fact, Kuhlbach was the experienced sergeant who objected to the disastrous tactics being employed against the I & R platoon.)

As Peiper had suggested to Bouck, there were indeed forces that would not forget. Unable to find steady employment and perhaps unhappy with the influence of "certain organizations"—he called German society bankrupt—he chose an unlikely place of refuge, a small French village, Traves, eighty miles from the German border. With his own hands Peiper built a small house on two acres and, seemingly, supported himself translating military history tomes for a publisher in Stuttgart. Occasionally, his wife, children and grandchildren visited him in Traves.

Three years after he settled there, an enterprising newspaper reporter, alerted by the Communist party, broke the story of an accused war criminal living quietly in France. When journalists approached Peiper, he responded with his customary arrogance. "If I am here, it is because in 1940, the French were without courage. There are threats to burn down my house. I thought France was a democratic country that respected human rights." His sneers hardly calmed the turbulent waters.

A series of threats failed to move Peiper, who insisted he had nowhere else to flee. And as Bastille Day 1976 arrived, at midnight, explosions like firecrackers or gunshots echoed from the woods where he lived. A glow in the night sky brought the villagers. Flames engulfed Peiper's rough-hewn home. In the morning, searchers, sifting the charred ruins, discovered a burnt corpse and a few spent cartridges. The assumption was that Peiper died defending his homestead, although a few continued to claim, à la Martin Bormann, Josef Mengele and even Adolf Hitler, that it was a hoax, with the alleged victim pulling off a successful disappearing act.

In 1977, the toll imposed by his wounds and a total of thirty-six operations finally killed Bill James. The story and a campaign to honor him with a Congressional Medal of Honor gained new impetus after a Parade magazine piece by Jack Anderson. James's congressman, Richard Ottinger, spoke up for his now-dead constituent. New York Yankees owner George Steinbrenner read Anderson's piece and invited James's widow to throw out the first ball for his club. She called Bouck, pleading, "I can't throw a ball." He urged her to accept the invitation in memory of her husband and for the pleasure of her sons.

When Steinbrenner learned of Bouck's support, he personally telephoned the chiropractor. After further conversation, Steinbrenner contacted all fourteen survivors of the I & R platoon and eventually arranged for twelve of them, with their spouses, to be flown at his expense, first-class, to New York. The party wined, dined and slept in luxury. Bouck was nervous about the response of the impatient spectators to the announcement that a widow of a World War II hero was to toss out the first ball while his group lined up behind home plate. "I figured for sure the Yankee fans would say, 'Get those old farts out of there and play ball.' But there was no sign of any derogatory reactions.'

That year, the effort to memorialize the I & R platoon reached the House of Representatives. A number of the men, including Bouck and the former Major Kris, appeared as witnesses to the feats of Tsak, which necessarily included material on the entire group. The House committee recommended the Secretary of Defense award the Congressional Medal of Honor to William James.

The final resolution came at a valor ceremony in 1981. Bill Slape, Bouck's platoon sergeant who remained in service until retirement after thirty years, Risto Milosevich, a contractor in civilian life, and Tsak, posthumously, won Distinguished Service Crosses. Lou Kahlil picked up a Silver Star, Lyle Bouck added a DSC to his Silver Star. The others all won Bronze Stars.

West Pointers Bill Boyle and Alan Jones, Jr., resumed their military careers following V-E Day. Boyle confounded those who first believed he would not live and then that he would be invalided. Ben Sullivan, the battalion surgeon, recalls that initially Boyle's two arms were so weak he could barely turn a doorknob. He was a prime candidate for a pension but Boyle refused to quit.

When the Korean War broke out, Boyle became a member of the 187th Airborne Regimental Combat Team. "I didn't know the men as well but I respected the junior officers. However, I felt the top side, the commanding general, the exec and most of the staff were incompetent. For three months I served directly under an officer I considered incompetent."

"I belong to the 517th Association and attend reunions because these are my men whom I loved and protected where I could, and when I was severely wounded, they did at least the same for me. They represent a major part of my life. I don't attend meetings of the 187th."

From his experiences in the two conflicts he has drawn some conclusions. "The Battle of the Bulge was my toughest combat, especially in Hotton. We were as close as 100 feet to the German positions. Whenever I crossed the bridge in Hotton, I was under small arms fire during the day. One night, four of us were in a building when a Tiger tank rolled up to the window. We had no antitank weapon. More than a few times artillery shells hit walls just above my head. During the attack south of Soy, I was fired upon by members of the U.S. 75th Division.

"I define courage or bravery as the ability to overcome fear. Heroism is more likely an action taken in answer to specific situations. Becoming a hero is in part due to circumstances. There must be a situation that demands extraordinary action. Training and discipline contribute, teaching us to react to particular stresses in specific ways. Camaraderie helps. Anything that enables soldiers to develop confidence in their fellow men is important.

"The West Point motto and honor system helped me. As a leader, I was taught to set the example. Some *commanders* do not do this and I don't consider them leaders. I differentiate between leaders and commanders. General Schwarzkopf was both. Generals Walton Walker [Korea] and William Westmoreland [Vietnam] were more commanders than leaders. General Ridgway was a leader as well as commander.

"I don't question the existence of post-traumatic stress but I don't believe it is anywhere near the level the media seems to believe. I look at most World War II groups and find little of it. During World War II you fought until wounded, killed or the war ended. There was no rotation home [as in Korea and Vietnam]."

Boyle retained his blunt honesty. "One of the battalion commanders whose companies I had to command, because he wasn't there or in control of his unit, became a major general." Perhaps because of his uncompromising integrity, Boyle never received a general's star. He retired to upstate New York as a full colonel.

When Alan Jones, Jr., returned to duty in the States after V-E Day, he was given a slot at the Pentagon. "The surface effects of my time as a PW were that I swore I would never restrict my eating or smoking, something I regretted many years later. I swore to myself I would never allow myself to surrender, even if surrounded I would try to shoot my way out.

"I had been exposed to some of the weakness of humans. I met some brave and some cowardly men and learned that how they will behave is not predictable from appearances. I also learned a great deal about soldiers under stress."

But he continued to speculate about the events that led to his capture. He tried to write a monograph for army use describing what happened to his 423rd Regiment. "Although Descheneaux and Cavender talked to one another, they had only limited information about what was happening. I think the surrender was a mistake. They should have gone into a defensive position. While the regiments would have suffered many casualties if they fought, we also lost many men from prison camp conditions and the bombing raids."

During his time at the Pentagon in Washington, D.C., he saw his father, Gen. Alan Jones, Sr., a number of times. "He was still recovering from his heart attack. I know he was deeply hurt by what had happened to the 106th. He had activated it, trained it and brought it into battle. But we never got around to talking about what went on with the different orders, the other commanders. After he died, I regretted not discussing the matter with him. I think he might have wanted to talk about it and I may have let him down by not bringing it up. Maybe I felt that it was too painful and that's why I never raised the subject." Conceivably, son and father may have feared what truths might have surfaced.

When the Korean war broke out, Alan Jones, Jr. went into battle with the 9th Infantry Regiment of the 2nd Division, an organization seen in the Ardennes when it held Elsenborn Ridge. A feeling of *déjà vu* would have been appropriate when the North Koreans lunged at Jones's regiment along the lower Naktong River in August 1950. "Our regiment reached a high-water mark in casualties. We threw every soldier into the line, the cooks and clerks took up rifles. The Fifth Marines saved us."

After the outfit recovered its poise, men and equipment, it headed north, to the Yalu River. The Chinese poured over the Yalu and overwhelmed the American infantry. "I saw the Chinaman behind a machine gun as he shot me in the foot. I was lying in a ditch, freezing to death, when Lucian Truscott III, whom I knew from high school, came by on a jeep and picked me up."

With his wound healed and the Korean "police action" ended, Jones served in various posts, even making a three-week inspection of conditions in Vietnam for the Pentagon before retiring as a full colonel in 1973.

Jones and his wife settled in a comfortable, total-service complex at Fort Belvoir, Virginia, designed for retired military and foreign service officers. Heart disease curtailed his regimen for a while but Jones busies himself on the golf course, traveling and trying to learn the functioning of a word processor in order to keep up with the grandkids. He lunches regularly with other former military men. "The rules are we don't talk about wives, children or sex. The proscription on war stories is occasionally violated. Politics, business, golf and what's happening to old friends are the staples."

The subject, apparently too painful for father and son, troubled many veterans of the Bulge. British accounts, which often presented a less than complimentary view of American efforts, criticized the conduct of the 106th. In U.S. veteran circles tales circulated of the 106th as the "Hungry and Sick" who cut and ran.

John Kline, a member of the division who became a PW, said, "We received some very bad press after the war. The British writers were the cruelest, made us out to be cowards. I've talked to guys who said they would walk into a Legion club to have a drink and somebody would say, 'Oh, you were with the 106th? You were one of those guys who let the Germans through the Bulge.' "

Self-serving memoirs from some other outfits denigrated the performance of the 106th and these served as research for still more books. In 1980, author Charles Whiting published *Death of a Division*, which, in essence, painted the 106th troops as not only green but also cowards who panicked and bugged out, creating a gridlock that prevent the 7th Armored from saving them. John Eisenhower's *The Bitter Woods* relied on the same derogatory sources.

Since more than 650 men from the division were KIA, 7,000 GIs from the 422nd and 423rd who had been on the Schnee Eifel had been surrendered, the 424th survived after hard fighting, the 81st Combat Engineer Battalion and remnants of the 589th and 590th Field Artillery engaged the enemy, wholesale retreat of thousands of panicky soldiers obviously seems incorrect.

One reader outraged by Whiting's book was Frank Raila, who,

after his months as a PW from the 423rd Infantry Regiment, returned to the States and had become a physician specializing in radiology. He drafted an eight-page letter to Whiting in which he savaged Whiting's characterizations of his fellow Golden Lions. Raila made good use of Whiting's own description of fire fights to contradict the writer's conclusions. He heaped scorn upon Whiting for using the word "rabble" to describe his fellow GIs, pointing out it was the same term used by a Nazi general. Raila assigned the blame for the demise of the 106th to its officers, particularly General Jones and Colonels Cavender and Descheneaux.

Ralph Hill, who had been a field artillery captain and a military government officer in the Ardennes that terrible winter, became a champion of Golden Lions vets. He corresponded with many of the individuals who were on the scene, pored over After Action Reports, official papers containing march orders and the like. Anyone who showed the slightest interest in Hill's study of what happened around St. Vith was bombarded with copies of his letters. Unfortunately, since one only sees the missives authored by Hill, often couched in vituperation, it is not always clear that an event has been accurately described. And in some instances Hill's springboard to a conclusion is constructed from an interpretation rather than a fact.

Ultimately, Hill concluded that the chief villains were 7th Armored brass, particularly CCB commander Bruce Clarke, whom he indicted for "incompetence, insubordination and lack of integrity," and some of his subordinates. Hill constructed a timetable of events, demonstrated the apparent failure of Clarke to acquire proper intelligence on enemy deployment and argued that the traffic jam that slowed the arrival of reinforcements occurred because 7th Armored officers mishandled the flow of largely legitimately retreating heavy engineering, supply and medical vehicles. Clarke, incidentally, after recovery from his gallstone attack during the Bulge, followed his military profession to distinguished heights during the Korean War.

Whatever the possible defects of Hill's research, it helped convince Charles MacDonald, the former youthful CO of rifle companies with the 23rd Infantry Regiment of the 2nd Division, that the conventional verdict damning the 106th was an error. MacDonald, the soldier who began World War II toting his portable typewriter, after being demobilized, translated his understanding of war and his literary talent into a career as a U.S. Army historian.

He produced official narratives of a number of World War II campaigns and captured his personal experience in *Company Commander*. In *A Time for Trumpets*, his recounting of the Battle of the Bulge, MacDonald placed the unhappy story of the 106th Division in a reasonable context and scrubbed off much of the opprobrium smeared on the Golden Lions.

MacDonald's report revived the drooping spirits of men like John Kline. "The book shows that the Germans took three days to chew us up, and in those three days they lost their impetus. They used up a lot of gas and men." From the moment he came across *A Time for Trumpets*, Kline began to search for others from the division. He joined the 106th Association and became editor of its quarterly magazine. The annual reunions draw good-sized crowds and the association is one of the strongest of its kind.

There is little doubt, however, that the retreat before the German onslaught was not always orderly. Witnesses like Abe Baum of the 4th Armored Division saw artillery pieces and vehicles left by units that broke, Charles La Chaussee of the 517th Parachute Regiment, came upon soldiers who had quit their posts, the scene described by Curtiss Martell of the 30th Division and Charles Mac-Donald himself, from the 2nd Division, whose reputation in the Bulge received the highest burnishing, spoke in *Company Commander* of men running away. At the very least, in isolated situations, soldiers from many different organizations abandoned their equipment and bolted.

Unless one has been in their shoes, it is difficult to condemn them. Jack Agnew, the pathfinder for the 101st, however, had no sympathy for anyone who quit. "When I came home, I had my job waiting for me, a very good job but they had gone on strike while I was in service. I knew I would do nothing but fight with those employees, especially ones who shirked their duty using war work as an excuse and I had to find employment elsewhere.

"I felt the same about those in the service who surrendered without a fight or whose units ran and caused so many other men to get killed, wounded or maimed for life. I am especially put out with those who acted this way and today place themselves in the limelight. If it were not for their wives and families I would do my best to make asses of them. A Bronze Star to any man who laid down his arms and surrendered out of fright is an insult to those who fought gallantly and to those that died fighting."

But even Agnew softens his condemnation. "I found a buddy

recently who seems to have real problems. He was in an aid station in Bastogne when the Germans overran it and he was captured. Only seventeen when he enlisted, he thinks we will not accept him because he was taken prisoner. He even reenlisted but still feels this way, no matter how we try to convince him. He won't change until he forgives himself."

Half a century before the bleeding began in the Ardennes, novelist Stephen Crane produced *The Red Badge of Courage*. His "episode of the Civil War" encapsulates the testing of men under fire and their fear of cowardice. The protagonist, "the youth" Henry Fleming appears first full of patriotic bravado tempered by fear he will not measure up. Full of shame when he flees his first battle, Fleming in a second encounter performs credibly. He seemingly reconciles himself to the nature of war and the reactions of men caught up in it, temporarily. But Crane skillfully insinuates that Fleming fools himself and that every battle will elicit the same dilemma of survival versus cowardice and shame.

The accounts of experiences and the attitudes of those who fought through the Bulge demonstrate how life follows art. Many who surrendered in the 106th, the 99th and the 28th Divisions, to name a few of the more prominent groups in the stalags, never had much of a chance to show their mettle in combat. They followed the orders that committed them to the mercies of the enemy. But their accounts of survival as captives are also tales of fear, shame and courage.

Chapter XIX

OLD SOLDIERS

THE LAST OF THE Johnnys from the Ardennes marched home or, in the cases of Glen Strange and Arnold Albero, rode stretchers on hospital ships back to the States. As Phil Hannon typified, they wanted to get on with lives interrupted by military service. They would pursue civilian jobs or, in a few instances, remain soldiers, professionals. They would marry, have children, divorce, lose spouses and remarry, sicken, die or live on through more war and peace, refracting their interpretations through memories drawn from the time in the Ardennes.

Paratrooper Jack Agnew, unwilling to work alongside people who struck during the war, accepted a position as a telephone installer with Western Electric, retiring after thirty-six years on the job. John Collins, one of the PWs from the 106th, developed a certain wanderlust, satisfied with positions that took him to Iran, Libya, Egypt, Thailand and even Vietnam. Nathan Ward, who had been part of the same group as Collins under Lt. Col. Thomas Riggs in the defense of St. Vith, employed his talents as a civilian with the Post Engineers at Fort McPherson, Georgia, for more than twenty-five years. Ward was among several who maintained a military connection through membership in the reserves.

Joe Colmer of the gliderborne 325th Regiment plied the trade of the welder, drawing a paycheck from International Harvester when he hung up his torch. Jerry Nelson, the 7th Armored Division gunner, settled in Two Rivers, Wisconsin, where he operated a barber shop in close proximity to his favorite recreations of fishing and hunting.

When Ed Uzemack, still in uniform, came back to Chicago, he blew a $2,500 opportunity to sell his memoirs as a 28th Division replacement and then PW to the Chicago *Tribune*, out of loyalty to his premilitary employer, the Chicago *Daily Times*, which paid him a princely $100 instead. Once a civilian, Uzemack occupied a rewrite slot at the *Daily Times* before moving into the public relations field with the American Medical Association and, subsequently, other health groups before retirement.

Lyle Bouck credits his military career with giving him an opportunity to develop leadership talents and confidence in himself. The humble chiropractic clientele that "didn't provide a pot to sit on" grew to the point where he became a prominent member of the St. Louis civic and business world, serving on county boards dealing with traffic and parks, acting as a member of the local Selective Service Board and being appointed a bank board member.

Richard McKee, part of the PW "Death March," established himself as a printer and publisher of two newspapers, along with commercial work. Abe Baum, the 4th Armored Division leader of the last mission to Bastogne before it was totally shut off and of the Hammelburg Raid, went into business with his father in the Major Blouse Company. He tried early semiretirement in Florida, and after financial reverses while in his mid fifties, went on the road selling in the West.

A number of former GIs, like Nathan Ward, continued to draw wages from the government, although as civilians. Clifford Broadwater, who had been part of the civil service, transferred from Washington, D. C., to a veteran's hospital in Oregon. After he reached the pensioner's age, Broadwater took a series of short-term posts before full retirement in 1980.

Dee Paris, from the 14th Tank Battalion, who had worked for the federal government before the war, renewed his affiliation, as an employee of the VA. He maintained his fascination with armor through the reserves and, as a baritone in good standing, lent his skills in public relations to the Society for the Preservation of Barbershop Quartets.

Congressional Medal of Honor awardees Frank Currey and Mel Biddle both accepted opportunities with the Veterans Administration. Currey, an upstate New Yorker by birth, heeded the invitations of fellow members of the 30th Division and took up residence in South Carolina. The division, originally a National Guard outfit drawn from Tennessee and South Carolina, traces its roots to Andrew Jackson. Currey converted himself into such a strong facsimile of a local boy that he became the first nonnative son to become president of the Andrew Jackson Society.

Biddle returned to Indiana to marry the girl whose agreement to write him at a parachute training camp stimulated his enlistment in the 517th. He worked for the VA in his home state for almost thirty years before retirement.

An architectural firm hired Jim Mills, the resident of Slaughterhouse V, as a draftsman. Under the GI Bill, he received four years of on-the-job training and made a career as a field supervisor for various phases of construction in Dayton, Ohio. Another Buckeye, Bill Dunfee, the 82nd Airborne trooper, accepted an offer from his prewar employers to teach him the lumber business. When he accepted early retirement in 1983 he was the company's general manager.

Some who came home dedicated themselves to making up for lost good times. Schuyler Jackson, the roisterer of the 101st Airborne, squandered about $8,000 left from the loot he took from the Germans, his terminal leave pay and his GI unemployment benefits. "I enjoyed myself for two years, and the one constructive thing I did was to get a pilot's license." When forced to find an income, Jackson started a business hauling bricks which he built into a very profitable operation. Dick Byers also satisfied a thirst for aviation. "I farted away my GI bill, learning to fly on the premise that I'd never be a foot soldier again. My main occupation became a heating and air-conditioning business."

Glen Strange had to wait out more than two years of treatment for his injury in military hospitals before he could get back to the "sand and black jack" of Oklahoma. When he finally was mustered out, Strange attended classes until earning a B.S. degree. He worked for manufacturing companies for a while, then became the Postmaster of the Tonkawa, Oklahoma, Post Office. "This was in the days of political appointments and it wasn't easy for a Republican to be appointed to anything in Oklahoma. But this was during the Eisenhower years and we had one Republican congressman from my area." He also held the post of municipal judge.

And there were some who found a home in the U.S. Army. William Desobry, the major from the 10th Armored who disappointed his West Point father with a concentration on foreign service studies at Georgetown, decided to stick with the military. Desobry attended the Command and General Staff College in 1952, served a 1965-68 tour in Vietnam as an advisor to the local ARVN forces and eventually retired with the rank of major general. Charles LaChaussee from the 517th Paratroops elected to remain in service and Marcus Dillard from the 4th Infantry Division similarly chose to become a "lifer." Dillard retired as a master sergeant. La Chaussee finished as a colonel.

Listing their post-World War II pursuits, of course, offers a superficial view of their lives. The matter of how their time in the Ardennes or in the entire war affected them is another matter. The question of psychological effects from a hammering on the anvil of war dates far back. In this century World War I produced "shell shock," World War II "battle fatigue," the Korean War "combat neurosis" and Vietnam "post-traumatic stress syndrome."

Paratroop commander William Boyle remarked that post-traumatic stress syndrome—depression, various physical ailments and mood swings—is a notion overblown by the media, and a number of other vets of the Ardennes, like John Collins of the 81st Combat Engineers, agree. On the other hand, Richard McKee, who endured the infamous Death March of PWs, draws a ten percent disability pension for PTSS.

While many seemed to pick up their lives without hesitation after they came home, others showed perceptible influence from their experiences. Barney Alford, Eric Wood's gun-section sergeant who earned a battlefield commission, changed his vocational plans. Oddly, although he endured the bitter winter in the Ardennes, Alford discovered a taste for the outdoors. "They gave me a desk job before sending me home. I realized the indoors was not for me. I had thought of becoming a dentist but instead I became a horticulturist, and I've enjoyed every minute of that profession. I owned and operated a nursery and greenhouse business before selling it to become Director of Grounds for the Bok Tower Gardens of Lake Wales."

Tanker Jerry Nelson believed his years as a soldier changed him. "I'm a more patient guy than I was and I appreciate the little things in life. I'm more patriotic, too, and try to do things that help people and causes. I belong to civic groups, mainly Kiwanis, but my big interest is conservation, fish and game groups." Nelson has been an officer in the local conservation club and county fish and game association for almost thirty years. "On the eve of December 16 when it all started, I have a very difficult time falling asleep." And nearly fifty years after the Bulge, when Nelson wrote about the personal losses incurred in the Ardennes, he wept.

Alan Shapiro's six weeks in the combat zone and his opportunity to study while a convalescent shifted him towards an academic orientation. "The turning point came during the summer/ fall of 1945 while I was at Shrivenham, England, and had a lot of time for reading. Sports journalism lost its significance. I began to feel as if I had to do something to make wars like World War II impossible. I didn't know what. During my 1947–48 college year at Adelphi University, when I came under the influence of Pickens E. Harris, dean of the education school, I found out. He made me feel teaching was the socially significant career I had been looking for."

While still a student, Shapiro received a summons to appear for a medical exam to determine if he qualified for a pension. He ignored the matter until an even more peremptory demand arrived by mail. "I went to Governors Island [in New York harbor] for a medical examination. I was there for almost the entire day, and when four o'clock and quitting time came, they were not through with me. I was told I'd have to come back. I said to hell with this.

"Subsequently, I was ordered to return. I was not going to waste another day and I threw away the letter. Some time later I received an official announcement, stating I had been found eligibile for something like a 10 or 15 percent disability. I started receiving a monthly check of $7.50."

When Shapiro completed his studies, he became a teacher of English and social studies for almost forty years in the public school systems of New York State. Shapiro also tried to work for peace through active membership in the United World Federalists, a post-World War II organization that sought to create a framework of international law and procedures to make it prevail. Since retirement from teaching he has worked on projects for Educators for Social Responsibility, arranging workshops to instruct teachers about nuclear problems, and in exchange programs with teachers from Russia and Poland.

Shifts in careers might be expected among any group of young men. But there were also some psychological effects that cut deeper. Some of the survivors of the Malmédy massacre, even nearly fifty years later, cannot speak of what happened. Life has been bumpy for Jim Mattera, who provided a graphic eyewitness account. And there are former soldiers, like Cy Blank of the 11th Armored, who still blot out their memories.

Curtiss Martell, of the 30th Infantry Division, frankly admits to a drastic change in his life and personality. "I entered military service as a mild, meek, compassionate young man. I returned home just the opposite; hard, callous, mean, a difficult person to live with. I would jump at the slightest unexpected noise. At night I would lie in bed and cry. I also have very severe stomach cramps. My immediate family recognized the disorder but hesitated to even mention it for fear of my violent temper.

"Even as late as ten years ago [1982], I had to go for psychiatric treatment as a private patient. I was told by two doctors that my problems were all the result of my war experiences. One even wanted to file a disability claim for me. I told him to forget it; it is much too late. I currently take tranquilizers."

Dee Paris professed no conscious sense of any aftereffects of his time in combat. But he added, "I never remembered dreaming but some of my bed companions right after the War told me that I'd start screaming, 'Get out, get out,' as if the tank was on fire."

Mel Biddle, the Medal of Honor winner, was another who faced night terrors. "My wife told me that I would have nightmares and scream in the first few months after we were married."

Harry Martin, the private with the 424th Infantry Division, who momentarily lost control of himself when masses of German infantry charged his company, had been wounded after the Bulge. After V-E Day he continued to defy his superiors, refusing to perform work or carry out orders for a period of three months. Eventually, without any punishment imposed, Martin received an honorable discharge, but his final medical examination diagnosed him as having an "anxiety neurosis." Forty years after his time as a rifleman in the Ardennes, Martin toured the area. "With the fog and deep shadows, it brought back the scene that I had seen so many times during the Battle of the Bulge. I felt the woods would suddenly erupt with screaming Germans trying to kill me. I still have nightmares about the Germans trying to kill me. In these dreams I keep yelling for help until I wake myself up. I get out of bed and turn all the lights on."

Phil Hannon was enough of a blithe soul to enjoy his honeymoon, two years after he gained freedom, atop an Idaho mountain as a fire watcher. However, he had no doubt that post-traumatic stress syndrome exists, said, "I know some came out of the PW camps with extreme physical and mental damage. I'm sure it was even worse for guys who were prisoners of the Japanese, the North Koreans or the North Vietnamese. The fact that the Oriental people think differently than the Europeans is bound to add stress."

However, Hannon believed he personally escaped any deleterious consequences. "At heart, I am an optimist, always three or four feet emotionally higher off the ground than others. I am an up person. It was never so bad that I couldn't stand it. I am constantly amazed by what the human mind and body can take. And I never had any flashbacks from my experiences."

Frank Raila, like Jerry Nelson, develops anxiety toward the middle of each December. "I feel a little nervous when December 16th comes and the week gives me a strange feeling despite all the years. Christmas has never been the same for me since 1944. I still feel somewhat guilty for being captured but what I think helped me was escaping. It erased much of my guilt. It was the least I could do for myself and my country at the time. During the late 1940s and early 1950s there were times when I had some bad emotional outbursts but those days are now long over."

For Abe Baum, the residue from World War II showed both in the way others thought of him and in how he treated people. As the newly-declared state of Israel geared up for war with the Arabs over what had been Palestine and the surrounding territory, it sought help in financial, material and human resources in the U.S. Baum's reputation as a soldier, even with the Hammelburg raid under wraps, made him particularly attractive.

"They wanted me to come to Israel to replace Mickey Marcus, the American colonel who graduated from West Point and had been killed. But I couldn't go. I had just gone into business with my father and if I left, it would have collapsed. And it would have been too tough for my family. They had received telegrams that I had been killed in action, wounded in action, and that I was missing after Hammelburg.

"Teddy Kollek [mayor of Jerusalem for many years] was the liaison here and he brought Moshe Dayan to see me. We met in the small office I had on 38th Street and 7th Avenue, over the Pine Tree, a vegetarian restaurant. They spread out a map of Palestine and Dayan explained to me that he wanted to capture the airport at Lydda and what tactics would I suggest.

"I said, 'You put your artillery battalion here, move your tank battalion through here.' Dayan and Kollek burst into laughter. Dayan told me, that for armor, he had one tank mounted on a truck. All I could instruct him were the lessons I learned under Patton and with the 4th Armored."

According to Dayan, in one of his biographies, Baum instructed him to forget about preliminary patrols that might tip-off strategy. Only after moving out should the recon units go ahead—as Task Force Baum operated during the Hammelburg mission. Furthermore, Baum counseled, said Dayan, "the moment you come to an obstacle, you open fire in all directions with whatever you have, machine guns, mortars. You shoot and drive, shoot and drive." Again the tactics mirrored those of the task force.

Six days after their meeting, an emissary arrived to see Baum and bussed him, with the explanation, "That's from Dayan. He wanted me to tell you, Abe, we took the airport."

Old comrades from the military establishment summoned Baum for intelligence on what made the Israeli forces so successful. They represented the same military apparatus that had denied Baum when he asked them for help on behalf of Israel's Hagganah. Gen. Bruce Clarke invited Baum to an uncomfortable luncheon attended by various fiscal and industrial potentates at a club that proscribed membership by Jews. A furious Baum later sought out Clarke to demand an explanation. Clarke answered, "I just wanted to make them aware people like you existed, Abe."

When Baum sought to use his celebrity to gain a concession from the bureaucracy that controlled the scarce supply of textiles, he obtained the necessary priority through Omar Bradley, after a four-hour rambling conversation about the war. Afterwards, he discovered the document carried no weight with the cloth manufacturers, busily profiting through gray- and black market business.

Subsequently, a potential source of materials called on the plant owned by Baum and his father. It quickly became apparent the man represented a black market operation. "I picked up a flatiron. 'You see this, I'll kill you with it if you ever approach me again.' My father was at a cutting table about thirty feet away and after the guy left he said to me, 'What did I raise, an animal?' "

Another postwar phenomenon that defies easy determination is attitude towards the former enemy. Curtiss Martell, who admitted to suffering long-term effects from his infantry service, bears no ill will toward those most responsible for his experiences. "I have no animosity towards the Germans. In fact, I married a German woman." Jim Mills, who cheered for American bombs even as they threatened his own life, also married someone from Germany.

Marcus Dillard, as a sergeant who gave the army twenty-six years of service, is another who chose a bride from his former enemy's country. Dillard says he never generated hostility toward the German people. "They had leaders who took them to war, just like ours did in Korea, Vietnam and Saudi Arabia." Dillard was angrier about officers in his own army. "What struck me was how they were treated. Their beds were made for them, shoes shined for them, their barracks or BOQs serviced by a private on duty all the time. They never had to take care of their personal gear."

Dee Paris claimed no current enmity towards the former foe. However, he says, "I think I did hate the Germans at the time. Men who hated the enemy, I think, were better soldiers. We'd see a German lad, nice chubby face, blue eyes and then I could see him sighting a rifle with those blue eyes, killing Americans."

"I really do not believe I ever hated the German people," said Glen Strange. "I did have a hate and a passion to kill many of the people, like Hitler, some of his officers, especially the SS. By the same token I respect some German officers, and most of the soldiers were only doing what they had been trained. However, knowing the history of the German people, I do not take them for granted. I believe in years to come they could be led down the primrose path once again."

Jerry Nelson harbored similar sentiments. "I have no hard feelings towards the Germans or the Japs—but I will always know who and how the war started. And we will never have to apologize for dropping the bomb at Hiroshima."

For Frank Raila, the issue was who was trying to kill whom. "I didn't dwell on what they were like and never had hatred for the enemy. The Germans are basically good people. However, there is some genetic perversity in a small segment of them that is peculiarly dangerous to mankind as a whole, foreigners and Jews in particular. If that group gets control, the entire business will be repeated." Raila's persistent dislike focuses on the officers he believes brought disaster upon the enlisted men of the 106th.

John Chernitsky, the antitank sergeant from the 28th Division, worked for a number of retail concerns before obtaining post supervising an assembly line. He, like Raila, accused officers of failing their men, the generals of seeking to celebrate Christmas while ignoring the peril of the troops.

Ex-paratrooper Bill Dunfee was less forgiving than others. "I will not buy a German or Japanese auto. I must confess, I resent those who do." He adds, "We buy as few foreign-produced items as one can today."

Whether the former GIs now incline toward pacifism or still believe the sword makes plowshares possible, they all considered the war against the Third Reich justified. "Aggression of the Hitlerian variety had to be stopped, " said Alan Shapiro.

Jack Agnew expressed a common ambivalence. "World War II was the second crusade to free the world from an ungodly oppression. No war is worthwhile. Those that were our enemies we helped rebuild and now strain our economy."

They felt little or no guilt for their roles in hurting or killing their fellow men. "I'm not happy about some of the things that I did," said Leonard Weinstein. "I have no love for war and destruction. But for the grace of God, I might have been the other guy. I share the view of a few others in my company, 'I'm glad I was able to do it, but I would never want to go through that again.' If we hadn't done what we did, those who survived would not live in freedom."

To Wallace Swanson, "World War II was worthwhile and necessary. Any life lost is a waste of a human being but a lot more would have been lost if we did not become involved."

"Was World II worth it?" Jerry Nelson answered his question, "The summer I graduated from high school, the Nazi yoke was in control of over 400 million people. From the English Channel into Russia, from the Baltic Sea south to Africa, and all the ancient capitals in Europe were gone, Paris, Prague, Amsterdam, Brussels, Warsaw, Vienna—everyone, and Britain stood alone. How could it be stopped? We had to get involved."

Glen Strange in his own pithy style probably spoke for all. "I don't think we have ever come out of any war with bona fide results that make world peace and end all wars. However, I was completely indoctrinated to the point where I believed World War II was a just war for our entrance into it along with all our allies.

"Hitler was a no-good bastard but he came along at a time when the German people were ripe for a change and needed a leader and this prick had the ability to take over. He had to be stopped, as he was in the process of trying to enslave all of Europe, and what he did to the Jews and to the free people of the countries they captured could not be tolerated in the free world.

"Yes, he and his kind has to be stopped; there is no place in this world for bastards who set themselves above God and everybody. Power-hunger, greed and plunder of one's fellow man cannot and must not be permitted. It was a very costly war, not only to us, but also to everyone, every country involved.

"I am sure if another dictator would do the thing that rat bastard did, I would once again volunteer to do what I could to help stop him."

The vets appear agreed on the rightness of the U.S. role in World War II but unanimity splinters with later military engagements, just as it did for much of the U.S. A kind of middle ground was voiced by Clifford Broadwater, "I think war is a terrible thing but sometimes it seems we have no alternative action unless we just fold and give up."

Glen Strange does not equate subsequent wars with the one that cost him the use of his legs. "I have made quite a turnabout in my thinking. There is no question but what I was a hawk, even after World War II and up through the Korean conflict. I helped bid my old National Guard unit at Tonkawa farewell for its trip to Korea. I was furious and really upset to hear about the many losses there and to note the political influence on conduct of the campaign. It bothered me to know that Gen. MacArthur was not given authority to carry the battle to a win situation.

"As far as I am concerned, there is no damn use fighting a war unless you intend to win, and why in hell fight a limited war? I am now not so damn sure we should have ever been in Korea, Vietnam or Panama. Look what happened in Korea. We still have too damn much involvement and think of all the expense. Vietnam was a no-win deal. Just think of lives lost, injuries and costs.

"Desert Storm—God, I don't know what to say. I am pissed off to a fare-thee-well we still have that prick in power in Iraq. And the people in that country are starving, being mistreated and suffering. In Kuwait, who in the hell do you think is in power, the same god damn pricks who were in power before the war and the same bastards that led a life of luxury while we were over there trying to save their damn necks. The people in Kuwait are worse off now than before. And to tell the truth, they were being treated like dirt before the war by their own people in power. A case again of the very rich and poor.

"Of course, I can better understand now people who oppose

wars. I am sure we don't know the outcome if there never was a war, but one wonders what good comes out of one."

Jim Mills contrasted subsequent military encounters to his time in Europe. "We had no choice but to enter the war with Germany and we did it the way we should. If you're going to fight a war, everybody must be involved. The way I feel about Korea and Vietnam is that if it is important enough to send men out to fight a war, then the whole country should get behind them and go all-out to win."

"I was too busy raising a family to become emotionally involved about Korea," said Dick Byers. "With Vietnam I started out a hawk but ended up realizing we were fighting the wrong war with the wrong weapons against the wrong people for the wrong reasons. I felt damn sorry for the Nam GI, with one year rotation vs. our two years of training as a unit. We knew and watched out for one another. Panama and Grenada were sickening! 8,000 medals for 7,000 soldiers in Grenada against 500 Cuban workers. It was a cynical farce put on to take the public's mind off the marine barracks bombing, and it worked.

"I have deep doubts about Desert Storm. There is the law of unintended consquences, and I am very disturbed by the control of the press. Facts are still coming out that reveal how things were manipulated. It is extremely difficult to put such power into the hands of the military."

"I am a hawk at heart," declared John Collins, "when they mess with the U.S. The time for us to be a paper tiger should never be. Politicians ruin our image."

"I accepted that North Korea, supported by China and the USSR, was being agressive beyond doubt," said Alan Shapiro. "At the same time, I felt I had a more realistic understanding of what combat was like than people who hadn't been there. Warfare, regardless of reson, made and makes me feel disgusted with human stupidity and compassionate for the people suffering.

"Stupidly, I worked for LBJ in the 1964 election campaign, helping to register voters by going door-to-door, because Goldwater's jingoism represented everything I despise. How was I to know what LBJ had in mind? I knew the war in Vietnam was wrong, gradually realized however it was no 'mistake.' I felt a lot of anger about U.S. aggression, as I saw and see it, participated in many antiwar activities, including refusal to pay taxes for several years. Ho Chi Minh was a lot of things but he wasn't Hitler and I resented the analogy. World War II seemed necessary but that didn't mitigate its horror. Vietnam was unnecessary and horrible. What's worse, the U.S. became, to me, the bad guy.

"As for Desert Storm, my World War II experiences continued to affect my attitudes and thinking. I don't know what the U.S. should have done about Iraq's military adventurism, but I know earlier U.S. policies contributed to it. Bombing civilians puts us in the same class as Hitler and I know, further, that strafing helpless soldiers is technological barbarism."

Carmen Capalbo, who has enjoyed a successful career in New York both as a producer and director of major theater pieces (*The Threepenny Opera, The Potting Shed, A Moon for the Misbegotten*), was anti-Vietnam, anti-Desert Storm. "I'm not a strict pacifist. If our country were attacked, I'd do everything possible to defend it. But, otherwise, wars, to me, are senseless."

Jim Buck, the court clerk who may have bumped into Eric Wood outside of St. Vith, worked for oil companies in Latin America and the U.S., insurance concerns. He then settled in Tustin, California, operating a travel agency and several women's clothing stores with his wife. Buck, from his taste of war and his immersion in war-crimes trials, became an all out pacifist. "I am totally anti-war. I don't think it accomplishes anything. I was against the Vietnam involvement, and in Kuwait all we did was destroy a kingdom run by a dictator."

"In my judgment," said Bill Dunfee, "Korea and Vietnam were fiascos of politicians misusing the military. Panama wasn't much better. Desert Storm was definitely in our interest, but with due respect to those involved, to call a ground action of four and one half days a war is stretching it a wee bit. They stopped this action about two days too soon. To allow fifteen divisions to escape when you have them almost encircled was incredibly stupid."

Frank Raila perceives differences in the status of the GI over time. "A soldier's life in World War II and Korea was much cheaper. You could be shot if you didn't obey orders. That was less true in Vietnam. There, a man could defy an officer or perhaps even kill him if he were particularly stupid or dangerous. I'm sure that occasionally occurred in the earlier wars, but in Vietnam I believe it was more common, fragging officers as they called it. The wall containing the names of soldiers from World War II missing in the Pacific, at the Punch Bowl cemetery in Hawaii, lists about 30,000, a large number. In Vietnam the total dead and missing totals around 50,000. Nobody comes to lay any flowers at the Punch Bowl wall. On the other hand, we discussed in my family the poor treatment of the Vietnam soldier who did not get a fair break. The idiots in Washington got a lot of people killed by trying to orchestrate the war instead of letting the military handle it their own way.

"In Desert Storm it was possible to avoid going. A soldier could practically hire a lawyer to keep you from going and no one was shot or thrown in jail. Just discharged. In World War II, at the least you'd be court-martialled and thrown in prison or the stockade for God knows how long. A significant number of Allies and GIs were killed by friendly fire in Desert Storm. There were thousands killed in World War II by so-called friendly fire."

Lyle Bouck, who enjoyed serving on his local draft board, was among those who enthusiastically backed his country in Korea and later in the Middle East. But Vietnam troubled him. "I couldn't understand what was happening. After Creighton Abrams took charge and he couldn't finish it, I figured something was very wrong."

The schism created by the U.S. involvement in Vietnam rocked some of the former soldiers' families. "I was 100 percent for our role in Korea," says Schuyler Jackson, "and I still figure we should have been in Vietnam, but should have allowed the generals to run it, not the goddamn politicians. My oldest daughter, though, protested the war in Vietnam, which pissed me off. It took us awhile to become reconciled."

For Alan Jones, Jr., a professional soldier from West Point, the resistance of one son to the war in Southeast Asia brought difficult times. "He was so opposed that he might have gone to Canada if drafted. There were very hard feelings between us and we didn't talk until a few years ago."

"The Battle of the Bulge," says Cy Blank, "in fact, the whole war, gave me cause to wonder about the obscenity of men killing other men. Living through it made me wonder why me and not so many guys whose names and faces I still remember. I have opposed every war that this country has been involved with. I just do not believe that war is a solution. In fact, I think war movies should be X-rated because they are more obscene than any other films.

"Probably I am a total pacifist, so much so that when my sons were very young, I forbade them from owning anything resembling a gun. No cap pistols, no water pistols, no imitation rifles, nothing. I could not see them sneaking around bushes and yelling, 'Bang! You're dead, ' with their friends, even if it was only playing. Peer pressure was a strong problem but the war and its effects on me were even stronger. I am not sure how my sons feel about this today, but I would hope they understand the depths of my feelings."

What most children tend not to understand or even know much about is what their fathers did and felt during the war. Part of the problem is summed up by Frank Raila, "No one can appreciate combat or the PW experience without having been involved first hand. You can read and write for a hundred years on combat, and unless you were in it, you won't really know it."

Abe Baum remarked, "I didn't think my children were interested and I didn't want to boast or try to tell them that I was a war hero." A similar opinion was voiced by Jerry Nelson, who, as a barber, often engaged in conversation with customers, but ordinarily left the subject out of his chats. "Only one soldier to another will talk about it."

Alan Shapiro produced his memoirs in letter form while stationed at Bremen, less than six months after his frozen feet removed him from the Ardennes, although he never mailed the journal home. "I don't recall my precise motivation when I sat down evening after evening writing what happened to me during the war. I know, however, that I felt I had an extraordinary experience, that memories of it would inevitably fade and I had to get it down." His father read the account the summer after Shapiro returned to the States. He is uncertain whether his wife, a high-school sweetheart, went through the manuscript. According to her, he never talked about what happened with her, nor have his children or grandchildren ever read the material.

A former marine captain who fought in Vietnam wrote: "I have to admit that for all these years I had also loved it [the Vietnam war] and more than I knew. I hated war, too. [Most other vets] would have to admit that somewhere inside themselves they had loved it . . . War is a brutal, deadly game, but a game, the best there is . . . But if you come back whole, you bring with you the knowledge that you have explored regions of your soul that in most men will always remain uncharted . . . The love of war stems from the union, deep in the core of our being, between sex and destruction, beauty and horror, love and death . . . One of the most troubling reasons men love war is the love of destruction, the thrill of killing . . .''

To a man, the American veterans of the Ardennes challenge the authenticity of this description for themselves. Jim Mills specifically scoffed, "War is not a game." Cap Capalbo dismissed the view. "I saw no exhilaration in anyone. I never heard any person express sentiments remotely resembling those." Abe Baum regarded the comments as typical of marine indoctrination, citing a formerly mild relative who returned from his marine training spouting enthusiasm for blood and gore.

Interpreting the remarks of the survivors from the Ardennes, it would appear that the ex-marine captain confused the instinctive reaction of a human to danger, the rush of adrenalin that may serve to preserve existence. Phil Hannon recalled "a higher sense of being when under fire." Others talked of a feeling of excitement but that is a state that accompanies terror as much as pleasure.

While some seem to have permanently disconnected their memory banks dealing with the Ardennes, others constantly seek to recharge them. Ted Kiendl went back to the site twice to pay homage to the fallen Eric Wood and to another officer beneath one of the thousands of white crosses and Stars of David. Jerry Nelson has not returned to the Ardennes, as so many others have, but he has visited other World War II sites. "The holiest place on earth for me is the cemetery on Omaha Beach and the view of the English Channel at the overlook. Van Tine's grave would be the most emotional for me."

Arnold Albero remained in contact with Belgian families he met in the Ardennes and visited them several times. Glen Strange retraced his steps in Luxembourg and Belgium, and developed strong friendships with residents. Schuyler Jackson, who destroyed much of a small village because of an infestation of booby traps, nevertheless was greeted with affection by the very people whose homes he blew up.

In 1988, Jean-Louis Seel and Jean-Philippe Speder, two young Belgians, searching for remnants from the battlefield, heard a telltale beep from their metal detector. They dug into the ground and uncovered a GI mess kit. About a yard deeper into the ground they found a snow boot, with a sock and footbones. The pair unearthed a billfold, rosary, Bible, five religious crosses and two dog tags. Eventually, from what had been a foxhole, they exposed the still-clothed, seated skeleton of Pfc. Alphonse Sito, a Baltimore machine gunner from the 394th Infantry Regiment of the 99th Division. A bullet hole in the helmet explained Sito's death in action on the first day of the German offensive.

Sito was one of nearly 80,000 men from World War II carried as MIAs, compared to more than 8,000 from Korea and 2,300 plus from Vietnam. Eventually, Dick Byers learned of the finding of Sito's remains. Byers organized a small committee through the 99th Division Association to hunt for others. Using names carried as missing by the American Battlefield Monuments Commission in Brussels, the group solicited information about the MIAs through the 99th Association's newspaper, *The Checkerboard.*

Byers recruited Rex Whitehead, a mortar man from the 99th, who drafted a map, based on the memories of men on the scene, indicating the approximate location of a KIA. Byers personally carried the chart to Belgium and delivered it to a search team. The body of Lt. Lonnie Holloway was found close to the place shown on the map. Byers and his associates continue to seek MIAs from the 99th.

Schuyler Jackson said of his time as a paratrooper, "I had some of the best and some of the worst times of my life." To some extent the phenomenon of "euphoric recall"—memories of the happiest moments of an experience while blocking out the dire ones—governs attitudes long after the fact. Phil Hannon believed that men seeking to recapture the "heightened excitement" of their war explains why many join the military associations. Joe Colmer drops in at the Legion for a drink and an opportunity to hash over "old times."

Looking for sources of material on what happened to men caught in the Ardennes and their reactions, one quickly becomes aware of the hundreds of alumni organizations for units that participated. All but three of the Americans who contributed their Bulge memories to this book belong to veterans organizations. Immediately after World War II, many joined the American Legion, Veterans of Foreign Wars and Disabled American Veterans, which provided leverage for benefits.

For the most part, the battles of old soldiers from World War II for their due from the government and society is now over. The interest seems much more oriented toward the alumni associations of their military outfits. Not only do the vets belong but they publish newspapers, newsletters and bulletins on their military history and their lives since; they attend reunions, visit the Ardennes, and engage in projects to erect monuments to the fallen or the achievements of their fellow GIs. Indeed, a growing organization is the Veterans of the Battle of the Bulge, which publishes a quarterly, *The Bulge Bugle*.

Based on their own words, behind the hunt for the missing by those like Byers, the pilgrimages to the graves of the dead, the building of memorials, the retracing and recall of the Bulge, lies an explanation for what kept them in the fight. In his book, *The Face of Battle*, British historian John Keegan, comparing battles, from Agincourt through the Somme in World War I, speaks of a number of influences on "the will to combat." According to Keegan, alcohol, hopes for plunder, religion, coercion or leadership and unit pride have been the major factors.

Liquor, which in the past was issued to men at war to dull fear, was not employed for these purposes to any significant extent during World War II. There were rations for officers, as Lyle Bouck recalled, but there was nothing like the traditional tot of rum given British seamen before engagements.

Some U.S. soldiers collected trophies, cameras, pistols and later artworks and household goods, when they overran Germany, but this was not on anyone's mind either before or during the fighting. The black market profiteering was an unfortunate piece of serendipity that accompanied victory.

World War II was the last war that saw Americans willing, even desirous to participate. While those who fought in the Ardennes were all there because their country required their presence, there was no genuine resistance to military service. Some were volunteers through enlistment or by joining an ROTC program. But that only put them in uniform sooner than if they had awaited the draft. However, it is apparent from comments by those who could have earned deferments that this was a war in which men wanted to serve. There was a general awareness that Hitler's Germany was a genuine threat. The belief in the American system could be classified as a secular kind of religion.

But during the crunch, nobody advanced under fire with the motivation of striking a blow against tyranny or to preserve the Stars and Stripes. And as far as the traditional, spiritual form of religion is concerned, according to several witnesses, it sustained them, but it was not a motivator for combat.

Leadership certainly entered into the equation. Commanders like Gen. James Gavin, Col. Robert Sink, Lt. Col. Bill Boyle, Maj.

Abe Baum, Capt. Charles La Chaussee, Lt. Lyle Bouck, S. Sgt. Frank Currey and, to a different degree, Gen. George S. Patton, Jr., to name a few, are cited by those who followed them. These officers and noncoms pushed men to do more than what might ordinarily be expected of them.

But above all, the testimony given here on the motivation to combat spells the word: "Camaraderie." That sums up the critical element in the GIs' makeup. Camaraderie is a kinship with others, where self-esteem stems from a reciprocal affection. It is a synonym for the sociology/psychology syndrome of bonding. Theorists delving into differences between Western men and women, claim that females, because of their oppressed status, tend naturally to bond. Men, on the other hand, freer to express themselves, supposedly have less incentive to relate closely to their brothers.

Whether that stands or not, it is certainly apparent that individuals, thrown together for a common purpose, bond in almost direct proportion to their interdependence for success. The power of symbiosis to produce strong ties translates in varying degrees to cover other group endeavors, space missions, government agencies, businesses, political and social movements. Indeed, it is a partial explanation for the strength of families.

An overblown description of professional football called it "the moral equivalent of war." Compared to war, football may well occupy a higher ethical plane, although on its own the sport's claim to probity is dubious. However, the microcosm of the game offers an insight into the explanation of men under fire. The basic approach of pro football says winning is everything, which, in war, sanctifies the worst that humans can inflict upon one another. Winning requires the player to perform up to a certain level if he and his teammates are to succeed. There is a common foe, opponents who figuratively aim to destroy the squad. The team factor is enhanced by considerable time together, the discipline of training camp, shared meals, common housing and time together even during off-duty hours.

The analogy delineates the glue that keeps soldiers together. Like pro football, soldiering means submission to higher authority, uniforms in common, eating together, sleeping together. But in war, the commonality extends to sharing the worst living conditions imaginable, a nonsexual intimacy (in the Ardennes men held one another for warmth and perhaps security) which may have exceeded the closeness of a marriage. In combat, the hideous dimension of winning as the *only* thing plays out in a context where your life often depends upon the man beside you and vice versa. Men risk their own destruction rather than jeopardize their standing with their fellow soldiers, an unwillingness to let comrades down.

From this boiling brew inevitably rises the compound of camaraderie. When war's terrible juggernaut crunched down upon the soldiers, the intellectual perception that Hitler needed to be stopped was hardly adequate to overcome a desire to flee. Confronted by the awesome destruction of modern weaponry, a soldier may or may not have drawn comfort from his religion, but nothing in the Book impels a man to advance under fire. Training taught the soldiers how to operate their weapons, instilled an acceptance of commands and the tactics for fulfilling orders. But camaraderie provided the strength to hang in there. Wellington was not far off the mark when he ascribed his victory to the playing fields of Eton.

Dee Paris boiled it down, "I never saw a man who wasn't frightened. And I've seen cowards. The difference is PRIDE! Two kinds of pride—your personal pride in your conduct and second, you don't want others to see you are a coward."

Jerry Nelson quoted Samuel Johnson, "Every man thinks meanly of himself for not having been a soldier."

Camaraderie, however, extends to both sides in a war. In itself, that bonding does not justify what is done by virtue of its power. War creates the most terrible dilemma faced by humans—with women coming to the front lines they, too, confront the specter—kill or be killed. Those Americans who were in the Ardennes were mostly young, many no more than boys on the edge of maturity. Their innocence drowned in blood, but the survivors know that because of them some order came to chaos, the strange new beast halted.

BIBLIOGRAPHY

Archer, Clark (Editor). *Paratroopers' Odyssey* (Hudson, FL: 517th Parachute Regimental Combat Team Association, 1985).

Baron, Richard, Abe Baum, Richard Goldhurst. *Raid!* (New York: G.P. Putnam's Sons, 1981).

Blair, Clay. *Ridgway's Paratroopers* (Garden City, NY: Dial Press, 1985).

Blumenson, Martin. *The Patton Papeers 1940–50* (Boston: Houghton Mifflin, 1974).

Bradley, Omar. *A Soldier's Story* (New York: Henry Holt and Co., 1951).

Breuer, William. *Geronimo* (New York: St. Martin's Press, 1989).

Cavanagh, William. *Krinkelt-Rocherath—The Battle for the Twin Villages* (Norwell, MA: Christopher Publishing House, 1986).

Chernitsky, Dorothy. *Voices from the Foxholes* (Uniontown, PA: Dorothy Chernitsky, 1991).

Cole, Hugh M. *The Ardennes: The Battle of the Bulge* (Washington, D.C.: U.S. Government Printing Office, 1965).

Downing, David. *The Devil's Virtuosos: German Generals at War 1940–45* (New York: St. Martin's Press, 1977).

Dupuy, R. Ernest. *St. Vith—Lion in the Way* (Nashville: Battery Press, 1986).

Eisenhower, David. *Eisenhower At War 1943–45* (New York: Random House, 1986).

Eisenhower, Dwight David. *Crusade in Europe* (Garden City, NY: Doubleday, 1948).

Eisenhower, John. *The Bitter Woods* (New York: G.P. Putnam's Sons, 1969).

Elstob, Peter. *Hitler's Last Offensive* (London: Secker & Warburg, 1971).

Foley, Charles. *Commando Extraordinary* (Costa Mesa, CA: Noontide Press, 1988).

Forty, Goerge. *Patton's Third Army At War* (London: Arms and Armour Press, 1976).

Gavin, James M. *On to Berlin: Battles of an Airborne Commander 1943–46* (New York: Viking Press, 1978).

Giles, Janet Holt. *The Damned Engineers* (Boston: Houghton Mifflin, 1970).

Hart, B. H. Liddell. *The German Generals Talk* (New York: Quill, 1979).

Infeld, Glenn B. *Skorzeny, Hitler's Commando* (New York: St. Martin's Press, 1981).

Irving, David. *The War Between the Generals: Inside the Allied High Command* (New York: Congdon & Lattes, 1981).

Keegan, John. *The Face of Battle* (New York: Viking, 1976).

Kessler, Leo. *SS Peiper* (London: Leo Cooper in Association with Secker & Warburg, 1986).

Lee, Ulysses. *The Employment of Negro Troops* (Washington, D.C.: U.S. Government Printing Office, 1966).

Leinbaugh, Harold P. and John D. Campbell. *The Men of Company K* (New York: William Morrow, 1985).

MacDonald, Charles B. *A Time for Trumpets* (New York: William Morrow, 1985).

MacDonald, Charles B. *Company Commander* (New York: Bantam, 1987).

Marshall, S.L.A. *Night Drop* (Boston: Little, Brown and Co., 1962).

Marshall, S.L.A. *Bastogne* (Washington, D.C.: Infantry Journal Press, 1946).

McMillan, Richard. *Miracle Before Berlin* (London: Jarrolds, 1946).

Merriam, Robert. *Dark December* (Chicago: Ziff-Davis, 1947).

Niedermayer, Walter. *Into the Deep Misty Woods of the Ardennes* (Indiana, PA: A.G. Halldin Publishing Co., 1990).

Nobecourt, Jacques. *Hitler's Last Gamble: The Battle of the Bulge* (New York: Schocken Books, 1967).

Pallud, Jean Paul. *Battle of the Bulge, Then and Now* (London: Battle of Britain, Prints International Limited, 1984).

Pergrin, David E. with Eric Hammel. (New York: Ballantine Books, 1989).

Reichelt, Dr. Walter E. *Phantom Nine* (Austin, TX: Presidial Press, 1987).

Robichon, Jacques. *The Second D-Day* (New York: Walker & Co., 1969).

Stawson, John. *The Battle for the Ardennes* (New York: Charles Scribner's Sons, 1972).

Toland, John. *The Story of the Bulge* (New York: Random House, 1959).

Toland, John. *The Last 100 Days* (New York: Random House, 1966).

Weigley, Russell E. *Eisenhower's Lieutenants* (Bloomington, IN: Indiana University Press, 1981).

Weingartner, James J. *Crossroads of Death* (Berkeley, CA: University of California Press, 1979).

Whiting, Charles. *Death of a Division* (New York: Stein and Day, 1980).

Whiting, Charles. *Patton's Last Battle* (New York: Stein and Day, 1987).

Whiting, Charles. *Ardennes: The Secret War* (New York: Stein and Day, 1985).

Winter, George. *Manhay, The Ardennes, Christmas 1944* (Winnipeg: J.J. Fedorowicz, 1990).

INDEX